THE GREATER GAME

The Greater Game

India's Race with Destiny and China

DAVID VAN PRAAGH

McGill-Queen's University Press
Montreal & Kingston • London • Ithaca

© McGill-Queen's University Press 2003
ISBN 0-7735-2588-2 (cloth)
ISBN 0-7735-2639-0 (paper)

Legal deposit fourth quarter 2003
Bibliothèque nationale du Québec

Printed in Canada on acid-free paper.

McGill-Queen's University Press acknowledges the
support of the Canada Council for the Arts for our
publishing program. We also acknowledge the financial support of the Government of Canada through the
Book Publishing Industry Development Program
(BPIDP) for our publishing activities.

All photographs by David Van Praagh

National Library of Canada Cataloguing in Publication

Van Praagh, David
    The greater game : India's race with destiny and China
/ David Van Praagh.

    Includes bibliographical references and index.
    ISBN 0-7735-2588-2 (bnd)
    ISBN 0-7735-2639-0 (pbk)
    1. India – History – 1947–.   2. India – Politics and
government – 1947–.   3. India – Foreign relations –
China.   4. China – Foreign relations – India.   I. Title.

DS480.853.V35 2003   954.05   C2003-902428-8

This book was typeset by True to Type in 10/13 Sabon

This book is dedicated to my children,
Shauna, Jaya, and Peter,
who have all experienced Asia
and are striving in their own ways
for a world of human freedom

Contents

Preface

This book marks the culmination of a long voyage of discovery. I was first drawn to India as a young journalist more than four decades ago. *The Greater Game* is meant to shed light on and provoke thought about a country that resists easy understanding by Westerners – or even other Asians – and that has long inspired love-hate feelings. India is changing in ways that increasingly affect a world facing new challenges which demand both the exercise of democracy and the defence of freedom.

I've written this book as a journalist (and journalism professor) acutely aware of the freedom and responsibility of the press – and aware that history does not begin when a journalist arrives on the spot. It brings together first-hand coverage of events and people over many years with analytical reporting and historical narrative. It is also a political book and a book by a non-Indian. Writing as a journalist, I have not used scholarly matter such as endnotes but have included a bibliography. I also try to convey what I have learned and felt as an individual engaged with India and Asia over more than four decades.

One thing I've learned is that there are no simple or easy answers. India is finally changing in a democratic way. But the Bharatiya Janata Party with its high-caste Hindu identity is not ideal as the inescapable main vehicle of change. Economic levels are going up and reforms are taking hold. But poverty is still pervasive for new reasons as well as old. India may or may not equal or surpass China in this century as a great power. But it deserves recognition as a major power that, after many lost years and much mutual suspicion, is eager to work with the United States and other Asian and Western democracies to preserve and protect peace and freedom on the world's most populous continent.

I'm deeply grateful to McGill-Queen's University Press for supporting a book that, like good journalism in general, aims at informing interested general readers in many countries, as well as scholars, policy-makers, and people in public affairs.

Writing a book about India was first suggested to me when I returned briefly to Toronto in 1968 after three years as the New Delhi–based correspondent of *The Globe and Mail*. But I moved my base to Singapore the following year in order to cover a much wider area, including India as well as the Vietnam war, and hardly had time to do more than plan books on India and the countries of Southeast Asia. After I started teaching international reporting at Carleton University in 1972, I returned to Asia nearly every year as a journalist, gathering and reporting relevant information. But it wasn't until the 1990s that I made substantial progress on the India book, which was to appear at the time of the fiftieth anniversary of Indian independence in August 1997. But the years immediately after the anniversary were so full of momentous developments – the Hindu nationalists coming to power in Delhi, their making India an avowed nuclear power, the United States and India coming together as strategic allies, and the war against global terrorism – that I was compelled to broaden the book's scope to provide perspectives on what indeed became The Greater Game. It is being published in 2003, fifty years after I became a journalist.

Many people have helped me in covering India, and by extension in writing this book. I want to thank all of them although I can name only a few.

Going all the way back, Bonbehari Nimbkar, my roommate at George School in Bucks County, Pa., first infected me with the Indian bug, and later he and his wife Jai opened Indian agriculture and their village of Phaltan to me during three visits. When I was based in Delhi in 1961–62, the late Paul Grimes of *The New York Times*, for whom I often filled in, gave me useful tips. Sol W. Sanders is an American journalist who has shared India experiences with me as a friend and colleague over many years. Mark Tully of the British Broadcasting Corporation was a good person to check in with during visits to Delhi. Pran Sabharwal, a distinguished Indian journalist, has been a friend and confidante for many years, and he and his wife Ruby always made me feel at home in Delhi. Vishnu and Rita Mathur are friends of long standing in both India and Canada.

Once in a great while a journalist's source becomes a friend with whom much more than the usual can be shared without comprising either's independence. In India, Canadian agricultural economist W. David Hopper – who later was the first president of Canada's International Development Research Centre and then vice-president of the World Bank for South Asia – was one such person. Another was the late Ambassador Chester Bowles of the United States, a true friend and critic of India, along with his wife Dorothy (Steb) Bowles. Yet another was the late Indian General Joyanto Nath Chaudhuri, an engaging military commander. In a category all by himself was the late Chakravarti Rajagopalachari, India's grand old man. Canadian diplomats in Delhi who were particularly helpful were Richard V.

Gorham and High Commissioner Roland Michener, before he was appointed Canada's governor general. David Henry, a Canadian University Service Overseas volunteer during the Bihar famine, was of great assistance.

The late Richard J. Doyle, then editor-in-chief of *The Globe and Mail* (and later a senator), and Clark W. Davey, then managing editor, were very supportive during my years as a correspondent in Asia, particularly in fighting the Indian government's attempts to deny me access. So were Newbold Noyes of the late *Washington Evening Star,* and its foreign editor, Burt Hoffman. Fran Cutler of the Canadian Broadcasting Corporation kept me doing many radio commentaries from India. As international-affairs analyst for CJOH-TV Ottawa in recent years, I've done a number of commentaries on India with the encouragement of Max Keeping, in charge of news and public affairs. A number of articles in *The Globe and Mail* in 1998–99 and *The Toronto Star,* where my editor was Vivian Macdonald, in 2001–02 gave me a first crack at new material for this book. Carleton University has given me time to travel and write, and talking about India to my students has helped focus my thoughts for the book. The National Endowment for Democracy in Washington, D.C., and its president, Carl Gershman, also afforded me a different perspective on India by sending me there and to other Asian countries in December 1984–January 1985 as its Asia consultant.

Diane Winter, my first wife, accompanied me twice to India, including our driving across Afghanistan in 1961, and she and I first explored India together. Pat Bell, my second wife, experienced India with me while raising our first two children in New Delhi, and returned to India as a journalist, expecting our third child, when I was barred from entering. Sunanta Janvitaya, my third wife, patiently encouraged me during the years needed to complete this book.

McGill-Queen's University Press has stood behind *The Greater Game,* and its publication would not be possible without the unwavering support, understanding, and guidance of Philip J. Cercone, the executive editor. His staff members in Montreal were invariably helpful and friendly. David Schwinghamer, my editor at MQUP, made many valuable suggestions to enhance this book.

In some ways, India is easy to write about. Except in remote villages, where I needed an interpreter of Hindi or another Indian language, I could always find someone who spoke English. In more ways, India is difficult to write about. It is virtually impossible to generalize about anything Indian. But India lends itself to comprehensive, continuing coverage, for non-Indian and Indian readers, and that's what I've tried to offer in *The Greater Game.*

Chapters 1 and 2 present India informally and personally, and explain India's race with destiny and China. Chapter 3 describes how the war against international terrorism has magnified India's importance, and in this connection tells a little about Pakistan and Afghanistan as keys to the Subcontinent. Chapters 4 and 5 provide an idea of India's history, culture, and economy. Chapters 6 to 14 tell how the Nehru dynasty and the Congress Party wasted precious decades for the most populous democracy, nearly destroying it, and how Hindu nationalists and the Bharatiya Janata Party have emerged as India's only realistic political alternative. Chapters 15 to 21 then describe India's wars and conflicts with neighbours, critical situations in Nepal and Kashmir, and India's shift from practising hypocritical "non-alignment" to being a nuclear-armed ally of the United States "in the cause of democracy" and potentially against China. Finally, chapter 22 puts these momentous events over more than fifty years, often misunderstood and largely underplayed in the West, into brief historical perspective.

Prime Minister Indira Gandhi restrains a tiger cub.

Prime Minister Indira Gandhi in Darjeeling

Prime Minister Lal Bahadur Shastri, Jawaharlal Nehru's immediate successor, spinning, a traditional act on Mahatma Gandhi's birthday.

Sheikh Mohammad Abdullah, the Lion of Kashmir

Three captured Pakistani infiltrators into Indian-held Kashmir

Canadian-designed nuclear power reactor – and source of
weapons-grade plutonium – under construction in
Rajasthan

The Chogyal and Gyalmo of Sikkim and Prince Palden before India's takeover of the tiny Himalayan kingdom

Rajasthan women and child

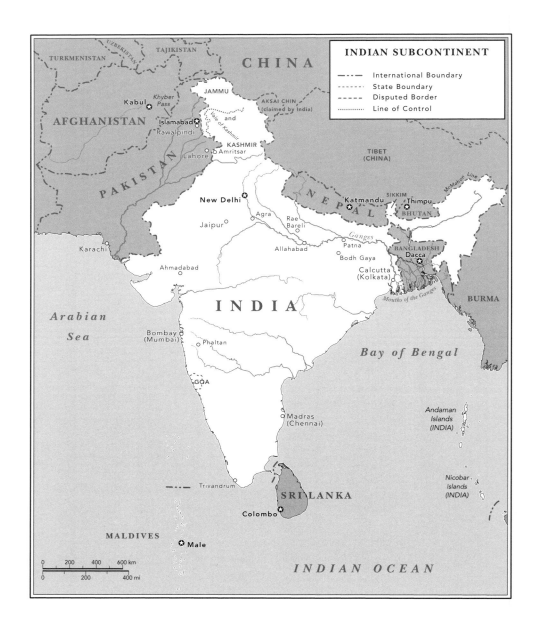

INDIAN SUBCONTINENT

International Boundary
State Boundary
Disputed Border
Line of Control

TURKMENISTAN
UZBEKISTAN
TAJIKISTAN
CHINA
JAMMU
Kabul
Khyber Pass
AKSAI CHIN (claimed by India)
AFGHANISTAN
Islamabad
Rawalpindi
Vale of Kashmir
and
KASHMIR
TIBET (CHINA)
Lahore
Amritsar
McMahon Line
PAKISTAN
New Delhi
NEPAL
Katmandu
SIKKIM
Thimpu
Jaipur
Agra
BHUTAN
Rae Bareli
Ganges
Karachi
Allahabad
Patna
BANGLADESH
Dacca
Ahmadabad
Bodh Gaya
Calcutta (Kolkata)
INDIA
Mouths of the Ganges
BURMA
Arabian Sea
Bombay (Mumbai)
Phaltan
Bay of Bengal
GOA
Madras (Chennai)
Andaman Islands (INDIA)
Nicobar Islands (INDIA)
Trivandrum
SRI LANKA
Colombo
MALDIVES
Male
INDIAN OCEAN

0 200 400 600 km
0 200 400 mi

THE GREATER GAME

1

A Tryst with More Than Destiny

On a sunny day in February 1958, during my first visit to India, I witnessed a democratic election. It was not one of the general elections I was to cover later in the Indian Union, when as many as a half-billion people or more were eligible to vote. It was a local election in the large dusty village of Phaltan, North Satara District, state of Maharashtra, more than 250 kilometres southeast of Bombay via winding roads through the Western Ghats or hills and Pune, then spelled Poona and a less crowded city than it is today.

A few hundred men wearing either dirty white dhotis – extended loincloths – or baggy homespun trousers, and women in faded green, yellow, red, or orange saris, pressed together in separate long lines. They were waiting on the equivalent of the village green, except that it was stark tan, to cast ballots for members of the Phaltan municipal council. The almost certain winners were candidates backed by the former Maharajah of Phaltan, a short stout man who had become the Congress Party boss in the small, old, princely state after trading in his elephants for the village's first jeep.

Still, I thought to myself how splendid it was that poor, illiterate peasants could take part in democracy in this seemingly remote setting. I was startled when a man standing in line to vote abruptly asked me, "Why can't Negroes do this in your country?"

To disbelieving stares, I stammered a reply to the effect that discriminatory voting requirements in states of the American South were almost gone, and black persons in the United States enjoyed the same privileged franchise as these Indian villagers. The man's question in Marathi and my answer in English were translated by Bonbehari Nimbkar, a progressive farmer in Phaltan and the son of wealthy parents in Bombay. A decade earlier Bon and I had roomed together at George School, a Quaker prep school outside Newtown, Pennsylvania, one of America's oldest villages.

In 1958 I couldn't be sure whether Phaltan's untouchables (now called *dalits*), the poorest and most despised people in the village, were voting as freely as caste Hindus. But the unexpected exchange taught me two lessons early on in my encounters with Asia.

One was that the sceptical, patronizing attitude taken by many Westerners toward people in economically poor countries exercising their democratic rights is unjustified as well as unhelpful. The other lesson was that people living in countries on every continent hold something precious in common: they are shaping, or trying to shape, national destinies.

India was not then, and is certainly not now, the only Asian country where people have the right to vote and do vote in meaningful elections. But if one Asian country symbolizes democracy, it is India as its one billion people enter a new century with thirteen parliamentary elections behind them. Whether or not democracy will ultimately succeed in India is another matter – India may also illustrate better than any other country anywhere how imperfect democracy can be. But popular elections somehow work in India, as do democratic institutions, even if much else doesn't.

This phenomenon is at the root of a race that Americans hear virtually nothing about any more, even after India exploded five nuclear bombs underground, including a thermonuclear device, in May 1998. It is the race between the two most populous countries of Asia and the world: democratic India and Communist China.

More than a half-century after India kept what Jawaharlal Nehru, its first prime minister, called "a tryst with destiny" by peacefully winning independence from the British Raj on 15 August 1947, this race is more important than ever. More than a half-century after Chinese Communists took power on 1 October 1949, following a massive civil war with Chinese Nationalists who then retreated to Taiwan, comparisons between the two leviathans are more than ever in order.

Yet many Americans and other Westerners wouldn't dream of putting India in the same league as China. Their television and newspapers condition them to think of China as a big if sometimes puzzling story, and of India as a marginal and often irritating story. China has long been a major, direct concern of U.S. foreign policy and much American business, India a minor, distant concern. Many East Asians, particularly, also think of India and the Subcontinent as separate, and apart from the rest of their continent. Even if they too are trying to make democracy work, that's where they would prefer to keep India. While other Asians fear Chinese aggression, they resent Indian intrusion.

But China appears to be changing for the worse. And there is impressive evidence that India is changing for the better.

The Chinese threat to stability and freedom in Asia and the Pacific is growing despite American and Asian efforts to "engage constructively" the unyielding Communist dictatorship in Beijing. Indian voters have put a new set of rulers in New Delhi who are eager not only to raise economic levels at home but also to work collectively with the United States and other powers to prevent China's domination of Asia.

The race between modern-day India and China goes back to a contrast in philosophies that could hardly be greater. During the Indian independence struggle, Mohandas K. Gandhi relied on the religious concept of ahimsa or non-violence. During the Chinese civil war, Mao Zedong held the materialist conviction that "power grows out of the barrel of a gun." Other long-standing differences between the two countries – the two civilizations – are also dramatic.

India is a democracy and China a dictatorship. Indians enjoy the rule of law, although government has often overridden law, and Chinese largely do not. India is an increasingly pluralistic society, while Chinese society is still monolithic. India has more divisions based on language, religion, or caste than does China, where one race – the Han, meaning Chinese – is more dominant than any single group is in India. But China has separatist movements – in Tibet and Xinjiang – as India does.

Farmers in India were free and on their own from the onset of independence, although they long received low government priority. Only in recent years have China's farmers escaped communes and other forms of rigid government control. Over many years China's economy has grown faster and attracted much more foreign investment than India's economy. That is the central reason why most of the rest of the world, notably including the United States under President Bill Clinton, has paid much more attention to China than to India. But the Chinese economy slowed down steadily after the onset of the Asian economic crisis in mid-1997, while other East Asian economies stayed above crisis conditions or in time started rising above them, and India's real economic growth rate at the turn of the century may have exceeded China's.

There are more striking similarities between India and China, however, than there are differences.

Both countries have huge populations: India's, one billion at the end of the twentieth century, will surpass China's, then 1.3 billion, before the middle of the twenty-first century. Finding enough food for all these people is a chronic problem in both countries. Despite their economic growth, both India and China are still mostly poor. Both lack sufficient oil, power, and transport. Both have many engineers and scientists but suffer shortages of skilled managers and technocrats, with state-owned enterprises holding back both. In both India and China, economic gaps between different regions are growing rapidly.

India has a defining religion in Hinduism that puts one group, high-caste Brahmins, above all others. China has a similarly elitist set of beliefs in Confucianism that, in its latest guise, puts Communist Party members above all others. As outgrowths of these value systems, India and China each have a strong central bureaucracy that has effectively run the country but not efficiently. But political power is starting to devolve to the states of India and the provinces of China.

Both India and China have national leaders of normal human stature following the giants of earlier years: Mahatma Gandhi, Nehru, and Indira Gandhi; Mao, Zhou Enlai, and Deng Xiaoping. One political party has long dominated each country. But here a new crucial difference emerges. India's Congress Party has fragmented and lost power under the Nehru family dynasty, and the Hindu nationalist Bharatiya Janata or Indian People's Party is consolidating itself as the nation's new paramount political force. China's Communist Party may have started to fragment but it still holds absolute power, and what might replace it has not yet taken shape.

Corruption has become a hallmark of both Indian and Chinese politics, a key reason for the growth in both countries of popular cynicism about rulers. But again their two paths have diverged in recent years. Indian voters successfully rejected the Congress Party in elections in 1996, 1998, and 1999 – after doing so earlier in 1977 and 1989 – and put the BJP in power partly on its promise to fight corruption. Chinese pro-democracy protesters in Beijing's Tiananmen Square in 1989 failed to oust or even change the Communist Party, and tanks and troops of the People's Liberation Army overwhelmed them.

Indians traditionally see their country as Bharat, the centre of the world. Chinese traditionally see their country as the Middle Kingdom, the centre of the world. India is striving to become a superpower, which most Westerners find irrational. China is striving to become a superpower, which most Westerners find reasonable. Both India and China threaten smaller neighbours – Pakistan and Taiwan, respectively, are the most obvious examples but not the only ones. Both India and China claim substantial areas of the Himalayas, the world's highest mountains, where their armies fought each other in 1962.

Each country has a large, growing, and increasingly modern army, navy, and air force. Each projects its missiles far beyond its immediate neighbourhood. Each is a formidable nuclear power, although India did not avow this status until 1998, thirty-four years after China did, and its nuclear-weapons development trails China's.

Finally, India has considered the United States a rival and a potential enemy even though both countries are democracies, and U.S. moral support for Indian independence and economic aid once it was established gave major boosts to India. And China has considered the United States a rival and potential enemy despite the friendly relationship initiated by President Richard M. Nixon, and the "strategic partnership" sought by Clinton when he went to Tiananmen Square in June 1998, nine years after the massacre of hundreds of pro-democracy students there.

But, once more, a significant difference has developed. China's attitude toward the United States is hardening, as is the attitude of many Americans toward China, as points of potential conflict come into focus. India's attitude toward the United States is softening to the extent that mutual recognition of areas of potential co-operation – political, economic, and strategic – informs U.S. policy under President George W. Bush.

Despite Clinton's tilt to China and his sharp criticism of India's open development of nuclear weapons, his visit to India in March 2000 marked the beginning of what he and Prime Minister Atal Bihari Vajpayee called "a closer and qualitatively new relationship" between the world's most powerful democracy and its most populous one.

In an extraordinary "Vision Statement," largely ignored by American journalists who focused on Clinton's viewing the Taj Mahal with his daughter, Chelsea, and on whether the president also would visit Pakistan, the two leaders declared: "In the new century, India and the United States will be partners in peace, with a common interest in and complementary responsibility for ensuring regional and international security. We will engage in regular consultations on, and work together for, strategic stability in Asia and beyond ... the United States and India are and will be allies in the cause of democracy."

Despite this unprecedented joint commitment, and the keen interest in India as a prospective major partner shown by Bush and his advisers months before the presidential election of 7 November 2000 and its result thirty-six days later, India, like China, is difficult for Americans, other Westerners, and other Asians to understand.

Nonetheless, it is apparent that China's advantages over India may not be as great as many have presumed. Unresolved problems, widening gaps, and popular discontent are clear and present dangers in both countries.

But a Communist dictatorship continues to rule China without regard for democracy and human rights, and with a burning ambition to reestablish historic Chinese hegemony over wide stretches of the most populous continent and adjoining waters, from the Korean Peninsula to Central Asia, and from the East China Sea to the Persian Gulf.

India's thirteenth parliamentary election in September 1999 strengthened a new ruling coalition committed to respecting democracy and improving poor living conditions as well as reviving Hindu culture, and anxious to contain a perceived threat from China in order to maintain Indian pre-eminence in the Subcontinent.

Cracks in the unity of either or both civilizations may prove more decisive than democracy in India or dictatorship in China. It is impossible to ignore the military threats, conventional and nuclear, each poses to other countries, and the distinct possibility that Indian and Chinese arms will clash again over disputed lands and spheres of influence. But these contingencies reinforce rather than contradict an inescapable conclusion.

A Greater Game started near the end of the most turbulent century in the history of the human race and will continue well into the twenty-first century. In two ways, it goes far beyond the Great Game played by the British Raj in the nineteenth and early twentieth centuries to keep India out of the hands of Russian imperialists, and described by Rudyard Kipling in his novel *Kim*.

The Greater Game involves political, economic, and cultural forces as well as military and intelligence moves. And it encompasses all of the vast and vital region of Asia and the Pacific: the Indian Subcontinent a half-century after independence; the People's Republic of China a half-century after the Communist victory; Russia after the Cold War; Japan and the Koreas after the Second World War; Indonesia, Thailand, and the other countries of Southeast Asia after the Vietnam war; even countries of Central Asia and the Middle East, including Israel; and certainly the United States and the other Western countries – Canada, Australia, and New Zealand – on the Pacific Rim.

This is a bigger ball game, in short, than just the United States and China. As even the Sinophile Clinton and the Indian nationalist Vajpayee came to realize, the time has come to talk about a democratic alliance or something close to an alliance, a word long shunned in Asia and the Pacific, where collective security is conspicuous by its absence. It would not be a Sino-U.S. alliance, which Clinton in his multifarious relations with the Chinese leadership seemed to have had in mind as the end result of a "strategic partnership." It would be a joint security arrangement directed against the Communist dictatorship still brazenly exploiting Clinton's embrace as a key part of its calculated scheme to make China a superpower early in the new century. Logically, India – whose BJP government prefers not a formal military alliance but "collective engagement" with the United States and other Asian and Western powers – would be a major, essential part of such an undertaking "in the cause of democracy," whatever it is called, in order to restrain the ambitions of China across Asia.

Let there be no mistake: China is seeking to emerge rapidly from Asia's chaos as the undisputed lord of 60 per cent of the world's population. Clinton obliged the autocrats in Beijing by downgrading democratic Japan as the most important U.S. ally in Asia and the Pacific, at first condemning democratic India for meeting the Chinese threat with nuclear weapons, failing to take advantage of the democratic potential in Indonesia after the fall of President Suharto, and siding with the Chinese Communist leadership against democratic Taiwan in ruling out any formula for coexistence except blind adherence to "one China." A de facto U.S. alliance with a supreme China would undercut democracy and democratic capitalism, and make economic recovery more difficult throughout Asia. Collective security measures against genuine threats – particularly the foremost one posed by China – would be impossible.

Asian nations in the past have balked at even talking about an alliance out of reluctance to be openly identified with the United States in their defence. This is even true of some countries with bilateral defence agreements with the United States. During the Cold War, India took the lead in insisting on non-alignment with both the United States and the Soviet Union, although in practice this holier-than-thou stance heavily favoured Moscow. But the new Indian leaders, along with feeling the need to make a nuclear statement, consider Nehruvian non-alignment "not very relevant," in the words of Lal Krishna Advani, Prime Minister Vajpayee's closest political associate and probable successor, who said this in an interview with me six years before the Bharatiya Janata Party came to power.

New Indian and U.S. interest in strategic cooperation not only increases the possibility of wide-ranging, flexible security measures coming into being, but also enhances the inviting prospect of a democratic alliance in Asia and the Pacific.

Despite the new ties with India forged by Clinton, such an alliance was inconceivable as long as a U.S. president used China, and was used by China, for his own purposes and China's. It is feasible with George W. Bush, who has made plain he considers China not a "strategic partner" but a "strategic competitor," who sees democracy as "the foundation for a better and more stable world," and who is seeking creative new forms of collective security with U.S. allies. The more tough-minded U.S. approach to threats to peace, the challenge of international terrorism, the growing Chinese danger, and the deep economic holes that Asian nations dug themselves into in the late 1990s are transforming the Asia-Pacific equation.

These nations need collective defence, including new or strengthened ties with the United States, in order to gain both protection and time. Increasingly, they also recognize democracy as a common denominator. Chinese dictators want nothing to do with democracy. But democracy is comfortably familiar to Indians. They have been at it for a long time, and after many discouraging setbacks democracy may finally be working, however imperfectly, the way it should in India.

2

India Beyond Midnight

Like most international flights into New Delhi, Swissair Flight 194 from Zurich touches down in the middle of the night. Most flights out of Delhi also take off in the dark lonely hours of early morning or late night, as if India is suspended in a black hole separate from the normal activities of the rest of the world. In or out, many planes are late, often by hours.

Surprisingly, my plane lands on schedule at twenty-five minutes before midnight of 31 May 1999. But in order to get from Baku, Azerbaijan, to the capital of India – a trip of three or four hours by a direct flight if there were one – I've had to catch a 4:40 AM flight of six and a half hours back to Zurich, from where I'd flown to Baku on the Caspian Sea one week earlier; wait six hours at the Zurich airport; and then fly for seven hours to Delhi: a total of nineteen and a half hours.

Since my first visit in 1958, I've experienced India many times and have lived in India nearly five years altogether. Prime Minister Indira Gandhi, for whom Delhi's airport is named, personally barred me in 1970 for more than seven years because she didn't like what I was reporting as a newspaper correspondent. I don't expect anything about India to be easy or direct or even logical as, with hundreds of others, I grope in the heat and dust and airport chaos of a May-June Delhi night searching for a car to take me to a hotel.

But I find on this second of two visits in the 1990s that changes that were becoming clear in January–February 1992 are becoming profound. And it occurs to me that India had only appeared to arrive at midnight, instead became lost following a roundabout route, and only now has overcome a seemingly insurmountable barrier to go beyond midnight toward the dawn of a new day.

Jawaharlal Nehru eloquently proclaimed India's independence in the middle of the night of 14–15 August 1947: "At the stroke of the midnight hour, when the world sleeps, India will awake to life and freedom." But only at the turn of a new century and a new millennium is India starting to "step out from the old to the new," as the man who became its first prime minister put it in his famous midnight speech. His timing was off by a half-century.

One of history's great ironies is that this didn't happen until the Indian people put the Nehru family dynasty behind them (Nehru, his daughter Indira Gandhi, her son Rajiv Gandhi, and his Italian-born widow Sonia Gandhi) and turned to Hindu nationalists who were widely assumed to represent India's past, and India's worst. But it is not only the change from the Nehrus and the Congress Party to the Hindus and the Bharatiya Janata Party that defines the new India.

It is also the change from Pakistan to China as India's main adversary and the country India is measured against. Indians have looked on China as their natural rival at least since the Himalayan war between the two countries four decades ago. It is long past time for the rest of the world to stop equating India and Pakistan – politically, economically, or militarily – and to start realizing that India under the BJP is ready and willing to play a major role with the United States and other Asian and Western powers in preventing China from dominating Asia and the western Pacific.

The Nehru dynasty stood squarely in the way of India's fulfilling the "destiny" set out by Pandit Nehru. During the thirty-seven of the first fifty-six years of independence when he, Indira, and Rajiv were prime ministers – indeed, until nearly the end of the twentieth century – India did not really reach midnight or life and freedom. Instead, India lost its way in a maze of red tape, hypocrisy, famine, ties to the Soviet Union, wars with Pakistan, and the pervasive arrogance of one family. A population that grew to one billion, and showed in one election after another how to make democracy work, could not escape deep and widespread poverty.

This began to change only when more and more Indians realized their destiny did not lie with the Nehrus but with the nature of their predominantly Hindu civilization – as long as the tolerant side of human nature was encouraged instead of the intolerant. This is a big "if" in any society but particularly in India, where religious, caste, language, and ethnic lines are tightly drawn.

This condition explains why what happened a few months before the beginning of the twenty-first century was a large miracle in a complex place. But most of the world paid little attention or got it wrong.

More than 350 million people in an economically poor Asian country voted freely. Actually, it was the thirteenth such democratic election in fifty-two years: the voters of India have elected a Parliament that many times since they won independence in 1947. The election in September–October 1999 was the biggest miracle of all because it enabled Indians to complete the transfer of power from one major political party to another through the ballot box instead of the machine gun. They did so not by sharpening the hostile edges of competing communities in an infinitely diverse society but by smoothing them with a new kind of coalition politics.

China has come nowhere near such an achievement. On the contrary, in 1999 it celebrated fifty years of unbroken Communist dictatorship with a huge display of triumphalism. Indonesia's chance to build a democratic society nearly drowned in a series of bloodbaths ordained by the army, and it is starting again almost from scratch. Japan, prosperous and democratic beyond most Asians' dreams, appears thoroughly confused about where it wants to go in the new century. The day before India installed its new popularly elected government, Pakistan's army carried out a military coup. The failure of Pakistani democracy, and very likely of Pakistan itself, got more headlines in the West than the historic Indian election.

India took too long to move from the Congress Party to the Hindu nationalist BJP as the paramount political force it needs in order to keep its many religious, caste, language, and ethnic parts from flying apart. Whether the BJP with its built-in religious and cultural biases can perform this essential task is still uncertain. Partly because of the decades wasted by the Nehrus, much can still go wrong to arrest or disrupt the forward progress of the world's most populous – and often disappointing – democracy.

But over the years, against daunting odds, Indians have never given up on finding the right democratic track.

Following my experience with the 1958 Phaltan election, in 1962 I covered India's third general election. Over several days I saw women and men wearing faded but still colourful saris and dirty white dhotis line up for hours in a number of villages, cities, and states to mark X's on paper ballots.

Because most voters couldn't read or write, they first made thumbprints to identify themselves when they reached the head of a line. Then they stepped behind a clumsily erected cloth curtain to peruse a list of pictorial symbols on the ballot standing for the candidates for the Lok Sabha or lower house of Parliament and a state legislature – a bullock cart, a spinning wheel, an oil lamp – and made their choices. Finally an official at the polling station stamped an indelible mark on the voter's hand. This showed that he or she had exercised the right to an input in India's future, and couldn't do it again that day.

Something in the bearing of most individuals when they put the carefully folded ballot in the box – a gleam in the eye, a straightening of the back, a self-conscious walk – reflected an inner realization of the importance of the act. Each person did count, and continued to count.

In 1967, three years after Nehru's death and one year after his daughter Indira Gandhi became prime minister, Indian voters protested for the first time against the Congress Party of the emerging family dynasty. It was the beginning of a process of political attrition that should have changed India in five or ten years at most but lasted thirty-two years.

Poor illiterate Indians all over the country patiently waited both to hear what candidates had to say and then to vote. They literally sat in the dusty streets of countless villages and towns for the campaign rally of one party, then moved a few hundred feet to sit down in the dust for a few more hours and listen to another party's speakers. They all talked among themselves about the election. If they could read, they read all they could. When the time came to make themselves heard, they did so with resounding selectivity, dismissing from office many central and state government ministers who had betrayed their trust.

A little more than a year earlier, I'd asked Information Minister Indira Gandhi – her family name came from her estranged husband Feroze Gandhi, a member of Parliament – why the government was deliberately delaying the spread of television in India beyond Delhi. She replied frankly and petulantly that widespread access to TV would raise the people's expectations dangerously.

Mohandas Gandhi – unrelated to Indira or Rajiv or Sonia in any way – had sensed the yearnings of the Indian masses. He knew they wanted a say in the way they were ruled, and they knew he knew. It was not simply a matter of Gandhi being a saint. The Mahatma observed: "Those who say that religion has nothing to do with politics do not know what religion means." In Gandhi's view, God is Truth, and Truth is essential in politics.

Gandhian non-violence defined the struggle for a free India. But it was an India little changed from the India of the British Raj. A country of "clarks, coolies, and commission agents," so the saying went, became a country of "clarks, coolies, and Congresswallahs." Moreover, the healthy connection between religion and politics that Gandhi engendered often turned vicious with brazen exploitation of religious and Hindu-caste loyalties and differences.

Sarvepalli Radhakrishnan, the Hindu philosopher and teacher who served as president of India, pointed out both the positive and negative sides of the Hinduism defining Indian civilization. In a 1961 Harvard lecture entitled "Fellowship of the Spirit," he observed: "The religious tradition of India ... has throughout its history been faithful to the idea of unity in diversity. It respects distinctions and autonomous individualities of social groups so long as they cooperate and fit into the social pattern which has been woven across the centuries." But in his book *The Hindu Way of Life*, first published in 1927 and continuously reprinted, Radhakrishnan wrote of Indians: "Our class conflicts are due to the fact that a warm living sense of unity does not bind together the different groups ... We are today drifting, not advancing, waiting for the future to turn up. There is a lack of vitality, a spiritual flagging."

Which side of Hinduism would prevail was starting to become a key question when I returned to India in January 1992, soon after the election of the last Congress Party government, the only one lacking a clear parliamentary majority. India's two modern lifelines had been suddenly and unexpectedly cut.

The one to the Nehru dynasty snapped when Rajiv Gandhi, voted out of office in 1989, was blown up by a terrorist bomb in the south during the May 1991 campaign for India's tenth parliamentary election, six and a half years after his mother's assassination. Delhi's economic and military axis with Moscow, carefully nurtured by the Nehrus, was severed when the August 1991 Stalinist coup against Mikhail Gorbachev failed and the Soviet Union subsequently collapsed following the loss of its empire in Eastern Europe.

As my old Indian journalist friend Pran Sabharwal suddenly exclaimed as we sipped fresh orange juice on his verandah under the north Indian winter sun, "India is in a crisis!"

In this extended crisis, Lal Krishna Advani, then the leader of the BJP and the official leader of the opposition, almost casually anticipated India's turning away from the Nehrus and toward his party, perhaps as soon as the next election. He seemed like a tall and pleasant older school teacher as he sat at his desk at home and talked with me. Above his head was a framed photograph of Sardar Vallabhai Patel, the no-nonsense Congressman of peasant stock who many believe should have been India's first prime minister, but who had been compelled to take second place to the sophisticated Jawaharlal Nehru when India became independent.

Advani gently rejected the widely held notion of the BJP as "fundamentalist" but accepted its definition as "Hindu nationalist." He emphasized that his party was committed to the nation's secular constitution – "Theocracy is alien to India's culture" – and denied that it intended to make minority Muslims second-class citizens. But, asserting that "the Hindu feels he's a second-class citizen," he made no apologies about the BJP's drive to reclaim the Ayodhya mosque in northcentral India that would be demolished by Hindu fanatics before the end of 1992. Advani said, "Religion gives ethical content to human behaviour." He didn't answer when I asked if he agreed with the link between religion and politics delineated by Mahatma Gandhi, who was assassinated in 1948 by a former member of the Rashtriya Swayamsevak Sangh, the militant Hindu organization that gave rise to the BJP's nationalism.

The BJP leader dismissed the Nehru dynasty as "marginal" to Indian culture and "unhealthy for democracy and the Congress Party." He said the party's past socialist economic policies, before the reforms introduced by the Congress government then in power, were "so wrong and we were so critical." When I asked Advani about matters of war and peace, and insurgencies against India, his voice took on a steely tone: "If it's war in the Pun-

jab and Kashmir, it's a proxy war waged by Pakistan." Before his remark
that Nehruvian non-alignment was irrelevant, Advani advocated unequivocally a declared nuclear deterrent for India. More than six years before
India did make such a declaration with its nuclear tests in May 1998, he
said this was not because Pakistan posed a nuclear threat – he didn't think
it did – but because Delhi would exercise "greater leverage in international affairs if India has nuclear power."

When I walked into the stifling heat of a Delhi June in 1999, it was shortly
before a BJP-led alliance of twenty-four parties headed by Prime Minister
Atal Bihari Vajpayee – now the moderate party leader, with his closest colleague Advani the home minister – won a decisive parliamentary majority.

In power then for fifteen months as a result of precedent-breaking but
shaky ties with regional parties, the BJP had taken India out of the nuclear
closet in response to a perceived Chinese threat. It had started to intensify
economic liberalization. Its new brand of coalition politics had begun to
give representation in Parliament to many Indians who might otherwise be
in the streets protesting. In the freezing cold of Himalayan ridges, Indian
troops, artillery, and planes were attacking Pakistan-based armed intruders
entering Indian-held Kashmir.

Pointing out the highlights of a terrain map of the remote combat zone,
Foreign Minister Jaswant Singh told me that India was determined to drive
out the intruders in the short term. In the long term, he volunteered, India
was ready and willing to explore "collective engagement" with the United
States and other nations aimed at strategic containment of China. One of
Prime Minister Vajpayee's confidantes, the tall courtly member of a Rajput
ruling family, left me in no doubt that the BJP was staking its reelection
hopes on quickly attaining its objective in the Kargil sector of Kashmir, but
without escalating fighting to a full-scale war.

I understood then that India was about to go beyond midnight. The
questions went beyond whether or not the BJP would keep power and
soften its hard, high-caste Hindu edge, and whether India's economic
reforms would become big enough and come soon enough to avert turmoil
among one billion people. They went deeper than the old questions of
whether or not India would break up, and whether another war with China
or Pakistan – which was on the verge of national failure – was inevitable.

Was Rabindranath Tagore, the rational Bengali poet, right when, like
Radhakrishnan, he warned even before independence that Indians were in
danger of getting stuck in "the dreary desert sand of dead habit?" Or was
India awakening at last, in its own ponderous and indecipherable way, in
what he had dared to call a "heaven of freedom?"

These questions had to do with India's very meaning. But in little more
than two years, they took on even wider and deeper relevance with India's
involvement in the global war against terrorism.

3

"Terrorism Is Terrorism"

On 11 September 2001, when word reached New Delhi that suicide bombers had crashed hijacked jetliners into the World Trade Center towers in New York City and the Pentagon outside Washington, D.C., the government of India said simply: "We stand with the U.S."

It was a historic statement. It would not have been made even eighteen months earlier and reflected a sea change within the world's most populous democracy, and in how the world's most powerful democracy and Delhi viewed each other. But within hours India felt like a bride left standing at the altar. The United States, the object of its new-found affection, seemed to have suddenly eloped with India's long-time rival, Pakistan, in anticipation of fighting a war in Afghanistan, the gateway to the Subcontinent.

The situation was not simple but complicated, as love stories and wars usually are. But despite the frustrations created by Pakistan, one billion Indians could be confident that the Bush administration remained loyal to its strategic thinking because of – not despite – the daunting challenge of international terrorism. Indeed, when India was dramatically targeted by Pakistan-based terrorists twenty days after 9/11, President George W. Bush asserted: "Terrorism is terrorism."

He meant that there is no such thing as good terrorists and bad terrorists; that all terrorists need to be rooted out whether they attack America, India, Israel, or any other country. But perceptions of terrorists do differ. Americans and many other people were shocked more by the deliberate destruction of the World Trade Center towers, causing 3,000 deaths, than they had been, or would be, by a suicide bomber blowing up a bus in Jerusalem; by a suicide squad attacking India's Parliament on 13 December 2001; or by another that killed forty people in an assault on the legislative building in Srinagar, the capital of Indian-held Kashmir – the event on 1 October that provoked Bush to equate all kinds of terrorism. Similarly, defeating the fanatical Taliban protectors of the Al Qaeda leadership in three months in Afghanistan is not the same as years of effort to rid the world of Saddam Hussein and his weapons of mass destruction in Iraq. Despite the Taliban's direct connection to Pakistan, getting rid of them in Afghanistan is different from reducing the influence of military and religious elements in Pakistan, an influence that effectively made Pakistan a terrorist state even while it posed as a "crucial ally" – a common journalistic description – of the United States in the struggle against terrorism.

Bush's comment proved to be deadly accurate before the end of 2001. Three battles against terrorism, politically related and geographically close, but previously seen as largely separate, converged as strikingly parallel actions in a world war against terror.

The United States, aided by Britain, Canada, Australia, and other allies, went after Al Qaeda terrorists and the Taliban regime in Afghanistan. Israel struck back at Hamas and Islamic Jihad terrorists and at the Palestinian Authority in the West Bank and Gaza. India threatened to retaliate against Pakistan-based Islamic terrorist organizations and the Pakistani military regime. Indian armed forces were built up so rapidly that many people did not realize India was taking part in a common war against terrorism and feared only an India-Pakistan nuclear exchange.

After the terrorist assault on the Indian Parliament building in New Delhi, resulting in the death of the five heavily armed attackers and nine other people, the Bush administration increased pressure on Pakistan to curb the activities of Islamic militants seeking to detach Kashmir from India. Even while lauding Pakistan's role as an ally, the administration made plain, as it had since taking office in January 2001, that it favoured India over Pakistan. But Indian jealousy turned to angry resolve when evidence revealed that the goal of the assault on the heart of Indian democracy on 13 December – the equivalent of 11 September to Indians – was to kill government leaders, and the attack could be traced to Pakistani military intelligence. The United States had little choice but to intensify its pressure on Pakistan to stop the operations of two organizations – Lashkar-e-Taiba (or Army of the Poor) and Jaish-e-Muhammad (or Army of Muhammad) – and at the same time caution India not to go to war.

In reality, India had no intention of going to war at that time, as long as Pakistan arrested these groups' leaders and members and froze their funds, which is what the military regime finally did do at the end of 2001 under U.S. prodding. But India had made its point dramatically: military action against terrorist bases on Pakistani territory or Pakistan itself would be an option as long as organized terrorism continued. Delhi pressed this point even harder after another bloody terrorist attack in Kashmir in May 2002.

But by early 2003 it was increasingly clear that at least some high-ranking Pakistani military officers, realizing that they were not going to get what they wanted from the United States for ostensibly joining the fight against terrorism – mainly all Kashmir – were again aiding, comforting, and possibly directing terrorists within their country as well as Afghanistan. Armed militants easily crossed the mountainous border in both directions despite Pakistani assurances to the United States to the contrary. New video-taped messages from supreme Al Qaeda terrorist Osama bin Laden strongly indicated that he had escaped from Afghanistan and was alive and well and living in Pakistan, quite possibly under the protection of the notorious Inter-Services Intelligence (ISI), Pakistan's military intelligence.

Resentful Indians complained that Washington gave Pakistani leader Pervez Musharraf unjustified credit for closing down terrorist operations. Out of deference to Pakistan, U.S. officials kept close defence and intelligence co-operation between India and the United States a virtual secret. Nevertheless, the United States stood with India as a major democratic ally as much as India stood with the United States.

India and Pakistan accounted for one of the few positive foreign-policy achievements of President Bill Clinton during his two terms. He went to Delhi in March 2000 and ended the longstanding, dangerously counter-productive U.S. equation of the two countries that had gained independence with the end of British rule of undivided India. He proclaimed, with the new Hindu nationalist prime minister Atal Bihari Vajpayee, that the United States and India were "allies in the cause of democracy." But Clinton did not give up his vision of the United States and China as "strategic partners," and he opposed deployment by India of its nuclear weapons.

Bush and his team of tough-minded foreign-policy advisers in the White House, the Pentagon, and the State Department, although not always thinking alike, have quietly moved the United States much closer to India than the intuitive Clinton. Although they have sought Beijing's cooperation in the struggle against global terrorism, they have retained their perception of China as a "strategic competitor." When Bush met Vajpayee at the White House on 9 November 2001, he committed the United States to a "fundamentally different relationship with India" – the clearest sign of many that he accepted India as a friendly de facto member of the nuclear club.

Indeed, sanctions imposed after India's 1998 nuclear tests have come to an end. Senior officials of the Bush administration moved quickly in late 2001, even before the terrorist assault on Parliament, to sign agreements with India on regular defence consultations, joint military exercises, and the sale of U.S. military equipment, including fighter planes, challenging Russia as India's main military supplier. In May 2002, U.S. paratroopers had a bird's eye view of the Taj Mahal as they jumped over Agra in an exercise with Indian paratroopers. Later in the year, Indian troops took part in exercises in Alaska.

One reason given for the two suitors now embracing is that a strong military relationship deters India from engaging with Pakistan, due to escalating conflict over Kashmir or terrorism, in what would be the fourth war between what are now nuclear powers. India, however, has acted responsibly and firmly on these fronts – most notably in mid-1999 in the face of a major Pakistani-backed infiltration of Kashmir, as well as after attacks on the Kashmir legislature, Parliament, and women and children at a military base in Kashmir – and thereby earned U.S. approbation.

The real reason for the new and profoundly important relationship between India and the United States – still largely unnoticed in 2001, 2002, and early 2003 by the American people and media – does not have to do directly with Kashmir or even with the unexpected war against terrorism. It has to do with the expected or at least potential war against China.

The United States under the second President Bush is making India, Japan, and Israel its main allies outside Britain, Canada, and its other partners in the North Atlantic Treaty Organization, some of which – such as France and Germany during the U.S.-led drive to disarm Saddam Hussein – may turn out to be less reliable or even disruptive in combatting the challenges of the early twenty-first century. Russia, apart from strengthening its ties with NATO, could complement this select group of Asian powers, but only if Moscow does not play a double game with China and the United States, does not delay collective action in Iraq and against other dangerous outlaw regimes, does not hamper a U.S. missile-defence system, and does make democracy work. In contrast to Russia, India has joined Japan in welcoming Bush's proposed missile defence, calling it "a strategic and technological inevitability." In addition, India, Japan, and Israel are all democracies, whatever their imperfections, and Indian democracy is finally working better than it did during decades of domination by the anti-American Nehru-Gandhi family dynasty, with coalition politics now reflecting the country's many parties and peoples.

The second Bush administration would have taken steps toward an alliance or collective-security arrangements among democratic nations in Asia and the Pacific even if the war against terrorism had not been forced upon it by the horrific events of 11 September. Along with the U.S. Pacific fleet, Japan and India are natural bulwarks against China. I see no persuasive reason to believe that changing Communist leaders in China will rein in their evident drive toward superpower status and wide-ranging "hegemony" – what they accuse America of pursuing – by joining economic globalization rather than just profiting from it to build up their country's military forces.

Intervening global war against terrorist networks can slow down or even cripple execution of the longer-range, still mostly undefined strategy to prevent China from expanding its already broad sphere of control or influence. Or fighting and overcoming international terrorists and rogue regimes can speed up and enhance an alliance for democracy against an arrogant Chinese leadership practising state terrorism toward China's peoples, particularly Buddhists in Tibet and Muslims in Xinjiang. After initial uncertainty, the Bush administration chose the fast-track, anti-all terrorists route, especially when Israeli-Palestinian and Indian-Pakistani relations sharply deteriorated.

Instead of putting the onus mainly on Israel for making concessions for peace with hostile Palestinians, Bush joined Prime Minister Ariel Sharon in condemning terrorist attacks on innocent people and in rejecting Yasser Arafat's Palestinian leadership. By putting aside the demands of Arab nations in the vague "coalition" against terrorists to put pressure on Israel, he avoided the double standard of leading the American attack on Osama bin Laden's Al Qaeda terrorists while blaming Israel for going after terrorists.

Japan's reluctance to do anything that might be construed as aggressive – similar to Germany's – presents a different kind of problem. By encouraging Japan to contribute naval combat ships to the Arabian Sea flotilla during the new war in Afghanistan and later the Iraq conflict, Bush persuaded the Japanese to take one more step away from the "no-war" constitution that would prevent their participation in a meaningful Pacific alliance beyond the U.S.-Japan mutual security treaty. North Korea's defiant threat to make nuclear warheads for its missiles was an even greater incentive for Japan to do more to defend itself. As for the perpetual puzzle of Russia, its joining the war on terrorism was offset by its resistance to collective action to remove Iraq's biological, chemical, and potential nuclear weapons.

But the most critical test, or tests, in the immediate wake of 11 September involved India, Pakistan, and Afghanistan. Although Bush initially lost time by listening to Pakistan's General Musharraf, he passed the tests with flying colours before the end of 2001 by providing decisive air support to Northern Alliance fighters who broke the Taliban's back in Afghanistan, ignoring or rejecting self-serving demands by Pakistan, and forging close if unheralded ties with India that will have an impact on South Asia – and all Asia – long after the war against terrorism is won.

For more than a thousand years, Afghanistan has been the gateway to India, the route of conquerors and would-be conquerors who made historic impacts on the Subcontinent. So it is at the beginning of the twenty-first century. With all the vivid words and especially pictures that came out of Afghanistan in late 2001, 2002, and 2003, Westerners, and even other

Asians, cannot fit Afghanistan into what they imagine a country to be. Yet it is as true as ever that to grasp what is going on in India, one must appreciate Afghanistan.

I first experienced Afghanistan when driving across the rugged, primitive country on mostly non-existent roads in 1961 and nearly not making it to the Khyber Pass and the plains of the Subcontinent. Later in the 1960s, I watched in justifiable disbelief as under King Muhammad Zahir Shah the Afghans went through a brief period of modernization – building roads, allowing women to go unveiled, even holding constitutional elections.

However, a series of tragic events jolted them back to the Middle Ages: a Soviet-backed coup in 1973 overthrowing the king, a Soviet-backed Communist coup in 1978, a decade of Soviet invasion and insurgency by U.S.-armed mujahedeen before the intruders left in 1989, three more years of war against a brutal Communist regime, civil war among victorious mujahedeen, Pakistan's creation of an army of benighted Islamic extremists called the Taliban that conquered most of the country by 1996, and then a steady, unresisted invasion by Al Qaeda terrorists led by Osama bin Laden. Finally, on 9 September 2001, in what may well have been the signal for what happened on the other side of the world two days later, Ahmed Shah Massoud, the legendary commander of the Northern Alliance who had defeated the Red Army in the Panshir Valley northeast of Kabul and had blocked total Taliban conquest of Afghanistan, was killed in a terrorist suicide bombing.

But the Afghans are tough tribesmen who for 2,500 years have fought invaders going back to Alexander the Great. They inhabit the rough land of the Hindu Kush – the Killer of Hindus – and they come by their suspicion of *ferengis* (foreigners) naturally since Genghis Khan came close to obliterating Afghanistan in the thirteenth century. Three times in the nineteenth and early twentieth centuries they defeated would-be British conquerors who were smart enough to make Afghanistan a classic buffer state between the Raj in India and Russian imperialists in Central Asia in what the British called "The Great Game."

After 9/11 the Afghans quickly adapted to a phase of a Greater Game put in play by the Americans. Their country shared only devastation with the World Trade Center. But they seized the way out of oppressive Taliban rule that was blasted open by American bombs and a temporary American invasion by CIA agents, special forces, a few Marine battalions, and, later, by elite paratroopers supplemented by British Marines and Canadian troops – all aimed at destroying Al Qaeda and its Taliban protectors.

The Afghans are still finding it hard to rebuild a nation that Sir Henry Rawlinson, the first Westerner to describe Afghanistan in detail, called in 1875 "a mere collection of tribes." But now, as then and in centuries past, peace among Afghan tribes – the Pushtuns, the Tajiks, the Uzbeks, the Turkmen, the Hazara descendents of Genghis Khan – is inextricably linked to stability in the Subcontinent. These victorious but wary armed tribes have been symbolically "held together, more or less closely," in Sir Henry's words, by Zahir Shah, the reformist king who in 1933, following the assassination of his father, assumed the Pushtun Durrani family throne dating back to 1747. In June 2002, at the age of eighty-seven, he convoked a *loya jirga* or grand gathering of the Afghan tribes in Kabul that, at U.S. insistence, confirmed Hamid Karzai, a highly educated tribal chief related to Zahir Shah, as leader of the Afghan government. With moderate Northern Alliance figures who had been Massoud's lieutenants holding key posts in Karzai's cabinet, both before and after the loya jirga, a start toward establishing a democratic government has been made. But rivalries persisted among traditional tribes and local warlords in a society in which most men carry guns and often use them. And Pakistan continued to interfere in Afghanistan even after Al Qaeda operatives were forced to move their world headquarters from Kandahar to Karachi.

In contrast to Afghanistan, whose failures over many centuries have been due to invading outsiders, Pakistan has failed on its own as a Muslim nation artificially carved out of predominantly Hindu India little more than a half-century ago. Following two miraculous liberations, the Afghans stand a good chance of succeeding as a nation if the United States continues its close – but not too close – support after ousting the terrorists instead of pulling out as it did after the Soviet withdrawal and Communist defeat. Ironically but inevitably, the Pakistanis face continued failure in large part because of the triumph in Afghanistan of the forces fighting global terrorism.

This triumph deprived them of their one success in fifty-six years of political, economic, and military failures: creating the Taliban and putting them in power in Kabul, and so ensuring that Pakistan had a friendly Afghanistan on its western border while confronting its inescapable enemy, India, to the east. But their friends gave sanctuary to Osama bin Laden, who then converted Afghanistan into the centre of world terrorism. When 9/11 made the Taliban an international problem in a way that repression of women and destruction of ancient statues of Buddha could not, Pakistan did not really have the choice that U.S. Secretary of State Colin L. Powell at the time told Musharraf it had: that of being either for or against the United States. With India immediately "standing with the U.S." and offering bases, Pakistan risked losing its last connection to the West if it did not come on board by providing air space, bases, and intelligence for military operations against the Taliban. But these same Taliban had been educated in hate in *madrassas* (Islamic religious schools) on Pakistani soil, armed and commanded by Pakistani officers, and propped up economically by a Pakistani lifeline.

Musharraf received some sympathy for his cruel dilemma and much positive, if unquestioning, media coverage. He might have deserved both were it not for the way he had come to power and the double game he played to control events.

In October 1999, less than three months after the failure of the major infiltration into Indian-held Kashmir which he commanded as army chief, he seized power in Islamabad in Pakistan's fourth military coup, effectively ending any pretense of real democracy in Pakistan. Appointing himself Pakistan's president before meeting Prime Minister Vajpayee in India in July 2001, Musharraf blocked any improvement in Indian-Pakistani relations by demanding a quick resolution of the complex fifty-four-year-old Kashmir dispute.

Having told 140 million Pakistanis that the war against terrorism had forced him to stand with the United States as the "lesser evil," Musharraf then tried to dictate the course of war in Afghanistan and the composition of the next Afghan government.

When U.S. bombing started on 7 October 2001, he called for its immediate end, and for four weeks persuaded the Americans not to hit the Taliban defenders of Kabul hard. When they were hit hard and retreated, he tried unsuccessfully, with Bush's support, to stop advancing Northern Alliance troops – mostly Tajiks, Uzbeks, and Hazaras, all backed by Russia, India, and Iran, as opposed to the Pushtuns he favoured – at the gates of the capital. When the Northern Alliance took control of Kabul, Musharraf worked with the British to fly in an international force to take it away – a bold ploy the Americans vetoed. During the siege of Kunduz, the last Taliban stronghold in the north, planes from Pakistan mysteriously flew Pakistani Taliban out. Other Pakistani Taliban – and possibly the Taliban leader Mullah Muhammad Omar – escaped into Pakistan from Kandahar when it became the last city to fall. During the last major assault in Afghanistan, on the mountains and caves of Tora Bora southwest of Jalalabad, Pakistani troops ordered to the nearby border failed to intercept fleeing Al Qaeda "Arab Afghans" – probably including Osama, the chief "Arab Afghan."

Pakistan, which never recovered from losing two wars to India over Kashmir in 1947–48 and 1965, and losing East Bengal in a third war in 1971, desperately seeks security. With as many Pushtuns or Pathans living on the Pakistani side of the arbitrarily drawn Durand Line as on the Afghan side, it is a constant reminder that creation of a Pushtunistan – once promoted vigorously by Afghanistan with Soviet support – would break up what was West Pakistan before the 1971 war giving birth to Bangladesh.

So some of Musharrif's tactics may have been excusable. He could not be excused, however, for ISI's betrayal of Abdul Haq, a rival Pushtun leader who was caught and executed by the Taliban when he went into Afghanistan to buy tribal support with CIA funds. Hamid Karzai, the American candidate for leadership of all Afghanistan, nearly met a similar fate but was plucked from the hands of tipped-off Taliban pursuers by a U.S. helicopter and closely guarded in Kandahar by U.S. special forces. Nor is it possible to dismiss the fact that two Pakistani nuclear scientists, detained for questioning only due to U.S. pressure, were in close touch with Al Qaeda operatives in Afghanistan who were eager to learn how to make or get their hands on weapons of mass destruction.

Only on 7 October, the day U.S. bombing started and nearly one month after Musharraf had pledged support to the war against terrorism, did he remove the pro-Taliban general commanding ISI, which has often been described as "a state within a state." But on 8 October and 12 October, ISI-authorized convoys of trucks loaded with Pakistani arms for the Taliban passed through the Khyber Pass into Afghanistan. Only after the convoys had gone through were ISI operatives and Pakistani military advisers withdrawn from Taliban forces, in all likelihood also due to pressure from Americans who were becoming aware of Pakistan's continuing support of the Taliban.

One reason for the military coup that had put Musharraf in power two years earlier was ISI fear that civilian Prime Minister Nawaz Sharif would weaken or reverse Pakistan's pro-Taliban policy due to U.S. concern about Osama's presence in Afghanistan. Whether Musharraf had to bide his time to get rid of pro-Taliban elements in ISI for fear of a coup against him, or was mostly pretending to cooperate with the United States, Islamic extremists remained in positions of power and influence in Pakistan's army and society, and the general could not hide his two faces.

Bush rewarded one face by promising an economic-aid package worth $1 billion to Pakistan's collapsing economy and lifting most sanctions. But he recognized the other face when he met Musharraf in New York City in early November and turned down the two things the Pakistani leader most wanted: U.S. mediation in the Kashmir dispute with India, and release of twenty-eight F-16 jet fighters withheld by the United States when Pakistan was moving toward acquiring nuclear weapons.

Especially after the attack on India's Parliament on 13 December, Bush and his advisers left no doubt that they viewed repeated acts of terrorism in Kashmir and even Delhi by militant Islamic groups as originating in Pakistan. Due partly to India's military buildup, they officially listed these groups as terrorist organizations and pressed Musharraf to render them inoperative. But as long as the United States also held up Pakistan as a valuable ally, a status it had enjoyed during the Cold War, the Islamic nation that had taken uncertain root after partition of the Subcontinent in 1947 could not easily be identified publicly as a failed state whose handful of nuclear bombs made it even more dangerous.

This made it easier for Musharraf to play the kind of double game over terrorism in Kashmir he had played in both opposing and backing the Taliban in Afghanistan. Publicly he condemned terrorism, ordered leaders of militant Islamic groups arrested, and directed the ISI wing supporting these groups in Kashmir to cease operating. But the last move exposed previous Pakistani denials of ISI involvement as lies. Musharraf released Muslim extremist leaders soon after they were detained. And by intimating that ISI's role in relation to Kashmir starting in 2002 would be limited to helping groups with local roots attack only military targets, Musharraf kept the door open to continued terrorism against India, with all the risks of war it now entailed. He even boasted at the end of 2002 that he had threatened India with a nuclear response if its troops went after Pakistan-based terrorists. Pakistan's nuclear bombs were designed by China and acquired illegally. In exchange for providing equipment to North Korea to make nuclear weapons, Pakistan has received medium-range missiles from Kim Jong Il, and its army has targeted Indian cities with them.

Appropriately, Musharraf has presented himself in a number of guises. The outfit he wears – a tailored army uniform, military fatigues, a Western business suit, a long black Pakistani coat, casual white Pakistani pajamas – conveys the impression he wants to make on his audience of the day. But he appears more clumsy than clever. His campaigning in various native accoutrements, including outlandish turbans, ended in nearly 100 per cent approval of him in a hastily rigged referendum in April 2002 – so one-sided and unreal that many Pakistanis ridiculed his claim that this was a step on the road to democracy. Within weeks, the general was humiliated by President Bush's virtual order to him to halt terrorist incursions into Indian-held Kashmir: "He must do so," said the president. In late 2002, however, terrorists invaded two Hindu temples in Kashmir, killing fourteen people. And the Pakistani army manipulated all-but-meaningless elections to ally itself effectively with pro-Taliban parties that took control of the two provinces bordering Afghanistan – the legendary Northwest Frontier and Baluchistan – making it virtually impossible for U.S. law-enforcement agents to continue tracking down Al Qaeda agents in Pakistan.

Musharraf may have best summed himself up at a meeting of South Asian leaders in Katmandu, Nepal, in January 2002. The armies of India and Pakistan were on alert and confronting each other. When his turn to speak came, he strode dramatically across the floor and offered his hand to Prime Minister Vajpayee. The Indian leader, who after his talks with

Musharraf six months earlier had said the general showed little awareness of the Subcontinent's history, politely rose and shook hands. But when it was his turn to speak, Vajpayee said that not symbolism but substance was required to fight terrorism.

If the Bush administration aimed to prevent Pakistan from fully becoming a terrorist nuclear-armed authoritarian state during and after the war in Afghanistan, its bottom-line objective with India even before 11 September was to enlist this huge democracy as a major ally in countering China's weight in Asia. While events compelled the Pakistanis to give the appearance of joining America in the fight against terrorism, the Indians were eager to ally themselves with America against both terrorism and China.

Like Israel has done in its cities as well as the West Bank, India has long waged its own war against terrorism in its cities as well as Kashmir. In sharp contrast to Pakistan's proudly calling China its best friend, India has regarded China as its main enemy at least since the 1962 Himalayan war between the world's two most populous countries. This distinction does not belong to Pakistan despite the myth to this effect, again trotted out by many journalists in December 2001 when Indian and Pakistani forces faced off along a 3,000-kilometre border as a consequence of Pakistani-sponsored terrorism.

In April 2001, just weeks after his inauguration, Bush took the unusual step of inviting a foreign minister, India's Jaswant Singh, into the Oval Office for a long chat. This made headlines in India but American media gave it scant notice, as they had Bush's emphasizing during his election campaign that India was an important but ignored country, and they had Clinton's democratic alliance with India. In May, following India's enthusiastic approval of Bush's plan to build a missile-defence system and cut the U.S. nuclear arsenal deeply, Deputy Secretary of State Richard L. Armitage went to Delhi and said the United States was worried about Pakistan's nuclear capability. He did not mention India's greater nuclear capability. In July, General Henry H. Shelton became the first chairman of the U.S. Joint Chiefs of Staff to visit India. In late August, just sixteen days before 11 September, unidentified administration officials finally made a noticeable impact on the media by revealing that the United States would soon lift nuclear-related sanctions as part of a move to engage India as a major strategic ally and trading partner.

These were some of the building blocks that led to India's confident declaration of solidarity with the United States in response to the terrorist attacks. But the whole framework for momentous policy shifts by both nations suddenly seemed to shake and come close to tumbling down when Washington turned to Pakistan for help in finding and destroying terrorists in Afghanistan.

Many Indians, still suspicious of the United States, feared that Washington – like Islamabad – was reverting to Cold War habits at India's expense. They wondered how America could hold hands with Pakistan, which they had no doubt was a terrorist state, while fighting terrorism. Like many Israelis, they accused the United States of employing a double standard. The terrorist assault on the Kashmir legislature on 1 October aggravated these feelings. The day before, a full-page open letter in *The New York Times* from Prime Minister Vajpayee to the United States and the "brave citizens" of New York City had spoken of a "joint fight" against terrorism: "The people of India know the challenge of terrorism ... That is why we share your shock and disbelief as our own; we understand the anger that you feel; this, too, we have lived with for long."

But the Bush administration did not do anything foolish, such as agree to the blatant Pakistani demands for mediation on Kashmir and delivery of the F-16s, that would have enflamed Indian opinion and opened a hard-to-close divide. With one exception that seemed risky at the time – but was repeated on a much larger scale in December, with at least initial positive results – the Indian government did not make a public show of its frustration.

The exception came on 15 October when Secretary of State Powell was in Islamabad and scheduled to fly to Delhi the next day. He was conferring with Musharraf when each man received word that India had opened a barrage of mortar, rocket, and machine-gun fire across the "line of control" dividing Kashmir. It was India's way of being noticed and making clear that its views could not be ignored. Bush had no such intention. But now the president warned, "It is very important that India and Pakistan stand down during our activities in Afghanistan." Powell did not improve matters when he went along with a Musharraf demand that "moderate Taliban" be included in a new Afghan government – something that did not happen and could not have happened because there was no such thing. But he reassured the Indians, who asked that the United States not resume arms sales to Pakistan, and within days Bush turned down Pakistan's request for the F-16s.

When Secretary of Defense Donald H. Rumsfeld flew from Islamabad to Delhi on 5 November, what he said and what was happening on the field of battle in Afghanistan sent a strong message to the Indians that the United States was living up to its commitment not to equate Pakistan with India and was rejecting Pakistani military advice. He stressed that U.S. military cooperation with Pakistan would not be at India's expense. He spoke of the agreements on close U.S.-Indian military ties and sale of U.S. military equipment, including fighter planes, that would be signed before the end of 2001. Meanwhile, the heavy bombing of the Taliban defenders of Kabul, which Pakistan had delayed for nearly one month, had started and was taking its toll of both Afghan Talibs and Pakistani fantasies.

Another high-level U.S. military visit to India soon followed, by Admiral Dennis C. Blair, then the commander-in-chief Pacific, whose vast region extends to India while Pakistan and Afghanistan are covered separately by U.S. central command, then under General Tommy R. Franks. Earlier, when Bush met Vajpayee at the White House on 9 November – in the same room where Bush had met Great Britain's Prime Minister Tony Blair to wage war on terrorism – the president asserted that together the United States and India would fight both terrorists and those who harbour terrorists. His emphasis since 11 September on going after countries harbouring terrorists had already been elevated to the "Bush doctrine." His reiterating it in Vajpayee's presence became a key point after the 13 December terrorist attack on India's Parliament building in New Delhi.

As with Israel at the same time, and in contrast to the past, there was no public U.S. call on India to exercise restraint. Instead President Bush telephoned Prime Minister Vajpayee to offer counter-terrorism assistance. Powell, despite his concern for coalition-building, said the United States understood that India would act in response to the attack by "murderers." Despite political pressure to do so immediately, and Vajpayee's pledge to "fight a decisive battle against terrorism to the end," his coalition government did not take precipitous military action. It waited several days before assessing full blame. With the United States pressing Pakistan to restrain Muslim militants, India had an opportunity to capture the moral high ground by defining the Kashmir dispute in terms of fighting terrorism rather than in terms of granting self-determination, as it had been defined for decades. Moreover, the Vajpayee government, like the Bush administration after 9/11, was in a stronger political position to fend off carping opposition critics after 13/12.

Five days after the attack, Home Minister Lal Krishna Advani accused Pakistan's ISI and the two Islamic groups with the most insurgents in Indian-held Kashmir of "the temerity to try to wipe out the entire political leadership of India." Vajpayee, reflecting a widespread feeling among Indians, observed, "Truly, our restraint has been understood as weakness."

Only peculiarly Indian conditions averted much greater human carnage at Parliament than the death of fourteen people, including the five assailants. A typical Delhi power failure prevented an accomplice from informing the gunmen – armed with grenades and explosives as well as automatic rifles – that the lower house of Parliament had adjourned five minutes after convening. The five drove onto the grounds in a VIP Hindustan Ambassador, a standard Indian car modeled on a 1950s Morris Oxford and requiring skill in shifting gears from the steering column – skill the gunman behind the wheel apparently didn't have, because he reversed the car into a collision with a similar vehicle in the arriving vice-president of India's motorcade. When the discovered terrorists stormed entrances to the vast circular building, guns firing, a wounded unarmed guard closed one gate before he died, and the other eleven gates then slammed shut before any of the gunmen could get inside, where hundreds of legislators, ministers, aides, and journalists were milling about.

A senior official, revealing that India was considering military action, declared, "This time we are determined to put an end to terrorism." Musharraf – in Beijing, where he hailed Pakistan's "time-tested" friendship with China – called this response "very arrogant ... knee-jerk." On Christmas day, Vajpayee signalled India's military buildup on its borders with both Pakistan proper and Pakistani-held Kashmir with these words: "We do not want war, but war is being thrust on us, and we will have to face it."

As rhetoric escalated on both sides, along with movement of troops, guns, tanks, missiles, planes, and ships, so did U.S. pressure on Pakistan and Pakistani arrests of terrorists, indicating that Indian military pressure was starting to have results. Recalling the Bush administration's hard reaction to the 11 September attacks, India resisted U.S. calls for talks with Pakistan, reinforcing Vajpayee's emphasis in Katmandu on the need for concrete actions against terrorists rather than empty words. War was unlikely unless someone made a mistake, a distinct possibility in the Subcontinent. But real peace was just as unlikely unless Pakistan effectively put an end to terrorist activity in Kashmir and India originating from Pakistani soil, where the Taliban movement and indeed Al Qaeda had also sprung up.

During brief visits to India and Pakistan at the beginning of 2002, Prime Minister Blair spoke for the United States, as well as Britain, when he declared in Delhi that there was "no halfway house" in dealing with terrorists: "There must be a complete rejection of terrorist acts and the support of them in any form." This unqualified demand and his bluntly calling on Pakistan in Islamabad to condemn the attacks on the Indian Parliament and the Kashmir legislature made it harder for Musharraf to continue supporting the halfway house of "freedom fighters" in Kashmir. So did Bush's categorical assertion in Washington at the same time: "I think it is very important for President Musharraf to make a clear statement to the world that he intends to crack down on terror."

Almost daily telephone calls from the president and his top advisers made crystal clear that the United States considered not territory but terrorism the key issue between India and Pakistan. They also conveyed to Musharraf the message that he had better act against terrorists before they acted against him, especially with the danger of radical Islamic escapees from Afghanistan transferring their jihad to Kashmir. At the same time, the Americans asked Vajpayee to be patient and urged a pullback of his troops from the borders. For his part, in his New Year message the Indian leader quietly offered to walk "more than half the distance" in discussing disputes with Pakistan, including Kashmir, in return for an end to terrorism. He had long suggested that Kashmiris could expect more autonomy if India's sovereignty over its part of the Muslim-majorty state were recognized, as difficult as this would be for some Pakistanis to accept.

The simmering crisis suddenly deepened when terrorists disguised as Indian troops attacked an army camp outside Jammu in Kashmir on 14 May 2002, killing thirty-four people, most of them women and children belonging to military families. One week later, an important Kashmiri moderate, Abdul Ghani Lone, who was considering taking part in what the Indians called a "free and fair" Kashmir election in October, was shot dead in Srinagar.

Without warning, nagging worries about a fourth war between India and Pakistan and vague fears of a nuclear exchange exploded into loud drumbeats. Vajpayee told Indian troops to prepare for a "decisive battle." Musharraf warned that Pakistan would retaliate with "full force" against an Indian attack. Pakistan tested new short-range missiles. The Pentagon made public an assessment that a full nuclear exchange would kill up to twelve million Indians and Pakistanis. American and other Western diplomats and their families in India and Pakistan were ordered to leave, and 60,000 other Americans in India were urged to do so due to the "definite possibility" of war. Senior U.S. and British officials undertook new rescue missions to the Subcontinent.

It is unlikely that these alarms were entirely genuine as it is not clear that India was on the verge of attacking terrorist bases in Pakistan's part of Kashmir. Nor is there evidence to support reports that Pakistan had prepared a nuclear response, then or at the time of the armed incursion into Indian Kashmir in mid-1999, although it is possible that Pakistani leaders would consider such suicidal action if their country was collapsing completely. There is no reason to believe that there is such a thing as an effective Pakistani nuclear deterrent.

But there is reason to believe that the Bush administration dramatically escalated its warning about nuclear conflict because it wanted to force Musharraf to curb again the actions of terrorists he had freed in the months following their detention at the turn of the year. This would account for Bush's stronger-than-ever message to Musharraf to "stop the incursions." One intent was to prevent a war. Another was to avoid exposing Pakistan as a terrorist state or make it easier for Pakistan to succeed Afghanistan as the centre of world terrorism. Musharraf, aware of the full consequences of backing terrorists again, did do as Bush said, and there was no war.

It is also not clear whether the United States and India coordinated their warnings. No U.S. official would say, even without direct attribution, what India's Jaswant Singh said at the time: "The epicentre of international terrorism is located in Pakistan." Indian officials continued to express impatience with the United States for not pressing Musharraf hard enough. But in the end, the tough American message to Pakistan was the same as the tough Indian message. Following fresh visits by Deputy Secretary of State Armitage, who called India "a great democracy," and Secretary of Defense Rumsfeld, who noted signs of Al Qaeda in Pakistan, Vajpayee said, "India was prepared for nuclear war but we were confident [Pakistan] would not resort to such madness."

It is possible to say that U.S. diplomacy pulled India and Pakistan back from war. It is also possible to say that the strategic alliance between the United States and India worked in its own mysterious way. Whatever the Bush administration's worries about war and proposals for peace, it did not go back on its core conviction that, as the president had put it and Blair had repeated in the Subcontinent, "Terrorism is terrorism." With or without the war against terrorism, India has become a far more important ally of the United States than Pakistan is or ever could be.

Some words matter, and perhaps those that best described President Bush's warm feeling for India – and should have eased doubts in Indian minds if not put them entirely to rest – were quoted by his ambassador, Robert D. Blackwell, in Bombay on 6 September 2001, just five days before 11 September. Blackwell, a Harvard professor and China specialist, had been one of Bush's closest foreign-policy advisers during his election campaign. He recalled the president's response when told about how democracy works in India with one billion people. Deeply impressed – and clearly interested in what this could mean for U.S. policies – Bush had mused, "Isn't that something?"

Imagining India's democracy is one thing. India as an ally of the United States, as unlikely as this once seemed, is also imaginable. India's poverty, which democracy is striving to overcome, remains, however, almost unimaginable.

4

Caste and Crass

The shriveled old woman squatting in the scorching noonday sun of eastern India in May tried to move into the shade of a building. She was stopped by one of the men about to dispense a grey gruel, with visible hairs and other bits of inedible matter in it, from a large pot. He forced the woman with her shallow metal pan to join more than a hundred younger starving persons. They had been squatting a half-hour or more in ragged rows on the blistering concrete surface of a fenced-in courtyard in blinding heat of at least 40 degrees Celsius. She would be served last.

Suddenly a tall man with a long wooden stick strode across the courtyard. He casually hit several men and women waiting for their only daily food. In the self-centred Hindu belief that his charity in this life would enhance the status of his next life, he had come a long way from Bombay to establish the temporary soup kitchen in the famine state of Bihar. His angry appearance signalled that the handouts could begin. His sullen assistants doled out the unidentifiable grey slop. They allowed no one to eat or leave until everyone had been served, ending with the old woman still holding up a thin shawl against the sun in Bodh Gaya.

Nearby was the bo tree under which the Lord Buddha preached right conduct and brotherly love 2,500 years ago. Its compassionate shade also went unused that day in 1967. Most people living and dying in the Subcontinent have shunned its message for many years.

The images are lasting, reflecting the realities.

Six months later, the little boy was curled up asleep, so peacefully that he might have been between the clean white sheets of his bed at home. But he had no clean sheets, no bed, and no home. His only possessions were the filthy straw mat he was lying on, the rag that half covered him, and whatever made up the small black-cloth bundle he was using as a pillow.

The dust-coated child, no more than four or five years old, was sleeping in the middle of the sidewalk of Jawaharlal Nehru Road, one of Calcutta's busiest thoroughfares. Most Indians who walked to one side or the other of the still figure must have noticed him. But they didn't really see him. He was but one of thousands of men, women, and children who performed the functions of life on the sidewalks of India's then most populous city, and still do. It was difficult to blame the Communists who had come to power in West Bengal earlier in 1967 for that boy, or for his equivalent – perhaps his son, if he survived somehow – more than a generation later. Human beings have been sleeping, begging, and scrounging for food in the smog and dirt of Calcutta's chaotic streets for decades.

In East Bengal – still East Pakistan, later Bangladesh – some days earlier, the old chocolate bars were locked up in a glass case. There were no customers at the new ice cream stand. And the candy man offered a tiny pack of Dutch lemon drops for two rupees, then worth nearly fifty cents or more than two days' average wages. In the "new bazaar" of Chittagong, the alienated east wing's largest port, a woman partially covered by a rag and holding two naked children and a tin plate stood silently, begging. Her eyes testified even more vividly to deep poverty, to the subordination of dignity to need, than the inaccessibility, to all but a monied few, of sweets bought every day by other Asians.

After three months in the comparatively luxurious world of Southeast Asia – Vietnam war and all – I was back in the Subcontinent. The kind of sub-life to which it is too easy to become hardened while living in India suddenly assaulted my senses. At Chittagong's docks, miserable little wood-and-straw houseboats bobbed alongside my newly tied-up, passenger-carrying, Norwegian freighter. Men and boys standing in them imploringly held up bottles upside down. They didn't want something to drink. They wanted the ship's empties to sell. A bearded old worker in a dirty Bengali wraparound found a colourful cookie tin on the freighter, empty. He humbly asked permission to take it home that night. When someone signed a piece of paper for him, he grinned like a child who has been presented with a boxful of cookies.

Back at Bipani Bitan, the new bazaar a jolting, hired-scooter ride away over a rutted road, a sign at the entrance to the three-story yellow stucco building said: "In the interest of the customers and the public in general squatters are strictly prohibited within the premises." Many persons – presumably members of the "public in general" but probably lacking the ability to read – squatted within feet of the sign. Most were men in the checked cottons worn by Muslims in the Subcontinent. But crouched in a dark corner were two children, one naked and the other wrapped in two rags. The only persons a brown-uniformed policeman chased out into a pouring late

monsoon rain were the erect begging woman and her two children. He hit
her on the arm with a stick, just as I put a few coins in her tin plate.

Possibly her children and the two in the corner were fortunate. In West
Pakistan in 1967, hundreds of teenage boys were suddenly discovered digging irrigation canals in *begar* or slave labour camps in the desert. They
had been kidnapped from their families, held in chains – in some cases
more than five years – tortured, whipped, branded, fed a narcotic called
bhang, and forced to work fifteen to twenty hours a day without pay. The
reason for the exposé, including a flurry of police raids, statements by high
officials, and the freeing of some boys, was not clear. The government had
known about the camps since Pakistan's independence in 1947. It probably connived in their operation by awarding petty construction contracts to
men known as Kharkars who ran them. The boys, and young girls abducted
and forced into prostitution, came from families of Pathans in the old
Northwest Frontier Agency, whose children are famous for fierce self-
reliance when they grow up. What was clear then and now is that the
medieval concentration camps were not eradicated. Bonded and child
labour continue in both Pakistan and India to this day.

On Christmas night of 1968, as India prepared to observe 1969 as the
centennial year of Mohandas Gandhi's birth, forty-two Indians burned to
death in a hut in Tanjore district of Madras state, now Tamil Nadu. Like
the assassination of Gandhi by a Brahmin fanatic on 30 January 1948 for
preaching tolerance, the incident starkly illuminated an India very unlike
the kind of country for which the Mahatma had worked. The victims –
three men, nineteen women, and twenty children – were untouchables, or
what he had called Harijans (Children of God) or *dalits*, the latter word
meaning broken people and what they call themselves now. They were
rice-growing peasant labourers and their families, the kind of suffering
people who Prime Minister Nehru had declared at the outset of independence must be served in a free India. They were attacked by *goondas*
(goons) brought in by high-caste landowners who refused to share the
benefits of the Green Revolution with deprived people. In some Indian
villages, Brahmins stop dalit youngsters from going to school by tying
them up.

It was in 1968 that Gunnar Myrdal, the Swedish economist, followed up
An American Dilemma, his classic work on inequality of whites and blacks
in the United States, with a more extensive one on the lack of social and
economic justice in South Asian countries, particularly India. In his three-
volume *Asian Drama – An Inquiry into the Poverty of Nations*, he
observed: "India is still far from being controlled by the majority of its people or even from having its policies devised so as to be in the interests of
the masses."

Three months into the Mahatma Gandhi centennial year, and three years after Indira Nehru Gandhi became prime minister, a 1969 dispatch by United News of India underlined Myrdal's point:

New Delhi, March 15 (UNI) – A target date for the provision of basic amenities, such as food, clothing and shelter, to the people was among the important suggestions made by the Cabinet to the Planning Commission during the day-long discussion of the draft Fourth (Five-Year) Plan today.

Some senior Ministers are reported to have suggested that if this objective could not be reached by 1975–76, as visualized in the Bhubaneswar Congress declaration of 1964, a fresh date could be fixed, say, 1980 or so.

The dispatch could as well have been filed in 1989 and informed readers: "if this objective could not be reached by 1995–96 ... a fresh date could be fixed, say, 2000 or so."

It was the great Bihar famine in 1966–67 that brought me and others face-to-face with the timelessness of India's desperation. Or, perhaps more accurately, the desperation of India's timelessness. Indians starved. Indians died. Many people around the world cared. Few other Indians cared. Callous indifference was evident especially among those elected or appointed to care. In the end, even a couple hundred thousand deaths from starvation or from diseases caused by starvation produced hardly a blip in the relentless surge of India's population toward the one-billion mark and beyond. Before television cameras defined such tragedies virtually by themselves, the Bihar famine offered one of the second half of the twentieth century's most striking lessons in the nature of the human condition in general and the Subcontinent's condition in particular.

The soup kitchen at Bodh Gaya wasn't the worst part. People weren't dying there when I visited it, although if they were, a trace of human kindness probably would have been just as difficult to find. Mathiani thirteen kilometres to the west was more appalling. Seen from the road in a distant sun haze, the dry mud-and-straw huts of Mathiani merged with the dry, bare earth like countless other villages trapped in the famine country of Bihar and eastern Uttar Pradesh. But this was a death village.

Fourteen of Mathiani's seventy human inhabitants – eight children, four women, two men – had died in the previous five weeks when I went there in May 1967. A dozen cattle had also died. Some of the barely moving skeleton figures of women, children, and cattle almost surely would die soon. Most of the peasants of Mathiani were lucky if they had a scrap of *bajra*, a coarse millet, to eat each day. They had tried, without help, to dig their own well to relieve a severe water shortage. But it had collapsed on them and they did not have the energy to try again.

Smallpox – since theoretically eradicated worldwide – had come to Mathiani. All fourteen people who had died had had smallpox first, had seemed to recover from the dread disease, then had grown thinner and expired. They probably died from secondary infections or dehydration or meningitis. Their lack of nourishment left them nothing with which to resist disease. Three more villagers of Mathiani – a mother, father, and son – were recovering from smallpox. If the monsoon didn't fail in late June and July as it had the past two years, it would bring cholera and other intestinal diseases with a higher direct mortality rate to Mathiani and thousands of other famine villages before it brought crops.

Ramdani, the village headman, paused before he walked to a job helping to dig a well in another village, paying eight annas to a rupee (then eight to sixteen cents) a day. A pained expression on his face, he asked his wife Lachia to come out of their mud hut. She emerged clutching a baby the size of a normal two-month-old infant. It was their one-year-old daughter, Batia, one of their three children. Other sights in Mathiani were more wrenching: an eight-year-old boy who was too ashamed of his toothpick arms and knobby knees to speak; an old woman crouched in the parched dirt, sick, moaning; and the smallpox family staring with eyes full of fear out of the entrance to their hut.

"We are like a cow," said Ramdani, forty-five, comparing the poor villagers to the holy animal that, as Hindus, they would not eat. "When we're sick, we cannot move, and we cannot work so we can earn money to buy food." As the owner of two acres of land, he was too proud to accept a dole at one of the free kitchens run by the Bihar Relief Committee like the one at Bodh Gaya. "I want to save my people," he continued in Hindi, "but I will take food only by working for it." He had to wait to sow wheat and rice until the time came, and then only if he could get seed. Now he rationed out small measures of water for the villagers each day from the unclean bottom of an existing well. But he didn't know when it would go dry.

Later that day, thinking it was not too late to save lives, I told the subdivisional administrative officer in charge of the area that fourteen people had died there. He replied with an arrogance suggesting this was none of my business: "I doubt if that many persons died and if they did, they died of smallpox, not starvation." In any case, he wasn't going to find out for himself or see what he could do to help.

"If these people are saved, it will be you foreigners who save them," a retired army brigadier had informed me in New Delhi in the clipped British accent cultivated by Indian and Pakistani military officers. "You don't expect Punjabis or Madrasis or Brahmins from Uttar Pradesh to care about a couple of million tribals in Bihar, do you?"

He might have added that among Indians not caring about peasants and Adivasis (tribal people) of Bihar were other Biharis – prosperous members of high castes, bureaucrats who couldn't be bothered to distribute foreign food aid, operators profiting from famine relief. Indeed, lack of genuine concern was detectable up to the highest levels of the Congress Party government of Prime Minister Indira Gandhi. The fact that American, Canadian, British, and United Nations volunteers, money, and resources were performing vital tasks in the hard job of saving human lives in Bihar suggested dire Indian spiritual shortcomings as well as shortages of food and water for more than 35 million people in 18,000 villages.

The Indian government thought nothing of diverting 300 tons of Canadian milk powder meant for children and expectant or nursing mothers in Bihar to the army for troop rations. After Mrs Gandhi promised the army would dig wells in Bihar on a mass emergency basis, a few platoons showed up with the excuse that the army had few well-drilling rigs or men with the experience to operate them. But more than a hundred rigs had come in from outside India, and U.S. Peace Corps and Canadian volunteers with no background in well-drilling were taken from their regular jobs to run them. An Indian geologist told a foreign relief agency not to drill in a rocky area, where the need for water was greatest, because it might reflect on his competence if he advised drilling and no water was found.

Jayaprakash Narayan, the head of the Bihar Relief Committee, was known for his devotion to needy Indians. But the response of other Indians to his appeal for funds was so poor he was compelled to entrust famine-relief kitchens to shady characters like the tall, stick-swinging autocrat from Bombay.

When asked why no other students from her huge institution were in nearby Bihar to fight a famine threatening to wipe out millions of people, a University of Calcutta student helping Bihari villagers replied: "I don't think most of them have heard about it."

Dwarko Sundrani, who ran an ashram whose Indian and non-Indian members went out to villages to organize manual-labour projects, said: "We have to take grain directly to a village – we're not sure it would get there if we entrusted it to anyone else."

On a project, a labourer could eat forty ounces of grain a day working in the hot sun but he couldn't manage to keep working on less than twenty-five ounces. In New Delhi, a government official justified with a maze of figures and graphs the supply of grain to Bihar that theoretically worked out to eleven ounces a day per person – but less in practice. He explained: "It's not realistic to ask for more."

Indira Gandhi herself admitted: "There is an awakening among farmers; they are demanding these things – fertilizers, hybrid seeds, irrigation – and we are unable to supply them." Yet she complained that not the problems but the publicity in Bihar was new.

It was not as if there had been no warning that a large swath of east central India would be stricken. When I had accompanied Mrs Gandhi in August 1966 on a trip to an army base below the eastern Himalayas, she had told me as we flew over Bihar about the impending famine after two bad monsoons.

Three months later, as the sun went down in the village of Sangatpur ninety kilometres south of Patna, the state capital, a small group of peasants stood sullenly at the edge of their grey mud huts and gazed at barren brown fields.

"This has never happened before," said Donanard, a landless labourer.

"There is no hope of it getting better," said Bajunandon Mathi, who was already obtaining grain in the black market to sell to his fellow villagers because they could not grow any themselves. "Slowly, slowly, people will start dying soon."

A young farmer with one acre of land, Shaban Kumar, echoed the rising sound of approaching death: "All our wells but one have dried up – when that one goes, we will die." "

"We have begun to sell our cattle," said Shamraut, an older farmer. "But not our children."

Another peasant said: "Come in, come in and see a poor man's home." Inside the straw-thatched hut, there was hay to sleep on, a small clay cooking stove, an oil lamp with a wick the size of a birthday candle, and a bucket of water. Inside a brass pot over a cow-dung fire was about one pound of rice with a handful of dal or split peas. Even at that early stage of the Bihar famine, that's all there was for eight persons to eat that night.

That November in eastern Uttar Pradesh (UP), India's most populous state – together UP and adjoining Bihar then held 140 million people – conditions were a little better but deteriorating rapidly.

In Ramnathi, a cluster of three villages two kilometres off the Grand Trunk Road and seventy kilometres west of the Hindu holy city of Banaras, women smiled shyly and children played under the shade of mango trees. It was a pleasant spot, almost primitive but clean and cheerful, in the heartland of India – and free of sadhus or Hindu holy men, the well-fed Brahmins who bathed in the dirty water of the Ganges at Banaras. Some peasants even went out to their long untended fields to plow after a little rain, the first in more than three months.

But Laudhar, his small but well-built frame bare above his dirt-stained dhoti, expressed little hope as he halted the slow progress of his two bullocks and ancient pointed wooden plow. "I lost my corn, my *kharif* [fall] crop," he explained in Hindi. "There is really not enough water for my wheat, my *rabi* [spring] crop." He said he had had to buy grain in the market for his wife and two children because the ten acres owned by himself and his two brothers had produced almost nothing. "There is enough food left for fifteen days, maybe longer," he added matter-of-factly. "Then I'll try to find work in a brick factory or some other place nearby. My brothers will go to the city."

Next to Ramnathi is the village of Bhiti, one of many in the district engaged in the cottage weaving of Mirzapur carpets. In a small, dark hut, half taken up by a large wooden loom, sat four men completing a multi-coloured carpet on which they had worked twelve hours a day for twenty-five days. They were bent over in a narrow space between the loom and the single small window giving them light. There was no electricity in Bhiti or Ramnathi.

Matasaran, who had been making beautiful carpets for thirty-six years and looked at least fifteen years older than his forty-five years, peered through the string warp of his loom. After several questions, he said in an uncomplaining tone: "I make thirty to thirty-five rupees (then four to five dollars) a month after my expenses in buying wool. This year with high prices it is not enough to buy food for my family. I have one meal a day now."

The year before, the grey-haired Matasaran had had two meals a day. But he was reduced to starting his twelve-hour work day with only a *gur* or brown sugar drink. Most of his evening meal was a *roti* or large unleavened wheat bread. He was a member of a Hindu joint family of fifteen individuals. His income of about one rupee or fifteen or sixteen cents a day was the average paid to a master weaver by large carpet manufacturers in buying up the products of hundreds of villages. Matasaran was paid not for his time but for how much carpet he made for eventual sale in New York or London or Toronto at astronomically higher prices.

The UP agriculture minister, Shyam Dhar Mishra of the Congress Party, was aware of conditions in both Bithi and Ramnathi because he lived nearby. He had told peasants he was sorry he couldn't provide more tube wells for irrigation but he was too busy with his carpet factory.

In Patna in early February 1967, no politicians were present as dalit and low-caste women and children squatted in the dirt near the railroad tracks and watched as wheat was unloaded from a train from Calcutta. Their thin bodies and the rags over them covered with dust, their eyes dull, they edged closer as coolies moved like zombies to waiting trucks. Each coolie carried on his head a burlap sack stenciled unclearly with the words Gift of the People of the United States.

Suddenly several of the women dashed forward with little wicker dust-pans. A sack had split slightly as it landed in the back of a truck and precious grains of wheat had slid to the ground. A coolie hit one advancing woman in a ragged sari whose colour could still be distinguished as green, and they exchanged angry words. Another woman swiftly put her dustpan near a truck tire, pushed more grit and dung than grain into it, and got away unscathed. A little sweeper boy was even luckier. Somehow he had talked a railway guard into letting him pick up the droppings in an empty freight car. His grin was almost as big as the rag in which he had tied the dirty grain as he ran to tell his family.

These desperate people were not the first concern of the Congress Party rulers of Bihar. The politicians' first worry was to get themselves reelected in India's elections a few weeks hence. They were campaigning not primarily by providing food to the people but by making crass appeals to caste loyalties among them. The next concern of the Congresswallahs lording it over 52 million Biharis was maintaining law and order. Along with limited amounts of grain, extra police – four battalions from the Central Reserve and adjoining UP – and Bren guns from Calcutta were being imported in case the people got out of hand. Chief Minister K.B. Sahay, who was running in a Patna constituency, said: "It is unjust to make critical remarks about the administration. I have toured the drought-affected areas and talked to many persons, including non-officials. No one has confirmed reports of starvation deaths. The government will ensure that no one dies of hunger."

"There's no question about it, people are starving," said Rev. Robert M. Donahue, the American director of Catholic charities in Bihar. "They've been dying of starvation for two months, in some cases for six months. People are already going five to six days without food."

In New Delhi in late May 1967, after I had returned from Bodh Gaya and Mathiani, and Patna again, the newly elected Parliament debated the famine in Bihar. Despite large Congress Party losses, forty-seven MPs, including three cabinet ministers, decided this was a good time to revive the Parliamentary Heavyweight Club for members weighing at least 200 pounds in summer dress.

The overweight members of Parliament gleefully vowed not to diet for any reason on pain of expulsion from the club. Although food austerity regulations affecting mainly the poor had been in force for eighteen months, they agreed to gorge themselves at club get-togethers every two weeks in the office of Parliamentary Affairs Minister Ram Subhag Singh. Then they sat down to a lunch of nearly a quart of milk and two pounds of food each, topped off with enormous watermelons.

This was as much milk as four children in Bihar received daily under a CARE feeding program, and half as much food grains by weight as an ordinary adult in many parts of the country, including New Delhi, received weekly on a ration card. Fruit was an extra feature of the no-diet special for the well-padded MPs, including four women, who flaunted their rolls of fat.

Singh turned over the presidency of the Heavyweight Club, started ten years earlier, to Piloo Mody, a bulky member of the free-enterprise Swatantra Party who outweighed him. Other members of Mrs Gandhi's cabinet who partook were Labour Minister Jaisukhlal Hathi and Education Minister Triguna Sen. The patron of the hilarious proceedings was the new vice-president of India, V.V. Giri, who presided over the Rajya Sabha or upper house and also was noted for his girth. At least sixty-five members of the two houses of Parliament or nearly 10 per cent of the membership qualified for the club. Food Minister Jagjivan Ram, a dalit who easily tipped the scales at 200 pounds, didn't show up for the meeting. In the debate, however, he told Parliament he had no reports of famine deaths from Bihar or any other state.

In November 1967, a year after the peasants of Sangatpur had all but given up hope, the great Bihar famine was over. Fields had miraculously turned green and pools of precious water dotted the once parched land. Men and women worked in the fields and little boys rode the backs of water buffalo. They all dipped gratefully into the water as often as they could, to wash themselves, their clothes, and their animals, and even to do a little fishing. Bullock carts loaded with bags of grain after the new *kharif* or fall crop trundled along dirt roads. Peasants stood straighter, moved more quickly, and smiled more often than they had a few months earlier.

More than 35 million Indians at risk of death had survived – "unexpectedly," as Father Donahue put it. But many had died unnecessarily. How many, no one knew. About 800,000 Biharis normally died in the course of one year. In the year ending with the first good monsoon in three years, up to one million died if projections from a medical survey of a famine district were correct. But Bihar's population still grew by one million during the famine year if the normal birth rate prevailed. Even 200,000 famine deaths wiped out only six days of normal population gain in all India, whose inhabitants numbered nearly 600 million then, nearly 900 million a generation later, and one billion at the turn of the century. A major famine can strike an impoverished but growing population, in short, and its toll may hardly be noticed except by decimated families and wandering journalists.

After two years of cruel drought, the weather had still played tricks. The monsoon was three weeks late and hope again faltered. After normal rain in late July and August, a deluge came in September, flooding Patna with twenty-two inches of rain in forty-eight hours, making thousands homeless, wiping out standing corn along the Ganges, and water-logging many rice fields. Finally the last phase of the monsoon, the gentle Hathia rains of early October, didn't occur at all. So what had looked like a bumper crop in September was only a good fall crop, and Bihar ran its normal food deficit.

Still, a new foundation for more productive agriculture was laid in Bihar by emergency aid in the form of wells, irrigation pumps, high-yielding hybrid seeds, and chemical fertilizers. A crash U.S. water survey of the upper Gangetic plain, conducted to find places to drill wells and save lives, revealed the existence of an underground lake not far below the surface that may be the largest and potentially the most productive in the entire world. Farmers have known about this vast pool of water for centuries. But it has never been tapped for irrigation of a land acutely vulnerable to the vagaries of the weather. Bihar possesses other underground riches in coal and other minerals. Experts agree it simply is not necessary for fields and human beings to dry up when the monsoon fails, for forests and soil to be denuded for firewood, even for the state's huge population to be engaged almost exclusively in agriculture. The one resource that should be drastically weeded out, Bihar's emaciated cattle, continue to pillage the countryside.

The question in the mid-1960s was whether lessons learned during the crisis – lessons about years of human neglect that lead to famine and then deepen its effects – would be applied. It remained unanswered when 2000 arrived. Bihar, one of India's oldest civilized areas, is still one of its most backward states. Most of its people are no less malnourished or undernourished. Ironically, many Biharis ate better during the great famine than they usually do. This was because of free food handouts not at Indian-run soup kitchens but through CARE's providing one nutritious meal a day – a mixture of corn, soya, and milk or CSM – to five million hungry children and mothers.

Yet there is another side to Indian agriculture. Starting in the late sixties, the Green Revolution transformed whole districts and the living standards of their inhabitants almost overnight. A visit to an average Punjabi village today, for example, reveals productive farm families with more wheat than they know what to do with, refrigerators and TV sets in their front rooms, tractors for road transportation as well as field cultivation, and confident pride in their own achievements. In villages as much as in cities, India is full of contradictions as well as surprises.

India is a country of mass poverty. India is a country of individual dignity. India is an ancient Asian civilization belonging to itself, peculiarly faded and pockmarked by signs of decadence. India is a modern nation with strong links to the West, exhibiting refreshing vigour in high technology. Indians are often maddeningly arrogant. The same Indians can display a deep inferiority complex. Some Indians are cruel and callous to fellow human beings. Other Indians are kind-hearted and sensitive. India is many nations, which helps to explain some of its contradictions. Except when thoughts and feelings come tumbling out, often violently, India is a state of mind – or soul – more than a scene of action.

This repels many Westerners and usually leads to mixed emotions, making for frustration on the part of those who are initially attracted. One does not have to become a mystic, however, to recognize the universality of the very movements of human beings crammed into Calcutta, starving in Bihar, voting in Phaltan, riding tractors in the Punjab, wearing flowers in their hair in South India, even driving stop-and-start taxis in Delhi.

Mahatma Gandhi, the father of the nation, must have personified India in that universal way. Otherwise he could not have generated the human force he did without ever seeking political office. His life really was his message. He spoke for the hungry majority of his countrymen and women when he promised: "I shall work for an India in which the poorest shall feel that it is their country in whose making they have an effective voice." His is a fitting definition of the democracy that has been bruised, battered, and scorned in the independent India he brought about.

If Indian civilization is irretrievably decadent, if casteism with all it implies is so entrenched it can never be uprooted by peaceful means, then both political freedom and satyagraha – the truth force mobilized by the Mahatma – will die. Then all that the world has seen over more than half a century is the occasional bright flickering of embers soon to be doused by an upheaval arising out of a repeatedly betrayed hungry majority. What Jawaharlal Nehru, reveling in his own tryst with power, called India's "tryst with destiny" will end in India's unavoidable, probably violent fragmentation.

Indian society is traditional and backward-looking, after all, more than modern and forward-looking. Hinduism, its religious and cultural core, is unreformed. Buddhism, the movement with the best chance of changing India, never took root in the land of its birth. The humanitarian efforts of the Mahatma, the individual rights written into the Indian constitution, and the development of scattered elements of an industrial society have not prevented the Hindu concept of caste – and popular acceptance of caste inequalities – from remaining decisive in the organization of life still based on primary agriculture.

India is frequently explained to this day by generous interpretations of the British Raj. To a significant extent, this is due to the interest of the last British viceroy, the late voluble figure grandly titled Admiral of the Fleet the Earl Mountbatten of Burma, in perpetuating positive imperial memories, especially of himself. In historic fact, the Indian caste system and the British class system neatly complemented each other for the better part of two centuries.

The elite of each social system neither swallowed nor resisted the other but coexisted at a distance. Each in their own way, the members of both saw as little of India as they wanted to see, and methodically transmitted their non-egalitarian values to those below them. Only the Indians at the bottom of the heap, the untouchables or the non-Hindus considered untouchables in villages and cities, got kicked without being able to kick someone else.

Those few Englishmen and women who allowed themselves to get close enough to feel a love for India often became twisted in time by hate. Beyond the archaic charm of Kipling's verse, *The Nightrunners of Bengal* by John Masters is a deeper portrayal of the limited English-Indian interface than E.M. Forster's *A Passage to India*, which explores Indian Muslim character but merely caricatures Hindu personality. When the British left in 1947, ninety years after the Mutiny by sepoys of the Indian army they had created, their parting contribution was to divide India into a predominantly Hindu but constitutionally secular state and an Islamic nation calling itself Pakistan. The white colonialists thereby showed both Indians and Pakistanis how to undo the unity the Raj had established by building railways, establishing the Indian Civil Service, and introducing the English language.

Political independence resulted not from violent revolution or even from healthy evolution. There was plenty of violence, but it was violence spawned by hatred between religious communities and borne of poverty and despair. If Gandhi's ideas on abolishing caste, requiring Hindus and Muslims to live together in one nation, and building from the village up had been adopted, the crust of an aging society might have been broken. Instead, India's new rulers used Gandhian non-violence first as a pretext for altering as little as possible internally, and then as a cover for pursuing by increasingly violent means the imperial ends of an artificially fabricated, xenophobic nationalism.

To make matters much worse, while Nehru with his elitist Eton-

Cambridge conditioning naturally took Britain as the political model for independent India, he looked to the Soviet Union for economic example. A succession of five-year plans concentrating on the creation of state-run heavy industries and promotion of science and technology hardly touched India's backward social and economic structure. Nearly two decades passed after the country had won political freedom before an all-India plan for increasing food output and improving the lives of the rural four-fifths of the population took effect. Without a readiness for what development economists call "distributive justice" at upper levels of Indian society – the exception being egalitarian Sikh wheat growers in the Punjab – initially many rich farmers got richer and many poor peasants were squeezed off the land and into already overcrowded cities.

Together with deep social and economic inequity, the other compelling force in India's present and future goes back beyond the Nehrus, Mahatma Gandhi, the two centuries of British domination and, before that, two centuries of Moghul rule in the north.

While Hindu culture has pervaded more than three thousand years of Indian civilization, only one Indian ruler has succeeded in uniting and ruling the whole Subcontinent, and then only for a mere thirty-eight years. Asoka did so from 270 to 232 BC, and he was a convert to Theravada Buddhism. Instead of relying on Brahmin priests, he tied the virtues of his religion to the legitimacy of his rule through Buddhist monks. The nightmare lurking in the back of the Indian collective mind is the breakup of India. It started to become real with British-induced partition in 1947. Although to India's immediate advantage, it loomed again with the breakup of Pakistan in 1971 and the creation of Bangladesh. It is connected to India's determination to hold on to the breathtakingly beautiful Vale of Kashmir. If the withering away of Indian nationalism ever goes past the point of no return, even military intervention to restore order is unlikely to stop the emergence of smaller nations based on language, region, or religion.

More than 800 languages or dialects are spoken in India, derived from twice that number of mother tongues. The constitution recognizes fourteen major Indian languages, and English is the second official national language after Hindi. Since 1960, when Bombay state was broken into Maharashtra and Gujarat, states of the Indian Union have been associated by law with major language groups. This has reduced the potential for language conflict – but not language chauvinism – within state boundaries. It probably has increased the tension between speakers of ten major Sanskrit-based languages in north and central India and speakers of four Dravidian languages in the southern states of Andhra, Karnataka (formerly Mysore), Kerela, and Tamil Nadu (formerly Madras). Many Indians opposed or cool to the northcentral language of Hindi as the national language – on the ground that it is spoken by 40 per cent of the population at most, and lacks the literary traditions of languages such as Tamil, Bengali, Marathi, and Urdu – live in the south. They prefer English as the "link language." Indians who understand English make up only 2 or 3 per cent of the population. But they are scattered throughout a vast and diverse country whose states in many ways are as dissimilar, or similar, as the nations of Europe.

Divisions among religions and among castes and subcastes of the predominant religion of Hinduism are also endemic in constitutionally secular India. The most glaring is the one between more than 800 million Hindus and more than 120 million Muslims, nearly the same number as those in Islamic Pakistan and more than those in Bangladesh. The division is aggravated by the historical fact of Muslim dominion over northern India before the British came along. It lies at the root of the conflict with Pakistan over Kashmir as the only Muslim-majority state in India.

Christians and Sikhs also make up important religious minorities in India, followed by Buddhists, Jains, Parsis, and Jews. India's share of the Punjab after the 1947 partition was redivided to give Sikhs a state they could call their own, on the legal basis not of religion but of their Punjabi language. This did not prevent a violent campaign for independence by Sikhs who were deeply alienated despite close Hindu-Sikh personal ties and the fact that they belong to the most economically advanced religious group in India except for the Parsis centred in Bombay.

At the same time, many Hindus, especially in the south but increasingly in the north as well, are hostile to members of the highest caste of Brahmins, whom they see as a self-appointed ruling class. But India's widest social chasm separates the four Hindu varnas or caste groups from more than 160 million outcastes or Harijans or – their preferred name, meaning "broken people" – dalits, who are largely restricted to doing "dirty" jobs no one else will do despite constitutional guarantees of equality. Entrenched discrimination against these Indians, who are literally untouchable to orthodox Hindus, overlaps religious bias. This is because many caste Hindus consider Muslims and Christians to be converts or descendents of converts from Hinduism who sought escape from the otherwise inescapable stigma of lacking caste status.

When Indians speak of "fissiparous tendencies," they are using not only stilted English but also a euphemism for deep-seated mutual distrust with profound political implications. Given the sharp differences among them, "Indianness" as an all-embracing cultural identity is almost a miracle. But considering that it extends to people living in Pakistan, Bangladesh, Sri Lanka, and Nepal – although many of these people would deny it – Indianness is clearly not an unbreakable shield against further fragmentation of India. The common characteristics it embraces provide protection against fresh partition. But they are not proof of lasting political unity.

This has been apparent in recent years in chronic rebellions in four distinct parts of India, in a sharp deterioration of the line of peaceful co-existence between Hindus and Muslims nationwide, and in unprecedented organized protests on the part of deprived dalits and low-caste Hindus.

In Tamil Nadu, the central Indian government succeeded for a while in diverting a Tamil separatist movement from its main goal by training minority Hindu Tamils from nearby Sri Lanka for insurgent warfare against the Buddhist Sinhalese–dominated government in Colombo. When Indian troops went into Sri Lanka in 1987 on the pretext of keeping the peace but actually to exert New Delhi's regional dominance, they ended up fighting extremist Tamil Tigers who had been supported from Indian soil. So India not only set another precedent dangerous for its own unity by aiding separatists from another country; by killing Sri Lankan Tamils, it also antagonized many of its own Tamils, who have turned again to removing real and perceived constraints imposed by Hindi-speaking northerners.

In Assam in India's remote northeast – made more so by the central government's placing the state and adjacent areas off-limits to foreign journalists – indigenous people, including large Muslim and Christian minorities, demand autonomy in the face of an influx of Hindus from nearby West Bengal. New Delhi has long resisted this campaign with political and economic carrots and military sticks. Use of force against separatist movements is a proven but not often witnessed method in eastern India. Indian forces have employed bombing, napalm, and search-and-destroy missions, all reminiscent of U.S. tactics in the Vietnam war, against Baptist Naga rebels and Mizo tribal insurgents laying claim to homelands adjoining Assam.

In Kashmir, a peaceful Muslim movement for self-determination evolved into an armed Muslim uprising against Indian control during the half-century since a United Nations–imposed ceasefire ended the first war between India and Pakistan over the divided state. This evolution was due partly to the death of the long-imprisoned, moderate Sheikh Mohammad Abdullah, the Lion of Kashmir. It was partly because of arms and insurgents from the Afghanistan war supporting Kashmiri militants through Pakistan-backed terrorism. It was perhaps mostly due to cruel repression of Kashmiris by Indian police escalating to massive retaliation by the Indian army. In 1965, India decisively defeated an attempt by Pakistan to seize the Vale of Kashmir in the second war between the two countries. In the late spring and early summer of 1999, troops, artillery, and planes drove heavily armed Muslim intruders, including Pakistani army elements, out of western Himalayan redoubts in India's part of Kashmir in what proved to be another dangerous miscalculation by Pakistan. Divided Kashmir and the passions it evokes may still hold the key to the future of the entire Subcontinent.

In the Punjab, a brutal campaign of counter-terrorism by Indian police succeeded in doing what the Indian army had failed to do with its unprecedented armored assault on a religious sanctuary, the Golden Temple in Amritsar, in June 1984. Operation Blue Star against the most sacred shrine of the Sikhs led to the assassination of Prime Minister Indira Gandhi by her Sikh bodyguards four months later, an immediate murderous retaliation against the large Sikh community in Delhi at the behest of her son Rajiv Gandhi, and an organized Sikh campaign of terror against Hindus in the Punjab. Well-armed Sikhs indiscriminately killed hundreds each month in the name of an independent Sikh state to be called Khalistan. When political negotiations did not bring about a permanent settlement, ruthless police agents imposed a temporary one. With the Punjab also then barred to foreign journalists, they broke the back of the terrorist movement through mass imprisonment and the assassination of real and suspected militants. But millions of Sikhs in and out of the Punjab remain alienated from the mainstream of Indian life to which they contribute richly as productive farmers, efficient technicians and entrepreneurs, and staunch military officers. The direction they ultimately take also will influence India's destiny significantly.

As important as these regional conflicts are, India's survival in its present form depends at bottom on whether Hindus across the country will respect the right of Muslims to secure lives, and the right of outcaste dalits and other desperately poor persons to better lives. To assure both, political will is necessary. Even more so is economic opportunity. Standards of living will have to rise before a readiness to share expands. Poor and rich Indians alike somehow will have to get over their ingrained fear that gain by others means loss by them.

The noble goal of all the people of India or at least a decisive majority of them going forward together can only be reached by democratic capitalist practice replacing democratic socialist theory no later than the first years of the twenty-first century. With political domination by the Nehru dynasty and the Congress Party fading into the past, the Hindu nationalist

Bharatiya Janata Party alone is in a position to provide the needed tolerance, political will, and economic opportunity for the future. This may be
ironic considering its past record of caste and religious discrimination. Or
it may be appropriate because familiarity qualifies the BJP to deal with
this evil. But it is the only perceptible way India will stay together and
thrive.

5

Dung and Decency

If India had stayed together in 1947, in all likelihood it would have done better in giving decent, fair lives to its people.

The challenge would have been tremendous with Muslims making up a minority of close to one-third of the population instead of 10 or 12 per cent. But the problems and the compromises needed to resolve them probably would have been preferable to what has transpired in a truncated India and an illogical Pakistan, even after the creation of Bangladesh from East Bengal. Mutual, natural antagonism between the two countries has been both a cause and a result of ruinous internal politics exploiting explosive religious differences and dangerous economic inequities.

Mohandas Gandhi, a firm believer in both building a nation from the village up and overcoming religious and caste barriers through example and non-violence, adamantly opposed partition. Jawaharlal Nehru went along with it, fearing that the price of a deal between the Indian National Congress and the Muslim League to keep India undivided would be a Muslim and not himself as its first prime minister. The League's Mohammad Ali Jinnah, who died soon after the creation of his distorted Pakistan, insisted on carrying out the "two-nation" theory: separate nations for Hindus and Muslims although India remained home to more than a third of the Subcontinent's Muslims and adopted a secular constitution. Lord Louis Mountbatten, a potential conciliator as the last British viceroy, was eager for a *fait accompli* that would be hailed as a historic achievement, not least by himself, and he heedlessly rushed the partition of Bengal in the east and the Punjab in the west months before a settlement was necessary.

The result was catastrophic: an immediate loss of human life, the first war between India and Pakistan, and most of all, Hindu and Muslim – and Sikh – actions and passions reinforcing old suspicions and hatreds and laying the groundwork for new ones. Unexpectedly the division of Bengal went quietly. To deter the most feared outbreak of violence, Gandhi returned to where one of his "fasts onto death" had helped stop the mass killing of Hindus and Muslims by each other in 1946. But the division of the rich farmlands of the Punjab, close to the cradle of Indian civilization, was accompanied by primitive massacres. More than 10 million people moved from one country to the other, mostly on foot, and perhaps one million of them died during or after their ordeal. Hindus and Sikhs descended on defenceless Muslim men, women, and children and slaughtered them indiscriminately. Muslims were no less merciless in raping and killing innocent Hindus and Sikhs as revenge followed retaliation. When there was a question of identity, men were knifed as Muslims if they were circumcised, as Hindus if they were not.

Independent India and Pakistan were born in an avoidable bloodbath. It is arguable that those who died horribly on their way to new homes, or lived in misery for months or even years after they reached their destinations, were victims of the personal ambitions of Jinnah, Nehru, and Mountbatten. There is no doubt that the two nations set out on their new paths with traumatic wounds carved into the psyches of their Hindus, Muslims, and Sikhs as deeply as the cuts that destroyed the integrity of undivided India and the best chance in more than two thousand years to keep India whole under native rule.

"Pakistan's obsession is India," said Dorothy Thompson in a rare American insight into foreign countries, "and India's obsession is India." For Pakistanis, this has meant failure after failure in trying to keep their artificial country together in the name of Islam. For Indians, no matter what their religion or caste, it has meant an acute consciousness of Hinduism as the core of a civilization that some consider stagnant. As economic conditions improved slowly or not at all or even deteriorated, and political choice narrowed under the dynasty started by Jawaharlal Nehru, a Kashmiri Brahmin, religious politics and communal violence grew. The link between religion and politics was not the inclusive, positive kind forged by Mahatma Gandhi in the independence struggle and envisioned by him for a free India. It would not have been characterized by mounting resort to violence if it had been. The connection was repeatedly narrow-minded and negative.

It was evident in local clashes between Hindus and Muslims, usually in towns of the crowded, impoverished northcentral Gangetic plain or Hindi belt, and growing out of real or perceived religious insults or student agitation. It became the focus of appeals for votes by state political leaders who pandered to caste and religious loyalties instead of rising above them or trying to reconcile them. Religion was behind the drive for an independent Punjab by Sikh extremists, who shifted their alliance from Hindus to once despised Muslims, and the fascist-like Shiv Sena movement of Marathi-speaking Hindus in Bombay. The Congress Party, whose monopoly on power in India's states but not New Delhi was broken in early 1967, fought Kashmir's Muslims at the same time it relied on Muslim and dalit support nationwide.

A few months before, on 7 November 1966 – twenty-six years before Hindu fanatics razed the Babri mosque in Ayodhya in northcentral India on 6 December 1992 – the frightening power of Hindu revivalism first asserted itself. Hundreds of half-naked or wholly naked ash-smeared, long-haired sadhus or self-anointed holy men, wielding small axes and hurling stones, assaulted Parliament itself in New Delhi with the intention of ending Indian democracy.

In a wild melee at the entrance to the grounds of the graceful circular building, police on horseback firing tear gas and rifle bullets managed to repulse the wild-eyed holy men, whose ostensible aim was an absolute ban on the slaughter of cows sacred to Hindus. An orange-robed member of Parliament, Swami Rameshwar Anand, suspended by the speaker for ten days after forcing a thirty-minute recess, had shouted to the mob at the gates: "I closed Parliament for half an hour. Now go in and close Parliament forever."

The bizarre sadhus failed at the time to "cut at the very roots of our democracy," as Prime Minister Indira Gandhi angrily put it. They and their followers could indulge only in an orgy of looting and burning when they were turned away from Parliament. But Anand was a member of the Jan Sangh, which organized the demonstration and was the forerunner to the Hindu nationalist Bharatiya Janata Party. A generation later the BJP assembled a larger mob at Ayodhya whose members succeeded in destroying the historic 430-year-old mosque unprotected by the police. Hindus believed the site to be the birthplace of Ram, an incarnation of the god Vishnu. But the Muslim place of worship was a nationally recognized symbol of the secularism guaranteed by India's democratic constitution.

Some argue that such obscene events are few and far between in independent India's history. The first, on 30 January 1948 in New Delhi, was the assassination of Mahatma Gandhi, who also was virtually unprotected by the police. His killer was Nathuram Godse, a Poona Brahmin and a former member of the Rashtriya Swayamsevak Sangh or RSS, which included Hindus who held Gandhi in contempt for his tolerance of Muslims. Thrown into deep shock, many Indians at first believed a Muslim had shot Gandhi at a prayer meeting. To deter mass communal killing that almost certainly would have crippled India more than had the partition slaughter in the Punjab the year before, All-India Radio added an all-important

sentence to its grim 6 PM announcement of the awful act: "Mahatma
Gandhi was assassinated in New Delhi at twenty minutes past five this
afternoon. His assassin was a Hindu."

At the time, five and a half months after independence, Hindu political
extremism was outside the mainstream of Indian life. Nearly nineteen years
later, when the sadhus flung themselves at Parliament, the Jan Sangh was a
significant but minor opposition party. In December 1992, when Hindus
triumphantly tore apart the Ayodhya mosque, the BJP was the main opposition in and outside Parliament to a weak, minority Congress government.
On 26 January 1992, India's Republic Day, a BJP procession that had been
allowed to make its way to Srinagar, the besieged capital of Muslim-majority Kashmir, raised the Indian flag there. It was another outrageously symbolic, deliberately provocative act, predating Ayodhya, and could have easily and widely ignited communal passions and even started another war
between India and Pakistan.

The Hindu militancy associated with the BJP stems directly from the RSS
and its Indian version of Nazi brownshirts. With destruction of the Babri
mosque, BJP militants finally triggered widespread and bloody Hindu-Muslim violence, usually at the expense of minority Muslims. This was especially so in Bombay in the weeks and months that followed. Shiv Sena
goons targeted not only poor Muslims but also well-to-do Muslims who
had long enjoyed a special respected place in the culture of India's most vigorous and sophisticated city. The goons burned, looted, and killed not with
police caught unaware but with the active connivance of police who, witnesses said, pointed out where prospective victims could be found. The
fanatical Hindu assaults on Gandhi, Parliament, and the Ayodhya mosque
in 1948, 1966, and 1992, respectively, targeted tolerance, democracy, and
secularism in India.

In Bombay in the weeks following the Ayodhya incident, the Hindu
extremists' objective was to demoralize the most dynamic part of the country's business community, and in some cases they succeeded temporarily.
However, Indian businessmen are not noted for their soft hearts. They are
capable of bringing about the higher economic levels essential to saving
India from medieval savagery, if they are allowed to do so by government
and are confident of stability. In fact many businessmen are among the new
supporters of the BJP as the political force most likely to bring stability and
reduce stifling government controls, even as the party's militants pursue
their destabilizing campaign to undercut the nation's modern secular
framework. Trapped in India's political, economic, and social morass, Hindus who would not normally turn to a revivalist party for national salvation have joined Hindus who would not think of looking anywhere else.

While a battle rages within the BJP over whether to drop its inherently anti-Muslim message for good or only appear to do so, anti-dalit feeling among Indians is so wide and persistent that it does not require tacit endorsement by a party with roots in Hindu culture. In 1969, a parliamentary committee found after a four-year nationwide investigation that untouchability was "virulent" all over India despite efforts to end it during more than two decades of independence and a legal ban on it enacted in 1955. Days before, the Jagadguru Shankaracharya or great and learned teacher of Puri, considered one of India's holiest men, had publicly criticized the ban and declared that people are born unequal, justifying the caste system and placing some outside it.

Another honest parliamentary inquiry would have to conclude that crass discrimination against dalits – more hurtful and demeaning in many ways than the apartheid system abandoned by South Africa – is hardly less malignant after more than five decades of independence. At the end of the 1990s, a report by the New York-based organization Human Rights Watch, drawing on interviews with more than 300 dalits, found, in the words of its Indian author: "Untouchability is not an ancient cultural artifact, it is a human-rights abuse on a vast scale." In many places in India during the decade, dalits, low-caste Hindus, and Christians, individually or in groups, were burned, beaten, stabbed, stoned, or shot to death for daring to seek better lives, for violating ironbound caste rules about marriage, or simply for being different.

Three decades after the deliberate Christmas 1968 burning to death of forty-two dalit villagers in South India's Tanjore district, a sickeningly similar massacre took place in the village of Shanker Bigha in the northern, famine-prone state of Bihar. On the night of 25 January 1999, the eve of India's Republic Day, more than fifty upper-caste landowners with guns burst into the mud huts of sleeping dalit farm workers and their families. They shot dead twenty-two men, women, and children before fleeing into the village's wheat fields. In their eyes the crime of the landless peasants, punishable by cold-blooded execution, was to demand the right to cultivate small pieces of the wheat fields under long-existing but unenforced land-reform laws.

Soon after the BJP took office in Delhi in March 1998, militant Hindus launched a number of attacks on Christian clergymen, churches, and recent converts to Christianity, especially among Adivasis or tribal people living in the western state of Gujarat, once Mahatma Gandhi's home. But the most shocking incident took place in a village in the eastern state of Orissa in January 1999: Graham Staines, an Australian evangelical missionary, and his two young sons were killed when a mob attacked them as they slept in their jeep, then setting the vehicle on fire. Reports of this assault and others in Western media, played up much more than stories about common

Hindu-Muslim clashes in India, implied that the Hindu nationalist government had organized a violent campaign against the country's 23 million Christians. A judicial inquiry later concluded that an individual Hindu had instigated the mob in Orissa, not a group associated with the BJP. The incidents were disturbing enough without drawing sweeping conclusions.

They strongly suggested that with the BJP in power avid Hindus felt fewer constraints in going after Christians they believed were threatening their way of life by actively seeking converts to Christianity. The World Hindu Congress affiliated with the BJP openly opposes mass conversions and promotes Hindutva, an all-embracing culture for India centred on Hinduism, while considering the country's secular constitution "unIndian." But Congress Party governments had long discouraged large-scale conversions to Christianity with little controversy, and the BJP government showed its sensitivity to the danger of a serious problem becoming worse by curbing anti-Christian Hindu militants.

In September 1998, however, the government could not prevent the killing of Srichand, a forty-five-year-old dalit known as a *balmiki* because he performed the lowliest job of cleaning toilets in Meerut northeast of Delhi, by other untouchables called *jatavs* who are descended from cobblers and carry out tasks considered slightly higher. The jatavs took vengeance because a girl belonging to their group had left the town with a balmiki boy.

Nor could mob violence be averted in March 1999 in Shimla northwest of Delhi two days after Nirmala, seventeen, and Desh Raj, twenty-three, both dalits, had eloped. With the enthusiastic approval of Shimla's caste Hindus and dalits alike, fifteen members of the girl's family killed the couple with sticks and scythes simply because they both came from the village, and therefore were deemed to have broken a rule in Haryana state against marriages within a clan.

In July 1999 in a village outside Lucknow, capital of the most populous state of Uttar Pradesh, upper-caste Hindu men abducted, raped, and burned to death Siya Dulari, forty, a lower-caste woman, because her fifteen-year-old son had eloped with the seventeen-year-old daughter of a high-caste family. Police, arriving too late to stop the human bonfire watched by hundreds of villagers, charged eight persons with murder.

Many policemen and other officials and even state governments remain unaware or unheeding of the law banning untouchability. The orthodox Hindu view of this pernicious practice certainly has not changed, and clearly in the eyes of some Hindus it has been reinforced with the rise of the BJP. But what has started to change is the fatalism of most dalits in morosely accepting the status of "sub-humans." So also has the indifference of the central government in paying little more than lip service to a law that is almost meaningless unless it is enforced.

For any dalit to gain the self-confidence to protest is not easy. The caste system is maintained less by violence than by non-violence, once employed by Mahatma Gandhi in a vain attempt to break caste discrimination along with colonial servitude.

Caste Hindus refuse to let Hindus below them draw water from village wells, enter village temples, and eat the same food in the same places with them. Dalits have no choice but to live in the meanest huts in the most primitive part of most villages. Dhobis or laundrymen, who make up their own subcaste, will not wash their clothes. Until recent years, panchayats (elected village councils) would not let them attend meetings. In one area of Madhya Pradesh in northcentral India, dalit men are traditionally prohibited from turning up their moustaches. Students who belong to castes have successfully boycotted teachers who are dalits. Nor is use of force to prevent dalit children from going to school unusual.

In cities, restaurants and hotels post signs reserving the right of admission, which everyone knows means keeping dalits out. In villages, a Brahmin considers himself or herself polluted if touched by the shadow of a dalit, let alone touched physically. Throughout India, many caste Hindus treat dalits like nothing more than the trash left behind by workmen for them to clean up. They are literally the sweepers of a society that has not broken with its past, the bottom rung of an intricate and inexorable system of human oppression. The pitiful brooms they use are deliberately kept short so dalits lose their dignity when they must stoop or squat to do their work – unspeakably dirty work by strict Hindu definition.

Yet groups of dalits have organized in some parts of the country to demand recognition and fairness. They have campaigned for a larger number of guaranteed government jobs, one of the recommendations by the parliamentary committee in 1969. They keep pressing for education of their children so coming generations can hope for better lives than their own. They joined tribal people, who are treated no better, and environmentalists in resisting a huge dam project in westcentral India that would inundate the villages of 170,000 people. Unless the Narmada power-and-irrigation project was halted, the protesters threatened, they would resort to mass suicide by drowning.

When an anti-Congress coalition came to power in New Delhi in 1989, Prime Minister Vishwanath Pratap Singh showed sensitivity to the needs of poor Indians by acting to increase the number of jobs in the central government "reserved" not only for dalits but also for low-caste Hindus. This caused violent reactions by higher-caste Hindus in many parts of the country, including hysterical demonstrations and the beating and burning of dalits. But a precedent was set for widespread government intervention – what would be called affirmative action in the United States – on behalf of the most downtrodden Indians.

In 1993, under a minority Congress Party government, Parliament adopted a constitutional amendment reserving one-third of village pan- chayat seats and village chiefs' positions in all India for women, and many of those for low-caste women. By the end of the decade, nearly one million women had been elected to the local governing councils to the dismay of high-caste men. At the same time, low-caste and dalit Indians sometimes have taken matters into their own hands. Soon after the shooting death of twenty-two members of dalit peasant families in a Bihar village in January 1999, a radical Maoist gang took revenge by killing at least thirty-three upper-caste villagers in the district.

Quotas are at best a partial answer to India's religious and caste divi- sions, however, and violence is no answer at all. Nor is restraining normal progress through government controls the way to narrow economic gaps. Only economic development that benefits all groups in a complex society will take the edge off mutual antagonism and create a larger pie in which everyone can share in the long term. As the conservative economist Milton Friedman argues, India offers compelling evidence that this economic growth can happen only if the government gets out of most of the econ- omy and lets a free market operate. Outside the former Communist world – although in many ways it was effectively inside that world for years – India is a glaring example of the disaster that government control of the "commanding heights" of an economy can bring. At the same time, too rapid a privatization of state industries and removal of subsidies to farm- ers can cause losses of jobs, economic shocks, and popular protests in the short term – results of what has come to be called globalization.

By mid-1991, when the Congress Party returned to power as a parliamen- tary minority under Prime Minister P.V. Narasimha Rao and Finance Min- ister Manmohan Singh, the nation was on the brink of bankruptcy as a consequence of more than four decades of the government's controlling the commanding heights. They had no choice but to begin to loosen the bureaucracy's stranglehold on Indian industry. A decade later, it is still unclear whether this change of course is sustainable – even or especially as it is intensified – or is too little and too late. What is certain is that India, as an overwhelmingly rural land like most developing countries, first must solve its food problem through the free enterprise of its farmers if it is to have a real chance to succeed.

It started to do this late, too: at the end of 1965, when Prime Minister

Lal Bahadur Shastri gave agriculture the logical priority denied it during nearly two decades of independence by Jawaharlal Nehru and his Soviet-style five-year plans. That change of policy was too late to stave off the Bihar famine, and too little to prevent the rest of the economy from grinding to a halt twenty-five years later. But it's in the dung-littered fields and villages of India that long-held hopes for bringing decency and respect to the lives of ordinary Indians will rise or fall.

Starting with my four-week stay in the large village of Phaltan in Maharashtra in 1958, and during subsequent visits in 1962 and 1966, I learned this primary lesson long before the Green Revolution took hold in scattered parts of India in the late 1960s. The related lesson I learned in Phaltan during the local election of 1958 – that the poorest and most remote people want to have a democratic say in the shaping of their society – is ultimately consigned to the dust if they cannot produce enough food to eat and earn enough money to spend.

When I encountered India the first time through Phaltan's heat and dust and farmers and animals, my friend and former schoolmate, Bonbehari Nimbkar, had to smuggle packets of hybrid seeds in from the United States because the Indian government discouraged anything but traditional, inadequate farming. Other cultivators had not heard of progressive agriculture. Although Phaltan had its first telephone and first motor vehicle, in most respects it could have existed with little change 200 or even 2,000 years earlier.

Swinging long sticks in unison, women beat piles of jowar (sorghum), the area's traditional grain, from chaff. Raising clouds of choking dust, shepherds drove flocks of goats through village lanes. Bonbehari teased me about my warily avoiding heaps of cow dung all over the place. Few people ate anything but flat sorghum cakes, a vegetable or two and, if they were lucky, milk from a water buffalo. Even at the modest home of Bonbehari and his wife Jai, we had meat from a goat only once in the four weeks, and she ground her own spices. As in most of the rest of India, bullocks did all the field work. A few open stalls sold only necessities such as metal utensils and bolts of cloth, and the weekly bazaar offered little else in the way of basic commodities, what there was laid out neatly but sparsely on the ground.

When I returned in 1962, it was with a spectronic colorimeter I had smuggled into India for Bonbehari's tiny lab, where he analysed samples of grain for the few local farmers who had joined him in progressive agriculture. Phaltan was growing as the centre of a farming area more than 250 kilometres southeast of Bombay. But its ancient rhythms were immediately familiar and hardly changed.

In April 1966, Phaltan was experiencing the same severe drought that

was to devastate Bihar in eastcentral India. Bonbehari greeted me with
the grim news that it hadn't rained since 12 September 1965. Although
this part of Maharashtra was used to dry weather and dust, crops had
never been as bad in the memory of many farmers. But they were showing the kind of tough initiative exemplified by Shivaji, the legendary seventeenth century Maratha warrior who waged guerrilla warfare against
Moghul conquerors. By resourcefully using the craggy land and sturdy
people, he mounted a revolution that resulted for a time in a defiant
Maratha kingdom.

Two small revolutions were going on in Phaltan three centuries later.
They were drawing on the same individual self-reliance demonstrated by
Shivaji, and defying or at least ignoring government edicts as he had.

One was a consumer revolution. Now dozens of open-air, clumsy little
shops were thriving. Many featured non-essential items such as the four or
five portraits of John F. Kennedy still sold each month by one stall (two and
a half years after his assassination) along with colourful pictures of Hindu
gods and goddesses and photographs of Indian political leaders (none yet
of Indira Gandhi, three months after she had become prime minister). Well-
stocked shelves of cottons and woollens – including ready-made clothes,
unheard of a few years before – children's toys, soda pop, and many more
cooking utensils were evidence that, given incentives, a backward Indian
community can begin to pull itself up by the bootstraps. It's true that Phaltan still exhibited disturbing poverty, dirt, and ignorance. But even in a
poor crop year, the jumble of shops showed that people had money and
wanted to spend it.

Even more important was the food revolution going on in Phaltan. Its
people were switching from sorghum to corn as their staple grain.

For food most Indians depend largely on the major grain grown in their
area. That is one reason their diets are not balanced and they suffer from
poor nutrition. A vicious cycle develops: a combination of hot climate and
not enough good food keeps a peasant plowing the same furrow with the
same bullocks and the same seeds year after year, impoverishing the land
and himself, and expecting and wanting little more than enough grain to
feed his family. Phaltan's peasants were beginning to break this cycle.

This was not because corn was particularly more nutritious than jowar.
It actually requires more precious water. But corn made use of irrigation
water that previously went to waste when peasants grew only one sorghum
crop a year, sowing in September when a little rain could be expected. As
a new crop, corn was being grown from improved hybrid seeds, which
were unknown in Phaltan until Bonbehari began distributing them. It had
expanded from twenty-five acres in 1962 to 6,000 acres. But in 1966 corn

was not yet the major crop it would be in another five years. The change was that two kinds of grain were now growing in quantity.

At first people in Phaltan said corn bread did not fill their stomachs. Then they said it caused diarrhea or it didn't taste good or it caused weakness. Their one legitimate complaint was that corn required double-grinding to be made into bread. But in 1966 more and more villagers said they liked corn better than sorghum because it tasted sweeter and the flat corn bread cakes were good even cold. If the conservative Indians who lived in Phaltan were switching to corn as their basic food, corn's by-products would benefit the area in the long run by diversifying its economy. Fats, waxes, oils, and medicinal alcohol can all be derived from corn. A co-operative starch factory using locally grown corn was planned as a first for India, whose two starch factories used corn imported from the United States as aid.

Phaltan's revolutions were happening despite the Congress Party governments of India and Maharashtra rather than because of them. Even more than in 1958 and 1962, the officials who came to Phaltan and the directives issued in the name of Congress democratic socialism in 1966 and as late as 1996 did more harm than good.

"Progressive farmers in Maharashtra are far ahead of any program of Mr Subramaniam," said Bonbehari, then thirty-four, referring to an intensive-cultivation scheme announced by Indian Agriculture Minister Chidambara Subramaniam. Sadashiv Shrikhande, fifty-five, an educated but not so well to do progressive farmer, when asked what he thought of the New Delhi plan, shrugged, "No, I don't know anything about that."

These two farmers, although they had suffered setbacks such as the 1966 drought, were leaders in Phaltan's quickening forward march. Since 1958 its population had grown from 12,000 to more than 20,000. The population explosion had created its own problems. But Phaltan was the centre of not only a 500-square-kilometre farming area but also a booming sugar-refining industry. Eight refineries in the area processed locally grown sugar cane, the main cash crop. Covered by the Koyna hydroelectric project, Phaltan had seen electric power spread from a few users for four hours a day in 1958 to hundreds of homes full-time. It had boasted twelve telephones in 1958. Now there were a hundred, and a waiting list for more than a hundred. Phaltan had had four automobiles in 1958. Now there were twenty-five cars and fifty trucks. There were also several primary schools, two high schools, and even a small college.

Apart from the natural obstacle of the Western Ghats or hills along the Arabian Sea coast that keep most of the monsoon rains from reaching the area – normal annual rainfall is only fifteen inches – Phaltan has had to overcome two directly related political hurdles. One was its past as a princely state, a small one but nonetheless characterized by the backward popular attitudes found wherever a maharajah once ruled. The other was the fact that the ex-maharajah, Naik Nimbalkar, had become the local Congress Party boss when independence had ended princely rule. He had rented his former palace to the new college for temporary quarters. But state funds entrusted to him to build permanent college buildings had somehow been lost after the foundations were laid.

Laxman Kshirsagar, thirty-nine, admitted that as an unprogressive farmer he had been licked by the odds against productive agriculture in Phaltan. He and his two brothers had given up cultivating their two acres because their well had run dry and there was no irrigation. "Even so, we have too little land for three brothers," he said, reflecting a widespread condition in India. Even as a member of the *mali* or gardener caste, he knew nothing of chemical fertilizers. Instead he used dung from the family's two bullocks, and said he would use hybrid seeds only if there were "plenty of water."

His comment about getting assistance nonetheless said something about the government's attitude as well as his own: "I never sought government help because help is usually given in the form of a loan. If we're not making anything from the land, it is better not to ask for anything. No government official ever came to the farm." He had found a job tending the cattle of another farmer, so he would not have to seek work on a government famine-relief project. Asked how he would vote in the coming elections, Kshirsagar promptly mentioned the "Raje Sahib," as the former maharajah was still deferentially known, and the Congress, and added, "There isn't anybody else."

Shrikhande's world was much wider but still precarious and still not enhanced by the government. A white grub pest had nearly wiped out his fifteen-acre operation a few years earlier, and he could find no official who knew more than he did about combatting it. With his hybrid corn stunted now due to "not enough water," his annual income would be cut in half to the equivalent of $650,* and the number of his irrigated acres reduced from eight to two. Shrikhande, a Brahmin, read all he could about farming but worked in the fields himself with his two hired men and eight hired women (who received two rupees or forty-two cents and one rupee or twenty-one cents a day, respectively). He grew hybrid seed for wheat and jowar, as well as corn, and also some grapes and cotton for marketing.

Seated on a crude chair in one of two small stone buildings he shared with his wife, three of their six children, and his brother, and surrounded

---

* All dollar amounts are in U.S. dollars.

by calendar pictures of Kennedy and Nehru, Hindu gods and Soviet farm tractors, Shrikhande quietly explained some of his problems: "In the last four years I have not had enough water. Fertilizers and insecticides are in short supply. I have to pay two rupees more for fertilizer on the black market. The government wants us to grow cotton but won't grant import licences for insecticides."

Bonbehari Nimbkar, who had introduced high-yielding hybrid seed to Phaltan, received his agricultural training at Rutgers and Arizona Universities and brought a modern Western approach to the dry, cracked soil of the area. From the start, he had run into outright government opposition. He suggested one new kind of cotton, for example, while the state government proposed another. His variety was accepted by other farmers and was now grown on 30,000 acres. The government belatedly recognized it as superior and distributed seeds, but only to co-operatives, not to individual cultivators.

The lanky Nimbkar farmed seventy acres, rented from an 800-year-old Hindu temple. But the hybrid seeds he had brought to Phaltan or developed on his own were grown on nearly 500 acres by other farmers, including Shrikhande, and were sold to many other farms in Maharashtra and neighbouring Mysore (now Karnataka) state. "In the beginning they were against the hybrids, too," he said of the government. "They felt that the poor ignorant cultivator would not be able to cultivate hybrids."

But at last this attitude was changing at the highest levels of the central government. Agriculture Minister Subramaniam had announced in December 1965, after a wrenching debate in the Shastri cabinet, that farmers would apply hybrid seeds and other modern agricultural inputs to 32 million acres or 10 per cent of India's cultivated land. Delhi's long overdue concentration on food grains output grew out of the success in the early 1960s of the Ford Foundation's "package program." This demonstrated in eight different farming districts of India – including a wheat-growing area of the Punjab and rice-growing Tanjore district in Madras (now Tamil Nadu) but not the Phaltan area – that a variable package of inputs, including hybrid seed, chemical fertilizer, irrigation, and insecticide, would double, triple, or even quadruple grain production. New dwarf varieties of plants would be able to take application of fertilizer and other inputs without "lodging" or falling over, as traditional tall plants do.

Still stuck on five-year plans, the government set a target date of 1971 for achieving national food grains self-sufficiency. Even Nehru, who had insisted on giving priority to building heavy state industries, had said that democracy was not possible if people's stomachs were empty. But it was not until nearly two years after his death in 1964 that the world's most populous democratic country at last made a start on expanding freedom from hunger by banking on the common sense of India's individual peasants. It was the beginning of the Green Revolution.

The Green Revolution was not confined to India. The hybrid wheats that were so successful in the Punjab had been developed in Mexico by Norman Borlaug, an American. The more difficult task of finding new rice varieties to suit diverse conditions was carried out mainly at the International Rice Research Institute in the Philippines, established by the Ford and Rockefeller Foundations. The Indian experience, however, not only bought vital time for hundreds of millions of people who would otherwise have gone hungry or starved; it also demolished the doom-and-gloom school of thought rooted in Malthusian refusal to admit that technology and food output can stay ahead – and historically have stayed ahead – of population growth in developing countries. It is also in stark contrast to the experience in China, where the Green Revolution did not take hold until much later. The Communist leadership had moved beyond low-output state collectives, but instead of going forward by encouraging the individual farmer, it had gone backward by regimenting peasants in huge communes.

The Malthusians will always be with us. They are almost as inventive as agricultural scientists in coming up with new varieties of their staple. But their underlying miscalculation was plain to see in a fashionable prediction at the time that India would face collapse in 1975 with mass starvation. That was the year India achieved what turned out to be a steady food grains surplus of at least 20 million tons, more than three times as much grain as the United States used to ship India annually under Public Law 480.

Indian farmers proved that "the process of rural development springs not from an answer to the question of how do we induce people to adopt new technologies, but from the question how do we find new technologies people will adopt." The words are those of W. David Hopper, a Canadian agricultural economist with the Ford and Rockefeller Foundations in India and later vice-president of the World Bank for South Asia. The shift in India, he pointed out, provided the "intellectual underpinnings" of the Green Revolution. Hopper and his pragmatic colleagues rejected the commonly held notion that the Indian farmer had not changed in a thousand years. As he put it with a logic supported by the tangible transformation of much of the Indian countryside, "No one has ever met a thousand-year-old farmer."

Despite dramatic increases in food grain production in some parts of India, and the bitter lessons of the famine in Bihar, Indians nevertheless continued to debate the wisdom of relying on growing numbers of progressive, informed cultivators for economic growth. Without parallel liberalization, Indian industry turned out mainly economy-depressing import substitutes. Politicians and bureaucrats instinctively denied, delayed, or diluted any economic measures except deadening government controls.

Inevitably, the time initially gained by the Green Revolution ran out without an across-the-board reform of the economy. India still managed to combine the worst aspects of socialism and capitalism: red tape preventing the birth of a broad market economy, and rapaciousness by entrepreneurs who could profit only by operating in a black market or at best a grey one. An Indian businessman reputedly kept three sets of books: one for the government, one for associates, and the real one for himself.

Shastri and Subramaniam pushed the new food policy through the cabinet over the stiff opposition of Finance Minister T.T. Krishnamachari, a doctrinaire-socialist Nehru holdover. When the prime minister unexpectedly died a month later, in January 1966, Indira Gandhi declared upon succeeding him that providing food to the people was still India's number one priority "in this year of scarcity." For the same reason she had opposed the spread of television as information minister, she never had her heart in giving free rein to India's peasants. The political risks were too high.

Congress Party chief ministers from India's states eventually lined up behind her outward support of modernized agriculture, although K.B. Sahay of Bihar actually told his people, "Let them eat flowers," when they didn't have enough grain to eat. But Indira failed pitifully to contain an embarrassing floor revolt against the new policy at the annual Congress convention in Jaipur a month after she became prime minister. A key element of that policy – letting Tata of Bombay, the most responsible large Indian private corporation, build a huge complex for domestic production of chemical fertilizers – never received government approval.

J.R.D. Tata, the distinguished Parsi who was recognized as India's most enlightened industrialist, pointed out that if the number of rural Indians who could earn enough money to buy manufactured products increased by only 10 per cent a year, "a staggering 50 million new consumers [would] be added to the present market potential." Now the figure would be more than 75 million. But Tata's dream had not come true when he died in 1993. Even today India's middle class has grown to perhaps 20 per cent of the total population – roughly 200 million people, including wealthier farmers – but up to half of the other 800 million Indians live in stark, unimaginable poverty. India's food grains surplus grew to 58 million tons in 2002 but part of it rotted and not enough reached hungry or undernourished people in remote areas.

By 1968, the Green Revolution gave rise to record-high crops, and to widespread hopes that the agricultural breakthrough would lead to overall economic progress by a deeply conservative, caste-ridden society. But it was clear even then that India's rich were getting richer and the poor were getting poorer.

"Production statistics confirm the growing abundance for a fraction of the population, at one end, and the fall in the level of living suffered by millions of families, at the other end," noted B.R. Shenoy, a leading Indian economist. Per capita consumption of essentials such as food grains, edible oils, sugar, and cotton cloth was steadily declining. Spending on cars, radios, electric fans, air-conditioners, air travel, and resort vacations, all far beyond the reach of ordinary Indians, was steadily rising. People in some rural districts were starving even in a year of plenty, while people in other districts prospered as never before.

The political-bureaucratic class clearly could not cope with the prospect of popular economic success. The nearly unlimited potential of the 80 per cent of Indians who lived in the countryside was starting to be tapped, with food grains output shooting up dramatically by 30 per cent in one year. But the government's fourth five-year plan starting in 1969 projected continued low levels of growth and consumption – targets that legions of mindless bureaucrats exercising countless controls would follow. It set the annual growth rate for agriculture at only 5 per cent, and overall growth before population and price increases at 6.5 per cent – in real terms, 2 to 3 per cent, even lower than what appropriately came to be called the "Hindu rate of growth."

"While Indian farmers have shown they can move ahead at a much faster pace," wryly commented an Indian agricultural expert, "government officials are already out of breath." But deficit spending by state and central governments continued unabated. Waste and inefficiency in government-owned industries, especially steel, continued to be a national scandal. Prime Minister Gandhi was on her way to nationalizing the nation's banks. Unemployment and underemployment kept going up. Exports barely moved. What was aptly called the "permit-licence raj" reigned supreme.

Some still said that more foreign aid was the answer to India's problems. But major injections of U.S. and other Western aid never prevented the Indian government from increasingly responding to Soviet advice and pressures on running the economy. Shenoy observed that India's economic sickness, far from being cyclical, was due to years of deficit spending, exchange controls, import licensing, and crushing taxation: "Indian planners, duly supported by expert advice from developed countries and United Nations agencies, have unwittingly created ... not the promised socialist millennium but near-ideal laboratory conditions for the spread of communism. The stepping up of foreign aid is no solution ... Massive aid, together with domestic savings, is being massively misdirected."

Communism – in India, rule by high-caste Communist politicians hardly distinguishable from self-serving Congress politicians – did not spread beyond the states of West Bengal and Kerala. But massive mismanagement by central and state bureaucracies, like that by the Communist-created apparat in the Soviet Union, maintained a backward momentum of its own. The crunch came in early 1991, when India's foreign-exchange reserves dwindled to the point of covering one month's worth of imports. Many feared the government would default on interest payments on the $70 billion it owed for international loans, the main form of aid to India.

The election-campaign assassination of Rajiv Gandhi in May delivered another blow to Indian stability, if only because he was known internationally. But it led to unexpected and desperately needed economic change. The Congress Party chose Narasimha Rao, a seventy-year-old Brahmin from Andhra who was considered no more than a party warhorse, to head a minority government as the first prime minister from South India. He made Manmohan Singh, a fifty-eight-year-old Punjabi Sikh economist who had spent his working life as a senior government official, the finance minister. Nothing the veteran politician and the career bureaucrat had done before suggested they would begin to dismantle the insidious apparatus that had crept inexorably out of Hinduism's ordered discrimination, the British East India Company's monopoly trade, and Nehru's socialist dogma. The question a decade later was not whether Rao and Singh cut off the tentacles of the central bureaucracy. They did not. The question was whether they and their successors had really intended to, and if so, whether doing so would have even been possible.

Rao asserted that India was "making history" with the economic reforms his government had set in motion. Singh said it had been clear by the late 1970s that "the whole system had outlived its usefulness." But the prime minister, still entranced by Congress ideology and fearful of a political backlash, refused to dispose of grossly counter-productive state industries, cut subsidies to farmers, or modify legislation barring the layoff of workers. The finance minister, still hooked on bureaucratic habits, did not anticipate a growth rate of more than 5 or 6 per cent but did sanction still greater deficit spending.

Some claim that market reforms in the present are possible only because of five-year plans in the past. Human Resource Minister Arjun Singh, Rao's main rival in the cabinet, who later was ousted from the Congress for seeking the prime minister's dismissal as party leader, was one of the politicians who expressed this self-serving point of view. There is some truth in it. As a new form of familiar Indian rationalization, however, it goes squarely against the overwhelming evidence cited by an American economist in New Delhi who told me in 1992 that four decades of central planning had "screwed the broad mass of the Indian people."

Rao deserves credit for having tried to extend the Green Revolution to eastern India, and for spending more on rural public works. Singh succeeded in devaluing the rupee, cutting impossibly high income taxes and tariffs, boosting $1 billion in foreign exchange more than $15 billion in four years, beginning to attract foreign investment, and increasing exports. Two other gains in the first half of the 1990s owed little or nothing to the government: the food grains output of nearly 200 million tons in 1995–96, double the record crop twenty-eight years earlier; and the burgeoning of a computer software industry centred on the southern city of Bangalore and drawing on the large number of Indian engineering graduates.

In 1991 India took its biggest step away from paralysis and breakdown since its partial acceptance in 1965 of the ability of farmers to use and profit from high-yielding seeds. But compared with strides by East Asian "tigers" and would-be "tigers," at least until the region's economic crisis starting in 1997, or compared with India's potential instead of its past, this progress is not yet the "ongoing economic revolution" that the government and even some Bombay businessmen proclaimed at its outset.

If the reforms of the early nineties had come instead soon after Indian farmers first dramatically expanded food grains production in the late sixties, they would have provided an industrial impetus for raising incomes and spreading benefits. But coming a whole generation later, the effect of the reforms was limited to making Indian industries competitive with those of East Asian countries that were once far behind India and had since moved far ahead. David Hopper, the agricultural economist who was at the centre of the Green Revolution, summed up the situation fairly and frankly when he returned to India at the end of 1993 for a debate on its development.

"By any assessment it is India, not China, that should have taught the world that a large nation can attain high economic growth rates [beneficial to] all its citizens," he asserted. But its planners had held India back, he maintained, because they distrusted "the inherent wisdom of the collective marketplace decisions of its citizens" and treated businessmen as "piranhas" instead of "contributors." With the grip of socialist ideology on a new generation of leaders still unbroken, Hopper continued, the new reforms were too weak to shake the "many political-bureaucratic-business alliances" resisting change. He predicted that India's economic transformation would take an indefinite period of time because beliefs do not change quickly in a democracy.

In contrast, in what is essentially a dictatorship in China, Deng Xiaoping and Zhu Rongji apparently did more than Rao and Singh to begin breaking old economic forms through what they called "market socialism." The opening of markets started in 1978, annual rates of growth until the Asian economic crisis were two to four times those projected or achieved by India, and foreign investment totalled $15 billion by 1993, when New Delhi was happy to attract less than $1 billion.

But even during and after several years of double-digit growth in the mid-to-late 1990s, before a slowdown induced partly by the East Asian economic crisis, the Chinese economy suffered from serious human and structural problems. We know far less about these problems because mainland China is still largely a closed society compared with India. It would have been impossible, for example, for Western journalists to visit drought-stricken Chinese villages freely the way they went into afflicted Indian villages during the Bihar famine. Starting in 2000, it was extremely difficult for foreigners to witness first-hand increasingly frequent, angry protests by farmers and workers in remote villages and cities against Communist Party corruption, and the swift suppression of these demonstrators by police or troops. Even the full extent of the brutal crackdown by the People's Liberation Army on pro-democracy students and other Chinese in Beijing's Tiananmen Square in June 1989 remains unknown.

What is known is that economic benefits have reached only a fraction of all China's citizens, and are concentrated mostly in the southeast: the coastal hinterland of Hong Kong and Taiwan. It is significant that soon after the British crown colony of Hong Kong became a special autonomous region of the People's Republic of China in mid-1997, an erosion of its limited political freedoms became evident along with signs that the party leadership favoured directly controlled Shanghai as China's future main entrepôt. Along with the mainland's near-total absence of political freedoms, and the party's swift repression of any breath of dissent, China lacks a legal institutional framework like India's that can regulate an overheated economy, or an under-achieving one, and offer long-term guarantees to investors.

Believers in the unstoppable liberalization of China – first economic, then political – pin their expectations on its being tied into rules-based globalization through membership in the World Trade Organization, a membership made more attractive thanks to incentives offered by the Clinton administration and supported by George W. Bush as a presidential candidate. But the phenomenon of more than 100 million peasants and workers roaming the countryside looking for work is destabilizing the country. In India, villagers moving into cities and making them overcrowded is an old story, but the breakdown of traditional Chinese society has never been so intense and tension between the people and their government is rising. The "iron rice bowl" – a guaranteed safety net – has shattered in China, but not the autocratic regime that ordained the end of basic family security. It never existed in India, so popular resentment probably is lower; and in any case Indians have the freedom to protest and pressure government to produce. The governments of both China and India look with trepida-

tion on the consequences of a promised privatization of large and small
state enterprises. How millions of temporarily unemployed workers
respond, and what the authorities do for them and to them, is a crucial test
of human development and national resiliency in each country. So is the
creation of new small businesses and entrepreneurs, where progress is
apparent in both countries. But while China is far ahead in exports, even
flooding India with its cheap products, India does not have China's problem of getting the army out of businesses.

In the end, Chinese market socialism could prove superior to democratic
capitalism, or at least to the changing Indian combination of democratic
socialism and capitalism. On the other hand, it could turn out to be the
elaborate oxymoron that some sober analysts and burned investors in
China deeply suspect it is: a camouflaged version of the crony capitalism
still holding back many Asian countries, but without even a pretense of
political liberty.

The Chinese Communist leaders may be no more willing to risk a
cooled-off economy and large-scale unemployment than they are ready to
entertain organized opposition and free dissent. Their bottom line in both
cases would be the same: repression of the people, not reform of the system. If political tyranny is threatened by economic liberalization, and if
popular discontent continues to spread, there is mounting evidence – most
dramatic in protests in China at the time of the mistaken NATO bombing of
the Chinese embassy in Belgrade in 1999 – that these worried leaders are
quite willing to resort to rampant Chinese nationalism. State socialism,
after all, drives the People's Republic of China, not laissez-faire capitalism.
If prosperity or the promise of prosperity flags or fails, the legitimacy of the
rulers crumbles. Then there is nothing else to bond them to the Chinese
people. The only way they can hope to sustain their bottom line is by
indulging in Chinese nationalism.

For these reasons, some suggest the Indian tortoise will win the race
against the Chinese hare. Another scenario is that both tortoise and hare
will drop out and self-destruct before the race is done. Each in its own way,
India and China could prove incapable of combining democracy and capitalism so that nearly everyone gains and national unity is assured.

In India's case, this would be much more likely if the Congress Party
were still in power. It has lost touch with the Indian people, and the bond
between the Nehru dynasty and the people is gone. But India has new
rulers in the Bharatiya Janata Party. Out of necessity as well as choice, Indians have switched to Hindu nationalists who assailed the nation's secular
foundation in the past, but whose bonding with the people rests on history and culture as well as economics. Apart from everything else, democratic India may have more time than Communist China.

If China was moving ahead too fast economically until 1998 and not progressing at all politically, India's economic progress until near the end of the nineties was too slow to prevent the aggravation of age-old religious, caste, and language tensions, even in a democratic setting. Wider, deeper, and faster reforms generating more money and improved living conditions would have a good chance of heading off the kind of violent intolerance the world witnessed at Ayodhya and in Bombay. On the other hand, economic change that is too sudden and has too great an immediate impact could raise tensions and widen gaps further between jealous groups.

A battered Congress Party avoided an early parliamentary election soon after destruction of the Babri mosque in late 1992 only because it was not routed in state elections in the north following New Delhi's contrived dismissal of BJP governments. But later election setbacks in key states – including Maharashtra, where a defiant Shiv Seni-BJP coalition came to power – weakened and further divided Narasimha Rao's Congress government. Pressures against further economic liberalization from within and outside the party, plus the prime minister's own instincts for political survival, intensified as the 1996 parliamentary election approached. But nothing could prevent an overwhelming Congress defeat in that popular vote. Rao was later indicted and convicted for corrupt practices. At the time the BJP could not maintain a minority government for more than days, and a shaky Congress-backed, leftist coalition took over the central government temporarily.

In this highly fluid situation, unhappiness and anger grew or festered among high-caste Hindus, low-caste Hindus, dalits, tribal people, Muslims, Sikhs, Christians, Hindi speakers, southerners, Bengalis and Marathas, Punjabis and Kashmiris. For many Indians, the easiest single answer was a Hindu *raj* or rule, especially if the BJP gave the benefit of its belief in free enterprise to bona fide caste Hindus. To some, despite past Hindu extremist assaults on civilized society, the only alternative to trying BJP rule was India's breaking up into warring sects larger than most established nations, and the Subcontinent's becoming a caldron magnifying the tragedies afflicting other lands whose peoples envy and despise each other.

This could still happen. But dangerous economic and social conditions in India created a political imperative that led to the election of the Hindu nationalist BJP in New Delhi in 1998 and again in 1999, on the eve of a new century and a new millennium.

Meaningful democracy and unity based on secularism can coexist in India with what the BJP calls a "common Hindu culture." For that to happen, more needs to be cut than the endless red tape that still requires a private company to file dozens of different reports to officialdom. More needs to be done than to enlarge a middle class isolated from the 400 million

Indians who exist in the dust on a dime a day plus inflation and do not have the capability to do more because they lack the necessary education and health care. The narrow bureaucratic mentality that determines so much in India may never disappear but neither can it be allowed to dominate. The human compartmentalization that grows out of fatalistic Hindu dharma at least needs to lose its sharp lines. Faith in the capacity of individual Indians needs to become the touchstone of government policy and implementation. Care and compassion for others need to work their way through antagonistic castes, classes, and communities.

What is required is nothing less than a change in the nature of Indian civilization. Such a change is possible but only through political will. Long years ago, Mohandas Gandhi started to create this indispensable instrument for nation-building. The Nehrus squandered that precious political will and the Mahatma's legacy.

6

The Nehrus

The Nehrus, the most celebrated family of Asia for more than a half-century, have covered India like a fine, suffocating blanket.

Widely admired for what millions think was their opening of vistas, they have stunted India's democratic evolution as well as its economic growth so drastically that this ancient civilization may have run out of time to enter the modern world. If not for four generations of a family that jealously considered itself the ruling dynasty of India – and did rule during thirty-seven of India's first fifty-six years of independence – one billion Indians would be significantly better off and freer than they currently are more than a half-century after their country slipped away from the British Raj on 15 August 1947.

A small irony is that much of the outside world, and many Indians, wrongly associate the last two of the family's ruling generations with the name Gandhi. What the Nehrus have stood for and done is far removed from the innately Indian principles and practices of Mohandas Karamchand Gandhi, the twentieth century's apostle of not only non-violence and tolerance but also popular participation in political and economic development.

A much larger irony – Indians would call it fate, and they might be right – is that no less than nine times did the Nehrus stay in power or regain power when by all odds they should have been banished to India's political wilderness. There will be a tenth time if long overdue economic reforms, initiated by the torn remnant of the Congress Party left by the shamelessly selfish Nehrus, prove unable to overcome the family's influence. If the reforms are not enough, either intolerant rule by revivalist Hindus or a violent breakup of India could rock Asia. Neither need ever have been close to happening. Neither ever would have been, in all likelihood, if not Jawaharlal Nehru but Vallabhbhai Patel, a man much closer to the earth and the people of India, had become the first prime minister in 1947.

If that accession to power is included among those when the princely
Nehrus should have been out of power but inveigled their way in, the count
is already ten. India may be knocked out without knowing it and will never
get to its feet.

Interestingly, a photograph of the decidedly unaristocratic Sardar Patel,
who organized the Indian National Congress as a political party in the last
days of the Raj, hangs above the head of Lal Krishna Advani, second in
command of the ruling Hindu nationalist Bharatiya Janata Party and
almost certain to be its next leader, when he sits at his desk at home. With
the BJP torn between exerting power as a Hindu party devoted to diversity
or as a nationalist party devoted to Hinduism, the framed portrait strikes
me as a poignant reminder of the valuable decades the Nehrus wasted for
India. Historically, it is a time to start all over on an unmistakably Indian
track – but it is too late to do so with a political party completely discon-
nected from religion in the driver's seat.

Pandit Nehru's brilliance long blinded many persons. I was one of them.
Worse, in July 1978 I was briefly taken in by the petulant charm of his
daughter, Indira Gandhi, when I returned to India after having been personally barred by her for more than seven years for my reports on her cynical policies in the famine state of Bihar and the Muslim-majority state of
Kashmir. I should have realized what was happening two decades earlier on
my first visit to India.

In February 1958 I was walking in the centre of Bombay when an Indian
businessman I had never seen before literally pulled me off the sidewalk.
Correctly identifying me as an idealistic young American, he astonished me
with a lecture on how Nehru was ruining the country. I argued that Indians should be proud of what a wonderful leader they had. I should have
listened. Like others, I should have looked clear-eyed and unemotionally at
the nature of India and the logical way for Indians to attain their goals
beyond political independence. Both Indians and non-Indians who should
have known better let themselves be seduced by the wiles of the dashing,
Kashmiri Brahmin Nehrus.

As we shall see, other larger-than-life political figures, as well as they,
define the nine or ten times the Nehrus were in when they should have been
out. The political battle shifts from New Delhi to Calcutta to Bombay to
Madras to village India and back again, and rages on all fronts at once. The
dynasty finally comes to a tragic end in 1991, in the forty-fourth year of
India's independence, although some Indians believe it will resume when
non-Nehru forces exhaust themselves.

But at the beginning of a new century, Jawaharlal Nehru, who once personified not only India but what was called the Third World, seems to be

little more than a broken idol. Indira Gandhi, his daughter, may be remembered most for breaking up the historic Indian National Congress, and allying with Communists, in order to save the dynasty. Her sons Sanjay Gandhi and Rajiv Gandhi, viewed in perspective, are rough and smooth sides of the same family coin. Now they are all gone, and the hope of those who would revive the dynasty lies, absurdly, in Rajiv's Italian-born widow Sonia, or, beyond her, their daughter Priyanka or son Rahul. The obsession with one family that came close to destroying India, and may yet still, lives on in a dwindling number of Indians as a kind of suicide wish, and in some Western journalists as a compulsion to take over-simplification to ridiculous lengths.

Only Jawaharlal died of natural causes, in May 1964, although the disastrous Himalayan war between India and China in the fall of 1962, and his failure in his last months to reconcile India and Pakistan in a compromise on Kashmir, broke his heart and ultimately his body. Indira and Rajiv were brutally assassinated, in October 1984 and May 1991, respectively. Sanjay was killed in a stunt plane crash in June 1980. As Jawaharlal understood, India goes on. But can India go far enough and fast enough to escape the mystique of the Nehrus?

"I too, like all of us, am a link in that unbroken chain which goes back to the dawn of history in the immemorial past of India," wrote Nehru in his last will and testament ten years before his death at the age of seventy-four on 27 May 1964. Then at the height of his influence and prestige, seven years into his seventeen as prime minister, he sought to refute the idea that the chain would break when he died and India would fall apart. Yet in many other ways he conveyed his conviction that India's fate and his own – and the Nehru family's – were inextricably linked.

Jawaharlal converted his father, Motilal Nehru, a wealthy Allahabad lawyer who fastidiously followed British ways and means, to the Indian independence movement. Motilal, the first of the four generations of Nehrus who took upon themselves the natural right to rule, had made his money representing propertied families in land-dispute cases that dragged on for years. He lost much of it, and many British affectations, in devoting more and more time to the Congress cause. But in becoming number two to Mahatma Gandhi in the fight for India's freedom, Motilal implicitly supported Jawaharlal as India's political leader when that fight was won.

As early as 1937, ten years before independence and five years before the wartime Quit India campaign by the Congress, Jawaharlal described in detail his vision of himself in that position. He did so anonymously and critically in an extraordinary article published in Calcutta entitled "The Rashtrapati" – "The Ruler." But there is no mistaking the aristocratic mindset of a man who is dead certain about the "tryst with destiny" he would spell out when he and India achieved their aims at the same time.

He memorably disavows any notion that he will be a fascist when he gains power: "Private faces in public places are better and nicer than public faces in private places." Yet he acknowledges putting on a smiling "mask" for adoring crowds, and that "men like Jawaharlal, with all their capacity for great and good work, are unsafe in democracy." Cocksure he will become not so much the philosopher as the historian as king, Nehru displays stunning insight into the future: "Jawaharlal cannot become a fascist. And yet he has all the makings of a dictator in him – vast popularity, a strong will directed to a well-defined purpose, energy, pride, organizational capacity, ability, hardness, and, with all his love of the crowd, an intolerance of others and a certain contempt for the weak and inefficient ... His conceit, if any, is already formidable. It must be checked. We want no Caesars."

Even if Nehru's conceit had been checked, it may be asked how any leader of the Indian people can be contemptuous of the weak and inefficient. Even had he not been an intellectual elitist educated at Harrow and Cambridge, one must wonder how an Indian with no apparent connection to Hinduism except his Brahmin caste could lead the nation. In another time or another setting, Nehru might have been nothing more than a member of the Indian Civil Service or a parlour socialist or even a dilettante. As India's political leader, he was able to do two things that inevitably undercut the popular respect he instilled for the parliamentary institutions he had learned about in England and that began operating in India under the Raj.

He entrenched the myth of indispensability he had warned about before independence. He enforced the affection for state industrial enterprises and five-year plans he had acquired from the Russian Revolution. The first meant that the shade from the banyan tree to which Nehru was likened continued to retard the growth of a healthy democratic spirit even after he died. The second kept economic levels unnecessarily low for ordinary Indians, especially farmers, preventing the widespread sense of participation in nation-building that Gandhi had emphasized is essential for democracy to work. At the dawn of independence at midnight of 14–15 August 1947, Nehru had said: "The ambition of the greatest man of our generation has been to wipe every tear from every eye." But this Gandhian ideal never could come close to realization under the policies Nehru pursued once he had become a Caesar in all but name.

Nehru had a way of hiding his hardness by putting himself softly and self-consciously at the centre of tough issues confronting the world as well as India. When he came back to New Delhi in the fall of 1961 after discussions with Premier Nikita Khrushchev in Moscow, he stood on the first grass beyond the airport tarmac and talked as if to himself about nuclear bombs with a small group of reporters, including myself, around him. As he spoke, his fine tan face edged in white homespun cotton, Nehru picked the petals one by one from the flower he was holding, as if he were ticking off the world's chances of survival.

At an interview soon after with the half-dozen American correspondents in New Delhi, his words seemed more associated with the autographed photograph of Gandhi on the desk of Nehru's office in the Ministry of External Affairs than the carved ivory tiger next to it. It was the eve of his departure for Washington and talks with President John F. Kennedy, who was among those who initially held Nehru in something like awe as well as esteem.

But Kennedy, who was becoming a charismatic hero in his own right to many Indians, was disillusioned by the aloof refusal of India's "non-aligned" leader during the early November visit to the United States to show an open mind about U.S. Cold War policies. Disillusionment turned to sharp disappointment just a few weeks later, in mid-December. That was when Nehru, at the urging of Defense Minister V.K. Krishna Menon, displayed his hardness and a certain contempt for the United States in ordering Indian troops to invade and seize the 400-year-old Portuguese colony of Goa on India's west coast below Bombay. The blatant use of force, at odds with Gandhian non-violence and Indian non-alignment, did nothing to deflate the holier-than-thou attitude of Nehru and India toward international issues. But it helped open the eyes of Americans and the rest of the world to the real nature of both.

Undeterred, Nehru delightedly welcomed Jacqueline Kennedy to India on a private visit in March 1962. She was in Delhi during Holi, the Hindu festival of spring when Indians throw coloured water on each other. In addition to the distinctive red rosebud he always wore in his lapel, the prime minister appeared at a press conference with a precious dab of pink just over his heart on his otherwise spotlessly white *achkan* or Nehru jacket. "Jackie did it," he announced with a smile of quiet triumph. To Nehru it was a mark of the compatibility of the naturally ruling families of India and America notwithstanding their political differences. They could play together even if they didn't see the world the same way.

Nehru's attraction to Jacqueline Kennedy was a mere flirtation compared with his infatuation, and quite possibly more, with Edwina Mountbatten, wife of the last British viceroy of India, fifteen years earlier. There is little question that Nehru's enchantment with the elegant Viscountess

Mountbatten made it easier for Lord Louis Mountbatten to bring about partition and independence less than five months after their arrival in Delhi. Whether deliberately or perhaps because he wanted to succumb, Nehru was cajoled into going along sooner than was right or safe: he became prime minister of a considerably shrunken and blood-soaked India.

Nehru's wife, Kamala, had died of tuberculosis in Switzerland in February 1936, when he was forty-six. He had two sisters, Vijayalakshmi and Krishna, and one devoted daughter, Indira, to whom during the Raj he wrote the letters from prison that became the impressive book *Glimpses of World History*. Indira left her husband, Feroze Gandhi, a Parsi – to whom she owed the name Gandhi – in order to care for Prime Minister Nehru at his home in "Teen Murti," the spacious former residence of British commanders of the Indian Army, and now the Nehru Museum. But the woman the handsome Jawaharlal could never escape – and could never charm into submission – was India herself.

He observed that India had feminine qualities. Perhaps he was thinking of irrationality, fickleness, unpredictability. But it was India's earthiness, vulgarity, and warmth that clashed with his detachment, sophistication, and cool. Opposites attract, and Nehru and India were fascinated with each other. But he never knew her fully, and she eagerly came to see him but not to hear or understand what he had to say.

Jawaharlal spoke and wrote beautiful English but his Hindi was poor and most Indians couldn't read. He was a highly educated, socialist, Brahmin lawyer. It was said with truth that Nehru's presence was necessary to resolve the crises of his own dilemmas. India was an uninformed, self-indulgent, low-caste peasant. Yet India was more complex than Nehru, stronger and, in the end, self-reliant. She was too much woman for the Prince Charming who wooed but never won her. But she grew older and used to him as he entertained and diverted her with baubles such as public sector steel mills and friendship treaties with Communist powers. Further captivated and sapped of energy by Jawaharlal's family heirs after he finally departed the stage, India will find it difficult even with different, more compatible men in charge to summon the vigour needed to snap the spell cast by the Nehrus and fulfill her vast potential.

It is painful to write these words. In the fifties and early sixties, my heroes were Adlai Stevenson, Jawaharlal Nehru, Dag Hammarskjold, and Canada's Lester Pearson. They were all committed democrats and internationalists. When President Kennedy was shot on 22 November 1963, I was covering a story in a Toronto hotel and a spreading buzz made me aware that a terrible event had occurred. The worst thing I could imagine until I learned the truth was that Nehru had died. When he did die six months later, I wrote that he had made democracy the basis of India's economic development. It was a distortion, like Indian democracy.

Political democracy does not have to wait for economic prosperity. The people of India, far more than Nehru or any other politician, have demonstrated that. But without economic freedom, political liberty means less and less as years pass. By strengthening a remote central bureaucracy that had grown out of the caste and class of Hinduism and the British Raj, Nehru denied economic freedom to Indians who were politically free for the first time.

He and a united Congress Party went through three national elections, in 1952, 1957, and 1962, attracting fewer than half of the popular votes cast in each. With the opposition divided, however, the Congress won roughly three-quarters of the seats in the Lok Sabha or lower house of Parliament each time, and every state legislature except the one in Kerala, where Communists first came to power in 1957 one year after the state on India's southwest coast was formed. Repeated Congress victories were fair political play in those early years, and Nehru could feel vindicated in providing Indians with both the ballot box and national stability.

But the timing of elections with the start of Soviet-style five-year plans revealed more than a simple ploy to give the government a campaign edge. It exposed Nehru's overriding priority of making sure the government held the "commanding heights" of the economy through a "permit-licence raj" that could hardly have been better calculated to mix the worst aspects of socialism and capitalism instead of the best. It was a paradise for clerks at all levels who exulted in entangling prospects for progress in dingy red tape, and for profiteers who gleefully discovered crooked ways to get around stultifying controls. Neither had any interest in the common good.

If Vallabhai Patel with his kulak roots – many Patels in the westcentral state of Gujarat are prosperous peasants by definition – had become India's first prime minister in 1947 at the age of seventy-two, he might not have had much time to make Indian capitalism respectable and legitimate. But he would have blocked the monopoly on power by the socialist wing of the Congress that had ensured Nehru's preeminence when Mahatma Gandhi unaccountably declined to endorse Patel for party president before independence. When Nehru became prime minister as undisputed leader of the party, he continued to benefit from the flow of financial contributions to the Congress by large landowners mobilized by Patel. But he did nothing to encourage the free market that would have allowed India to leap ahead of China and provide an example to Asia and the world of dynamic democratic development.

India's economy crept ahead instead. The only big increases were in the number of grossly inefficient state enterprises and the number of poor Indians who were shut out of development altogether. Combining what was called a "one-party-plus" political system and an economic stranglehold by the bureaucracy, India in important respects was more like a Communist country than a democratic one. When the nation's first prime minister died in May 1964, it was the first real opportunity for healthy change – for India's pursuing her own "tryst with destiny" – in seventeen years. That was because it was the first time the Nehrus should have been out of power for good.

Lal Bahadur Shastri started out as prime minister of India after Nehru's death much as Harry S. Truman did as president of the United States after Franklin D. Roosevelt's death. No one quite thought the void could be filled or was sure the country could go on. The patrician hero who had long held the nation in his hand was suddenly replaced by a common man of the people whom no one knew very well. The new leader, a political lieutenant of the old one, was himself the product of political compromise. He spoke clear words and pointed a forward direction for his country but the words were a mere echo and the vision a poor shadow of the eloquence and style that had gone before. His first task in 1964, like President Truman's in 1945 near the end of the Second World War, was to hold party, government, and country together at a critical time. As was the case with Roosevelt's successor, many believed that Shastri – the name, meaning a graduate of a Gandhian university course, was adopted like the middle initial in Truman's name – would not be up to new problems and would soon fall by the political wayside.

As Indians got to know their new leader, however, he proved surprisingly decisive, again as Truman had. He made two bold decisions within weeks of each other in the fall of 1965: to go to war with Pakistan over control of Kashmir and to switch India's economic priority to agriculture and its farmers. Nehru would have hedged on or ruled out both. But Shastri was unable to extend the parallel with Truman to his first big political test. In 1948, Truman had lost the extreme right and left wings of the Democratic Party and still won an election. In January 1966, a year before the first election in India without Nehru, Shastri, sixty-one, died of a mysterious heart attack after only nineteen months as prime minister.

If he had lived to hang on at the polls and serve another term, as Harry Truman did, Lal Bahadur Shastri in all probability also would have led his people into a new era in which their own chances of survival were greatly improved. Instead, he met his end at Tashkent, the capital of Uzbekistan in

Soviet Central Asia, where he had travelled to meet President Mohammad Ayub Khan of Pakistan and the Soviet premier, Alexei Kosygin, and ratify the results of the successful war he had waged. He was surrounded there by Indian and Soviet officials who had a stake in preserving not only India's military victory, but also the statist economic road for India laid out by Jawaharlal Nehru. There is no material evidence that Shastri was murdered in a strange land far from home. Neither is there conclusive evidence that he indeed suffered a fatal heart attack. The only certainty is that his totally unexpected death opened the door to the return of the Nehrus in the person of Indira Gandhi.

Nehru had probably had Indira in mind as his eventual successor. Asked at a press conference five days before his own fatal heart attack about who would succeed him, the ill Prime Minister Nehru replied, "My lifetime is not ending so very soon." In the preceding year, he had induced some cabinet ministers and state chief ministers to resign. The good reason was to let them work exclusively for the Congress Party. The real reason was to push away from the *gaddi* or seat of power some contenders Nehru didn't like, particularly Morarji Desai, who as central finance minister and earlier chief minister of the old state of Bombay was in Patel's mold. When Nehru's physical condition took a turn for the worse in January 1964, he brought Shastri back into the cabinet. With Nehru and Indira, the former home minister had chosen Congress candidates for the 1962 election. His many political contacts and the new blessing bestowed by Nehru made likely the party's choosing him as leader and therefore prime minister when the time came. If Nehru had seen him as a caretaker until Indira was ready, Shastri quickly showed that he was his own man. He brought Nehru's daughter into his cabinet as information minister. But he established a distinct and popular identity very different from that of the elitist Nehrus.

I met Shastri in a suite of the Chateau Laurier Hotel in Ottawa on 12 June 1965. President Lyndon B. Johnson had undiplomatically cancelled visits to Washington by the Indian leader and Pakistan's Ayub at an anxious time when the United States was on the brink of committing combat troops to the war in Vietnam. India was chairman of the International Control Commission in Vietnam, set up by the 1954 Geneva Accords to supervise what had become a non-existent truce between North and South, and Canada and Poland were members. Shastri went ahead with a scheduled visit to Canada to show his independence and to offer his views on the crisis in Southeast Asia as well as on the rapidly growing prospect of India and Pakistan's going to war for the first time since the 1947 conflict over Kashmir. His few days in Ottawa, Montreal, and Niagara Falls were his first exposure to the West and, except for attending a Commonwealth

Conference in London immediately afterward, his only one. Just before my interview with him for *The Toronto Globe and Mail*, he conferred privately for twenty minutes with B.K. Nehru, the Indian ambassador to the United States and a cousin of the late Jawaharlal, who had made an unannounced trip to Ottawa to outline U.S. policy on Vietnam to Shastri and deliver a confidential letter from President Johnson to the Indian leader.

As I took the seat next to the prime minister vacated by the ambassador on a sofa in the grandly decorated suite, Shastri seemed far more nervous than I. Just over five feet tall, he was dressed in his customary white cotton cap, brown herringbone tweed achkan – too heavy even for Ottawa in June – and white dhoti or flowing Hindu loincloth. His face was a study in composure. But his strong brown hands moved constantly as he kept twisting his fingers around each other while he searched for answers to my questions, usually waiting long moments before slowly and carefully expressing himself. It was not a problem of language: his English was clear and precise. Nor was it unfamiliarity with his position: he had been prime minister for a full year. Looking back, I think it was more than anything a difference in cultures. Shastri was shy about representing India in a Western setting. In contrast, Jawaharlal Nehru had been sure about expressing himself in a Western manner in an Indian setting. It's tempting to say Shastri was no less firm. In reality, he was stronger and more open-minded than Nehru at the same time.

He warned that use of U.S. combat troops in Vietnam "might lead to dangerous consequences." But when I asked him whether the problem in South Vietnam was caused primarily by civil war or foreign intervention, Shastri replied: "The main problem is that of intervention – there is intervention on both sides." He added that he had found on a recent visit to Moscow that the Soviets would "continue to give arms and equipment to North Vietnam." Shastri emphasized that "each country," North Vietnam and South Vietnam, "must decide its government and ideology for itself" through popular votes. He would not comment directly on the letter he had just received from Johnson or what B.K. Nehru had told him but he said: "As far as my information goes, the United States is willing to have a talk [with North Vietnam], even if it takes place early or late. The United States may have to take other steps also before the talks can begin." What steps? Shastri smiled but did not reply. He made clear later he had in mind a pause or halt in the U.S. bombing of North Vietnam, something Prime Minister Pearson of Canada had proposed two months earlier, angering Johnson. Although he didn't say so explicitly, the prime minister of India had to be concerned about the danger of a wider war in Indochina prompting intervention by

China, whose troops continued to confront Indian troops in the Himalayas.

Toward Pakistan, which China supported, Shastri was unusually conciliatory. He warned, however, that hostilities between India and Pakistan in the Rann of Kutch, a western desert where India's Gujarat state touched Pakistan's Sind province, "might take a serious turn." They did, and this clash was followed in the fall of 1965 by the second war over Kashmir. Shastri did not depart from the policy of non-alignment invented by Nehru. But he was willing to criticize the Communist side as well as the U.S. side, Nehru's often exclusive target. He was both tough and flexible with India's enemies, in a way that was different from Nehru's uncompromising vacillation.

Most striking was Shastri's self-conscious willingness to meet anyone on equal ground in contrast to Nehru's discrimination toward others bordering on disdain. After he eagerly leaned so far over the parapet at Niagara Falls that Canadian police feared his small figure would tumble into the gorge, the next time I saw him was on 2 October 1965. It was Gandhi's birthday and Shastri (whose own birthday was 1 October) was sitting on a low platform near the Mahatma's samadhi or memorial on the banks of the Jamuna River in Delhi and spinning on a simple wooden wheel with scores of others, the custom on that day for Congress workers (Nehru never did it and Indira didn't know how). I simply walked up to him – security for Indian leaders was not nearly as tight as it became later – and recalled our meeting in Ottawa. Shastri's eyes shone in recognition, and he grasped my hand and asked what I was doing in India. I told him I had arrived a few days earlier to cover the end of the India-Pakistan war as a resident correspondent, and we chatted for a few more moments. His uneasiness had disappeared in what hardly could have been a more Indian tableau, and he greeted me naturally as a friend. Such a casual approach and warm response in public would have been unthinkable with Nehru. They had been normal with Gandhi – his assassin came right up to him at a prayer meeting because he knew he could – and Shastri was a Gandhian.

In March–April 1930 he had taken part in the 24-day, 390-kilometre march to the sea at Dandi led by the Mahatma, whose deliberate breaking of British law by gathering untaxed salt was the beginning of the end, according to the poet Rabindranath Tagore, of the white man's moral superiority and the Raj. Shastri had been a village school teacher in Uttar Pradesh. After working in the Congress movement for independence, he had laboured to strengthen the Congress as a political party. As a pragmatic politician rooted in the soil of India, he succeeded in rising briefly to the top where the intimidating Vallabhai Patel had failed. As a devoted child of Gandhi, Shastri handled for too short a time the irrational woman of many parts that is India where Jawaharlal Nehru as a detached colleague of Gandhi had failed.

He did this by quenching her thirst for revenge by soundly defeating Pakistan in a major war, and by satisfying her hunger for food by allowing a long-blocked agricultural revolution to go ahead. During Shastri's time, Indians proudly shouted, "Jai jawan, jai kisan!" – "Victory to our soldiers, victory to our peasants!" Neither triumph was easy.

To make free farmers the catalysts of Indian economic development, Shastri had to discard the Nehruvian dogma that public sector bureaucrats must come first. His own experience reinforced the logic of Gandhi's conviction that ordinary Indians need to build the nation from the village up. He did not break the permit raj's grip on India in the mid-1960s. But he loosened it enough to buy time – perhaps as much as a generation – before wider liberalization could no longer be delayed. The question remains whether the delay until the early 1990s was too long.

In an interview with me two months before she succeeded Shastri, Indira Gandhi said, "I don't know if Pakistan would have attacked" India in September 1965 if her father Nehru were still prime minister. She may have had a point. The fact remains that, by ordering an invasion of Pakistan proper for the first time, Shastri acted swiftly to prevent Pakistani forces from cutting off Indian troops in Kashmir. Apart from how far Indian forces could have advanced into Pakistan – some Indians contend they missed a chance to destroy Pakistan – their British- and Soviet-model tanks prevailed over U.S.-made Pakistani tanks in the biggest armoured battle since the Second World War. From then on, without question, India was militarily predominant in the Subcontinent. The outcome somehow seems not subtle enough to have suited Nehru, who resisted clearcut answers.

In late June 1965, following his visits to Ottawa and London, Shastri attended a summit conference of Afro-Asian countries in Algiers. On arrival, he worked with his officials all day and night and into the small hours of the next morning to define India's position on a variety of issues. When the exhausted prime minister returned to his hotel suite, he bumped into Indonesia's President Sukarno, whose suite was on the same floor because the name of his country also started with the letter *I*, and who also was coming back for a few hours of rest after a heavy night. But Sukarno had been following his well-known predilection not for briefing papers but for beautiful women. With a leer, he asked, "You too, Shastri?"

Shastri didn't reply, according to the senior aide who related the incident, and in all likelihood he didn't know what Sukarno was grinning about. He was not that kind of man, and not just because he was very close to his wife, Lalita, and had his hands full with feminine India. He was square. He was open. Like Truman, there was nothing frivolous or devious about him. It may be unnecessary to add that he was not a Brahmin.

At Tashkent in January 1966, he agreed to withdrawal of Indian troops to prewar positions because India had kept control of the treasured Vale of Kashmir. This fig leaf for Pakistan was one of the things that some Indian politicians and officials held against him. When the Soviets refused to grant me a visa to cover the Tashkent summit – some of these same Indian officials, displeased with my stories on Kashmir, advised them not to – I looked forward to talking with Shastri again in the capital of Afghanistan. He planned to visit Kabul on his way back to Delhi although the Afghan government, fourteen years before the Soviet invasion, sided with Pakistan. But he never left Tashkent alive. He died early in the morning of 11 January. I flew to Delhi from Kabul via Rawalpindi, then the capital of Pakistan, where a returning President Ayub was plainly shaken by the sudden loss of his generous adversary.

On 12 January more than one million Indians, many wailing with grief, lined the route of Shastri's funeral cortege through New Delhi and Old Delhi. The tiny body in repose, showered with marigolds, was taken to a cremation site near Gandhi's and Nehru's on the banks of the Jamuna. "May Shastri live forever!" shouted thousands as the flame was lit. Shastri's distraught wife, Lalita, comforted by Dorothy (Steb) Bowles, wife of U.S. ambassador Chester Bowles, accompanied his ashes on a train across the northern heartland of India before the ashes were scattered in the Ganges. The first thing in India that Pat, my wife then, and our infant daughter Shauna encountered was the masses of common people at Shastri's funeral paying devotion to a common man. In what we had thought would be a happy reunion, I had met my family in Karachi, Pakistan, on their way from Toronto to our temporary home in India's capital. We arrived in Delhi too late to see Lal Bahadur Shastri leave, for the last time, his plain house of red brick and white trim at 10 Janpath – 10 People's Way.

Exactly one week later, on January 19, Indira Gandhi stepped onto the stage of world history in her own right when Congress members of both houses of Parliament elected her as the first woman prime minister of India. The answer to what had been the classic question in Indian politics – After Nehru, who? – had been Shastri. But less than twenty months after Nehru's death, his daughter firmly assumed the seat of power. After sudden war, sudden peace, and the sudden death of Shastri, the Nehrus were suddenly back.

How did it happen? Why did Indira, forty-eight, a widow now as well as

Nehru's only child, possessing virtually no experience in government, easily dismissed as a lightweight candidate for prime minister when her father died, sweep to victory with only one obstacle in her path? The bottom-line answer to these questions is political cynicism. In that dangerous game, a small group of Congress bosses known as the Syndicate decided to use Indira as a mere plaything. She soon turned the tables on them by showing she could play the game better than they or anyone else. But by far the biggest losers in the game were the people of India.

The single obstacle to Indira and a return to Nehruvian leadership was Morarji Desai, then sixty-nine. Few political figures in the world ever endured more constant defamation than Morarji (Indians commonly refer to him by his first name, as they do to Indira Gandhi and her sons, even after their deaths). He represented a conservative Congress tradition that Nehru and his socialist supporters had denigrated even as they were forced to coexist with it. He came from Gujarat, the home state of Mohandas Gandhi and Vallabhai Patel. Like Shastri, he was a Gandhian, but stiff-necked about it. He had been a strong central finance minister and chief minister of the former Bombay state, encompassing what is now Maharashtra and Gujarat, and so was widely called "authoritarian" and "old-fashioned."

Pushed aside by Nehru, Morarji had reluctantly dropped his candidacy for leadership of the party when the first prime minister died, for the sake of unanimity in the selection of Shastri. Despite heavy pressure by the all-powerful Syndicate and the certainty of defeat, he refused to withdraw his name when India's second prime minister passed into history. In the secret ballot by Congress members of the Lok Sabha and Rajya Sabha, the appointed upper house of Parliament, Morarji surprisingly received nearly a third of the votes, 169, to Indira's 355.

Some analysts and academics acclaimed the many consultations and the peaceful election for enhancing the stability maintained during the first transition in leadership. But the selection process came down to raw politics. The Syndicate wanted to take control of the Congress Party and it wanted the Congress to win the national elections due in a year's time. Indira Gandhi – attractive, intelligent, apparently sensitive, a modern woman despite her pro-Soviet sympathies, above all a Nehru – seemed to suit both purposes splendidly.

The acknowledged leader of the Syndicate was K. Kamaraj Nadar, a shrewd, low-caste Tamil, who continued to dominate Madras politics after having been chief minister. While Nehru was still alive, the "Kamaraj plan" under which senior Congressmen resigned their government posts had been named after him. All the contacts and consultations to choose a successor to Shastri, including talk of Kamaraj himself as prime minister, revolved around him. But while he stolidly went through these intriguing motions, Kamaraj was unequivocally behind Indira from beginning to end, and knew she would win.

Some of his colleagues in the Syndicate may have been less enthusiastic at the beginning. But in the end they too recognized the apparent advantages to them of another Nehru. They were Atulya Ghosh, the Congress leader in Calcutta whose huge girth and dark glasses made him seem like a caricature of a political boss; S.K. Patil, the hard-nosed, no-nonsense, pro-business Congress boss of Bombay; N. Sanjiva Reddy, who had gone from being chief minister of the southern state of Andhra to joining Shastri's cabinet; and Siddavanahalli Nijalingappa, chief minister of the southern state of Mysore, later Karnataka. Oddly, the wholly unofficial Syndicate contained no member from the populous, Hindi-speaking, economically backward, northcentral Gangetic plain – a region so key politically that Chet Bowles used to say that Indian politics was like American politics would be if the Deep South were the decisive part of the United States.

Kamaraj and the Syndicate engineered Indira's election on the basis of two assumptions about her. One was that her image and Nehru family background would be popular and possibly decisive in India's fourth general elections due in early 1967. More important was the belief that she was weak as well as inexperienced, and would prove a pliant tool in the hands of the Congress bosses.

The first assumption was partly valid. Considering the heavy election losses the party suffered one year later, however, it probably was greatly exaggerated. The second assumption was dead wrong. Where members of the Syndicate erred was in thinking that "the girl" – the way they and other older male Congresswallahs referred to Indira – would put the party first. She fiercely put herself and her family first, at the expense of the nation as well as the party. Her mixture of pride, petulance, paranoia, prejudice, charm, tactical canniness, and plain vindictiveness came close to annihilating both. But in the bright January sunshine of the garden outside her yellow stucco bungalow at 1 Safdarjung Road, where she met reporters following her historic election as the leader of all India, no one could imagine the damage she would do in the years to come.

Indira had been tense and unsmiling when she emerged in a crush of well-wishers from the huge central hall of Parliament, where the Congress MPs had voted and she had been declared the winner. It was only when she reached home that she visibly relaxed. Wearing a plain white cotton sari and a plain brown shawl, she joked with reporters in the manner of her father and her eyes flashed. But the famous Nehru temper almost flared when another mob scene developed, delaying the start of the press conference. She was taking personal command as if her genes dictated it.

The first question from a Western reporter was how it felt to be a woman prime minister. Indira snapped: "I don't regard myself as a woman. I regard myself as a person with a job to do ... I'm the first servant of the land."

In her acceptance speech in Hindi and English in the circular high-domed central hall, with portraits of India's immortals looking down from the walls, she had said India faced enormous problems and pledged she would follow in the path of Nehru and Shastri. Now she welcomed as a "first step" the Tashkent Declaration by Shastri and Ayub promising peaceful relations between India and Pakistan, adding: "We should try and create what my father called a climate of peace. We should honour the spirit of Tashkent." She said she was in favour of U.S. peace moves on Vietnam but they would have to be accepted by the other side to be effective. She did not respond to Morarji Desai's entreaty in defeat: "I hope and pray that in the future an atmosphere of fearlessness will be cultivated in the party and in the country."

The first time I met Indira Gandhi, in 1962, my impression of her was similar to that formed by Indian politicians: she was close to Nehru but not a leader in her own right, more dallying than decisive, engaging but not deep. My interview with her when as Shastri's information minister she ruled out widespread introduction of television in India because it would raise popular expectations added an element of cynical calculation.

When I did a TV interview with her in early March 1966 for the Canadian Broadcasting Corporation, she was already comfortable in her new job as prime minister as well as in her home. Unable to take over the mansion of her father, which was to become a museum, she had made clear she preferred to live in her bungalow as prime minister instead of moving into the larger but more plebeian house at 10 Janpath that Shastri had occupied. The forty-five-minute interview took place in the book-lined, tastefully decorated drawing room. Photographs, sketches, and paintings of a brooding Jawaharlal Nehru seemed to cast a spell. When I asked if she felt bound by her father's political and economic ideas, Indira defiantly replied: "I very much have my own views on all matters."

She displayed a sharp knowledge of these national and international issues confronting India but a reluctance to commit herself on any of them. Asked who she thought was to blame for the war in Vietnam, for example, she remarked with a little laugh: "No, I'm not entering into this kind of controversy." Apart from again invoking the Tashkent spirit, generated by the Soviet Union, she added that India as chairman of the International Control Commission in Vietnam could only work toward peace if Canada and Poland, the Communist member, went along. She said "it would be a good thing" if she and Ayub "met at some point" but the United States and other nations had to understand that India would have to defend itself against further "Pakistani aggression." She briefly expressed the belief that India should not develop an atomic bomb.

With the effect of the 1965 drought on the availability of food grains evident, but not yet the impact of the drought of 1966, Indira asserted, "I don't think it's a question of starvation and, quite frankly, I don't approve of this attitude of begging" for food from the United States and other countries. About to press President Johnson to resume full U.S. economic aid suspended during the 1965 India-Pakistan war, she admitted that her government did not have a clearcut food policy since the onset of drought had upset Shastri's emphasis on agriculture. Her only positive suggestion was that "rather rigid and tradition-bound" Indians should be "more flexible" in their eating habits: "I may like rice but if rice is not available, there are so many other things I can eat and keep well on."

I next interviewed Indira eight months later, in November 1966, under unusual conditions. One foreign correspondent was usually designated to travel with the prime minister on her trips within the country in an HF-24, a small, twin-prop-engine government transport plane built in India to a British design. It was my turn when she flew east from Delhi to visit Indian troops at the northern end of West Bengal, among the forces facing Chinese troops along the disputed Himalayan border four years after the Sino-Indian war. After some time, I was summoned to her mid-plane compartment, where she was sitting alone, and she smiled and motioned to a seat across from her. But the engines just outside were so loud that she had trouble hearing my questions and I couldn't understand her answers. She asked if I wouldn't mind sitting on the floor of the plane next to her seat, so she could talk directly into my ear. Surprise at this strange arrangement with the prime minister of India soon gave way to wonder at what she kept talking about.

As we flew over Bihar, she pointed to the barren land below and told me what her government had not acknowledged in Delhi: a major famine afflicting tens of millions of people was inevitable now that the monsoon had failed two years in a row. But Indira quickly turned to political matters. She regaled me for the better part of an hour with tidbits about Congress personalities she claimed were inept, and details of party intrigues she insisted were directed against her. This kind of pettiness did not make for copy a serious Western journalist, or even a responsible Indian one, could easily produce. A few months before the 1967 elections, Indira's chatter directly into my right ear did reveal her obsession with politics. The only other person I had met with such an intense preoccupation with politics – and a compulsion to share it – was Richard Nixon. Politics was also mother's milk to Bill Clinton, but he was not known for whispering secrets into reporters' ears. Indira seemed much more caught up in politics than in the impending Bihar famine or the forward Indian forces she was going to inspect. But when her plane landed, she obviously enjoyed flying from one army encampment to another in a huge Soviet-built helicopter even louder than her plane.

Step by deliberate step, Indira was then establishing her own preeminence in the Congress Party and making herself as popular as possible with voters. She was performing an intricate balancing act with a series of foreign as well as domestic ploys. By August 1966, she had charmed Lyndon B. Johnson in the White House, broken with the Syndicate, stared down her opponents in Parliament, and kicked off the 1967 election campaign by taking on the Communists in Kerala. It was a gutsy performance involving calculated risks and therefore not certain of success. Little wonder Indira couldn't stop talking about politics when she had my ear.

As for her seeming even more casual than Shastri, and in that way different from Nehru, I think this was more a reflection of aristocratic guile than of natural warmth. But I believe that Indira Gandhi was a lonely woman who instinctively and plaintively talked to people she thought might understand her. She was determined to persuade them that what she was doing was right or at least unavoidable. She also needed to convince herself.

Indira told Johnson she was willing to take his word that the United States wanted peace in Vietnam. At home, she pressed for ending emergency regulations, in force since the late 1962 Himalayan war, that denied full democracy. She most pleased the United States and the World Bank by not only promoting Shastri's agriculture-first policy and hinting at looser industrial-import restrictions but also devaluing the rupee. The unexpected, precipitous drop in its longstanding value of 4.21 to the U.S. dollar to 7.5 provoked predictable howls of protest in India. No less a figure than the Syndicate's Kamaraj led the leftist charge against Indira for defying him as well as Congress socialist doctrine. This was just what she had counted on. She calculated that her daring action would dramatize her independence at the same time renewed U.S. aid revived India's economy, enabling her to lead the Congress to electoral victory and keep her job afterward.

By launching her campaign with a direct assault on the Kerala Communists, who alone had broken the all-India Congress monopoly on power, Indira reinforced the impression that she was at least open to the conservative wing of her party. Just before a key meeting of the Congress working or executive committee in Delhi in early July, she spent three days in the sweltering monsoon heat of the southern state pumping up Keralite Congressmen to "fight against overwhelming odds" and putting down Communists for threatening to "disrupt every house in the state." This helped her overcome the challenge to her economic policies at the Delhi meeting: she emerged as the strongest individual in the party.

In early August she cemented this triumph by easily defeating a motion of non-confidence in her government introduced in the Lok Sabha by Communists and other opposition leftists because of the rupee's devaluation and Indira's soft stance on Vietnam. The anticipated outcome of the vote – 267 to 61, with about 175 members absent – was not nearly as impressive as the way Indira imposed her discipline on the unruly lower house. Clad in a yellow sari, she scored sarcastic debating points in the manner of her late father. She threw back at Communist MPs the same criticisms of her economic measures that many Congress members had expressed outside Parliament. She lashed out at leftist extremists for threatening Indian democracy with violence in the streets and in the Lok Sabha. When several opposition members tried to shout her down, she defiantly stood her ground, at one point by leaning forward with her arms straight down on her desk and glaring back for long moments. "Some members of the opposition," she declared when the shouts had died away, "are trying to break the hope and self-confidence of India."

It was Indira Gandhi at her noble best as prime minister. But it was not the real Indira Gandhi. And her best as ruthless politician was yet to come. She savaged in later years every principle she stood for in 1966 after her first weeks in power. She carried to perilous extremes the very abuses she attacked in the months before her first election.

Instead of reforming the Congress Party, Indira broke it up. Instead of fighting the Communists, she effectively joined them. Far from seeking peace with Pakistan, she went to war. Rejecting fairness toward the United States, she embraced the Soviet Union. The dove on a nuclear bomb for India became a hawk. Instead of relaxing economic controls, she maintained them. Far from opposing anti-democratic emergency powers, she proclaimed an emergency of her own that nearly killed Indian democracy. The leader who claimed to speak for the people of India acted against the people. Her ideas were not different from her father's but virtually the same.

But while Nehru had coated his politics with hope and had coexisted with conservative Congressmen, Indira soon rooted her politics in the fear that Morarji had warned against. For her, it was a matter not of politics first but of politics always, and not for the sake of principles but in order to win or keep power for the Nehrus. The first time she bet the family's political future at the polls was in February 1967.

7

Winning at Any Cost

Two weeks before Indians voted in February 1967, Indira Gandhi rode frantically from village to backward village in a jeep. Wherever the jeep skidded to a stop in a cloud of dust, she reminded the poor people of Rae Bareli, her constituency, that the Congress Party had won independence for India.

Usually frowning, her sari streaked with the unavoidable dust, she was campaigning in her first bid for elective office. But she could offer little more than continued sweat and struggle to gain the elusive economic fruits of freedom. After nineteen years of Congress rule – all but one under a Nehru – she blamed attacks by China and Pakistan, poor monsoons, and caste rivalries for the lack of progress in Rae Bareli district and in India generally.

"Don't think that by voting for Congress all your ills will be cured immediately," she told men, women, and children sitting on the hard ground and looking up respectfully but quietly at her. "You can't purchase food and water with money if the food and water are not there."

About 1.4 million Indians, all dependent on the dried-out land for their livelihood, eked out a day-to-day existence in Rae Bareli, a 5,000-square-kilometre parliamentary constituency. At its centre, the non-descript North Indian district town of the same name is about one hundred kilometres south-east of Lucknow, capital of India's most populous state of Uttar Pradesh. The prime minister, still a member of the appointive Rajya Sabha or upper house of Parliament, had chosen Rae Bareli to run in for the Lok Sabha or lower house for family reasons. Her aunt and Nehru's sister, the distinguished retired diplomat Vijayalakshmi Pandit, was running for re-election in Nehru's old Phulpur constituency – which she had won in a by-election following his death in 1964 – near the family's home city of Allahabad.

With 300,000 persons expected to vote in Rae Bareli, a burgeoning Congress organization was counted on to produce a huge margin of victory for

Indira over seven opponents. The most notable of these were a religious Hindu candidate of the Jan Sangh – the predecessor of the Bharatiya Janata Party – and an untouchable backed by the Socialist Party. The Jan Sangh had raised the issue of a ban on cow slaughter, and had started a whispering campaign among conservative peasants about Indira's association with the nattily dressed Dinesh Singh, the former raja of adjoining Kalakankar. The pro-Soviet Singh was then the prime minister's closest adviser on foreign affairs although he was only a minister of state in her cabinet, and she was waiting to give him the top post of foreign minister.

In her short talks to villagers, Indira seemed to contradict her acknowledgment of persistent poverty by observing that if they worried about the slaughter of holy cows, "things can't be so bad." Betraying her abiding belief in socialism, she said it was up to the government to draft economic plans, and up to the people to carry them out without argument: "If we work hard together, our troubles will be over. But if we fight and quarrel with each other, our troubles will get worse."

In one village a kneeling elephant was among her listeners. In another she was greeted by a small brass band that usually played at weddings. In Sataon, a local poet sang her praises, calling her the embodiment of *satyam*, *sivam*, and *sundaram* – truth, purity, and beauty. Wherever she went, her closed jeep plowing through billows of fine dust, she heard the practised slogans: "Long live Indira Gandhi! Victory to Indiraji!" She received few cheers but plenty of attention and, thanks to heavy security, no hecklers. Villagers grabbed eagerly for flowers and garlands as she tossed them about after she spoke. But her primary message – "It was hard to face the lathi (stick) charges of British days" – probably meant little to most of them when nearly a whole generation had grown up in the mean villages of Rae Bareli tasting dust of free India as bitter as that of the colonial Raj.

One other interesting fact about this remote corner of India was not known to the handful of foreign correspondents who followed Indira around Rae Bareli district. It was the temporary home of Svetlana Alliluyeva, Joseph Stalin's daughter.

Svetlana was living at the home of Indira's friend, Dinesh Singh, in Kalakankar after having brought the ashes of her late common-law husband, Brajesh Singh, an Indian Communist who was Dinesh's uncle, to India from Moscow on 20 December 1966. She had met Indira when the prime minister came to Kalakankar on 16 January and was among those who listened when she gave a campaign speech on behalf of Dinesh, who was the Congress candidate for the Lok Sabha in that district. Afterward she personally told the prime minister that she wanted to stay in Kalakankar as long as possible. But her presence in India somehow remained a secret outside the Soviet embassy – which was pressuring her to return quickly to Moscow – the highest levels of the Indian government, and the small circle of Indian friends and acquaintances she had made in the Kalakankar area.

So did the fact that Dinesh Singh had cruelly rejected a heartfelt request by Svetlana Alliluyeva for asylum in India because granting the request would have provoked great Soviet anger. Singh and then–foreign minister M.C. Chagla later denied this was the reason, but Stalin's daughter confirmed it in a letter that was read in the Indian Parliament. It is not known whether Indira was involved directly in the cold decision to bar Svetlana. She had wished the Russian woman good luck in Kalakankar. But it is reasonable to believe, on the strength of both her official and personal ties to Dinesh Singh, that she knew about the denial and did nothing to stop or revoke it.

On the evening of 6 March 1967, after Svetlana had been compelled to return to the Soviet embassy in Delhi in order to fly back to her homeland, she took a small Hindustan Ambassador taxi driven by a Sikh to the U.S. embassy next door. She climbed the long marble stairs. Once inside, she identified herself to the Marine guard as Stalin's daughter and said she wanted to defect to the United States. The Marine's initial reaction is not recorded. A few hours later, however, on the initiative of Ambassador Chester Bowles, the strong-minded Svetlana was on a plane to the West. The secret of Svetlana in India then exploded into an international sensation.

But while she waited in Switzerland to enter the United States, an Indian diplomat presented her with a draft of a letter to Dinesh Singh for her signature. Written by Singh himself and obviously meant to quell Soviet suspicions, it said no one in India had helped Svetlana to "flee." Because this was true, she signed it. In turn, she entrusted the senior diplomat with delivering through the Indian embassy in Moscow a long letter she had written to her two children in the Soviet Union explaining her actions. They never received that letter. There is good reason to believe the Indian government turned it over instead to the Soviet embassy in New Delhi.

When the Svetlana story broke after the 1967 elections, in the minds of some Indians it increased doubts about Indira's good faith. Others had fought her tooth and nail during the campaign as the arrogant personification of an ideology that in their minds was destroying free India. Her anti-Communist, pro-capitalist gestures fooled them not at all.

As early as 1959, five years before Nehru's death, the Swatantra Party, dedicated to free enterprise as well as democracy in India, was founded in Madras. It was the first secular national opposition party to the right of the

Indian National Congress. It lasted until 1974. If Swatantra had hung on until Indira took all political power into her hands the following year, quite possibly the Hindu nationalist Bharatiya Janata Party would not have surpassed the Congress as its main rival, and conceivably a conservative coalition with few or any links to Hinduism would be ruling India at the beginning of a new century. Notwithstanding Swatantra's fate, three of its leaders, who together represented an alternative to the Nehrus in the critical 1967 elections, suggest not only what might have been but also the kind of leadership needed to save India now.

One was a truly beautiful maharanee. Another was a worldly Bombay intellectual. And then there was India's grand old man and "great dissenter" at one and the same time.

Gayatri Devi, the elegant Maharanee of Jaipur, once one of India's most sumptuous princely houses, took Indira on in a bitter political battle for Rajputana, famous for valiant deeds of mustachioed, turbaned warriors. But their fierce rivalry really had to do with who had the right to rule India. Although both Congress and opposition camps had attracted royal personalities, the maharanee's impact on Indian politics as a Swatantra candidate highlighted the desire of some traditional rulers to free India from the clutches of a new family dynasty. Reacting instinctively as a Nehru, Indira scorned Indian royalty as belonging to the distant feudal past. The issue was a lively one in the northwestern desert state of Rajasthan, which as the successor to Rajputana with its many princely houses offered Swatantra the best chance to capture a state government.

In the 1962 elections, Gayatri Devi had run for Parliament in the pink city of Jaipur and won a bigger majority of votes from her former subjects than any other candidate in India. I met her then at the comparatively modest estate where she lived after the polo-playing maharaja and she had let the old Ram Bagh Palace in Jaipur become a hotel. Apart from her classic beauty, I was taken with her articulate criticism of one-party rule in India. She readily acknowledged that local loyalty to the royal house of Jaipur was the source of her popular support. But the maharanee, who had come to Jaipur from the former princely family of Cooch Behar in eastern India, gracefully decried the distance between the Congress and the people.

In 1967, still a striking vision at about fifty years of age, Gayatri Devi offered this simple advice to Rajput peasants: "If you want to end your worries, throw the Congress out of power." Pulling her sari coyly around her head, the maharanee told villagers seated respectfully on the ground around her: "Last time I sought your votes to build a strong opposition in Rajasthan. I seek your votes this time to form a Swatantra government with the help of the Jan Sangh." She was running for the legislature as well as Parliament, and if such a coalition were formed, she would stay in Jaipur to keep it together although not necessarily as a cabinet minister.

The very idea infuriated Indira, who inherited her father's revulsion at rajas (except Dinesh Singh), big landowners, industrialists, and Hindu fanatics. Heckled at a Congress rally in Jaipur, she shouted angrily at her listeners: "Go and ask the maharajas how many wells they dug for the people in their states ... Do we want to make India a modern nation or do we want to go back to the sixteenth century?" But the Congress raj had failed to provide Rajasthanis with enough food and water, to stop rising prices, to allay suspicions of corruption, or to inspire them to look forward instead of back.

M.R. (Minoo) Masani of Bombay also was a classic and rare Indian: an anti-Communist intellectual who broke with socialists to become president of Swatantra, leader of the opposition in Parliament after the 1967 elections, and editor of an outspoken journal called *Freedom First*. Like others of his kind in other lands, he had been repeatedly disillusioned but had never given up hope for his country or for democracy. I vividly recall an encounter with the angular, sensitive Masani that could be a metaphor for his India.

I bumped into him at the airport in Srinagar, Kashmir, at the end of June 1968, and we sat together on an Indian Airlines Viscount flying back to Delhi in late afternoon. As the plane approached the capital, two surreal things happened at once. The setting sun cast a roseate glow throughout the cabin. And the monsoon due to begin at that time of year broke over Delhi, shaking the aircraft so violently that it appeared to be increasingly out of control. We stopped talking. An unearthly quiet enveloped us except for the dimly heard whine of the engines. We could see nothing outside the window but pink clouds. The erratic plane seemed to enter another world. I'm sure Minoo contemplated his immediate fate as deeply as I did mine as the glow faded. But it didn't suddenly turn black. With no warning, the plane touched ground smoothly instead of breaking up on contact. It was like India stopping just short of disaster after a rough journey when its glowing ideals seemed certain to disintegrate.

A few excerpts from Masani's last, appropriately entitled book, *Against The Tide*, published in New Delhi in 1981, give an idea of the nature of that long trip as he experienced it: "Nehru was a noble failure. Given the prejudices and the attachments he had formed by the time India became independent, he could hardly have behaved very differently, but it is to his credit that he did not suppress the voice of dissent ... On the other hand, there is no doubt that he made communism respectable. He broke down the barrier against communism which Gandhiji had built."

On Shastri's reply when Masani asked him why he had named Indira

Gandhi to his cabinet, Masani wrote: "He smiled benignly and said he did not think there was any harm in what he had done. On the other hand, he said, if he had left her out of the cabinet she might well have become a rallying point for disgruntled Congressmen and the Communists. That was something he had wished to avoid."

Minoo Masani concluded *Against The Tide* with these words: "Since our politicians are by and large beyond repair, if India is to be saved, it will have to be saved by the small man, particularly the middle class of the cities and the landed farmers of the countryside who are the backbone of the nation. These classes have suffered cruelly under the so-called 'socialist pattern' that Nehru imposed on the country and which is still rampant, but their back is still not broken ..."

Chakravarti Rajagopalachari did far, far more for India than found the Swatantra Party when he was eighty years old. Indeed, it was because C.R. – or Rajaji, as he was even better known – had stood with Gandhi, Nehru, and Patel in the struggle for independence that his break with the Congress was profoundly significant. He had been the statesman, in many ways the brain, and in other ways the conscience of the Congress movement. So his withering assault on the permit-licence raj that it spawned under Nehru – he coined the term – was devastatingly credible. Instead of going gracefully into retirement as the grateful nation's grand old man, he never stopped dissenting from established policy and pretension with greater grace and wit.

I am extremely fortunate to have sat literally at Rajaji's feet a half-dozen times in his cottage in Madras when he was in his late eighties, and listened to him discourse incisively but gently on the problems of India and the world. Alone with this small bent man, who was set off as cleanly by his words as by his simple white garments, his dark-framed spectacles, and his famous walking stick, I knew I was in the presence of greatness. Even as he talked, I felt I was taking part in a human dialogue, not a mere interview. His words instilled peace of mind.

Once, returning from Madras, I ran into Morarji Desai at the airport in Delhi and mentioned I had just had a meeting with the first major defector from the Congress Party. "Rajaji," mused Morarji, who accepted few others as equals and was still a staunch Congressman, "is smarter than all of us." It was a Brahmin's tribute to a Brahmin. But Rajaji, like Mohandas Gandhi, recognized that barriers dividing castes had to fall if fairness and democracy were to have a chance in India.

Perhaps the most notable single instance of this happening was the marriage of Rajaji's daughter Lakshmi and Devadas Gandhi, a son of the Mahatma, who came from the Vaisya or merchant caste. At the insistence of their fathers, the couple first stayed apart for five years as a test of their love for each other. Their joyful wedding in Poona in 1933, just nine months after a nearly fatal fast by Gandhi on behalf of untouchables, set a precedent for intercaste unions, provided an exception to the Hindu rule of arranged marriages, and demonstrated the closeness of Rajaji and Gandhi, as well as of their children.

This intimacy came close to producing a historic political result when Gandhi, during painful negotiations on the terms of independence from the British, urged the Muslim League's Mohammed Ali Jinnah to accept what was called for its author the "C.R. formula." This compromise between an undivided India and two nations would have established a confederation of India and Pakistan, with defence and foreign affairs as the joint concern of the two countries. If Hindus and Muslims had met on this middle ground, said Rajaji, "the Asian Subcontinent would have stood on rock and been a powerful, peaceful democratic confederation today." He wrote those words in December 1971, when the separate Islamic Pakistan that Jinnah had demanded and got in 1947 broke into two itself with the creation of Bangladesh. As Leonard Mosley observed in *The Last Days of the British Raj*, Rajaji even then "spoke too forthrightly and too soon to be heeded."

He probably was too smart and too much of a maverick to be chosen as India's first prime minister, even if Gandhi had not made the worst of his many irrational decisions in choosing Nehru over Rajaji as well as Patel as his political successor in the Congress. But after serving as chief minister of the old Madras state before the British left, Rajaji became the nation's first Indian head of state as governor-general or representative of King George VI when Mountbatten departed in June 1948, ten months after partition and independence. Although he kept a small office in the big old Viceroy's palace, he naturally eschewed the trappings of state.

When India became a republic in January 1950, Nehru wanted Rajaji to stay in Rashtrapati Bhavan as India's first president. But other Congress voices prevailed and a safe, conventional party member, Rajendra Prasad, was chosen. Rajaji served as appointed governor of West Bengal briefly before returning to Madras to become chief minister again, and then giving up office to become India's full-time gadfly. He actively led Swatantra after founding the pro–free-enterprise party in 1959. As the leader, but also simply as C.R., he crisply expressed his views in a weekly column in *Swarajya* or Freedom, a plain English-language magazine – he was an avid champion of English as the only link language for India – published in Madras. In 1962 Rajaji went to the White House and so impressed Kennedy with his plea for abolishing nuclear arms that the president pushed harder for ending nuclear testing.

I first met Rajaji earlier in 1962 during the campaign for India's third national elections. When he realized I was covering a Swatantra rally in

Madras addressed in Tamil by him, he repeated some of his more pungent phrases in English. Later, at Kancheepuram, he saw to it that delicious South Indian coffee was poured in an amazing stream from cup to bowl and back again, to cool it off and make me feel at home. That night, thousands of people seated on the ground chanted, "Rajaji! Rajaji!" In response, a patriarch wreathed in white and carrying his long cane like an Old Testament prophet picked his way among them to the platform. He delivered a spontaneous, delightful drumfire attack on the powers that were, at least five years before Indians throughout the country began to realize how right he was about the Congress Party he had left behind as unworthy of support.

To mark Rajaji's ninety-third birthday on 8 December 1971, a commemorative volume was published. Honoured to be among hundreds of persons who were asked to contribute, Indians and non-Indians alike, I wrote:

Rajaji's voice has been one of the clearest for years in speaking out against government encroachments on basic human rights. He has naturally dealt mainly with India and the 'permit-license raj' (but) Rajaji's warnings ring out far beyond India ... He is one of the few men – virtually a miracle among public figures – who can establish a rapport with whomsoever he is speaking to and cut through the myths and misconceptions of politics to the eternal verities at the same time ... He almost invariably uncovers a commonsense reason, a moral basis or an historic necessity for taking a stand in defense of the exploited little man, of integrity in public and private life, of reliance on peace instead of power, of the individual instead of the State. Any journalist would be proud to have exposed a fraction of the faults in the permit-license raj that Rajaji has brought to light, and to have done so half as clearly ... It is true he has often been disappointed in his labors. But he has never let himself sink into bitterness or personal spleen. He has kept an open mind, a big heart and, incredibly, hope for the future.

Finally I quoted Rajaji himself: "We thought that democracy was the way to welfare, justice and progress. But as the years have passed, careerism has replaced genuine patriotism ... We cannot give up democracy. We have cut off all other paths and we must stick by democracy and Parliament, and make the most of it."

If Rajaji had become India's first president, he surely would have made the most of it. Nehru might well have regretted endorsing him and even attempted to remove him.

Under the constitution that was adopted by the Constituent Assembly on 16 November 1949 and came into effect on 26 January 1950, making India a republic, the president, chosen by an electoral college consisting of members of Parliament and state legislatures, enjoys wide powers. These powers have never been fully defined, and many of them were not tested until the late 1980s or 1990s. They are akin to those of the British monarch, who has no substantive authority. But there also are similarities to executive powers in the U.S. system: the president of India is the commander-in-chief of the armed forces, and takes an oath to "preserve, protect and defend" the constitution with its fundamental human rights. A key question has been whether the president must accept the "advice" that the cabinet headed by the prime minister is required to give him. A constitutional provision that the cabinet will hold office only "during the pleasure of the president" has also been subject to varying interpretations.

In the Constituent Assembly, an ambiguous Nehru said the president was not to have "any real power" but neither was he to be "a mere figurehead." As prime minister, however, he made clear he would brook no opposition from the president. Rajendra Prasad had said as president of the Constituent Assembly that the constitution did not "lay down that the president is bound to accept the advice [of the cabinet]." But as president of India, he did whatever Nehru advised him to do. Many expected more independence from his successor, Sarvepalli Radhakrishnan, an example of philosopher as king if ever there was one. But the distinguished interpreter of Hinduism never went publicly beyond the symbolic authority of his office. I was unable to draw him out when I interviewed him informally as president at Rashtrapati Bhavan. Over time Radhakrishnan made no secret, however, of his talking privately to Nehru about many matters – without revealing the nature of his counsel – or of his unhappiness with abuses of political power after Indira became prime minister. As a moralist who was aware of the potential of his office, he might have exerted real authority on some controversial questions, particularly in resisting Indira's manipulation of presidential powers to further her own ends. But he was not a political or even a public man.

Rajaji was both, and did not believe in hiding his views. If he had felt the need as president to stand up to Nehru, he certainly would have done so, as he did out of office. If he had occupied that exalted position even for a single five-year term and had set positive precedents, or if President Radhakrishnan had been willing later to speak and act publicly, Indira might not have gotten away with her crippling undermining of the institution of the presidency, and of much else precious to Indians, after the 1967 elections.

Her determination to remain prime minister was so strong that, before the vote, she did not support V.K. Krishna Menon in his bid to run for re-election to the Lok Sabha as the Congress candidate in an important Bombay

constituency. Menon, then seventy, the one-time confidant of Nehru and
the all-time critic of the United States, had been denied a place on the Congress ticket in Northeast Bombay by S.K. Patil, the party's pro-business,
pro-Western, Bombay boss. Indira, once Menon's protege and still his ideological soulmate, spurned his appeal to her, partly because of the different
image she was then cultivating but mostly because she wanted Patil's support after the election. Having broken with the Syndicate – its leftist leader
Kamaraj backed Menon – she was angling for an alliance with its one
member who was sympathetic to the economic policies she had temporarily espoused. Menon, a dark wraith whom Nehru had been forced to fire
as his defense minister after the debacle of the Himalayan war with China
in late 1962, finally resigned from the Congress and ran with fervid Communist support as an independent candidate. Northeast Bombay was part
of an ethnically diverse area where, with Nehru's strong endorsement, he
had easily defeated earlier in 1962 an anti-Communist candidate put up by
three conservative parties.

Further north on India's west coast, not far from where Mahatma Gandhi
had staged one of his most successful non-violent protests, forty village
leaders, including one woman, sat cross-legged on the floor of a small
room. Most wore white caps of khadi – homespun cotton popularized by
Gandhi and adopted by the Congress Party as a puritanical symbol of
adherence to his ideals. The *sarpanches* or chairpersons of village governing councils offered proof that many conservative Indians were still sticking with the Congress.

Two weeks before the election, their designated leader, with a tiny low
wooden table in front of him, asked the others how the campaign was
going in the Valod *taluka* (bloc of villages). "The opposition could not even
organize a meeting," one reported eagerly. An old man meekly admitted,
"In my village, 25 per cent of the people will vote for Swatantra." Another sarpanch said, "The people do not want other masters." Most nodded
before receiving fresh instructions on how to keep the state of Gujarat –
home of Gandhi, and Patel and Morarji – in Congress hands. Along with
adjoining Rajasthan and Orissa in eastern India, it was one of three states
where Swatantra was mounting a strong challenge.

The story was similar in Surat, Morarji's constituency. Zinabhai Darji,
president of the district panchayat or council, expressed confidence the
Congress would withstand the free-enterprise, anti-statist appeal of
Swatantra to Gujarat's self-reliant peasants, even when 6,000 villages with
one-fourth of the state's 22 million people were suffering from their third
straight poor monsoon. "There are many social workers still from Bapu's
(Gandhi's) day and they work for the poor," he explained. "Of all the Congress workers, 30 per cent are also social workers. The poor are satisfied.

They have trust in us." Darji, a big man seated at a big desk below photographs of Gandhi and Sardar Patel, added between answering telephone
calls: "There is one leader and the people all have faith in the leader – and
that is Morarji."

A few days in the Valod area were enough for one to understand the
impact of continuing popular equation of the Congress with good works. I
also caught a glimpse of the kind of India that Gandhi had envisioned and
worked for but was almost impossible to find elsewhere.

It was simple but it was clean. It had no big government steel mills, but
industrial enterprises started by farmers were more efficient. Whole villages
consisted not of huts but of pukka houses. At least some Indians were helping other, less fortunate Indians. It was still far from being the peasants'
paradise that perhaps Gandhi and Patel dreamed of in 1928 when they
launched in nearby Bardoli a farmers' struggle against the British for non-
payment of land taxes. But at Anand, in Kaira district south of Gujarat's
modern capital of Ahmadabad with its privately owned textile mills, a
modern dairy processed milk collected daily on a fair-price, cooperative
basis from 110,000 farmers – most with only one or two water buffalo –
in 588 villages. Congress leaders wisely and untypically kept their hands
off. They realized that the best way the party could benefit was through a
continually rising standard of living in the villages serving the dairy.

"Those who don't work with the people are only politicians," observed
Darji with simple logic. "They'll lose power some day."

The first such day for many politicians, particularly Congressmen
throughout India who had lost touch with the people, was 16 February
1967. In Ulhasnagar, a rapidly growing industrial city sixty-five kilometres
northeast of Bombay, it was hot. At the end of a dirt lane crossing a foul-
smelling ditch, a refugee woman with a baby in her right arm had a little
round ink mark put on her left index finger, and was handed a pink slip, a
white slip, and an X stamp. Then, clutching her child, she went in succession behind two small cardboard partitions carrying notations in Marathi
and English of "Assembly" and "Parliament." After a brief pause behind
each, she came out and put her ballot in the slit of a green metal box of prescribed size under the watchful eye of an election official. Having stamped
her X's next to a depiction of a pair of bullocks, an oil lamp, a bullock cart,
a hut, a lion, or an elephant – the symbols of the contesting parties or independent candidates in her constituency – she became one of the first voters
in India's fourth general elections, the biggest democratic exercise in history
at that point.

Most of the people who lived in Ulhasnagar were refugees from Sind in
West Pakistan. Polling station No. 1, where the woman was among the
nearly half of 1,220 registered voters who had cast ballots by early after-

noon, was in the school of one of five refugee camps of solid buildings that had become permanent. Voters in Ulhasnagar were among the more than one-third of those in Maharashtra who went to the polls on the first day of the elections along with some of the voters in each of seven other states. Balloting was to continue in different areas for seven days until 21 February, when the counting of votes was to begin.

Large numbers of women voters were evident on the first day not only in rural Maharashtra but also in Gujarat and Madras city, and voting was heavy in the famine state of Bihar but light in Rajasthan. At Kamba, a tiny crossroads hamlet outside Ulhasnagar where two polling stations across a dirt road from each other were serving three villages – no Indian voter is supposed to walk more than five kilometres to vote – an election official inside the makeshift tent that housed one poll said only 120 of 705 registered voters had cast ballots one hour before closing time, and another in a school reported only 98 of 626. But as the latter talked, four wives of Maharashtrian peasants, their saris typically bound tightly around their legs above the knee, moved quickly to the poll to exercise their franchise.

"It's very peaceful," said a Congress worker. "It's absolute democracy."

But democracy in India was undergoing a profound change. It was not just that Indian voters strongly protested for the first time. It was not only that disaster overtook the once invincible Congress Party. A severe realignment of political forces started in villages and towns across the country in February 1967.

Widespread ferment in the months before the voting had pointed toward the replacement of India's only truly national party by something else. What that something might be and how fast the change would come were unclear. When naked ash-smeared Hindu holy men organized by the Jan Sangh had tried to assault Parliament in early November 1966 in the name of protecting the cow, they dramatized the drift toward lawlessness in Indian society. When the astonishing election returns came in, followed by breathtaking political manoeuvres as Indira Nehru Gandhi desperately resorted to unprecedented methods to cling to power, the loss of democracy itself loomed as a distinct possibility.

Analysts had calculated that if the Congress lost only Kerala and 50 parliamentary seats – dropping in the Lok Sabha from 361 seats to about 310 out of 520 – Indira would remain prime minister with Kamaraj's grudging support. But if the Congress lost several other states and the number of its Lok Sabha seats fell significantly below 300, they had agreed, India would have a new prime minister and his name probably would be Morarji Desai. If that happened, many believed, the nature of the party and indeed the political system would change while remaining democratic.

Government by consensus, with Congress bosses and state chief ministers joining central cabinet ministers to reach necessarily watered-down decisions, might give way to government by a strongman who, unlike Nehru, would tackle longstanding economic and social problems. This in turn might be the start of a healthy two-coalition if not two-party system, with Congress leftists and the two Communist parties in opposition to a private enterprise–oriented government of Congress conservatives, Swatantra, and responsible members of the Jan Sangh.

Even leading Congressmen admitted, usually anonymously, that the party had deteriorated so much that it mocked words once spoken by Nehru: "We wanted no change of masters from white to brown, but a real people's rule by the people and for the people, and an ending of our poverty and misery." One astute Indian analyst summed up the malaise afflicting India this way: "There is a crisis in character, there is a food crisis, there is an economic crisis, and there is a crisis in leadership."

If the Congress share of the popular vote had dropped from 45 per cent in 1962 to 35 per cent, a realignment of parties would have happened fast enough in all likelihood to protect democracy, and easing of these crises would have followed. With 153 million Indians voting – a highly encouraging record 61 per cent of eligible voters, up from 130 million or 55 per cent five years earlier – the proportion backing Congress fell sharply, but only to 41 per cent. The party took just 283 seats in the Lok Sabha for a loss of 78, with only 99 of its winning candidates capturing more than 50 per cent of the popular vote in their constituencies. But this was still enough for a small majority. The southern states of Kerala and Madras quickly fell to opposition coalitions, the first led by Communists, the second by the Tamil Dravida Munnetra Kazhagam or Dravidian Progressive Party. In the Madras outcome, masterminded by Rajaji, even Kamaraj lost his race for a legislative seat. In no less than seven other of India's then sixteen major states – Bihar, Gujarat, the Punjab, Orissa, Rajasthan, Uttar Pradesh, and West Bengal – the once dominant Congress managed no more than a standoff with different combinations of ambitious opposition parties. But these indecisive state results, and the opportunities they opened up for buying off venal politicians, soon proved to be assets for Indira.

By the second night of counting, on 22 February, the party she had taken over from Nehru and Shastri was in shock and disarray. Under her leadership, it had nearly lost control of Parliament and verged on losing control of half the states of the Indian Union, including three of the four most populous. Eight of her cabinet ministers, including Food Minister Chidambara Subramaniam, and four Congress state chief ministers, including the leader of famine-stricken Bihar, had gone down to ignominious defeat. Amazingly, Bombay boss Patil and Calcutta boss Ghosh had lost their parliamentary seats, although Patil's man in Northeast Bombay had defeated Menon. Indira's heavily-financed campaign in Rae Bareli had netted her only 55 per cent of the popular vote, compared with Morarji's 66 per cent in Surat. But she savoured the unexpected defeat in Jaipur of Gayatri Devi for the Rajasthan legislature, although not for the Lok Sabha.

If Indira was in bad shape, the Syndicate was shattered. If the Congress had lost valuable ground to Swatantra, the Jan Sangh, and the Communists, it still survived as the largest party. Just enough was left of the party for the prime minister to salvage her own job if she were cunning enough.

Wearing a purple sari, a small blue cornflower, and a brave smile, Indira made a stage-managed appearance 24 February at election press headquarters in Hyderabad House, once the New Delhi home of the Nizam of Hyderabad, reputedly the world's richest man, who had died of unrelated causes that day as the mounting returns from across India nearly but not quite killed the Congress. Someone asked if she were a candidate to succeed herself. Nehru's daughter replied tartly: "What do you think?"

To any citizen who cared deeply about India, to any member of the Congress who wanted to save the integrity of the party that had won the nation's independence, there was only one sane and logical answer to her question. Indira had to go. It was the second time the Nehrus should have been out of power for good.

But precious little sanity, logic, or integrity was evident in the chaotic Indian political scene in the coming days, and largely for that reason in the coming years. Whether a disintegrating Congress Party was too shocked or too corrupt or too set in its ways to do otherwise, or all three, it simply ignored the people of India. At the first clear signal in twenty years of momentous change in the popular mood, the Congress responded by first continuing to put its destiny and India's in the hands of discredited and now defeated party bosses, and then entrusting a weakened central government to a plainly self-centred woman whose principal claim to leadership was still that she was the daughter of India's first prime minister.

It was not as if the alternative was to surrender power in New Delhi to other untested or suspect parties. The alternative was to form a Congress government that would reflect the people's clearly expressed desire for change, co-operate with new state governments of varying complexions, and begin to do something about long-neglected economic and social inequities that were keeping most Indians poor. More than 150 million voters had made it possible for India to embark on a meaningful reform program in 1967 instead of a full generation later. For this to materialize, the Congress had only to choose as its new leader and India's prime minister the man the party had twice turned down before: Morarji Desai.

By the end of February, as the Congress bosses started doing business at their same old stand as if nothing had happened, Morarji sketched out policies for a new government of India designed to address the main causes of the voter revolt: food shortages, rising prices, and arrogant bureaucracy. It was his way of again challenging Indira without explicitly saying so. Instead of speaking out directly, he did so through an unnamed source close to him, V.Y. Tonpe, his suave, intelligent top aide.

"We should put the fourth five-year plan with all its frills in cold storage, lock the door, and throw the key in the Indian Ocean," Tonpe told me anonymously. "The Congress high command has not yet pulled itself together but it is not too late to set definite priorities and make sure they're carried out."

Morarji's first priority was good government. He was prepared to cut bureaucratic red tape ruthlessly and to keep any Congressman with the hint of a shadow of corruption over him out of office, emphasized Tonpe. The second priority was keeping prices down. Morarji was ready both to offer incentives to industrialists to increase long-stagnant production and if necessary flood the market with goods. Another priority, picking up on Shastri's after a gap of more than a year with Indira at the helm, was to increase food grain output through intensive, small-scale, local irrigation – the most crying need in the famine state of Bihar.

Although most Western journalists described Morarji Desai only as ascetic and puritanical, and ignored his thinking, he also wanted relations between New Delhi and new non-Congress state governments to be friendly and co-operative instead of hostile and suspicious, said Tonpe. As he emphasized Morarji's openness, pro-Beijing Communists were on their way to forming a coalition government in West Bengal as well as the one in Kerala; Swatantra was coming to power as the main party in Orissa; and other anti-Congress coalitions were taking over Bihar and the Punjab in addition to Madras.

The most important political point made by Morarji through Tonpe was that he refused to accept the number two position in the cabinet under Indira. This seemed to make another contest between the two of them inevitable when Congress members of the new Parliament met in caucus 12 March.

Two days before, an avuncular Morarji stood under a big tree in his garden and declared: "I've decided ultimately to contest. I consider I'd be the better leader." Standing behind him was Vallabhai Patel's thin, white-haired sister, Maniben, a member of the Rajya Sabha. But despite his words and ideas, a deal between Morarji and Indira was in the making. And Kamaraj, whose new distrust of Indira did not match his old dislike of Morarji, was again the would-be broker. The seventy-one-year-old Desai, who would have been in an excellent position to achieve his aims as prime minister, was willing to become India's first deputy prime minister since Sardar Patel's death a year after independence. Negotiations that went on into the early morning hours of 11 March focused on whether he also would become home minister, as he wanted in order to be able to deal with the states, or finance minister once more.

Morarji's tactics, his good faith, and his strategy all come into question. Should he have said on the record what Tonpe had said for him on background, and so seized the high ground in the eyes of the nation before political opportunism took over? Was he angling for an accommodation with Indira all along? Or did he have longer-range goals in mind? His words immediately after he announced his candidacy for the leadership hint at some answers: "I am doing this as a duty, but I am considering the country's interest even more than the party's."

This sounds like mere self-serving rhetoric. But Morarji's initial aim apparently was to wake up the Congress without limiting its willingness to change by equating the party with his own ambition. Beyond what Tonpe had said for him, he publicly warned members of the Congress that failure to heed popular sentiment would jeopardize the party's very survival. When they disregarded his warning, and another victory for Indira in another contest was all but certain, Morarji may have done his "duty" and announced his candidacy anyway. This would improve his bargaining position to become the strongman in her government and pursue his objectives in that capacity. If this didn't work, or if her government collapsed within two years as many political analysts were predicting, Morarji would still be acceptable as the leader of a new conservative coalition. Creation of a united non-Communist parliamentary opposition was the aim of Rajaji, who looked to the day when it could form a government with Congress conservatives.

Portents filled the air when Congress MPs finally convened in the Central Hall on 12 March, and when President Radhakrishnan swore in a new government at Rashtrapati Bhavan the next day.

Although Morarji had agreed to nominate Indira as part of the deal that had been struck, Kamaraj took no chances. He announced: "We are here to elect Mrs Indira Gandhi unanimously as leader of the Congress Parliamentary Party." Morarji then moved the nomination. The entire process took four minutes, ending with 168 Congress members of the Rajya Sabha joining the sharply reduced number of Congress members of the Lok Sabha in pounding their desks to acclaim the triumphant Indira. Garlanded with marigolds and jasmine, she wore a Nehru rose, but a pink blossom, not the red bud always affected by her father. When the cheering subsided, Morarji wryly commented: "It is a crown of thorns that we have put on her head."

Undismayed now that she had attained her single goal of reelection as prime minister, Indira no longer had to try to be someone she was not. In international affairs, she asserted, the new government would follow the path of non-alignment set out by her father "because that is where our interests lie." At home, she proclaimed: "We have no choice but to follow a policy of left of centre because the prime problem of this country remains the poverty of the mass of the people and that problem can be met only by such a policy." Indira thereby lost no time in tripping up her unwanted number-two-to-be. Morarji had courteously refrained from circulating a letter to MPs seeking their support for the leadership, and suggesting that ineffective statist policies contributed to mass poverty.

On 13 March Indira duly named Morarji deputy prime minister and finance minister. She reappointed Yeshwantrao Chavan of Maharashtra, who had cleaned up the mess in the defence ministry left by Menon, to the key home ministry, Morarji's first choice. She gave the vital food ministry to Congress veteran Jagjivan Ram, a leader of untouchables now known as dalits. She promoted her friend and adviser, Dinesh Singh, to commerce minister. There was some new blood but it was largely an unimaginative cabinet.

Singh would rise to foreign minister under Indira. Ram would eventually challenge her, and Indira's reaction would devastate the country. Chavan's first act as renamed home minister was to impose president's rule or central administration on the state of Rajasthan through the person of Radhakrishnan. As party nabobs had haggled in Delhi, ordinary Indians rallied by a determined Gayatri Devi had poured into the streets of Jaipur to protest when the politically appointed governor asked the Congress to form a government although it had failed to win a legislative majority.

As for Morarji, he didn't know it but he was on his way out the moment he had decided it was best to go into the government again. Already, Indira was plotting how to get rid of him.

8

The Soul of a Nation

On New Year's Day of 1969, I rose at the back of a crowded New Delhi room at Prime Minister Indira Gandhi's first press conference in a year and asked: "How long do you expect to remain prime minister?"

It was a deliberately provocative question and she gave a predictably petulant answer: "I don't think there's any commission sitting on this yet."

But the people of India were sitting in increasingly appalled judgment on their leader and her performance three years after the daughter of Jawaharlal Nehru succeeded Lal Bahadur Shastri as prime minister of India, and nearly two years after she managed to survive their first protest vote against the ruling Congress Party. At the rare press conference, she angrily defended her record with words that revealed more than she intended: "There is no indecision at all ... policy is no hodgepodge at all ... I stick to the policy I believe to be right whether it costs me my life or anything else."

Indira, then fifty-one, probably meant her political life. But more than anyone could have realized at the beginning of 1969, her own life, and the life of all India, as an enormously complex country trying to overcome centuries of human oppression by democratic means, were on the line.

In the short run, simultaneous February elections in four important, politically unstable states – what Indians were calling a little general election – would provide the first big test of Congress popularity and opposition staying power since the watershed elections of February 1967. In the long run, the ability and the right of the Nehru family dynasty to run the world's most populous democracy were open to serious question indeed. So were the vibrancy and effectiveness of Indian democracy and economic development as long as the Nehrus dominated both.

At the heart of these questions was the soul of a nation.

"A moment comes, which comes but rarely in history, when we step out from the old to the new, when an age ends, and when the soul of a nation, long suppressed, finds utterance."

The words are Pandit Nehru's just before midnight of 14 August 1947 when he said India was keeping a "tryst with destiny" in gaining independence from the British Raj at long last. But that magical moment did not really come then. More than a half-century later, it still has not fully come. It will happen only when India is fully free of dependence on Indians past and present who limit human potential and constrain human hope.

India has distanced itself from the Nehrus in recent years. But the vast country is just starting to step out from the old to the new. A glance at any of its hundreds of thousands of villages and towns confirms that caste-conscious Indians have not yet left behind familiar inequality let alone embarked upon an age of unfamiliar equality. The long political battle in India is taking new forms. It will be decided only when the soul of the nation, still suppressed, either surrenders to habitual authority or breaks completely free. On that historic day its true nature will be revealed. Meanwhile, the battle continues.

Two brief comments by India's grand old man indicated its character following the 1967 debacle for the Congress Party. "Majority rule," observed Chakravarty Rajagopalachari as Indira's willingness to stop at nothing in order to stay in power became clear, "is not the same as democracy." Fighting into his nineties for individual freedom and a responsible opposition in India, Rajaji pointed to the most dire consequence of a wholesale abuse of democracy: "Prestige is fast going up in favour of the Communists." Under the woman who increasingly called herself Indira Nehru Gandhi, a cliché nearly came true. India nearly went Communist.

Even more than during the election campaign, the prime minister was obsessed with the details of personal politics when it was over. She disdainfully brushed off a growing credibility gap with the Indian political class, the press, and the people. Her hypocrisy in the matter of India's denial of asylum to Svetlana Alliluyeva, Stalin's daughter, contributed to this distrust. When she said she was moved by starving peasants in Bihar but her government offered little help, some Indians wondered about her honesty. Opposition MPs were emboldened enough to accuse her on the floor of Parliament of accepting gifts from foreign leaders such as the king of Saudi Arabia and Soviet chairman Nikita Khrushchev when her father was prime minister. But Indira had her eye on benefits more valuable to her than diamond necklaces or sable stoles. She was engaged in a reckless operation to destabilize state governments formed by non-Congress parties. This was her chosen way of shoring up her own crumbling foundation in New Delhi.

Indian federalism always has been heavily one-sided in favour of "the centre." But Indira's tactics amounted to a selective attack by her central government – which existed thanks only to a small parliamentary majority – on individuals, parties, and coalitions in state capitals that were not in her camp. One weapon was inducing legislators to defect to the Congress, in many cases by monetary bribes. Another was to use the constitutional provision of president's rule to dismiss ruling coalitions not because they failed to maintain law and order – the legal criterion – but because they were not friends of Indira. To do this repeatedly, Indira had to be sure of a rubber-stamp president of India who would carry out her "advice" as prime minister with no questions asked, despite the fact the constitution gives wide but untested powers to whoever holds the position of head of state. If she lost her own parliamentary majority due either to a new election or defections from the Congress, as seemed likely, she especially wanted a protector in Rashtrapati Bhavan.

The retiring president, Sarvepalli Radhakrishnan, had deferred to Nehru publicly on controversial matters, and had for the first time imposed central bureaucratic rule on a state at Indira's bidding after the 1967 elections – on Rajasthan when popular protests greeted an attempt to install a minority Congress government. But the dignified Hindu philosopher had recently made known his abhorrence of Congress mismanagement. If he had remained in office, he surely would not have let himself become a puppet as politicization of the presidency intensified.

Many of the early post-election doubts about Indira focused on her determination to elevate Vice-President Zakir Husain to Radhakrishnan's place despite widespread objections within and outside the Congress. She even threatened to resign as prime minister if she did not get her way. Considering how the unembarrassed head of government was to cheapen the presidency – the highest office in the land, symbolizing India itself – party leaders should have taken her at her word. Instead, she won her most notable victory over Congress boss K. Kamaraj Nadar in obtaining the party's endorsement of Husain.

In principle, Nehru's daughter could not be faulted for insisting that as president the Muslim educator would underline predominantly Hindu India's secularism. But her real motive in wanting Husain was that, especially as a vulnerable Muslim, he was expected to be a pliant tool in her hands. On 6 May members of Parliament and state legislatures cast votes, weighted on the basis of population, in India's first contested presidential election. They chose Husain by a wide margin over the candidate of seven non-Communist opposition parties, Koka Subha Rao, who had established a reputation for independence and liberalism as chief justice of India's Supreme Court. The real winner was Indira in gambling that Congress electors would not desert her whatever their misgivings. It was the first in a series of moves on her part that were tactically brilliant, politically dangerous, and highly destructive of the integrity of the Republic of India.

By the end of May, Indira's government had moved to counter a more widely recognized threat to the nation: a possible Communist bid to take over West Bengal. It named a tough new governor of the eastern state with its seething capital of Calcutta. It demanded that the newly elected, Communist-dominated, United Front government stop workers from laying siege to management in factories and offices instead of tacitly supporting these lock-ins, called gheraos. And Indian troops restored order in Calcutta when police could not stop street violence.

The new governor was Dharma Vira, a highly respected top civil servant close to security officials in Delhi and experienced in administering president's rule of a state unable to rule itself. In 1966, he had presided over partition of the Indian Punjab, demanded by militant Sikhs, and then had served as joint governor of the new states of the Punjab and Hariana until president's rule gave way to elected non-Congress governments in both. Vira's transfer to Calcutta was a clear warning to Bengali Communists that Delhi would not countenance insurrection. In West Bengal's case, the prospect of president's rule had to do with more than Indira's own political ambitions. Ironically, however, legitimate concern in her government about Communist aims in specific states came to coexist with a Communist strategy for takeover of all India that included Indira.

West Bengal was by far the most significant of these states. With a history of radical revolutionaries, and Calcutta's still simmering resentment at having been abandoned as the capital of British India in 1911 in favour of Delhi, it was separate from the rest of the country and yet had a crucial bearing on independent India's direction. "There is hardly any aspect of the Bengali existence today," wrote Bengali author Nirad Chaudhuri at the time, "which does not exhibit a preference for the unreal."

Bengal's unreal part in the malaise gripping India in the wake of its most encouraging democratic exercise started to hit me in Calcutta in mid-November 1967. A small, immaculate man in a white dhoti, sitting behind a big, horseshoe-shaped desk in the Writers Building, said bitterly then: "We have no guns against the army." He paused and repeated slowly: "We don't have the guns."

It was the only time during an interview that a flicker of emotion contradicted the cold voice and face of Jyoti Basu, the most powerful Communist in West Bengal. Except for his reiterated statement of fact, he did not sound like a revolutionary. The desk belonged, after all, to the deputy chief minister and finance minister of a state of 40 million people at the time that was of immense strategic and industrial importance to the rest of India. The Writers Building was named for the *babus* or government clerks who had scribbled on papers, pushed them around, or tied them up with red tape for decades. As leader of what were called the left Marxist Communists in West Bengal, Basu had come to power when an anti-Congress front led by his party jubilantly joined another grouping led by the right pro-Moscow Communists to form a fourteen-party United Front government headed by Chief Minister Ajoy Mukherjee, an idealistic, non-Communist rebel opposed to the Congress.

But when I met Basu, this leftist government had ostensibly just lost its legislative majority due to the resignation of another veteran non-Communist ex-Congress minister, Prafula Ghosh, and the withdrawal of support by sixteen other legislators. Basu, the deputy chief minister, and other suspicious Communists were not alone in imagining that Delhi had engineered the defections with the aim of forming a new state government that would include the unpopular Congress and, if need be, clamp president's rule on West Bengal and enforce it with the army Basu feared.

A further factor in this shadowy cat-and-mouse game was a third group of Communists called Naxalites. While workers in the Calcutta area were shutting down factories, tribal peasants in the tea gardens of Naxalbari in northern Bengal were seizing land. The United Front government refused to send state police but consented to Delhi's dispatching two companies of central reserve police to put down the uprising. This split the Marxist Communists, the largest party in the ruling coalition. The far left Naxalites demanded an end to participation in what they called a "turncoat" government and called for an official promotion of Mao Zedong–inspired peasants' revolts throughout India. The radical Naxalite agenda eventually turned out to be a blessing in disguise for Basu and his avowedly law-abiding Marxist colleagues, who claimed their comparative moderation qualified them to rule West Bengal. For this reason, some believe the whole Naxalbari movement was an invention of Communists who had more attainable objectives in mind than Indian rural revolution.

But on 21 November 1967 Governor Vira dismissed the United Front government and named Prafula Ghosh as chief minister. Ghosh was seventy-five and had been West Bengal's first chief minister as a Congressman. The United Front's immediate reaction was a two-day hartal or general strike, marked by frequent clashes between demonstrators and police. But a much bigger confrontation loomed when the legislature met 30 November at the call of the new chief minister. In addition to his 16 legislators, Prafula Ghosh would need the support of 130 Congress members loyal to the party's widely despised boss in Calcutta, Atulya Ghosh – of no family or political relation – in order to secure a majority in the 280-seat house.

Communists prepared for a mass march on the plain, neo-Gothic, legislative building, next to the more imposing Raj Bhavan or governor's palace and the multi-pillared Calcutta High Court, although emergency regulations banning assembly of more than four persons were in force in the area. Inside the legislature, Communist members would challenge the constitutionality of the session, backed by a speaker who had rejected Prafula Ghosh's request to permit police in the chamber to curb violence by members. Supported by the governor, the chief minister was expected to seek adjournment as soon as the session's legality was established by virtue of the legislature's convening.

The night before, the unreality of Bengal was palpable in the dim streets of Calcutta. Democracy, Communists, law, order, revolution, and anarchy were all involved, but it was impossible to be sure what any of these terms meant or who stood for what. In a city accustomed to terror among its masses, people at all levels were caught up not so much by present tension as by a past that made violence a necessary accompaniment to any change. Fear hung over Calcutta as thickly as the smog from hundreds of thousands of tiny cooking fires lit by its poor.

Hundreds of persons were arrested as reinforced police cut off the city and its environs by forming concentric rings around them in an effort to contain violence. At Lal Bazaar – meaning Red Bazaar, another unreal Bengali touch as the name for central police headquarters – hundreds of brown-uniformed policemen carrying ancient .303 Lee-Enfield rifles stood by glumly, ready to go into action in an uneven collection of trucks and jeeps. A senior police inspector told me in a calm voice that did not hide his anxiety: "We not only expect trouble. We know we'll get it tomorrow morning. They've given an order to their people to march."

The next day, the blood that ran in the streets of Calcutta was real enough. So was the fighting among elected representatives that broke out on the floor of the legislature. But Bengal scenes then and later were no less unbelievable for being predictable.

Policemen charging demonstrators with lathis or metal-tipped staves is standard procedure in India. Still, I was unprepared for Calcutta police catching up with an old man a few feet away from where I was standing. He was among the thousands of people marching on the legislature until they were forced to retreat. Several enraged policemen hit him relentlessly with their lathis until blood poured from his broken head. Then his limp body was carelessly carried away. When the sweating, frightened police managed to keep the marchers at bay several hundred feet from the legislative building, the action shifted inside.

As if on cue, Communist Solons blocked the doors to the legislative chamber and lay down on the floor to keep other members from entering. When that didn't work, the house came to calculated disorder, as well as mandated order, as its leftist members shouted slogans, punched other members, and threw objects. The lamp on the desk of the grey-haired Prafula Ghosh, knocked over by a hurled paperweight, hit the pensive chief minister on the forehead and he slumped down in his seat. The lean, gesticulating, pro-Communist speaker in his dhoti did his best to stop the session as soon as it started. The stout Governor Vira, representing in his Western suit the authority of the government of India, stood up on a chair to avoid scuffling legislators. He then proceeded to read a few pre-arranged words of a speech that could then be taken as read in its entirety – and therefore as having legitimized the new state government of West Bengal, its source.

Eighteen days later, after a second Marxist-led hartal, the ousted chief minister, Ajoy Mukherjee, was arrested outside Raj Bhavan as he started a civil disobedience campaign like those conducted by Mahatma Gandhi against the British. Mukherjee, sixty-six, was under no illusions about his Communist partners in the United Front. He later in writing attacked them scathingly for having cynically exploited the hopes of Bengal's masses. But neither was he prepared to accept blatant manipulation of the law in furtherance of political interests in Delhi. Protesting injustice was an old story with Mukherjee: in 1942 his Indian "national government" at Tamluk in Bengal had defied the Raj, and in 1965 like Rajaji he had broken with the Congress Party. Late on the night of 18 December 1967, he was released and sent home by a magistrate who declined to press government charges against the old Indian freedom fighter.

The next day, Calcutta police arrested more than 200 women continuing civil disobedience by violating the ban on public assembly. At the same time, Parliament in Delhi began debating a government bill authorizing fresh curbs on anyone deemed to be preaching or carrying out secession by a part of India. Home Minister Yeshwantrao Chavan, rejecting opposition charges that the Congress government aimed to use the broad new powers against its many opponents, said the bill would place "reasonable" – but, if necessary, secret – restrictions on the freedoms of speech, expression, assembly, and association anywhere in the country. Indira Gandhi, head of that government, had retreated a long way since the time when she had urged the lifting of emergency powers routinely used against alleged enemies of India.

Soon after these events, a Congressman defeated in the nationwide 1967 protest vote recounted how he had taunted Basu for failing to set Calcutta on fire. The embittered Communist replied: "It will take another hundred years before India is set on fire."

The masses of India were already suffering from malnutrition of both body and mind. Now the nationally ruling Congress Party, by moving lazily into the vacuum it had created, was paralyzing the body politic as well.

Individual politicians could not be blamed for inactivity. To open a newspaper each morning was to read a scoreboard of defections to and from the Congress in various states, with some particularly agile legislators jumping back and forth two or three times in a week. But the only discernible activity by the central Congress government was to attempt to drown islands of opposition as they popped up, starting with dismissal of the United Front government in West Bengal. It had no significant program, no popular mandate, and no vigorous leaders. Indira tightened her grip on the prime ministership by doing as little as possible as prime minister. She turned India's top political position into an end in itself rather than a means to govern decisively. As one analyst put it, "Mrs Gandhi has learned how to hit dead center every time."

This cynical political drift in a country crying out for meaningful economic action to relieve the poverty of hundreds of millions was never so apparent as at the seventy-first annual meeting of the Indian National Congress, in Hyderabad in January 1968. The delicious decadence offered to delegates (and journalists) by the young Nizam of Hyderabad, nephew of the late Nizam, unintentionally struck just the right note. At a stand-up banquet, guests partook of traditional Hyderabadi curries and condiments prepared for days, placed on solid gold plates, and topped off by vanilla ice cream and chocolate sauce flown in from Paris. At the "working" sessions, fat old men, tired women, and a listless rank and file were served up with a dearth of fresh ideas.

Indira said before the session that the path of Indian democracy did not have to follow the British or U.S. example. But where was the democracy in a one-party-plus system when the one party was going outside the law to do away with the plus, expanding police powers at the expense of guaranteed human rights, and ignoring the voice of the people? The new Congress president, Siddavanahalli Nijalingappa, notable earlier as a member of the party's Syndicate of bosses, admitted that popular dissatisfaction was greater than before independence. He confessed that none of the historic Congress ideals set by Mohandas Gandhi and often reluctantly concurred in by Jawaharlal Nehru had been attained – land to the tiller, *swaraj* or freedom of the spirit, a new deal for Indians known as untouchables, Hindu-Muslim harmony, a place for cottage industries, clean villages, even non-violence.

Indira's only apparent aims were to outmanoeuvre her main rivals for the party leadership, Finance Minister Morarji Desai and Home Minister Chavan, and to bring down non-Congress state coalition governments. At

Hyderabad, the Congress casually proclaimed the end of the era of coalitions. The regimes of diverse parties that had supplanted Congress rule in half of India's states in 1967 were often illogical and could not easily last. But in the most populous states of Uttar Pradesh, Bihar, and West Bengal, they offered the only possible basis for the beginning of political change when there was not yet another truly national party in sight. Their misfortune and India's, as even some Congressmen acknowledged privately, was that this possibility had not taken hold in Delhi. Congress majority unity in Parliament permitted party leaders to place the full blame for growing violence in India on state opposition parties. It never seemed to occur to Indira and many of her colleagues that lawlessness flowed largely from popular desperation at not finding remedies for economic and social wrongs within the law and particularly within India's retarded party system.

I soon found myself fighting a wrong done to freedom of the press in India and to me personally. On 4 April 1968, a week after my current one-year visa as a resident newspaper correspondent had expired and more than seven weeks after I had applied for a new one, I was handed a brief typewritten letter at the grimy Foreign Regional Registration Office in New Delhi. Signed by the officer in charge but formalizing a decision made somewhere in the morass known as the government of India, it said: "Your extension (of stay) will expire on 28-4-1968 and no further extension can be granted to you. You are requested to make arrangements to leave the country immediately and not in any case later than 28-4-68."

My shock and hurt were temporarily overcome by anger at the sneaky way the order was carried out. No one ever gave me a specific reason. External Affairs officials had told me the Press Information Bureau, the government's propaganda arm, was unhappy with some of my dispatches, particularly on the Bihar famine. But they had seemed to accept my assurance of fair reporting. A notification mailed 1 April to our home in Jor Bagh, one of New Delhi's residential colonies, saying I should come in for "grant of further extension of stay," contained no inkling of the expulsion order.

On a bright, warm day at the beginning of North India's long, cruel summer, I went to the fenced-off barracks near the circular Parliament building where foreigners who were not British subjects were kept track of. A pleasant man I had encountered before stamped my U.S. passport with a new visa, then motioned me with a nervous smile into another room while he kept the passport. Here a fat, oily man I had not seen before said, "Please take your seat" – a seemingly polite expression used by bureaucrats the world over but especially in India to signify you will have to wait for them

– and gave me a battered copy of an old American newsmagazine to read.
When he finally presented the letter limiting my stay in India to twenty-
four more days, I stormed into the office of the head of the Foreign Regional Registration Office and indulged in a practice that most foreigners in
India cannot avoid at one time or other: shouting at officialdom. I knew it
was useless in an office where everyone was employed by the Criminal
Investigation Division, the Indian equivalent of the FBI, as detective-clerks.
But there are times in India when one is compelled to express oneself loudly and clearly, if not altogether rationally, as a human being. When I went
back to the first room to recover my passport, I found that "CANCELLED"
had been stamped in black ink at least fourteen times over my new visa.
For the time being bureaucracy was triumphant.

What I didn't think to question at the time was my being given twenty-
four days instead of twenty-four hours to leave India. If not twenty-four
hours, the usual limit, why not three days or one week or even one month?
My guess later was that somewhere in that deep, dark bureaucracy I had a
friend who had substituted "days" for "hours" and the change had slipped
by unnoticed. Or perhaps "28-4-1968" was a clerical error. Whatever the
reason for the odd deadline of twenty-four days hence, it gave me, my editors, and other friends enough time to get the expulsion order rescinded at
what turned out to be, another oddity, the very highest level of the government of India.

Never before had an order been served on a Western correspondent to
leave independent India ostensibly because of his reporting. At least one
attempt was made to leak news of the order against me to the leftist Indian
press. It failed, and by a minor miracle the action was kept quiet. The government never would have reversed itself if it had had to do so publicly.
When the expulsion order was quashed – one day after the 28 April deadline for my departure – so was an attempt to set an insidious precedent in
the largest Asian democracy. But this did not stop the individuals behind
the order from trying again, more broadly, publicly, and with more success,
later.

I decided immediately, and was supported by the editors of *The Toronto
Globe and Mail* in a flurry of cables, that it was worth fighting privately to
save my position in India instead of giving it up in a blaze of publicity.
They, the editors of *The Washington Evening Star*, Ambassador Chester
Bowles of the U.S., several Canadian officials, and General Joyanto Nath
Chaudhuri, retired chief of staff of the Indian army, who was then India's
high commissioner or ambassador in Ottawa, made repeated diplomatic
and not-so-diplomatic assaults on three Indian cabinet ministers and at
least a half-dozen senior officials. When a favourable decision finally
resulted, I assumed the prime minister's secretary as head of the civil

service had made it. But in the end the internal affairs committee of the cabinet, including Indira, Morarji, and Chavan, the big three in the Indian government, decided the issue.

I was stunned to find this out when I telephoned V.Y. Tonpe, the quietly astute secretary to Desai, to say I had been granted a six-month extension of stay (later extended by another full year). Tonpe informed me that he knew all about it because the committee had been the court of last resort. A few days later I received a note from Morarji, who in an earlier letter had declined for the record to intercede on my behalf, that concluded: "I am happy to be assured that you would ever continue to remain a friend of India." In a brief letter to the deputy prime minister and finance minister, who, I am convinced, was the most important friend of mine in this matter, I had written: "I feel strongly that if there has been any prejudice on my part in reporting developments in India, as had been charged, it was in favor of India rather than against."

On 4 April, the day I was ordered to leave India as the only representative of a Canadian newspaper, Indira paid tribute to retiring Prime Minister Lester Pearson of Canada with these words in the lower house of Parliament: "The friendship between Canada and India rises above the routine … It is founded on mutual regard and understanding." The next day, in response to complaints by MPs about adverse coverage of the Bihar famine, the prime minister told the Lok Sabha: "Our image abroad will inevitably be a reflection of our situation at home." At precisely the same time, officials close to her, who became more identifiable later, were moving to get me out of India because of stories having to do less with famine in Bihar, I discovered, than with repression in Kashmir and decay in Delhi.

The country's drift and moral decay had advanced enough by the beginning of 1969 that, as a re-established resident correspondent, I presumed to ask Indira about the duration of her stay as prime minister. In early February, as 40 per cent of India's voters trooped to the polls in Bihar, the Punjab, Uttar Pradesh, and West Bengal in the tenuous hope of electing stable state governments, a high Congress official's calm assessment of the situation did not hide the panic invading party circles. Sadiq Ali's anonymous remarks even before the votes were counted amounted to recognition that the national political realignment signalled by the elections two years earlier could no longer be put off. The longtime party secretary and strategist told me on a plane flying from Bihar's capital of Patna to Lucknow, capital of Uttar Pradesh, that the once omnipotent Congress was prepared to enter coalitions with other parties immediately in state capitals and eventually in New Delhi.

"In 1967 the mood of the people in many states was for coalitions of opposition parties," said Ali, an engaging, worldly Muslim who stood for the party's old ideals. "They didn't work and now the mood is for coalitions of Congress with other parties."

He was trying to make a virtue of necessity, and he ruled out Congress deals with the Jan Sangh, the forerunner to the Hindu nationalist Bharatiya Janata Party. In all likelihood Indira underlined this exclusion as she met other party leaders at the same time in Tirupathi, near Madras, to discuss possible coalition partners in the four contested states. When Jan Sanghis had jeered her in Patna at the last of the more than 250 rallies for Congress candidates she had addressed, she had shouted emotionally: "I will never tolerate this and will crush them with all my might!"

Nehru's daughter did not express herself as intensely, if at all, on barring the Congress from coalescing with Communists. But then no one expected her party to make a bargain with any Communist party either. A year after decreeing the end of coalitions, at least she and the demoralized Congress were taking a step or two toward the real world. This long overdue, still tentative awakening appeared to make a coalition government in New Delhi following the next parliamentary election, due in early 1972, a distinct possibility if not a probability.

But the focus in early 1969 was on four key states temporarily under president's rule imposed by Zakir Hussain on Indira Gandhi's "advice."

In West Bengal, army-backed administration through the Delhi-appointed governor, feared but also provoked by Jyoti Basu, had supplanted in February 1968 the Congress-supported regime of Prafula Ghosh when Communist members prevented the legislature from functioning.

In caste-riven Bihar and the new Sikh-majority Punjab, Congress-engineered defections had toppled coalition governments formed after the 1967 elections. Apart from president's rule, this had led to political appeals to caste or religious loyalties that were even crasser than usual.

In Uttar Pradesh with its then nearly 90 million people, politicians of all stripes at all levels had contributed to the breakdown of normal government and imposition of central rule. Although the Jan Sangh posed the main challenge to the Congress, a breakaway party led by an overly shrewd farmer politician named Charan Singh had exploited political stalemate: he had defected from a weak Congress regime after the 1967 elections to head a coalition government that subsequently split apart itself. One of the ironies in the "little general election" was that good Congress showings in Uttar Pradesh and West Bengal might shorten Indira's political life. Two of her bitterest enemies were C.B. Gupta, party boss in her home state, and Atulya Ghosh, Calcutta Congress boss.

The election results, and coincidental events in Madras and Bombay, went far beyond state politics or political personalities in their impact. On top of the nationwide protest vote in 1967, they demonstrated that fires of deep discontent were burning out of control in India, especially in vital areas outside the country's stagnant Hindi-speaking heartland. Far from emerging from the 1969 state elections with a stronger hand, the Congress and Indira came out in worse shape at the hands of bitterly disillusioned Indians. It was clearer than ever that the party and its leader were holding the unity of free India and quite possibly its survival up for ransom. As the normally pro-government *Times of India* put it editorially when the votes came in, "The choice is not between a strong centre and strong states – the choice is between a national polity and complete disintegration."

Bengalis inflicted the worst punishment on the Congress. After fifteen months of interference in West Bengal by the central government, they opted overwhelmingly for the devil in Calcutta they knew over the devil in Delhi they had distrusted for more than a half-century. The Communist-dominated United Front won 214 seats and the Congress only 55. The Marxists led by Basu captured 80 seats as the largest party in the dramatically redeemed Front, and the pro-Moscow Communists another 30.

In the Punjab, India's most agriculturally productive state, the militant Sikh Akali Dal, or Party of God, easily defeated Indira's secular Congress. More a religious movement than a political party, the Akali Dal nevertheless formed a ruling coalition with the Hindu Jan Sangh. This enabled Sikh farmers to attain their old dream of a government of their own. The anti-Congress vote and government pointed to the violent movement that was to come among Punjabi Sikhs for an independent Khalistan.

Voters in Bihar forgot neither the famine that had recently ravaged their state nor the caste divisions that have long made it the most backward in the Hindi heartland. The non-caring Congress took little more than one-third of the legislative seats. But with many Biharis dispersing their votes on the basis of caste, no other party came close. Continued instability and lack of progress, marked by periods of president's rule, were unavoidable.

Only in Uttar Pradesh did the Congress win a victory of sorts with a rout of the Jan Sangh. This temporarily halted gains by the Muslim-baiting Hindu party, which had been making gains nationally since the 1962 general elections. But the UP Congress still barely managed to break even in legislative seats. This left the balance of power in dissident Charan Singh's hands, and little room for economic gains in the giant state. Another UP result of note was the outcome of a parliamentary by-election in Jawaharlal Nehru's old constituency of Phulpur. With his sister Vijayalakshmi Pandit having resigned the seat in late 1968 after holding it for four years, a Socialist Party candidate defeated a prominent leftist put up by the Congress.

Wild scenes in Madras at the beginning of February provided a prologue to the election returns in northern states. Hysterical crowds of Tamils mourning the death of C.N. Annadurai, state chief minister and populist hero, testified vividly to the widespread appeal of a defiance of central authority and promotion of cultural regionalism. His Dravida Munnetra Kazhagam, or Dravidian Progressive Party, catering to low-caste Tamils, formed the most solid anti-Congress state government in the country. Neighbouring Andhra Pradesh, one of the last Congress strongholds in south India and indeed in all India, was gripped by a violent movement for a separate Telengana, a depressed rural area where revolutionary Communists had tried to seize power twenty years earlier.

As votes were tabulated in the north, a fascist-like organization instigated the worst mob violence until then in the history of Bombay, the country's commercial capital and most cosmopolitan city. More than fifty people were killed by police bullets in wanton pillaging by young goondas of the Shiv Sena, a group harking back to the seventeenth century Maratha warrior Shivaji and demanding the state of Maharashtra for Maharashtrians only. This was the first step in a violent campaign that was to escalate to even more destructive rioting by the Shiv Sena in Bombay in 1992, when Hindu toughs targeted Muslim homes and families for burning and killing, and were abetted instead of opposed by the police.

Prime Minister Gandhi's immediate reaction to this shattering series of events was not to seek reconciliation or reform but to strengthen her own hand in the shambles of her Congress Party. At the unusual hour of 1:00 AM 14 February, just hours after the full extent of the Communist victory in West Bengal became clear, she announced the promotion of her favourite young cabinet colleague, Dinesh Singh, to the position of foreign minister, a move previously blocked by other Congress leaders. In freeing herself from this portfolio and again asserting her independence, Indira said cryptically that she wanted to devote more time to "higher direction" of the government, particularly in economic matters.

Considering her virtually full-time obsession with politics – and Singh's strong Soviet ties – it is reasonable to conclude she had a deeper motive. Dinesh had shuttled between the Soviet embassy and Indira in the denial of asylum to Svetlana Alliluyeva in early 1967. There is every reason to believe that Indira wanted him as her liaison with Moscow in carrying out a whole new political strategy in the coming months. This startling concept differed sharply from the potentially healthy idea of Congress coalitions with middle-of-the-road non-Communist parties. With the near collapse of the Congress, Indian Communists were already drafting this daring strategy. Indira wanted to be certain that the united or popular front government the Communists envisioned in New Delhi was led, thanks significantly to Soviet help, by no one but herself.

With the defeats of early 1969 piled on top of those of 1967, she was as aware as the Communists of the perilous plight of the Congress. The party was reduced to just keeping its head above water in the states of the impoverished Hindi belt. Generally more progressive states as near to Delhi as the Punjab and as far as West Bengal, Kerala, Tamil Nadu, and Orissa – where the free-enterprise Swatantra Party was effectively running the government – were turning to parties more closely expressing their special character. Under Indira, the Indian National Congress had failed not only to relieve India's chronic economic woes, but also to respond to anguished cries of protest from all corners of the country.

If the party were going to collapse entirely or split irreparably, however, she was determined to command an alternative of the left that would be ready to take the place of the Congress in New Delhi. Indeed, she might well have felt more comfortable leading a leftist coalition than in her present role, especially if by so doing she could block a conservative alternative of the right from coming to power nationally. The nature of this potential coalition of the left, and how Indira might connect with it, became clear when I visited the palm-fringed southwestern state of Kerala a few weeks after the little general election of 1969.

E.M. Sankaran Namboodiripad, the sports-shirted Marxist Communist chief minister of Kerala and architect of the stunning Communist electoral victory in West Bengal, willingly revealed to me a grand design for a Communist takeover of all India, and possibly half of Pakistan as it then existed. In an interview in his huge office in the capital of Trivandrum on the Malabar coast near India's southern tip, he confidently predicted that a national united front of "left democratic and socialist elements" would take power from the devastated Congress Party following the 1972 general election.

Asked if his Communist Party and he personally would lead the coalition, E.M.S. – the initials by which he was known throughout India – replied in the stutter that made even critics sympathize with him: "It is too early to say." But people close to him left no doubt that his becoming prime minister was the fondest ambition of the high-caste Brahmin whose national position had been vastly enhanced by developments in West Bengal and Kerala.

The design he patiently described could be traced back to his own state. Since 1962, Communists had been in and out of power in Kerala, whose population – 18 million in 1969 – is the most densely packed and the most literate in India. They had been the first opposition group to defeat the

Congress at the state level. But only since E.M.S.'s Marxist-dominated front had won a big majority in the 1967 elections had confrontation between the Congress central government and Kerala's Communists all but ceased. This was because the leftist coalition government generally respected the law and even encouraged private business and investment. The stark contrast with its disruptively anti-capitalist counterpart in West Bengal, first elected at the same time, had been evident to me during an earlier trip to Trivandrum in February 1968.

Family planning workers, high school students, bank employees, public grass cutters, and students of Aryuvedic medicine were all demonstrating then for more or better-paid jobs. But their protests were peaceful and the government was trying to meet their needs instead of further stirring them up. Inside the long, green-and-white Kerala legislative chamber, as forty ceiling fans continually whirred, E.M.S.'s government casually defeated by a vote of eighty-nine to thirteen a motion of non-confidence brought by a handful of Congress members. Violence and obstructionism, common in the West Bengal legislature, were absent. Even then Namboodiripad and his fellow ideologues kept developments in India's states in an ambitious national perspective. One of them termed Delhi's ouster of the United Front government in Calcutta at the time "not a tragedy [but] a changing phase – we want Kerala and West Bengal as bases for establishing socialist equity in India, with the Communist Party embracing all India." "

Now that Jyoti Basu's Bengali Communists had swept spectacularly back into power in 1969 with much greater popular support, the next phase called for them to emulate E.M.S.'s Kerala Communists in gaining respectability by seeming to uphold law and order. The extremist Naxalite Communists, originating in Bengal, had started to make the Marxists look good. This red herring, together with the transfer of popular Bengali hostility from local Communists to the Congress central government, and the example of stable Communist rule in Kerala, were all parts of the master plan designed by E.M.S.

He told me candidly that he looked forward to an Indian version of the classic Communist popular front that would bring together his Marxists, the pro-Moscow Communists, socialist groups, state parties such as the Dravida Munnetra Kazhagam of Tamil Nadu, dissident groups that had broken away from the Congress in West Bengal and Uttar Pradesh, and individual Congress rebels. It was unnecessary to add that once such an extreme leftist front came to power at the centre in Delhi, it was certain to reverse Communist demands at the time for more state powers.

A proposal by West Bengal's new rulers suggested that another Communist goal was what Frank Moraes, the hard-headed editor of *The Indian Express*, sarcastically called a "red Bengalistan" under China's auspices.

The Calcutta United Front had asked Delhi's permission to send a "good-will mission" to East Pakistan to "normalize relations" between the two separate parts of Bengal, historically the Subcontinent's most radical region. At the time, two years before oppressed East Bengalis broke away to form Bangladesh, Pakistan's political future was in more serious doubt than usual, with President Mohammad Ayub Khan about to retire in the face of massive popular protests in both of the country's wings. Communist parties were outlawed in Pakistan but a major force in East Bengal was Maulana Bhashani's pro-Beijing National Awami Party. The NAP was an appropriate candidate for a popular front extending even beyond India: one dominating all Bengal with its more than 100 million people even then.

Bold confidence on the part of Namboodiripad, the national Marxist leader, and his Bengali friends contrasted with demoralization in Congress ranks and disarray among non-leftist opposition parties. Responsible Indians talked openly of the breakup and disappearance of the Congress now that its historic role in unifying the country before and after independence in 1947 seemed to have ended with the freely acknowledged loss of touch with ordinary people, and with growing corruption. It was taken for granted that the Congress would not win a parliamentary majority in the next election. The belief was growing that some Congress leaders, especially Indira, who like her father saw forces on the right as her main enemy, would desert the party if a new national leftist coalition offered a better chance of continuing to rule India.

Distrust of Indira increased not only because she had quickly brought Soviet sympathizer Dinesh Singh to her side politically after the 1969 state elections; she also lost no time in seeking a compromise with the Bengali Communists once they had come back to power decisively. At the same time E.M.S. was telling me about his prospective national front, the prime minister all but caved in to their demand for an immediate recall of their nemesis, Dharma Vira, the centrally appointed state governor. The transfer soon thereafter of Vira, a staunch anti-Communist and one of India's most respected civil servants, amounted to unprecedented appeasement of Indian Communists by the Congress leadership. It dealt a heavy blow to the Indian Civil Service – the "steel frame" of India established by the British – and to a tradition of government administrators immune to political interference. These assuredly were Communist objectives in line with the grand strategy outlined by the chief minister of Kerala. But Indira's eagerness to deal with the triumphant Calcutta Marxists also signalled that E.M.S. had a formidable rival for leadership of a popular front designed to turn India into a Communist country.

From Trivandrum I flew north to Bombay. I found that members of India's most sophisticated business community were far more fearful about the formation of a national popular front by the Communists, and possibly the daughter of their old bugbear Nehru, than they were about the recent local reign of terror by the Shiv Sena. "We will recover from the violence of the rightists," wryly commented one businessman. "What we are more worried about is the non-violence of the leftists."

Still, Bombay had learned a useful lesson about the far right. An executive with a leading industrial firm told his story of having seen the documentary film *The Rise and Fall of The Third Reich* shortly after Shiv Sena thugs took control of the streets for several days in their vengeful drive to rid Maharashtra of outsiders. When the screen showed Nazi stormtroopers in Berlin in the 1930s, his wife suddenly turned to him and exclaimed: "My God, that's what happened here!"

Bombay had nonetheless quickly resumed its fast, free pace. The inner suburbs where most of the riot damage had taken place were sending commuter-packed electric trains into the city on schedule again. Marine Drive with its rundown but still impressive apartment buildings curved as if in perpetuity around the sands of Chowpatty, where people strolled, bought coloured drinks and peanuts, or simply watched the Arabian Sea as if nothing had happened. If a national conservative coalition were going to challenge the prospective leftist front, it would spring in large part from this sprawling port city with its dingy old shops, shiny new skyscrapers, and unashamed profit motive.

Many of its inhabitants were wrong in believing that Bombay had seen and survived the worst: still to come was sectarian violence even more traumatic, and the Shiv Sena's actually coming to political power as the Nazis had in Germany. But Bombay still felt in 1969 that it belonged to itself. The problem was that it was less sure than ever who India belonged to. It was used to absurdly heavy taxes and ridiculous red tape, and willing to run its private business in tandem with public planning. But Bombay was no longer very willing to invest its money in West Bengal. And it was beginning to have an uneasy feeling about the future of free enterprise in all India if politics did not soon become more rational.

As is often the case when a crisis turns on a suspect individual – Watergate and Richard Nixon, for example, or integrity in government and Bill Clinton – the irrational Indian crisis revolving around Indira Gandhi was even more serious than anyone imagined. This became apparent when I returned to Delhi for my last few weeks in India as a resident correspondent before voluntarily shifting my base for covering South Asia and Southeast Asia, including the Vietnam war, to Singapore in April 1969.

Indira launched a relentless campaign to discredit Finance Minister Morarji Desai and Home Minister Yeshwantrao Chavan, both of them her senior cabinet colleagues, and other moderate or conservative Congress Party leaders. Congress members of Parliament, particularly other women, openly attacked the prime minister. The party desperately tried to paper over the wide cracks that were coming close to destroying it. And Indira's camp hinted she might call the next parliamentary election long before early 1972, when it was due if the normal five-year interval following the last one held.

The Congress working committee adopted on 13 March a resolution criticizing "a growing tendency of party members to make personal allegations against each other." Despite its failure to name names, this amounted to a reprimand of Indira as well as an attempt to keep the party's dirty linen out of the public eye and avert a final split. It was no secret she was behind charges of impropriety leveled against Morarji by S. Chandra Shekhar, leader of the "Young Turks" among Congress MPs, on the floor of the Rajya Sabha. The unsubstantiated allegations, following similar Communist charges against the finance minister's son, suggested Morarji had profited from contacts with the Birlas, one of India's leading industrial families and a favourite leftist target. He responded to these charges, as Indira must have known he would, by threatening to retire from politics unless some measure of party discipline was restored.

In the Congress caucus of MPs, however, the prime minister found herself on the defensive. Morarji did not directly accuse her of being behind Chandra Shekhar's charges but he told Indira: "If he accuses me of dishonesty and I continue as deputy prime minister, I do not do any honour to you or to myself." Tarkeshwari Sinha, a striking and outspoken woman MP from Bihar, led an unprecedented assault on the prime minister for trying to isolate Morarji and Chavan, who as home minister had opposed taking Governor Vira out of West Bengal. Mrs Sinha – who later told me privately that the Congress under Indira had "developed a kind of death wish" – demanded to know why the prime minister had not condemned Chandra Shekhar. Another prominent Congresswoman, Sucheta Kripalani, declared: "I am sorry to say the leader is not functioning." Suresh Desai, unrelated to Morarji, asked Mrs Gandhi: "Madam, may I ask what sort of a government you are presiding over?" Indira gave no answers to her fellow caucus members. As for Chandra Shekhar, who would blatantly serve the Nehru family again at the expense of public morality, he refused to apologize even when Indira felt compelled to ask him to do so.

Despite the willingness of some Congress members to hold Indira to account, they were not able to agree on anyone else for prime minister. As long as this was so, the party's infighting was increasingly ideological as well as political. With the Communists out in the open about forming a national united front, this was exactly the way Indira wanted it. Polarization increased with the return to Parliament in May by-elections of Congress rightist S.K. Patil of Bombay and her old radical family friend V.K. Krishna Menon, running as an independent in West Bengal with United Front support. If Indira could call an early parliamentary election, she might profit sooner and more decisively from her deliberately leftist stance than anyone expected.

But the anticipated course of politics has a way of being interrupted by the unexpected. On 3 May 1969, President Zakir Husain, seventy-two, died of a heart attack, three years before the expiration of his five-year term. Suddenly Prime Minister Gandhi was deprived of her own man in Rashtrapati Bhavan.

Indira had repeatedly used Husain as her constitutional instrument to replace state governments composed of parties opposed to the Congress, as he would establish president's rule until Congress regimes could be formed. She had depended on him for her own protection if her position were challenged. If the next election, whenever it took place, did not produce a Congress parliamentary majority but Indira could form a government with Communists, other leftist parties, and her supporters in the Congress, she could have counted on Husain to ask her to do so instead of turning to a right-of-centre coalition. Without him, she was in greater danger of isolation within the Congress if the party agreed on a successor to Husain who was not her friend, and might be her enemy, and that person were elected.

Vice-President Varahagiri Venkata Giri, a Congressman and trade unionist who had previously distinguished himself as patron of the Parliamentary Heavyweight Club, was sworn in as acting president. But under the constitution a new president had to be elected within six months to a new term of five years by the electoral college of members of Parliament and state legislatures. This probably would happen during the monsoon session of Parliament in August. If Indira were going to save herself and keep the Nehru dynasty intact, she would have to move quickly and boldly.

She did so not once or twice but three times. Her staggering moves and the reaction to them offered a biting commentary on political will, human nature, and the state of the Indian Union.

On Saturday, 12 July, Indira lost the first round to her adversaries, and what could have been the last round, on the key question of Husain's successor. At a meeting of the Congress Parliamentary Board in Bangalore, other party leaders, including Morarji and Chavan, overruled her nomination of Giri for a five-year term as president of India. They then turned down by a formal vote of four to two her second choice of Jagjivan Ram, the food minister and dalit leader, whose name she had put forward as a compromise. The vote was in favour of N. Sanjiva Reddy, the genial speaker of the Lok Sabha and Andhra Pradesh Congress leader, and formerly a member of the party's now broken up Syndicate, as the Congress candidate for president. Responding with her usual angry petulance when she didn't get her way, Indira warned that the decision could have "serious consequences." It should have been the other way around. The party's repudiation of her on such an important question was cause enough for Indira to resign as leader and therefore as prime minister. But this was not her way. Instead she launched a sweeping offence as her best defence.

Her initial tactic was meant to look as if it were Giri's. Denied Congress endorsement for a full term as president, the seventy-five-year-old former labour leader resigned as acting president to stand as an independent candidate. This meant a candidate of the left. Both Communist parties, eagerly awaiting a Congress split as a major step toward their planned popular front, immediately supported him. It also meant that India was without a president, an acting president, and even a vice-president. Only someone holding one of these constitutional positions could bring order out of probable chaos when not just the Congress but all of India's political forces were on the verge of bitterly dividing into right and left. Indira was acutely aware of both factors. She also made sure that Giri's resignation did not take effect until just before the monsoon session of Parliament convened on Monday, 21 July.

On Wednesday, 16 July, Indira made her first bold move. She fired Morarji Desai. A letter she wrote to the old Congress stalwart and her chief rival, informing him without warning that he was out as finance minister, dared the stunned party to get rid of her as prime minister. Indira allowed in the letter that Morarji could remain deputy prime minister but without a portfolio. This, as she well knew, was adding gratuitous insult to grievous injury. He promptly and proudly resigned, saying the prime minister had no confidence in him.

Her excuse for sacking Morarji as finance minister was their differences over nationalizing India's privately owned banks, an issue then nagging the Congress. He was strongly against putting them under state control, and she seemed ambivalent at the time. But whatever the pros and cons of this issue, Indira reneged on the political agreement after the 1967 elections that had made her prime minister again and had designated Morarji as number two on the understanding he would work toward economic liberalization.

Indira's betrayal of the already disillusioned Desai, then seventy-three, stood in mean contrast to the integrity of a man who probably could have become prime minister soon after the 1967 protest vote by leading a revolt of moderate members of the Congress. Morarji preferred to remain loyal to Indira. To him, loyalty to the Congress leadership was one of the legacies of another Gandhi called Mahatma.

The prime minister also came close at that point to dismissing Chavan as home minister because he had favoured Reddy for president. According to Minoo Masani, the well-informed leader of the Swatantra Party then, she may have held back because her Soviet advisers had cautioned her that he could still be a valuable leftist ally. This proved to be the case when Chavan also executed a political double-cross.

Realizing the crunch in India had come, I flew back to New Delhi from Singapore on Friday night, 18 July. Man was about to walk on the moon for the first time. But my telescope was still focused on India. I cabled my editors at *The Globe and Mail*: "Appreciate moonlanding competition but looks like Indira Gandhi may either be out by Sunday or woman dictator with Communist support."

9

Nearly Going Communist

The first story I filed from New Delhi, at 1:15 AM Saturday, 19 July – nine and a half hours ahead of Eastern Daylight Saving Time – led: "The boys are back and they're out to get the girl who has dominated India's politics for three and a half years."

The Congress Party bosses of the old Syndicate, plus Morarji Desai and Yeshwantrao Chavan, reunited in the steamy capital for a showdown with the fifty-one-year-old woman many Indians still called "the girl." Prime Minister Indira Gandhi's opponents were planning to bring a motion of non-confidence against her when the Congress parliamentary caucus met Sunday, 20 July. To pass, it would require two-thirds of the 431 Congress members of both houses, or 288 votes. But there was strong support for the betrayed seventy-three-year-old Morarji to succeed her, or for a deal whereby he would serve as prime minister for a year or two before giving way to Chavan, fifty-seven.

Siddavanahalli Nijalingappa, the Congress president, flatly warned Indira in person that she faced the risk of a humiliating loss of her job if she did not make an "early" decision to reinstate Desai as finance minister. He said later he found the prime minister "courteous, cool, calm, and receptive." Other party leaders pressing her to avoid a final split were K. Kamaraj Nadar of Madras, S.K. Patil of Bombay – two of the majority of four in the Congress Parliamentary Board who had voted for N. Sanjiva Reddy as the Congress candidate for president of India – and Atulya Ghosh of Calcutta. Including Reddy, the virtual president-designate, these five men remembered vividly how contemptuously Indira had treated them as members of the Syndicate after the 1967 elections. They were ready to pay her back with interest. Congress leftists supporting her were clearly outnumbered at this stage. They were led by Foreign Minister Dinesh Singh, who had rushed back from Washington to be at her side in her gravest hour.

Undeterred by the increasing odds against her, Indira Nehru Gandhi made her second breathtaking move later that Saturday, 19 July, three days after she had fired Morarji as finance minister. She nationalized India's fourteen major commercial banks.

Her timing was minutely calculated, and deadly. Minutes after she had accepted Morarji's resignation as deputy prime minister, Indira summoned her cabinet in late afternoon and had it authorize the sweeping decree. Immediately, a compliant V.V. Giri signed the ordinance just before his resignation as acting president took effect.

Indira had promised a few days earlier not to take such a drastic step without further debate. Bringing the ponderous government into one of the few economic fields it did not control killed any hope of desperately needed liberalization. It put her squarely on the side of the Communists. Moreover, it was patently illegal despite Giri's signature: Parliament, which alone had the constitutional power to make such a major change, was to meet in two days.

But Indira's move pre-empted the motion of non-confidence in her in the Congress caucus the next day. She abruptly gained the psychological advantage and therefore the political upper hand. Pushed to the edge of India's political galaxy, the girl kept her cool and her job, dividing and scattering the boys who had thought they finally had her number. India's founding political party was split down the middle in all but name. So was the bewildered country. But a Nehru remained prime minister. For the time being Indira maintained the Nehru family's orbit around India, or what her many despairing critics called India's orbit around the Nehru family.

She emerged from the historic cabinet meeting in Parliament House beaming and arm-in-arm with Dinesh, dapper as always and more cocky than ever. The prime minister threw a knowing, triumphant glance at Chavan. The stocky home minister went from the cabinet meeting to a meeting with the angry would-be Congress bosses – Nijalingappa, Kamaraj, Patil, and Ghosh – but not Morarji. An Indian journalist asked Chavan when he came out if he would stay in the cabinet. Grinning enigmatically, he snapped, "Of course." Later he hailed Indira's bank nationalization for opening the way to "radical economic transformation." Chavan fulfilled and probably exceeded Soviet expectations of him, which probably were conveyed by Dinesh to Indira. He was the key figure in a monumental piece of political double-dealing that ensured at least her immediate future as prime minister.

The most powerful man in the government after Morarji before the latter resigned as deputy prime minister, Chavan had privately promised Desai he would resign himself if Indira did not give back the finance portfolio as demanded by the top Congress leaders. If as the party's Maharashtra leader he had supported Morarji, Indira in all likelihood would have had no choice but to resign, and Chavan would have been in a position to succeed her, if not immediately then after a short period with Morarji as prime minister. Instead, he supported Indira's nationalization of the banks, and by so doing shored up her shaky position.

In a conversation with Minoo Masani early Saturday afternoon, 19 July, when the Swatantra leader was unaware of the imminent cabinet meeting and he appealed to Chavan to oppose Indira, Chavan emphasized that as a "leftist" he was compelled to go along with her bank nationalization. According to Masani, the home minister said a majority of the members of the Congress parliamentary caucus would vote for a motion of non-confidence against Indira if it were brought, but action against her should wait until Reddy's election as president of India.

Chavan's leftist roots went back to Phaltan, the village in Maharashtra where I had witnessed one of the beginnings of the Green Revolution in India. He had hidden there from British authorities as a suspected Red. Whatever his ideology, he never showed the courage of a Maratha warrior that many Indians thought he possessed. If Chavan anticipated that Indira ultimately would hand him a political prize for having knifed Morarji and supported her, he did not have long to wait before receiving a knife in his own back, and wielded by her.

Even the once all-powerful Kamaraj, who had led the drive against Indira, was among many Congress supporters of the takeover of the banks. Advised by Dinesh Singh, Krishna Menon, and Soviet specialists in Indian affairs, she had cleverly chosen an issue that most Congresswallahs, brought up in the hopelessly impractical school of Nehruvian socialism, could not resist. By making the issue of Morarji's dismissal passé, Indira saved her own skin. In a broadcast over All-India Radio, which she kept strictly under her control, she declared that her sudden strike at private banks with nearly $4 billion in deposits was necessary to attain the Congress goal of "a socialist pattern of society."

When the Congress parliamentary executive met Sunday, 20 July, Morarji's supporters did not introduce a resolution urging his reinstatement, simply because Indira said its adoption would amount to a vote of non-confidence in her. When the full Congress caucus met that night, fear of a formal party split stopped the anti-Indira leaders from going ahead with the planned non-confidence motion. They wanted members united at least on paper in support of Reddy for president in the election four weeks away. Morarji told his fellow Congress MPs that the prime minister had treated him "more shabbily than a clerk." But after hearing him and Indira, the caucus broke up without even considering action against her.

Having disposed of her main political opponent and dealt a crippling blow to India's economy, Indira stayed up early Monday morning, 21 July – Sunday, 20 July, in the United States – to listen to the All-India Radio relay of Apollo 11's safe descent to the moon's surface. When the monsoon session of Parliament convened later Monday, she graciously told the Lok Sabha: "We are now able to see our world in better perspective and see new beauty in it."

The world was also able to see India in better perspective. But there was not much beauty in it. Morarji told the lower house of Parliament that the prime minister's actions endangered "the sacred principles of democracy." Communists gleefully heckled him. Indira's calculated strokes had succeeded brilliantly. But they left her party and her country in a shambles. The lead on the story I filed from New Delhi on Tuesday, 22 July, read: "While man landed on the moon, a woman became near-dictator of one-seventh of earth's inhabitants."

Frank Moraes, the fearless editor of *The Indian Express*, spelled out the ramifications in a front-page editorial:

It is the youth of India who must decide whether the extreme leftist policies now being pursued by Mrs. Gandhi and her juvenile hatchetmen are in the best interest of India. Under the prime minister's stewardship the country is being deliberately mortgaged to the Soviet Union whose growing influence is perceptible not only in the conduct of our foreign affairs but in the trend of our internal policies ...

Internally there is political chaos and economic deterioration. In the public sector never has so little been done by so many for so few. A government, unable to run relatively small public undertakings efficiently or profitably, is now attempting to swallow up and fritter away the bank savings of millions of small, defenseless people to bolster its discredited economic policies.

India's Supreme Court, one of the last barriers to government by decree, stayed the bank nationalization ordinance on 22 July following an appeal by the Swatantra and Jan Sangh parties. But this only underlined the supremacy of political expedience, by provoking Indira and her cabinet into railroading through Parliament by 9 August a bill embodying the terms of the ordinance. Ironically, the chief justice of the Supreme Court then had little choice but to sign it as acting president. A further opposition appeal to the court served only to delay the inevitable implementation of the retrogressive legislation.

Prodded by Congress "Young Turks" and Communists who had little time or thought for democratic niceties, Indira was moving by 25 July to consolidate her near-stranglehold on decision-making machinery. Chavan learned of his reward: imminent breakup of his home ministry giving the prime minister control of internal intelligence – India's secret police – and centre-state relations, and stripping him of effective power like Morarji earlier.

Indira also planned to break up the finance ministry to bring economic policy and coordination under her direct control while relegating strictly financial matters to a subordinate minister. Already in charge of economic planning as planning minister, she would bring international trade under her new economic department. To help her wield power unequaled since Nehru's time, she relied on a few leftist ministers – Dinesh Singh and Industries Minister Fakhruddin Ali Ahmed – and a handful of apparatchiks, all with their ears open to Soviet advice.

But Indira still had one major piece of political business to transact in 1969.

The man she wanted for president of India, V.V. Giri, the Communists' official candidate, was still the underdog in the 16 August election as long as Congress ranks held for N. Sanjiva Reddy, the choice of leaders who had been confounded and routed in every other confrontation with Nehru's daughter. They offered a truce: if she provided them with a few cabinet seats after Reddy's accession, the erstwhile bosses and the new president would not threaten her position for two or three years, until the next parliamentary elections.

Kamaraj, Patil, Ghosh, and Nijalingappa also took what they thought was the precaution of guarding their rear. They solicited second-choice votes for Reddy from the Swatantra and Jan Sangh parties, which had put up their own candidate for president, C.D. Deshmukh, a former Congress finance minister. If no candidate won a majority of votes – cast by the members of Parliament and state legislatures, and weighted by the number of people they represented – second preferences expressed by electors who had voted for candidates who were subsequently eliminated would come into play. In this three-cornered contest, if first-choice votes did not produce a clear majority, the second choices of those who had voted for Deshmukh would be distributed to either Reddy or Giri, putting one or the other over the top.

India's most sagacious mind had a simple proposal for reducing the danger that another pawn of the prime minister, one also backed by Communist parties, would sneak into Rashtrapati Bhavan. If non-Communist opposition parties had heeded the advice of Chakravarti Rajagopalachari, they would have had a better chance of containing Indira Gandhi's mushrooming autocracy. From Madras the old man urged Swatantra to support the conservative Congress candidate as its first and only choice for president. Unconditional endorsement of Reddy by Rajaji's party as the lesser of two evils would have been a signal to other parties to follow suit, and might well have hastened the formation of a right-of-centre coalition to challenge the leftist front rapidly taking shape.

But the liberal idealist Masani would not accept Rajaji's sensible advice. It was the worst mistake of his career. Swatantra, along with the Jan Sangh and Charan Singh's party of breakaway Uttar Pradesh Congressmen, ostensibly put principle over pragmatism at a time when this was a decidedly risky thing to do in Indian politics. The three parties decided to nominate Deshmukh, who had no chance of winning, and to seek second-choice support for Reddy from members of these three parties, a moderate Socialist party, and the Dravida Munnetra Kazhagam in Tamil Nadu.

Veteran Congress leaders had just discovered the hard way that fair play didn't pay against Indira's vicious brand of calculated risk. Her opponents in and out of the Congress recognized that India was at a political crossroads. Most understood that the country's salvation lay in free economic enterprise. But they treated this grave crisis as if it were somehow on a non-political level. Their inertia and naïveté were inexplicable and inexcusable.

Indira might have been goaded into what she did next by the Congress leaders' appeal for Swatantra and Jan Sangh second-choice votes favouring Reddy. Allowing her prejudices against capitalism and organized religion to take flight, she might have imagined a dark plot by reactionaries and fascists to force her out of power immediately despite the leaders' assurance on this score. Much more likely, their tactic gave her the excuse she had been seeking to embark on her most brazen gamble yet.

On the eve of the presidential election, Indira called publicly for a free vote by Congress members.

In firing Morarji and nationalizing the banks, she had stayed within the broadest definition of her rights as Congress prime minister. But now Indira as Congress leader deliberately ignited a revolt within her own party with the aim of electing the candidate of Communist parties. If Reddy won despite her refusal to back him, the least she could expect from her vindicated but shaken party would be a stiff reprimand. The most she could fear would be loss of power after all, long before the next elections. But if her latest wild risk succeeded on top of her earlier ones, Indira would stand astride the ruins of the party that had put her into power and her father before her. She would be in an unchallengeable position to consort with Communists and other leftists to establish a new raj for India far worse than the British one or even the permit-licence raj.

On Saturday, 16 August, Indira's third and crowning move paid off. Her Communist-supported candidate for president of India defeated the Congress candidate.

The first count of the weighted votes made clear that large numbers of Congress members had followed Indira in defecting from the party. Giri received 401,641 electoral votes to Reddy's 313,878 and Deshmukh's 112,915. But this was 12,577 votes short of the absolute majority required. And supporters of Deshmukh had been instructed by their party leaders to cast their second-choice votes for Reddy.

The second and final count showed that many of them – more than one in every six – also defected or didn't bother to express second preferences. Giri received 420,077 votes, Reddy 405,427. The Congress candidate gained 91,549 votes from Deshmukh. But the 18,436 votes gained by the candidate backed by the Communists and Indira gave Giri his narrow margin of 14,650. If Reddy had attracted only 7,500 more votes from non-Communist opposition parties – votes he had every right to expect, just as he should have been sure of nearly all Congress votes – he would have won.

Instead, the outcome left the party of Mahatma Gandhi and Indian independence prostrate and irreparably split. Non-Communist opposition parties were shattered: it turned out that some of their electors had cast their first votes for Giri, while Charan Singh and his UP dissidents had all betrayed the cause in a sign of things to come. Only the Communists and Indira's leftist followers in the ruined Congress cheered, along with her Soviet advisers. Other Indians could only wring their hands in shock and dismay after failing to exert the intelligence or the courage to stop her. The potentially victorious forces arrayed against Indira, skillfully outmanoeuvred and shamelessly divided by her, missed the best chance to be done with the dynasty – the third time the Nehrus should have been out of power but ruthlessly contrived to stay in power.

The events of July-August 1969, following the elections in 1967 and early 1969, marked a great divide in the life of independent India as well as the Congress Party. Indira Gandhi was to do even worse violence to Indian civility, and Indian civilization, in order to maintain the dominance of the Nehru dynasty. But her later assaults would not have been possible without her astonishing victories in 1969 on the verge of defeat. From then until the early 1990s, India's hungry majority fell even further behind in its race to develop in freedom. A culture of tyranny and fear, directly nourished by Communist forces, closed its grip on the nation without India's technically falling under communism. As the agents of this cancer intensified their war against their natural enemies, including free and responsible journalists, I became one of their victims.

My return visit to New Delhi upon Morarji's dismissal demonstrated that the India story demanded more frequent reportage than my editors and I had anticipated when I moved my base to Singapore in April 1969 to cover a vast region. I had informed Indian officials dealing with foreign journalists that I would be moving but continuing to report on India, and had returned in July on my one-year multiple-entry visa, which didn't expire until October. They said nothing relating to the attempt to expel me as a resident correspondent in 1968, or about a new intent to keep me out of India. On 16 January 1970, anticipating a trip to India the next month, I immediately obtained a visa for entry as a journalist at the Indian embassy in Jakarta during a visit to Indonesia. But in February I was assigned to go to Japan instead to write an extensive series of articles during Expo '70, and the Indian visa expired.

These details are relevant only because of the tissue of lies the government of India concocted when I finally flew from Colombo, Sri Lanka (then Ceylon), to Madras on 14 September 1970. My initial objective in India at the time was to cover a state election in Kerala. Following the voting on 17 September, Indira's Congress Party was expected to be caught red-handed in a formal alliance with the pro-Moscow Communist Party of India for the first time.

I had first applied for a fresh visa at the Indian high commission in Singapore (members of the old British Commonwealth maintain high commissions instead of embassies in each other's capitals). The high commissioner, Prem Bhatia, a former prominent journalist, had left for India for a visit by Singapore's Prime Minister Lee Kuan Yew; on two occasions just before he did, he had told me, "I'll see you in Delhi." Other officials said they would have to refer my application as a journalist to New Delhi, but if necessary I could enter India as a tourist without a visa for up to three weeks. Although I planned to be in India less than three weeks, I decided after arrival in Sri Lanka that it was best to apply for a tourist visa. I did so at the Indian high commission in the Fort or central area of Colombo on Thursday morning, 10 September. Again I was advised I could enter India as a tourist without a visa, but to leave my U.S. passport and come back in the afternoon for the stamped visa in it, not an unusual procedure at consular offices. My intention was to tell the Madras office of India's Press Information Bureau of the circumstances immediately upon my arrival, and obtain accreditation. The editor-in-chief of *The Globe and Mail*, Richard J. Doyle, had informed the head of the PIB in Delhi, M.L. Bharadwaj, of my impending visit in a brief letter on 7 July. I had no reason to believe anything was amiss.

When I returned on Thursday afternoon to the visa section of the Indian high commission and asked for my passport with the visa, an official said even my application as a tourist would have to be referred to Delhi. I asked to see the high commissioner, knowing that a head of mission has the authority to issue visas without reference, but received no clear reply from any of the dozen or so bureaucrats in the room. Then I noticed that my passport was being taken to a desk in the back. I politely asked for it again, pointing out loudly and clearly that it was the property of the U.S. government, and no other government had the right to put anything in it that was not requested, or required on entering or leaving a country. When this entreaty was ignored, I said I would have to report any abuse of these conditions to the U.S. ambassador to Sri Lanka. Again there was no response. An unpleasant memory clicked in my mind: the Indian official in Delhi who, behind my back, had blacked out a visa in my passport on 4 April 1968, while I was being served with an expulsion order. I walked into the Indian visa office in Colombo from the reception area and simply picked up my passport from the rear desk.

Two officials tried to rip it out of my hands. They and two or three other Indians assaulted me, knocking me down. At least two of my assailants were plain goondas, not clerks, if ever I've seen Indian goons. A painful blow to my back left it cut and throbbing but I managed to hold on to my passport. One page had a stamp saying "VISA APPLIED FOR" – a tipoff to immigration officials at any Indian entry point – but no official had succeeded in dating or signing it. I got up and asked a Sri Lankan named Stanley Pelpole, who had accompanied me as an interpreter and had caught a punch on the mouth meant for me, to run to the nearby Fort police station and report what had happened. No one stopped him or tried further to restrain me.

Before I left, I told the Indian civil servants in the room what I thought of their astonishing behaviour. I don't remember my exact words because I was hurting too much at the time. But I then witnessed the extraordinary phenomenon of a dozen or more Indian heads hung in obvious shame. Upon reaching the street, I met Pelpole with a police sub-inspector named Amarasakate. I provided details to the officer, who took notes and expressed concern. But he recommended dealing with the incident through diplomatic channels before making a formal complaint, because legally it had happened on Indian territory. The next day an official of the Indian high commission found Pelpole and warned him not to say anything about what he had witnessed.

The behaviour of Indian diplomats, and their superiors, turned out to be even more incredible than that of Indian clerks. I immediately and fully informed both the U.S. embassy and the Canadian high commission in Colombo of the scene in the visa office. Both contacted the Indian high commission. K.P.S. Menon Jr., deputy high commissioner (and son of a well-known Indian diplomat who had made his mark as ambassador in

Moscow), responded after a perfunctory "investigation" that I had assaulted an unnamed high commission employee. In a long talk with his Canadian counterpart, George Seymour, about my wish to enter India as a *Globe and Mail* correspondent, Menon said that any visa application by a non-resident of Sri Lanka had to be referred to Delhi and an answer would take at least ten days.

This was patently untrue: I had quickly obtained an Indian visa in Jakarta as a non-resident of Indonesia. But the informal conversation with Seymour was a perfect opportunity for Menon to convey knowledge of any order barring me as a journalist from entering India. If the Indians didn't want to tell me directly, he could safely assume the Canadians would. Menon certainly would have known or could have quickly found out about any such edict, which would have been circulated to Indian diplomatic missions in other countries. But he, like his colleagues in Singapore, said nothing.

Two Sri Lankan doctors examined my injured back, and one of them dressed the cut. Sri Lankan, American, and Canadian friends, including Sydney Schanberg, the New Delhi correspondent of *The New York Times* who was then in Colombo, sympathized with my predicament. I'd received negative but not definitive signals from the Indian missions in Colombo and Singapore. Exclusion from India, or inability to reverse such a bar again, was still inconceivable to me. I decided to fly to Madras without a visa, as the two Indian missions had said I could do. Four days after I had been assaulted at the one in Colombo, on Monday afternoon of 14 September, I boarded an Indian Airlines plane for the short flight to Madras.

Indian officials apparently knew in advance what plane I was on. As soon as it landed and I entered the terminal building and presented myself to an immigration official, a half-dozen burly Indian men in plain clothes surrounded me. I felt very alone and afraid of another physical attack, with no chance of recourse this time. I was assaulted instead with a copy of a home ministry order signed by Indira Gandhi, who was now home minister as well as prime minister. The order barred me from India. It was dated 30 January 1970, fourteen days after I had received the Indian visa in Jakarta. In the intervening seven and a half months, no representative of the government of India had informed me, my editors, or the U.S. or Canadian governments of this unprecedented order against a foreign newspaper correspondent. Nor was a specific reason given for the order, then or later. But it clearly reflected a new and much stiffer official policy toward foreign news media covering India.

On 29 August, sixteen days before implementing the secret order against me, Indira's government had closed the British Broadcasting Corporation's office in New Delhi. Officials had complained that a BBC series of television documentaries produced by Louis Malle depicted Indian conditions of poverty unfairly. They had gone back ten years to come up with offending excerpts from BBC news broadcasts. The PIB's Bharadwaj denied that new rules, including a requirement that TV film had to be officially approved before leaving India, constituted censorship. But India's most respected newspapers – *The Hindu* of Madras, *The Hindustan Times* of New Delhi, *The Indian Express* of Bombay and New Delhi, and *The Statesman* of Calcutta – sharply criticized the new policy. *The Statesman* had commented in a prescient 1 September editorial: "India is still a long way from being a closed society but any semblance of a restriction on free reporting would be a first step toward that totalitarian condition. When foreign journalists are condemned according to criteria held in some ministry or other in New Delhi, it is a dangerously near thing to regimenting newspapermen at home."

Bharadwaj and other Communist-leaning bureaucrats had failed in taking what there is every reason to believe was that first step in April 1968, when they couldn't make the expulsion order against me stick. But the drastic change in India's political climate in July-August 1969 had given them much greater power. Now they were carrying out undisputed directives from above, with no Morarji or Chavan in the cabinet to neutralize or moderate Indira's vindictiveness against critics and opponents. The BBC was logically the first institutional target among foreign media, considering its prestige and its influence with Indians. It looked like I had the unwanted distinction of being the first individual target. Many more journalists and news organizations, foreign and more so Indian, were to fall victim to what soon became an uninhibited and unashamed policy of censorship. My immediate problem, however, was what to do as a prisoner of Indian officialdom at the Madras airport.

I asked the chief immigration officer, who declined to give his name, if I could telephone the U.S. consulate in Madras. He refused. I persisted. Finally he said I could make one telephone call. The consulate dispatched a vice-consul as soon as I reached it. When he arrived at the airport, I unrealistically told him I thought the order could be lifted if we could just get through to Delhi. The helpful U.S. official, whose name was Dane, told me that long-distance telephone lines were down, not an unusual occurrence. "And you know from your own experience," he patiently added, "that the government of India is not likely to make a decision in hours or days or even weeks." He promised to fully inform the embassy in Delhi of the exclusion order.

The Indian official said normal procedure was to send barred persons back where they came from. That would have meant my spending the night under guard at the airport and flying back to Colombo on the first plane the next day. But he said I could take the first flight out of India from Madras. That happened to be an Air India plane to Singapore leaving at midnight. I reluctantly bought a one-way ticket home. The first time I relaxed in five days was after two double Bloody Marys, brought to my seat in the dark by one of Air India's sari-clad flight attendants. Back in Singapore, my doctor found I had a badly bruised rib and nerve damage as well as a lacerated back from the Colombo incident, and my whole system was suffering secondary shock. He ordered three days of complete rest.

First, I started another battle for continued access to India, with cables to my editors in Toronto and Washington. We still had the advantage of no publicity, as we had had nearly two and a half years earlier. It disappeared Friday, 18 September. The Indians had apparently tipped off the outgoing BBC man in Delhi, Ronald Robson, about my being barred, and he told a British colleague, who got confirmation from the U.S. embassy in Delhi. A two-column headline over a staff-written story datelined Delhi in *The Times* of London and run on page four with a front-page notice read "India bars entry of American journalist." A similar news story appeared in *The Statesman* of Calcutta.

The spokesman for the Indian foreign ministry, S.K. Singh, confirmed the *Statesman* story. He said the decision to bar me was "based on a review of his reports between 1967 and 1969 written from India which are distorted and in many instances wrong." He denied existence of "a new policy to refuse admission to foreign correspondents." Syd Schanberg of *The New York Times*, who was back in Delhi and had respected my cabled request not to file a story about my being barred, wrote me that Singh had then told some Indian journalists "off the record" that I had been involved in a "fist fight" at the Indian high commission in Colombo, implying I had started it. Indian officials had actually leaked my being refused entry as early as the day after it happened. A 15 September Press Trust of India story datelined Madras, reporting I had been barred as an "American national" who "described himself as a correspondent of *The Globe and Mail*, Toronto, Canada," turned up 16 September in *The Patriot* of New Delhi, a daily newspaper known as a Communist mouthpiece, two days before the fuller *Times* of London and *Statesman* stories.

The Globe and Mail waited as long as it could before running a news story Tuesday, 22 September, under the headline: "India bars Globe correspondent – Protest lodged." It waited until Monday, 28 September, two weeks after execution of the order against me, to run a lead editorial, headlined "The unwelcome journalist," decrying the Indian government's arbitrary actions against the BBC and me. The editorial concluded: "These two acts place the entire foreign press community in India in invisible bonds. No correspondent can now know what he may write and what he may not without courting expulsion. He must inevitably suspect that unpleasant reports, however true, may draw upon him the condemnation of the Indian Government. It is not freedom of the press as that term is defined in democracies. It is most depressing."

My editors and I nonetheless continued to press for cancellation of Mrs Gandhi's order. Our efforts at least yielded more pieces of incriminating evidence of the mindset of highly placed Indian bureaucrats and politicians.

In Ottawa, the Indian high commission – no longer headed by retired General Joyanto Nath Chaudhuri, who had intervened on my behalf in 1968 – extended an invitation to *The Globe and Mail* to send another correspondent to India. The managing editor, Clark W. Davey, rejected the offer with the contempt it deserved. In Delhi, the government spread the story that it had informed me when I moved to Singapore that I would receive no further visas, and also had told the U.S. and Canadian missions. But there was no such indication at the time I moved in April 1969; I had returned to India in July on a valid journalist's visa; and I had received another in January 1970.

From colleagues in Delhi, I learned that the coterie of senior Indian officials behind the anti-free press policy included, in addition to Bharadwaj as chief information officer and Singh as foreign ministry spokesman, Information Minister Inder Kumar Gujral – who was to become prime minister in 1997 after serving as ambassador to Moscow and foreign minister – and Foreign Secretary T.N. Kaul. All were known for their leftist views and pro-Soviet sympathies. David Loshak, Delhi correspondent of *The Daily Telegraph* of London, described these men in a despairing letter to me as "a powerful group ... who want to curb the foreign press and other media in India at any cost, and simply do not care what anyone thinks about it."

Without question, they carried out the calculated policy – the enthusiastic orders – of Indira Gandhi and Dinesh Singh, her chief adviser and the conduit between her and the Soviet embassy. The numerous Soviet and Soviet Bloc members of the Foreign Correspondents Association of India, who enjoyed official diplomatic privileges, blocked protest by Western journalists through the group. In Moscow, a savage attack on *The Globe and Mail* by *Pravda*, the Soviet Communist Party newspaper, may not have been unconnected to events in Delhi.

One of the Indian officials I wrote to was T.N. (Ticky) Kaul, the foreign secretary or top civil servant in the foreign ministry, who also had made his reputation as ambassador to the Soviet Union. He didn't bother to reply. But I learned from *The Washington Star*, whose editors had contacted the Indian embassy in Washington on my behalf, that he was particularly peeved by a front-page story I had filed 27 July from Delhi.

On the eve of a two-day visit by President Richard Nixon – a reason for my returning from Singapore apart from Indira's political machinations – I had reported that the United States had conveyed to Kaul its disappointment with India's truce supervisory role in Vietnam as chairman of the International Control Commission, and its unwillingness to support a new role unless the Indians were more decisive in exposing Communist violations. I had attributed the story to "U.S. sources."

In an interpretive wrap-up on page three of *The Star* that I had filed 1 August, emphasizing that Nixon appeared to have had a brush with the Soviet concept of Asian collective security in his talks with Indira, I had reported official Indian denial – by Kaul – that U.S. unhappiness with India's Vietnam role had been expressed before the president's arrival. The source of my first story, although it could not be revealed then or for long after, was Ambassador Kenneth Keating, formerly U.S. senator from New York. He told me in a background interview that he had personally delivered the gist of the strongly held U.S. position to Kaul. The foreign secretary's reaction to U.S. displeasure with India's performance becoming public was another example of the Soviet-style hypocrisy and disinformation pervading Delhi.

An official Indian desire to publicize the exclusion order against me as a warning to other journalists – or simply the letters, cables, and telephone calls that Indian officials kept receiving about my case – may have been responsible for an extraordinary and unprovoked exchange on the floor of the Rajya Sabha or upper house of India's Parliament on 18 November 1970. During question period, a leftist member initiated a series of fourteen queries and eleven responses taking up more than ten minutes by asking an apparently planted question: "May I know ... whether it is a fact that some foreign intelligence agents get into India in the garb of foreign correspondents? In this particular case (of David Van Praagh), I would like to know what was the bar for this representative of *The Toronto Globe* to get his visa for India."

Foreign Minister Swaran Singh, a conformist Punjabi Sikh politician chosen by Indira to assume Dinesh Singh's position now that the latter presumably had more important things to do for her, never specifically replied that I was not a spy, even when his questioner referred to "other intelligence agents ... in the garb of foreign representatives of newspapers." Swaran Singh said the home, information, and foreign ministries had decided to keep me out because, in his words, I had "persisted" in writing dispatches "tendentious and heavily prejudiced against India" despite "numerous warnings" by the PIB's Bharadwaj. He then repeated the false story about my being barred when I moved to Singapore. Another member asked for examples of my "prejudiced reports." The foreign minister answered: "I have not got the details of that. He is a very distinguished journalist and (the member) can look up some of the files of (his) newspapers." At another point, a testy Swaran Singh said: "According to our constitution, ours is an open society and there is freedom of the press, and we do not want to put any unnecessary curbs on anyone, foreigner or Indian."

Despite what *The London Daily Telegraph*'s David Loshak called the foreign minister's prepared "slanderous aspersions" on me, I legally entered India less than two months later – for five days. That was the length of a visit by Prime Minister Pierre Elliott Trudeau of Canada on his way to a conference of Commonwealth heads of government in Singapore. How I got back into India 9–13 January 1971, and what happened when I did, offer some revealing insights into politicians, diplomats, and editors.

I had assumed a *Globe and Mail* reporter would accompany the prime minister from Ottawa, and I'd help cover him only in Singapore. Instead *The Globe* instructed me to meet Trudeau's Canadian Armed Forces plane when it landed in Rawalpindi, West Pakistan, and join the twenty-five journalists travelling with him. Meanwhile, Canada's national newspaper arranged with Trudeau for Indira to be officially informed that I was a member of his press party, and so should be allowed to enter India like the others. In this way, my editors succeeded in putting Indira and her flacks on the spot: keeping me out would be a slap in Canada's face.

They also wanted to isolate the Canadian high commissioner in Delhi, one of too many Western diplomats who take leave of the values they are supposed to represent. Both in April 1968 and September 1970, in contrast to his U.S. counterpart, James George had seemed to show more sympathy for the government of India than for freedom of the press when asked to support my access. Swaran Singh was apparently referring to him when he told Parliament that "diplomatic representatives" had "appreciated" the order barring me. At the end of 1970 I had reported to Clark Davey, *The Globe*'s managing editor, that George had written a letter to me saying an attempt on my part to cover Trudeau in India "might raise further questions in Parliament, which could cause some embarrassment to both governments." In a return letter, I had strongly rejected this unsolicited interference.

James George's warning could not have been better calculated to raise the hackles of the proudly independent *Globe and Mail*. It reinforced the editors' determination to demonstrate that some things are more important than official face. On Wednesday, 6 January, I received a cable from Davey in Rawalpindi saying the Indian government had informed the Canadian government that I could enter the country with Trudeau on a "one-shot basis," and suggesting I apply for a visa. I did so at the Indian high commission in Rawalpindi, where I was treated civilly. Predictably, my passport – with an Indian visa valid for the five days amazingly stamped in it by the Indian consulate in Karachi – did not reach me until I was at the Karachi airport minutes before Trudeau and the reporters accompanying him left for India late Saturday, 9 January. But that made me one of them. A short but satisfying story in *The Statesman* that day, datelined New Delhi, was headlined "India to Lift Ban on U.S. Journalist."

When Trudeau's plane landed that evening at Delhi's Palam airport, Indira warmly received him by putting a traditional marigold garland around his neck. The dashing Canadian, who delighted in doing the unconventional, took the garland off and put it around her neck. The reception Indira accorded me was distinctly cooler.

Reporters had deplaned first and I had almost bumped into her as she went to greet Trudeau. I smiled and gave her a *namaste* – palms brought together in a kind of salute. Indira instinctively smiled in return and brought her hands up for a return *namaste*. Then she recognized me. Her smile instantly became a scowl. She sharply brought her hands down as she swept by. Welcome to India.

Trudeau graciously went along with my unexpected presence on Indian soil. When I posed a question at his press conference in Delhi, he gave me a quizzical look and asked, "What are you doing here?" Lesser Canadian officials were less at ease, partly because, apart from the special Indian visa in it, my U.S. passport was clearly distinguishable from those of my Canadian colleagues. At a signing ceremony attended by the two leaders, only one journalist representing Canadian print media could attend, and we drew lots to determine the pool reporter. When I won, George's deputy, Geoff Pearson, son of former prime minister Lester B. Pearson, approached me uncomfortably and asked me to withdraw. I declined on the ground that I had entered India specifically as an equal with the other journalists covering Trudeau. Pearson understood. Nothing untoward happened at the ceremony. At no time during the five days did I attempt to discuss future access with Indian officials.

Trudeau's schedule in India was so crowded that I hardly had time to think about my status, or about Indian politics. In addition to his talks in Delhi with Indira – he urged her not to let Canadian nuclear technology provided to India for peaceful purposes be used otherwise – Trudeau paid homage to the Taj Mahal in Agra, and communed separately with a Hindu mystic and Roman Catholic brothers of a Quebec monastic order in the Hindu holy city of Benaras. On the next-to-last evening in Delhi, sitting two rows behind Trudeau, Indira, and the British prime minister, Edward Heath (also on his way to the Commonwealth Conference in Singapore), at a brilliant classical Indian dance recital by the seductive Yamini Krishnamurthi, I nearly fell asleep, after having filed a long story on Trudeau's activities that day without taking time to eat dinner.

But the leftist Indian officials conspiring against disliked foreign and Indian journalists didn't forget my case. Back in Singapore, I received a letter dated 25 January from S.K. Singh, the foreign ministry spokesman. Ostensibly answering letters I had written to Indira and Foreign Secretary Kaul the previous November, Singh made clear that despite my having been allowed into India for five days "as a gesture of goodwill for the prime minister of Canada" the edict barring me stood after "careful" review. He then indicated the Indian government stuck by its version of the events leading to the order signed by Indira.

Nevertheless I wrote again to the prime minister of India on 21 April 1971. My brief letter didn't mention the barrier that had come down again but offered congratulations on her stand in defence of the persecuted people of East Bengal in what was shaping up as another India-Pakistan confrontation, and on another political victory. I received a personal note dated 25 April in reply. Indira's words, and her writing at all to a perceived enemy, hinted at the complexity of the woman who ran India. The note read: "Thank you for your letter. It is not often that one gets understanding from newspaper correspondents. The grim tragedy that is being enacted so close to our border is indeed a cause for great concern. With good wishes, Yours sincerely, Indira Gandhi."

The political victory by Indira I had acknowledged should not have been a surprise by the time it happened, although it was to many. Her opponents had continued to show the same timidity and vacillation that had allowed her to get away with her coups in 1969. They had failed to form an effective non-Communist coalition, which alone could have stopped or slowed her forward momentum.

Still, Indira caught many Indians off guard when, on 27 December 1970, she dissolved Parliament and called an election for March 1971, one year earlier than scheduled. She had repeatedly warned she would call a snap election. But this was the first time India's pattern of parliamentary elections every five years was broken. The voter turnout was significantly lower than in 1967, and the Congress – now formally branded with an *I* for Indira – received the lowest percentage of the popular vote it had ever captured. But Indira stunned the nation when she and her rump of the party won an overwhelming majority of the seats in the Lok Sabha. Her victory was a dramatic throwback to those of her father in the three parliamentary elections before the 1967 protest vote. Indeed, its scope far exceeded her own fondest dreams.

For that reason and that reason alone, Indira did not enter into a national popular front with the Communists and other leftist groups following the parliamentary election, as she had been fully prepared to do before the vote.

On top of her successful support of the Communist-backed candidate in the 1969 presidential election, Indira had set a clear precedent at the state level for coming together with Communists in a leftist front. Her party joined the pro-Moscow Communist Party of India in a ruling coalition in Kerala following the September 1970 election which I had wanted to cover in India in the expectation this would happen. After the March 1971 parliamentary election, however, she found herself with enough Congress supporters in the new Lok Sabha to remain prime minister legitimately without Communist allies in the government. This situation did not last as long as she thought it would when the election returns signalling her latest coup came in. But by unexpectedly consolidating her position as the leader of the Congress (I) party, she made it four times the Nehrus had stayed in power when given the circumstances they should have been denied power.

Before the end of 1969, there were efforts to stop this very thing from happening. In March 1970 Rajaji, at the age of ninety-one, defined the non-Communist opposition's objective in a Swarajya article entitled "My Hope for a Grand Coalition." The main elements in this conservative front were to be his free-enterprise Swatantra Party, the Hindu nationalist Jan Sangh, Charan Singh's Uttar Pradesh Congress dissidents, and a sizable national faction of breakaway Congressmen led by Morarji Desai, who had chosen the unfortunate name of Congress (Organization) Party, or Congress (O), to differentiate it from Congress (I).

These groups, holding nearly 150 parliamentary seats, could present a clear alternative to Indian voters if they were able to forge a bloc in Parliament before the next election. The prospects looked promising when Swatantra's Minoo Masani drafted a joint platform at the urging of Morarji and the Jan Sangh, and the Congress (O) as the largest group approved a final version in late June with little outward opposition. The platform spelled out the threats to Indian democracy posed by Indira and her would-be Communist allies. It declared that only unity of democratic forces could stop Communist subversion and bring about rising economic levels.

But that was as far as unity against Indira and the forces backing her went at that time. Even the emphasis on democracy was soon lost. Within days, Congress (O) leaders balked at forming a multi-party bloc at the monsoon session of Parliament in August, let alone fielding common candidates in all constituencies in the next election. Rajaji, quickly sizing up the situation as usual, wrote to Masani: "I have done my utmost, and what else is there but to submit to misfortune and look upon my efforts as mere foolish vanity?" Minoo said later he was dealing with a bunch of "dithering old men who just could not make up their minds."

Their self-defeating paralysis was never so apparent as on 3 January 1971, one week after Indira called her snap election. Three aggressive members of the radical Socialist Party with links to the Communist Marxists made Siddavanahalli Nijalingappa, Congress (O) president and former Syndicate member, a prisoner in his own home. They browbeat him and the Jan Sangh's Atal Bihari Vajpayee into taking out any reference to democracy or common policies in the prospective front's platform. The Socialists thereupon joined the coalition, and Masani took Swatantra out of the coalition. Partly at the insistence of Rajaji, who may have taken political pragmatism too far this time, Swatantra came back into the nameless front. In a matter of days after Indira's election call, however, the coalition's challenge to her had plainly become a bad joke. By the time the coalition was inaccurately named the Democratic Front, Indira was on the verge of soundly defeating her hapless adversaries once again.

The election posed a problem for me. There was no way I was going to be allowed to enter India to cover it. But it was too important to *The Globe and Mail* and me to leave coverage entirely to wire services. I suggested that Patricia Bell, my wife and a journalist who had worked for *The Globe*, go to India to gather information for colour and interpretive stories, and that I write them under a joint by-line on her return to Singapore. My editors agreed and so did Pat, who, although more than six months pregnant with Peter (our second daughter Jaya had been born in New Delhi in March 1967) flew to India in early March 1971.

Delhi's taxiwallahs provided one tipoff to the election outcome. Mostly Punjabi Sikhs, they flew the flag of Congress (I) for days before the voting, and on election day more than 500 of them gave their services and little cars free to transport voters for Indira's party to the polls. Or the pundits might have listened to the north Indian villager who explained cryptically: "The poor vote for the poor." Asked whom he intended voting for, he replied: "Indira Congress – the old Congress wants the rajas to remain rajas and the poor to remain poor."

In Bombay, the cosmopolitan centre of business opposition to Indira's socialist policies, thousands of people gazed overlong at signs that read: "You Too Can Become A VIP – Vote Indira to Power." In Madras, a modest South Indian said simply: "We don't like this Dump Indira thing –

politicians shouldn't speak so harshly about our prime minister." His voice proved to be louder than those of two of India's shrewdest political minds. Rajaji and former Congress boss Kamaraj, long enemies, met in the same city to plot a new political strategy whereby the two Congress parties would reunite and choose a new prime minister. It proved as futile as the Democratic Front.

Back in India's capital, a little shopkeeper said firmly: "We want food, not fountains." This was a sarcastic reference to civic improvements in New Delhi made by the municipally ruling Jan Sangh, which as a member of the Democratic Front pitched its appeal to lower middle-class people like himself. An illiterate Hindu voter made the same point even more cogently. Told by a Jan Sangh worker he would hurt holy animals if he stamped the cow and calf ballot symbol assigned to Congress (I), he replied that if he stamped the *deepak* – the Jan Sangh's oil lamp symbol – it would be snuffed out.

Apart from the ineffectiveness of the Democratic Front – the anti-Indira vote was still divided among an average of more than four opposition candidates in each constituency – Indira had three things going for her.

One was a popular backlash against the narrow "Indira Hatao" or "Remove Indira" slogan raised in the end by the non-Communist opposition. Another was her own slogan, no less simplistic but more positive, of "Gharibi Hatao" or "Remove Poverty." Perhaps most important, for the first time people in all states but three had only to vote for a parliamentary candidate instead of both a parliamentary candidate and a state legislative candidate. This lowered the turnout, and left out the local grievances brought to the polls by many voters. By carrying out her threat to call an early election, Indira had not only unnerved her opponents, although more time may not have helped them, but had also focused the whole electoral process on herself, taking another calculated risk that this would pay off. As usual, she won her gamble.

Only 55.3 per cent of 274 million eligible voters went to the polls, down sharply from the record 61.3 per cent in the 1967 parliamentary election. Congress (I) captured 43.7 per cent of the popular vote, and the opposition Congress (O) another 10.4 per cent, compared with 40.8 per cent for the undivided Congress in 1967. But while the Congress under Indira had won only 283 Lok Sabha seats out of 520 in February 1967, or 55 per cent – and Indira had held on to a minority of only 228 at dissolution after the party split – Congress (I) swept 352 seats out of 518 in March 1971, or 68 per cent. This gave Indira virtually as big a majority, more than two-thirds of the seats, as Nehru's 364, 371, and 361 seats in the Lok Sabha after the elections of 1952, 1957, and 1962, respectively. Indian politics seemed to be back to square one. Despite the nation's economic setbacks and political contortions since her father's death in 1964, and Indira's de facto alliance with the Communists, the Nehrus still reigned supreme with a Congress Party they had co-opted.

On the left, the Marxists and pro-Moscow Communists maintained in 1971 their small but steady electoral advances, winning a total of 48 parliamentary seats with nearly 10 per cent of the popular vote. But their ambitious scheme to compel a desperate Indira to join them in a popular front shattered on the rock of her big new Congress (I) majority.

On the right, the dissident Congress (O) won only 16 seats, including Morarji's. The other members of the Democratic Front fared even worse. The Swatantra Party, once envisioned by Rajaji as the core of the non-Communist opposition and government in waiting, took only 8 seats, compared with 44 in 1967, and its share of the popular vote plummeted from nearly 9 per cent to a little more than 3 per cent. The Jan Sangh dropped from 35 seats and more than 9 per cent of the popular vote in 1967 to 22 seats and 7.4 per cent in 1971. After making the non-Communist coalition give up its meaningful message, the radical Socialists saw their seat total cut from 23 to 3 and their popular vote halved to 2.5 per cent. Leaving aside the Socialists, the three national non-Communist opposition parties won a pitiful total of 46 seats with less than 21 per cent of the popular vote – 2 fewer seats than the two Communist parties won with less than 10 per cent of the popular vote.

Even taking into account the distortions caused by the first-past-the-post system that India, like Canada, had inherited from Britain – Indira winning her two-thirds-plus majority of seats with less than 44 per cent of the votes cast – it was clear she had a mandate she could use to continue her authoritarian ways without having to rely on Communist support. In her victory speech, the newly radiant prime minister declared: "The entire people voted for a direction in which they want the country to go."

This was patently untrue. But who was to stop Indira Nehru Gandhi from taking the country in her direction?

A Delhi bookseller who had voted for the Jan Sangh advised Pat to buy a book of cartoons about "that lady" immediately because he expected not to be allowed to sell it soon: "Mrs Gandhi's heavy majority in the Lok Sabha is very dangerous – now she can become a dictator if she chooses." V.Y. Tonpe, the aide to Morarji, who would be the only opposition figure of stature in the new Parliament, said philosophically: "Indira has the power. May she have the courage and wisdom to guide this country. But she has often shown bad judgment and little reasoning." Frank Moraes of *The Indian Express* wrote even before the election returns came in: "Mrs.

Gandhi ... seems bent on retaining the prime ministership for some decades like another Queen Victoria clutching the imperial crown and diadem of India."

As a visitor to India during the election period, Chester Bowles looked for a silver lining as he twice had as U.S. ambassador under Democratic presidents: "Mrs Gandhi is the country's only hope at the moment – especially because she is trying to go it alone without Communist partners." But like many others he was worried about the high popular expectations that her promise to get rid of poverty had aroused. On this score *The Statesman* of Calcutta commented: "The central point that mass poverty cannot be attacked without a higher level of economic growth has been successfully obscured [by Indira] ... what remains is the slogan in all its alluring isolation."

Indira's fresh triumph did nothing to change the unrelieved poverty, bureaucratic constipation, dying nationalism, and regional fragmentation afflicting India. Nor did it lessen Moscow's heavy investment in keeping India on the road to regimentation in the name of democracy. If Indian Communists were still limited to holding or sharing power in West Bengal and Kerala, it mattered little to the Soviets, and the United States was less likely to be alarmed at the trend in India as an unfavourable aspect of the Cold War. With Indira enjoying a two-thirds majority of her own party members in the Lok Sabha, she could amend the constitution to strengthen her own powers and weaken the Supreme Court of India, which had delayed her nationalization of the banks and her depriving ex-maharajas and maharanees of privy purses promised at the time of independence. She could even take away the constitutional right to property.

The most disturbing explanation of Indira's electoral success came from an astute, well-informed, Bombay businessman: "She got money from the rich – mostly by selling favours and business licences – and sympathy from the poor." To whatever extent his observation was true, her new deficit-ridden government lacked funds to tackle such urgent necessities as an efficient and fair national birth control program. She and her economic advisers gave little indication of understanding that the Green Revolution could revolutionize industrial production and dramatically expand domestic markets as well as increase food grains output and ease hunger. India's business community, disappointed at the failure of the right-of-centre coalition but relieved that the prime minister did not need Communist support to stay in power, waited to be convinced to put money into profitable production as well as conspicuous consumption.

But Indira was still dedicated, as her misguided father had been, to what independent economists had long substantiated: discredited socialist ideals, woefully unrealistic five-year plans, and tremendously wasteful public-sector enterprises. Her advisers were "London School of Economics types" at the time, their heads in the air. On the ground, half of India's children suffered from malnutrition, only 20 per cent of farmland was irrigated, and most Indians' incomes had long stagnated at unnecessarily low levels.

By December 1971, Prime Minister Gandhi made an impact outside domestic politics. But it was not in the economic field. By sending the Indian army into East Bengal to end the oppressive West Pakistani presence and establish Bangladesh, Indira succeeded not only in breaking Pakistan in two, but also showed she was capable of pursuing power in the larger, dangerous arena outside the Subcontinent. This gave a shot in the arm to Indian nationalism. Referring mainly to the United States, and making a racial allusion, Indira asserted one day before India's third war with Pakistan broke out: "The times have passed when any nation (faraway) could give orders to Indians on the basis of their colour superiority ... India has changed and is no longer a country of 'natives.' "

Her action provoked President Nixon into ending what Henry Kissinger called the long U.S. "honeymoon" with India. After resorting to gunboat diplomacy and cutting economic aid to India in support of Pakistan's generals, Nixon called Indira a liar – with respect to how the two-week war had started and ended – and she vigorously returned the compliment. With Moscow strongly backing New Delhi, the conflict did what Indira's Soviet-supported or engineered political coups had not done: tip India into an adversarial relationship with the United States in the Cold War. But Indira's bottom line, as ever, was maintaining power at home. She had decided it was good domestic politics to make India an increasingly important player in the developing equation of Asian power.

Her statement of India's clout acquired an exclamation point on 18 May 1974, when Indian scientists set off a "nuclear device" beneath the Rajasthan desert. It was a "dirty" nuclear event but Indira's government – she held the atomic energy portfolio in the cabinet, as her father and Lal Bahadur Shastri had – claimed it was an "implosion" rather than an explosion, and was solely for peaceful purposes.

In reality, India had used nuclear technology, provided by Canada for strictly peaceful purposes but with few safeguards, to move toward becoming a de facto member of the exclusive club of nuclear powers. Although there was only one test at the time, and Delhi concealed its true purpose, it served notice on China and what was left of Pakistan of India's intention to make nuclear weapons. Flying crudely in the face of the non-violent ideals of the other, nearly forgotten Gandhi, Indira exploited this perilous technology not so much for security as to inflate the xenophobic marks she had won with the Indian people by tearing away Pakistan's east wing.

From the election in early 1971 until mid-1975, she could take credit for little else but India's most decisive armed victory over Pakistan and the nuclear detonation. At the end of 1972, Chakravarti Rajagopalachari, the most persistent as well as the wisest Indian of them all in the pursuit of human freedom and decency, died in Madras at the age of ninety-four. On 18 March 1974, two months before India's first nuclear test, Jayaprakash Narayan began to assume Rajaji's moral mantle in opposition to the regime of Indira Gandhi.

The widely respected but theretofore remote figure did so by identifying himself with a student-led campaign in his native Bihar against the inept, corrupt Congress (I) state government, whose police that day reacted to an attempt to hold the legislature captive by shooting protesters and sacking the offices of critical newspapers. But JP, as the old freedom fighter was familiarly known to Indians throughout the country, held himself above politics or at least above political parties, both in Bihar's capital of Patna and when he transferred the growing popular movement against cruel and cynical government to Delhi. In this respect, he was more like the Mahatma than his fellow Gandhians Rajaji or Morarji, with whom he joined in what soon became a full-scale assault on Indira and her style of rule. He was therefore more to be feared by Indira, who from the time she was a little girl had witnessed the effectiveness of non-violent, religion-based agitation against oppressive government.

JP did nothing new in adopting a deliberately lonely stance. He had broken with the old Congress Party soon after independence. When Nehru was alive, Narayan had dismissed himself as a potential successor. He was an avowed socialist but had always distanced himself from India's Communist parties. JP had last attracted national attention during the Bihar famine in 1966–68, when his individual effort to raise money to feed starving people provided an early contrast with the lethargic disinterest of both the central and state governments. Now he proclaimed nothing less than a "total revolution." What was new, as he readily acknowledged, was a change in conditions: "Revolutions happen. All that the leader does is to give it direction."

On 8 April 1974, three weeks before he underwent a dangerous prostate operation in South India, JP continued to provide direction by leading a silent protest march in Delhi. Then he presided over a convention in the capital that formed an organization innocuously named Citizens for Democracy. Appropriately, it was in the Nehrus' home town of Allahabad in the Hindi heartland of Uttar Pradesh that JP, still weak from his surgery, explained his goal in a speech in June to a youth conference:

We want the entire system changed; we do not want the ruling party to be simply replaced. My interest is not in the capture of power but in the control of power by the people. People now have only one right left, the right to vote. If that also is denied or falsified, what remains? In [developed democratic] countries ... there are many checks on those in power: the press, the academic institutions, the intellectuals. There is strong public opinion. We have no such foundations and we will take time to develop them. I wish to give the people's movement a revolutionary direction so that the people can develop their own power and become the guardians of democracy.

How precisely this was to happen, and to what extent JP would be compelled to ally with opposition political parties to bring it about, remained unclear. But there was no mistaking his indictment of not only the Nehrus but the entire system for lack of political evolution during nearly twenty-seven years of Indian independence. Combined with the changing conditions he had been quick to recognize, India's new mahatma and his soul-stirring message must have been little short of terrifying to Indira.

Almost from the day of her 1971 election triumph, high popular expectations, as predicted, had been disappointed. Inflation following the war with Pakistan had jumped almost out of control with the worldwide oil-price crisis in 1973–74, making fuel for irrigation pumps four times more expensive and the price of oil-based fertilizers ten times higher. The Green Revolution consequently faltered before it had spread widely to poor farmers, and famine returned to several areas. In early 1974, when JP was launching his populist movement in Bihar, Indira cracked down massively on striking railway workers. Police arbitrarily jailed more than 30,000 union members, breaking their strike and enabling vital trains to start moving again. This deterred only temporarily more strikes by workers and demonstrations by students.

It was an example, however, of the draconian action the embattled prime minister was prepared to take to preserve her control of the nation. As she continued her habit of destabilizing and dismissing state governments of political opponents through the device of president's rule – in 1974 she easily put a new presidential pawn in Rashtrapati Bhavan, Fakhruddin Ali Ahmed, in place of the retiring V.V. Giri – protests by all opposition parties except the pro-Moscow Communists reached a desperate pitch. One of their ploys worked, resulting in Indira's conviction for breaking election law during the 1971 campaign in her Rae Bareli constituency.

This personal embarrassment coincided with Jayaprakash Narayan's relentless non-violent appeal for fair and decent government, the fresh emergence of Morarji Desai as a political rival, and a revolt against the prime minister within her own party. Indira Nehru Gandhi reacted by letting loose an avalanche in June 1975 that all but buried democracy in India.

10

Presuming Too Much

Early in the morning of 26 June 1975, agents of the government of Prime Minister Indira Gandhi secretly cut the power lines to India's national daily newspapers in Delhi, preventing them from publishing that day. Under cover of the same darkness, actually starting shortly before midnight of 25 June, police acting on Mrs Gandhi's orders secretly raided the homes of hundreds of her political opponents. They arrested Jayaprakash Narayan, Morarji Desai, Gayatri Devi, leaders of opposition parties except the pro-Moscow Communists, and even distrusted members of the ruling Congress (Indira) Party and clapped them into unidentified jails.

Indira herself, following her penchant for acting in the dead of night when she felt acutely threatened, was busy in the early morning hours of the darkest day in independent India's history. First she went in secret to Rashtrapati Bhavan. There she got Fakhruddin Ali Ahmed, the third president of India willing to forego his powers and automatically do her bidding, to sign a proclamation of "Emergency." Then she secretly convened her cabinet to approve her *coup d'état* from within the government. Its members obediently did so, asking few questions about the indefinite suspension of the constitutional liberties and individual freedoms that distinguished India as the world's most populous non-Communist country.

A decade before Jawaharlal Nehru became India's first prime minister in 1947, he had written anonymously that "private faces in public places are better and nicer than public faces in private places," adding ominously: "The fascist face is a public face ... Jawaharlal cannot become a fascist. And yet he has all the makings of a dictator in him." Now, under the cloak of night, his only child, Indira, unashamedly displayed these dictatorial traits. On her personal command, public faces intruded in unprecedented ways in private places. Her robot-like operatives violated the most elementary human rights. She willfully tore up the constitution that was her father's proudest legacy. Indira Nehru Gandhi contemptuously cast aside the civilized respect that, at least at upper levels of society, set India apart from most other poor nations: those run by despots.

"This woman, who is a xerox of Hitler and Stalin combined, has subverted a majority of the people's faith in themselves, their belief in an open society, their hopes that men and women could live in a country free of secret police, of hidden surveillance, of persecution of political ideas, with that cunning device, the weapon of the dictator – deception of openness to camouflage the truth."

Those chilling words are from a letter written by an Indian in Bombay to friends in North America in late 1976. The writer, whose identity was necessarily hidden, described a picture of "insidious oppression" that brought to mind George Orwell's *1984*, with an important difference: "This country is ruled by her and her toadies with the aid of statistics – figures which nobody believes any more since actual facts are different ... this goes on day in and day out, in our media, on our radio, on TV, on huge posters all over the city showing the 'Big Mother' watching us, a figure on a poster, frozen in a rhetorical pose, towering over us."

The real image of the Big Mother as distinct from Orwell's fictitious Big Brother! It was terrorizing innocent people not in a ruined London of the future but in the present-day villages and cities of an impoverished Asian country that for nearly three decades had tried to distinguish itself from China regimented under the gaze of Mao Zedong. To some Britons, harking back as they always do to their own Raj, Indira became the Empress of India, as a more benevolent Queen Victoria had once been. To many Indians, she was the embodiment of Kali, the dark Hindu goddess of destruction. Nirad Chaudhuri, the most incisive Indian commentator on his society, reported that some Hindus actually identified her with Sakti – power personified.

Mrs. Gandhi's slogan, constantly repeated on posters on its own or accompanying the omnipresence of her angry face, was "India is Indira and Indira is India." She gave every indication of believing it was true. As her father's daughter and the mother of Sanjay Gandhi, her closest partner in carrying out the Emergency, she apparently thought she had succeeded to the hereditary right to rule India previously belonging to the dethroned princely families. She saw herself as a vital link in an unbroken chain of reigning Nehrus.

Identification of Indira with India's survival was one gross "deception to camouflage the truth." The *r* inserted in "India" stood only for repression of perceived enemies of one family. The need for an Emergency ending India's constitutional safeguards was another Big Lie. Untrammeled journalists were in a position to expose both, together with the obscene means used to perpetuate both in a country where Mohandas Gandhi had stressed the sanctity of means to attain worthwhile ends. Therefore, a primary target of Indira throughout her Emergency was journalists, Indian and foreign. She not only stopped India's major dailies on Delhi's Bahadur Shah Zafar Marg from reporting the nation's sudden conversion to a police state until it was a done deed, complete with strict censorship of print media to go along with continuing government control of All-India Radio. She also threatened all Indian journalists with taking away their livelihoods or even their homes, and intimidated all but a handful of them into silence or conformity. She imposed rigid "guidelines" on foreign correspondents, so that a number of them who refused to comply, or were suspected of intending to report freely and fully, were expelled from India or were refused admission or left voluntarily.

During the summer the Emergency started, I visited several Asian countries. It was my second return trip to Asia since leaving my Singapore base as a correspondent. But under the conditions in force in India, it would have been useless for me as an already barred journalist to attempt to enter and report on the shocking developments set in motion by Indira's Emergency proclamation. My frustration was sharpened by the knowledge that the same men who were killing freedom of the press in India on her orders had tried unsuccessfully in 1968 to expel me as a resident correspondent, and in 1970–71 had succeeded in keeping me out as a regional correspondent except for the five days I had covered Trudeau's visit. It was clearer than ever that I had been a test case – and that Indira herself had been behind this trial run for her coming crackdown on all journalists covering India. Notwithstanding worldwide protests against her press restrictions, it also was clear that finding out, reporting, and analysing events during the Emergency, as and when they happened, would be difficult at best and often impossible.

The first question about the Emergency was Why? Why did Indira take all power into her own hands in June 1975 by effectively doing away with law, when she had decisively won an overwhelming parliamentary majority – big enough to amend the constitution legally if she wished – in her snap March 1971 election?

The next question was What? What was the Emergency's impact on the nation's politics and economy, on Indira's political associates and her political opponents, on middle-class Indians and poor Indians – and on India as a civilization?

The most important question had to do with its outcome. Was this the end of the line for India's pretensions to being a democratic, progressive, and for that matter unified nation, as many Indians and well-wishers assumed? If not, how would a way be found out of the Emergency? And would Indira allow Indians to take it now that she had those who opposed her not only on the run but behind bars?

All the answers had to do with the nature of Indira and the Nehru dynasty and the distorted knot in which they had tied India. Jayaprakash Narayan characterized these answers in the rhetorical question he put to Indira in a letter he wrote 5 December 1975, nearly six months after she had made India a personal dictatorship, and several weeks after he was released as her most important prisoner because of a serious and debilitating kidney condition.

"You are reported to have said that democracy is not more important than the nation," wrote JP. "Are you not presuming too much, Madame Prime Minister?"

The frail Gandhian in his seventies continued: "You are not the only one who cares for the nation. Among those whom you have detained or imprisoned there are many who have done as much for the nation as you. And every one of them is as good a patriot as yourself. So please do not apply salt to our wounds by lecturing to us about the nation.

"Moreover, it is a false choice that you have formulated. There is no choice between democracy and the nation."

Indira Nehru Gandhi was indeed presuming too much, as her father had before her. They not only equated themselves with India, but put themselves above India – she even more than he because, despite all her political triumphs, she was much weaker politically and did not have Jawaharlal's respect for law. As JP pointed out in his letter, it was the Congress Party led by the Nehrus that had failed to deliver on the constitutional promises of "Justice, Liberty, Equality, and Fraternity" to all Indians: "It is precisely because of that failure that there is so much unrest among the people and the youth. Repression is no remedy for that ... It only compounds the failure."

Indira presumed too much in proclaiming the Emergency and dismantling Indian democracy, and in finally providing a partial way out after twenty-one months. All her acts were predicated on the conviction that Indira's remaining in power as the representative of a family dynasty took precedence over all else. In her view, this was more important than not only her party, as she had demonstrated in 1969, but also both democracy *and* the nation.

The irritant that rankled with Indira more and more, because it put into question the very legitimacy of her holding office, went back to the election in 1971 that otherwise had gone almost all her way. She had been re-elected to the Lok Sabha in Rae Bareli with two-thirds of the popular vote and a huge margin of 112,000 votes over her nearest rival. But that candidate was a gadfly named Raj Narain, one of the radical Socialists who had intimidated the Congress (O) leader before the election and so helped to undermine the anti-Indira electoral coalition. Immediately after the election, he filed a suit charging the prime minister with fourteen violations of the 1951 electoral law. She denied the charges, testifying in court in her own defence for more than seven hours in early 1975.

The processes of law in India grind exceedingly slowly, as they had when Indira's grandfather Motilal Nehru won big legal fees in drawn-out property-dispute cases in the Allahabad area. On 12 June 1975, more than four years after the Rae Bareli vote, Justice Jag Mohan Sinha of the Allahabad High Court found Indira guilty of two of the allegations of corruption, and of not having told the truth as a sworn witness. The two counts upheld by the judge were that she had employed an official from the prime minister's secretariat in her election campaign, and had used local officials to set up loudspeakers and other equipment for political rallies.

These were trivial offences compared with the illegal practices, including excessive fundraising, indulged in by many if not most candidates for both the Lok Sabha and state legislatures. But they involved the prime minister of India, and by finding her guilty the judge dramatically underlined the democratic nature of the nation's political system, including the tarnished but still intact independence of the judiciary. Judge Sinha reserved his biggest impact for the punishment he imposed: he sentenced Indira to surrender her seat in Parliament and to forfeit her right to hold elective office for six years.

She appealed to the Supreme Court of India, where she could expect to win partly because she had appointed the chief justice. But British parliamentary tradition, on which India's system is based, demanded that she also resign as prime minister before the court's decision. Some informed Indians say she contemplated taking this course. It would have been a temporary expedient if the Supreme Court decided in her favour with greater speed than usual, and she would have partially regained the moral high ground with a shock of her own. But three important political developments converged at the same time as the Allahabad High Court decision. Even without them, it could not have taken much persuasion by Sanjay and the closest members of her legion of hangers-on for Indira to decide she was larger than the law. After all, she had refused to resign as leader of the Congress Party, and therefore as prime minister, when it had rejected her candidate for president of India in July 1969, and had gone on to her greatest political victories.

By refusing to resign in June 1975, however – by staying in power the fifth time the Nehru family should have been out of power – Indira handed the political forces coalescing against her an extraordinary issue such as they never had had before. This burning issue of immorality in government both focused on her and went far beyond her in a way Mahatma Gandhi would have seized on instinctively. It was an issue that pitted the long deprived hungry majority of Indians against a ruling minority clearly identified with the Nehrus.

Partly on Narain's urging, JP, the new mahatma and also an old radical, prepared to move once again from Patna to Delhi. This time he would lead a mass rally in the capital on the evening of 25 June demanding Indira's resignation and launching a national campaign of satyagraha or passive resistance to bring it about, including if necessary a gherao or lock-in of the prime minister at her residence. But she was already confronted with two other related problems, and they were even more pressing than the bad news out of her home town of Allahabad and the coming civil disobedience campaign by thousands and perhaps millions of Indians.

On 13 June, the day after her conviction, a coalition of anti-Congress (I) parties in Gujarat called the People's Front, led by Morarji Desai and blessed by JP, easily won a state election. Indira had allowed the election by lifting president's rule in Gujarat in response to a "fast unto death" in April by Morarji, an old Gandhian. Just eight or nine months before scheduled parliamentary elections across India, this result in one of the states – Mahatma Gandhi's own – closely contested between pro-Indira and anti-Indira forces since 1967 indicated a possible national trend. It brought together the two formidable figures of JP and Morarji as the leaders of an increasingly confident opposition just when Indira had suffered a serious personal setback.

The events in Allahabad and Gujarat, together with renewed and rising unease and discontent throughout the country before they occurred, had a special impact on members of the Congress (I) Party. As usual, loyalties within her own party were Indira's paramount concern. Roughly one-third of the then 361 Congress (I) members of the Lok Sabha were known to disdain her continued leadership. As many as 60 sympathized with JP and his avowedly above-politics movement. At least 60 others, fed up with Indira's socialist nostrums, openly pushed for Jagjivan Ram, the rotund formerly untouchable leader whom she had unsuccessfully put forward for president of India and who was then minister of agriculture, to replace her as prime minister before the 1976 elections. The feelings of other Congress (I) MPs, as opportunistic as other Indian politicians, were not known.

There is a good reason and a real reason for almost every public act. The real reason for Indira's Emergency was her fear that she would lose the leadership of her party to another unless she moved first. Her response to Jagjivan Ram's challenge was consistent with her reactions to Morarji's challenges in 1966 and 1967, and to the reconstructed Syndicate's challenge to her in 1969. Regardless of laws, conventions, and consequences, she had done what she felt she had to do to put down each challenge and so keep control of her Congress Party. In June 1975, Indira probably felt more cornered than ever. On top of rebellion within her party came the stinging Allahabad court ruling, the disturbing Gujarat outcome, and JP's impending mass mobilization against her. As always, she relied first of all on her instincts as a political infighter.

Indira must have surmised that if she had resigned as prime minister upon her conviction for corruption, Ram would have been in a position to enlist the party support to oust whomever she designated as a temporary replacement. Without question, she proclaimed the Emergency to prevent the ambitious Ram from succeeding her under any circumstances. In this sense she took another of her bold calculated risks to save her political life. Only this time she subverted the very system legally sustaining her and other Indian politicians.

Sanjay, her twenty-eight-year-old younger son, previously known for his unsuccessful efforts to build a factory with public funds to make an "Indian" automobile, was reported to have advised her to suspend the constitution and take all powers into her own hands in order to teach her many opponents "a lesson they'll never forget." Whether or not this is true, by the evening of 25 June and JP's big rally against Indira in Delhi, all the state machinery was in place to implement all the details of the most outrageous act ever performed in independent India's history.

When Jayaprakash called publicly for Indira's resignation, he also urged soldiers and policemen to ignore government orders offensive to their consciences. In so doing he unknowingly gave her the good reason she sought to make herself a dictator. Quickly accusing JP of preaching mutiny, Indira substituted her Emergency proclamation for India's constitution in the middle of the night, and threw him and hundreds of her other tormentors into jail before the sun rose on Delhi the next day. Nearly two years later, when ordinary Indians got the chance, they accused and convicted Indira of far more than election malpractice or a threat to the nation. They charged her with destroying free India not to save it but to save power for herself and her family, and they punished her accordingly. During the darkness of 25–26 June, however, Indira was able to arrange things in India the Nehrus' way more than ever before.

A few days earlier, *The Statesman* had quoted her as saying: "My eyes were set on my country. I have done no wrong for I have not done anything for myself." At least others were then free to express publicly their views of her actions and motives.

Under the Emergency, she arbitrarily put into effect an ordinance covering "publication of objectionable matter." It made foreign as well as

Indian journalists subject to fine and imprisonment for anything printed that the government considered "embarrassing" to itself or likely to "bring into hatred or contempt or excite disaffection toward the government (so as to) cause or tend to cause public disorder." In short, only Indira Gandhi and her henchmen could determine and propagate the truth about her actions and motives, and anyone else who reported anything contrary to that version could be severely penalized. Perhaps I had left India at the right time: the comparatively mild measures meant to keep me out of the country marked the beginning of a path leading to denial of press freedom worthy of a Communist or fascist regime.

Some foreign journalists in India or able to gain admission partially evaded the restrictions or gave up trying. But other journalists went along with Indira's line that curbing a dangerous opposition had been necessary to save the country, and that the people welcomed dictatorship in the realization that only "strictest discipline" could "remove poverty" and ensure safety. A reader of their stories might have gained the impression that the Big Mother had changed the chaotic nature of India and the individuality of most Indians as suddenly as she had taken away their inherent rights.

The reaction of all but a few Indian journalists to the Emergency was more depressing, even after the Bombay High Court in April 1976 courageously struck down most "objections" by the censor to printed matter on the ground that the rule of law was intact in India in spite of Indira's edicts. They acted like so many sheep in doing what her arrogant bureaucrats demanded of them, and more. This was partly because they feared for good reason that they would lose their jobs, and their homes in the case of many who lived in government housing for journalists, if they defied her by trying to tell the truth.

One editor who did defy her – and as a result had his small four-page Bombay weekly called *Opinion* closed down by the authorities – wrote: "In the last resort, the free press rests on the character of the journalist, his personal integrity, his love of the truth, his independence of mind." A.D. Gorwala, who had started *Opinion* after retiring as a civil servant, told his readers in bidding them farewell: "The current Indira regime, founded on 26 June 1975, was born through lies, nurtured by lies, and flourishes by lies." Minoo Masani, the former Swatantra Party leader, suspended publication of the journal *Freedom First* rather than submit to censorship, and as its editor brought the suit that led to the Bombay High Court's gratifying decision. The publisher, editors, and some writers of *The Indian Express* were among noted exceptions to the conformist rule among journalists working for daily newspapers.

After Indira had received her comeuppance from the people, Khushwant Singh, who as editor of the magazine *Illustrated Weekly* could have done more himself to stand up to her brazen denial of press freedom, wrote in April 1977: "The vast majority [of Indian journalists] knuckled under [to Information Minister V.K.] Shukla's draconian laws and did his bidding – suppressing, distorting news, praising those he wished to praise, denigrating others he wished to denigrate." Shukla's successor as Indira's information minister scornfully told these journalists: "When you were merely asked to bend, you chose to crawl." Their performance did not bode well for the future of Indian democracy when it was restored; they did little or nothing to bring it back themselves, and most may have too easily believed it would never return.

To be fair, much evidence supported this belief. All India succumbed so quickly to Indira's preplanned subjugation of the nation, and to further atrocities when she and her goons encountered so little resistance, that many wondered how the Indian tryst with democracy ever could have inspired such hope. To those who were already convinced that Indian civilization is decadent, the apparently wide acceptance of personal despotism was proof positive. The darkness spreading over the land was far more pervasive than that seen by an anguished Nehru when Mahatma Gandhi was shot dead at a prayer meeting in New Delhi on 30 January 1948. Indira had her apologists abroad as well as at home. But most Westerners and many Indians resigned themselves to the failure of Asia's great democratic experiment, as they had given up earlier on attainment of the Gandhian goal of peacefully building an equitable society from the village up.

Exploiting India's two best crop years until then, Indira repeatedly insisted with no possibility of contradiction that her authoritarian measures were helping the poor. In reality, a small minority of middle-class and upper-caste Indians grew richer during her Emergency, and the enormous gap between the smug haves and the mostly unseen have-nots widened. Along with fundamental human rights, her uncontrolled regime brutally assaulted whatever good and decent was left in Indian civilization, and whatever hope remained that a peasant could value and improve himself or herself.

No longer could the sticky sprawling apparatus headed by her be termed a legitimate government. Partly for that reason, it operated with an officious hypocrisy that revolted decent Indians. Like Hitler, Mussolini, and Stalin, Indira turned truth on its head so that black became white and white became black. She claimed that autocracy as embodied by her saved democracy and economic development in India, and that constitutional democracy – including individual freedoms, opposition parties, the courts, and the press – was leading to national destruction. Whether or not anyone believes such gratuitous lies, a leader who recites them and acts on such patently false assumptions plainly holds the people as well as the law in deep contempt.

By invoking article 352 of the constitution, providing for rule by emergency decree of the central government, Indira effectively removed the constitution from everyday life in India. The "external" emergency going back to the December 1971 war with Pakistan culminating in creation of Bangladesh was still in effect when she proclaimed the much more drastic "internal" emergency. She then rammed a series of constitutional amendments through Parliament, where she had the two-thirds majority to adopt them even if many MPs were not in jail or boycotting what became a parliamentary farce.

The first one barred the judiciary, which she obviously considered one of her enemies, from challenging the Emergency's legality. Another nullified the prime minister's conviction for election corruption; it not only ruled out judicial review of the results of any election but also granted immunity to prime ministers from civil or criminal prosecution for violations of the law before and while they held office. Still not sure she was off the hook, the paranoiac Indira pushed through a bill killing retroactively the specific charges on which she had been found guilty. A compliant Supreme Court of India, unable and apparently unwilling to decide on the key question of the government's right to change the very nature of the constitution, then formally threw out Indira's conviction for electoral dishonesty.

Not content with having transformed the Parliament of India into a plaything, Indira clamped president's rule on Tamil Nadu and Gujarat, the only two remaining states where Congress governments loyal to her were not in power. Unwanted central administration helped convince Tamils and other South Indians that the Emergency was directed specifically against them, and Gujaratis that their votes were worthless.

Going beyond provisions for preventive detention existing since British days, Indira had new legislation adopted allowing police to jail any person for two years without charges or trial. Unrestrained, the hand of the central bureaucracy reached into and squelched local government. Power radiated solely from the prime minister's office. Indira created her own intelligence network, innocuously named the research and analysis wing – but feared by Indians as RAW – and a paramilitary corps loyal to her in the border security force. By screening and choosing top military officers, she assured herself control of the million-man armed forces. Even before the Emergency, police officials responsible to her opened the mail of senior generals in order to detect any hint of disloyalty or threat of a military coup.

Rigid censorship and the penalties incurred by honest reporting were not enough to slake Indira's vindictiveness toward journalists. One of her ordinances repealed immunity against prosecution for journalists reporting what was said on the floor of Parliament; they had enjoyed this protection – traditional in parliamentary democracies – by virtue of a law sponsored by Feroze Gandhi, Indira's late husband, when he was a Congress MP. Not satisfied with muzzling major newspapers from outside, Indira gained internal control of several by forcing boards of directors to accept majorities of government appointees who then got rid of independent editors. She combined the country's two wire services – the government's partially independent Press Trust of India and the private United News of India – into one government propaganda agency (apart from All-India Radio, widely known as All-Indira Radio) called Samachar.

Indira's minions simultaneously dictated what was to be printed, decided what was not to be printed, and claimed the Indian press was "free from any type of interference." The prime minister of India even attempted to extend her version of freedom of the press to other developing lands. Telling delegates from avowedly non-aligned countries at a Delhi conference in July 1976 that Western reporting of her Emergency "as an onslaught on democracy or an abrogation of our constitution was not at all correct," she proposed clones of Samachar in other nations. These agencies would "pool" official accounts of events that would take the place of stories from "colonialist" Western news agencies.

The government's newly created monopoly on information in India spawned an Orwellian newspeak that reflected Indira's attitude toward truth, and would have been ludicrous had it not been so insidious. Dictatorship was termed "freedom." The "discipline" of the "New India" was called more democratic than the "indisciplined" old India. Inevitably, words assigned meanings opposite to their real meanings – lies and innuendos – became weapons against Indira's real and imagined enemies. For example, one government pamphlet linked JP to Naxalite and Marxist Communists, and by extension to violent revolutionary acts. Another associated the "fanaticism" of a Muslim political party with "fascist forces." Seeking to create bugbears for the Indian people, and fearing any religious movement that conceivably could develop into a Gandhian-like protest against misuse of authority, Indira's regime directed a particularly nasty stream of abuse against a Hindu sect called Anand Marg or Path of Bliss, whose growing ranks included many civil servants. The campaign's managers publicly accused the fringe movement and its leader of performing rituals of torture and death, and maintaining ties with both "Nazi ideology" and the CIA. Then they had him and some of his followers charged and convicted of murder in an atmosphere of fear and intimidation of defence witnesses.

On 2 November 1976 – the day Jimmy Carter, a champion of human rights, was elected president of the United States – Indira Nehru Gandhi's Lok Sabha effectively destroyed India's suspended democratic constitution, the pride of Jawaharlal Nehru with its guarantees of individual freedom and dignity to all Indians. Elected in early 1971 for a maximum of five years, the lower house of Parliament at the time was nearly a year beyond its term, with no new elections in sight. It was boycotted by all opposition members except pro-Moscow Communists, and its once lively debate was a thing of the past. It obediently voted to pass what Indira called the forty-fourth amendment bill, and the Rajya Sabha and the state legislatures automatically followed suit with similar two-thirds majorities.

This bill went much further than previous crippling amendments to the constitution during the Emergency, and even went beyond a proposal by a Congress (I) Party committee headed by Swaran Singh – who, among other services rendered to Indira, had slandered me in Parliament as a journalist – to deprive the courts of the power to review a constitutional amendment. It not only took away this power from all courts, including the Supreme Court of India, but also barred all courts except the Supreme Court from deciding on the constitutionality of any law, and specified that the Supreme Court could strike down a law only by a two-thirds vote. Moreover, the bill gave the prime minister the right, through the figurehead president and without cabinet consultation, to put any state under emergency rule at any time.

By passing this crowning legislation proposed by the illegitimate Indira regime, Parliament sealed its own fate as well as that of the judiciary. It left the governing of India solely to a self-obsessed bureaucracy headed by a woman considered mad by some Indians for whom her self-serving acts provoked comparisons with Hitler's cynical methods of consolidating Nazi power in Germany in the 1930s. India's lawmakers, abdicating their public responsibilities and their private consciences, mindlessly unmade law in favour of arbitrary recklessness with hundreds of millions of human lives.

As with other official reigns of terror, the harm the Emergency actually inflicted on people from its inception was even worse than the damage it did to their constitutional protection.

No one outside the government could keep count, and Indira's regime put out no figures, but the hundreds of individuals thrown into jail for no specific reason quickly became thousands. Estimates ranged from 30,000 to 250,000 but the prime minister said in 1976 only that the number was "very small, relative to India's whole population." If 1 per cent, say, this could have been 6 million in a population then over 600 million. India's khaki-uniformed equivalent of Nazi stormtroopers banged on doors and dragged men and women away in the middle of all the nights of Indira's darkness. In many cases, the very loss of habeas corpus – the agony of not knowing where they were being taken and what would happen to them, for both these instant prisoners and their legions of friends and supporters – was more painful than the physical treatment they received.

JP's sudden disappearance during the night of 25–26 June, hours after his lawful appeal to Indira to resign, caused great concern and wild rumours among his followers considering his poor physical condition. With her operatives having stopped publication of major newspapers until they could be controlled by censors, many Indians only learned that JP and virtually all other opposition political leaders had been seized by listening to the British Broadcasting Corporation news on short-wave radio. In response to a cabled appeal to Indira, a statement signed by doctors at the All-India Institute of Medical Sciences in Delhi was put out, saying JP had been treated at the hospital and had left in satisfactory condition. Only later was it learned that he had been transferred to the Post Graduate Institute of Medicine in Chandigarh northwest of the capital, where he was kept incommunicado and in solitary confinement. On 7 November his brother was allowed to visit him and was so alarmed at his physical state that he wrote the prime minister. On 11 November an order was issued to release him because of ill health. The last thing Indira wanted on her hands was the death of JP as her prisoner, giving all India a beloved martyr to her despotism.

Yet this nearly happened due to typical bureaucratic insensitivity and delay. When the weak JP was finally freed on 16 November, he wanted to go to Bombay. But the prime minister's office directed for no good reason that he be taken to Delhi first. When he finally was admitted to Bombay's Jaslok Hospital on 22 November, his condition had deteriorated so much that doctors urgently put him on an artificial kidney. JP had come so close to dying he agreed to make a notarized statement that would leave no doubt about his political position when the end came. After noting that his kidneys had been "very badly damaged" during his four and a half months in solitary confinement, he affirmed at the beginning of December: "My views about the situation in India are precisely what they were on 25th June 1975 ... Indeed, all the ugly things that have happened since have only confirmed my apprehensions ... I hope the people of India will be able before long to liberate themselves non-violently from the present tyranny."

Other political prisoners did not receive special treatment – or, if they did, it was not to take tardy account of illness but to break their bodies and their spirits. Most remained in detention for nineteen months, and many were tortured. The International League for Human Rights documented, on the basis of eyewitness reports, beating and burning of prisoners, stretching of their spinal cords, hanging them by their feet, and putting live electric wires in their bodies. Morarji Desai was a proud prisoner throughout this period, as was Raj Narain, who had dared to sue the prime minister and win.

One of Indira's special detainees was Gayatri Devi, the beautiful Maharanee of Jaipur who had led the anti-Congress opposition in the desert state of Rajasthan and had helped form the now-defunct Swatantra Party. Because she personified the princely class and free enterprise in India – and probably also because she was a woman – she was forced to endure cruel and unusual punishment in a bare jail cell far removed from the more comfortable accommodations available in Indian jails for noted prisoners. It was as if Indira wanted to humiliate her outspoken rival by stripping the maharanee of any trace of her status, her wealth and, if possible, her beauty.

Personal vindictiveness also played a part in the relentless pursuit by Indira's police of George Fernandes, a radical Socialist colleague of Narain and leader of the railway workers' union that had defied the prime minister by striking in 1974. Arrested then but later released, Fernandes had gone underground when the Emergency was proclaimed. Meeting foreign journalists at different hideouts, he sniped at Indira for nearly a whole year, especially on behalf of south Indians, calling her "a dictator from Kashmir." On the night of 1 May 1976, frustrated police arrested his younger brother Lawrence at their mother's home in Bangalore. They slapped him, kicked him, whipped him, and beat him with clubs in an unsuccessful attempt to find out where George was. Three weeks later, Alice Fernandes, the mother, found out where Lawrence was – in a cell, semi-paralyzed, and "looking dead" after being shuttled between hospitals under a false name, according to a letter she wrote to the president of India pleading for a judicial inquiry into "this barbaric torture."

The only response, from the home ministry, was an egregious illustration of the ease with which Indian officials can lie: "Allegation of torture ... is totally false, baseless, and mischievous." It came after George Fernandes was finally captured in Calcutta on 10 June. Holding him up as an example, Indira had him indicted and tried for incitement and sabotage to overthrow the government violently. However unjustified she was in bringing these charges, her doing so contrasted sharply with her holding of thousands of political prisoners for months without charges or trial.

The government maintained it had the right under emergency provisions not only to arrest and hold these persons but also to keep its reasons for detaining them "confidential matters of state." No less than seven state high courts disagreed in upholding habeas corpus for a total of forty-three prisoners, including four members of Parliament. It was no wonder that Indira pushed through the legislation emasculating these courts. But her stacking of the Supreme Court of India with her pawns again paid off for her.

On the government's appeal of the lower court decisions, the Supreme Court by a vote of four to one ruled in effect that fundamental constitutional rights to life, liberty, equality before the law, and habeas corpus could be suspended by the government's determination of an "emergency," without its specifying a "clear and present danger," in the classic words of U.S. Supreme Court Justice Oliver Wendell Holmes Jr. Except for a lone dissenting opinion, India's highest court abjectly surrendered to Indira's capricious authority by unquestioningly accepting the good faith of her bogus government. As did the sheep-like compliance of frightened journalists, this shameful act by craven jurists raised the disturbing question of how deep India's democratic instincts went.

But Justice H.R. Khanna wrote his dissent with the ringing clarity of an opinion upholding civil liberty by Justice Holmes or Justice Louis D. Brandeis, or by a Canadian judge upholding the freedoms in the Canadian Charter of Rights and Freedoms: "The power of the courts to issue a writ of habeas corpus is regarded as one of the most important characteristics of democratic states under the rule of law. The principle that no one shall be deprived of his liberty without the authority of law was not the gift of the constitution. It existed before the coming into force of the constitution." Without court protection of this basic human right, he courageously continued, any "malicious petty official" could arbitrarily arrest and detain innocent people: "In a purely formal sense, even the organized mass murders of the Nazi regime qualify as law."

As the seniormost justice on the Supreme Court, Khanna was due to become chief justice in early 1977. Not surprisingly, Indira passed over Khanna and named one of his cowardly colleagues to succeed A.N. Ray, who as her last appointed chief justice had done her bidding as scrupulously as any of the presidents of India – Hussain, Giri, and Ahmed – who effectively served under her when constitutionally they should have served over her.

It took a man who could fairly be described as a "malicious petty official," although he held no government position, to do in Indira Nehru Gandhi politically. That was, however, the furthest thing from the mind of Sanjay Gandhi, her younger son and heir apparent.

Sanjay also unwittingly served an even greater purpose. Lacking the refinement of his grandfather Jawaharlal Nehru and the shrewdness of his mother – and all but rudimentary education – he exposed as never before the contempt of the Nehrus for the people of India. It was not simply a question of each generation of the family being more crude than the one before. Indira's elder son Rajiv proved smoother than his brother when his political turn came. It was a question of a dynasty's obsession with itself regardless of the human cost to others. Sanjay made this unequivocally clear by assaulting the right of ordinary Indians to their own bodies even if they had not been put behind bars without cause or legal redress.

Before the Emergency, he had become a focus of popular attention through two new names linked to the Nehru family – Maruti and Maneka. With government funds he had deviously obtained, Sanjay promoted an Indian car of the future he called Maruti. His engagement and marriage to a wealthy Punjabi model and would-be journalist named Maneka Anand, who at the time seemed equally unaware of principles, suggested the making of another blindly ambitious generation of the Nehru dynasty. Sanjay was neither elected nor appointed to an official post until December 1975, when he joined the executive committee of the Congress (I) youth wing six months into the Emergency. But he built a power base of his own with a growing band of followers consisting mostly of young Punjabi men known, as he was, for brusque surliness. They were a different, more openly frightening lot than the suave Kashmiri Brahmins, known as the "Kashmir mafia," with whom Indira surrounded herself. One of Sanjay's friends, Bansi Lal, who had established a reputation for corruption when he was chief minister of Haryana, was named defence minister at the same time Sanjay got his party job.

None of this would have been possible without the indulgent help of Indira. Her commitment to socialist ideals contrasted with Sanjay's belief in capitalist methods. But she doted on her "political" son – Rajiv, an Indian Airlines pilot, showed little interest then in ruling India – even more than most Indian Hindu mothers favour their male offspring. Sure of her affection and protection and, it is safe to say, his succeeding her as prime minister one day, Sanjay was said to be cruel at times to his mother. Whatever the nature of their intense relationship, he clearly influenced the political decisions she made, including proclamation of the Emergency itself.

But Sanjay soon came up with his own four-point plan for transforming India without democracy. His outward aims, unexceptionable in themselves, were to increase literacy, abolish the dowry system impoverishing many families, beautify the country, and control population growth.

A propaganda campaign paralleling the one exalting Indira and her broader objectives for India promoted Sanjay and his goals. But it didn't become evident until the spring of 1976 what Sanjay specifically had in mind, particularly for improving appearances and keeping the number of babies down. Bulldozing squatter communities of makeshift huts and forcibly moving their inhabitants to remote locations – as Imelda Marcos was doing at the same time with Manila slum dwellers under her husband's martial law in the Philippines – turned out to be one of Sanjay's specialties. Compulsory sterilization, mostly of men but also of women, made a much bigger impact on Indians, many of whom might have been willing to believe in the supposed benefits of the Emergency.

The first practice, forcibly taking people's homes away from them, was confined largely to Delhi. Violation of the most basic right of human beings – the right to have children, precious to poor Indians who have virtually nothing else – was widespread in the backward Hindi-speaking belt of northern India. More than anything else, it led to a revolution against the Nehrus. The wonder was not the revolution itself but that it was non-violent, with one exception, in the best Gandhian tradition.

In the old city of Delhi in April, the first protest was in fact tragically violent. Fearing that volunteers mobilized by Sanjay to raze their homes, take them away, and force men to undergo vasectomies were carrying out a Hindu plot to prevent Muslim families from having more children, poor Muslims rioted in the Turkman Gate area. In typical Indian fashion, police charged the desperate slum dwellers with lathis and shot them down with .303 rifles, killing more than fifty and injuring hundreds. When resistance ceased after several hours, the destroying of homes and the sterilization of men and women continued there and in other communities as if nothing had happened.

From the beginning, callous excesses marked Sanjay's birth control program, as if the lives, the feelings, and the future generations of poor Indians mattered not a whit. Even before the central government finished drafting a bill requiring all men with more than three children to be sterilized, state governments had started implementing a massive intrusion of public faces into the most private places. Under the proposed legislation, failure to comply would mean a fine and imprisonment. But in Delhi, government workers were threatened immediately with loss of their housing and pensions if they did not show up for an operation by 1977.

Having a vasectomy suddenly became a prescribed duty for men all over the country, regardless of the number of children they had, and in many cases even if they had none. Artificial quotas took precedence over real lives. Old men were dragged in off the street to vasectomy clinics under bright *shamianas* (tents) that had blossomed in Delhi and many other cities and villages. So were young unmarried boys. Some men returned again and again. A "bonus" – really a bribe – for undergoing a vasectomy was sixty rupees (eight dollars then) in cash, or a cheap tran-

sistor radio, or a tin of cooking oil. On some days, teachers and policemen each had to bring in four people for sterilization or else not be paid
for that day's normal work. A man whose family had been forced out of
a squatter colony risked losing his food ration card or not getting a loan
to build a new shelter if he did not present himself at a vasectomy clinic
at his new location.

The operation on a man, cutting of the vas deferens or sperm duct, was
short, simple, and technically reversible. For a woman, a tubal ligation or
tying of a fallopian tube was more complex but far less frequent. Neither
was new in India. Since independence, 16 million people or about 800,000
a year had been voluntarily sterilized. After the emotional protests at Turkman Gate and elsewhere, Indira distanced herself from the compulsory sterilization bill. Like her father, she had made a special political appeal to
Muslims and dalits, and did not want to alienate them. Following the
Emergency she even insisted that no Indian had been compelled to undergo
a birth-preventing operation.

But Sanjay's sterilization squads and statistics told a different story. From
April to September 1976, two million people were sterilized, five or six
times the earlier rate. According to alarming rumours that spread throughout India, the number of people forcibly sterilized on Sanjay's orders and
made impotent – and, more important, the number to come – were far
higher. In all respects, the sterilization campaign was a vast human disaster
from beginning to end. Demographically, it was counterproductive because
it created a backlash among families whose willingness to accept voluntary
birth control methods was diminished for years. Politically, it changed
India's history.

On 18 January 1977, Indira jolted the nation by dissolving the Lok
Sabha and calling new elections for March. Her startling announcement
provoked a spate of speculation, which continued a quarter-century later,
about her motives, her timing, and her intentions. She declared at the time:
"Let us go to the polls with the resolve to reaffirm the power of the people." A little verse in Hindi that swept through the villages and towns of
the northern Gangetic plains soon after her election call expressed concisely
how most Indian people intended to use their power, and the main reason
why: "Indira hatao, indiri bachao!" The English translation was just as
direct: "Get rid of Indira and save your penis!"

Despite her belated misgivings about compulsory sterilization, Indira
could not have been fully aware of how the Sanjay-induced wave of vasectomies was affecting ordinary families. There is no reason to doubt that
when she talked about "the power of the people," she firmly believed it
would vindicate her and permit her to continue her domination of India. It
may be an over-simplification – but in all likelihood it is not – to say that,

like other dictators, she primarily wished to legitimate autocracy. In India that could only mean a fresh democratic election.

In February 1976, a month before her 1971 electoral mandate ran out, Indira had had Parliament postpone the next election for a year. In November 1976, she had had Parliament put it off again until November 1977. Yet two months later she changed her mind. Perhaps she sensed growing popular realization that the Emergency, including the sterilization campaign, was a fraud and feared that this awareness and a possible poor monsoon in 1977 made waiting for a vote until late 1977 unwise. Almost certainly, if an election had been held as scheduled in March 1976, she and the Congress (I) Party would have won easily again, whether or not she let her political opponents out of prison to contest it. But the Emergency would have had only nine months to show results.

When Indira surprised everyone by calling an election for March 1977, she lifted neither the Emergency nor government censorship. She eased already relaxed restrictions on the press, she allowed political rallies, and she finally let her army of political prisoners breathe the air outside fetid jail cells. But her police-state apparatus was still in place, and could have been used to revoke an election outcome unwanted by her. The strange thing about India's new democratic election was that it went ahead when India was not a democracy. This was good reason for opposition leaders to refuse to take part in it. But just as Indira took another calculated risk – but one whose final result she had the power to determine – they decided to take her on again despite the long odds against them.

Perhaps because of these odds, and the knowledge that this would not be a genuinely free election, non-Communist opposition parties quickly succeeded in doing what they had not been able to do before any previous national vote: they effectively united. The new Janata or People's Party was really a coalition of the Congress (O), the Jan Sangh, the radical Socialists, and Charan Singh's dissident Uttar Pradesh party. In contrast to tactics leading to their joint fiasco in 1971, these disparate parties divided up Lok Sabha election districts to minimize splitting of anti-Congress (I) votes. Moreover, Jagjivan Ram, whose presumptive challenge to Indira in 1975 had propelled her into the Emergency, shocked her in 1977 when she took the election route by defecting from her party and forming the Congress for Democracy in league with Janata.

Some of the men and women who emerged from Indira's torture racks and prisons, such as Gayatri Devi, were too hurt or broken to take active part in what seemed at first a hopeless fight against her. Jayaprakash Narayan, still the moral leader of this struggle, was tied to a dialysis machine and could not campaign full-time. Minoo Masani of the old Swatantra Party, although he had not gone to jail, did not have the heart to wage another campaign against Indira. But Morarji Desai, who seemed to thrive on adversity, assumed vigorous political command of the opposition at the age of eighty-one. Atal Bihari Vajpayee of the Jan Sangh proved reassuringly moderate in appealing to Indian voters for change. Raj Narain recalled Indira's past illegal conduct. George Fernandes ran for Parliament from the jail cell where he awaited trial for criminal conspiracy. Charan Singh asked the many small cultivators of UP for a fresh show of loyalty. The appeals of these expected leaders were amplified by the words of welcome additions: the dalit leader Ram, former Indira foreign minister M.C. Chagla, and Vijayalakshmi Pandit, who was her aunt and Nehru's sister and held his parliamentary seat. The impressive Madame Pandit left no doubt of her meaning when she said that the individual freedoms encouraged by Mahatma Gandhi had been "suffocated" during the Emergency.

Notwithstanding these encouraging moves and inspiring messages, the forces arrayed against Indira, Sanjay, and their political and police phalanxes appeared to have too little time, too little money, and too little support to pull off a miracle. This was just what the prime minister was counting on. Less than eight weeks after opposition leaders and workers had been out of action and out of contact with each other, they would have to challenge at the polls her formidable party organization, bolstered by twenty-one months of uncontested propaganda. They would have to raise campaign funds from scratch while she and Sanjay had received major contributions from fawning Indian industries for months. Despite protests, many state and local workers for opposition parties remained in jail even when Indians cast ballots 16–20 March. In contrast, Congress (I) workers not only paid voters and got them to the polls but, along with police and paramilitary units deployed throughout the country, flexed the muscles that could rig the results.

Indira left nothing to chance. Thinking better of a plan to replace veteran Congress (I) candidates with headstrong recruits from Sanjay's youth wing, she kept experienced party men on. Reports of the backlash against Sanjay's sterilizations apparently filtered through the layers of sycophants and bureaucrats surrounding her, because she restricted her son's campaigning to the presumably safe rural UP district of Amethi, where he was running for Parliament for the first time and right next to her own Rae Bareli constituency. This had the added advantage of appeasing her consistent Soviet supporters, who were nervous about Sanjay's pro-capitalist utterances.

The prime minister herself crisscrossed the vast country as she had in past campaigns, tirelessly addressing hundreds of rallies, once again holding up her family and her party as the saviours of India, plaintively asserting that she could not be a dictator if she held elections. But she sternly warned voters that, as a Congress (I) statement put it, the Janata Party offered "no alternative to the Congress" but an "explosive combination of incompatibles of extreme ideologies" that if elected would "finish once and for all the great purposes upon which we are embarked." At the same time, Indira coyly promised to "abide by the verdict" of the voters. The Indian writer Ved Mehta wryly commented that it was "as if, in truly democratic elections, she would have any choice."

Fear was the unexpressed but palpable leitmotif of Indira's campaign. She went through the motions of democracy but she meant to exploit mass fear of herself and the monster Emergency state she had created. JP fully understood what she was doing and where it would lead if she succeeded. In his last *cri de cœur* to the people of India, before his illness compelled cancellation of his appearances in the final days of the campaign, the nation's last mahatma warned: "This is the last chance. If you falter now, nineteen months of tyranny will become years of terror."

JP dared not presume they would opt for freedom and an untried opposition over the state and a dictator with the mystique of a goddess. No matter on what side they were on, middle-class and upper-caste Indians everywhere were stunned when lower-class and lower-caste or non-caste Indians made their choice clear. All-India Radio, a willing tool of Indira, couldn't bring itself to announce the astonishing election returns until after many Indians had learned them in other ways, usually by going in person to tightly guarded vote-counting centres that took on the aura and excitement of *tamashas* or folk festivals.

The myth that political liberty means nothing to a peasant, that he or she is concerned solely with a hand-to-mouth existence, went out the window along with Indira in March 1977.

In villages across the breadth of northern India, peasants put one rupee or two rupees or five in Janata collection baskets, often the same money they had been paid by Congress (I) workers, because they said it wasn't right that the freedoms of all but the rulers had been taken away, and a man or woman could be put in jail without receiving a fair trial. When the time came to cast ballots, the peasants not only thrashed Indira in Rae Bareli, but singled out for special punishment her ministers responsible for castrating the constitution and gagging the press, and of course Sanjay, the "boy" who wanted to castrate them and had delusions of grandeur they did not think justified.

India's intellectuals and its Gandhians, although by no means all members of either group, talked about saving democracy. Only agricultural labourers, little farmers, and penniless workers could save democracy and possibly the nation, and they did not falter in doing so. They demanded their due and they defined their dream for India. The hungry majority of unseen Indians forced recognition from the unseeing, who had acted all along – but more than ever under Indira and her Emergency – as if only their own comforts and privileges mattered. The most convinced detractor of India had to admit after 1977's watershed election that more than a spark of life remained in a weary civilization. In the years to come, it seemed certain at the time, the most cynical politician could ignore the needs and aspirations of India's awakened masses only at his or her peril.

By permitting the election, Indira provided a partial out from the Emergency that she was sure would give her not only legitimacy but also carte blanche for years to come. Instead, she inadvertently produced her own exit from office and, most Indians felt confident, from politics.

This time she miscalculated massively. The opposition achieved unprecedented unity. The widely perceived threat to Indian manhood turned out to be an even more potent issue against Indira than her gross abuse of power, corruption, and empty economic promises. The Election Commission of India was honest, carrying out admirably its mission of running a nationwide poll in a non-partisan manner. In the end there were some officials Indira couldn't subvert. In the end, too, the many reports of Indians' unthinking deference to her and her Emergency, and of their willingness to forsake democracy in a poor country, proved vastly exaggerated. The whole thing was altogether too much for civilized people everywhere to hope for. The lesson of March 1977 in India was momentous far beyond the Subcontinent.

More than 194 million Indians voted – 60.5 per cent of the electorate, only slightly lower than the record 61.3 per cent in the 1967 protest vote, and significantly higher than the 55.3 per cent in the 1971 vote returning Indira. With 542 Lok Sabha seats at stake, the Congress (I) Party hung on to a mere 154 – a staggering 198 fewer than in 1971 – or less than 29 per cent. Its share of the popular vote plummeted to 34.5 per cent, compared with 40.8 per cent in 1967 and 43.7 per cent in 1971.

This was by far the worst electoral showing by the ruling Congress Party in the three decades since India's winning of independence. But it was the logical next step after the anti-Congress vote in 1967, and underscored the anomaly of the 1971 result. Just as voters in 1967 had ousted Congress governments in important states for the first time, those in the nation's sixth parliamentary election ten years later did something that had never been done before in India: they threw the Congress Party out of power at the national level. Moreover, the pro-Moscow Communists, Indira's de facto allies, captured only 7 seats, sharply down from 23 in

1971, while the Communist Marxists, who opposed her, slipped only 3 to 22.

The Janata Party won the election with a clear and convincing Lok Sabha majority of 295 seats or more than 54 per cent, and 41.3 per cent of the popular vote. This was an astonishing achievement for a party that hadn't existed two months earlier, and whose components plus Swatantra had taken only 49 seats and 23 per cent of the popular vote in 1971. But it was a matter of applying the lesson learned in 1967 that the opposition's path to power lies in preventing fragmentation of protest votes. In Uttar Pradesh, the most populous state and the one where the politically deadly rhyme against vasectomies resonated most, Janata captured fully 68 per cent of the popular vote; Congress (I) won only 25 per cent, and failed to take a single seat. Sanjay, with barely one-third of the vote in his race, was soundly beaten in Amethi. In Rae Bareli, Indira paid dearly for her sins, both local and national, in the eyes of her constituents: Raj Narain gleefully buried her by 55,000 votes.

The rout of the Nehrus was plain by 20 March. But Indira did not concede defeat or make a public appearance when the last polls closed that day. She could have used her Emergency powers to nullify the election results with as much or as little justification as she had had in nullifying the constitution twenty-one months earlier. Many Indians feared she would do just that. This would have amounted to saying the Indian people had to be saved from themselves.

But such an act of defiance was beyond even Indira. Possibly she experienced pangs of conscience over the damage to Indian democracy she had already inflicted. Much more likely, she recognized that the democratic imperative, once it has burst artificial bonds such as those imposed by her, is irresistible. In one way, however, she ran true to form. Just as she had had the Emergency proclaimed in the middle of the night of 25–26 June 1975, she ended it at 4 AM on 21 March 1977. That was when she drove to the home of Vice-President B.D. Jatti, who had become acting president upon the death in February of President Ahmed, an early bad omen for her. Indira advised him to revoke the Emergency. This time the nation breathed a collective sigh of relief at a presidential order originating with her. Then she resigned as prime minister of India.

It was the normal thing to do in a parliamentary democracy following an election defeat. Except for the nineteen months when Lal Bahadur Shastri had been prime minister in 1964–66, it was also the first time that India found itself without a Nehru at the helm. But there was a crucial difference. Most Indians had mourned the loss of Jawaharlal after his seventeen years and three parliamentary elections as prime minister. Following her eleven years, three parliamentary elections, and twenty-one months of dictatorship as prime minister, Indira stepped down in public disgrace.

Her resignation marked no less than the sixth time the Nehrus should have been out of power. Now, however, they actually were out of power for the first time since the brief Shastri government. Almost everyone, except Indira herself, assumed they would stay out of power for good.

11

Back to the Past

Three decades after India won independence, Indians rejoiced at what they thought was both the end of the Nehru era and the demise of Indira Gandhi's detested Emergency. But the new era owed much to the past.

Morarji Desai became prime minister in March 1977 after having tried and failed when Jawaharlal Nehru died in May 1964, when Lal Bahadur Shastri died in January 1966, and when the people first protested against Congress Party rule in February 1967. At eighty-one he assumed the reins of a government made up largely of ex-Congresswallahs like himself. These men and women had given up on a Congress Party shaped by Nehru and his family heirs. Morarji's finally attaining his personal goal was not simply a matter of his stubborn perseverance finally paying off like the Gandhian *charka* he liked to use, the seemingly outdated home spinning wheel.

Desai's patience and even more so the spiritual leadership of Jayaprakash Narayan reflected the old Congress spirit, the all-but-forgotten Gandhi, the rudiments of a way of life that is starkly non-Western yet more at home with Western nations than with the Communist despotisms that Nehru and Indira had cultivated. Hardly had the election results been announced than the members of the new Janata majority in the Lok Sabha gathered at the samadhi where the slain Mahatma's remains were cremated in 1948. There they pledged "to serve our people and give our best to the weakest among them."

Naturally some members of Morarji's coalition cabinet did not come out of the Congress tradition – the Socialists George Fernandes (freed from jail) and Raj Narain, for example, and the Jan Sangh's Atal Bihari Vajpayee, who as foreign minister pursued a constructive policy of regional co-operation with India's neighbours and even-handed dialogue with the United States and the West. But former Congressmen predominated in the Janata government that immediately revoked the "external" emergency dating back to the 1971 war with Pakistan, and set about repealing all the ordinances, laws, and constitutional amendments passed during the "internal" emergency.

Concurrence of two-thirds of the state legislatures and the Rajya Sabha was needed to quash an amendment. So new elections had to be held first in many of the states that Indira had effectively taken over. Within three months the central Janata government forced elections in ten states, including seven in the north whose voters had demolished Congress (I) parliamentary candidates as if they represented the plague. The decimation continued with Janata capturing absolute control of the seven Hindi-speaking states, including UP and Bihar, and coming to power in the Punjab with the Akali Dal of the Sikhs. In Tamil Nadu, a Tamil party returned to office, and in West Bengal the Marxists regained power at the head of a new leftist coalition.

Indian politics got back on track, in short, as the gross distortions induced by Indira going back to 1967 but especially since proclamation of the Emergency in 1975 were ironed out of the system.

The larger Janata aim beyond personal ambitions, if the promises of Morarji and his lieutenants were serious, was to bring "bread and liberty" to the people. It was to use India's revived democratic framework to change the direction of economic policy so the rural masses, the poorest peasants who had voted Congress out, finally would benefit fairly. The historic implication was even more profound than India's miraculously finding its democratic footing again.

It was that India was back where it should have been years before. If this were correct, Indira had bucked the tide of modern Indian history that was released by Mohandas Gandhi and had found channels in democratic institutions. Nehru himself, while he championed these institutions, had been outside the Gandhian wave in stressing Soviet-style industrialization. Both father and daughter, therefore, had been anachronisms. During the time that Indira had found ways to keep herself in power, India may have stood still for more than a decade while its population raced ahead by about 15 million people a year. During the time her father had been likened to a banyan tree in his domination of the country, India may have lost nearly two more decades.

If the new, freely elected rulers of India meant what they said about going back to first things such as food output, rural jobs, and village industries first, it was as if Shastri had lived – the little man with the big heart who, in his tragically short time as prime minister after Nehru, gave agricultural production the priority it deserved. Or as if Morarji, the old Hindu puritan, had directly succeeded Shastri. Or, to go farther back in India's past, as if Vallabhai Patel, the patrician peasant from the same part of the country as Gandhi and Desai, had even blocked Nehru's tryst with destiny. But it was not 1947, 1964, or 1966. It was 1977. Possibly, it was already too late for India and nobody realized it. But neither could anyone doubt that India had a lot of catching up to do.

India also had a seemingly golden opportunity to capitalize on a new birthright and an old one at the same time. Indira's iron rule had had to end for India to rekindle its democratic spirit. To give that spirit the substance it had lacked in years past, the Janata or People's Party would need to live up to its name and heed Mahatma Gandhi's message about giving the poorest Indians a voice in the building of their own country.

There was reason to doubt this would ever happen. Nirad Chaudhuri, a peasant-caste Bengali writer who was more blunt about the pattern of Indian society than any Western critic, saw two classes vying for dominance. In his view, Indira represented an Anglicized, urban, upper middle class intent on preserving its privileged status far above that of most Indians. And the former Congress politicians who had wrested power from her belonged to an unsophisticated, rural, lower middle class that traditionally exploited small or landless peasants.

Nehru had tolerated this rustic class for the benefit of mutual political profit. Indira had curbed it, not out of a social consciousness on her part but an unwillingness to share power beyond her own family-oriented clique. She found Morarji particularly distasteful. Indeed, it would have been hard to find a more appropriate leader of the new ruling group with its old suspect roots than Desai, a kinsman of the rural Patels of Gujarat, the most prosperous kulaks in India. It would have been harder to find a more authoritarian-minded Brahmin for prime minister than the crochety octogenarian. But here is what Morarji, a smile hardly crinkling his eyes behind thick glasses, said within one month of taking office in a speech about economic planning in India:

In a free democratic country, the government is not run for the benefit of those who are running it, but for the benefit of the people, for giving them happiness, for giving them justice, for enabling them to be fearless ... We should not think that we know everything and have nothing to learn ...

The goods needed by every person in society can be more conveniently produced, more easily produced, and produced with much less capital, per capita or per man employed, in small and cottage industries than in the big factories ... Because of lopsided emphasis on heavy industry, though industries have grown, unemployment has also gone up. I do not think there can be more convincing proof than this of planning going astray ...

Considerable harm has been done to this country by the neglect of agriculture ... Unless we improve our agriculture, whatever we do is not going to give us happiness or a sense of fulfillment ... Our land can produce three times or even more what it is producing today ... But this can happen only if we help the small cultivator, who forms 70 per cent of our agriculturists, to increase production ...

In March a new kind of silent revolution came about in this country. It was a peaceful revolution. It was not merely an election and a change in government. The people have shown great capacity, farsightedness, and placed a trust in me and my colleagues and this trust has to be justified ... We have to make a change in our planning, its processes, and its implementation. But it must be a harmonious change. I do not want a violent change, because it is not possible to switch over immediately from one thing to the other. But the change must be quick. It should not again take, as it sometimes takes in many government transactions, endless time ... We have got to meet the hopes of the people. It is in the service of the people that we can derive more satisfaction than in anything else.

Morarji's statement was extraordinary for its lack of arrogance, its grasp of what had gone wrong and what needed to be put right, and above all its respect for ordinary Indians and their rising expectations. It combined wide-eyed realism, urgency, and a kind of mellowness – qualities usually not associated with an Indian ruling minority or, in the last case, with the stern Desai.

It would have been rash to assume that his promises were more likely of fulfillment than Indira's opportunistic pledge in 1971 to remove poverty. But Morarji struck a more humane, less contrived chord. His government quickly started moving toward his economic objectives as well as removal of all traces of the Emergency, and an international stance that did not inspire fear among India's neighbours and distrust in Washington. It is reasonable to believe that if the Janata government had received a fair chance and a full five-year term, it would have willingly put India on the road to essential economic reform thirteen or fourteen years before a minority Congress government did so out of desperation in 1991. In all likelihood it would have done so on a broader scale and with more popular support.

Even before euphoria over the Indian people's election victory faded, much of the international press treated the Janata government as an aberration and Morarji as some kind of a freak. Some foreign journalists seemed to resent not having the Nehru raj to report on any more. Almost all those who wrote about India's new prime minister discussed his vegetarian diet and supposed inclination to drink his own urine before getting briefly into his policies.

To me, Prime Minister Desai represented not only a new beginning for India but also an entree into a country I had been barred from visiting since January 1971. I'd technically, and hopefully, entered India on 16 June 1972 as an airline transit passenger with the intention of spending a few hours in Delhi. But officials had cancelled the arrival stamp in my passport when they checked my identity. They had forced me to spend twelve hours under guard in the airport, stifling at that time of year, before my outgoing flight.

I contacted Morarji through his trusted aide and my old friend V.Y. Tonpe. Although the leftist politicians and officials who had carried out Indira's vendetta against the press were gone, it took weeks for Indian bureaucracy to lift the ban and grant me an entry visa in June 1978. On 26 June, three years to the day after Indira's Emergency started and fifteen months after it ended, my wife Pat and I were excited but a little nervous as our plane, skimming over fields under monsoon clouds about to break, approached Delhi's airport. Once on the ground and officially admitted to India, we were relieved and waiting for our baggage when a policeman approached me and asked, "Are you David Van Praagh?" Instantly recalling my being surrounded at the airport in Madras in September 1970, and my being kept under guard at this same Delhi airport in June 1972, I pleaded guilty as my heart sank. But the tan-uniformed policeman did not eject or arrest me. Instead he smiled and promptly handed me a note that said I had an interview with Morarji the next day. It was the best welcome to India I ever had.

The buoyant mood I sensed among Indians was confirmed when we were ushered into the prime minister's office. Several officials sat around casually, not to record the interview or to make sure he didn't say the wrong thing but to hear what he did have to say. Morarji himself was positively jovial. When I recalled that I had interviewed him on several occasions in the past, he responded playfully, "But not when I was prime minister!" In contrast to his old stiff aloofness I had sometimes experienced, he didn't mind showing he could be a warm human being. When I turned on my recorder to tape part of the interview and it didn't work immediately, Morarji made a good-natured joke about foreign technology. Like a solidly built school teacher, he reiterated his goals for "the people," cited evidence of progress in reaching them, and emphasized India's intention to be a friendly Asian nation, partly by re-examining the Nehruvian policy reserving its right to become a nuclear power.

But it was not so much what Morarji said as the conviction with which he said it, and the apparent confidence and commitment that pervaded his government, that were at odds with the disenchantment starting to characterize the Indian press as well as foreign coverage of India. I was also favourably impressed by Foreign Minister Vajpayee, who in another friendly interview logically and informatively explained India's new positive regionalism and friendship with the West. Apparently other journalists were not listening to Janata leaders, or not hearing what they wanted to hear.

One hot and humid Delhi morning, we went to Indira's house. So did scores of Indians, mostly women, at a time when security at the homes of public figures in India was almost non-existent, and visitors could expect to have *darshan* (a personal audience) in due course. I had seen little point in making a written request for an interview in advance. Sending my card inside, I had no idea how Indira would react to the unexpected material-ization on her doorstep of a journalist she had banished from India. Once she came outside in a multicoloured sari and arranged a group of women for a photograph with her as if they were so many ducks in a row. While we were waiting, Sanjay strolled by in summer whites, his expressionless face as indifferent to others as ever. Presently we were summoned into the house.

Indira apparently had not remembered or even looked at the name of the foreign journalist asking to see her. But she immediately recognized me in person and started momentarily, as she had when she had last encountered me at the Delhi airport with Trudeau on 9 January 1971. Possibly because of Pat's presence, however, she graciously motioned for us to sit down on a sofa with her. I couldn't help recalling another time she had stared hard at me, after an interview in Toronto before she became prime minister, and thinking that perhaps my physical appearance reminded her of her late hus-band, Feroze Gandhi.

Whatever had happened in the past, Indira's gaze was set firmly on the future. Whatever stories I had written before that she didn't like, she made no attempt to hide her angling for one that would put her in a positive light. She went on for more than an hour about how Indian voters had been misled into voting against her, and how Morarji and the Janata government were betraying their trust. She blithely contended that the sterilization cam-paign had been wholly voluntary and shamelessly exaggerated, and that Sanjay was a "good boy" who had been repeatedly wronged. She cleverly brushed aside questions about a methodical denial of democracy and harsh imprisonment of political enemies during the Emergency. Indira gave the impression of taking us into her confidence, partly by revealing what seemed to be intimate family details, as she had once told me about per-sonal intrigues in the Congress Party. She nearly succeeded with me in gen-erating sympathy for her plight. When we left, I said to my wife, "She's not so bad after all." Pat, a journalist who was used to sob stories, retorted, "I can't believe you said that after all that's gone on and the way you've felt."

She was right, of course. Like the strand of white running provocatively back from Indira's forehead through her black hair, the former prime min-ister's charming side had made me temporarily forget the dark side of the woman who had reveled in being Empress of India. What was clear was that if she could no longer control journalists, she could convince them. She evidently was persuading others that somehow a historical mistake had been made in her being compelled to give up power, and in a government without Nehrus taking over. It was even clearer that she meant, through every device available to her, to rectify that unforgivable error in her eyes as soon as possible.

By the time I returned to India on 27 December 1979, Indira, astonishingly, had almost succeeded.

She had reaped favourable publicity beyond her wildest expectations when Morarji foolishly made a martyr of her by putting her in a jail cell briefly for her conviction on past election-law violations. Her suffering for a few days was trivial compared with the agony the thousands of Indians she had thrown into jail without charges or trial went through for months during her contrived Emergency. But she made the most of it, successfully turning back on Morarji the accusation of vindictiveness against her.

Indira's most lethal weapon, however, was the same one that had been used against her Congress Party in a number of states following the 1967 protest vote: defections by ambitious politicians who were then in a position to help form new governments. For this she had the perfect foil in the Janata home minister, Charan Singh, the leader of an Uttar Pradesh party of ex-Congress dissidents who had shown himself to be a master of political defection.

I had interviewed Charan Singh when he was chief minister of UP. As a Jat, a member of a caste of small farmers, he had expressed practical ideas about helping poor Indians. But a certain slyness seemed to substitute for any sense of moral principle. Indira knew just the man to go to when she felt the time was ripe to break up Morarji's Janata coalition.

Charan Singh withdrew his parliamentary support in the summer of 1979 with the aim of becoming prime minister himself, just as he had become chief minister of UP by depriving state governments of legislative majorities. With all eighty-five members of the Lok Sabha from UP belonging to his party, owing to the 1977 anti-Indira electoral sweep of the state, the rest of Janata was left without a majority in the lower house. Predictably, this led to the resignation of Morarji, whose sense of moral principle was stronger than ever. Charan Singh briefly became caretaker prime minister, supported by Congress (I) as part of his deal with Indira, betraying the millions of UP men and women who had voted to get rid of her and Sanjay.

But Charan Singh's party and hers combined did not make a Lok Sabha majority either. So Indira got what she wanted: calling of a new election less than three years into what should have been a five-year Janata term. Ironically, the president of India, N. Sanjiva Reddy, whom the Janata government had installed in that position after he had been defeated as the Congress candidate in 1969 by Indira's candidate, saw no choice but to dissolve Parliament, opening the way to her return to power.

All the major political events that have since happened in India flow from the unexpected and unnecessary breakup of the Janata government in 1979. For the first time, an Indian central government represented a coalition of different parties as well as a consensus of diverse interests. It did so more effectively than any government following it at least until 1999. In contrast to governments dominated or decisively influenced by the Nehrus, Janata's two and a half years of rule combined Gandhian idealism with Hindu culture, and the free enterprise of farmers and industrialists with Congress socialism. Possibly Janata could not have lasted long without a party at its centre stronger than a group of refugees from the Congress Party. But after the Indian people had miraculously escaped from their worst nightmare by freely breaking the bonds of Indira's Emergency, they lost their best opportunity to overcome their awesome problems. Everything that followed should not have been surprising. But it was often shocking.

Most Indian and foreign analysts blamed squabbling within Janata for its split. But dissension was less the cause than a result of manipulation by Indira, who proved as unscrupulous out of office as she had been in power. Morarji and his associates needed more time to bring India out from under the shadow of the Nehrus. Indira made sure they never got it.

In September 1979, when she and Charan Singh had succeeded in toppling Morarji, Indira peddled an old line in Bombay: "Unity and stability are the first requirements of the country – democracy comes later." This had been her smug rationale for imposing the 1975–77 Emergency and cancelling guaranteed human rights and freedoms. If Indians should have learned anything, it was that only through real democracy did they have a chance of finding social unity, political stability, and economic prosperity.

On 8 October, as if on cue, Jayaprakash Narayan finally died, mercifully without seeing an end to his dream but surely knowing it was coming. The practical genius Chakravarti Rajagopalachari, who like JP had turned away early from the catastrophic path the Nehrus were leading India down, was long since gone. Rajaji's old Swatantra colleague, Minoo Masani, demonstrated not classical liberalism as he claimed but hopeless naïveté, when he ostentatiously refused to choose between Janata and Indira after having refrained from endorsing the first promising alternative to the permit-licence raj. Morarji, once he was caught in the Indira-induced whirlpool of accusations and counter-accusations, ran out of chances as well as good humour, and did not even run in the new election. The Jan Sangh, once it was no longer covered by the Janata mantle, was on its way to flaunting Hindu chauvinism as the Bharatiya Janata Party.

Indians went to the polls during the first week of January 1980. An unexpected event in the neighbourhood drew much more worldwide attention: the Soviet invasion of Afghanistan beginning in the last week of December 1979. But I had come back for India's seventh parliamentary election, and I resisted the temptation to be overly distracted. This time, only 57 per cent of the electorate cast ballots, although for the first time more than 200 million Indians voted. With the non-Communist opposition hopelessly divided now into three groups, and two of them claiming the Janata name, Indira brought the Nehrus back into power with an ease that belied her family's seeming to have lost it for good in March 1977.

Her Congress (I) won only 42.7 per cent of the popular vote, one percentage point less than in 1971 but more than eight percentage points more than in 1977. It was enough to hand her an overwhelming majority of 353 seats in the 542-seat Lok Sabha, one more than in 1971. Indira and Sanjay breezed to victories in Rae Bareli and Amethi, respectively, with Raj Narain not challenging her again. The pro-Moscow Communists dropped to 5 seats and the Marxists rose to 29. As for the parties that had been proudly united and victorious in renewing democracy in India thirty-four months earlier, they were in total disarray: they could capture a total of only 85 seats with a combined 33.7 per cent of the popular vote. If Indira had needed the handy Charan Singh to form a government, she might have approached him again. But he had served his usefulness to her. She ignored the scheming turncoat who had brought down the Janata coalition at her bidding as much as she derided the loyalists who had bravely tried to use the coalition to take India into a brighter future.

The woman who had managed to drag India back to a dreary past was never more exultant. At an impromptu press conference outside her house, where I had listened to her plead for sympathy in July 1978, Indira poured scorn on her defeated opponents and jubilantly declared: "The voice of the people has finally been heard."

Her words clearly implied that the people of India had not truly spoken in 1977. But what she had said a few months earlier about democracy coming after other priorities contradicted her sudden expression of faith in the people. Many Indians expected Indira to reimpose the Emergency. But until the next crisis arose, it wasn't necessary for her to take extreme measures to have things all her own way once more.

Even before Indira was sworn in as prime minister again, bureaucrats in India's foreign ministry publicly condoned the Soviet seizure of Afghanistan. In so doing they correctly anticipated her position and disregarded criticism of Moscow by the Janata government in its last days. Considering the huge Soviet investment in Indira going back to 1966, Soviet troops seized control of the gateway to the Subcontinent in order to influence events in India as well as to sustain a shaky Communist regime in Afghanistan. Like the Russian Revolution in 1917, the period connecting their invasion and Indira's fresh triumph was "ten days that shook the world," or at least a good part of the world, at the beginning of the 1980s. Together, the two events mightily set back democratic development in South Asia and Central Asia.

The only defeat Indira suffered in 1980 was a bitter, personal one. In June, Sanjay Gandhi was killed when the stunt plane he was flying over Delhi with an instructor crashed. I happened to be in Nepal at the time and could easily pick up news of the tragedy over All-India Radio. The broadcasts reflected the anguish of a mother who had carefully groomed a son to take over her political responsibilities at the appropriate time, representing the third generation of family rule. By the time I went to India in the second half of July, it was clear that Indira was already preparing her elder son Rajiv for the political career he had avoided as an airline pilot. She wanted to be sure he could continue the Nehru dynasty in Sanjay's place when the time came. Again, her single-minded devotion to herself and her family, above the people and a free India, was on display for all to see.

When I returned to India in June 1981, Indira appeared more determined than ever to keep opposition parties out of power in every state capital as well as New Delhi. She had resumed her abuse of the constitutional device of president's rule, dismissing state governments not because they couldn't rule but because she wanted to give her followers an advantage, unfair or not. Her return to power had done nothing to bring economic dynamism to India, bound as it was by wasted decades of barely loosened red tape. The majority have-nots and the minority haves, and the tremendous gap between them, all continued to grow.

For my visits to India in mid-1980 and mid-1981, I was gratified but a little surprised when I had no trouble obtaining triple-entry visas even though Indira was back in power. A strange thing happened on my way to Delhi, however, on 23 June 1981.

As on 14 September 1970, I flew from Colombo to Madras that Friday to enter India. Nearly eleven years earlier, without a visa, I was surrounded at Madras airport by officials who told me I was barred on Indira's orders, and they forced me to fly to Singapore. Now I had a valid visa and had visited India three times since 1978. But no sooner had I landed than several officials intercepted me and, in a weird replay of the distant past although they were polite, ordered me to "take my seat" while they "checked with Delhi." Seized by a sickening sense of déjà vu, I explained what had happened back in 1970 and asked them to look at stamps in my passport as proof that I had been allowed back into India. An answer from Delhi on short notice on a late Friday afternoon was doubtful at best.

After twenty minutes, the officials returned and said the exclusion order signed by Indira was still on file at the airport but they had verified that it had been superseded and I could enter India. Had they really checked with Delhi by a means whose speed was utterly unknown to the public in India? Why was an eleven-year-old order still in effect, if it was, until it could be shown to be invalid? Had anything really changed? I was allowed to go on my way, but the incident was an eerie indication that Indira's power in the past still mysteriously applied in the present.

She faced no serious challenge in Parliament at that time in the absence of a coherent national opposition. But Indira not only insisted on the right of a single family to rule the vast country of India, she also demanded that the diversity of Indian civilization, as reflected in states more populous than most nations, conform to a political pattern she alone defined.

Compared with the federal systems of the United States, Canada, and other Western countries, the federalism of the Union of India has always leaned heavily toward the central government. Moreover, at first the nationally ruling Congress Party under Nehru held power in virtually all the states. Then the central government under Indira regularly wielded its power to intervene in state affairs through president's rule. In the early 1980s, Indira went one big step farther and attempted to do away almost entirely with political self-determination by India's states. Her support fell steadily in a number of states as she tried to impose her will on them, jeopardizing her chances of winning a new parliamentary election due by the beginning of 1985. What Indians called "the Punjab problem" was particularly acute.

Since the Raj, the Punjab had been divided twice. At independence the British-ordained partition giving East Punjab to India and West Punjab to Islamic Pakistan was bloody. Division of the Indian share into two states, Sikh-dominated Punjab and Hindu-dominated Haryana, was peaceful and, technically, not along religious but language lines, the determinant of most Indian states: the Punjabi language, while virtually identical to Hindi, uses a different script. But Sikh sectarian demands were behind the second split, and militant Sikhs continued to agitate for a separate nation of their own to be called Khalistan.

Conflict springing from communal, caste, or language differences or passions is not unusual in many parts of India. But the Punjab and the Sikhs have long held special importance. Both the proximity of the Punjab to Delhi – northwest of the capital along the Grand Trunk Road – and its prosperity due to the Green Revolution in growing wheat in its fertile fields have a major impact on India's politics and economy. Sikhism grew out of Hinduism, and Sikhs make up less than 2 per cent of India's population. But the religion has done away with caste, and Sikhs, spread throughout the country as well as concentrated in the Punjab, have demonstrated a rugged egalitarian self-reliance that has made them good farmers and soldiers and injected a certain toughness into Indian political culture. India cannot afford to lose the Punjab, its breadbasket and the historic homeland of a vibrant ethnic as well as religious minority.

Yet this danger loomed ominously as Indira blindly pursued her own objective in the intricacies of Punjabi politics. This was to manoeuvre her Congress Party into power at the expense of the Sikhs' traditional Akali Dal or Party of God. It was a foolhardy venture by Indian political criteria, which always are influenced by religious considerations, and unwise in the extreme in the volatile Punjab. It led to heavily armed Sikh separatists turning the Golden Temple, the heart of Sikhism in Amritsar, into a fortress under a fundamentalist preacher, Sant Jarnail Singh Bhindranwale.

In June 1984, Prime Minister Gandhi made the biggest mistake of her life. She ordered Indian army troops and tanks to assault the Golden Temple to search for and if necessary destroy the insurgents. Operation Blue Star 3–7 June, whatever the political and security motivations for it, was an unprecedented military invasion of a religious sanctuary in India: the holiest shrine of the Sikhs.

Militarily, it was successful. In every other way, it was a disaster. Approximately one thousand people were killed, including Bhindranwale, giving the Khalistan movement a martyr. Moderate Sikhs, the great majority, were deeply hurt by the armoured attack on the Akal Takht, which symbolizes the temporal authority of God. Many Sikh soldiers mutinied. Indians of all religions were shaken by what turned out to be the first in a series of profound blows cracking the country's secular foundation.

Operation Blue Star also activated two elements long present in the Punjabi Sikh psyche: desire for revenge no matter how long it takes, and a willingness to use assassination to achieve it. The classic example until 1984 came twenty-one years after the historic massacre of hundreds of defenceless Sikhs demonstrating for Indian independence at Jallianwala Bagh in Amritsar in 1919. In London in 1940, a Sikh shot and killed Sir Michael O'Dwyer, who as British governor of the undivided Punjab in 1919 had supported the action by Gurkha troops under the command of Brigadier-General Reginald Dyer, although later it was officially censured and Dyer was court-martialed.

Less than five months after Operation Blue Star, in New Delhi on Wednesday morning, 31 October 1984, Indira Nehru Gandhi, then sixty-seven, left her yellow stucco bungalow at No. 1 Safdarjung Road. She had moved back to the small house she was especially fond of when she became prime minister of India again at the beginning of 1980. She started to walk with a few aides to a nearby bungalow serving as an office, for a television interview with the actor Peter Ustinov. She never left her garden alive.

At 9:18 a waiting senior police bodyguard, a Sikh, drew his revolver and fired point-blank at her. Another police bodyguard, also a Sikh, fired a clip from his automatic weapon at her as she fell to the ground. Her slight body riddled with bullets, she died before anyone could come to her aid.

It was the first time a prime minister had been assassinated in India, and she had been prime minister for sixteen years in all. Whatever she had done to India, the cold-blooded murder of the woman all Indians knew as Indira was the most shocking event in the nation since a Hindu extremist had shot and killed Mahatma Gandhi in New Delhi on 30 January 1948.

Other policemen immediately captured the two Sikh assassins and hustled them into a guard room, where the senior one, Beant Singh, a converted former untouchable, was shot dead. The younger one, Satwant Singh, was also shot, but he survived to be questioned and to stand trial. There was no question, however, that the killing of Indira was revenge for the carnage at the Golden Temple of the Sikhs caused by Operation Blue Star.

Within hours, two more unprecedented events took place in New Delhi. Without consulting the Congress (I) Party as a whole or its parliamentary caucus, cabinet colleagues of the slain prime minister met and designated the inexperienced Rajiv Gandhi, forty and her surviving son, as her successor, and he was sworn in by President Zail Singh, a Sikh. On Rajiv's orders, the Congress (I) Party then secretly organized a massacre of innocent Sikh families in the capital that went on for three days and three nights.

As police stood by, up to 4,000 Sikhs were killed and 200,000 were made homeless as goondas burned their houses and shops. It was the worst wave of violence rooted in religious discrimination in India since the partition of the Punjab and independence in 1947. But the government instigated it instead of trying to stop it. Following Indira's military assault on the Golden Temple, in quick succession, her revenge assassination and the counter-revenge campaign of terror covertly mounted by Rajiv Gandhi, the nation's new prime minister, again shook India to its foundations.

A few days before her assassination, Indira had said in her last address to the Indian people: "I do not worry whether I live or not. As long as there is any breath in me, I will go on serving you. When I die, every single drop of my blood will give strength to India and sustain united India."

Many interpreted her words to mean that she had had a premonition of her violent end. When I learned of her death, I felt a sudden void and a disbelieving sorrow more painful than I would have rationally expected. Many Indians experienced similar feelings, only more so, and combined also with an inchoate fear for the future of their country. Instantly, they transferred their hopes for India and for themselves to Rajiv Gandhi. Weeks before the nation's eighth parliamentary election in late December

1984, he became in their hearts and minds a larger-than-life hero who had accepted the dreadful death of his mother with apparent calm and strength of character and could do no wrong himself.

The problem was that, except for the grief that overcomes human beings on the loss of a familiar figure, none of this made sense. It illustrated nothing but the transcendental accomplishment of the Nehrus in instilling the irrational belief in hundreds of millions of people that only one family could rule their lives. Considering that these same people had consciously and decisively rejected the Nehru dynasty seven and a half years earlier, this psychological feat was all the more extraordinary. It amounted to reducing Indians from individual thinking adults to regimented helpless children. The comparison may be unfair but the phenomenon was similar to the spell that Hitler cast on the German people.

Unless Indira had changed her very essence, there was no reason to believe she had given up fighting for what she deemed to be right, namely, perpetuation of India's ruling family, until her last, natural breath. Some saw her keeping her armed Sikh bodyguards when she was at grave risk of Sikh retaliation as a kind of death wish. Much more likely, it was an extreme form of hubris: her conviction that as a Nehru she was above or untouched by normal Indian concerns proved to be tragically fatal. As during the Emergency, she was presuming too much.

But the Rajivmania that swept over India when Indira miscalculated for the last time was even more deeply ironic. Not only was Rajiv wholly unprepared to be prime minister of India, his sudden and arbitrary elevation by the cabinet went against the tradition of broad consultation and democratic succession that seemed to have been established in India beginning with Nehru's death in office from natural causes in 1964. Rajiv's very first act as the nation's leader was to deliver a devastating blow to the "united India" that his mother had gravely undermined when she was alive. Indeed, the deliberate and vicious Congress (I) onslaught against the Sikhs, violent at first and then political during the election campaign, was reminiscent of organized Nazi terrorism and propaganda directed against the Jews in the pre-war years.

Indians throughout the country also presumed too much. They turned desperately to Rajiv to save India precisely at the moment the Nehrus, who for the seventh time should have been out of power, were tearing India to pieces.

When I returned to India on 24 December, it was in time to see an immaculately dressed Rajiv, standing far above an awed outdoor crowd on a heavily guarded platform, confidently address his last Delhi campaign rally. This time, soon after Indira's assassination, I had had trouble getting an

Indian entry visa for unexplained reasons. I had asked the newly established National Endowment for Democracy in Washington, D.C., for
which I was travelling to East Asian countries and India as Asia consultant,
to obtain it for me at the Indian Embassy in the United States.

What struck me in Delhi far more than the handsome figure of Rajiv and
the unusually quiet preparations for the elections was the sullenness of all
the Sikhs I encountered, from taxi drivers to professional men and their
wives. Smoke from the fires that had gutted Sikh homes and shops targeted
by Hindu goons employed by Rajiv's Congress Party (I) had long since
drifted away, and the bodies of Sikh men, women, and children stabbed,
clubbed, or burned by mobs were gone. But hurt and dismay remained in
the eyes and words of Sikhs whose infectious goodwill had helped define
the life of the capital. The pride of Sikhs as individuals had given way to
the fear of members of a scapegoat community. Intermarried Sikhs and
Hindus, common in Delhi, lived under the shadow of widespread Hindu
indictment of Sikhs as somehow un-Indian because they were too rich or
too smart or both.

Punjabi Sikhs did not get a chance to vote then because the government
declared their state and Assam in the northeast – scene of another armed
ethnic insurgency that had blossomed under Indira – too enflamed to allow
election of members of Parliament. In all other states but two, there was
virtually no contest.

Sixty-two per cent of eligible voters went to the polls, slightly above the
previous high of 61.3 per cent in 1967. For the first time, one party won 50
per cent of the popular vote – and the other 50 per cent went to an opposition that was more divided and dispirited than ever before. Rajiv's Congress
(I) amassed a record majority of 402 Lok Sabha seats. A total of only 105
seats went to other parties or independent candidates, and voting was not
held or was countermanded for 35 seats, including the Punjab's 13 and
Assam's 14. A language-based state party, Telugu Desam of the southern
state of Andhra, became the largest opposition party in the Lok Sabha with
28 seats. Only one other opposition party won more than 4 seats from one
state: the Communist Marxists with 18 from West Bengal. Candidates running under the Janata banner were virtually wiped out. With Hindus in the
north voting heavily for Congress (I) and its blatantly communal message,
the Hindu nationalist Bharatiya Janata or Indian People's Party, running for
the first time in place of the Jan Sangh, captured only 2 seats with 7.4 per
cent of the popular vote. In Amethi in UP, Sanjay Gandhi's old district, his
brother Rajiv easily defeated his widow Maneka Gandhi; a Congress slogan
used against her was: "She is the daughter of a Sikh – a nation of traitors."

A popular wave of sympathy for Rajiv and foreboding for India swept
all else before it. He overwhelmingly won the parliamentary election his

mother might well have lost. As the magazine *India Today* put it: "He seemed to have stepped straight out from the stars, the Peter Pan of Indian politics ... The youth, the looks, the idealism, the dynamism."

That was in November 1989, near the end of Rajiv's five-year term as prime minister with a larger parliamentary majority than his mother or even his grandfather had enjoyed. The cover story was headlined "The Promise That Failed." *India Today* continued: "The transformation in Rajiv Gandhi is so vivid and so drastic that five years now seem a lifetime ... [The] real Rajiv [is] a hard-headed politician in the mold of his late mother, opportunistic, uncaring of public opinion, disdainful of political propriety."

Other responsible Indian newspapers, magazines, analysts, and ordinary men and women made the same kind of appalled comments by then. What had gone wrong? To be fair, the "transformation" was partly in perceptions of Rajiv. But the man himself changed under the pressures of public office and critical exposure by Indian journalists, who in many cases made up for their cowardice in not challenging Indira during the Emergency. Rajiv had made a conscious decision to stay out of politics, to remain on the periphery as a cleancut airline pilot. When the untimely deaths of first Sanjay and then Indira thrust him into Indian politics at their apex, Rajiv reverted to family type. He showed he was a Nehru. In addition to repeating his mother's mistakes and biases, he also provided another reason the dynasty was unfit to govern India: his alleged involvement in corruption.

Rajiv seemed at first to be a modern-minded man who could bring about technological breakthroughs in India. He was like Sanjay in this respect, but possessed the kind of outward charm his younger brother had hardly been noted for. Interestingly, this image never faded in the West as it did in India. While Rajiv talked about economic liberalization and achieved some cosmetic reforms, in reality nothing changed. India was locked as tightly into bureaucratic gridlock and sterile de facto alliance with the Soviet Union under him as it had been under Indira and Jawaharlal.

But the two mistakes of Indira that Rajiv most prominently duplicated had to do with the Sikhs and the press. He waged war on both. Moreover, he unintentionally created dangerous tensions between Hindus and Muslims, partly by making the disputed mosque at Ayodhya – later destroyed by BJP-encouraged fanatics – a much larger issue than it needed to be. Rajiv's running battle with major newspapers was both a result and a cause of the allegations of India's biggest corruption scandal. Unlike his mother, he lost his feud with journalists.

From the beginning to the end of his political career of less than seven years, Rajiv could not escape the Sikh issue. For one thing, he was under heavy guard day and night against another revenge assassination, and this prevented him from coming into contact with ordinary Indians until near the end. But his role in the retaliation against Delhi Sikhs for Indira's murder was never publicly acknowledged. This helped him make a deal with Punjabi Sikhs in July 1985, just six months after his election, that survived the assassination of the Akali Dal leader who signed it, and let the Akalis take power in a state election. But then Rajiv got cold feet because he feared the award to the Punjab of the modern city of Chandigarh, designed by the French architect Corbusier and until then the joint capital of Haryana and the Punjab, would alienate the Hindus of Haryana. As it turned out, cancelling the agreement didn't help him with Haryana's voters or those of more crucial Hindi-speaking states. It hurt him with the Sikhs, and his imposing president's rule on the Punjab in mid-1987 angered them even more.

This set up another perilous Golden Temple scenario. Sikh separatists again turned the sacred shrine in Amritsar into an armed fortress. Operation Black Thunder was Delhi's response this time. It was carried out in May 1988 not by the army but by the police, commanded by a tall, white-bearded, cold-blooded Sikh officer named K.P.S. Gill. He estimated that only 30 people were killed in forcing the surrender of the separatists, who were shown to have desecrated the Golden Temple themselves. At least 22,000 people died in attacks on civilians by armed Sikh extremists and in a later, ruthless, counter-terrorist campaign run by Gill that broke the back of the separatist movement in the Punjab. But Rajiv refused to allow a state election that would have let Akali Dal moderates come back to power. He suffered the consequences in the next parliamentary election, when nine of the thirteen Punjab seats were won by Sikh militants, including the widow and the father of Beant Singh, one of Indira's assassins, and a senior police officer facing charges of involvement in her murder.

Rajiv demonstrated no more sensitivity, backbone, or political savvy in what was called the Shah Bano case. This eventually led to the deep crisis in Hindu-Muslim relations over Ayodhya. It also marked the first time the Indian press went after a prime minister with a doggedness it had never shown before.

In 1986 the Supreme Court of India struck a blow for women's rights by ruling that a divorced Muslim woman was entitled to maintenance by her former husband under Indian law, and the period of support should not be limited to the three months prescribed by Islamic tradition. The ruling Congress (I) Party welcomed the decision. Muslim religious organizations howled in protest. That was enough for Rajiv to decide that the "fundamentalist position made better sense for the Congress." The government introduced a bill in Parliament absolving a Muslim man of all responsibilities to his former wife upon divorce. A progressive male Muslim member of Rajiv's cabinet resigned. *The Economic and Political Weekly* commented: "The bill is ill-considered, retrograde and anti-woman ... [it focuses] attention on the Rajiv Gandhi style of government – undemocratic, hasty, confused and ... irresponsible."

When the bill was passed, Rajiv thought he would make amends by allowing Hindus to worship at the Ayodhya mosque, which they believe stood on the birthplace of the Hindu god Ram. That was enough to bring a back-burner issue to the front burner. Rajiv later made matters even worse with both Muslims and Hindus by first permitting a Hindu organization to lay the foundation stone of a temple at Ayodhya, then preventing construction from going ahead.

The first clear indication of Rajiv's distrust of India's free press despite its earlier adulation of him also emerged in 1986. A report by a commission headed by Supreme Court Justice M.P. Thakkar inquiring into Indira's assassination normally would have been laid before Parliament as a public document. It described a possible conspiracy and lapses in security and intelligence. The prime minister had his Lok Sabha majority pass a measure allowing his government to keep the report secret.

His reputation for inappropriate conduct grew in 1987 when, at a press conference, he angrily fired the seniormost career official in the foreign ministry, A.P. Venkateswaran, for supposedly overstepping his bounds during a visit to Pakistan. Rajiv's breach of etiquette shocked the entire civil service. One of India's most respected analysts, Romesh Thapar, wrote: "What is happening suggests an unconscious wrecker at work, a person who imagines that he and his family are here to rule over some private property."

In March 1987, *The Indian Express*, which along with *The Statesman* had been the sharpest journalistic thorn in Indira's side during the Emergency, published a letter purportedly written by the Sikh president of India, Zail Singh, to the prime minister. In it Singh disputed Rajiv's assertion in the Lok Sabha that he was keeping the president informed about affairs of state. Indira had always made sure her man in Rashtrapati Bhavan did what she wanted but she had briefed him regularly, as a British prime minister briefs and may consult Queen Elizabeth II. The possibility of a rift between Rajiv and the president, and the intrusion of the press into normally confidential precincts, were obviously explosive.

The matter was never publicly resolved. But police raided the home of Ramnath Goenka, proprietor of *The Indian Express* and long-time critic of the Nehru family, and arrested the newspaper's financial adviser. The latter was charged with violating the Official Secrets Act – another British legacy – by writing an earlier series of articles alleging that Rajiv's government had granted questionable concessions to a suspect textile company called Reliance Industries. Few believed the government's explanation that it had acted against *The Indian Express* because of the Reliance case and not the Zail Singh issue.

President Singh was not finished making waves, and the next time he did so directly instead of through a leaked letter. Rajiv steamrolled a measure through Parliament innocuously entitled the Indian Post Office (Amendment) Bill. It merely gave the central and state governments the authority to intercept, detain, and destroy any books, periodicals, newspapers, and private mail going through the post office. The legislation opened a back door to the kind of arbitrary controls Indira's censors had exercised during the Emergency. *The Economic Times* of Bombay warned: "The assumption of such powers leads to the violation of a fundamental right ... namely the freedom of expression."

Zail Singh apparently thought so, too. He returned the bill to Rajiv's government, unsigned, for "reconsideration." Never before had a president of India shown the independence to do what he had every constitutional right to do: reject "advice" from the government of the day that he considered unsound. The Post Office Bill was never reintroduced.

In the course of 1987, the year marking forty years of India's independence, three scandals broke and spread. They threw into doubt as never before the integrity of a central government and opened a new phase in the country's contorted political evolution. They sounded the death knell of the last phase of the Nehru dynasty.

The first scandal began as an apparent offshoot of the *Indian Express*–Reliance affair. The government produced a letter from an official of a private American investigating firm named Fairfax saying the newspaper's proprietor Goenka and a rival Bombay textile magnate had hired Fairfax to verify foreign bank accounts belonging to the owner of Reliance and other wealthy individuals close to Rajiv. Indians are legally barred from depositing money abroad. The letter was a forgery. Finance Minister Vishwanath Pratap Singh admitted in Parliament that it was he who had hired Fairfax as part of an investigation of alleged economic criminals. His admission amounted to an open declaration of war on Rajiv by the second most powerful person in his government.

V.P. Singh withstood a torrent of criticism within the ruling party. As a veteran Congressman with a reputation for probity, he recognized that the prime minister was politically vulnerable but faced no challenge from an opposition figure of stature. Rajiv moved him from finance to the defence ministry, where V.P. Singh promptly launched another investigation. This one resulted in the second scandal: charges that persons high in government had received illegal kickbacks from the purchase of four German submarines for the Indian navy.

In April V.P. Singh was forced to resign from the cabinet, and the third and biggest scandal erupted. A Swedish radio correspondent reported that Bofors, the huge arms manufacturer in Sweden, had paid kickbacks and large sums of money into Swiss bank accounts to make sure that Indian political leaders and defence officials approved a contract for selling how-itzers to the Indian army. Newspapers in India, especially *The Indian Express* and *The Hindu* of Madras, took up the story from there. They could not prove the involvement of Rajiv or any of his close associates, given the stonewalling by Bofors, Swiss banks, and the Indian and Swedish governments. But investigative journalism came into its own in India with a relentless stream of embarrassing exposés. Rajiv Gandhi's denials, like Nixon's in Watergate, fed widespread suspicions that he was covering something up and steadily eroded his popular support.

But it was his instinctive desire to retaliate against the press, inherited from his mother, that more than anything else convicted Rajiv in the court of public opinion. Paranoid about journalists and political opponents in and out of his party ganging up on him, he introduced legislation in Par-liament in 1988 transforming India's libel law into a government weapon. The Defamation Bill shifted the burden of proof from a person claiming he had been libelled to the newspaper printing an allegation. Editors would be required to attend secret summary judicial hearings anywhere in the coun-try; they would need to present original documents as proof; and they would be subject to imprisonment if found guilty of wrongly accusing a person of a criminal offence such as accepting illegal kickbacks. It was an Emergency measure without the emergency. India's press exploded into indignant protest.

The Hindu termed the Defamation Bill an "insult to the collective intel-ligence of the people." *The Hindustan Times* of Delhi asserted that it "bla-tantly goes against freedom of expression and of the press." *The Indian Express* declared that it was designed to "intimidate the press into silence." Even the pro-government *Times of India* said that it "reveals the totalitar-ian temptation lurking beneath the surface of Indian democracy." On 6 September journalists throughout India went on strike for one day against the bill. *The Statesman*'s editor, Sunanda K. Datta-Ray, observed later: "The bill was a retrograde measure ... and it was intolerable to the Indian people."

Indian journalists did themselves proud in getting up off the floor where Indira had knocked them cold during the Emergency. They fought back like American journalists do when the latter believe the First Amendment is in peril, or like they did against Nixon during Watergate. More than Vish-wanath Pratap Singh, who moved into a vacuum waiting to be filled, jour-nalists delivered the decisive blow to Rajiv once they thought they had a "smoking gun." Three weeks after the Lok Sabha adopted the Defamation Bill during the August monsoon session, the government announced that it would not be enacted into law.

Rajiv nevertheless continued to harass his main journalistic tormentors. He never seemed to learn that this only drove the press and the otherwise weak political opposition into each other's arms against him, particularly when he accused them of having foreign backers. Indira had often resorted to this ploy, and had sometimes mentioned the CIA by name, but this was only one of her many ways to keep journalists and opposition politicians in disarray. When V.P. Singh inevitably broke with Congress (I) – the *I* never disappeared, as if Indira personally still controlled the party – for Rajiv the handwriting was on the wall.

In the parliamentary election in December 1989, Congress (I) under Rajiv lost more than half its Lok Sabha seats, capturing only 197 with 39.5 per cent of the popular vote. V.P. Singh, having stolen the halo of incorruptibility from Indira's surviving son, led a party called the Janata Dal – another name for People's Party, and made up of recent and past defectors from the Congress – to victory in 143 districts with 17.8 per cent of the popular vote. The BJP, capitalizing on its appeal to Hindus with Congress (I) again on the defensive, made its first big gains, taking 85 seats in northern states with 11.4 per cent of the popular vote. Communist parties increased their total of seats to 45. For the first time in independent India's history, no one party came close to winning a majority of Lok Sabha seats.

But non-Communist opposition groups including state parties had made election deals to oust Rajiv, and they united after the vote to make the crusading V.P. Singh prime minister at the age of fifty-eight. A chastened Rajiv assumed the unaccustomed position of opposition leader, and the role of spoiler his mother had played to perfection following her election defeat. It was the eighth time the Nehrus should have been out of power. But unlike the Janata Party in 1977, the alternative to Congress (I) as the 1990s dawned lacked the coherence to last in power, even without being undermined.

Instead of digging deeper into the corruption scandals that had brought Rajiv down, or undertaking needed economic reforms, V.P. Singh tried to create a meaningful identity for his government by helping low-caste Hindus get government jobs. His version of affirmative action aimed to raise the economic levels of some poor Indians. But it also played caste politics and underlined the role of bloated bureaucracy in Indian life. In August 1990, the prime minister set aside 27 per cent of central government positions for members of low castes, in addition to the 22 per cent already reserved for dalits and members of tribal groups. With nearly half of these sought-after jobs no longer awarded on merit, high-caste Hindus demonstrated emotionally in many north Indian cities and towns, and some youths even committed suicide. The V.P. Singh strategy not only aggravated serious divisions in Indian society, but also backfired politically.

The new prime minister was seeking to head off a rival in the Janata Dal named Devi Lal. An elderly Jat from Haryana, Lal threatened to turn on V.P. Singh, as Charan Singh had stabbed Morarji Desai in the back. But it was another ambitious ex-Congressman, Chandra Shekhar, who was enticed by Rajiv into betraying V.P. Singh. As a Congress "Young Turk," Chandra Shekhar had been a willing tool of Indira's in her smear campaign against Morarji, and for his pains had been jailed by her at the outset of the Emergency. On 6 November 1990, however, he again put himself at the service of the Nehru family by leading a revolt of fifty-six Janata Dal members of the Lok Sabha. The eleven-month-old government headed by V.P. Singh fell on a vote of non-confidence.

Rajiv rewarded sixty-three-year-old Chandra Shekhar by briefly extending Congress (I) support for his becoming prime minister, just as Indira at no cost to herself had paid back Charan Singh for subverting the Janata Party government. But if the Nehru family's destabilizing a ruling coalition was old hat, another disturbing political phenomenon was new. The BJP also withdrew its support for the hapless V.P. Singh, because police had fired on and killed dozens of party militants taking part in a chariot march on the Ayodhya mosque in late October. If he could appeal to low-caste Hindus, the BJP – elated by fervid popular response to television dramatizations of the Hindu epics Ramayana and Mahabharat – could make a pitch not just to members of high castes as in the past but to all Hindus.

One horrifying event obscured the shifting tectonics of Indian politics and culture as well as the results of a new parliamentary election in late May 1991, less than a year and a half after the last election, and following Chandra Shekhar's resignation in March. It was the assassination of Rajiv Gandhi on the night of 21 May as he was campaigning in Tamil Nadu.

Unlike his mother, who in her last moments may have glimpsed her Sikh assassins and their guns, he never knew who or what killed him. A woman suicide bomber approached Rajiv, then forty-six, and literally blew him up along with herself as he prepared to address a Congress (I) rally he had almost been unable to attend. She was not a Sikh separatist but an agent of the secessionist Tamil Tigers of Sri Lanka, who deeply resented the Indian troops whom Rajiv as prime minister had dispatched to their island in 1987 as "peacekeepers." Expected to side with the minority Hindu Tamils against the majority Buddhist Sinhalese, the since departed Indian soldiers had engaged in bloody fighting against the radical Tigers.

Suddenly the last political Nehru, or the man who seemed to be the last political Nehru, was gone. Again Indians were deeply shocked, only six and a half years after Indira's assassination. Because Rajiv had met his awful end in the south, many people in that part of the country were especially sympathetic. But reaction in much of the rest of the world suggested that India itself had come or was coming to an end. Few non-Indians seemed to remember that Rajiv was no longer prime minister, and hardly anyone that he had been implicated in major corruption and sectarian strife when he was.

Mark Tully, the BBC correspondent in Delhi, later wrote that he had had to contend with "experts in London" who were sure Indian democracy had died along with Rajiv. My former newspaper, *The Globe and Mail* of Toronto, ran a banner headline across the top of the front page: "Gandhi Assassinated." That headline would have been appropriate the morning after the Mahatma's death in 1948, but not on 22 May 1991 following the murder of a Nehru. When I did a TV commentary in Canada, I said the deaths of both Rajiv and Indira were tragic partly because they grew out of conditions the two generations of the Nehru dynasty had largely created.

Rajiv had been optimistic on the election trail. He had shaken off his heavy security detail, letting him come into physical contact with ordinary Indians for the first time. Without adequate protection, he was vulnerable to a fatal attack. But he had used up the store of goodwill the Indian people had given him when his mother was killed. If he had lived, there was little chance he would have repeated Indira's miracle and led the Congress (I) to a comeback victory or even to a place in a coalition government. The Hindus in India's northern Hindi-speaking heartland had become too alienated from the Nehru raj for that to happen. It was mainly because of sympathy in the south following the assassination in Tamil Nadu that the Hindu revivalist BJP did not score a bigger electoral breakthrough than it did. Only this southern support allowed a stunned Congress Party to form a shaky minority government without the Nehru family for the first time.

Many distraught Congressmen found the prospect of a party without Nehrus so inconceivable that they had begged Rajiv's grieving widow Sonia, an Italian woman and a Roman Catholic who had no connection to India except through her marriage, to become their leader. Nothing could have better illustrated the bankruptcy of the party that had won and consolidated India's independence. Nothing did until 1998 and 1999, when Sonia Gandhi actually did become Congress leader and ran in effect for prime minister in two elections.

In 1991, it was only because of the coincidence of India's economic bankruptcy that the new Congress government found a platform to stand on. Jawaharlal Nehru, his daughter Indira Gandhi, and her son Rajiv Gandhi would not have approved of even its hesitant economic reforms. Many party members still shared their doctrinaire socialist views. Rajiv's assassination was the ninth time the Nehrus should have been out of power. For India's sake, I hope it stays this way. But India had not escaped their ideas, or even the absurd notion that Rajiv's widow, Sonia, or their daughter Priyanka, who bears a close resemblance to Indira, or their son Rahul would take over some day. Indian democracy did not die with Rajiv. The Nehrus, including Rajiv, came close to killing it. They might yet succeed if India does not find the common sense and the energy to make a lasting, clean break with them.

The Congress (I) share of the popular vote in the May 1991 election dropped to 36.6 per cent, not much higher than the party's record low of 34.5 per cent in 1977 after the ravages of the Emergency. It won 226 Lok Sabha seats, more than the 197 it had captured in 1989 with 39.5 per cent of the popular vote, but significantly short of a majority. Only 58 of these seats came from the Hindi belt, its traditional stronghold, where 225 seats were on the line. But of 129 seats at stake in South India, Congress (I) took an unusually high 86, including all 28 it contested in Tamil Nadu, the scene of Rajiv's assassination.

In contrast, the BJP nearly doubled its share of the popular vote to 20 per cent compared with its performance in 1989. Never before had a distinct opposition party with no Congress dissidents done nearly so well. It won 117 seats, a big gain over its 85 in 1989, and a huge one over its 2 seats in the 1984 election. Of these, 81 were from the Hindi-speaking north, where the party did not fare better only because of low-caste support for the Janata Dal, especially in Bihar. In the south, despite the Rajiv sympathy vote, the BJP became a factor for the first time, taking 5 seats. V.P. Singh's Janata Dal could capture only 56 seats overall, for a staggering loss of 87, with 11.3 per cent of the popular vote. The Communist parties won 48 seats with their usual share of roughly 9 per cent of the popular vote.

When Sonia Gandhi had the good sense to say "No" as the shattering election campaign came to a close, the Congress (I) Party unenthusiastically chose as its new leader P.V. Narasimha Rao, a veteran Brahmin politician from the southern state of Andhra, who at the age of seventy-one suffered from a heart condition. After the voting, Rao was able to enlist enough members of small parties to be reasonably sure of bare majority support in the Lok Sabha, and he became, if Indira is counted twice, India's tenth prime minister. Later, through conversions and by-elections, his party attained a razor thin majority. More important, the taciturn Rao brought in a non-political Sikh bureaucrat, Manmohan Singh, as finance minister to initiate and implement economic liberalization. But their reforms were too long overdue and not nearly broad enough to bring quick or lasting benefits to poor Indians. And more urgent forces were changing India's political arithmetic.

As the next parliamentary election, due by May 1996, approached, the Congress Party remained unsteady as it underwent new divisions and defections. Prime Minister Rao appeared more and more indecisive, and no vigorous younger leader was in sight. The Janata Dal, the only non-Communist, non-Hindu opposition by any name, was pushed almost as much to the fringe of Indian politics as the Communist parties. That left the BJP.

The Hindu nationalists could not yet claim to be a national party. They suffered reverses in some state elections after the 1991 vote, partly because people were frightened by the new hammer blows at Indian secularism represented by destruction of the Ayodhya mosque in December 1992 and the anti-Muslim violence that followed. But under the leadership then of Lal Krishna Advani, whom some considered a comparative moderate and others a dangerous extremist, the BJP held out the shining promise of a Hindu raj to the hungry majority of Indians who had been consistently deprived under the Nehrus. Many Hindus not only had seen pledges of prosperity and democracy broken but also, as Advani claimed, had come to feel like second-class citizens in their own land.

India's contradictions and dilemmas were plain when I returned in January 1992 – with a five-year entry visa! – to try and put them in some kind of perspective. How to resolve these perplexing problems was not. With Indira Gandhi's Emergency behind them, at least the vast majority of Indians were not contemplating the kind of autocratic answers that the leaders of China and other East Asian countries, Communist and non-Communist, arbitrarily enforced. In their own anarchic, slow-motion way, they had been a large part of the post–Second World War global democratic revolution from the very beginning. One couldn't say Indian democracy always worked. But it was possible to say that the people, soon one billion of them, were the biggest plus India had.

In 1992, they had been through ten parliamentary elections, and who knows how many state elections. They had sat in the dust of tens of thousands of election rallies, listened to candidates of a bewildering array of parties make promises, and then decided whom to trust and whom not to trust. They had been deeply disillusioned, they had been badly betrayed, and once in a while they had been modestly rewarded. The people had it in their power to give a Congress Party without Nehrus more time to deliver, or to entrust India's future and their own to a Hindu party claiming to reflect the Indian soul. Or they could go off in different directions, depending on what religious faith they followed, what caste or sub-caste they belonged to, or what language they spoke. Whatever they did, the people of India would do it in their own time: if not in the 1996 election, then in an election or two or three later, or by resorting to non-democratic methods.

Mohandas Gandhi taught Indians not to resort to violence. How well politicians absorbed his message about this and other essentials may be gauged by a *Times of India* cartoon some years ago. Laxman, the country's most cutting political cartoonist, depicted a stout Congressman in a Gandhi cap trying to figure out the identity of a familiar figure in a framed portrait. The little *babu* or clerk, who is Laxman's trademark, whispers in the Congressman's ear: "Gandhiji, sir." Tragically, most Indian politicians – not all – have forgotten Gandhiji: his lessons about giving the people a real say, building the country from the village up, and communal harmony as well as non-violence. The last is reasonably assured only if the others come to pass.

Panditji – Jawaharlal Nehru – his daughter, Indiraji, and her sons, Sanjay and Rajiv, blocked natural political evolution in all India and its many distinct parts, and devalued democratic elements that were not Indian to begin with in order to keep their self-created dynasty in power. They wasted four decades of the people's lives by tightening the screws of Soviet-style central planning and bureaucratic ineptitude. When popular discontent flowed inevitably from the Nehrus' political and economic blunders, Indira and Rajiv encouraged dissension among religious communities and even indulged in organized violence themselves. One wonder was not that the BJP with its inherently anti-Muslim message had attracted wide support but that the pro-Hindu party had not disavowed the democratic route to power.

By carrying out in 1977 what Morarji Desai called "a new kind of silent revolution," the Indian people revived democracy as a viable option. India showed then it was not Indira – or Morarji, or even JP, or any other individual, family, or party. Rajaji understood this in trying to build a broad non-Communist alternative to the Nehrus. Lal Bahadur Shastri knew that only better living conditions for peasant families ultimately sustain democracy in a developing country. When I saw Morarji in Bombay in January 1985, he shook my hand with a firmness suggesting a younger Gandhian who has never lost faith in the future, not a defeated warrior about to turn eighty-nine. He died in Bombay on 10 April 1995 at the age of ninety-nine, still fighting for life. But many perils have always confronted India, including a plethora of lesser nationalisms within her bosom. They are sure to grow if, to recall Desai's words, the great capacity of the people to employ democratic methods is ignored, if their trust is betrayed, and if the silent revolution fails.

12

The Only Option

Indian popular protest against the Congress Party, still linked with Nehrus who were no longer living, entered a new stage with the eleventh parliamentary election in April–May 1996. Indeed, political developments, moves, counter-moves, embarrassments, and denouements in the year and a half before the fiftieth anniversary of India's independence in August 1997, and the six years after it, marked the beginning of India's redefinition. They reflected glaring and possibly fatal weaknesses but also abiding and possibly saving strengths.

More than 340 million voters – 57.9 per cent of the 590 million eligible – cut Congress strength fully in half in the 545-seat Lok Sabha, from 271 seats (including 45 secured after the 1991 election) to 136. In contrast to the heydays of Jawaharlal Nehru, Indira Gandhi, and Rajiv Gandhi, when levels of less than half the popular vote produced large parliamentary majorities, the prevailing political arithmetic worked against Congress candidates. Although they had prudently gone back to running under the Indian National Congress banner rather than the *I* for Indira designation, they captured only a quarter of the seats with 28.8 per cent of the popular vote, compared to 36.6 per cent in the 1991 election. Both the Congress seat total and percentage of the popular vote were record lows. India's voters inflicted devastating defeat on a party that until recently had assumed victory as a matter of right and still identified itself with India's independence struggle.

Conversely, the 1996 election marked another historic but not yet decisive leap forward for the Hindu nationalist Bharatiya Janata Party. From 117 seats won in the 1991 election, when it would have taken more were it not for the pro-Congress southern sympathy vote following Rajiv's assassination, it zoomed to 185 with its allies, including the fascist-like Shiv Sena's 15 Maharashtra seats. Although the BJP's share of the popular vote rose only by three-tenths of 1 per cent to 20.3 per cent and its strength was still concentrated in four northern states plus Delhi and Bombay, it captured a third of the seats, far more than any other party. This was nearly 90 seats short of a majority. But for the first time Hindu revivalists, who once had assaulted the gates of Parliament, threatened the secular foundation of India's federal constitutional democracy from within Parliament.

The third force in Parliament was heavily weighted to the left. It had grown out of Vishwanath Pratap Singh's Janata Dal, which had ousted Rajiv and the Congress at the polls in 1989 but had stumbled in the 1991 election. The National Front–Left Front, a loose coalition of thirteen parties, won 20 per cent of the popular vote and 125 seats or 23 per cent of the total, although some members later defected, compared to 96 seats in the last Lok Sabha. The Janata Dal held 46 of the 125 – down from 56 – the Marxist Communists 33 and the pro-Moscow Communists 12. Unlikely ever to gain a majority on its own, the NF-LF permitted the kind of coalition politics that would have been healthy in New Delhi as well as state capitals nearly three decades earlier but was too late now to bring about quick, badly needed positive change.

A few other figures told more about the political climate in Delhi and throughout India than seat totals or voting percentages. Far more than the unpopularity in some quarters of the P.V. Narasimha Rao government's economic reforms, the figures explained the sharp Congress setback and the failure of both the BJP and the NF-LF to take fuller advantage.

When voters went to the polls, sixty-five top politicians were under investigation for corruption, including seven Congress ministers in the central government, BJP leader Lal Krishna Advani, and the Janata Dal president, Laloo Prasad Yadav. Rao, the increasingly remote prime minister, now seventy-four, was suspected of official wrongdoing. With few signs of responsibility or morality among politicians and bureaucrats, the Supreme Court of India had taken it upon itself to play a more powerful role in the pursuit of justice. The people of India were fed up with most of their political leaders, and cynical about the whole political process.

It was against this dark background that intrigues and manoeuvres began with the purpose of forming a new government out of the most fragmented political picture ever to emerge in Delhi. Fragmentation was nothing new in virtually all the states of the Indian Union, ever since the Congress Party began to fall apart in 1967. As prime minister, Indira Gandhi had encouraged or even ensured fragmentation once the Congress could no longer dominate most states on its own. But except for Morarji Desai's underestimated Janata Party government in 1977–79 after two years of Indira's vindictive Emergency rule, and the Janata Dal government in 1989–91 as a reaction to Rajiv's apparent and alleged abuses, the Congress had always easily formed a government by itself at the "centre" after winning an undisputed parliamentary majority or, in 1991, coming close to doing so. The stranglehold in Delhi, like the fragmentation in the states, was due to the baneful influence of the Nehru dynasty.

After the 1996 election, however, the best the Congress could do was hold the balance of power by giving a temporary working majority to an NF-LF government. Being Congressmen and women, party members assumed this would soon lead to their coming back to power. Despite the clear thumbs-down message from the voters, they unanimously re-elected Rao as leader of the Congress caucus. Showing no intention of even moving out of the prime minister's official residence, he left no doubt he shared their expectation.

The first task was to prevent the BJP from coming to power. The good reason was that it menaced Indian secularism. The real reason was that it put in peril the notion of the Congress ever again forming a government. But a deal providing Congress support for an NF-LF government proved impossible to reach in days and nights of haggling. Many leftists wanted Rao out as a condition of their entering into an alliance with the Congress, and Rao refused to leave. Moreover, NF-LF members had trouble choosing a leader who would become prime minister with Congress backing.

V.P. Singh declined on the ground that he was ill with leukemia. Jyoti Basu, the longtime Marxist Communist chief minister of West Bengal, now eighty-one and as tough as ever, teased MPs with a Hamlet-like perfor-mance – seeming to covet and abhor the leadership at the same time – and probably would have been elected if his party's politburo had not turned down the idea. Apart from what the world would have thought of a radi-cal Communist as prime minister of India, Basu certainly knew he would not have had the clout that he and his party had once pursued in a leftist united front government with Indira that came close to fruition before her first electoral triumph in 1971.

The NF-LF finally chose as its leader a political nonentity unknown to most Indians. He was H.D. Deve Gowda of the Janata Dal, an amiable sixty-three-year-old farmer from a dominant peasant caste who had been in national politics only three years before serving as chief minister of the southern state of Karnataka, formerly Mysore, for sixteen months.

But the president of India, Shankar Dayal Sharma, an old Congress warhorse, had no choice but to invite the leader of the party with the most seats in the Lok Sabha to form a government. On 16 May, Atal Bihari Vaj-payee, seventy, the avuncular leader of the BJP, his white hair contrasting with a saffron scarf around his neck, took the oath in Hindi rather than English as the eleventh prime minister of India (if Indira is counted twice). He had taken over from the still active Advani earlier in 1996 because the latter was under investigation in the corruption scandal, and in order to soften the party's image. As foreign minister in the Janata government of 1977–79, Vajpayee had pursued a policy of regional co-operation with

India's neighbours, including Islamic Pakistan. Despite his long association with the BJP and earlier with the Jan Sangh, he was known and respected throughout India.

Vajpayee was hard and conciliatory at the same time. He reaffirmed BJP stands in favour of making India an avowed nuclear power, making Muslim-majority Kashmir an Indian state like all others, applying civil laws to India's more than 120 million Muslims, and building a Hindu temple on the site of the demolished mosque at Ayodhya. He clearly approved of the BJP concepts of Hindutva (Hindu culture) and Hindu Rashtra (Hindu land). He also accepted the anti-Western as well as anti-Muslim coalition government of the Shiv Sena and the BJP in Bombay, capital of Maharashtra. He appointed a leader of the extremist Rashtriya Swayamsevak Sangh, a former member of which had assassinated Mahatma Gandhi, as defence minister. But he included a Muslim, a Sikh, a low-caste Hindu, and a tribal in his twelve-member cabinet. When the party objected to his making the Muslim home minister – that key post instead went to the militant M.M. Joshi, who had led the 1992 BJP march to Srinagar – Vajpayee named the Muslim foreign minister in place of himself. He assured Pakistan of peaceful intentions. Although the BJP was opposed to Kentucky Fried Chicken outlets in India, he endorsed economic reforms designed to attract productive foreign investment.

Vajpayee's positive gestures were all in vain. Respect for him as an individual did not translate into willingness to give the BJP a crack at running India. Non-Communist MPs of other parties called it "chauvinistic" and "extreme," and Communists accused it of "Hitlerism," charges difficult to refute as well as hurtful. Vajpayee's government could not be sure of the support of more than 194 MPs when it faced a mandatory vote of confidence in the 545-member Lok Sabha. Vajpayee had observed at the outset: "Democracy is a game of numbers and the numbers are not on our side ... I don't see our government lasting very long."

It lasted twelve days. He resigned 28 May instead of letting the vote go ahead. Nevertheless, the precedent of a BJP government of all India was established.

Many Indians and Westerners instinctively condemned the Hindu party's prominence and reassured themselves with the quick fall of its government. But Vajpayee's gentlemanly conduct in the face of provocative attacks, and the BJP's remaining far closer than any other single party to a parliamentary majority, suggested confidence and strength otherwise lacking in Indian politics.

Now it was the NF-LF's turn to step front and centre in India's clearly unstable, rapidly changing political scene. The meek Deve Gowda was sworn in as prime minister 1 June. With promised Congress support, his government won a formal vote of confidence in the Lok Sabha. But the thirteen-party leftist coalition, commanding only 116 seats, appeared anything but strong, coherent, or lasting.

It had nearly fallen apart over the allocation of cabinet posts to members of the reduced Janata Dal, the two Communist parties, and regional parties from Andhra, Tamil Nadu, and Assam. Eight of the thirteen cabinet ministers finally chosen were from South India. Significantly, none of the thirteen and only one of twenty-one lower-ranking ministers of state was a Brahmin. The finance minister, Palaniappan Chidambaram, had served as commerce minister under Rao and could be counted on to continue the essential but still limited economic reforms started by Manmohan Singh. The defence minister was a former corrupt chief minister of Uttar Pradesh. The foreign minister, Inder Kumar Gujral, had held that job in V.P. Singh's 1989–91 coalition after serving in 1976–80 as ambassador to the Soviet Union, a position usually awarded to an Indian who would be ideologically comfortable in Moscow.

Deve Gowda, whose caste name in his Kannada language means "people of the plow," said he was the first farmer to become prime minister: "I am a peasant ... and my priorities would be rural development, social welfare, and prominence to the agricultural sector." But his own brother said that like all politicians he ignored ordinary people, and another former chief minister of Karnataka, the high-caste Ram Krishna Hegde, called Deve Gowda "clannish, petty, and vindictive." At five o'clock one morning, the time appointed by his astrologer, the new prime minister moved unannounced into the official residence, surprising P.V. Narasimha Rao, who was still there.

In policy matters, it was difficult to distinguish the NF-LF from the Congress, or from the bureaucrats accustomed to working with Congress politicians. Despite Deve Gowda's emphasis on agriculture and his pledge to maintain economic liberalization, there was more official concern with industry and avoiding the sell-off of wasteful state enterprises and the layoff of workers in unproductive jobs. Although the inexperienced prime minister looked forward to renewed dialogue with Pakistan in an exchange of letters with his counterpart, Benazir Bhutto, India continued to develop missiles and to block a comprehensive nuclear test-ban treaty in the United Nations.

Politics and corruption, however, obsessed Indians. The two words had come to mean the same thing to both the people and the politicians. But while popular anger was rising at the venal abuse of power, politicians were blithely stepping up their illegal pursuit of money. To make matters worse, politics was grounded more than ever in caste. On gaining power, a political leader no longer bothered to cover up the distribution of jobs and funds to fellow caste members, and the dismissal of members of rival castes.

Perhaps more than at any time since Indira's Emergency in 1975–77, Indian democracy was in jeopardy. It had miraculously recovered from that sudden, nearly fatal blow, only to be squeezed by Indira again, then her son, and now other cynical politicians lacking the Nehru mystique. Without another catharsis like the 1977 election, producing a decisive and positive result, democracy's survival was at risk from the creeping cancers of corruption and casteism – almost all that was left of the Congress legacy.

In August 1996, police found more than $1 million in rupees stuffed in nooks and crannies of the Delhi home of a Congresswallah named Sukh Ram, who as Rao's commerce minister had taken bids on the installation of 10 million as-yet-to-materialize new telephones in India. Also discovered was a diary implicating a number of politicians in questionable transactions. In September, Rao resigned as leader of the Congress Party after he and his astrologer were charged with cheating an Indian known as the "pickle king" of Britain of $100,000 when Rao was prime minister. The party chose its longtime, previously low-profile treasurer, a dalit named Sitaram Kesri, as temporary leader while Rao hung on to his leadership of the Congress parliamentary caucus. But he was forced to quit his last party position in December as demanded by Kesri, whose devious master plan to return Congress to power with himself as prime minister became clear by the beginning of 1997.

By then, taking a leaf or two from the Congress book, the NF-LF government had invoked the constitutional device of president's rule to prevent the BJP from coming to power in the most populous state of Uttar Pradesh although it held the largest number of legislative seats, and to dismiss a BJP government in Gujarat. In UP a coalition of leftists and a party of dalits took over, in Gujarat, a Congress-led coalition. In Assam in the northeast, meanwhile, renewed separatist violence broke out.

Kesri, a small man who at seventy-eight had waited a long time to make his move, aimed to buy off enough MPs of small parties and independents to push the number of Congress seats just above the 162 held by the BJP without its allies. Then the Congress would abruptly drop its support of the NF-LF coalition, and he would demand that the president of India invite him as the leader of the largest party to form a government. Kesri calculated that the leftists, although deprived of power, would back the Congress in preference to the BJP, and he would be prime minister on the fiftieth anniversary of India's independence.

On 30 March 1997, after just ten months, the Congress withdrew its support of the NF-LF government, which lost on a motion of non-confidence by a vote of 338 to 90 when BJP and Congress MPs came together to support the motion. But Kesri controlled no more than 140 MPs, too few to claim largest-party status, and his scheme was so blatant that it stirred up a hornet's nest – although some politicians undoubtedly would have restrained their anger if a Nehru were the mastermind. To his credit, Deve Gowda stood up to Kesri, calling him "the old man" who played "dirty politics," and refused to drop the official investigation into Congress corruption, before offering to resign as NF-LF leader. The Congress was forced to declare publicly that it did not seek immediate power. But it called on the NF-LF to choose a new leader as the price of renewed support. Above all, Congress members feared a new election that could further decimate the party. If it could not manoeuvre itself into power without an election, Kesri's ambitions would have to be curbed, and Deve Gowda would have to be the sacrificial lamb.

After considering Marxist militant Jyoti Basu again, the NF-LF decided on another man familiar with Communist ideology and tactics as its new compromise leader, although he was considered a political lightweight. On 21 April, Inder Kumar Gujral, seventy-seven, who had been ambassador to Moscow and twice foreign minister, who was openly and viscerally anti-American, and who sported a bantam figure and a goatee that some likened to Lenin's, took the oath as prime minister of India.

Before switching from the Congress to the Janata Party and then the Janata Dal, Gujral had gone from being a member of the underground Communist party to Congress membership, picking up two Ph.Ds along the way. Many remembered him as Indira Gandhi's information minister – one of the hatchet men responsible for carrying out her vindictive campaign against freedom of the press and Indian and foreign journalists before and during the Emergency. Indira had promoted him to Moscow in 1976 a year into the Emergency. He had managed to survive as ambassador during the 1977–79 Janata government following Indira's defeat, until she returned to power in January 1980, ten days after the Soviet invasion of Afghanistan. Partly on his advice, although she hardly needed it, she condoned that action.

Gujral's credentials were undisputed: his Marxist mindset, his sympathy with Russia, his animus against the United States, his backing of Saddam Hussein's Iraq in its invasion of Kuwait and the Gulf War in 1990-91 when he was foreign minister, and his eagerness to do the bidding of the Nehru family. They entitled him to be called the Punjabi V.K. Krishna Menon. Moreover, the political implications of his selection were disturbing to say the least. In the short run, it provoked the temporary withdrawal of the Tamil party with its twenty seats and Finance Minister Chidambaram from the NF-LF, leaving the illogical coalition leaning more to the left than ever and economic reforms up in the air. In the long run, it was the clearest signal yet of the gradual coalescing of the remaining Congress members, Communists, and other leftists against the BJP.

Ironically, Western journalists chose not to concentrate on Gujral's political history, or perhaps many weren't even aware of it. Nor did they project political trends in India very far into the future. They focused instead on Gujral's having moved at the time of the 1947 partition from Pakistan to India, and new Pakistani prime minister Nawaz Sharif's having moved then from India to Pakistan, and how this long-ago parallel between the two Punjabis might somehow bring about Indo-Pakistani peace and reconciliation. This chimera was a red herring from the time Gujral as the NF-LF foreign minister began pressing for talks between India and Pakistan, which resumed in Delhi in March 1997 a few days before the Congress withdrew its support of the Deve Gowda government. By continuing to hold out the prospect of peace with Pakistan, on top of making pro forma pledges to support economic reform and oppose poverty and corruption, Gujral diverted attention from a key fact. In order to become prime minister with Congress support, he had promised not to pursue the investigation of official, pervasive, deep-rooted corruption.

In his first six months as head of government, Gujral did discuss "normalization" of relations with Sharif at a summit of South Asian leaders in the Maldive Islands, and again at the United Nations in New York, with talks in Islamabad by officials in between. He also concluded one long-negotiated and delayed agreement with Bangladesh on a diversion of Ganges River waters, and another with Nepal on developing hydroelectric power. His efforts to ease neighbours' suspicions of India recalled the actions of Vajpayee, now the leader of the rival BJP, when he was Janata Party foreign minister twenty years earlier. In November 1996, when Gujral was still foreign minister, India had even welcomed President Jiang Zemin of China to Delhi. The two governments signed an agreement to reduce or limit military forces along their still disputed Himalayan borderlands in the old Northeast Frontier Agency and the Ladakh bulge of Kashmir.

But India and China came no closer to resolving the substantive differences that had pitched them into a war in the world's highest mountains in 1962. Nor were India and Pakistan nearer to coming to grips with the crucial issue of Kashmir. In reality, India before and after Gujral became prime minister intensified its threats to neighbours – particularly Pakistan and China – resumed its major arms deals with Moscow, and pursued its goal of becoming a world superpower as well as the Subcontinent's dominant power.

The Soviet Union's collapse and near-bankruptcy in 1991 had forced India to curtail its steady military buildup going back to the 1962 Himalayan fiasco. But in late 1996, just before the Jiang visit, Delhi eagerly returned to Moscow (also a provider of modern military hardware to Beijing) as its main arms supplier. The first Indian order was for forty SU-30 fighter aircraft at $1.8 billion. Following the pattern of earlier MIG purchases, this would enable India to manufacture more than 100 SU-30s on its own. Russian deliveries to come were to include up to 100 jet trainers, newer tanks than the Soviet models already possessed by India, howitzers, submarines, and possibly an aircraft carrier. Despite U.S. objections, Russia also planned to sell two nuclear reactors to India, enhancing an ability to make weapons growing out of its Canadian-designed reactors.

Apart from short-range Prithvi missiles on the border with Pakistan that Delhi did not admit deploying because of U.S. pressure, the Indians also resumed development of the Agni missile, capable with its 2,500-kilometre range of hitting targets in China and Pakistan or for that matter Southeast Asia and the Middle East. Only U.S. pressure stopped Russia from selling long-range missile technology to India. Prime Minister Gujral reiterated India's refusal to sign the treaty banning all nuclear tests, thereby blocking a major international effort to obtain universal approval of control of nuclear weapons. This stand was in addition to India's familiar refusal to sign the Nuclear Non-Proliferation Treaty or go along with its extension. India's jet fighters, Prithvis, and Agnis are all potentially capable of delivering its nuclear warheads, which at that time were still secret.

Finally, at the same time as the celebrations of fifty years of independence in August 1997, Indian and Pakistani artillery on the 1949 Kashmir ceasefire line, now called the "line of control," engaged for days in the heaviest exchange of fire in years, resulting in significant casualties on both sides. Predictably, Gujral's government insisted that India was "committed to the peace process." When the two countries' prime ministers first met earlier, Pakistan's Foreign Minister Gohar Ayub Khan – the late Marshal Mohammad Ayub Khan's son – said Indian troops in Kashmir had "gone beserk" with killing, burning, and rape. None of this was exactly new. To Indira's old information minister and man in Moscow, it must have seemed like a sentimental trip back to the halcyon days of non-alignment and the Cold War.

But it was hard for Gujral to tear himself away from more mundane problems. Within a week of his becoming prime minister in April 1997, India's biggest scandal to date in monetary terms hit his party, the Janata Dal, making it difficult for him to keep his promise not to pursue corruption if he wanted to stay in power.

In what was called the "fodder scam," India's Central Bureau of Investigation (CBI) charged the already implicated Laloo Prasad Yadav, who was both president of the Janata Dal and chief minister of Bihar, with having stolen $285 million over twenty years. A huge amount anywhere, it was staggering in India. The funds had been allocated each year to the notoriously mismanaged state for the care and feeding of cattle. The cows, holy in India if real, were figments of Yadav's imagination. They never existed.

Claiming the money was meant to help poor Biharis, he refused to resign as chief minister. Much of the slush fund probably did go to Yadavs like himself, members of a low farmer caste, in exchange for their votes. Laloo, as he was known, went so far as to threaten mob violence if his state government was dismissed. Gujral, who had a legitimate reason to use president's rule to do just that, instead fired the CBI director for doing his job. When the Communists in the shaky NF-LF coalition in Delhi said they would withdraw their support if Yadav was not removed one way or another, he finally quit. Without apology, he then named his illiterate wife to succeed him as chief executive of a state with 100 million people divided by caste and plagued by poverty.

On the Congress side of the corruption ledger, the former prime minister, Rao, already charged in the "pickle king" affair, was indicted in June 1997 on charges of paying bribes totalling $800,000 to four MPs for their support in a non-confidence vote in 1993. Many thought the courts also should have gone after the overly ambitious ex-treasurer Sitaram Kesri. Instead, still with his eyes on the prize, he won a three-cornered race for the Congress presidency in another indication of the growing importance of caste voting. One of the defeated candidates was Sharad Pawar, the party boss and former chief minister of Maharashtra, and perhaps the only Congress leader with the backbone to become a strong prime minister some day.

The hopes of those who will never give up on the Nehru dynasty were raised in May 1997 when Sonia Gandhi, Rajiv's Italian-born widow, formally joined the Congress Party by paying the one-rupee membership fee. But in all likelihood her move, like earlier flirtations with the party when Rao was prime minister, had to do with past rather than future politics: it was no secret that she was anxious to prevent her husband's name from being tarred with misuse of a much larger sum of money.

She became a Congresswoman after Swiss authorities handed over documents to their Indian counterparts detailing $40 million in payments into Swiss bank accounts in connection with India's purchase of artillery from Bofors of Sweden. More than anything else, that still mysterious deal had brought down Rajiv in the 1989 election as the dynasty's last prime minister, and had made corruption the other side of the coin of Indian politics. With the Laloo and Rao revelations, corruption in India attained a certain sublimity.

Nevertheless, when a weak Congress Party had returned to power in 1991, the government headed by Rao started dismantling the stultifying socialist controls that the Nehrus had imposed on the economy, having no choice but to do so. Indians who hail these reforms, as many of them once glorified red tape, contend they are rapidly transforming India's economy regardless of changes of government, politics, and even corruption.

It is not that simple. Nothing in India ever is. There are hopeful economic signs and encouraging statistics. There are also distressing trends, and statistics in India are usually suspect. Moreover, the reforms slowed down before clearly reaching their potential.

In 1997, for example, Bombay – renamed Mumbai by its chauvinist Maratha Hindu rulers – boasted the highest office rent in the world at about $170 per square foot ($1,700 per square metre), ahead of Hong Kong and Moscow. Delhi was fourth at about $100 per square foot ($1,000 per square metre), ahead of Singapore, Beijing, and Shanghai. This might have indicated a thriving, cash-rich Indian economy. But the prime business areas where the rents were charged were far removed from Bombay's long-existing colonies of squalid huts and Delhi's *jhuggis* or squatter shacks. Bombay's top ranking might or might not have reflected the new phenomenon of extortion and murder by Mafia-like gangs in India's business capital. It might or might not have hinted at the hard time that the Maharashtra government then was giving major would-be foreign investors seeking to produce and sell much needed energy (America's later discredited Enron) or popularly desired cars (France's Peugeot).

Certainly it contrasted sharply with India's high ranking in another survey: percentage of population living on less than $1 per day from 1981 to 1995. India placed fifth at more than 50 per cent, behind only three of the poorest African countries, and barely behind Nepal. China came in at about 25 per cent. The percentages would have been higher if the new criterion of purchasing-power parity, cutting disparities with richer countries, had not been used.

Such comparisons may be unfair. They are no more so than some official Indian statistics. One claim is that the number of Indians living below the country's poverty line was cut to less than 19 per cent of the population by 1994. Others are that the number of Indians in the "middle class" – this figure keeps going up by leaps and bounds – has reached 20 per cent or 25 per cent or perhaps even 33 per cent of the population. Economists, politicians, and diplomats have many ways of devising figures. But this kind of rosy picture simply is not real to anyone who has experienced India.

Some figures can serve as guidelines. It is true that after creeping along from 1960 to 1990 at what is called the "Hindu rate of growth" – 4 per cent a year or less – the Indian economy picked up to 5 per cent or more in the first years of liberalization, and in 1995–96 broke the 7 per cent barrier. Presumably the percentage of Indians living on less than $1 per day dropped after 1995. If sustained and accelerated, this kind of growth can lead early in the new century to India's steadily keeping up with or even surpassing East Asian "tigers" it had fallen far behind, especially because these latter economies faltered in varying degrees starting in mid-1997.

But India's stepped-up economic growth was not sustained after the May

1996 election, and many analysts believed it would fall below 6 per cent and perhaps even revert to type. It slipped to 6.8 per cent in 1996–97 and 6.5 per cent in 1997–98. Impressive increases in industrial output, imports, and exports all slowed significantly despite a relaxation of some bureaucratic barriers, quotas, and restrictions. Earlier increases in agricultural production were not matched by later ones. Dramatic exposés of dishonesty in government threw a wet blanket over economic confidence. Leftists in governments in Delhi and some states were ambiguous at best and hostile at worst toward freer markets and the need to keep spurring productivity.

This became painfully apparent when the NF-LF government decided days after the "golden jubilee" in August 1997 to grant salary increases to nearly five and a half million government employees, and to pay for them by raising duties on all imports except petroleum despite its promise to lower tariffs further. The turnabout was a revealing example of how easy it is to succumb to old bad habits. The whole reform program appeared to be undercut.

Along with wage increases totalling some $4 billion, an independent commission had recommended cutting overtime and "casual leave," increasing the work week to six days, and reducing the central bureaucracy in stages by 30 per cent. The unions loudly protested. The Gujral government caved in. It ended up paying another nearly $2 billion to the paper-shuffling workers, keeping the bloated bureaucracy, and still allowing one day off a month apart from holidays. Hope that laws preventing the dismissal of unneeded employees in both the public and private sectors would be soon modified, and that wasteful Nehruvian state enterprises would be sold or closed, went out the window. Even China seemed to be doing more to lighten the heavy burden of state industries and businesses.

Without strong leadership willing to get rid of such sacred cows or at least drastically reduce their number, India's economy could find it hard to grow significantly. Realistically, at least 40 per cent of India's population of one billion at the dawn of the new century – 400 million people or more – are still desperately poor, earning the equivalent of $1 a day or less, and incapable of doing better. This is much better than the 50 to 60 per cent of two decades or so ago. But it is not the less than 20 per cent officially claimed. The "middle class" actually may number 20 per cent or more. This means perhaps 200 million Indians have something substantial they can call their own. This is roughly twice as many as two decades ago, but not nearly as great an improvement as claimed. It still leaves roughly 400 million people struggling between poverty and decency at the start of the twenty-first century.

More than ever, it is necessary to look squarely and honestly at India's demographics. India simply has too many people. This is not Malthusian theory but demonstrable fact. The reason India has too many people is that it has waited too long to stimulate economic growth. Historically, throughout the world, poverty produces more babies, and prosperity produces fewer babies.

India's population growth came down to 1.6 per cent a year by 2000, lower than the replacement level, with its fertility rate cut from 6 births for each woman of child-bearing age to 3.1. But Indians are so numerous that before the middle of the twenty-first century, there will be more than 1.5 billion of them, according to United Nations projections, and they will outnumber Chinese. By the end of the twenty-first century, there will be an estimated two billion Indians, more than twice as many as on the fiftieth anniversary of India's independence in 1997, and nearly six times as many as on the day India became independent in 1947.

As in the past but more so, most of them will be concentrated in the north, a region traditionally marked more than others by poverty, backwardness, and irresponsible rule. Better off, more progressive states, especially in India's south, are bringing their populations under control. But the populations of the four northcentral states of Uttar Pradesh, Bihar, Madhya Pradesh, and Rajasthan – totalling 400 million people in 2000 – are rising from 45 per cent of all Indians to 55 per cent.

These are the states where the BJP is strong. They are also the states where political parties appealing to low-caste and dalit Indians challenge the high-caste Hindu party. Whether human opportunity opens up in these states and others, or human stagnation prevails, depends to a decisive degree on their political direction. It is not certain yet which way the BJP will go, and the same is true of its rivals. Nor is it certain whether the BJP or what can be called populist parties will come out on top.

What is certain is that economic liberalization, if it is to continue and expand in India, will need to happen in the states as well as with a central government that is pushing India forward instead of backward. If economic and social reform fails to take hold in the states, especially those making up the northern heartland, and in Delhi as well, India will ultimately redefine itself not by competition and freedom but by confrontation and violence. More than ever, members of rival castes, religions, and language groups will be at each other's throats. Rich, middle-class, poor, and poorer Indians will fight for a smaller pie instead of a bigger one. India will be at greater risk of breaking apart in the third traumatic partition of the Subcontinent since independence, with better off states seeking their own distinct destinies and less fortunate states sinking deeper into poverty and despair.

There is no need for this to happen. But only a paramount political force that believes in both democracy and capitalism and is willing and able to break down the barriers dividing Indians can stop it from happening. At first glance, and at second, there seems to be no such force on India's landscape.

The Congress Party logically should have been that force. With the coming of independence, it had the necessary all-India scope and the required moral authority, even after the passing of Mahatma Gandhi. But Jawaharlal Nehru believed in socialism rather than capitalism, and all the Nehrus were wrapped up more in their own ambitions than in the nation's. As a consequence, progress toward higher economic levels and social equality was much more limited than it should have been during the thirty-seven years the Nehru dynasty ruled. By the fiftieth anniversary of independence in 1997, the Congress was a shadow of its former self and was stripped of its moral authority, thanks to the divisions set in motion by Indira Gandhi in 1969 and the corruption that had overtaken the party.

The Janata or People's Party logically should have become India's needed political and moral force when it was elected in 1977 on a wave of popular euphoria following Indira's draconian Emergency. It brought together under the same roof many former Congressmen and women, including its Gandhian leader, Morarji Desai, and Hindu nationalists before they went their own way and founded the BJP. But Indira cut short the Janata road to reform by reinstalling the Nehru dynasty. The worst mistake Indian voters made in thirteen national elections was to give her one more chance. Their bad judgment led to the assassinations of Indira and her son Rajiv, and more profoundly to the political splintering of India.

The fallout included the Janata Dal, a much more narrowly based party than the Janata Party. The Janata Dal drifted left to join Communist and regional parties in the National Front–Left Front government in temporary power in Delhi at the time of the fiftieth anniversary of independence. But without the remains of the Congress, the leftist front by any name is too weak and illogical to become a national force. Locked in an alliance with the Congress, it would be too tainted at least in the foreseeable future. With or without the Congress, it may champion less privileged Indians, but it does not have the required commitment to a free economy that alone can improve these people's lives over the long term.

That leaves the Bharatiya Janata or Indian People's Party. It certainly considers itself an Indian national force. But two major deficiencies seemed at first to block the BJP from becoming the widely recognized force that India needs. First, it had shown political strength almost exclusively in northern states. More serious, its adherence to high-caste Hindu or Brahmin values makes it suspect to many low-caste and dalit Hindus, Muslims, and devotees of other religions, and anathema to many secular-minded Indians.

Atal Bihari Vajpayee as foreign minister in the old Janata government and as prime minister of the short-lived BJP government in 1996 began to address these problems. However great its fervour for Hindutva, the BJP is committed to both democracy and capitalism. It had started to make political inroads beyond the Hindi-speaking heartland. It had allied with other parties at the state level, including the Akali Dal of the Sikhs in a Punjabi government in 1997. But its strength is its unity as a single party, in contrast to other parties aspiring to national status. The challenge facing the BJP is to reach out sincerely to Indians beyond its hard-core members – Indians these high-caste Hindus have traditionally despised – in the cause of a freer, more prosperous, and united India.

The very idea seems inconceivable, a contradiction of Indian culture. It flies against the Hindu caste system at the heart of Indian civilization. How can a party that has never disavowed the active fascist-like organization that condemned Mahatma Gandhi in 1948, and prodded fanatics to tear down a mosque in 1992, become a force that promotes the spread of economic benefits to all Indians regardless of caste, religion, language, or region? How can benighted Brahmins who exalt a militant, xenophobic Bharat Mata create a peaceful, tolerant Mother India in which all Indians share equally?

It could never happen if the Nehrus had not stunted India's economic growth, cultivated a climate in which corruption eventually flourished, stood in the way of India's healthy political evolution, and torn apart the Congress Party standing for a secular India.

The Congress option for India has dwindled to nearly nothing. As early as 1967, twenty years after independence, Indians used the ballot box to try to make the Congress more responsive to their needs. When this didn't happen, and Indira Gandhi came close to destroying India's democratic system with her Emergency, Indians freely chose a secular alternative to the Congress in 1977. The Janata Party was the non-Communist opposition to the socialist Congress that Chakravarti Rajagopalachari, the wise old intimate of the Mahatma and severe critic of the permit-licence raj, had known would have to be ready to take power at the opportune time. An outgrowth in part of Rajaji's old Swatantra Party, the Janata of Jayaprakash Narayan and Morarji Desai was, I believe, India's last and best chance to make a strictly secular approach work. But thanks to Indira's single-minded determination to resurrect the Nehru dynasty, it too failed. In contrast, the Janata Dal has no chance to hold India together on a secular or any other basis. Its handing out rewards to low-caste Hindus and petty clerks has widened the bitter divisions in Indian society. Its allying with radical Communists has made lasting economic liberalization almost impossible under its aegis.

Becoming India's guiding force is still not a *fait accompli* for the BJP. As the Hindu nationalist party attempts to dominate the north and extend its influence beyond the most backward states, it could still divide Indians irreparably by region, language, caste, and religion. It could bring about the separation of the "cow belt" – the Hindi-speaking northern states – from the rest of India.

But by 1998 if not 1996, the BJP had become the only national alternative left to Indians. The decades of independence wasted by the Nehru dynasty had made the BJP their only clearcut choice, dismaying as this was to many. The party had demonstrated blatant Hindu chauvinism – at the Ayodhya mosque, on the march to Srinagar, in the streets of Bombay. It had expressed distaste for secular policies that it claimed had made Hindus second-class citizens in their own country. But leaders of the BJP also had said for years that the party would not end constitutional secularism if it came to power nationally. Assuming democracy continues in India, this pledge is not as important as the party's continually having to compete for the votes of low-caste Hindus, dalits, Muslims, and South Indians, as well as high-caste North Indians.

While polls in India can be as unreliable as statistics, they are becoming more accurate. A national poll as early as mid-1997 indicated that if the twelfth parliamentary election were held then, the BJP and its allies would win 253 seats in the Lok Sabha, just 20 short of a majority, and the Congress barely 100. It became clear then that when the Indian people did elect a new Lok Sabha, probably before the end of the century, only a solid alliance of the National Front–Left Front and the Congress Party could possibly stop the BJP from coming to power for a much longer period of time than the twelve days its government had enjoyed in May 1996.

Even if such an alliance against the Hindu BJP were built around a defence of the secular principle, however, also clear was that the alliance would have difficulty coming or staying together for long. This was because prospective regional components of such an alliance would see the Congress as the enemy in important states. If the BJP did not gain a parliamentary majority on its own in the next election, it could attain one by extending to the national government in Delhi its demonstrated willingness to join with regional parties in state capitals. The Hindu nationalists had been unsuccessful in making such an offer after the 1996 election. In the next election, it was widely anticipated, a few key states outside the north-central plains could well tip the balance from a loose leftist coalition to an expectant Hindu camp.

13

A Historic Turning Point

The first battle of the next parliamentary election campaign still took place in the heartland, in October 1997. It signalled that Indians would go to the polls to elect a new Lok Sabha sooner rather than later, that emotions rooted in caste were so intense they could fly out of control, and that the Congress Party had learned nothing and forgotten nothing.

Members of the Uttar Pradesh legislature in Lucknow literally fought with each other on the floor. Indians throughout the country with access to TV witnessed scenes more violent than past confrontations in Parliament in Delhi or even the West Bengal legislature in Calcutta. But the Hindu nationalist Bharatiya Janata Party came out looking better and stronger than other parties.

The conflict arose when the Bahujan Samaj Party of dalits, having just headed the government of the state of 140 million people for six months under an agreement with the BJP, went back on the accord by refusing to back a government led by the high-caste Hindu nationalists for the same length of time. The BJP then offered cabinet posts to Bahujan Samaj and Congress legislators as incentives to defect, a standard practice in Indian politics for thirty years. Members of these parties responded by wildly assaulting BJP legislators on the floor and storming out. This allowed the stunned Hindu nationalists to win a confidence vote.

The next move by the Congress was as disturbing and revealing to many Indians as the deliberate resort to violence. It prevailed on Prime Minister Inder Kumar Gujral of the Nationalist Front–Leftist Front central government to recommend to the new president of India that he use his constitutional power to dismiss the BJP government in UP. The Congress did so by threatening to withdraw its support from the coalition government in Delhi if this familiar tactic was not employed.

But President Kocheril Raman Narayanan, a dalit and a constitutional scholar, did what presidents had not dared to do when Indira Gandhi or

Rajiv Gandhi was prime minister. He rejected the prime minister's "advice" on the ground that law and order in UP had not broken down to the extent that president's rule was justified. Narayanan not only kept the BJP in power in the country's most populous state, but also established his independence in the bitterly divisive politics enveloping India.

But it wasn't long before the Congress under the opportunistic Sitaram Kesri executed another destabilizing manoeuvre. Again, the party's action proved to be embarrassing and counterproductive.

In early November 1997, a judicial commission report about Rajiv Gandhi's assassination in Tamil Nadu in May 1991 said there had been "active connivance" in the killing by some leaders of the southern state's Dravida Munnetra Kazhagam (DMK) or Dravidian Progressive Party assisting Tamil guerrillas from Sri Lanka. Sonia Gandhi, Rajiv's usually quiet widow, demanded that the Congress react. The DMK was an important member of the NF-LF coalition government in Delhi headed by Gujral.

On 20 November, at Kesri's instigation, Congress members of Parliament voted to withdraw the party's support from the government unless the prime minister ousted the DMK from his coalition. The Tamil party, denying wrongdoing, angrily called the provocation "politically motivated." For three days running, Congress and DMK members shouted accusations at each other on the floor of the Lok Sabha in another blow to Indian parliamentary decorum, bringing proceedings to a halt and the speaker to despair. On 24 November, after an emergency cabinet meeting, Gujral rejected the Congress demand in a letter to Kesri. The Congress leader acknowledged he was again aiming for the formation of a government by the increasingly discredited Congress without a new election.

His admission came after the leftist coalition government resigned, making another election all but certain. Exasperated by the arrogant Congress demand, Gujral had gone to Rashtrapati Bhavan at midnight of 28 November to convey its decision to Narayanan. Earlier that day, the three leading associations of Indian businessmen had jointly urged Indian politicians to cease indulging in "political expediency and competitive populism" when prospects for continued economic liberalization, foreign investment, and growth were rapidly diminishing. *The Times of India*, once pro-Congress, commented editorially: "There have been political crises in the past but the spectacle being played out in New Delhi these days is by far the most sordid and cynical."

President Narayanan, at seventy-seven one of the few constructive elements in the fractious Delhi landscape, gave the political parties time to find a way of avoiding a fresh election less than two years after the last one. But this was beyond them. The BJP was not in a position to attract enough defectors to form a government. The Congress strategy, to obtain the United Front's backing after twice withdrawing support from the coalition, had badly backfired. On the night of 3 December – a few hours after Kesri had publicly whined, "Can't there still be a compromise?" – the United Front, along with the BJP, asked Narayanan to dissolve Parliament and leave it to India's voters to settle the issue. The next day the president ordered that a new Lok Sabha be constituted by 15 March 1998.

Almost immediately an ominous cloud of communal violence gathered over the coming election campaign, especially in South India. On 6 December, the fifth anniversary of the destruction of the Ayodhya mosque by Hindus linked to the BJP, two bombs exploded on trains in Tamil Nadu and a third on a train in Kerala, killing ten people and injuring seventy. A little-known group called the Islamic Defense Force claimed responsibility.

Indians anticipated and feared another indecisive election result, with no party capturing anything like the old big Congress majorities. But they fully expected the Hindu nationalists to win the largest number of seats in the 545-member Lok Sabha, as the BJP had done in 1996. The militant Hindu party had steadily advanced on its own from 2 seats in the 1985 election to 85 in 1989, 120 in 1991, and 160 in 1996. In order to continue its dramatic march and come close to a majority of 273 seats, or even win a small majority, however, either the BJP or new allies of the predominantly northern party would need to gain a significant number of the four southern states' 129 seats. The BJP also sought to broaden its voter base by wooing Muslims throughout the country with evidence that the number of Hindu-Muslim clashes had decreased in states where it held power. If South Indian Muslims were behind the bomb blasts, they appeared to be targeting the two new BJP thrusts.

But the eager Hindu nationalists quickly moved ahead on all fronts toward a solid if not a majority government, softening their image and causing panic in the hapless Congress camp. In December and early January 1998, the BJP put together alliances with eight regional parties, and persuaded some notable members of the Congress to join its ranks, including fifteen members of Parliament, former cabinet ministers, and state leaders. One prominent defector, Mani Shankar Aiyer, who had been close to the Nehrus, said that Kesri and the former prime minister, Rao, had taken "but six years to destroy a party it took 106 years to build." The Congress was close to splitting once again and for the final time.

What happened next was a godsend to Western journalists covering an election with no names widely recognized outside India and a plethora of strange parties. A well-known name was the only certainty about the entrance of Sonia Gandhi onto the disheveled stage of Indian politics.

Statements put out in Sonia's name in late December – naturally she was known, like other Indian political or would-be political figures, by her first name – said Rajiv's widow, fifty-one, would campaign for the Congress and would be joined by her recently married daughter Priyanka, twenty-six. Since Rajiv's assassination in May 1991, the Italian-born, Roman Catholic Sonia had lived in virtual seclusion behind the high metal gate of the family house in Delhi. It was not known when her impending emergence was announced, or later, whether she would help or hurt the Congress, although the battered party could hardly do worse. Nor was it known then or later what if anything she believed in, or why she was publicly entering politics after resisting sycophants of the family since her husband's death more than six and a half years earlier.

As the Swiss government continued to turn over documents to the government of India, there was not then or later any reason to change the widely held view that Sonia's chief motive was to prevent the surfacing of evidence showing that Rajiv as prime minister had had $40 million in kickbacks from the sale of Swedish-made Bofors howitzers to India deposited in secret bank accounts. As a BJP leader, Pramod Mahajan, put it: "Sonia Gandhi is an unopened envelope. Nobody knows what is written inside."

On 11 January, she nervously delivered her first campaign speech at Sriperiumbudur, the dusty town in Tamil Nadu where Rajiv had been blown up by a female Tamil Tiger suicide bomber in the 1991 election campaign. It was brief and in incongruous Italian-accented English, translated into Tamil for a disappointing crowd of less than 10,000 – small for an Indian political rally – made up almost entirely of paid Congress workers who had been trucked in and typically made to wait for several hours. Sonia moved stiffly in a dark green sari, and was always surrounded by armed guards. She did not announce her candidacy for prime minister or even for a Lok Sabha seat. By conventional Indian standards, her long-awaited political debut was inauspicious, even a failure if its purpose was to reignite popular enthusiasm for the Congress Party.

But there was nothing conventional about the reclusive doyenne of the faded Nehru family coming out into the open in India, especially because she was foreign, white-skinned, and Catholic. The moment Sonia emerged, she embellished a family myth that, however destructive of India, was inextricably tied up with fifty years of Indian independence. Her aim, or the aim of her handlers, most of them former aides of Rajiv, was to establish her connection to the family and the country as the ideal Indian widow, daughter-in-law, and housewife in the minds of the masses. This living link to the past, they hoped, would revive the dying Congress and cast doubt on the surging BJP. The intent of the simple sentences she read could not have been clearer:

I stand here today on this soil made sacred by the blood of my husband who died a martyr in the cause of the nation's unity and integrity.

I became part of India thirty years ago when I entered Indira Gandhi's home as her elder son's bride, and I have come to love India.

My devotion to our country and her people is unwavering and absolute.

I believe Congress is the only truly national party representing the whole country and all its people.

We do not want our people to be separated from each other because of caste, religion, or region. We prize our diversity.

Indira Gandhi had mouthed similar platitudes at the same time she cut up India, democracy, and the Congress Party. Rajiv Gandhi had shown how much he valued the nation's unity in his first act as prime minister: ordering Congress goondas to attack innocent Sikh families in retaliation for his mother's slaying. Yet time after time, starting with Jawaharlal, the Nehrus had gained power or stayed in power when there were compelling reasons to bar them or expel them from power.

Could history conceivably repeat itself through a seemingly taciturn woman who came from a European country, was not even a Hindu, and had no experience in politics or government? Could the Nehru dynasty rise up, reincarnated in an Italian woman with a Mona Lisa smile, from the very spot where it had died violently nearly seven years before? That was plainly what those behind Sonia wanted impressionable Indians to believe. They calculated correctly that many Indians would accept Sonia on the basis of the traditional practice of a married woman becoming part of her husband's family – in her case, a family that had once dominated India.

Indian analysts, conceding the Sonia factor could influence the election outcome, pointed out her limitations and the drastically changed political scene. Headlines in Western journals reflected a half-wishful, half-fanciful approach to the reality of India: "A New Gandhi Hopes to End The Chaos of India's Politics" (*The New York Times*); "Enter Sonia, with the Gandhi magic" (*The Economist*); "Sonia Gandhi emerges from wings to save Congress" (*The Globe and Mail*).

The words were unconvincing. But a photograph taken at Sriperiumbudur and featured in publications around the world was eerily familiar, and frightening to many. It showed Sonia and Priyanka standing side by side, the blandly handsome widow gazing indulgently at the unseen crowd, her lanky smiling daughter looking uncannily like Indira, their saris draped exactly the same way, their three-quarters-bare right arms raised high in exuberant, parallel salutes of greeting and victory.

Were the two women from successive generations of a family that wouldn't go away following in the footsteps of the Big Mother? Were they new embodiments of an old dynastic line dazzling to its beholders and tragic for India? Did Sonia's fascist-like salute, emulated by her daughter, imitate the admiration for Benito Mussolini demonstrated by her industrialist father?

By the end of January, Sonia Gandhi – or lifesize cardboard cutouts of her giving a prim namaste in a light-coloured sari – was a fast-moving blur on the Indian election trail. Like Indira in past campaigns, she gave five or six carefully prepared, increasingly impassioned speeches each day, and wore saris and winter shawls traditional to the area she was gracing with her presence. In the north, her ten-minute addresses were in Hindi she read from a Romanized script, still with an Italian accent, but often including an expression or two or a dialect intonation familiar to local people.

She drew larger crowds in Congress strongholds in northern India, where BJP support was higher than in the south but educational levels were lower. In Rohtak, a farming town north of Delhi known for a lawless element, she twice broke away from her security guards to mingle with admirers. On the vast Calcutta maidan, thousands shouted, "Sonia Gandhi zindebad!" or "Long live Sonia Gandhi!" There and at other rallies, she was accompanied by her son Rahul, twenty-seven, who had come home from a job in the computer industry in England to stand next to her in Congress whites, the unsmiling scowl on his face reminiscent of Sanjay's.

Told what to say – and not to answer reporters' questions – by Congress reformers seeking to save the party from its current leadership, Sonia began to get into policy questions. Tacitly acknowledging grievances against the Congress, she apologized publicly for the army's assault in 1984 on the Golden Temple of the Sikhs in Amritsar, ordered by Indira, and the destruction of the Ayodhya mosque in 1992 when the Congress was in power under P.V. Narasimha Rao. In her first known intervention in the party's workings, she overruled Kesri in vetoing candidacies for Congress members involved in either action, including Rao.

Meanwhile, Manmohan Singh, the non-political Sikh bureaucrat who had initiated economic reforms as Rao's finance minister, prevailed over Kesri in putting further growth-inducing measures, including privatization, into the Congress election manifesto. All these developments combined to create a possible scenario, seriously entertained in some quarters for a brief time, in which the Congress did well enough at the polls to form a government and Sonia designated Singh as "her" prime minister.

This was not being realistic about Congress's chances or Singh's. As for Sonia, she gave up the idea of running for a Lok Sabha seat anywhere, including Rajiv's former district of Amethi, two days before a conspiracy trial ended 28 January with the conviction of all twenty-six Indians and Sri Lankans charged with taking part in his assassination, and all now liable to be hanged. The verdict might have given her a springboard to a safe seat. But it was becoming clear by this time that, however much Sonia was enlivening her party's campaign and worrying BJP strategists, the Congress was past saving in this election.

Against the unexpected Sonia boom, the BJP's slogan for its leader seemed almost harmless: "Abki baari, Atal Bihari" or "This time around, Atal Bihari." Vajpayee personally refrained from directly attacking Sonia. Other BJP leaders warned that she threatened India with "Rome raj." One said: "She's like a dumb doll. No one knows where she stands. She reads from a piece of paper. It's pantomime." Polls made Sonia the second most popular choice for prime minister. But Vajpayee was still far and away the first choice.

Sonia's speeches reminded Indians of divisive BJP proposals: ending the separate Muslim legal code and Kashmir's special status, building a grand Hindu temple on the site of the Ayodhya mosque, and making India an avowed nuclear power. As party president, Lal Krishna Advani reiterated this nationalist agenda summed up in the BJP call for "one nation, one people, and one culture."

But Vajpayee made clear the party's program would be modified to take account of the wishes of its coalition partners. He sought particularly to assure Muslims fearful of suffering under a BJP government: "Just try us once. You won't be disappointed." On economic policy, in line with the slogan "Microchips yes, potato chips no," the BJP wanted to bar foreign investment in the consumer field, such as Kentucky Fried Chicken outlets, but to encourage it in infrastructure and high-tech projects. The Hindu nationalists, while favouring priority for Indian businessmen, had supported economic liberalization to overcome India's deep problems long before the Congress had. Many Indians were impressed by their pledge, hardly mentioned in foreign media, to provide clean, stable, efficient government.

"We will give new life to India," Vajpayee emotionally promised 150,000 listeners at one of his last campaign rallies, in his Lucknow constituency in central India, if the BJP finally attained power. "After more than fifty years of independence, the days of our national humiliation will be over, and India will fulfill the potential squandered by years of corruption and inefficiency ... Give us a parliamentary majority, and we will lead India to the greatness that is its destiny."

If the BJP did not win a majority by itself, it would need to rely on the new alliances it had made with leaders of state parties in order to come to power and to stay in power. One of these partners was not promising in terms of delivering expected seats but was intriguing as part of the BJP's southern strategy.

She was Jayalalitha Jayaram, a former movie star and mistress of the late legendary Tamil film star and politician M.G. Ramachandran. As chief minister of Tamil Nadu for five years, she had caused sensation after sensation by promoting popular worship of herself as a goddess, indulging in shocking extravagance including 10,000 saris and the $10-million wedding of her foster son for which she charged the state, and, on the other hand, bringing impressive rural, industrial, and social development projects to Tamil Nadu. Likened to Imelda Marcos of the Philippines, Jayalalitha had been thrown out of office by the voters in 1996 and charged with fraud estimated at $270 million. But, brazen as ever, she was attempting a comeback with her Tamil party by allying it with the BJP.

Apart from the BJP, its allies, and the Congress, the parties making up the National Front–Left Front were in disarray during the election campaign. They were looked on as potential members of a Congress-led coalition if the BJP could be blocked from coming to power. But the Congress, in seeking such an outcome without an election, had twice undercut NF-LF governments in the less than two years since the last time voters went to the polls.

One Front party, the Telugu Desam of the southern state of Andhra Pradesh, was led by a modern-minded chief minister whom many considered the Bill Gates of India. Chandrababu Naidu, forty-seven, the son-in-law of another legendary movie star turned politician, N.T. Rama Rao, had brought computer technology and international loans to Andhra. He had also put together the multi-party NF-LF in 1996 as a third political force. Now he saw the Congress as not only having brought down two Front governments in Delhi but also threatening his state government in Hyderabad.

Another Front party was unequivocally opposed to the BJP as the lesser of two evils in its eyes. Jyoti Basu, who had hardly shunned violence as Marxist Communist leader and chief minister of West Bengal, called the Congress "rotten to the core." But he identified the Hindu nationalists as "the main enemy" and as "barbarians who will attempt to divide us on communal lines." Basu had admitted earlier that his refusal at his party's behest to accept the NF-LF's tentative offer to become prime minister in 1996 had been a "historic blunder." Now the veteran Communist, eighty-three, said his Marxists would join a coalition of the Congress and Front parties, and, in what amounted to a wishful revival of the vision of a united front government, would agree to his heading it.

As usual in a nationwide election in India, voting was staggered over several days to allow election officials and security forces to shift from one part of the country to another. Most voters went to the polls 16 February, 22 February, or 28 February, and counting started 2 March, before voting for a handful of Kashmir and mountain seats on 7 March and in June. Just as the election campaign had been kicked off by an attempt to bring down the BJP government in Uttar Pradesh in the north and bombs exploding in Tamil Nadu in the south, so it ended with remarkably similar events in the same key states and with even greater impact on all of India.

On 14 February twelve bombs went off in the centre of the city of Coimbatore in Tamil Nadu, killing forty-three people, including a suicide bomber, and injuring more than 200. Six more people were killed by a bomb they intended to throw at security forces. If Advani had not been delayed in flying to Coimbatore from Delhi, and if a rally due to be addressed by the BJP president had therefore not been late, the toll might have been much higher. As it was, the violence was the worst during an election campaign since Rajiv's assassination in Tamil Nadu in 1991.

The state government banned two Islamic organizations in Coimbatore and arrested their leaders. Army troops were deployed instead of police, always a sure sign of an extremely dangerous situation. It was not improved when Kesri, the irrepressible Congress president, declared that the Rashtriya Swayamsevak Sangh, the extremist Hindu volunteer corps connected to the BJP, had set off the bombs as a protest against the party's endorsing secularism to attract votes. Other Congress members suggested the aim of the explosions was to create sympathy for the BJP like that generated for their party by Rajiv's killing in 1991.

One week later, in Lucknow on Saturday night, 21 February, the Delhi-appointed governor of UP dismissed the BJP government when twenty-two legislators defected from the ruling coalition. The move on the eve of the second day of voting in the state was clearly meant to embarrass the Hindu nationalists and make them look weak because of the loss of their major stronghold. There was no question it originated with Congress leaders and the United Front caretaker government in Delhi, specifically Mulayam Singh Yadav, a former UP chief minister charged with corruption and bitterly opposed to the BJP.

The implications were serious. The BJP had long believed that its control of the government in UP was an essential stepping stone to its assuming power in Delhi. Vajpayee, asserting that "a deep-rooted conspiracy" existed to deny national power to his party, started a "fast unto death" until the government's dismissal was reversed. But, as had been the case five months earlier, the anti-BJP ploy in India's most populous state backfired.

On 23 February the UP High Court in Allahabad voided the governor's order and the swearing in of a Congress-dominated government. The BJP chief minister, Kalyan Singh, then recaptured his office. The speaker of the legislature said he had the support of 225 members to his rival's 196. Vajpayee halted his fast. The BJP probably made a net gain of votes for the Lok Sabha from Indians who had not yet cast ballots. Some of the party's opponents were exposed again as crass opportunists whose "dirty tricks" did not stop short of risking bloodshed in the streets.

But a peaceful miracle in India was at hand. On 2 March, as counting of votes started and the first results were announced, several things became clear.

The first, although no one said so at the time, was that Indian democracy was working again. The people, the hungry majority, had decided what kind of government they wanted. No dictator, no ruling minority, was imposing a government on them. Despite all that had gone wrong and could go wrong, notwithstanding all the disappointments and setbacks they had endured, the ordinary people of India, half of them still poor and illiterate, were trying again and hoping again. Each man or woman who cast a ballot showed he or she was still eager to contribute to building a nation. Some middle-class Indians, perhaps camouflaging their intention to support the BJP, said they couldn't be bothered to vote. But as the independent election commissioner, Manohar Singh Gill, exclaimed before the polls opened: "Thank God the masses still have faith and have not become cynical."

The second thing to become clear was that the BJP was gaining in most parts of India, including even the south and West Bengal, while keeping its hold on the northern heartland. Maintaining its upward momentum, it was establishing itself as the country's strongest party. For the second time it would win the most seats in the Lok Sabha. But again it would not win a majority. In all likelihood the BJP would be able to form a government with its allies. But their support would be contingent on the party's not pushing its radical Hindu agenda. Even as the first returns came in, the Hindu nationalists showed they had become conciliatory by dropping their longstanding demand, directed against Muslims, for a uniform civil code for all Indians regardless of religion.

The early returns also established that the Congress would not gain appreciably, as it had hoped to do behind Sonia Gandhi. But neither would it lose dramatically, as it had done in 1996. Even districts and states where Sonia had drawn the biggest crowds were not producing many or any more Congress votes. Only where strong Congress organization combined with large lower-caste and Muslim votes did Sonia's appeals seem to have helped. The Congress was being shut out again in its former stronghold of UP, including Rajiv's old Amethi district. The Nehru family clearly no longer had the power to sway the Indian nation. But Sonia may have saved the Congress from another electoral disaster. Even before vote-counting started, the desperate party began talks with the United Front aimed at forming a coalition that could snatch victory from the BJP.

But the NF-LF was the big loser as votes were counted. In most parts of the country, its member parties suffered reverses that looked as if they would add up to a defeat nearly as devastating as the one sustained by the Congress in losing half its seats in 1996. The Janata Dal, the coalition's leading party, had split into three groups and was on the way to being wiped out in the south and eastern India. While Jyoti Basu's Communist Marxists held their own in West Bengal, the Front's two Tamil Nadu parties faltered badly.

One of the two big surprises in the returns was what was happening in Tamil Nadu, where the singular Jayalalitha Jayaram was leading her party out of the wilderness to victory as an ally of the BJP. The other surprise was in Maharashtra, where the Congress was making a decisive comeback against the Shiv Sena–BJP combination that controlled the state government in Bombay. Sharad Pawar, the strong Congress leader in Maharashtra and not a friend of the Nehrus, was scoring a bigger breakthrough for the party than Sonia Gandhi.

These developments in Maharashtra and Tamil Nadu were part of a wider trend against incumbent parties and MPs, demonstrating that Indian voters had not lost their ability to discern and defeat sitting politicians they believed were not acting in their interest. Jaswant Singh, then the BJP's finance critic, was one of a number of the party's candidates who went down to defeat in the western state of Rajasthan. In the Punjab, where the Akali Dal of the Sikhs came through as an ally of the Hindu nationalists, a film star running for the BJP ousted a five-time Congress MP from a seat the Congress had captured in all eleven preceding parliamentary elections.

In the twelfth parliamentary election, 344 million Indians cast ballots, 57 per cent of nearly 600 million eligible voters, almost one percentage point down from 1996 but still a healthy showing.

The BJP won 179 seats, a gain of 19 over its tally in 1996, or nearly one-third of the 545 Lok Sabha seats on its own. It attracted nearly 26 per cent of the popular vote, up about 5.5 points. Compared with 24 (later 33) seats from a few allies in 1996, the BJP's dozen allies in 1998 added 73 seats with 12 per cent of the popular vote for a total of 252 seats, a gain of 67 but still 21 seats short of a majority of 273. Jayalalitha's branch of the Dravida Munnetra Kazhagam, also divided into three groups, brought 18 Tamil Nadu seats into the BJP camp, the socialist Samata Party accounted for 12 seats, the Akali Dal added 8 Punjab seats, and the Shiv Sena managed to produce 6 Maharashtra seats.

The Congress captured 141 seats, 5 more than in 1996, again a quarter of the Lok Sabha on its own. But it drew only a little more than 25 per cent of the popular vote, down about 3.5 points from 1996 and more than 11 points from 1991: a second-place showing in share of the popular vote for the first time in Congress history. Allies added 26 seats to the Congress camp for a total of 167, or 28 more than after the 1996 election, but only 4 per cent of the popular vote. Without Sonia's short scripted speeches, some analysts said, the Congress by itself might have fallen below 100 seats.

The United Front's thirteen parties dropped sharply to a total of 96 seats with about 19 per cent of the popular vote, as against 125 seats and 20 per cent of the popular vote won in the 1996 election, and 173 seats after it had padded itself in power. The three regional branches of the Janata Dal, including one in Bihar led by Laloo Prasad Yadav of imaginary-cow fame, salvaged only 32 seats among them, compared with 46 for the undivided party in 1996 and 56 in 1991. The Communist Marxists also captured 32 seats, one less than in 1998. The Communist Party of India won 9, down from 12. The low-caste UP Samajwadi Party of the BJP-baiting Mulayam Singh Yadav took 20 seats. Chandrababu Naidu's Telugu Desam Party won 12 seats in Andhra Pradesh, down from 17 in 1996.

On paper, the Congress camp's 167 seats and the Front's 96 added up to 263, more than the BJP camp's 252, and only 10 seats short of a majority if the two sides came together. A total of thirty-nine parties – more than ever before – and six independents won seats, before the contests for the last five elective seats and presidential appointment of two Anglo-Indians. Theoretically the twenty-three MPs outside any of the three camps held the balance of power and could put either the BJP or the Congress into office.

But numbers weren't the only consideration as the slow intricate drama leading to the formation of an Indian central government shifted from hundreds of thousands of dusty polling places and often claustrophobic counting centres guarded by uniformed men with guns to a few shaded bungalows in New Delhi. Politicians from all parts of the vast country came and went at the bungalows, designated by the major parties for continuous bargaining and brokering, and frequently the scene of bickering.

By 4 or 5 March, a consensus had developed on what BJP leaders indeed called a government of "national consensus," as opposed to one of "division and fragmentation" ruled out by Vajpayee. The consensus seemed inescapable. And yet, as if India could not bring itself to break with the Nehrus or accept revivalist Hindus, it was not conclusive. By any realistic reckoning, however, memorable words uttered by Jawaharlal Nehru at midnight in August 1947, when India gained independence, were truer in March 1998: "The past is over and it is the future that beckons to us now."

The Hindu nationalists were ready to take power. The Congress was not, and neither was the United Front. Even without a BJP parliamentary majority, India was at a historic turning point.

Journalists, foreign and domestic, reported the BJP was selling its Hindu soul for the sake of support by regional parties that still might pull the rug out from under it at the first opportunity. But the only way the Hindu nationalists could safely come to power, and hope to stay in power in a country as diverse in India, was by broadening their ideas and bringing the states into a new Indian federalism. They were compelled to do both, or at least start the process of doing both. They could never rule for long, or at all, simply as a party of the north dedicated to enforcing Hindu culture.

In 1996, the Bharatiya Janata Party had become India's biggest political party. But virtually all other parties had shunned it and stigmatized it. In 1998, enough other parties associated with the BJP to allow it to begin to fulfill its potential of replacing the Congress Party as the paramount political force that India needs to survive as one nation. In order to succeed politically, the BJP needed not only to continue following the democratic path but also to make capitalism work in India and to bring Indians together instead of driving them apart.

Immediately after the election, despite all the publicity received by Sonia Gandhi, the Congress Party was no less and probably more divided and indecisive than before. The once dominant party's long fall may have been arrested, but there was no evidence its descent wouldn't resume. Congressmen couldn't agree on whether to do business with the United Front or resign themselves to an opposition role. The party was split among adherents of Kesri, Sonia, and Pawar. Even if the Congress had been able to form a coalition government, there was no designated leader or agreement on who would become prime minister. Such a government would have achieved little or nothing more than to push a frustrated BJP to the right and very possibly into the streets, bringing severe pressures on Indian unity.

As for the United Front, its role as a third force, able to help govern India if called upon to do so, was diminished at best, disintegrating at worst. Janata Dal survivors including Gujral made clear they preferred opposition to coming into a Congress-led government. Basu's Communist Marxists finally said they would support a coalition government only if it were not run by the Congress. Naidu's Telugu Desam formally targeted the Congress as its "first enemy," opening the way to a switch by the party's twelve MPs to the BJP camp, and making more likely the survival of a BJP government in the required confidence vote in the Lok Sabha that would follow its formation.

Notwithstanding all these signposts, the focus was on the Congress and Sonia during the second week after the counting of votes started. It was a week that should have seen the BJP take power but was marked instead by a sense of other players, including President Narayanan, waiting for something else to turn up.

On Monday, 9 March, Kesri said he would resign as Congress president and suggested that Sonia should take his place. His impending resignation was richly deserved although it turned out he didn't mean it. Her prospective accession was hailed as the return of the Nehru dynasty to Indian politics. But that had already happened, and the new twist underlined again the party's desperation.

On Tuesday, 10 March, a meeting of the Congress working committee broke up after eight minutes without even discussing the party president's resignation, although Congress officials still talked of blocking the BJP. Meanwhile, Narayanan invited Vajpayee not to form a government but to provide letters of support from political allies proving that he could form a "stable government." That night Vajpayee, expressing confidence in "making a majority," accepted the unprecedented request, formally contained in a letter from the president. The next day he went to Rashtrapati Bhavan with a bunch of letters from parties and independents allied with the BJP pledging their support.

But late Thursday afternoon, 12 March, Vajpayee returned to the presidential palace with the news that a key ally, the redoubtable Jayalalitha Jayaram of Tamil Nadu, had not met a 5 PM deadline to deliver her letter. She was holding out for a number of cabinet seats for her party, including finance, and for a promise that a BJP government would dismiss the Tamil Nadu state government through the president, thereby quashing the fraud charges against her. To his credit, Vajpayee had totally rejected her outrageous demands. But this meant he had to tell Narayanan that the BJP could be sure of the support of only 240 Lok Sabha members, 33 short of a majority.

The president responded that he would stay in touch with the BJP but would also open talks with the Congress and the United Front. He did so separately Friday, 13 March, amid speculation that two unpredictable women would snatch power from the BJP just as the Hindu nationalists were about to taste it at last. Jayalalitha could switch her support to the Congress, and Sonia could be acclaimed president of the Congress. Together these acts might give an anti-BJP coalition the impetus and feasibility its potential components plainly had not been able to generate.

On Saturday, 14 March, Congress MPs did elect Sonia unanimously as president of the party. Accepting a position she had turned down immediately after Rajiv's assassination nearly seven years earlier, she asserted as she had during the campaign that BJP policies threatened India's secular ideals. A colour photograph on the front page of *The New York Times* Sunday, 15 March, over the inaccurate caption "Gandhi Dynasty Revived," showed Congress supporters in Delhi celebrating with firecrackers.

But the party's outward unity did not hide its internal rivalries. Terming his removal "illegal," Kesri stormed out of a meeting of the Congress working committee after it had called on him to carry out immediately his promise to resign. Maharashtra's Pawar, who had led the party to its surprising capture of thirty-seven of the state's forty-eight Lok Sabha seats, tightened his hold on the leadership of the entire Congress caucus in Parliament that had bestowed the party's presidency on Sonia. And while the Congress was trying to put its house in order, the BJP was moving to within a step of power.

On Saturday the other woman in India's political dance drama, Jayalalitha, gave Vajpayee the letter of support on behalf of her Tamil Nadu MPs she had embarrassingly withheld. She dropped her demands but declared that BJP leaders had been "condescending, patronizing, and contemptuous" in reacting to them. Her provocative independence sent a message that she could easily withdraw her party's backing at a later opportunity.

Still, Vajpayee could tell Narayanan on Saturday night that the BJP could be sure now of the support of 264 MPs. After an hour's conversation at Rashtrapati Bhavan, however, the president still did not make a decision. He finally did so only on Sunday night, 15 March, the date by which a new Lok Sabha was supposed to be constituted, and two weeks after tallying of the election returns had started.

First he had met earlier that day with Sonia Gandhi, the new president of the Congress, who told him her party was not strong enough to form a government. This was hardly news to any half-informed person in India. Rightly or wrongly, Narayanan's not making up his mind until after he had solicited advice from Sonia, a political novice and a foreign-born member of the Nehru family, intensified questions during the drawn-out post-election period about the independence he had established for himself earlier.

Whatever the president's reasons or emotions in waiting so long to end suspense that was no longer justified, he hardly could wait any longer. That Sunday night he finally presented a letter to Vajpayee formally inviting the BJP leader to form a government.

India's prime minister-designate responded with characteristic grace and candour: "The results of the recent general election have not given a clear majority to anybody. But this flaw in the verdict can be overcome if parties set aside confrontationist politics and become participants in the noble task of nation-building."

Vajpayee was addressing apprehensions on the part of many Indians, probably including the dalit president, about high-caste Hindu nationalists coming to power a little more than fifty years after the assassination of Mahatma Gandhi by a Brahmin extremist. He also was expressing his own determination to avoid anything like his twelve-day government in 1996. A BJP spokesman conceded that running what had grown into a seventeen-party coalition with a "thin majority" would not be "an ordinary affair." But he added: "People want a stable government and they don't want the Congress to come back."

The Congress had been forced to accept the status of India's main opposition party even if it was not reconciled to this unaccustomed role. Following Sonia's meeting with Narayanan, in a rare reply to questions by journalists, she had said: "We have no numbers to form a government, so we are not staking a claim ... Basically, my priority is to work on restructuring the party so it can re-emerge as a strong party."

This didn't sound as if she would be mere window dressing in this endeavour. But it was not at all certain that Sonia could, or should, be a strong leader. Pawar in particular had the experience, the ambition, and the potential to lead the Congress in the new direction that was clearly necessary for its survival as a meaningful political force. If the party could rally around only Sonia, a person even more patently unqualified to lead the country than Indira and Rajiv had been, it risked keeping alive a family legacy that had tragically failed India. If the primary or sole objective of the Congress under Sonia was to bring down a BJP government at the first chance, and then succeed it by inducing defections, the reach of the Nehru dynasty might well extend to bringing about hopeless instability and incurable disunity in India.

Fears that such a scenario would unfold increased the very next day, Monday, 16 March, when Sonia still succeeded in overshadowing Vajpayee, who was putting together a cabinet and a policy statement. Although she did not hold a seat in either house of Parliament, the Congress working committee abruptly elected her leader of the party's parliamentary caucus in addition to having her as new party president. As fantastic as the notion was, this made her the likely prime minister of India if the Congress returned to power by upsetting a BJP government. It was a serious setback for Pawar, who was compelled to accept Sonia's appointment of him to the subordinate position of Congress leader in only the Lok Sabha. She named Manmohan Singh, the reformist former finance minister, as the party's leader in the Rajya Sabha.

Clearly, the former colleagues of Rajiv who had brought his widow into the election campaign still wanted her front and centre in the struggle to follow, although the Congress had lost in more than half the districts she had given speeches in. Just as clearly, for the sake of her own aroused ambitions or theirs or both – or, as Indian newspapers suggested, to continue to head off an investigation of alleged Bofors kickbacks to Rajiv as prime minister – Sonia was not going back into seclusion. In another pep talk that had all the markings of having been written for her, she asserted the Congress had to recognize it was to blame for the popular trend against it, and needed to "reverse this trend," if it was to "survive as a responsible political organization." Again she called for fighting "forces [seeking] to undermine our democratic and secular foundation."

This was exactly what the BJP was trying not to do. On Wednesday, 18 March, at a press conference in the garden of his New Delhi bungalow, Vajpayee released a "National Agenda for Governance" that bent over backward to be positive instead of negative, and to go "back to basics" in the nation's business. "Governance" had a nice ring, eliciting respect and suggesting that the BJP-led "Alliance," as incongruous as it might be, was settling in for the long haul. But Vajpayee's words in introducing the policy statement were more direct and reminiscent of Morarji Desai's moving pledge to meet the needs and aspirations of the people of India soon after the Janata Party (including Vajpayee) took office in 1977 following the popular rejection of the Emergency and the Congress Party of Sonia's mother-in-law.

Flanked by his old and certain colleague, Lal Krishna Advani, and his new and uncertain partner, Jayalalitha Jayaram, he declared:

This is a document of unity. Our goal is the good of India ... Above all, to bring peace, unity, well-being, and prosperity to the lives of all citizens of our country ... [Our Agenda] is not merely aimed at seeking consensus but also at ending the adversarial relationship between the ruling group and the opposition ... The nation cannot afford such adversity; we will replace it with co-operation and participation ...

The huge and ever-expanding number of unemployed people cannot be ignored. We will therefore seek to link economic growth with employment generation. Hence, our emphasis on Berozgari Hatao [Removal of Unemployment] ...

Ours will be a government that will take governance back to basics ... The biggest security for the common man, more so the poorest of the poor, is food security. We are pledged to providing this security. [We will] step up public investment in agriculture, rural development and irrigation ... Our aim: a better quality of life for the rural people and to enhance their purchasing power ... The unempowered need all assistance. . . Gender equality is close to our concerns ...

The people need a respite from violence in every form. Internal security will be of primary concern to us. We are committed to a riot-free and terrorism-free society. On the external front, there shall be no compromise on India's security needs. We will exercise all options, including the nuclear option, to protect India's sovereignty and territorial integrity ...

Strong states and a strong centre can co-exist. We will prove this ... We are committed to changing the content of governance, the thrust of governance. But, above everything else, we are committed to clean and transparent governance ... [We will ensure] that everybody who holds public office is accountable and his actions are open to scrutiny. We will also strike at the root of corruption in public life through comprehensive electoral reforms.

All political promises should be taken with a grain of salt. Journalists usually take several, searching for the controversial at the expense of the conventional. In this case, the words "nuclear option," and a no less vague reference in the policy document itself, provoked a spate of coverage and criticism that hid the BJP's new "thrust." Far from being temporary and dishonest, as some analysts implied, it marked out a whole new path of politics as well as governance.

The Hindu nationalists were saying they wanted to keep India united instead of divided. Their expressed aim was to ensure jobs, food, and justice for all Indians regardless of religion, caste, or region. They were saying they were committed to preventing communal violence instead of stirring it up. Their declared intention was to create a new federalism and to attack corruption vigorously. Vajpayee's emphasis on providing enough food and increasing the purchasing power of farmers was significant decades after both should have happened under Congress rule. "Strong states and a strong centre" was more than a facile slogan: it held out the prospect of groundbreaking partnerships in spreading the benefits of economic liberalization and growth.

The agenda itself added some specifics but was also notable for some omissions. The BJP's election pledge to provide "stable, honest, transparent, and efficient government" now targeted widespread police corruption. Commitment to continued economic reform emphasized both *swadeshi* – Indian self-reliance, a central tenet of Mahatma Gandhi – and the development of energy, power, and other infrastructure through foreign investment. Along with driving down unemployment, the BJP and its allies promised to bring annual economic growth, sinking back to 5 per cent, up to 7 or 8 per cent.

In addition to allocating 60 per cent of five-year plan funds to agricultural and rural development, they said they would stimulate cottage, handicraft, and other small-scale industries: another Gandhian priority. They made a commitment to endeavouring to end illiteracy and child labour, and to ensuring safe drinking water in all villages. Perhaps most important, a coalition headed by a Hindu supremacist party promised "truly and genuinely [to] uphold the practice and concept of secularism consistent with the Indian tradition of equal respect for all faiths and on the basis of equality of all."

In line with this unequivocal pledge, completely at odds with continuing Congress allegations of undermining secularism, three of the four most controversial BJP proposals were missing from the policy statement. In addition to leaving the adoption of a universal legal code in abeyance, it did not mention ending Kashmir's constitutional special status, or building a temple to the Hindu god Ram on the site of the destroyed Ayodhya mosque. Muslims strongly opposed these three demands by militant Hindus. But the BJP's determination to soften its platform and its image did not extend, at least not entirely, to the party's stand in favour of making India an avowed nuclear power. The agenda said that one military option to be explored by the government in undertaking India's first strategic review was to "induct nuclear weapons" into its armed forces.

The wording did not make this option a *fait accompli*. Nor did Vajpayee when he said in answer to questions, "There is no time frame – we are keeping the option open." But in reality the nuclear option already existed, although this was not acknowledged.

Since carrying out a single underground nuclear test in May 1974, which Indira Gandhi's government at the time claimed was for peaceful purposes, India had secretly built an arsenal of up to 200 nuclear warheads. A new BJP government could be expected to speed up the development of missiles and the acquisition of planes that could carry and deliver the warheads. It was not certain if India's declaring itself a member of the nuclear club would reinforce its existing obstruction of international efforts to stop the testing and proliferation of nuclear weapons. But its conducting another nuclear test would automatically prompt the United States to cut off its economic aid and veto World Bank and International Monetary Fund loans to India, at a time when the Indian economy needed all the help it could get.

A government headed by Vajpayee would have to weigh the certainties of this reaction and worldwide criticism against India's security considerations and the long-held Hindu nationalist desire to establish India as a prospective superpower. Predictably, Pakistan protested against the ambiguous policy pronouncement after Prime Minister Nawaz Sharif had written a conciliatory letter to Vajpayee. But it was China and a perceived "nuclear ring" it was forging in Pakistan, Tibet, and Burma that most concerned many Indians, not only the country's prospective new rulers. The danger was that the BJP, like the Congress before it, would resort to brandishing a nuclear sword against a foreign threat in order to unite the nation during a political or economic crisis, and to deter political allies from deserting the party.

On Thursday morning, 19 March, as the beginning of the long, hot North Indian summer competed with pomp and ceremony to suffuse the formal gardens of Rashtrapati Bhavan, Atal Bihari Vajpayee was sworn in a second time as prime minister of India. At seventy-two, his pleasant reassuring face set off by his silver hair and three layers of light-coloured traditional Indian garments – but not a Hindu saffron scarf as in 1996 – he was surer of his footing than he had been when he took the oath the first time twenty-two months earlier. But he had stayed up late the night before, trying to distribute cabinet seats to dozens of eager aspirants from a strange mix of parties, and he would not complete his delicate balancing act until the next day.

Vajpayee could look back with gratification on nearly six decades of personal political activity, more than three of them devoted to the struggle to bring a Hindu political force to power. Born in Gwalior in northcentral India in 1925, he was one of seven children of a Brahmin school teacher. He ended an early teenage flirtation with communism when he came into contact with the Rashtriya Swayamsevak Sangh, the ideologically pure fountainhead of the Jan Sangh, the first Hindu party he had worked for in the 1960s, and its successor, the BJP. But although he was in some ways a quintessential North Indian high-caste Hindu, Atal Bihari had followed his own predilections.

He had never married but had raised an adopted daughter, Namita Bhattacharya, now married with her own children and living with him in a plain government bungalow. He wrote Hindi poetry, and it often seemed as if he spoke Hindi poetry. Despite his close association with dogmatic Hindu extremists, he had always been openminded, moderate, and conciliatory, able to get along with many kinds of Indians. Unlike Advani, whose role model was Vallabhai Patel, Vajpayee was an admirer of Gandhi and Nehru. Unlike most Hindus, he ate meat and drank whiskey.

Indeed, Vajpayee seemed to have changed little since the time he was the debonair foreign minister in the Janata government of mostly ex-Congressmen twenty years earlier, working against odds for regional co-operation between India and its neighbours. Many still thought the odds were against him and the BJP. Vajpayee himself conveyed the impression that he knew the struggle for a new India was far from over. "I have a pledge to redeem," he said on the day he became prime minister again, "and a promise to fulfill."

His cabinet, although more diverse than he might have wished, was a start in that direction. It combined major BJP figures and representatives of contrasting pieces of the Indian mosaic, with some of the non-BJP members known nationally.

Vajpayee kept the foreign-affairs and atomic-energy portfolios for himself, as Nehru once had. He made Advani, seventy-one and his closest associate, the powerful home minister, thus putting Advani in a position to counter violence before or immediately after it started and to oversee the police although he was still under indictment for inciting the Hindu mob at Ayodhya in 1992. Murli Manohar Joshi, the ultra-nationalist third member of the top BJP trio, became minister of human resource development and also of science and technology, indicating that the emphasis on creating jobs was not just rhetorical. Another party leader, Ram Jethmalani, was appointed urban development minister. Vajpayee was urged by Bombay businessmen to give the finance ministry to the reformist BJP finance critic, Jaswant Singh, although he had been defeated in running for a seat from Rajasthan. But Vajpayee named a retired bureaucrat, Yashwant Sinha, who had been the last finance minister before the 1991 election and Congress-initiated reforms that stopped India short of bankruptcy.

The defence ministry went to Indira's old nemesis, George Fernandes of the socialist Samata Party, who had successfully campaigned as industry minister in the Janata government to kick IBM and Coca-Cola out of India. A Muslim, Sikander Bakht, one of two appointed, became industry minister, an important position. A Sikh leader, S.S. Barnala, became minister in charge of food, chemicals, and fertilizers, clearly another key position. A prominent former Congressman, Ram Krishna Hegde of the southern state of Karnataka, became commerce minister. The railways ministry also went to a non-BJP candidate. The only woman among the twenty-two full ministers was Sushma Swaraj, a lively and articulate former chief minister of Delhi, who took charge of information and broadcasting. Vajpayee could not assign jobs to the twenty-one ministers of state until 20 March. They included three more women, including Maneka Gandhi, the widow of Sanjay who had long since broken with the Nehrus, and was put in charge of welfare. A dalit became responsible for health and family welfare.

Now that the government was in place, the next challenge was to keep it there by winning the mandatory confidence vote in the Lok Sabha within ten days. In the style of President Bill Clinton, Vajpayee made a number of policy statements in his first days as prime minister. Instead of indicating departures from the past, however, they sent a message to Indians that there would be no unpleasant surprises.

In the debate leading up to the confidence vote, Congress, Communist, and other opposition MPs attempted to divide members of the BJP-led coalition by sarcastically recalling their past differences and extreme BJP demands. But Advani reiterated that the party's campaign manifesto did not apply to the new government. And Vajpayee, recalling his resignation in 1996 before a confidence vote could be held, smilingly replied: "But this time we have a majority, and we will prove it."

First the BJP took a dramatic step to demonstrate its new openness to all Indians, and thereby to guarantee the government that majority. Shortly before the confidence vote, the coalition proposed an MP from the Telegu Desam Party, still formally a member of the United Front, as the new speaker of the Lok Sabha. When G.M.C. Balayogi was elected to shouts of protest from the opposition benches, he was the first dalit ever to become speaker. It was a symbolic victory for the BJP and a practical one in turning the southern party with its twelve Andhra Pradesh MPs into a de facto government supporter.

On Saturday, 28 March, nine days after taking office, the Hindu nationalist-led Alliance won the confidence of the Lok Sabha by a vote of 274 to 261. The thirteen-vote winning margin wasn't much. But it was more than the predicted one vote or even ten votes – and a breakthrough.

14

Finally the Future Beckons

Over most of the next year, the political victory extracted by the Bharatiya Janata Party from a sceptical Indian electorate in March 1998 looked less and less like a breakthrough, except in one way. It was a big way: in May, India openly broke into the world's exclusive nuclear club with a bang – actually five bangs, the number of underground tests ordered by the coalition government headed by Prime Minister Vajpayee. But at home the BJP found itself up against a combination of disconcerting elements: three scheming women, the high price of onions, a slow start on new economic reforms, caste and religious violence, and Hindu extremism.

The conditions for a profound change in the way India is run, however, had not changed. In the year and a half between the 1998 vote and the thirteenth parliamentary election in September–October 1999, the BJP found its footing, responded to these conditions, and overcame the obstacles confronting it. Luck played a part, and so did Pakistan. But at the end of this exciting period, reflecting many of the changes in India, a country more diverse than ever had a government both reasonably stable and reassuringly moderate. With what should be the final defeat of the Nehrus, one billion Indians could believe that words uttered by Jawaharlal Nehru in 1947 on the eve of India's independence as a democracy were finally coming true: "it is the future that beckons to us now."

It is a future not dominated by one family, and not dominated by one political party that is convinced it owns the exclusive right to rule, as the Congress Party of the Nehrus traditionally has believed. One party will be dominant for the foreseeable future but it is open to smaller parties representing states, language groups, Hindu castes, and other religions making up the complex mosaic that is India.

The BJP needs these parties for what it appropriately calls the National Democratic Alliance to rule. These nearly two dozen parties need the BJP to have a share in ruling India. There are risks, as there are with any coalition government. But in the Indian context there are two huge, mutually reinforcing benefits. The Hindu nationalists cannot impose their divisive revivalist ideas on the country because their partners will not let them stay in power if they try. And the parties and politicians exploiting caste, ethnic, or language loyalties become less divisive and more cohesive as they are compelled to become part of a larger picture if they want to retain or compete for a share of national power.

Indian politics would become even healthier if the repeatedly divided and long demoralized Congress Party accepted the new rules of the game. Then, as the main opposition party, it might compete with the BJP to become the paramount political force needed by India to prevent everything from flying apart. But this is unlikely to happen unless the Congress chooses a new leader to replace Sonia Gandhi and also gives up the fantasy of resurrecting the Nehru dynasty. That means finding a leader who is not Priyanka Varda or Rahul Gandhi, the children of Rajiv and Sonia.

As Mahatma Gandhi emphasized, politics is a means to an end. As long as Indian politics was selfish, narrow, and distorted, opportunities for economic gains were unnecessarily and tragically limited. With the rise and transformation of the BJP and the fall of the socialist Nehrus and the archaic Congress Party, prospects for significantly reducing grinding poverty and raising economic levels have brightened. This will take time, and India has already lost far too much time. But the widening of political competition means more and more players are striving for fair shares of a pie starting to grow larger.

For a party that had waited so long to come to power, the BJP was hesitant to act on the aims outlined by Vajpayee after the March 1998 election, apart from the popularly acclaimed nuclear tests. Its first budget was disappointing, keeping protectionist controls in place and balking at privatization of state-owned companies. Finance Minister Yashwant Sinha rolled back price and tax increases before their benefits could take hold. With Tamil Nadu's tempestuous Jayalalitha Jayaram threatening as early as August to withdraw her party's support, the government was clearly reluctant to rock the boat.

It faced its first crisis in October when the price of onions, an essential ingredient in most Indian meals, skyrocketed as much as sevenfold due to a late monsoon in the north followed by floods. Other vegetables were hard hit but the onion became a metaphor for a widely perceived lack of *suraj* (good government) promised by the BJP. In Delhi and Rajasthan, the worst affected areas, thousands of people demonstrated or stood in long lines for subsidized onions. Too late, the BJP fired the chief minister of Delhi, removed the import duty on onions, and ordered an airlift of onions from South India and the Middle East. Calculating the impact on the government's popularity, the magazine *India Today* commented sarcastically: "The humble onion seems set to prevail over the nuclear mushroom."

The BJP paid a high political price in state elections in November. Congress Party landslides threw the Hindu nationalists out of their strongholds in Delhi and Rajasthan, and a vulnerable Congress government managed to stay in power in Madhya Pradesh. Suddenly, the BJP surge seemed to have stopped. Some jubilant Congressmen called for a non-confidence vote in the Lok Sabha. Party president Sonia Gandhi responded: "The government will collapse on its own." Still too weak to take power, the Congress was trying to build up its depleted organization for an election in early 2000.

Despite the BJP's efforts to minimize its cultural agenda, it was further embarrassed by Hinduism firsters. Shiv Sena militants in Bombay threatened to disrupt an India-Pakistan cricket match. They backed down only when Vajpayee threatened to dismiss the Shiv Sena–BJP state government in Maharashtra; Pakistan's cricket team arrived without incident in Delhi in January 1999. The BJP thought it could safely make the singing of Vande Mataram – a popular hymn to Mother India actually composed by a Muslim but accompanied by its singers bowing to the earth – compulsory for all school children. But when some Muslims complained, the prime minister prevailed on state governments to withdraw it. When Hindu extremists angry at Christian conversions engaged in destructive anti-Christian acts in Gujarat, Vajpayee flew there to express support for frightened Christians. On 30 January, the fifty-first anniversary of Mahatma Gandhi's assassination, he declared: "Such violence violates our tradition and culture of tolerance. It goes against everything that Gandhiji and our savants have taught us."

The BJP's response to another shocking incident of intolerance, and the Congress reaction to the BJP response, impressed on Indians the changing nature of both parties.

In Bihar, still the poorest state and still ruled by the thoroughly corrupt Laloo Prasad Yadav through his wife, the army of high-caste landowners responsible for the slaughter of twenty-two dalit peasants struck again, killing twelve poor farm workers on 10 February. Two days later, Vajpayee moved to oust the lawless nine-year-old Yadav regime through imposition of president's rule, and dispatched 16,000 police to Bihar.

But putting a state under central government control was no longer the automatic execution of the prime minister's political will it had been when Indira Gandhi held sway. Both houses of Parliament and the president would consider carefully any such move. The Congress Party, long the champion of dalits, opposed president's rule for Bihar on the ground the massacres did not justify it. The party had the votes in the Rajya Sabha or appointed upper house of Parliament to block the move. Nothing changed when Vajpayee met Sonia for forty-five minutes although she had said the Laloo government had lost the moral authority to govern.

The BJP had its own political motives in Bihar. But the Congress clearly betrayed the dalits in favour of its developing alliance with the arrogant Laloo, the leader of the low cowherd caste of Yadavs who was courting high-caste Bhumihar landowners. A principle of equality was involved as well as politics, and Vajpayee staked his government's survival on an affirmative vote in the popularly elected Lok Sabha on president's rule in Bihar. Then his government revoked the order rather than see it defeated in the Rajya Sabha. But Sonia and the Congress had made a bad moral and political mistake. Vajpayee and the BJP had begun to recover politically because they looked like they had a moral purpose.

On 20 February, Vajpayee made the second of three moves that month which helped the BJP re-establish itself as India's premier political force. He travelled to Lahore on the first bus between India and Pakistan since the outbreak of their second war in 1965. The forthcoming prime minister initiated a peace process with his Pakistani counterpart, Nawaz Sharif, that promised action on a long list of disputes, and gave Vajpayee the mantle of a statesman. Less than three months later, the Lahore bus trip also made him, unexpectedly, a martyr to peace.

At the end of February, finally, Finance Minister Sinha's second budget put the BJP and its allies on a clear reformist track. Inviting foreign investment in a number of fields, including insurance with its potential of generating investment funds, he raised taxes to cut the budget deficit, offered productive tax breaks, laid out specific privatization plans, and increased defence spending by 11 per cent. The Bombay stock market responded with a 20 per cent spurt.

On 19 March, BJP members from across India celebrated one year in power at the Hauz Khas Moghul ruins in Delhi. The party had turned around impressively after its early missteps. Some of its many critics were even predicting it would stay in power longer than expected. Vajpayee confidently told *India Today*: "Learning along the way, a year down the line, we have been able to settle down as a team."

But the very success of the Hindu nationalists in adapting to India's new conditions was about to bring their biggest crisis down on their heads. Like the witches of Macbeth, three women were stirring a brew that would lead to India's third parliamentary election in less than three and a half years. Very possibly for the same reason, Pakistani generals were preparing for a fight that easily could have led to the fourth India-Pakistan war in fifty-two years.

Sonia and Jayalalitha, in that order, were the first two of the three BJP-phobic women to show their hands. The day before Parliament reconvened on 15 April, Jayalalitha flew into Delhi with twenty cartons of clothing, linen, and towels, and moved into an entire wing of a luxury hotel. Then she went to a tea party in her honour. Sonia attended the tea and talked with Jayalalitha, thereby signalling the Congress president's objective of bringing down the coalition government immediately. Jayalalitha then carried out her longstanding threat to withdraw her Tamil Nadu party with its eighteen MPs from support of the government.

The avowed reason given by Jayalalitha for her action was the government's firing of the naval chief, Admiral Vishnu Bhagwat, four months earlier when he didn't accept the deputy assigned to him. She had demanded Bhagwat's reinstatement and the firing of Defence Minister George Fernandes, and Vajpayee had refused. Her real reason, as usual, had to do with the corruption charges against her from her time as chief minister of Tamil Nadu. She resented Fernandes for, in her eyes, going back on what she considered a promise to have the charges reduced, and she had it in for the BJP for not dismissing the current Tamil Nadu government and thereby quashing the charges completely.

Sonia's real reason for forming a tacit alliance with the duplicitous Jayalalitha was a switch in Congress strategy. Instead of taking time to build up the party and waiting for the government's mistakes to topple it, Congresswallahs had been alarmed by the reversal in BJP fortune and had decided they couldn't afford to wait while the Hindu nationalists grew stronger. If the BJP couldn't muster enough votes now to stay in office with its allies, the Congress hoped to persuade other parties to support it in power without going to a fresh election.

Politicians from all over the country descended on Delhi as they do when India is about to enter a new stage in its political development. They hardly paid attention when India tested a medium-range Agni missile, Pakistan responded with a medium-range Ghauri missile and a short-range Shaheen, and India ended the display with a surface-to-air missile test. When the Lok Sabha met, Vajpayee carried out an order from President Kocheril Raman Naraynan and introduced a motion of confidence. But he was reasonably certain that the BJP could mobilize enough support from small parties to stay in office now that it had bid good riddance to Jayalalitha. As he put it to fellow MPs: "What kind of government will come in my place, and who will lead it?"

Before the vote on Saturday, 17 April, the BJP had good reason to believe it had the support of 269 MPs. This was two short of a majority if everyone voted. But in addition to winning over three small parties outside the ruling coalition, the BJP had secured a promise from Mayawati, the woman who led the Bahujan Samaj Party of Uttar Pradesh dalits and low-caste Hindus, that her party's five MPs would abstain, ensuring the government's survival. When members voted electronically, the BJP did receive 269 votes. But 270 MPs voted against it, including the five controlled by Mayawati and one Kashmiri who broke with his own party.

By a margin of one vote, the Alliance government fell. Mayawati, the third woman out to get the BJP, had only one name but plenty of clout as she deliberately tricked the BJP. She was still furious following the dispute in 1997 over how long her party and the BJP, then partners in UP, should each hold power in the state. It turned out that in climaxing act one of India's new political drama, Mayawati had conspired with Sonia, who had launched the play with Jayalalitha. But acts two and three also held surprises.

Vajpayee resigned upon the non-confidence vote of 270 to 269. He was naturally disappointed but, looking back on his struggle to keep his coalition together, he also could say: "I feel free." The president asked him to stay on as caretaker prime minister for up to two weeks as efforts to form a new government went ahead. Vajpayee stayed for six months. It was one of the most decisive periods in modern India's history. Beginning with the vote defeating the BJP-led government, events and non-events from mid-April to mid-October 1999 consolidated the historic turning point in early 1998 when the Hindu nationalists came to power in New Delhi. They also greatly strengthened India as a responsible major power in Asia.

But now the ball was in Sonia's court. As thousands of Congressmen and women showered her with roses and marigolds at her home at 10 Jan Path, the house once graced by Lal Bahadur Shastri, she confirmed she would aim to form the next government. But she was really trying to do what the despised Sitaram Kesri had failed to do as the party's leader when it pulled the rug out from under two short-lived leftist front governments: manoeuvre the Congress back into power without a parliamentary majority, without a popular election, and without any other parties joining it in a new coalition. Under the latest member of the Nehru dynasty, the arrogance of the Congress Party was back for all to see.

As talks began, a Congress leader admitted privately: "We have a fractured mandate, and there are problems." But Sonia sailed full steam ahead, declaring on 21 April: "We have 272 votes and we hope to get more – we are confident we will get more."

She claimed the backing of at least twelve parties in addition to the 140 Congress MPs, and said she would give letters to this effect to President Narayanan. But later that day a meeting of all small parties offered her no support. Mulayam Singh Yadav, the bitterly anti-BJP leader of the low-caste, pro-Muslim Samajwadi Party of UP and a rival of Mayawati, said the only government he would support would not be led by the Congress and would include other parties.

With the Congress dream of again ruling India all by itself rapidly turning into a mirage, on 23 April Rashtrapati Bhavan gave Sonia more time. But on Sunday, 25 April, act two of the political drama came to a climax with a loss to Congress more severe than the one the BJP had suffered eight days earlier. Sonia informed Narayanan she had not been able to enlist enough support and was giving up. She confessed she had lined up only 239 MPs but made clear the Congress Party still was "not ready to bargain" for a multi-party coalition government.

The damage to Sonia's carefully nurtured image – her mystique as what one analyst called a "bride" among martyrs, a "patroness" of the poor, a "goddess" of secularism – was devastating. Whether she and her advisers had been bluffing or lying, or had miscalculated, Sonia had pulled down a coalition government just thirteen months after the election creating it, with no prospect of another government replacing it. It was the shortest time an Indian central government had lasted. Like Nehrus before her, she had put her party over the nation, and herself over the party. She, like her predecessors, would never lack for mindless Congress sycophants. But as *India Today* observed: "For the public as well as the party, Sonia is more a concept than a three-dimensional politician."

On 16 April Narayan dissolved Parliament, having "reached the conclusion that the time had arrived for the democratic will of the people to be ascertained once again."

The immediate question was when exactly this time would be. The election had to be held within six months. But if it were soon, the weather would be too hot. If it were a little later, the weather would be too wet. The BJP nevertheless pressed for a June election, not wanting voters to forget its recent achievements or Sonia's treachery. On 4 May, Election Commissioner Manohar Singh Gill, noting that temperatures in the north already were as high as 43 degrees Celsius, or 118 degrees Fahrenheit, said that voting would not take place until September and October, spread as usual over several days in order to concentrate election and security personnel in different parts of the vast country. Later, four dates in September and one in early October were set. The long delay proved to be a godsend for the BJP and its allies, still in office as a caretaker government.

Before the curtain went up on act three – to be scripted mostly by the people of India at 800,000 polling stations – two more unforeseen developments stunned the nation. One reflected the weakness of Sonia and the Congress Party and weakened them more. The other underlined the perils on India's borders and allowed the BJP to demonstrate its strength.

On 15 May Sharad Pawar of Maharashtra, the tough Congressman who had been instrumental in the party's winning 37 of its 140 Lok Sabha seats in 1998, asserted in a letter to Sonia that India should always have a native-born prime minister, and proposed a constitutional amendment to this effect. Pawar, fifty-eight and a potential prime minister himself, had disassociated himself from Sonia's grab for power. He was joined in his politically explosive demand by two symbolically important party colleagues: Tariq Anwar, a Muslim from Bihar and a senior Congressman, and Purno Sangma, a Christian from eastern India and a former Lok Sabha speaker.

Their move resoundingly split the Congress one more time, all but ensuring that it could not count on the major state of Maharashtra in the forthcoming election. It added respectability to the BJP view that India's consideration of a foreigner for its leader was a disgrace. It also amounted to a plea to the Congress Party to be done with the Nehrus once and for all. The three Congressmen expressed their argument in soaring rhetoric: "It is not possible that a country of 980 million people, with a wealth of education, competence, and ability, can have anyone other than an Indian, born of India soil, to head its government." Recalling Mahatma Gandhi's advice that India should be open to "winds from all over" but should not be "swept off [its] feet" by them, they proclaimed: "Our inspiration, our soul, our honour, our pride, our dignity [are] rooted in our soil."

Sonia Maino Gandhi responded in the rhetoric that, written by others, had come to be expected of her: "Though born in a foreign land, I chose India as my country ... I am Indian and shall remain so till my dying breath. India is my motherland, dearer to me than my own life." She also resigned the Congress presidency in a move plainly designed to rally support around her and to culminate in her changing her mind. Within hours women hysterically attempted to mob her with pleas to do just that. Later one woman tried to kill herself.

The Congress Party itself joined in the play-acting, making more obvious than ever its pathetic dependence on Sonia. Its top leaders and its few state chief ministers also resigned. Its working committee unanimously rejected Sonia's resignation, then expelled Pawar – the one person who could effectively lead the party as he had led its parliamentary caucus – and his two associates for six years. On 24 May, Sonia unsurprisingly announced she would continue as Congress president, earning her a front-page story and most of an inside page in *The New York Times*, apparently dependent on her for news of India. The next day rhetoric turned to soap opera with a fascist tinge as Sonia, "doubly resolved to lead the fight for our beloved country," returned in a staged show of mass adulation at Delhi's Talkatora Stadium. "Sonia Gandhi Zindabad!" chanted thousands clad in Congress white over and over again: "Long live Sonia Gandhi!"

Something more momentous than the last gasp of the Nehrus was going on in India, however, in the course of May and June and into late July. Indian troops, artillery, and planes were pushing back armed intruders from Pakistan from freezing Himalayan ridges on the India side of the "line of control," formerly the ceasefire line, in the disputed state of Kashmir. Bloody fighting in the strategically important Kargil sector between countries that had tested nuclear bombs one year earlier was connected to the campaign for India's thirteenth parliamentary election in ways that went beyond politics.

I discovered in Delhi in early June that, in a more profound sense than even testing of nuclear bombs could produce, the Hindu nationalist BJP was taking over from the Congress Party of the Nehru dynasty in defending the national security and vital interests of India. The BJP had not instigated the fighting to score political points. Indeed, Indian forces and intelligence may have been slow to detect the intruders. Pakistan had instigated the fighting. General Pervez Musharraf, the Pakistani army commander, wanted at a minimum to stop the Lahore peace process. His ambitions may well have extended to bringing about political outcomes in both countries: a military coup by himself in Pakistan, which happened in October, and defeat of the BJP at the polls in India at the same time.

Many conversations in Delhi indicated that the political performance of the Hindu nationalists was tied to the military performance of Indian forces in a way that could not be measured by pre-election polls. Foreign Minister Jaswant Singh, an intimate adviser to Vajpayee on political as well as international matters, made clear to me India's determination to completely drive out the intruders from Pakistan. But, sensitive to American concerns, the BJP caretaker government was carefully avoiding escalation of the fighting to a wider war beyond Indian-held Kashmir.

It came down to a matter of popular trust. Sonia Gandhi opened her Congress campaign in early August by blaming the BJP for the deaths of hundreds of soldiers due to negligence. At the same time, a BJP campaign poster, showing a determined Atal Bihari Vajpayee looking skyward as if to the Himalayas, said: "He can travel far to shake a hand, he can also crush it with a Kargil." By then, India had won decisively in the mountains of Kashmir.

The National Democratic Alliance, a coalition of twenty-four parties led by the BJP, was driving for a decisive win among the voters of India in early October. In contrast to the 1996 election, when hardly any other party wanted to touch the Hindu nationalists, and the 1998 election, when they expediently put together a jerry-built alliance, a highly respected, quietly heroic Vajpayee aimed to return to power at the head of a strong "coalition of parties" with a common, secular platform. The BJP contested only 330 Lok Sabha seats, leaving some 200 for its allies. Many Indians still distrusted it but its days as a pariah party were past, partly because it had shown in Kashmir that it represented not just Hindus but all Indians.

The Congress Party was selling itself as a "party of coalitions," meaning that it would rule if it could by itself, with support from other parties on particular issues. But, apart from the serious questions about Sonia's integrity, ability, and even her intention to lead, the only real Congress allies were the totally discredited Laloo of Bihar and Jayalalitha of Tamil Nadu. The Congress tried to fan fears of the BJP bringing instability and breaking up the country. But the days when the Congress was identified with Indian stability and unity were past, and it was in danger of becoming discredited itself. As for India's "third force," the National Front–Leftist Front that had provided a brief transition between Congress and BJP rule in 1996–98 had fallen apart, leaving only the two Communist parties and a few other radical parties in what was called the Left Alliance.

Unlike 1998, when Sonia campaigned but did not run for the Lok Sabha herself, she ran in not one but two constituencies in 1999. In what was meant to be a surprise, on 19 August she filed as a candidate in Bellary in the southern state of Karnataka, a presumably safe seat won by the Congress twelve straight times. A few minutes later, an eager, smiling woman named Sushma Swaraj filed for the BJP, declaring in a direct thrust at the Italian-born Catholic Sonia: "I have come here to fight for India's self-pride."

As the highest-profile woman in the BJP, Sushma was information minister, and had taken over as chief minister of Delhi during the onion crisis. She was not only politically savvy but an embodiment of Indian Hindu womanhood with her large *bindi* or forehead mark, nose jewel, and vermilion powder in her jet-black hair. Immediately Indians called the contest Sonia versus Sushma – the *videshi bahu* or foreign daughter-in law versus the *swadeshi beti* or Indian daughter.

Later Sonia also filed in Amethi in UP, her husband Rajiv's old constituency. Her campaign manager there was her daughter Priyanka, who looked like Indira Gandhi and attracted spellbound crowds as her grandmother had. Sonia still felt compelled to say in Amethi: "I feel completely Indian – well, I do have this accent and I don't blame people for making fun of it."

But it was not her Italian accent, which was less pronounced than during the 1998 campaign, that made it difficult for Sonia to establish a rapport with most Indians; nor was it the fact that she was no longer a novelty. Her handlers didn't make it easier as she swooped down in a helicopter to a Congress rally, read a short speech written for her in Hindi or English as she was surrounded by security guards, and flew away. The underlying reason, however, went deeper. Many people, especially middle-class Indians, did believe that Sonia's foreign background disqualified her to lead India, if polls could be believed. More important, they no longer believed that a Nehru had to lead India, especially one they knew little about.

Sonia was an issue for the BJP throughout the short campaign. At the end even Vajpayee, who was running as usual in the UP capital of Lucknow, questioned why, after coming to India as Rajiv's bride in 1968 at the age of twenty-one, she had waited fifteen years to become an Indian citizen, and whether she still held Italian citizenship. Some barbs were nasty. George Fernandes said Sonia's only contribution to India was "the two children she gave birth to – two people in 100 *crore* [one billion]." Another BJP minister asked: "If we are so keen on having a foreigner as prime minister, why not Tony Blair, Bill Clinton, or even Monica Lewinsky?"

Once the infiltrators from Pakistan were out of Indian-held Kashmir by early August, such comments enlivened an otherwise dull campaign. Competing polls predicted majorities of varying sizes for the BJP and its allies, who exploited a widespread desire for a result that would last, providing a respite from elections. With so many parties in a position to influence the outcome, state and local issues would have a greater impact than ever on a national election. But a key question was how many Indians would come out to vote.

On 5 September, the first day of voting, turnout was a respectable but not high 55 per cent of eligible voters in 145 constituencies in a number of states. It was only 23 per cent in Kashmir, where Islamic groups urged a boycott, and Pakistani-backed terrorists killed two politicians. Electronic voting machines were a novelty in areas with 25 million of the 160 million eligible voters that day. Election Commissioner Gill, reporting on the beginning of another miracle in India, characterized voting as "much cooler" than in past elections despite conditions in Kashmir.

Campaigning, including Congress and BJP claims of victory, continued through voting on 12, 18, and 25 September, right up to 3 October, the last day of voting. So did exit polls projecting a National Democratic Alliance majority of nearly 300 seats. Some analysts looked for a breakthrough by the Congress in UP, where with no seats it had nowhere to go but up. On 2 October, the one-hundred-and-thirtieth anniversary of Mahatma Gandhi's birth, both Vajpayee and Sonia paid tribute at the Rajghat memorial. Later the prime minister said in Hindi: "There is only one Gandhi and there cannot be another Gandhi." When the last votes had been cast 3 October, my friend Pran Sabharwal in Delhi told me it looked as if the Congress Party would have done much better without Sonia Gandhi at its helm.

Counting started after the last polls closed and the first results were announced 6 October. It was clear almost immediately that the Alliance would score a real victory across India.

Although Sonia defeated Sushma by 56,000 votes in Bellary and the

Congress was making gains in the Punjab and Karnataka, the BJP was on its way to a sweep of Delhi's seven seats – including defeat of former Congress finance minister Manmohan Singh – and, alone or through its allies, was headed for decisive wins in Bihar, Haryana, Rajasthan, Maharashtra, Gujarat, Orissa, Andhra Pradesh, and Tamil Nadu. Vajpayee, who came out of his house flashing the victory sign, defeated his Congress opponent in Lucknow, Karan Singh, the former Maharaja of Kashmir, by 124,000 votes. Foreign Minister Jaswant Singh, following his 1998 loss, defeated his Congress rival in Rajasthan by 113,000 votes. Home Minister Lal Krishna Advani won easily in Gujarat. So did Finance Minister Sinha and Defence Minister Fernandes in Bihar. For the first time Laloo Prasad Yadav lost in Bihar, to a Janata Dal ally of the BJP.

At midnight, the Alliance had captured 107 seats and was leading in races for 179 others for a total of 286 in the 543-seat Lok Sabha. The Congress Party was headed for a crushing defeat with fewer than half that number.

Late Thursday night, 7 October, with nearly all the returns in, Pran exclaimed over the telephone that Sonia should be "hounded out" of the Congress because the party had lost seats compared with the 1998 election and, in its worst showing ever, would end up with even fewer seats than in the 1996 election. Emphasizing that this was the first time a non-Congress prime minister had won re-election, he said the BJP-led National Democratic Alliance would "touch" 300 seats: "It was a good discerning vote."

It was a particularly sweet vote for Atal Bihari, who took traditional sweets symbolizing his victory from Sikh supporters. Sonia did not appear in person to concede defeat but put out a statement: "Congress reverses call for introspection, frank assessment and determined action ... We accept unhesitatingly the verdict of the people." As if the rejected Congress Party of the dismissed Nehru dynasty had any other choice.

About 363 million Indians cast ballots, 60 per cent of 605 million eligible voters – much higher than it looked at first.

The BJP and its twenty-three allies won 298 seats with 40.8 per cent of the popular vote, compared with 252 seats and 38 per cent of the popular vote captured by the BJP and its twelve allies in the 1998 election. Five more MPs supporting the Alliance brought its total to 303. The BJP alone won 182 seats and its allies 116, compared with 179 and 73, respectively, in 1998.

The Congress Party took only 114 seats, a loss of 27 from its 141 in 1998. Its allies won 23, down from 26. Together their total was 137, a loss of 30, but with 33.8 per cent of the popular vote compared with 29 per cent in the last election.

All other parties and independents won 25.4 per cent of the popular vote. The Left Alliance's five parties won 43 seats with 8 per cent, other parties 60 seats. In 1998 the United Front's thirteen parties had taken 96 seats with 19 per cent of the popular vote.

The Telugu Desam Party, led by the computer-age Chandrababu Naidu, which also was re-elected in Andhra Pradesh, was the BJP's largest partner with 29 Lok Sabha seats. Although it declined to join the cabinet, this offered much more stability than the unreliable Jayalalitha had. In the most significant political shift at the state level, a newly formed branch of the Janata Dal accounted for 21 Alliance seats after defeating Laloo and numbering his days as effective head of the Bihar government. Shiv Sena produced 15 seats from Maharashtra, where as expected Sharad Pawar deprived the Congress of its biggest base after forming a new party called the Nationalist Congress, which won 7 seats on its own. The ruling Dravida Munnetra Kazhagam in Tamil Nadu, Jayalalitha's enemy, won 12 Alliance seats; the Orissa Janata Dal 10; West Bengal's Trinamul Congress, a breakaway from Sonia's Congress, 8; and Haryana's Lok Dal 5. The Punjab produced only 2 seats for the Alliance following a split in the Akali Dal. Kashmir's National Conference, formerly close to the Congress, supported the Alliance with 4 seats. Altogether, 16 of the Alliance's 24 parties won seats.

The parties of Jayalalitha and Laloo, the two most disreputable politicians in India, were the only significant but reduced allies of the Congress, winning only 10 seats and 8 seats, respectively. In Uttar Pradesh with its 85 seats, where Sonia captured Amethi by 300,000 votes and her party won 9 other seats and its allies 2, the Congress failed to make a breakthrough with the BJP winning 30 UP seats, Mulayam Singh Yadav's Samajwadi Party 26, and Mayawati's Bahujan Samaj Party 14. In West Bengal and Kerala, Jyoti Basu's Marxist Communists won 33 seats and the pro-Moscow Communists 4 for the Left Alliance. Thirty-nine parties in all won seats, and three independents, including Maneka Gandhi, Sanjay's widow and Sonia's family rival, who again supported the BJP.

State results and the fortunes of regional parties were important because a whole new political pattern was taking hold in India, promising a wider spread of economic benefits as well as greater stability.

There was no longer any question about the BJP replacing the Congress as India's paramount political force. It also was clearer than ever that the Hindu nationalists' deals with and dependence on smaller parties had a positive two-way effect: the BJP could not push its old Hindu revivalist agenda, and parties based on caste or state could push for fair shares of a growing economy by looking outward. But the economy could not achieve higher growth without stability and co-operation between Delhi and the states as well as reforms cutting red tape. With the Congress still playing the one party–plus politics that belonged to the distant past, only the BJP and its allies comprised a coalition of parties that an increasing number of poor and middle-class Indians could support. In a word, democracy in India was working better than ever before.

Bihar in the north and Andhra in the south were striking examples.

Bihar was still the poorest state in the Indian Union – poorer even than it had been at the time of the famine in the late 1960s – due to the gross waste and corruption practised by Laloo. But for the first time many exploited voters rejected his negative brand of caste politics. This meant that the BJP-led central government, supported by a new, allied state party, could get rid of Laloo and his wife at last, and Biharis could hope to experience better living conditions.

Andhra was a mix of the old and the new. Its dynamic Chief Minister Naidu took account of the old by promising the tools and services wanted by poor peasants, but not the free electricity promised by his Congress opponents. He was creating the new by cutting subsidies and attracting World Bank loans and international investment for education, rural development, and high-tech enterprises. The Bill Gates of India soundly defeated the Congress and more closely allied his Telugu Desam Party with the BJP, which already was talking of a "second generation of economic reforms."

The BJP could have done better in some states. In UP, many members of its state party sat on their hands, and Vajpayee replaced the chief minister after the election. But the parties of Mulayam and Mayawati, appealing to low-caste, dalit, and Muslim Indians, limited Congress gains. In the Punjab, the BJP was hurt by the split in the Akali Dal of the Sikhs. But only in that northern state and Karnataka in the south did the Congress make unexpected gains.

One Congress leader admitted anonymously: "We've come back with our tail between our legs – it's a shameful defeat." Younger party members talked quietly of the need for Sonia to go. But other Congress leaders resigned to shift the blame from her. Asked about Sonia's resigning as party president, the party spokesman replied with familiar Congress arrogance: "The question does not arise." Astonishingly, the sharply reduced Congress parliamentary caucus unanimously elected Sonia as its leader, and she decided she would lead the opposition on the floor of the Lok Sabha as the MP from Amethi.

Once again, the Congress Party, or the men who intended to keep control of it through her, had learned nothing and forgotten nothing. But within days after the election returns, Sonia was painfully reminded of the past in two ways. The Supreme Court rejected the appeal of four people sentenced to hang for Rajiv's assassination in 1991. And a government prosecutor finally brought charges of illegal kickbacks from India's purchase of artillery against Rajiv, when he was prime minister in 1985–89, and against the former head of Bofors of Sweden and an Italian businessman named Ottavio Quattrocci who had been a friend of Sonia's late husband.

On Monday, 11 October, the president of India appointed Vajpayee as prime minister, saying a confidence vote in the Lok Sabha wasn't necessary because he was satisfied that Vajpayee commanded a majority of members, and Parliament should tackle economic issues as quickly as possible.

The whole process was much shorter and simpler than the consultations, suspense, and narrow vote of confidence that had dragged on for days following the 1998 election. Just nineteen months later, it reflected the popular acceptance of the BJP as India's ruling party with its allies. Vajpayee had been elected leader of both the BJP caucus and the Alliance caucus. An Alliance delegation had presented a letter to Narayanan claiming a majority of 304 members. The president had met Vajpayee for forty minutes and given him a bouquet of flowers as well as his constitutional blessing.

On Wednesday morning, 13 October, in a two-hour ceremony in the forecourt of Rashtrapati Bhavan, Narayanan swore in a seventy-member government, the largest in years. Vajpayee, seventy-three, in apparent good health, looking quietly exuberant, took the oath first. The United News of India reported that the installation "heralded an era of stable coalition government." Indeed, the BJP had reason to hope for the full five-year term that was highly unlikely before the blunders of its enemies bringing on the election.

The prime minister covered as much political ground as possible in naming fifteen cabinet ministers from the BJP and eleven from other parties, as well as thirty-one ministers of state from the BJP plus thirteen from other parties. There were no big surprises, correctly conveying the impression that the government was carrying on.

Advani remained home minister, Sinha finance minister, Jaswant Singh foreign minister, Fernandes defence minister, and M.M. Joshi human resources minister. A woman, Mamata Bannerjee of West Bengal's Trinamul Congress, became railways minister. Independent Maneka Gandhi took charge of social justice as a minister of state. Six other women became ministers of state as the government prepared legislation reserving one-third of the seats in Parliament and the state legislatures for women. A number of dalits and Muslims also joined the government.

"The NDA reflects the spirit of India in all its diversity," asserted Vajpayee with justification in an address to the nation on 16 October. "It also mirrors the fundamental unity in this diversity."

Pledging that his government would work to "create a kinder, gentler, and more tolerant society," he emphasized the importance of economic reforms, reiterated the goal of providing basic services in rural areas, and affirmed a policy of "zero tolerance" for terrorism and corruption.

On 12 October, one day before India's installation of its new democratically elected coalition government, Pakistan's army under General Musharraf carried out a military coup simply banishing the civilian government in place, arresting Prime Minister Nawaz Sharif, suspending the constitution and Parliament, and imposing martial law for the fourth time in the country's history. Musharraf had directed the intrusion by armed men into Indian-held Kashmir during the spring and summer, and its failure was a major factor in the coup in Pakistan as it had been in the election in India.

In outlining the Alliance government's policies when the new Indian Parliament convened on 25 October, President Narayan promised a "bold strategy" of economic reform creating 10 million new jobs each year. But most notably his address laid out India's views of its neighbours and the world.

He said that India would preserve its "strategic autonomy" as a nuclear power. He warned: "Pakistan must stop cross-border terrorism." He said that India would aim to strengthen its traditional ties with Russia and "continue our dialogue with China." But before coming to Russia and China, he declared on behalf of the new Hindu nationalist-led government: "India seeks to further deepen and broaden her relations with the United States of America, on the basis of the values and ideals we both share."

President Bill Clinton had struck a similar note when he telephoned Vajpayee on 15 October to discuss Pakistan and wrote in a subsequent letter: "As the leaders of the world's two largest democracies, you and I have a special responsibility to demonstrate that democracy provides the best foundation not only for domestic prosperity and stability, but for cooperation and harmony among democratic nations."

At most times in the past, words such as these between the United States and India would have been taken as futile rhetoric. Near the dawn of a new century, and at the beginning of a new era for India, its president effectively responded with this commitment in his address to Parliament: "My government will maintain and foster close understanding with our strategic partners."

15

Violence, Alignment, and the Bomb

The rise of the Bharatiya Janata Party and fall of the Nehru dynasty is transforming India's impact on Asia and the world as well as politics within India. Contrary to dire predictions when the Hindu nationalists came to power in March 1998 and openly tested nuclear bombs two months later, the change in both cases is positive rather than negative.

Just as the parliamentary election in September 1999 consolidated healthy coalition politics as well as the BJP in power, it was a stabilizing factor in Asia and gave India a new and constructive role to play as a democracy willing to join others to keep in check China's openly expressed ambitions to dominate Asia and the Western Pacific. In a word, India has become more honest in its dealings with other countries. As a consequence, the prospects for a needed democratic alliance in Asia and the Pacific are brighter.

In the past, no country had done more than India to project a certain image of itself to the rest of the world. No country's actions had contrasted more sharply with its desired image than those of India. But the image is disappearing as the Nehrus fade into history. And the reality is healthy for Asia, and global peace and security, as Hindu nationalists instead of the Congress Party make and carry out Indian foreign and defence policy.

Non-violence, non-alignment, and opposition to nuclear weapons: these terms described until recent years India's intended international image. They still have not entirely lost their resonance. They stem from the noble principles of Mohandas K. Gandhi, the sophisticated foreign policy of Jawaharlal Nehru, and the anti-nuclear stance inherent in both.

But India's actual role in the world and particularly in its neighbourhood has been very different. During more than a half-century of independence, India has regularly employed violence in waging five wars and a few mini-wars, and conducting lengthy anti-insurgency campaigns. India embraced alignment with the old Soviet Union, and still risks inertia in its relationship with Russia. India relies at bottom on possession and, if need be, use of the bomb.

By resorting to violence under cover of non-violence, by cloaking alignment in non-alignment, and by demanding that other powers give up nuclear weapons while secretly amassing warheads and the means to deliver them, India attempted to conceal its real nature. Moreover, these elaborate forms of camouflage, especially as they were deployed shamelessly and repeatedly by the Nehru dynasty, masked a larger fact about India.

Most non-Indians, and many Indians on the basis of their own experience, look on the second most populous country as mired in chronic poverty. Under the Nehrus, unneeded economic and political constraints did sap Indian energy and stunt Indian growth long after independence in 1947. But at the same time most Indians consider their country not only the dominant power in South Asia. They see India as a potential world superpower.

This deep-rooted Indian perception helps account for the confusion, tension, and finally betrayal felt by many Westerners who try to understand India. Attracted by India's claim to be the world's biggest democracy, repelled when they find much wrong with Indian democracy, they're dismayed by the discovery that such a poor country seriously entertains superpower ambitions.

Whether pursuing those ambitions or not, India has had many enemies over the years. Many outsiders see only Pakistan as India's enemy, and Pakistan is obsessed with perpetuating this myth as well as with India itself. But other nations in South Asia – Sri Lanka, Nepal, and even Bangladesh, which India created out of East Pakistan – have been India's enemies in a sense because they stand in the way of a Greater India. In a sense Japan is India's enemy because the former's economic success in Asia, despite problems in recent years, stands in stark contrast to Indian performance. Notwithstanding limited military co-operation soon after the end of the Cold War and the collapse of Delhi's Soviet patron, and much closer defence co-operation starting in 2001, the United States in another sense is India's enemy simply because it is the only full superpower. This hostility was never so evident as in December 1971, when Indians saw a U.S. Navy task force led by the nuclear-powered aircraft carrier Enterprise in the Bay of Bengal as interference in their third war with Pakistan, which gave birth to Bangladesh, and as a deliberate attempt to deny great-power status to India.

But China is India's real enemy. For good reasons, Indians believe that the Chinese directly challenge them for hegemony over a large slice of Asia. It took the coming to power of Hindu nationalists for India to meet China's challenge honestly and directly.

Historically, raw Hindu nationalism shaped hostile Indian attitudes to the outside world. Caste Hindus considered invaders from that world – Alexander the Great, Mahmud of Ghazni, the Moghuls, the British – as unclean aliens, sometimes to be resisted, usually to be tolerated with disdain and absorbed with time. Mohandas Gandhi violated orthodox Hindu tradition when as a young man he left the world of India and crossed the ocean to South Africa.

After return of the Mahatma and removal of the British Raj, the Nehrus refined the crude Hindu belief in Bharat or India as the centre of the world. They adapted it to post-colonial, Cold War conditions, and made an international impact in doing so. But they didn't change its essence.

In 1992 Lal Krishna Advani, then the leader of the BJP, expressed confidence to me that this cultural conviction soon would come back as government policy shorn of the camouflage of non-alignment and non-violence, and underlining India as a declared member of the nuclear club. When the Hindu nationalists did gain power near the end of the twentieth century, however, they unexpectedly modified the concepts that had guided India in breaking with the Raj in 1947. India did come out of the nuclear closet almost immediately, and one year later engaged in a mini-war started by Pakistan. But India kept the war limited, and as a nuclear power sought not superpower status but strategic co-operation.

Although the Hindu caste system survived and influenced various Moghul rulers over more than 500 years, and coexisted with the British class system for nearly two centuries, the fundamentalist believers in Bharat as the world's fulcrum were naturally anti-Muslim, anti-Raj, and anti-Western. If the pragmatic Vallabhai Patel, who came from Gujarati peasant stock, had been India's first prime minister, it is unlikely he would have let this negative outlook come in the way of a close relationship with the United States. But Pandit Nehru, as the worldly Brahmin leader of the Indian National Congress and independent India, altered these instinctive biases so they became anti-Pakistani, anti-colonial, and anti-American.

With a substantial Muslim minority remaining even after partition, and largely Muslim Kashmir still in dispute, predominantly Hindu but constitutionally secular India could not appear to be against Islam as a religion. With the British physical presence gone, a whole class of anglicized Indians felt freer to admire and ape British ways. With India on its own, Prime Minister Nehru was free to weave the web of deception that frequently characterized its foreign and defence policies.

From the beginning, usually implicitly but often explicitly, the Nehrus depicted the United States as India's ultimate adversary despite official and popular American sympathy for the Indian freedom movement, generous

U.S. economic aid to independent India, and Americans' adherence to democracy in common with that of Indians. During the Cold War, despite the Nehru family's repeated protestations of non-alignment, warm ties with the Soviet Union combined with this anti-American animus to make India a major ally of Moscow. The Soviets continuously interfered in and tried to direct Indian politics and economic development as well as foreign policy, and usually succeeded. Along with huge amounts of military hardware, the Soviets provided India with a model not of imperfect democracy but of despotic mismanagement.

At first Nehru was widely hailed in the West as an Asian leader who looked to all the world for inspiration and guidance instead of only Western civilization. Politically correct revisionists in the 1990s would have loved him. In the early 1930s, he had written an extraordinary series of letters to his only child, Indira, from prisons in India to which the British had sentenced him for his part in the independence struggle; updated and revised for a book called *Glimpses of World History*, they are nothing less than what he called a "rambling account" of the civilized world from its beginnings. Impressive for breadth and knowledge without benefit of reference books, *Glimpses of World History* also reveals a jaundiced view of the United States that Nehru never could rise above.

In a letter to Indira dated 3 January 1933, about the U.S. colonial presence in the Philippines, he spoke of the "invisible [economic] empire that the United States of America possesses" in many countries, and warned that this was the kind of "dangerous thing ... we must beware of." When Indian independence came in August 1947, Nehru's elegant "tryst with destiny" speech was striking in part not only because it took in the whole world but also because it left out common democratic values: "[Our] dreams are for India, but they are also for the whole world, for all the nations and peoples are too closely knit together today for any one of them to imagine that it can live apart. Peace has been said to be indivisible; so is freedom, so is prosperity now, and so also is disaster in this One World that can no longer be split into isolated fragments."

Nehru meant freedom from Western colonialism before any other. In any case he was not about to let the fragment of Kashmir, the homeland of his family, go to Pakistan or become independent through exercise of freedom. When the independence-minded Hindu maharaja of Kashmir felt he had to accede to India despite the adherence to Islam of most Kashmiris, and after tribal gunmen had entered the state to claim it for Pakistan, India went to war with Pakistan the first time. Nehru's government airlifted troops to Srinagar, the summer capital, just in time to save the beautiful and coveted Vale of Kashmir for India and win the war.

The United Nations ceasefire line that went into effect 1 January 1949, and was later legitimized further as the line of control between Indian and Pakistani forces, confirmed Delhi's attainment of its objective. In the UN Security Council, the Soviet Union consistently used its veto to support India's rejection of a popular plebiscite or referendum that would have allowed Kashmiris to exercise their internationally established right to self-determination. Most of the world still chose to believe that newly independent India was following Gandhian non-violence and strict non-alignment in the rapidly developing global confrontation between the Soviet bloc and the West. In reality, Nehru casually compromised these principles from the moment the Raj came to an inglorious end in arbitrary partition and religious violence, and he cleverly espoused a softer version of Indian chauvinism.

Following Delhi's protests against formation in 1954 of the U.S.-inspired Central Treaty Organization and Southeast Asia Treaty Organization – Pakistan eagerly joined both military pacts – any doubt that remained about India's double standard in the Cold War should have disappeared in November 1956. During the Suez crisis, Nehru strongly condemned Britain, France, and Israel for their military intervention in Egypt for strategic purposes. But he could not bring himself to criticize the Soviet Union for its simultaneous invasion of Hungary and brutal suppression of a popular movement for autonomy that would have been called anti-colonialist in Asia. The United States and Canada also found themselves joining Moscow in opposing the Suez adventure by their historic allies. But, in sharp contrast to Nehru and India, they labelled the tanks in Budapest as unmistakable evidence of aggression launched by the Soviet Union to maintain its empire in Eastern Europe, even if little could be done to stop it.

It was also in 1956, on 28 April, that India signed an atomic agreement with Canada. It called for construction, with Canadian aid, of India's first nuclear reactor. Although the agreement vaguely limited the reactor's use to "peaceful purposes," there were no specific controls, international or otherwise. The forty-megawatt heavy-water research reactor at Trombay, outside Bombay, "went critical" – set off its first chain reaction – on 10 July 1960, not quite four years before Nehru's death. Trombay was India's first deliberate step toward becoming a nuclear-weapons power. Later a plant was built adjacent to the experimental reactor for converting spent fuel from the reactor and from much larger Canadian-designed twin power reactors in Rajasthan into weapons-grade plutonium.

In late 1961, Nehru vividly demonstrated in his inimitable way that he no less than Hindu chauvinists considered India the centre of the world, impervious to international opinion. He struck a blow directly against

Western colonialism and indirectly against the United States. But it hurt India the most when it boomeranged.

After the British left India, the French had voluntarily withdrawn from their tiny territory of Pondicherry in the south. But the Portuguese had stubbornly stayed on in their enclave of Goa and two smaller territories named Daman and Diu on the Arabian Sea coast south of Bombay. Portugal's presence in the Subcontinent was nearly 450 years old, and its Roman Catholic and cultural influences had spread to Bombay and beyond. But India insisted that Goa, Daman, and Diu represented an unacceptable colonial intrusion on its land. Lisbon, under dictator Antonio Salazar, ignored Indian demands for a negotiated Portuguese withdrawal. In sharp contrast to the British Raj's usually non-lethal methods of dealing with Gandhian demonstrators, Portugal's troops had shot down Indians attempting to march non-violently into Goa.

Soon before he left for a long-anticipated meeting with President Kennedy at the White House in early November, Nehru summoned the half-dozen American correspondents in Delhi, including myself, to an interview. Seated comfortably at his long desk in his Ministry of External Affairs office, at his charming best, the prime minister noted philosophically that every nation saw the rest of the world from its own particular angle. His point was that India's view of Goa was naturally different from how faraway America saw the quiet Portuguese territory.

It was not Nehru's views on this subject that demolished Kennedy's admiring illusions about Nehru but the Indian leader's aloof unwillingness or inability at least to understand U.S. global policies. Soon after Nehru's return home, however, India shocked the United States and most other countries by removing the impediment in its world view through unprovoked use of armed force. Striking without warning on the night of 18 December, bombers hit key facilities in Goa – including the telegraph office, to delay word of the Indian invasion from getting out – and troops crossed the international border. An Indian army division quickly overcame light resistance and forced the small Portuguese garrison to surrender. India won its second war in thirty-six hours.

The days immediately before and after the takeover of Goa, Daman, and Diu were revealing in several ways.

The United States' Ambassador John Kenneth Galbraith, the liberal Canadian-born Harvard economist, was under instructions from Washington to prevail on India to give up thoughts of a military venture that could only harm its image and reduce its influence. He met almost daily with Nehru as journalists waited expectantly to see if the cat would jump. We knew it would when we learned that the Indian railways had cancelled regular passenger trains and were rushing tanks south. The canny Nehru was giving the impression that V.K. Krishna Menon, his radically anti-Western defence minister, was pushing him to go ahead with an invasion. But the prime minister had probably decided on the military action before he went to Washington, possibly long before. He had first publicly advocated such action in 1955. If he had any last minute doubts, they were dispelled by Galbraith, who told him privately that "Jack" – President Kennedy – would understand an armed Indian attack on the Portuguese colony. That was why it was India's turn to be shocked when Adlai Stevenson, the U.S. ambassador to the UN and twice the Democratic candidate for president, roundly and eloquently condemned the Indian aggression in the Security Council.

I was in Delhi for the invasion, acting for the *New York Times* correspondent who was trying to cover it on the ground, but I flew down to Goa soon after it was conquered. Two feats by Indian troops, in addition to their walkover victory, impressed me there. They had virtually cleaned out the wine shops where Portuguese rosé had sold for a pittance compared to the cost of any alcoholic beverage in India. And true to their British military tradition, they staged a musical march-past on the dusty parade ground of Panjim, the old colonial capital, to which Goans were invited.

Lieutenant General Joyanto Nath Chaudhuri, the dashing southern army commander who had executed the carefully planned military operation, jovially told me the two reasons for this stirring show of victory. It was meant to end any doubts on the part of the local population that the Indians were in Goa to stay and to inspire something akin to awe of Indian dominance. Intimidation of Goans by the Indian army, and eventual peaceful integration of Goa into the Indian body politic, nevertheless were a far cry from the Indonesian army's brutal invasion of Portuguese East Timor in 1975 and its mass killing of people for years, especially after they voted in 1999 for independence. Macao, the third bit of Asia held by Portugal for more than four centuries, passed peacefully under China's control at the end of 1999.

Nehru's reaction to criticism of the Goa operation was typical: "In spite of the fact that I've been called a hypocrite," he insisted, "I may say I work for peace." He explained that peace was different from non-violence; if India pursued Gandhian non-violence as a policy, he said, it could not even have armed forces.

On returning to the United States in mid-1962 following a year based in Delhi, I sensed that despite Goa and India's exasperating holier-than-thou non-alignment, many Americans still accepted Nehru on faith while despising Krishna Menon. They still identified India more with the saint represented on the prime minister's desk by a framed autographed portrait of Mahatma Gandhi than with the carved ivory tiger next to it.

In reality, in late 1961 and through most of 1962 the still hungry Indian tiger stalked the same enemy that the United States was trying to keep from overrunning Asia – Communist China. The tiger was mauled when it crept too far into the Himalayan lair of the Chinese. But the Indian tiger was then on the side of the good guys as far as the Kennedy administration and most Americans were concerned. Although many have forgotten it, this was a key precedent for the United States, India, other Asian countries, and other Western countries – all democratic – to ally against China early in the twenty-first century.

16

Debacle in the High Himalayas

The conflict between India and China along more than 4,000 kilometres of the world's highest and most glorious mountains goes back to the Raj at the turn of the last century. It is certain to continue at least well into the twenty-first century.

In 1904 the Younghusband expedition to Lhasa enabled the British to make Tibet under Chinese suzerainty a buffer state, like Afghanistan, against Russian expansion in Central Asia. By the First World War, however, China's presence in Tibet was judged a potentially greater threat to India. So the British established Himalayan boundaries that they hoped the Chinese would respect. At stake then, and now, were 130,000 square kilometres of remote disputed mountainous borderlands, and since the late 1940s, the prestige and strategic position of the world's two most populous nations.

The conflict reached a climax in October and November of 1962 in the only war India lost of the five it has waged. The war in the Himalayas at that time did not receive the attention it deserved in the United States and the West because it coincided with the Cuban missile crisis. But it was a watershed in modern Asian history, and easily could have joined the Soviet provocation in Fidel Castro's Cuba to bring a nuclear holocaust even closer to reality than it was.

One reason to recount the Himalayan war is that it starkly revealed Indian attitudes that were not clear at the time but, long after Jawaharlal Nehru, continued to characterize Indian thoughts and actions. India's relations with China have eased in the last four decades. But Indian humiliation and desire for revenge remain. More important, so does India's determination under a new kind of government to protect its national security, alone if necessary, but preferably with other powers in broad mutual security agreements. The wide-ranging border dispute between two countries that consider themselves potential superpowers has not been settled. Large numbers of Chinese and Indian combat troops still face each other across the cold, snowy high Himalayas. Since 1962 there have been several armed clashes and the two sides have come perilously close to wider hostilities. The war is not over.

It actually started in 1950, when newly triumphant Communist Chinese leaders sent the People's Liberation Army into Tibet to take over the vast plateau between Han China and the Subcontinent. This was a renewed threat to India's protective Himalayan shield as well as what became a systematic campaign of genocide against the Tibetan people. But Nehru refused to acknowledge either reality publicly until after the Dalai Lama's miraculous escape over the Himalayas to India in March-April 1959 as Chinese troops massacred his rebelling countrymen and came close to destroying Tibet's Buddhist culture.

Instead of resisting, condemning, or even openly recognizing a far more brutal case of colonialism than anything the Portuguese or British could have dreamed up, India's philosophical leader appeared determined to appease China in the name of Asian solidarity. He embraced with seeming naïveté what were called Panch Shila or the five principles of "peaceful coexistence" in a 1954 agreement with China on Tibetan trade. The following year these motherhood ideals were extended to relations among all Afro-Asian nations meeting at Bandung, Indonesia. But Chinese leaders practised exactly the opposite of peaceful coexistence as they blatantly broke promises to the Tibetans and the world about autonomy and civilized conduct, and with Nehru's help, long covered up their repeated atrocities in Tibet.

Regarding India for good reason with little more than contempt, China started pushing south in 1957 into what it considered its own territory, although the outside world didn't know it at the time. Meeting no Indian resistance, Chinese troops occupied the 59,000-square-kilometre eastern bulge of the Ladakh sector of Kashmir known as Aksai Chin, establishing the presence of a third power in the troubled state besides those of India and Pakistan. More important to China, this permitted the building of a road through Ladakh linking its extreme western province of Xinjiang and Tibet. Far to the east, the Chinese crossed the McMahon Line drawn by the British in 1914 and claimed by the Indians as the boundary dividing their Northeast Frontier Agency or NEFA from Tibet. Between these two mountainous areas where Chinese-controlled Tibet and India meet, China intensified pressures on the Himalayan kingdoms of Nepal, Bhutan, and Sikkim. The Han Chinese were attempting to translate into reality their traditional view of Tibet as a hand with five fingers – NEFA, Bhutan, Sikkim, Nepal, and Ladakh from east to west – all belonging to China.

India's formal response to this growing peril to its security was expressed in a long series of mostly polite notes to Beijing. The diplomatic exchanges between the two governments make up several thick Indian white papers. They set out in often exquisite detail their claims and counter-claims, charges and counter-charges. But, to most observers, India's stance seemed to be summed up by Nehru's comment in the Lok Sabha in 1959 that "not a blade of grass" grew on land in Ladakh claimed by India but used by China to connect Tibet and Xinjiang.

The clear implication was that Delhi considered the territory Indian but would not fight to retain or regain possession of it because it was too desolate to worry about. The aristocratic prime minister dismissed with horror the notion of bombing the Chinese road "out of existence," hopefully suggested by an opposition MP, as "not the way the government would like to function in such matters."

On the ground, however, the Indian government and the Indian army functioned in a way that was sharply at odds with Delhi's diplomatic line and opened to question nothing less than Nehru's honesty. India's method of finally meeting the Chinese challenge in 1962 was marked by shameless duplicity on one hand and incredible ineptness on the other. Nehru suffered a stunning political reversal as well as a devastating military loss from which he never recovered. As much as or more than any internal political event, this Himalayan debacle made continuation of the Nehru dynasty all the more irrational and catastrophic for the country. As much as or more than victories in other wars, defeat in this one underscored India's fantasies about itself as a world power then and for years to come.

"India ultimately will take effective action to recover our territory," the prime minister told Parliament in the fall of 1961. "But whatever action we take, we have to be strong enough to pursue it to its logical end."

Nehru meant unspecified moves in the Himalayas more than the impending invasion of Goa. Capture of the small seacoast territory from lackadaisical Portuguese defenders was a logical if questionable end in itself, and India had the military strength to achieve it quickly. Recapture of some of the world's most rugged and expansive terrain from well-equipped, highly motivated Chinese troops was an entirely different matter. Starting with his permissive response to highly provocative events in Tibet, Nehru had hopelessly confused in the public's mind the end sought by India, which in any case was simply not militarily strong enough at the time to "take effective action."

Nehru never fully abandoned his outward policy of appeasement of China going back to the Communist takeover of Tibet in 1950. But, starting in late 1961, India also pursued a secret "forward policy" of pushing back Chinese forces in the Himalayas.

Indian troops gradually built up mountain roads and military posts. They went around, leapfrogged, or surrounded isolated Chinese outposts. They thereby forced Chinese troops to pull back. By September 1962 the Indians had regained about 6,500 square kilometres of the 36,000 square kilometres in dispute in Ladakh and had eased the Chinese completely out of the bits they held of the 94,000 square kilometres of NEFA claimed by Beijing. They deliberately avoided armed confrontation.

But the forward policy rested squarely on the assumption by Nehru and his associates that the Chinese would do the same even if they were losing territory they considered valuable and their own. This assumption grew out of a conviction that first, India was wholly in the right in its border dispute with China, and second, no country except perfidious Pakistan would attack India, the champion of peace, non-alignment, and Asian unity.

Arrogance more than naïveté was at the root of the forward policy, and perhaps the appeasement policy – meaningless arrogance if India's military unpreparedness is taken into account. Both policies failed miserably when the leaders in Beijing decided they could put up no longer with Indian territorial gains and gratuitous insults, and needed to give Asia and the world a dramatic lesson in the use of military might to preserve China's hegemony.

The fact remains that India, however misguided and ill-prepared its government and armed forces were, took on China on its own. The outcome of the fighting in the fall of 1962 in no way mitigates this demonstration of Indian self-reliance. It was wildly unrealistic but it lessened the military burden on the United States in containing Communist China. It was tragically unjustified but it underlined India's pretensions at the time to superpower status. At the dawn of a new century, when many nations in Asia and the Pacific face the formidable challenge of resisting China, India's lonely action back then is a pointed reminder of the increasingly urgent need for collective determination and security.

As with the "liberation" of Goa, the menacing figure of Defence Minister V.K. Krishna Menon hovered like a dark shadow over India's military adventure in the Himalayas. Lieutenant General Brij Mohan Kaul, commander of Indian forces in NEFA, carried most of the first-hand blame for the fiasco, although he later defended himself better than he had defended Indian territory. Both men were intimate favourites of Nehru – "Bijji" Kaul, a Kashmiri Brahmin, was also a relative – and the prime minister had personally put them in key positions of responsibility.

But, again, as with Goa and the first war against Pakistan in 1947–48, the ultimate responsibility for Indian actions belonged to Nehru. It is highly unlikely that he was unaware of conditions on the ground. The evidence is overwhelming that he knew what was going on in the Himalayas and was fully aware of Indian objectives that went directly against professed Chinese aims. In the end, the failure of Indian arms and Indian policies must be placed at the feet of Nehru, who visibly aged overnight as much that he stood for crumbled.

Failure entailed a sudden loss of large swaths of land vital to the protection of India's heavily populated northern plains. It arose from fielding, and in many cases needlessly sacrificing, outnumbered, often demoralized soldiers who did not have the necessary experience, weapons, ammunition, or even clothing and boots for mountain warfare. It was due to petty bickering among Indian generals at a time of national crisis, and personal grandstanding by Kaul when he should have been commanding. It lay in gross miscalculation of the enemy's intentions and capabilities. It forced a temporary abandonment of non-alignment – in desperation and long after the time when an acquisition of modern weapons from Western powers could have prevented or lessened decisive defeat.

Failure in the Himalayas, considered by Indians until then their country's unsullied crowning glory, culminated in India's humiliation and loss of international face. Tactically, strategically, and politically, India under Nehru's morally discredited democratic leadership suffered a debacle at the top of the world at the hands of a clever, determined, tough-minded Asian dictatorship.

All this could have been avoided if Nehru had met Zhou Enlai even less than halfway when the Chinese premier came to Delhi in April 1960 for extensive talks on the border issue.

Red China had earned a reputation for taking a hard line on what it considered its vital interests from Korea and Taiwan to the long Sino-Soviet border. India was known for its soft line on Communist actions, particularly those in Tibet during most of the 1950s. So it was supremely ironic that Zhou showed a flexibility on the Himalayas question that Nehru was unwilling to match for the sake of a peaceful settlement.

The Chinese premier set out specific proposals in Delhi confirming Beijing's willingness to accept the McMahon Line as the border in the east although China did not recognize it, if India would accept the Chinese presence in Aksai Chin in the west; the "line of control" would prevail in both mountainous areas. Nehru rejected out-of-hand this simple formula, which would have meant India's giving up only an uninhabited stretch of land that he himself had described as remote and desolate but which was important to China. Moreover, moments after Zhou's plane left Delhi for Katmandu, where the premier signed a border agreement with Nepal as he had with Burma on the way to India, Nehru accused China of "aggression" in one of his more notable airport comments to the press.

India's usually conciliatory leader was applauded both at home and abroad for unexpected firmness throughout Zhou's stay. A Herblock cartoon in *The Washington Post* approvingly showed the Chinese premier encased in a block of ice following Nehru's frosty reception. Certainly the Chinese had been aggressive toward more than one adversary and could not easily be trusted. But the prime minister's stubbornness during the talks, and his provocative remark after they ended, were ill-timed and undiplomatic to say the least.

His attitude seemed uncharacteristic to many who had followed his career. But at bottom Nehru was as much an India firster as the most fervent Hindu nationalist, and his condescending stand should not have been surprising. He had long equated himself with India, and now he voiced concern he would lose his job if he conceded even an inch of Indian soil to China. He enjoyed a big parliamentary majority two years before the next election, however, and the last thing he had to fear was a vote of non-confidence.

It is not hard to find the real reason Nehru was unyielding and finally offending when he had a real opportunity to reach a fair settlement with Zhou, and to rescue what was left of the 1950s feeling of *Hindee Chinee bhai-bhai* (Indians and Chinese are brothers). He was getting ready to carry out the recently agreed upon forward policy in both Ladakh and NEFA. Without question he believed that India could get back all the land it claimed in both disputed sectors of the Himalayas without having to make a single concession and with hardly a single shot being fired. His monumental chutzpah grew out of a supreme vision of himself and India as number one, on morally higher ground than any other leader or nation. Pandit Nehru could not have miscalculated more grievously, especially after having "wronged" – the word the Chinese used – the shrewdly discerning premier who was second to Mao Zedong, whose People's Liberation Army held the physically higher ground.

Nehru persisted in his mindset despite the fact that the first armed clash between Indian and Chinese troops had taken place at Longju in NEFA on 25 August 1959, followed in October by an encounter at the Kongka Pass in Ladakh in which nine Indian policemen were killed. These incidents should have served as warnings to the Indian government of what was to come without a border settlement. Instead they served only to stir patriotic and political Indian emotions. This contagious jingoism gave Nehru at first an excuse and then a mandate for the combination of overt diplomatic intransigence and covert military advance that led inevitably to the wider fighting he was confident would not happen.

No formal document ever described the forward policy. Indeed, those behind it took pains not to put the bold scheme in writing. Rather it gradually took shape as a convergence of the self-serving views of several men, and then developed a disastrous momentum of its own.

Its military architect was General Kaul, although he disavowed his own claim in this regard when the plan failed due in large part to his bungling performance in battle. Kaul, whose delusions of individual grandeur nearly matched Nehru's, could not have helped create the forward policy if he had not been able to go over the heads of his military superiors and consult directly with the prime minister. Without this close personal and family relationship, Kaul, who had no field combat experience although he was a graduate of Sandhurst, also would not have been entrusted in early October 1962 with command of the army corps committed to the defence of NEFA. But one thing can be said for Kaul: he tried to impress on Nehru the necessity of India's obtaining modern military equipment from the United States and other Western countries before risking a confrontation with Communist China. His appeals fell on the deaf ears of a Brahmin aristocrat to whom non-alignment remained an article of faith – until it looked as if Chinese troops would sweep virtually unopposed into the Gangetic heartland of India.

Only one Indian figure could have been more adamantly opposed to Western military aid than Nehru, and that was his defence minister since 1957 and alter ego for many years, Krishna Menon. The devil the West and many Indians knew was closely involved in the evolution and execution of the forward policy. Although he naturally preferred Pakistan to Communist China as India's main enemy, he even argued after the policy's failure that it could have succeeded.

Krishna Menon's main contribution to catastrophe in the Himalayas was his vicious animus against Indian military officers following in the British tradition. His contemptuous treatment of such competent senior officers had compelled India's finest soldier, General K.S. Thimayya, to resign from the top military post of chief of the army staff in August 1959, days after two key events – the Longju clash and revelation of the Chinese road in Aksai Chin – had brought widespread demands for the defence minister's head. Nehru therefore persuaded Thimayya to withdraw his resignation. But Krishna Menon's promotion of Kaul to lieutenant general over the army chief's recommendation stood: a clear slap in the face of traditional officers who had little use for Kaul because of his lack of combat experience, his overweening political ambition, and his eagerness to exploit his channel to Nehru.

These officers, the nucleus of India's armed forces, were stung again in early 1961, when upon Thimayya's retirement Krishna Menon once more ignored his recommendations and named the less-than-assertive General P.N. Thapar as his successor and Kaul to the number two army staff position. The final step ensuring that Indian generalship at least in NEFA would be divided and incompetent was the appointment of Kaul in early October 1962 as commander of the new IV Corps, which actually consisted of less than one division, comprising as it did only two of the three brigades of 4 Division.

The choice of Kaul by Krishna Menon and Thapar greatly pleased Nehru, if the prime minister had not actually made it himself. One hour after the appointment was announced, while the forward policy was also going ahead in Ladakh with the aim of forcing the Chinese to abandon their strategic road, Nehru summoned Kaul and personally instructed him about finally pushing the Chinese out of NEFA and back into Tibet. One other official was also close to Nehru in framing and carrying out this irrational policy. He was B.N. Mullik, director of the intelligence bureau, who was obsessed with evicting the Chinese from every bit of disputed territory and avenging the loss of the nine policemen in the Kongka Pass. He repeatedly advised the prime minister that the Chinese would not resist.

At the end of 1959, China had told India in one of the many diplomatic notes exchanged between them that war between the world's two most populous nations was an "absurd idea." In mid-September 1962, with Indian troops under the forward policy biting into long established Chinese positions, especially in Ladakh but also at a key point in NEFA, Beijing warned ominously: "If the Indian side should insist on threatening by armed force the Chinese border forces who are duty-bound to defend their territory ... it must bear the responsibility for all the consequences arising therefrom."

By then Chinese troops were already counterattacking in Ladakh by standing in the way of further Indian advances and putting pressure on new Indian posts. And they were moving toward the first battle of the Himalayan war at Thag La ridge above the extreme western part of NEFA at the Bhutan border – "above" because even Indian maps showed Thag La five to seven kilometres north of the McMahon Line.

Despite Chinese protests, the proponents of the forward policy had arbitrarily moved the de facto border between NEFA and Tibet to the 16,000-foot ridge, the highest point in the area. In the first half of 1962, Indian troops had not only set up about two dozen new posts right on the McMahon Line, but had also established a post just below Thag La. When Chinese troops resisted at that point in the same way they were resisting at several places in Ladakh, the reaction in Delhi was that this was an invasion of India and they had to be driven out. Krishna Menon, representing India at the UN General Assembly in New York – Nehru was also abroad at this critical time – confirmed an order to oust the Chinese from the southern side of Thag La ridge, dismissing General Thapar's fears of a possible Chinese reaction in Ladakh.

Unlike senior army officers, Nehru and his defence minister deceived the Indian people and apparently themselves about both the location of the British-drawn boundary – accepted but not recognized by China in the absence of a joint survey – and the ability of the Indian army to carry out this task. Far from enjoying the military advantage in NEFA as claimed – in supposed contrast to Ladakh, where Chinese forces had the acknowledged advantage – Indian troops were scattered, unused with some exceptions to high altitudes, badly outnumbered and outgunned, and dependent for supplies on hit-and-miss air drops. Their Chinese counterparts were fully organized and acclimatized, and well and easily supplied by trucks traversing the Tibetan plateau. Yet Nehru directly ordered the Indian forces to spurn the last Chinese plea for brotherly friendship, conveyed across the Himalayas by a party commissar through a loudspeaker. He and his civilian colleagues in Delhi still believed the Chinese would retreat rather than open fire at advancing Indians.

When the thoroughly justified objections of Indian officers in the field delayed the Thag La assault through September, impatience in the Indian capital for an anticipated victory put added pressure on Krishna Menon and his increasingly nervous top generals. On 3 October they created the new NEFA corps from two-thirds of a division, and put Kaul in command to carry out the operation immediately.

Nehru then personally charged the familiar political soldier, his relative with no combat experience, to do the militarily impossible. The prime minister evidently was beginning to have some doubts. But the next morning Kaul, under few illusions himself, was on his way by plane to NEFA and what he later called "my doom." It was a fate shared by India.

Kaul's first order in the field was to dispatch reinforcements, recently arrived from the plains after long marches, to the Thag La area with inadequate supplies, summer uniforms, and fifty rounds of ammunition per man (some Indian soldiers had to fight in the Himalayas in 1962 with First World War Lee-Enfield .303 single-shot rifles). An undetermined number of troops died on their new forced marches over rugged terrain five kilometres high. It was the first instance of their new corps commander caring little for the lives of *jawans* or Indian GIs. It would not be the last.

Kaul himself reached the Indian post below Thag La on 7 October after being carried part of the way by a Tibetan porter when Kaul, too, felt the sickening effects of exertion at high altitude. There he saw at first hand and fully appreciated what officers before him, relieved by higher command or criticized by him, had understood: the forlorn situation of the Indian troops facing superior Chinese forces dug in above them and on the other side of a rain-swollen river. Bypassing the normal channel to the army's eastern command in Calcutta, Kaul signalled Delhi in effect that without much greater resources, including air power, he could not be responsible for the outcome if the Chinese responded forcefully to his planned attack on 10 October.

This almost instantly conceived operation, sending a battalion of Rajput troops to occupy a pass west of Thag La and higher, amounted to a suicide mission. Chinese guns could easily wipe out the unsupported Indian jawans as they climbed without cover to above 16,000 feet. If any of them reached that level, they would starve or freeze to death because there was no way to supply them. But when a large advance patrol of Punjabi troops did not draw Chinese fire, Kaul immediately jumped to the conclusion that the forward policy was working and his limited forces were about to take Thag La ridge unopposed. He sent another, distinctly different message to Delhi gleefully anticipating this personal triumph.

Early on the morning of 10 October, as the Rajputs started to move out, Kaul's fantasy was rudely shattered. So was the forward policy. So was peace in the Subcontinent.

A Chinese battalion supported by heavy mortars descended the ridge and attacked the patrol's position. The Punjabi troops repulsed the first Chinese assault, inflicting heavy casualties. But then they were forced to withdraw across the river, and no thought could be given to the main operation by the Rajputs going ahead. The underlying assumption by Nehru, Krishna Menon, and Kaul, that the Chinese would not use force to stop advancing Indian troops, had suddenly evaporated. Kaul's first reaction was to scurry back to Delhi and consult with Nehru personally. As he wrote later, "I had now fully understood all the implications of our predicament."

His words turned out to be an understatement. None of the framers of the forward policy grasped, or wanted to understand, what was happening. The "predicament" was largely Indian-made, not Chinese-made, and only Indians could mitigate it.

The logical – indeed, essential – thing to do now that the Chinese had unmistakably undercut Indian calculations was to exit as gracefully as possible from what was plainly a disastrous policy. With winter coming on, one easy step could have been Indian troops quietly abandoning the obviously provocative post below Thag La ridge. India also could have taken China up on renewed talks, on the grounds of avoiding further bloodshed and resolving border problems fairly and peacefully. Instead, Indian troops stayed above the McMahon Line near Thag La on Kaul's effective recommendation. Worse, two days after their telling setback, Nehru told India and the world that the Indian army was under instructions "to free our territory." He added pointedly that as long as China's "particular aggression" at Thag La continued, there was "no chance of talks."

Nehru made these unnecessary, self-destructive comments at another of his impromptu airport press conferences, before he flew south from Delhi to Ceylon (Sri Lanka) on another trip abroad as the clock continued to tick toward India's "doom" in the north. Kaul had returned to Delhi ill from his futile exertions in the Himalayas. But on the night of 11 October he had briefed a high-level meeting at Teen Murti, the prime minister's house and formerly the residence of the British commander of the Indian army. Less through action than inaction, or paralysis, the consensus at the meeting, strongly backed by Krishna Menon, was not to withdraw the beleaguered brigade from below Thag La. Although snow was already falling, the order went out to reinforce the brigade instead with more weary troops from the plains in summer uniforms. But Nehru contemptuously rejected Kaul's proposal at the meeting to seek immediate U.S. military assistance. With this rejection fresh in his mind, the prime minister's favourite general was dismayed on returning to NEFA, he claimed later, to learn of Nehru's airport remarks promising renewal of the Indian offensive.

Within five days, even more ill, Kaul was flown back to Delhi again for treatment at home. Apart from considering his physical weakness, one has to question whether at least part of his problem was psychological. But apparently no thought was given then to replacing even temporarily the IV Corps commander, or if it was it wasn't expressed. Instead, from his bedroom in Delhi, Kaul threatened officers in the field with removal or court martial if they did not carry out his orders to push units forward in line with Nehru's ill-considered comments. The forward policy again was becoming a suicide mission for hungry, freezing Indian troops. Brigadier John S. Dalvi did convey his intention to resign in a vain attempt to prevent the slaughter of his soldiers in an imminent Chinese attack.

Early in the morning of 20 October, confident, well-prepared Chinese troops heavily supported by artillery launched a division-size assault. Simultaneously, Chinese forces in Ladakh far to the west attacked Indian posts in the Chip Chap River valley and two other key areas. These advance positions were quickly overrun, Indian officers more professional than Kaul ordered evacuation of smaller posts, and the forward policy in Kashmir came to a dismal end.

But the Chinese drive in the eastern Himalayas was just beginning. Within hours PLA troops smashed through desperately resisting but vastly outnumbered Rajputs and Gurkhas in the centre of the thinly manned river line below Thag La, and easily bypassed other advance Indian positions. They sliced the forward brigade of IV Corps into bits, and captured Dalvi, its commander. As these Indian remnants attempted to retreat south toward the plains, the Chinese deliberately crossed the McMahon Line on 25 October and occupied the abandoned site of the Indian brigade's headquarters at Tawang about sixteen kilometres to the south. Then they paused.

At the same time in Delhi, on 24 October, the army gave command of what was left of IV Corps to an experienced lieutenant-general, Harbaksh Singh. But then, five days later, with the obvious connivance of Nehru and Krishna Menon, the corps command was handed back to the third major perpetrator of the failed forward policy, B.M. Kaul!

The prime minister was less successful in trying to save his defence minister. Faced with mounting protests against Krishna Menon by MPs and state chief ministers of the ruling Congress party supported by President Sarvepalli Radhakrishnan, Nehru took over the defence portfolio himself on 31 October but kept Krishna Menon in the cabinet by making him minister for defense production. When Congress MPs threatened for the first time to make Nehru himself the next target, however, he was forced to dismiss Krishna Menon entirely on November 8.

One other development significantly changed the political climate if not the military one.

Nehru had received expressions of support from the United States, the superpower he distrusted – Kennedy wrote him that "Our sympathy ... is wholeheartedly with you" – and Britain, the former colonial power. His instinctive reaction was to reject offers of military help from both. But India's de facto ally, the Soviet Union, was in the midst of a full-fledged crisis with the United States over its missiles in Cuba, and Chairman Nikita Khrushchev temporarily sided with Communist China. Even non-aligned countries qualified their backing for nominally non-aligned India, or did not extend it at all. Nehru was compelled to take account of these depressing factors as well as the impressive military capability China was showing in the Himalayas.

On 29 October the besieged Indian leader informed an eager Ambassador Galbraith that India would accept U.S. military aid. Within five days, U.S. cargo planes with needed military equipment began landing at Indian airfields.

With the last phase of the Himalayan war about to begin, Nehru's dropping of strict non-alignment and Krishna Menon were important policy and personnel changes. But there was no change of heart or mind at the topmost level of the government, or among ordinary Indians, when it came to inflexible insistence on the rightness of India's cause. Moreover, steps to improve the inferior status of Indian forces vis-à-vis the Chinese were too little and too late.

These forces were ordered to form a new line at Se La, a potentially strong mountain position. But Se La was only twenty-four kilometres from the new Chinese base at Tawang, and could be easily outflanked. It was too remote to be effectively supplied, and too high for reinforcements unused to thin, cold air to defend at full capacity. Crucial mistakes like those made at Thag La were waiting to happen again.

It would have been far better for Indian forces to make a fresh stand at Bomdi La, as an order in line with a strategically sound 1959 defence plan had stipulated. The order, however, was cancelled. Bomdi La was nearly one hundred kilometres beyond Tawang. But it was the northernmost point where Indian troops could be built up more rapidly than Chinese forces could be reinforced. At 2,600 metres it was two kilometres lower than Se La and easier to fight for and hold. The army's opting nonetheless for the forward position at Se La, a move that would be seen as conceding as little land as possible, once again reflected wishful political thinking, not realistic military calculation.

So did India's response to China's last bid to talk instead of shoot. Premier Zhou had written to Nehru on 24 October, making the first direct contact since their ill-fated Delhi meeting two and a half years earlier. He proposed that both countries withdraw their forces twenty kilometres from the "line of actual control" in November 1959; that Chinese forces then withdraw to north of the McMahon Line; and that the two prime ministers meet again to "seek a friendly settlement."

The Indian government rejected this overture the same day. It accused China of using territory gained by "aggression" as a "bargaining counter." It suggested talks only after Chinese troops withdrew to their positions before 8 September, when they had first confronted the Indian post below Thag La. Nehru reiterated this counter-proposal in a mildly-worded letter to Zhou on 27 October. But when another letter from the Chinese premier on 4 November elaborated on Beijing's proposal, Nehru sharply replied that agreeing to anything less than Indian troops returning to their forward posts both in Ladakh and at Thag La would amount to India's existing "at the mercy of an aggressive, arrogant and expansionist neighbour."

Apart from its advantage on the ground, this Nehruvian outburst gave China an excuse to resume its military operations. The introduction of U.S.-supplied guns into the conflict presented Zhou with both an opportunity to link India publicly with "U.S. imperialism" and a reminder that the PLA's Himalayan advantage might not last indefinitely. The little "phony war" that had followed the capture of Tawang on 25 October ended in mid-November with major Chinese attacks in two areas of NEFA.

The first overwhelmed Walong, an important position at the extreme eastern end of NEFA near the border with Burma, and cut another Indian brigade into fleeing bits and pieces. This assault might have coincided with the main Chinese move on Se La, like the simultaneous Chinese attacks in NEFA and Ladakh on 20 October. But the PLA took Walong in direct response to an uphill attack by reinforced Indian troops whose apparent aim was to give Nehru a present on his seventy-third birthday, 14 November, in the form of a military victory. Instead, in a repeat of the fiasco at Thag La, the attack failed with heavy losses and it was the Chinese who moved forward.

Kaul made no less than four visits to Walong to inspect the ground, watch the fighting, and witness the Indian rout. This was during the first part of November, when the newly reinstated corps commander would have been better engaged overseeing defence of the principal Indian stronghold at Se La. His flitting from one remote place to another in NEFA contrasted with concentration by officers of the Indian army's western command on building up an effective defence in Ladakh, although it was relatively easy for them to shift troops from the Kashmir ceasefire line with Pakistan to the obvious route of a renewed Chinese onslaught. On 18 November Chinese troops again attacked in Ladakh, quickly capturing in heavy fighting the last Indian posts in territory claimed by China in that sector. But they advanced no farther, and the lives of jawans were not needlessly sacrificed in Ladakh as they were in the eastern Himalayas with Kaul's seeking to gain or hold isolated patches of rocky ground.

The battle of Se La was lost by India more than it was won by China. Poor or non-existent generalship, demoralized troops, confusion, and cowardice on the Indian side rapidly coalesced in an unimaginable calamity. Militarily, Kaul and his personally chosen officers hardly could have handled more ineptly from beginning to end the deployment of what now was a full division. Politically, the credibility and prestige of India and Nehru hardly could have suffered more in the eyes of the world and, more important, of the Indian people.

With Se La instead of Bomdi La the focal point of the Indian line, it was necessary to spread out 4 Division from one end to the other of the hundred-kilometre mountain road between the two passes. Moreover, a trail to the east, discovered by the British in 1913 preparatory to their drawing the McMahon Line, bypassed Se La. Chinese troops came down the Bailey Trail on 17 November in much greater strength than the Indians had thought possible. Again they rolled over outnumbered and outgunned defenders. On the same day, while Kaul was still skipping over the lost battlefield at Walong far to the east in a helicopter – he later compared himself to Second World War U.S. General George S. Patton in his desire to be with his soldiers – the PLA mounted a frontal assault on Se La.

At first Garhwali hillsmen of the Indian army, who had panicked in the retreat from Tawang, repulsed repeated attacks. But with the Chinese from the Bailey Trail reaching the road between Se La and Bomdi La, and threatening the vulnerable division headquarters in between, the division commander feared that the main position at Se La would soon be cut off, reduced, and destroyed. He asked permission to take his troops out.

An earlier decision to withdraw would have permitted an orderly retreat and regrouping of Indian forces at Bomdi La, where they should have concentrated in the first place. A quick decision now still might have salvaged a large fighting force. But Kaul was not present to make a decision. And his superior officers – the army commander General Thapar and the eastern commander – who were present at IV Corps headquarters in Tezpur on the plains far to the south, and were at least as familiar with the situation as Kaul was, refused to make a decision.

When Kaul finally returned to Tezpur on the evening of 17 November, he was initially for Indian troops remaining at Se La at least through the night although Chinese envelopment was proceeding rapidly. Then, after a discussion with only three other senior officers – Thapar, the eastern commander, and the fawning director of military operations – he dispatched an order for immediate withdrawal to Bomdi La. A few minutes later, Kaul again reversed himself. Apparently realizing with the other senior officers the political implications of a militarily necessary retreat, he ordered 4 Division to hold at Se La. But Kaul also left it to the division commander to pull back from "untenable" positions. This was a transparent attempt to shift the blame from himself for what was now an impending disaster. The disaster unfolded as mutual recriminations among senior Indian commanders were replicated among field-level officers and between officers and men.

Shortly after midnight, a battalion unaccountably withdrew from a key position in the brigade defence of Se La. This had an unnerving effect on other troops and set off a retreat by the entire defending force at dawn of 18 November instead of the next night as planned. Chinese troops who moved into Indian positions captured hastily abandoned weapons, including U.S.-supplied automatic rifles in unopened crates. The Indian brigade, attempting to escape down the north-south road controlled now by Chinese troops, suffered heavy casualties and was hammered into pieces – the third brigade in NEFA to meet this fate – and its commander was killed. Next to flee were 4 Division headquarters personnel at Dirang Dzong. Troops there who would have been far better used in the defence of Bomdi La also scattered toward the plains.

The thin, remaining Indian brigade in NEFA still could have given the Chinese a fight at Bomdi La. But it was further weakened when Kaul ordered it to send out a column to relieve already lost Dirang Dzong. When the Chinese assaulted Bomdi La, these troops tried to get back to their positions but were caught out in the open. Overcoming stiff but brief resistance, the PLA captured the last Indian stronghold before the plains late in the afternoon of 18 November.

But Kaul was not finished displaying monumental military incompetence. Trying to reach his shattered forces, he ordered troops trying to regroup at Rupa, thirteen kilometres south of Bomdi La, to continue retreating instead. Then he ordered them to reverse course and make a stand at Rupa when it was too late to do so. The Indians fell back another twenty kilometres on 19 November to a place called Chaku. There the Chinese assaulted them from three sides soon after midnight, breaking up the fourth and last Indian brigade facing them in NEFA and sending the survivors straggling toward the plains.

General Kaul then believed that the PLA was headed toward the plains: the heartland of India. Incredibly, he saw himself as the commander of a vast new army to stop the Chinese. On 20 November, with this dramatic scenario in mind, he ordered most of his corps headquarters to retreat nearly 160 kilometres southwest from Tezpur to Gauhati on the other side of the Brahmaputra River. Then Kaul took to his helicopter again to survey the scene of the devastating Indian defeat in the mountains.

But 20 November marked more than the end of the historic battle for the Himalayas. For one thing, it was what Galbraith called "the day of ultimate panic" in Delhi.

The day before, a fatigued Nehru had informed an initially incredulous, then outraged Lok Sabha that Se La as well as Walong had fallen. He also had told the nation over All-India Radio that the situation was "very serious and very saddening." Wild rumours flew, including one that Kaul had been captured by the Chinese. President Radhakrishnan, wryly dispelling the report, said: "It is, unfortunately, untrue."

But Nehru's faith in Kaul remained unshaken. General Thapar had personally submitted his resignation to the prime minister on 19 November. The prime minister accepted it the next day, making Thapar an official scapegoat. Nehru then proposed that Kaul, the general most to blame for the whole Himalayan fiasco, succeed him as chief of army staff! Radhakrishnan dissuaded him, fortunately, and at the president's suggestion General Joyanto Nath Chaudhuri, the conqueror of Goa, became the new army commander.

Chaudhuri immediately ordered all troops in eastern India to stop retreating and stand where they could, and IV Corps headquarters to return to Tezpur. He removed Kaul from corps command, and replaced him with an experienced combat general, H.J.F. (Sam) Manekshaw, whom Kaul had once tried to blackball and Krishna Menon had rejected as commander of IV Corps in favour of Kaul. On 25 November, Kaul, fifty, requested retirement from military service. When it came through, Nehru wrote a "My dear Bijji" letter expressing his regret. Only after the depar-

ture of Kaul, who had advised officials in Tezpur and the Assam state government of the imminent arrival of the Chinese, was calm in eastern India
restored and a mass flight of civilians, with bureaucrats and politicians at
the head of the line, halted.

On 20 November, the central government ordered all state governments
to arrest leading members of the Communist Party of India. The intention
was to take out of circulation only those members who later formed the
pro-Beijing Marxist party. But, to Nehru's dismay, police also rounded up
pro-Moscow Communists temporarily. The prime minister's affinity to the
Soviet Union, however, did not prevent him from taking the most significant step in India that day.

Late at night the self-appointed paragon of non-alignment appealed
urgently to the United States for warplanes to strike advancing Chinese
troops and protect Indian cities. Nehru informed neither his cabinet nor the
foreign ministry of his desperate appeal through the U.S. embassy, and it
remained a secret until early 1965 after his death. But he specifically
requested fifteen squadrons, indicating that he might have been advised by
Kaul. Washington responded immediately: an aircraft carrier of the U.S.
Pacific fleet made for the Bay of Bengal.

The most extraordinary event of all on 20 November made Nehru's
revealing move unnecessary, and the carrier turned back. At the same time
it made India's debacle in the Himalayas even more devastating. Shortly
before midnight in Beijing, the Chinese government announced that at midnight of 21–22 November its forces would cease fire, and on 1 December
they would start withdrawing to twenty kilometres behind the 1959 "line
of actual control, that is, north of the illegal McMahon Line." These were
precisely the terms that China repeatedly had sought to negotiate peacefully
with India. Having demolished the forces that had stealthily carried out the
forward policy, Beijing now imposed these terms unilaterally, also warning
Indian troops to stay back twenty kilometres or risk further attack. In
effect the Chinese proclaimed magnanimously to Asia and the world that
they did not have to invade India to punish Indians who had dared defy
them.

For political reasons, India never formally accepted the Chinese terms.
For military reasons, India had no choice but to accept them. The Chinese
withdrew as promised, and carefully returned not only Indian prisoners but
also captured Indian equipment, including the unused U.S.-supplied automatic rifles. Delhi provided only in 1965 an account of Indian casualties:
1,383 killed, 1,696 missing, 3,968 captured. About 90 per cent of these
losses were sustained in NEFA. Hundreds of Chinese troops also were killed
but not a single prisoner was taken.

Many Indians deceived themselves with the notion that the PLA pulled back because Beijing feared a fresh Indian move. It is true that the farther Chinese troops advanced, the more tenuous their supply lines became. Deliberate disengagement came shortly before U.S. planes would have bombed increasingly vulnerable Chinese columns. But this was all part of a brilliantly conceived and executed master plan that added up to the most striking military triumph in the history of the People's Republic of China.

Defeat of India in the Himalayas was more decisive than Chinese "volunteers" throwing back U.S. troops advancing up the Korean peninsula in 1950, or the more limited, nearly failed "punitive expedition" mounted by Beijing against Vietnam in 1979 in reaction to Hanoi's invasion of Cambodia. In response to what China saw as a creeping threat to its hold on Tibet and its stake in Central Asia, three Chinese divisions in NEFA and a smaller Chinese force in Ladakh inflicted on numerically equal Indian forces a series of stinging, unequivocal, and finally humiliating setbacks. As a historic consequence, Jawaharlal Nehru and democratic India no longer could pretend to enjoy equal status with Mao Zedong, Zhou Enlai, and Communist China.

Predictably, they did so pretend. In reply to renewed personal entreaties by Zhou for negotiations, Nehru and the Indian government stuck to their original demands as if nothing had happened. They even got some non-aligned countries to front for India in an organized bid for resumed talks, when India as always had no intention of talking about anything less than China's accepting whatever Delhi claimed in the Himalayan borderlands. But India's stature in the non-aligned movement was sharply reduced, and India's own non-alignment in the Cold War was seriously compromised despite Nehru's denials and continuing solicitude for the Soviet Union (whose diplomats had joined his closest colleagues in telling the prime minister the Chinese would not use force against the forward policy).

The United States and Britain quickly put together a $120-million military assistance program (worth about $1 billion in 2003) split evenly between U.S. aid and Commonwealth aid from Britain, Canada, and Australia. In 1963, the Americans and British carried out the kind of joint air exercise in India that Nehru had secretly requested when a Chinese invasion of the central plains appeared to be underway. But Western sympathy for India, if not suspicion of China, then faded and came to a halt along with Western military aid when an enlarged and modernized Indian army went to war against Pakistan in the fall of 1965. Meanwhile, Congress Party politicians made sure a high-level military inquiry into the causes of the Himalayan disaster was limited and its findings were never made public.

Needless to say, Nehru did not resign for a calamity that would have brought down almost any other government following the parliamentary tradition. Before and after he died in May 1964, many Indians said he had been betrayed by close civilian and military advisers, who so accused each other, and by China.

It may be more accurate to say that Nehru betrayed himself and India at the same time. Whether or not he believed in the peaceful ideals he eloquently talked about, the policy he pursued in the Himalayas was warlike. Whether or not he considered China an enemy from the start, as his intelligence chief Mullik claimed, the prime minister thought India could attain its goals without the Chinese fighting back. The forward policy failed and Nehru was dead wrong. He was dishonest to himself in waging war. He was naive in assuming India's adversary would not wage war. He badly hurt India by thinking India was a nation like no other and could have war and peace at the same time. But his convictions also reflected India's preoccupation with itself as the centre of Asia and the world.

Jawaharlal Nehru had a dual obsession – with India, and with himself as representing India like no other. In the end this was what killed him, soon after India's obsession and his own shattered like the hapless Indian brigades on the remote slopes of the unforgiving Himalayas.

17

Talking Peace and Waging War

A disheartened Jawaharlal Nehru set his sights on one more international goal, however, and this time he dropped his usual pretenses. In his last weeks, he made a gallant effort to come to terms with India's inescapable enemy, Pakistan, over the emotional issue most dividing them: Kashmir.

The prime minister realized that a peaceful agreement to India's liking with a triumphant China, which had tightened its grip on Kashmir's Aksai Chin bulge, was out of the question for the foreseeable future. Partly due to the frustration this produced, partly because India had a less formidable alternative adversary at hand, it also was clear that popular Indian hostility toward Pakistan was bound to increase. Perhaps most of all, the ailing Nehru must have been agonizingly aware of his own mortality. He had little time to soften, through peace instead of war, the profound effects of independent India's crushing defeat in the Himalayas in the fall of 1962 – and undivided India's traumatic partition in the summer of 1947, historically a bigger mistake and an event with which he was also intimately connected.

"After seventeen years of bitter separation between India and Pakistan," began an analysis of mine in *The Globe and Mail* on 26 May 1964 under the headline "Mr. Nehru's Last Effort," "Prime Minister Jawaharlal Nehru has decided that reconciliation of the two countries is essential and is doing all he can to bring it about."

He had ordered Sheikh Mohammad Abdullah, the Lion of Kashmir and the hero of Kashmiris, released from detention on 8 April after ten years, and conspiracy charges against him dropped. He had eased out Bakshi Ghulam Mohammad, Delhi's puppet in Srinagar, as the premier of the state of Jammu and Kashmir, and then as the power behind the throne, and had seen to it that a more popular, less corrupt regime was installed. At Nehru's bidding, Sheikh Abdullah, following talks with the people of Kashmir and at length with Nehru, had then gone to Pakistan to talk with President Mohammad Ayub Khan.

The tall leader of the divided Muslim-majority state, at once charismatic and meditative like Nehru himself, had come out for joint Indian-Pakistani rule of Kashmir, including the beautiful Indian-held Vale, under either a condominium or a broad subcontinental confederation. Nehru had given his blessing to this seemingly revolutionary idea. Actually, he had himself revived the concept of confederation, first proposed by Chakravarti Rajagopalachari before independence and partition, and rejected by Nehru then.

Nehru, a Kashmiri Brahmin, had encouraged Abdullah, a moderate Muslim, to become a bridge to a deal with Marshal Ayub and Islamic Pakistan. One reason that Nehru favoured Abdullah was the Kashmiri leader's position on the key sticking point between India and Pakistan over Kashmir. At the time of the 1 January 1949 United Nations ceasefire agreement between the two countries, Nehru had suggested a plebiscite to allow Kashmiris to determine their own future. Since then, however, while Pakistan had demanded that such a plebiscite take place, India, fearing Kashmiris might favour Pakistan, had contended that necessary peaceful conditions for such a vote were not in place. Abdullah's own position was not to insist on a plebiscite. This major concession promised a new opening, leading not only to a peaceful relationship between India and Pakistan but also to joint defence against China.

By demonstrating their willingness to do away with the entrenched partition of Kashmir, tacitly accepted by both governments while each publicly demanded the whole state, Pandit Nehru and Sheikh Abdullah together made Indian-Pakistani reconciliation the *sine qua non* for a solution of the Kashmir problem instead of the other way around, and President Ayub agreed in principle to meet Nehru in this spirit.

Speaking to the All-India Congress Committee in Bombay, Nehru declared that unless a settlement were reached with Pakistan through Sheikh Abdullah, "India will carry the burden of continuing conflict with Pakistan." In words rarely heard in India, he continued in his soft yet compelling voice: "I hope that it may be possible for the two countries to develop closer and more intimate relations to the advantage of both ... At the present moment it appears difficult to change our attitudes toward each other. But I earnestly hope that an attempt to do so will bear fruit and ultimately may bring about the change we desire and work for."

One of the Subcontinent's most tragic ironies was that the man to whom all Indians once ran for decisions, although he usually found it difficult to make decisions, lacked the power now to carry this one out. Nehru, who because of a heart condition had been forced in January 1964 to leave day-to-day running of the government to a committee of lesser politicians and technocrats, was no longer dominant enough to enforce his will.

Elements in the Congress Party as well as outside it were emboldened by his illness to stir up deep-rooted Hindu sentiments against coming to terms with Muslims, especially over Kashmir. Pakistan, befriending the new enemy of its old enemy, had moved closer to China following Beijing's victory in the Himalayas. It had reinforced its intransigence against anything but a plebiscite in Kashmir, resulting in what it was sure would be Pakistani control of the state. Only a personal meeting of Prime Minister Nehru and President Ayub, if Sheikh Abdullah first succeeded in limiting the area of disagreement, might have overcome negative political pressures in both their countries.

The world will never know what would have come from such a historic encounter. On 27 May 1964, at the age of seventy-four, Nehru died in New Delhi. So did the best hope for reconciliation of India and Pakistan, and for resolution of the Kashmir question.

Abdullah returned empty-handed from a Pakistan determined again not to budge. Hindu nationalists prevailed in upholding India's paramountcy in Kashmir. To Nehru's everlasting credit, and with help from few others besides Abdullah, he had bravely managed to distance himself from these mutually destructive mindsets. But he was too late. He missed a tryst with destiny that would have gone a long way toward redeeming the one he had enunciated in August 1947, when at the very same time the Subcontinent was joyously freed from foreign rule and cruelly divided along religious lines.

After Nehru, India did not come close for many years to rising above insidious Hindu-Muslim division, Pakistan's raison d'être. The Kashmir problem symbolizing the division grew dramatically worse. China remained a feared enemy of India. But for some time Kashmir was more useful to India as an excuse for military measures that could more profitably be taken or threatened against Pakistan. One of these measures, which ultimately came to be directed more against China than against Pakistan despite a stubborn myth to the contrary, was the development of a nuclear-weapons capability.

India continued as a leader of the non-aligned movement, passing judgment on other nations' wars and Cold War battles in the name of peaceful coexistence, as Nehru had done regularly with his presumed moral authority. But except for brief periods, Delhi moved steadily toward and then effectively into the Soviet camp. This trend was both a cause and a result of sharpened Indian-Pakistani hostility, which erupted in two wars in September 1965 and December 1971. India won both of them decisively through violence and alignment. It was and is prepared to use or threaten to use the bomb if there is another major war with Pakistan, and certainly if there is another war with China.

As early as the end of 1964, seven months after Nehru's death and two months after China's first nuclear test, Indians were debating whether to create a nuclear deterrent for themselves at the same time as they renewed calls for nuclear disarmament.

The new prime minister, Lal Bahadur Shastri, reiterated Nehru's pledge that India would use nuclear energy for peaceful purposes only. But he dropped broad hints that India, despite its official non-alignment, would welcome a guarantee of nuclear retaliation from one or more of the nuclear powers – then the United States, the Soviet Union, and Britain – in the event of a Chinese nuclear attack. This was another way of saying that India's promise not to develop nuclear weapons might not hold if China joined the nuclear club. Some opposition political parties, especially the Hindu nationalist Jan Sangh, and individual Congressmen did not attempt to hide their nuclear hawkishness.

Homi J. Bhabha, chairman of India's atomic energy commission, all but declared himself in favour of an Indian bomb, and even made an All-India Radio broadcast about the supposedly low cost of developing a deterrent. This would be possible because of the Canadian-built research reactor at Trombay, which unlike a power reactor being built by the United States in India was not explicitly covered by provisions barring non-peaceful uses. Moreover, it is easier to make weapons-grade plutonium from the spent fuel of a heavy-water reactor of Canadian design than from a U.S.-designed reactor using enriched uranium.

India's intention to become a nuclear power almost certainly originated with Nehru. Just as he camouflaged India's aggressive forward policy in the Himalayas with repeated offers to China of peaceful settlement of territorial disputes on Indian terms, so India's promotion of peaceful nuclear uses at home and nuclear disarmament by other countries was meant to conceal real Indian nuclear aims.

Nehru was close to the widely respected Bhabha, the father of nuclear energy in India, and held the secretive atomic affairs portfolio in the cabinet himself, as Shastri, Indira Gandhi, and Atal Bihari Vajpayee did after him. He constantly emphasized the importance to India of a modern, scientific approach to its problems. If he never fooled himself about China as a rival of India, notwithstanding all the rhetoric about shared ideals, he surely understood that India could not sustain such a rivalry without nuclear weapons. India might not be able to surpass China in this esoteric field, either secretly or openly. But it had the potential capability of deterring Chinese nuclear threats. With its corps of nuclear physicists and international nuclear assistance, India also could be certain of leaping ahead of Pakistan and staying ahead.

Shastri's emphasis on Indian self-reliance in all fields ensured that India would continue to exploit its strong nuclear potential for many years. Building on an acquired foundation of foreign technology, India recorded impressive nuclear achievements on its own, overtly with power reactors not requiring direct assistance from outside, covertly with warheads and the missiles to deliver them. All these efforts, and the outlook of Nehru and his Congress Party successors, were predicated on a vision of India as second to none. But it was fully thirty-four years after Nehru's death, with the Bharatiya Janata Party's coming to power as the Hindu nationalist successor to the Jan Sangh, before this vision was unveiled for all the world to see.

When Lal Bahadur Shastri went to Canada in June 1965, it was not to discuss restrictions on Indian use of Canadian nuclear technology. If the subject came up in his discussions with Prime Minister Lester Pearson, it was not reported. In office for barely one year, Shastri had other purposes in mind, although they had to do with war, current or impending.

One was to send a message to President Lyndon B. Johnson that undiplomatic postponement of an invitation to him to visit the United States, along with similar treatment of Pakistan's President Ayub, had not deterred Shastri from coming to North America. When the little prime minister gazed on Niagara Falls from the Canadian side, he personified India's snubbing the United States in return. When he warned of the consequences of imminent U.S. military intervention in Vietnam in his talks with Pearson, who was then seeking an international formula to contain the war, and in his interview with me, Shastri asserted India's assumed prerogative of giving advice to the United States. At the same time, in contrast to Nehru's one-sidedness on global issues, he injected a note of fairness when he termed the Soviet-aided North Vietnamese intervention in South Vietnam part of what he called the "problem."

But Shastri had another international concern less than three months before the second India-Pakistan war. While he was publicly conciliatory toward Pakistan, he quietly observed that in view of the two countries' failure to agree on ownership of the Rann of Kutch on the Arabian Sea – a disputed desert area straddling the border between India's Gujarat state and Pakistan's Sindh province where tanks had engaged in battle in a mini-war – "the situation might take a turn for the worse."

More than a month earlier, in early May 1965, fully anticipating such a turn, Shastri had made a momentous decision. He had secretly given permission to General Joyanto Nath Chaudhuri, still the chief of army staff two and a half years after the Himalayan war, to invade West Pakistan proper if Pakistani forces attacked Indian-held Kashmir. Without explaining why, the army chief later specified 5 May as the date when "Pakistan's intentions to seize Kashmir before we got too strong became apparent."

India had sharply increased military spending for new equipment following the calamitous 1962 war with China. It planned to build up its army to 825,000 men by 1969. This would give it a better than two-to-one advantage over Pakistan, although Indian troops also faced the Chinese in Tibet. Preparations for war continued in both India and Pakistan even when Shastri, after his visit to Canada, met Ayub in mid-June at the Commonwealth Conference in London with the aim of settling the Rann of Kutch conflict. Prodded by British prime minister Harold Wilson, the Indian and Pakistani leaders signed a ceasefire agreement on 30 June providing for the return of both countries' forces to their positions at the beginning of 1965.

Although Pakistan made the next military moves, covert and overt, India shared the blame for a reckless slide into a war that the governments and peoples of two of the world's poorest nations seemed to want and clearly relished.

On 5 August, in a repeat of the tactics that had set off their first war in 1947, armed infiltrators under Pakistani army command started to slip into Indian-held Kashmir at a number of points. Others occupied about two dozen Muslim border villages in Rajasthan in western India. On 13 August India decided to retaliate in kind, and on 24 August Indian troops crossed into Pakistani territory. This tit-for-tat pattern was still strictly limited and largely unpublicized. Apart from the warning signal it sent up of what might come in the event of escalation, Pakistan had failed to draw major Indian forces in the Punjab, the main area of confrontation, hundreds of kilometres south to the Rann of Kutch battlefield. Moreover, the infiltrators had failed to incite a popular Kashmiri rebellion against Indian rule.

But men intent on a large goal often are undeterred by not gaining smaller objectives. On 1 September, a Pakistani army brigade supported by ninety tanks launched a major assault in southern Kashmir aimed at capturing Akhnoor on the Chenab River and then the city of Jammu. By slicing the road between Delhi and Srinagar, Islamic Pakistan sought finally to cut off the treasured Vale of Kashmir and its defenders from hated Hindu India.

It was Pakistan's boldest bid to assert its identity vis-à-vis India before or since. Marshal Ayub and his generals failed again.

Indian forces held in what became known as the Chhamb sector after initially giving up ground. On 6 September India executed the plan to invade Pakistan that Prime Minister Shastri had secretly authorized four months earlier. General Chaudhuri mounted a three-division drive along the Grand Trunk Road and two other roads westward toward Lahore, capital of Pakistan's Punjab and cultural centre of all the northern Subcontinent. Farther north, another Indian force struck for Sialkot, south of Jammu. In all, six divisions on each side were engaged. So were both nations' air forces in bombing raids and dog fights. In the dust-choked fields of Khem Karan south of Lahore, Indian and Pakistani tanks fought the largest armoured battle at that time since the Second World War.

Most soldiers on both sides were Punjabis. So the war was really between Punjabi Muslims and Punjabi Hindus and Sikhs. It lasted only twenty-two days. The United Nations Security Council passed a ceasefire resolution. That was not the only factor imposing a military standstill amidst the steady streams of propaganda from Delhi and Rawalpindi. Both sides were exhausted. But when Indian forces reached the forty-seven-mile-long Ichhogil Canal protecting Lahore, Pakistan had no choice. In order to save the country's most valued city and indeed its heartland, it had to give up its grab for Kashmir and plans for another thrust on 8 September into India's Punjab to cut off Indian forces it had wrongly assumed would not move from the border.

India won the war. It held on to the Vale of Kashmir, the prize Pakistan vainly sought. It gained 1,840 square kilometres of Pakistani territory: 640 square kilometres in Azad Kashmir, Pakistan's portion of the state; 460 square kilometres in the Sialkot sector; 380 square kilometres far to the south in Sindh; and, most critical, 360 square kilometres on the Lahore front. Pakistan took 540 square kilometres of Indian territory: 490 square kilometres in the Chhamb sector and 50 square kilometres around Khem Karan.

In military performance, Indian troops and equipment held a small but distinct edge over their Pakistani counterparts in Second World War–type operations. General Chaudhuri offered evidence to support this claim, modest when compared with most others on both sides, when I interviewed him in Delhi shortly after the fighting halted, and Western military attachés backed him up. I reported: "Assessments made by professional experts and detached Western observers, who cannot be identified further, said Indian victory claims are not groundless even if self-satisfaction sometimes accompanying them may be unnecessary."

In particular, Pakistani tank crews paid a high price when they did not follow U.S. training advice in deployment of their Pattons against India's British-made Centurion tanks. Many of them were not sufficiently educated to make full use of the Patton tank's gun sight and other sophisticated mechanisms. Indian radar-guided anti-aircraft fire against Pakistani F-86 Sabrejet raiders was accurate, bringing several down. Patton and Sabrejet became common terms of derision among Indians for Pakistan's U.S.-provided armour and aircraft.

More important than conventional assessment of warfare was the impact of the war on Pakistan and India. Pakistani forces not only failed again to take the Vale of Kashmir, the crucial objective they had confidently believed was within their grasp, but also failed to live up to the long-held myth that one Muslim soldier was worth four Hindus. With the number of troops on each side in the war roughly equal, at best one Pakistani soldier was equal to one Indian, and perhaps not even that. A widening awareness of these crushing failures among initially elated Pakistanis demoralized the nation.

The war's effect on Indians was more complex.

On one hand, the mass elation that grew out of initial worry about Pakistani inroads proved justified. India clearly won a major war with Pakistan after losing one disastrously to China just three years earlier. Moreover, India showed it was a nation like any other in defending what it considered its land and invading a neighbour it deemed an aggressor. Shastri was much more open and direct in taking on Pakistan than Nehru had been in challenging China, and he had better generals. On the other hand, some Indians, including other generals, made no secret of their conviction that India could have defeated Pakistan much more decisively, specifically by capturing and holding the city of Lahore. They wanted not a ceasefire establishing India's supremacy over Pakistan but continued warfare with the goal of destroying Pakistan.

Lieutenant-General Jack Jacob, who was to come close to achieving that objective six years later on the other side of the Subcontinent, was one of the army officers who was highly critical of General Chaudhuri's performance. Another, predictably, was the retired B.M. Kaul, whose public casting of aspersions on Chaudhuri gave vent to an old jealousy. Indeed, Chaudhuri disclosed much later that he had agreed to become army chief in late 1962 at the end of the China war on condition that Kaul leave military service. This accounts for Nehru's favourite general promptly doing just that following his unbelievably inept performance in NEFA.

In 1965, Kaul still imagined himself riding to India's rescue, this time against Pakistan. But he was obviously disappointed at the outcome of two revealing exchanges, and this explains his spleen against Chaudhuri. When Pakistani infiltrators entered Kashmir in August, Indira Gandhi, then information minister, inappropriately initiated the first exchange. Having apparently inherited from her father a fondness for "Bijji," the general in the family, despite the 1962 debacle, she astonishingly asked him whether he would be willing to come out of retirement and deal with the Pakistanis. Kaul readily assented. He must have eagerly anticipated his public vindication as a field commander. But he heard no more. The reason became clear when Pakistani troops invaded Kashmir at the beginning of September. Then Kaul wrote to Shastri to offer his services. The hard-headed prime minister immediately replied, in effect, thanks but no thanks.

Apart from personal bitterness, what rankled with Indian chauvinists, civilian and military, was not only Indian forces' hanging back from pressing their advantage but even more Shastri's agreeing with Ayub to a joint withdrawal of Indian and Pakistani troops from captured territory. India had a lot more to give up. In answer to a question of mine soon after, when she had become prime minister, Indira said Pakistan would not have attacked in 1965 if her father had still been prime minister. But if it had and Nehru had been in charge, one wonders what course he would have pursued.

After Nehru, certainly, it was not the intention of the Indian government or the objective of the Indian army to take Lahore or any other big city in a war with Pakistan. Military contingency planning in 1964 under Chaudhuri ruled this out along with an indefinite occupation of Pakistani territory. Long after the war, he put it simply: "To capture Lahore was not the aim of 1965 operations." The troops required to take and hold it were not available, and destruction of the city with its cultural monuments in inevitably heavy fighting would have poisoned already embittered India-Pakistan relations beyond repair. In Chaudhuri's words, India's military goal was "to destroy the Pakistani fighting potential." In this it largely succeeded, putting perhaps a third of Pakistan's armour out of action. Replacing these losses put a heavy economic strain on Pakistan, and this together with popular demoralization after the war led to Ayub's resigning as president.

It was true that "Muchu" Chaudhuri always seemed to be India's general in the right place at the right time: first, in 1950, in commanding the division that prevented the Nizam of Hyderabad from handing his state to Pakistan, then in executing the 1961 Goa operation, next in stabilizing the Indian army as its commander after its 1962 defeat at Chinese hands, finally in commanding the troops who beat the Pakistanis at their own game in the major if brief war in 1965. But as a strategist he was highly respected by some other Indian generals, including his capable friend H.J.F. (Sam) Manekshaw, who later was promoted to chief of the army staff. In sharp contrast to Kaul, Chaudhuri was also popular with both jawans and the Indian people.

This popularity caused nervousness on the part of Indian politicians who constantly feared a military coup; Manekshaw told me in Calcutta when he was eastern commander that Indian police routinely opened and read letters exchanged between Indian generals. As a consequence, Chaudhuri's term as army chief was not extended and he was asked to go to Canada in 1967 as India's high commissioner. I saw him in Ottawa in the summer of 1968, and thanked him for his help in killing the Indian expulsion order against me in April. At the end of a long conversation touching on many subjects, he asked me as a resident correspondent if I thought the army could seize power in Delhi. The question surprised me but seemed to spring from casual curiosity, not deliberate intent. I answered in the negative.

Because of dispatches I filed from Kashmir in October 1965 about Indian police repression of Muslim protesters, the Indian government even then secretly vetoed the granting of a Soviet visa that would have allowed me to go to Tashkent, Uzbekistan, in then–Soviet Central Asia in early January 1966 to cover a meeting of Shastri and Ayub arranged by the Soviet premier, Alexei Kosygin. It was at this summit that Shastri, before suddenly dying on 11 January, committed India to a joint withdrawal with Pakistan from ground gained since 5 August 1965 in accordance with UN Security Council resolutions. This was not the setback for India that critics of both Shastri and Chaudhuri alleged. While India kept its military superiority as well as the Vale of Kashmir, the pro-Indian Soviets enhanced their international influence by appearing even-handed. Most important, Shastri was honest and aboveboard in peace as he had been in war, projecting India as a powerful but good neighbour instead of the intolerant, unbudgeable centre of the world.

This spirit was evident in early February 1966 when I visited several battlefields in Pakistan where Indian troops were preparing to withdraw under UN supervision.

More than four months after the fighting had ended, the Indian flag still flew mockingly over the ruins of the town of Dograi, in full view of Pakistani troops still dug in on the west bank of the sixty-foot-wide Ichhogil Canal almost on the outskirts of Lahore. But Indian troops were standing up and relaxed. The last shooting over the canal had occurred on 25 January, when Pakistanis opened up on Indian army engineers trying to salvage two Patton tanks. Centurions in fields nearby, together with Pattons captured from the Pakistanis, soon would be gone. Old Indian Sherman tanks and artillery pieces had already been pulled back sixteen kilometres to the Indian side of the border. Soon the only trace of a foreign presence would be the word "India" scrawled in large English letters and Punjabi script on several walls by Indian soldiers, and in one place a crude caricature of Zulfikar Ali Bhutto, then Pakistan's foreign minister.

At Phillora in the Sialkot sector, near where hundreds of tanks had clashed, India's corps commander expressed his attitude toward the withdrawal of his troops in these clipped words: "I couldn't care a damn as long as I can get back to my fishing and whatnot."

Standing near withered sugar cane and cotton fields, where his men were filling in trenches with spades and lifting mines, Lieutenant-General P.O. Dunn made a striking military figure from his silver hair and Gurkha side-cap to his perfectly creased khaki cord trousers.

In contrast, a dust-covered jawan paused in his work and said in Hindi, as others nodded their agreement: "No, we are not happy about withdrawing. We would like this land to remain India."

"How does that poem go?" asked Major-General Mohinder Singh, commander of one of the three Indian divisions in the Lahore sector. "Theirs not to reason why, theirs but to do or die – that goes proverbially for every soldier, down to the lowest rank."

None of these statements exactly reflected the new Indian policy of conciliation with Pakistan. But both general and jawan were cheerfully carrying out orders to withdraw back to India in the coming days.

"There have been no incidents and Indians and Pakistanis have been very
friendly indeed – mind you, we've known each other for years, especially
the senior officers," General Dunn casually observed. He had been due to
retire at the time of the war but General Chaudhuri had asked him to stay
on because he was an armoured-warfare expert.

As he chatted, a number of Pakistanis watched curiously from trenches
a hundred yards from the small battered railway station at Alhar, the only
place where a Pakistani rail line had been cut by Indian forces. Meanwhile,
Indian troops on the other side of heavy barbed wire along the track vigorously emptied sandbags and shovelled dirt into foxholes they had recently
occupied. The last shooting in the Sialkot sector had come with the news
of Shastri's death: some Pakistani police shouted vulgar names across the
front line and fired their rifles in the air. But a Pakistani army platoon had
fired a volley into the air in honour of the Indian leader, which the jawans
much appreciated. The Indians had allowed Pakistani farmers to water
their brown, untended fields before returning to their deserted villages
upon completion of the military withdrawals.

"It's a fair thing," said General Dunn. "After all, the chaps have got to
live."

Live and let live, however, is a philosophy that is no more deeply rooted
among the peoples of the Subcontinent than proper use of the English language. It is "there," as an Indian would put it, but it is easily overcome by
baser instincts connected to individual, group, and national survival.

When Indira Gandhi succeeded Shastri in January 1966 immediately after
Tashkent, soothing words expected with the return of the house of Nehru
were there. Behind them were cynical calculations of how to ensure India's
regional dominance among perceived enemies, and how to keep fearful
groups within India united.

Indira quickly re-established the mythological link between the Nehru
dynasty's charisma and the nation's destiny. She solidified a foreign policy
that emphasized the Soviet Union as India's best friend, portrayed China as
India's looming new enemy, kept the United States at arm's length except
when India's survival depended on U.S. aid, and viewed Pakistan as India's
old but newly vulnerable enemy. India followed the familiar road of Nehruvian non-alignment, but with twists induced by the wars of 1962 and 1965.

With a relentless logic not readily apparent at the time, this twisting road
led within six years to another war between India and Pakistan in December 1971. Their third war culminated in a much more clearcut victory for
India than either of the first two.

It brought about nothing less than a second partition of the Subcontinent. Overwhelming Indian forces broke Pakistan in two and created the separate nation of Bangladesh out of what had been East Pakistan and was always East Bengal. General Jacob, a Calcutta Jew, led Indian troops on the ground in a lightning campaign against isolated, disheartened West Pakistani troops who had cruelly repressed and massacred Bengalis seeking provincial autonomy, but proved incapable of putting up an effective fight against properly equipped soldiers. But it was Indira Gandhi who masterminded the invasion from Delhi.

She saw a golden opportunity in the irreconcilable conflict between exploited East Pakistanis and arrogant West Pakistanis, and the flow of up to 10 million East Bengali refugees into India's West Bengal. She seized it in order to disprove the two-nation theory – the rationale for the Subcontinent's first partition, and for Pakistan as the supposedly undivided home of the Subcontinent's Muslims – and to cut Pakistan down to a size significantly smaller than India beyond all reasonable doubt.

Indira succeeded dramatically in attaining both aims and in consolidating her political position at home. Nehru's daughter also delivered an unexpected Cold War triumph to the Soviet Union, a stinging rebuke to China, and a slap in the face to the United States under President Nixon. Only with her greatest domestic political victories – splitting her own Congress Party in 1969, winning a snap election earlier in 1971, proclaiming her notorious Emergency in 1975, and returning to power in 1980 – did Indira revel in more glorious vindication at the expense of her enemies.

India achieved strategic superiority in the Subcontinent through a series of political, economic, and military moves that balanced the Soviet Union, the United States, China, and Pakistan against each other.

Even as Shastri spoke after the 1965 war of Indians and Pakistanis becoming "good neighbours," he warned ominously of Chinese "hostility" in league with Rawalpindi. At the end of 1965, even before the military pullbacks, Delhi recalled the 1962 war with China in charging that PLA troops had carried out fresh border incursions at Thag La and in Ladakh. In February 1966, India's new woman prime minister turned her charm on visiting U.S. Vice President Hubert Humphrey, who announced a resumption of economic aid cut off when India and Pakistan had gone to war. In May, Pakistan complained that India was acquiring 600 tanks from the Soviet Union and Czechoslovakia. This nearly doubled Indian armour after the 1965 war losses. More important, it confirmed that the Soviets, who had helped India increase its armed forces after the 1962 war, had become Delhi's main military suppliers.

When Indira went to Moscow in July, however, she found that Soviet support was no less unconditional than U.S. aid. She had persuaded President Johnson in Washington to loosen U.S. purse strings further, and had put into effect limited economic reforms including devaluation of the rupee wanted by the World Bank and the West. The Soviet premier, Kosygin, responded to India's not strictly toeing the Soviet line by brushing aside Indira's bid to end the Vietnam war through peace talks, and withholding automatic Soviet backing for India's case on Kashmir. Still, India was too big to be ignored. And it was in a position to begin playing its nuclear card.

In January 1965, Shastri had inaugurated the plutonium plant at Trombay next to India's Canadian-built research reactor. It was producing enough weapons-grade material from spent fuel for at least one Hiroshima-size bomb a year. For the time being all this plutonium was being stored, while India produced its own uranium. The government insisted that its nuclear activities were strictly peaceful: research into irradiation to extend the life of food, production of medical radioisotopes, and the building of reactors for needed power generation. But as early as 1963, the atomic energy department directly under Nehru had test fired rockets from the Thumba launching site on the Arabian Sea shore of the southwestern state of Kerala with French and U.S. collaboration. Soon India would make its own rockets, and later it would produce missiles.

Homi J. Bhabha, the guiding light of Indian nuclear development, was killed in an Air-India plane crash in the French Alps in January 1966, one day before Indira Gandhi became prime minister. Whatever his own ambitions for India had been, his loss and her rise a year before national elections removed whatever insulation had existed between the sacrosanct nuclear program and the exigencies of Indian politics. Soon after, China's third nuclear test sharpened the Indian political debate over whether India should make the bomb. The new chairman of India's Atomic Energy Commission, Vikram Sarabhai, said a "total commitment" was necessary once such a decision was made, and this could come only after India had built a strong industrial base. But Indian diplomats renewed appeals for international guarantees against Chinese nuclear attack, and warnings of a change in India's avowedly peaceful policy unless there was nuclear disarmament.

It was only a matter of time before Pakistan reacted to this dire threat and engaged in a come-from-behind effort to match or at least deter India in the deadly nuclear field. In late July 1966 I reported from New Delhi that Pakistan had told the Canadian government of India's intention to explode a nuclear device in the near future, ostensibly for peaceful purposes but in reality to claim membership in the nuclear club. At the time the Pakistanis put India's nuclear timetable far ahead of where it was, deliberately so in the hope of slowing Indian progress while they sought nuclear components wherever they could find them. But the Indian response only increased fears of a nuclear arms race in the Subcontinent.

Indira did not repeat past denials that India planned a nuclear test at some point. Nor did she reiterate the standing Indian request to recognized nuclear powers for protection against China. She indignantly told the Lok Sabha she fully shared the sudden Indian concern that the Pakistani protest was a cover for nuclear co-operation between China and Pakistan. With more foresight than she realized, she asserted: "If Pakistan explodes a bomb, it will be a Chinese bomb. We can only take steps to provide our own protection."

Before the end of 1966, Indira's government rebuffed probably the most serious attempt in the first half-century of Indian independence to include India in a possible alliance of Asia-Pacific countries to keep China in check. The U.S. ambassador, Chester Bowles, sought to enlist India's support against Chinese expansionism outside the Himalayas. Going beyond the positive U.S. response to Nehru's urgent call for help in the Himalayas in late 1962, his bold initiative reflected the pragmatism as well as the deep sympathy for India of a prominent Democrat who had served earlier as President Harry S. Truman's ambassador in Delhi. Bowles envisioned India and Indonesia as the most important strategic partners of the United States in Asia along with Japan. But he got nowhere with Indira.

On the much more immediate Vietnam question obsessing Washington, Indira dropped the hint of Indian impartiality injected by Shastri. Her government spurned a bid by President Johnson's roving ambassador, Averell Harriman, for Indian acceptance of the American view that an unconditional halt in bombing of North Vietnam was unrealistic. Instead Indira pointedly joined Presidents Josip Broz Tito of Yugoslavia and Gamal Abdel Nasser of Egypt (then part of the United Arab Republic) in a Delhi declaration demanding such a halt and recognition of the Vietcong.

Intensified anti-Western non-alignment did not prevent Indian troops, however, from engaging in the biggest firefights with Chinese troops in four years. In contrast to repeated Chinese victories in the 1962 war, jawans trained and equipped for high-altitude combat used U.S.-provided mountain artillery, deployed on higher ground than that of the guns of their adversaries, to decisive tactical advantage at Nathu La and Cho La near the Sikkim-Tibet border. Over several days each side took about 300 casualties – including a Chinese political officer whose head was cut off by a Gurkha wielding his kukri or razor-sharp curved knife – in a standoff that was a far cry from the Himalayan rout of Indian forces four years earlier.

In June 1967, the Nehru family's usually suppressed anti-Western venom came spewing out during the Six Day War in the Middle East.

Indian troops in the United Nations Emergency Force in the Sinai had helped open the door to that decisive conflict by moving out of the way of an imminent Egyptian invasion of Israel that was pre-empted by Israeli air strikes. Speaking just before Egypt stopped traffic in the Suez Canal, which was India's food-aid lifeline, Indira squarely and scornfully blamed Israel for the war. Her voice rising above shouts of protest in the Lok Sabha, she startled journalists in the press gallery when she condemned Israel for receiving U.S. arms like Pakistan, and declared that the birth of the Jewish state in 1948 had contained "the seeds of the current conflict." Repeating her father's line at the time of Goa's "liberation" that "non-alignment has never meant we should be neutral," Indira insisted her government was not for the destruction of any nation. Socialist Party leader Ram Manohar Lohia, long a bitter enemy of the Nehrus, replied: "Except our own."

During the same month Indira verbally assaulted Israel and the United States, she showed an entirely different face in not preventing, and in all likelihood authorizing, physical assaults on Chinese diplomats in Delhi.

Ostensibly in retaliation for the manhandling of Indian diplomats in Beijing by Red Guards carrying out Mao Zedong's Cultural Revolution, Jan Sangh–led mobs twice broke into the Chinese embassy compound. While police stood by, the intruders went far beyond officially sanctioned violence in China's capital. They badly beat eight Chinese, burned cars, broke windows, and smeared black paint on buildings. The government prohibited reporting within India of these events, and delayed stories about them filed by foreign correspondents. Indira's foreign minister at the time, M.C. Chagla, displayed Indian hypocrisy when he intoned in Parliament: "The Chinese may act in a barbaric manner but India as a civilized country cannot act in a like manner." Then he flew to the United Nations to press India's attack on Israel. When China tested a hydrogen bomb one day after the embassy incidents, Indira hinted self-righteously that an Indian bomb was closer to reality than ever.

India's steady move into the Soviet camp, and the spread of Soviet power and influence throughout the southern rim of Asia, were plain for all to see in 1968.

At the Republic Day parade in Delhi on 26 January, symbolizing as usual the direction of the world's most populous non-Communist country, Premier Kosygin and President Tito joined Prime Minister Gandhi in watching the first public display of Soviet-built Indian aircraft – MIG fighters, transports, large helicopters – and SAM anti-aircraft missiles. India had also obtained hundreds of tanks from Moscow but none of them took part in the annual parade. In addition to the exhibited aircraft, the Indian air force was taking delivery of more than a hundred Soviet-made SU-7 fighter-bombers as older British-built planes started to be phased out.

Kosygin was back in Delhi three months later, ostensibly to assure Indira – who cut off journalists' questions directed at the Soviet leader – that a major economic aid agreement signed during a much longer visit to Pakistan would not adversely effect the de facto Indo-Soviet alliance. To the Soviets, India was a big element but hardly the only one in their intensive efforts to establish a dominant sphere of influence from Istanbul to Dacca. Kosygin had visited Turkey and Iran as well as Pakistan – all Western allies then – and had strengthened Soviet links with still independent Afghanistan, while vigorously championing the cause of the Arab world in the wake of the Six Day War. In India, he received secret assurances that Soviet submarines operating in the Indian Ocean could use a base at Vishakapatnam on the Bay of Bengal built for subs soon to be delivered to India by the Soviet Union.

In her continuing campaign to mollify Moscow, Indira had informed the Lok Sabha that Soviet military supplies to the Communist side in the Vietnam war posed no problem because North Vietnamese and Vietcong forces were fighting for their "self-protection" against "aggression." In March 1969, a month after Indira had made her intimate pro-Moscow friend Dinesh Singh her foreign minister, he acknowledged that the Soviet Union was flying unspecified cargo and passengers to North Vietnam via India, with a refuelling stop at Calcutta.

On 31 July 1969, New Delhi was steaming under the glaring sun of the North Indian monsoon with no sign of cooling rain clouds. From an American perspective, it was the capital of a country whose domestic politics and foreign policy were going alarmingly against U.S. interests. Richard M. Nixon chose this day to step from Vietnam and Southeast Asia into the India of his boyhood dreams.

It was a brave act, whatever one thinks of Nixon. Sweating in his neat blue suit and starched white collar, he stood stiffly at attention in nearly 100 degrees of brutal heat while an Indian military band played the two national anthems. Then he stood up in his bubbletop car and waved at hundreds of thousands of smiling Indians who lined the eight-kilometre route from the airport to Rashtrapati Bhavan to catch a glimpse of the first American president to come to their country since Dwight D. Eisenhower had done so ten years earlier. As he liked to do, Nixon was entering the lair of an enemy, not the people of India but a government that by then had become almost as much of a Soviet client as the one in Hanoi.

The Nixon administration was under no illusions on this score. Ambassador Kenneth Keating made this abundantly clear to me after I had returned to Delhi from Singapore, partly to cover Nixon's one-day visit but mainly to report on Indira Nehru Gandhi's breaking up of the Congress Party and assuming the mantle of a near-dictator with Communist support. Shortly before the president's arrival, the former U.S. senator from New York had told me – naturally not for direct attribution – that the United States was strongly opposed to India's taking part in a new international truce-keeping organization that would be created to supervise a new Vietnam peace accord. Since 1954 India had repeatedly sided with the Communists as the supposedly neutral chairman of the International Control Commissions in Vietnam, Laos, and Cambodia; NATO member Canada and Communist Poland were the other members. My story in *The Washington Star*, as well as *The Toronto Globe and Mail*, revealing that Nixon would inform Indira Gandhi of this opposition, helped pierce the usual Indian sanctimoniousness toward the rest of the world and particularly the United States.

During the presidential visit, hypocrisy was not confined to the Indian side. Nixon stood with his eyes closed for nearly a minute under the punishing sun after he placed a wreath of white flowers on the samadhi of Mohandas Gandhi, the simple stone memorial marking the spot where the Mahatma's body was cremated following his assassination in 1948. As the president accepted India's gift of several books by Gandhi, he recalled that he had received from his Quaker maternal grandfather a biography of the apostle of non-violence as a high school graduation present. Nixon's self-conscious homage to Mahatma Gandhi, and his solemn words about pursuing peace, contrasted with the bombing of North Vietnam by U.S. warplanes on the president's orders at the very same time.

Nixon obtained from Indira, however, what he had primarily come to India for: a picture of the Soviet concept of Asian collective security, a key part of what came to be known as the Brezhnev Doctrine. In close touch with Kosygin, she briefly lifted the veil on what was then a Soviet secret weapon in Asia before quickly pulling it down so as not to be accused of speaking for Moscow. She made plain India's willingness to be part of a Soviet sphere of influence in South Asia – without losing U.S. economic aid – while a U.S. sphere of influence would include Southeast Asia and Northeast Asia. Obviously such an understanding would be directed against China.

But Indira followed directly in the footsteps of her father – except during the electric moment in the fall of 1962 when the Chinese had seemed on the verge of invading India and Nehru had begged for American military help – in expressing firm opposition to any military alliance or security arrangements backed only or mainly by the United States. This was the message that Nixon took away from his brief encounter, ending 1 August, with an India steeped in present-day realpolitik. The blunt exchange of views between the president of the most powerful democracy and the prime minister of, still, the most populous democracy started to set the stage for an Indo-U.S. confrontation little more than two years later. Then Indira's India broke up Pakistan with the full support of the Soviet Union while the United States under Nixon and China under Mao Zedong could do little but stand by and watch.

By June 1971, the prospect of a third war between India and Pakistan – sheer madness to Western minds – was assuming an inexorable logic in the minds of the leaders of both countries.

With West Pakistani troops continuing their brutal repression of majority East Pakistanis, Indira voiced publicly the acute concern she had expressed privately about the explosiveness of India's eastern borders. India had good reasons for intervention: an influx of some four million refugees – Delhi later raised the number to ten million, though Pakistan insisted it never went above two million – the threat of Hindu-Muslim violence, and the peril of Bengali Communists turning West Bengalis toward a revolutionary, poor, but eventually united Bengal. India's real reason for war was the establishment of an independent Bangladesh or Bengal nation, but only in East Bengal. It had what it needed to achieve this aim in a modernized million-man army that could easily overwhelm the Pakistani troops cut off in the alienated cities and towns of East Pakistan.

This increasingly likely denouement was not without appeal to many West Pakistanis. Zulfikar Ali Bhutto, inspired by the vision of a Pakistan led by himself as there would no longer be any danger of control by a Bengali majority, had instigated a split between the western part and East Pakistan's Sheik Mujibur Rahman. As a result of the country's first real democratic election, Mujib, as he was known, should have been prime minister of all Pakistan instead of a prisoner of the army. In the short run, losing East Bengal altogether would be a devastating defeat for Islamic Pakistan and a stunning victory for predominantly Hindu India. But West Pakistanis would be out of an impossible situation of their own making, and united in blaming India for the breakup of their country. Indeed, the only factor that headed off military conflict in mid-1971 was the long Bengal monsoon, which would have drastically slowed the progress of invading Indian troops.

In early November, as the monsoon ended, Indira went to Washington to see Nixon, exactly ten years after the visit to Kennedy by Jawaharlal Nehru in early November 1961 preceding the Indian takeover of Portuguese Goa by force in December. But an important difference was that India was backed up now by a recently signed treaty of friendship and co-operation with the Soviet Union. Before leaving Delhi, the prime minister had told her people it was important "not to speak or act in anger or in haste." But her government and armed forces had already drawn up detailed plans for seizing East Pakistan and handing it over to East Bengalis.

It was easy to blame President Yahya Khan of Pakistan exclusively for lowering the threshold to armed conflict by not finding a political solution to the deep division between the country's east and west wings. Many Western journalists, including myself, were influenced by steady Indian propaganda in making this mistake. In reality, Indira shared the blame. She had moved the two poor countries to the brink of war by rejecting appeals to cool the situation. She had authorized the arming and training of Mukti Bahini guerrillas from East Bengal. She had accepted more Soviet military aid than ever. She had ordered Indian forces to mass on the border. Meanwhile, U.S. military assistance continued to flow to Pakistan. General Yahya was seeking more weapons from China. And President Nixon was secretly preparing for a trip to Beijing and an understanding with the Chinese Communist leaders about the balance of power in all Asia.

Indian intentions toward East Bengal were telegraphed by the fact that the man plotting strategy in his new job as director of policy planning in the external affairs ministry was Durga Prashad Dhar, one of the most ruthless political operatives in the Subcontinent. For years Dhar, a Kashmiri Brahmin and former Communist, had been Delhi's agent in the Muslim government in Srinagar. From Kashmir he had gone to the United Nations and then Moscow as India's ambassador. As number two in the foreign ministry, he had negotiated the Indo-Soviet friendship treaty. After General Jacob's troops had conquered East Pakistan under the overall command of General Maneckshaw, then chief of army staff, Dhar went to Dacca ostensibly as India's ambassador. He was actually the temporary Indian proconsul of newly independent Bangladesh.

The scheme he had set in motion under Indira's direction began to unfold at the beginning of December 1971. Indian troops crossed the border into East Pakistan. Pakistani planes responded by attacking air bases deep inside India. With China's support, the United States introduced a resolution in the UN Security Council calling on India and Pakistan to cease fire and withdraw troops from each other's territory. The Soviet Union vetoed the resolution, which if implemented would have affected only invading Indian troops.

With fighting limited in the west of the Subcontinent, unlike the 1965 war, the only territorial gains were India's in the east. General Yahya desperately declared: "India has always tried to weaken and ruin Pakistan ... The time has come for the heroic mujahids [Muslim fighters] to give a crushing reply to the enemy." But Indira Gandhi defiantly proclaimed: "We have stood for peace but peace itself has to be defended. Above all we are fighting for the cause of human freedom."

India was fighting above all, and once again, for a Greater Bharat. But it won the propaganda war even before it won the ground war, which was over in one week.

With Bengal's plains dry, Jacob's forces swiftly routed the three scattered Pakistani divisions defending the eastern wing of the country, and made prisoners of the Pakistani troops upon their surrender. With Himalayan passes blocked by snow with the onset of winter, Chinese troops in Tibet could not move in the east toward West Bengal as they had in 1962, even if Beijing had wanted them to; and Pakistani troops in the west could not cross the mountains into Indian-held Kashmir as they had in 1965. The U.S. naval task force dispatched to the Bay of Bengal, comprising the nuclear-powered aircraft carrier Enterprise and seven destroyers, succeeded not in intimidating but angering India, although it may have secretly sunk an Indian destroyer that challenged it, and could have easily sent the nearby Indian carrier Vikrant to the bottom.

India's deliberate and violent sundering of Pakistan destroyed the myth of equality between the two countries, which the United States tried in vain to uphold in the Security Council and the Indian Ocean. India established itself as unquestionably the predominant power in the Subcontinent. At the height of the Nehru dynasty's pro-Soviet, anti-U.S. policies, India more than ever also saw itself as a potential superpower. But the ramifications of India's third and most decisive military victory over Pakistan immediately went far beyond the Subcontinent.

The third Indo-Pakistani war jarred the momentum toward an entente between the United States and China. It angered Richard Nixon and Zhou Enlai, who had been exasperated by Indira's father a decade earlier. The president of the United States and the premier of the People's Republic of China were not amused by Delhi's upsetting the balance of power in the Subcontinent. They were appalled at their mutual allies, Pakistan's generals, losing half a country – the blood-stained eastern half where West Pakistani troops, acting under the generals' orders, spilled more Bengali blood even as Indian troops entered Dacca. The U.S. and Chinese leaders were upset by the Soviet Union increasing its predominant influence in India and extending it to Bangladesh, a new independent nation even poorer economically than India and West Pakistan.

Henry Kissinger, who on two trips to Beijing facilitated by Pakistan had laid the groundwork for Nixon's forthcoming visit in February 1972 and ratification of a new balance of power in all Asia, led the administration's attacks on India. Reflecting the Nixon Doctrine, joint Sino-U.S. recognition of spheres of influence in Asia was designed both to make it easier for Nixon to withdraw remaining U.S. troops from South Vietnam without an immediate loss of non-Communist parts of Vietnam, Laos, and Cambodia, and to make him look like a world statesman in his 1972 re-election campaign. But India's ripping Pakistan's east wing away seemed to put this whole strategy at risk, and to give an edge to the Soviet plan for Asian security that Nixon had encountered in Delhi in 1969.

That was why Nixon and Kissinger engaged in a personal vendetta against Indira and India, and why they resorted to gunboat diplomacy on a massive scale. Nixon's claims to being on the side of the angels were more absurd than Indira's. First he contended he was about to persuade General Yahya to give autonomy to East Pakistan when fighting broke out. Then he maintained he had restored peace by persuading the Soviets to put pressure on India not to continue the war in the western part of the Subcontinent. In reality, Nixon handed much more influence to Moscow in the entire region than it deserved by turning his back on democratic India and going to extraordinary lengths to defend murderous Pakistani generals. In the end, the East Bengal war hardly hindered Nixon's progress on his road to Beijing via Pakistan. He had one more reason to embrace Zhou and Mao when he got there.

Nixon had considered India too poor and too weak to play a significant role in Asia. China's leaders regularly branded India as a "running dog" of the "imperialists" or of Moscow. To prove both wrong, and to brandish the ultimate weapon against China more than against Pakistan, the Indians had to do one more thing. They had to demonstrate a nuclear bomb belonging solely to India.

On 18 May 1974, a large, violent event broke the still surface of the Rajasthan desert in western India.

The Indian government called it a clean "implosion" of a "peaceful nuclear device." It was a dirty explosion of a warlike nuclear bomb. Indian scientists had meant to keep the test underground. They could not fully control it. At first Delhi denied that the material used came from the research reactor at Trombay – built by Canada and using heavy water provided by the United States – and had been processed at the adjacent plutonium plant. Then Indian officials admitted this was indeed the case. Canada immediately suspended nuclear aid to both India and Pakistan. It was a classic case of locking the barn door after the horses are stolen.

Starting as early as 1948, India had long since acquired the nuclear technology it wanted. In showing the world in 1974 it could tap this technology for military potential, India did not announce its membership in the exclusive nuclear club, or formally apply. That would not come until twenty-four years later, in 1998, under a new Hindu nationalist government. Typically, India under the Nehru dynasty sought to occupy the moral high ground, above that of the recognized nuclear powers: the United States, the Soviet Union, Britain, France, and China. But the message, especially to its enemies and its own people, was unmistakable: India would soon possess nuclear weapons of mass destruction.

This should not have come as a surprise. In 1966 Pakistan had warned prematurely that it was about to happen. China and the Soviet Union, for different reasons, kept careful track of India's military development. On the strength of exhaustive research in both India and Pakistan, I had written in early 1968 that the Indian government appeared bent on developing a nuclear capability for military purposes – probably one of the articles that motivated Indira to get me out of India or keep me out. In 1974, however, as in the years before and even after India became a de facto nuclear power, many people in the West found Indian ambitions hard to take seriously. This was due not so much to acceptance of the benign image India sought to project as to plain incredulity.

By the time Indians celebrated fifty years of independence in 1997 – a year before the Bharatiya Janata Party came to power – the time was long past when India's pretensions, in Asia and globally, realistic or not, could be safely ignored or shunted to the periphery of concerns about international peace and security. Although India was still nominally in the nuclear closet, it ranked with Israel and far ahead of Pakistan as an undeclared nuclear power. In 1995 the annual report of the U.S. Department of Defense to Congress pointed out that India had "the third largest military in the world," after the United States and China. This modern armed establishment continued to expand in a region whose many conflicts and problems had grown sharper or deepened since 1947, not softened or gone away. Military and political analysts quietly began to consider the Indian Subcontinent, rightly or wrongly, as the most likely place in the world for a nuclear exchange.

Several years before the series of Indian nuclear tests in May 1998, conservative estimates of the number of Indian atomic bombs, assembled or ready for quick assembly, varied from 60 to more than 100. Some experts put the number at more than 200, which would be roughly half the size of China's nuclear stockpile. All or nearly all of India's Hiroshima-type bombs – possibly 25 new ones every year – have come off a veritable assembly line starting with the Trombay research reactor, and created supposedly for the harmless purposes of irradiating fruit and supplying medical radioisotopes. Indian nuclear scientists had also designed a crude, not yet tested hydrogen bomb.

The number of delivery vehicles available for this secret nuclear arsenal also grew steadily and dramatically. In addition to its Soviet-built fighter-bombers, in 1988 India tested its own short-range Prithvi missile, and soon deployed a number of these missiles – capable of hitting targets 250 kilometres away – on its border with Pakistan. In 1989 it started testing the medium-range Agni missile, with the aim of developing it to threaten targets 2,500 kilometres away in China, the Middle East, or Southeast Asia. India was even working on a submarine-launched missile. Apart from its nuclear capabilities, it maintained stockpiles of chemical and biological weapons.

India pointedly boycotted the UN conference in New York in the spring of 1995 that voted to extend indefinitely the twenty-five-year-old Nuclear

Non-Proliferation Treaty. Its reason for continuing to refuse to sign the treaty, and later for refusing to sign a comprehensive treaty banning all nuclear tests, was that these agreements imposed "double standards" by dividing the world into nuclear haves and nuclear have-nots. India was a nuclear have, yet claimed to be a nuclear have-not.

India's conventional forces, as reflected in rising defence budgets, also grew more formidable even before a BJP government sharply increased spending on the military and defence research.

By the mid-1990s the army, continuing the buildup started after the 1962 China war, reached 1.2 million men. It deployed modern armour provided by the former Soviet Union or manufactured in India, tactical missiles, and electronic battlefield devices. India's air force, bolstered by two additional squadrons of MIG-29s bought for $2 billion from Russia and earlier MIG models assembled in India, became the fourth largest in the world, capable of carrying out a variety of missions. The Indian navy provided the most spectacular story of growth. Seventh largest in the world, it aimed to be fourth. Its expansion had started after the 1965 Pakistan war, when India possessed one old aircraft carrier, a dozen destroyers and frigates, and no submarines, and had taken off after the 1971 Pakistan war and the Enterprise incident. By the mid-1990s, the navy boasted two carriers with a third under construction, nearly fifty destroyers, frigates, and corvettes, and about fifteen submarines, although the Russians had taken back a nuclear-powered sub. Overall, Indian factories and shipyards turned out about three-fourths of the country's military needs. But India still spent more than $3 billion a year on procurement abroad.

In contrast to think-tank or private analyses of these trends, the public U.S. stance on India's burgeoning military power was unperturbed and even perverse in its lack of concern – until the Hindu nationalists kept their promise to make India an avowed nuclear power.

Washington successfully pressured Russia not to provide long-range missile technology to India. Until the Clinton administration signalled its intention in late 1995 to relax restrictions on the export of high-performance computers generally, pleasing American high-tech companies, it had opposed any transfer to India of advanced technology that could be used for military purposes. But even before the liberalization of controls on super-computers, U.S. administrations and the U.S. Congress had found it difficult to give up the long-obsolescent habit of judging India and Pakistan equally. In the past this had benefitted the Pakistanis. But more recently it had sharply penalized them because of greater dependence on the United States.

India possessed perhaps ten times as many nuclear warheads as Pakistan, and possibly twenty times as many. But under special legislation, in 1990 the United States cut off military aid to Pakistan, including the delivery of paid-for F-16 fighter planes purchased in order to keep pace with India's growing air force, until Islamabad would at least suspend its nuclear program. In contrast, Washington's entreaties to Delhi to exercise nuclear restraint were weak at the time and had little or no effect. The Clinton administration was adamant, however, in pressing China not to sell M-11 short-range missiles to Pakistan, in the hope this would persuade India not to deploy its Prithvis. In January 1995 the United States signed a military agreement with India providing for joint consultations, training exercises, defence research, and weapons production. Although the United States signed a similar agreement with its longstanding ally Pakistan at the same time, many Indians predictably contended that their country's new link with the world's only superpower reflected grudging U.S. recognition of India as the regional superpower in the Subcontinent and the Indian Ocean. It did nothing of the kind then. But it led to closer agreements in 2001, stepping up military co-operation that can be one foundation stone for a wider alliance or interlocking joint security measures against China.

Pakistanis naturally see India differently. Air Chief Marshal Zulfikar Ali Khan wrote in 1995: "The threat that Pakistan perceives from India is not a product of our fevered imagination or a 'phantom,' but a harsh reality. Nor is Pakistan alone in experiencing the predatory nature of India. India does not allow any country on the Subcontinent to undertake any action in foreign affairs or defence policy that India deems inimical to Indian hegemony. It has not hesitated to intimidate its neighbours through subversion, economic coercion, or outright use of military power."

Abdul Sattar, who as high commissioner in Delhi in 1992 had spelled out to me Pakistan's sense of unfairness on the part of the United States in stopping delivery of the F-16s, put the danger posed by India this way: "Pakistan's threat perception is not imaginary; it is founded in the experience of India's recurrent use of force to impose 'solutions' of its own preference upon less powerful neighbours. Moreover, India is continuing its military buildup for no apparent reason other than its aspiration to regional dominance."

General Khalid Mahmud Arif went even further in describing Pakistan's adversary: "[India's] ambitions are high. She looks at South Asia as if it [were] a region subordinate to her policies and aspirations in which she has a right to interfere in the affairs of her neighbours. She visualizes herself to be a global power in the making. She arrogates [to herself the right] to be the sole inheritor of all the rights and responsibilities once enjoyed by the British government in the Indian Ocean region during the zenith of the imperial Empire."

Pakistan is hardly blameless in the Subcontinent's cycle of conflict since 1947. Indeed, Pakistani ground or air attacks have started every one of the country's wars with India, even the one that was bound to end in the loss of East Bengal. If India is determined to be the region's top power, Pakistan seems determined to be the world's top troublemaker. But the Pakistanis have a point about India's enforcement of its aims over many years. Under the Nehru dynasty particularly, India repeatedly went it alone in pursuing its interests, and not only disregarded world opinion but tried to fool it.

In 1984, as Indira continued to uphold peace and non-alignment and a parliamentary election neared, she considered ordering an air strike to take out Pakistan's uranium enrichment plant at Kahuta when the Pakistanis were just starting down the road to nuclear weapons. In 1986–87, after her son Rajiv Gandhi had succeeded her as prime minister following her assassination and had easily won the election, India came close to going to war again with both Pakistan and China, although not at the same time.

Operation Brass Tacks, carried out for weeks by 250,000 Indian troops near the border with Pakistan, appeared to presage an invasion to cut the country in two, or to be designed to provoke a Pakistani military response. Neither happened. On the border between eastern NEFA and Tibet, Indian and Chinese forces in sight of each other nearly clashed in the disputed Sumdurong Cho sector. Only in 1995 did the two countries agree to pull troops back from four points in that remote Himalayan area.

Some analysts contend that in May 1990, with a sharp escalation in Indian-held Kashmir of both armed Muslim insurgency and heavy-handed repression by the army, India and Pakistan teetered on the brink of a nuclear exchange. Although U.S. intervention helped cool tempers, it is highly unlikely that a nuclear exchange was imminent. The evidence is sketchy, and Pakistan was not much further along at the time in its nuclear development. But then or soon after, India moved three army divisions facing Chinese troops to the scene of fighting with Kashmiri guerrillas.

Widespread violence in Kashmir at that time carried a constant risk of flaring into the fourth major India-Pakistan war, as I learned in Islamabad in early 1992 following the bombing of Indian police headquarters in the Vale. For years Indian and Pakistani troops have sporadically shot at each other from snowbound positions on the 15,000-foot-high Siachen Glacier, which neither country is prepared to abandon although the risk of death from frostbite is greater than from gunshot.

In December 1995, India appeared to be preparing for its second nuclear explosion, or another experiment with nuclear weapons, at the Pokaran test site in the Rajasthan desert, according to a story leaked by the CIA to *The New York Times* on the basis of U.S. satellite intelligence. Nonplussed Indian officials at first denied any such intention, then said merely that the report was "highly speculative." Privately, they implied the United States was attempting to embarrass India and prevent the Congress Party government from making a dramatic nuclear statement shortly before the parliamentary election in April 1996.

In all likelihood, that was so. But it was just as likely that such a popular step – or just confirmation of India's ability to take that one step closer to membership in the nuclear club – was precisely the intention of the hard-pressed government headed by Prime Minister P.V. Narasima Rao. Almost certainly, India meant then not only to threaten China and Pakistan but also to show the United States that it could undermine the extension of the Nuclear Non-Proliferation Treaty by thumbing its nose at the proposed ban on all nuclear tests. When Prime Minister Jean Chrétien of Canada urged Rao in Delhi in January 1996 to commit India to non-proliferation, Indian officials brushed him off with suggestions that Canada was too close to the United States on this key issue.

Although China and Pakistan come into all calculations by Delhi, they are not the only countries to have felt military pressures from India, and Kashmiris are hardly the only people to have been targeted by the Indian army.

In a swift operation recalling the conquest of Goa, Indian troops have taken over the tiny Himalayan kingdom of Sikkim. They have threatened the large Himalayan kingdom of Nepal, backing up an economic chokehold by Delhi on Katmandu for daring to flirt with Beijing, and maintained constant pressure on the Himalayan kingdom of Bhutan. Copying U.S. tactics in the Vietnam war, the Indian army has waged incessant anti-insurgency campaigns against rebel Naga and Mizo villagers in eastern India, using napalm widely.

After "liberating" East Bengal from Pakistan, India long antagonized Bangladesh by withholding vital river waters. It long interfered in Afghanistan by joining the Soviet Union in support of the former Communist regime against mujahedeen or Islamic guerrillas backed by Pakistan and the United States. After first arming and training minority Tamils from Sri Lanka on Indian soil, Rajiv's government sent the Indian army into Sri Lanka in 1987 as a peacekeeping force requested by the government in Colombo but opposed by the majority Sinhalese. The Indians, whose real objective was to control Sri Lanka, then waged a bloody war against the Tamil rebels. But they failed to attain peace, victory, or control, and withdrew in disgrace in 1990.

Only during the Janata Party government under Prime Minister Morarji Desai from early 1977 to late 1979 did India seek both regional co-operation with all its neighbours and narrowing of the nuclear option that other prime ministers, particularly the Nehrus, had kept wide open. In 1997 the leftist coalition government led by Inder Kumar Gujral also

cultivated better relations with India's neighbours. When Indira Gandhi
had returned to power at the beginning of 1980, she had immediately
backed the Soviet invasion of Afghanistan and swept away Morarji's policies of moderation and conciliation, which were rooted in the ideals of
Mahatma Gandhi.

In 1991 the U.S.-led victory in the Gulf War and the breakup of the Soviet
Union forced India to refocus its version of non-alignment, which Rajiv
Gandhi and his successors had kept alive, with limited military co-opera-
tion with the United States and the establishment of full relations with
Israel. But Rao's shaky Congress Party government was no less intransigent
toward Pakistan and China, and on the issues of Kashmir and the bomb.
Many feared that Hindu nationalists would be even more dangerously mil-
itant if they came to power.

Before that happened, the Indian way of looking at the world had not
changed despite major changes in the way the world impacts India.

In October 1994, A.P. Venkateswaran, the Indian diplomat who had
been unfairly dismissed as foreign secretary by Rajiv in 1987, talked at
Carleton University in Ottawa about international security. He warned of
"diktat" and the imposition of "double standards" by the United States as
the "sole superpower." He hailed Russia as possessing nearly the same
resources and military power as the old Soviet Union. He defended non-
alignment between two "equal blocs" during the Cold War as a means to
independence. He dismissed as a "total fallacy" the notion that peace after
the Second World War had been due to mutual nuclear deterrence.

Venkateswaran said India did not practise "self-denial" of nuclear
weapons and had a "right" to be a nuclear power as well as a permanent
member of the UN Security Council with a veto. He contended that India
as the "big" power in South Asia maintained "totally justifiable" conventional military force levels, and did not need to "please smaller countries"
like Pakistan. He rejected mediation on Kashmir on the ground that it
belonged wholly to India. He asserted that the presence of Chinese arms in
Nepal justified India's closing of the vulnerable kingdom's vital economic
transit points. In 2,000 years, he insisted, India has never gone outside its
borders. He did not define Indian borders.

His words might have come from almost any Indian diplomat, general,
or politician past or present. In particular, they might have been spoken by
any Nehru. Even more to the point, they might have been uttered unctu-
ously by any proponent of Bharat as the centre of the world.

18

Between Dragon and Serpent

In Katmandu at about 7:45 Friday night, 1 June 2001, in the royal palace of the Himalayan kingdom of Nepal, the crown prince shot to death his father the king, his mother the queen, and seven other members of the royal family. He then turned one of his guns on himself, and went into a coma he never came out of. He was nevertheless recognized as the new king of Nepal before he died from his self-inflicted head wound on Monday afternoon, 4 June. His uncle, the younger brother of the king who had been the first person shot by the crown prince, became Nepal's third king in four days.

Katmandu and Nepal have exotic reputations. But nothing so strange and unexpected as the Friday night massacre at Naranyahiti Palace had ever happened before. It was a Himalayan version of the last scene of a Shakespearean tragedy, with the major characters dying one by one at the top of the world. The slaughter of royalty was unmatched anywhere since the slaying of the Romanoffs in Russia in 1918. In Asia, the last regicide had been on 9 June 1946, when King Ananda Mahidol of Thailand was found dead in his palace with a bullet through his head. Like Thais then and now, Nepalese in a land also symbolized by its monarchy were thrown into shock and confusion, and did not know what to believe. Even before the traumatic royal killings, however, Nepal's survival was in question.

Since 1955, kings of Nepal have had rhyming first names, followed by the names Bir Bikram Shah Dev. So King Mahendra Bir Bikram Shah Dev, upon his death from a heart attack in 1972 at the age of fifty-one, was succeeded by his son, King Birendra Bir Bikram Shah Dev, then twenty-six. On 1 June 2001, Dipendra Bir Bikram Shah Dev, twenty-nine, was the crown prince who killed his fifty-five-year-old father Birendra and became king. Upon Dipendra's death on 4 June, his uncle Gyanendra Bir Bikram Shah Dev, fifty-four, assumed the throne. The portly businessman was little known to his people and distrusted by many of them. He faced not only popular dismay at the massacre but also widespread poverty, a new and faltering democratic system, and a growing Maoist revolt.

Dipendra's bloody rampage had nothing to do with Nepal's deep problems. He was driven to kill by women, Scotch whiskey, and drug-laced cigarettes. The chubby Eton-educated prince, who sported a short brown beard and moustache, had the means of his crime at hand in a variety of guns he collected personally and sometimes tested for the Nepalese army. He wanted to marry Devyani Rana, a beautiful young woman who came from the family that traditionally provides wives to kings of Nepal. But his father and especially his mother, Queen Aiswarya, herself a Rana, opposed Dipendra's marrying Devyani and had another Rana woman in mind as the next queen.

When the royal family was gathering for its monthly Friday dinner in the palace compound, this night in the crown prince's residence, Dipendra played billiards and got drunk on straight Famous Grouse whiskey and cigarettes containing, according to a 14 June report by a commission of inquiry, hashish and an "unnamed black substance," probably a form of heroin. Soon unable to stand, he was taken to his bedroom, before the king arrived, by four members of the royal family, including his younger brother Nirajan and his cousin Paras, son of Gyanendra, who was away from Katmandu. There Dipendra called Devyani three times on his mobile phone over a half-hour, finally telling her he was going to sleep. Instead he changed into combat fatigues, armed himself with at least two and probably three lethal weapons, and returned to the room where dinner was to be served.

Crown Prince Dipendra shot King Birendra first with a submachine gun, then turned another gun on his father. With Birendra dead, Dipendra was the king but he went right on shooting. Birendra's youngest brother Dhirendra tried to stop him but was shot in the chest, and died on 4 June shortly after Dipendra did. Dipendra then shot dead his sister Shruti, Birendra's sisters Sharada and Shanti, Sharada's husband Khadga, and Birendra's cousin Jayanti, and wounded Birendra's sister Shobha, Gyanendra's wife Komal, and Birendra's cousin Keytaki. Finally, in the garden, Dipendra's brother Nirajan tried to shield their mother and implored him not to shoot her. But he gunned down Nirajan first and then he killed Queen Aiswarya, apparently shooting her in the face. Only then did Dipendra shoot himself in the temple, falling into unconsciousness.

For days, few Nepalese knew what had happened, and few believed what they were told at first or later. The streets of Katmandu were the scene of both rioting and royal funeral processions to cremation sites. The people's feelings about Birendra and Dipendra had been mixed. But many Nepalese were particularly suspicious of Gyanendra, who became the regent for the short period between Birendra's death and Dipendra's.

This was partly because he was not in the palace during the shooting spree – but his wife Komal had been wounded. Another reason was his attributing the deaths to an "accidental explosion" – although neither Gyanendra nor any other Nepalese could call Dipendra a murderer while he was still alive and the king. Gyanendra was widely believed to oppose Nepal's struggling democracy, but this was not certain. Most of all, many Nepalese despised Gyanendra's only son Paras, thirty, for his involvement in four fatal hit-and-run accidents as the driver and his escaping prosecution as a prince – but Paras had shielded several women from harm while Dipendra was firing his weapons. Still, neither Paras nor his wife Himani had been shot. When Gyanendra became Nepal's twelfth king, Paras was not then designated crown prince and heir apparent, which would have been customary and normal. But many of Nepal's archaic customs seemed to have suddenly come under a dark shadow. And no one seemed to be sure anymore of what was normal and what was not in the sorely afflicted Himalayan kingdom of Nepal.

From the top of a hill just twenty-nine kilometres north of Katmandu, on a clear day one can glimpse the range of Himalayas from Annapurna in the west to Everest in the east. Rippling pines on the hill drop off into a hazy chasm extending many kilometres to an unbroken horizon of seemingly floating snow mountains. Looking north, the viewer fixes nearly on the centre not only of Nepal's 800-kilometre Himalayan barrier but also of the wall of mountains between China and India extending more than 4,000 kilometres. It is a gripping, exhilarating, other-worldly vision of the top of this world.

Less than eight kilometres from Katmandu, Nepalese jostle each other for a chance to heap flowers and coloured paste on a stone image of a reclining Hindu deity called the Sleeping Vishnu. In minutes, they see their offerings slide off in water poured on the black statue by self-anointed holy men. The primitive spectacle offers depressing testimony to the inability of human beings to lift their eyes from the ground. These Nepalese can breathe the clean fresh air of magnificent natural surroundings. Yet, like some people in many other societies both old and new, they prefer the rank smell of imposed superstition.

The two scenes tell much about a still largely secluded part of Asia that has become a cockpit of conflicting national ambitions. The everlasting enormity of the Himalayas dwarfs the men, women, and children living below them and the transience of their pursuits. How the world's two most populous nations attempt to gain advantage over each other in the world's

mightiest buffer profoundly influences the fate of isolated mountain kingdoms and peoples who had hardly started to blink at the twentieth century before it was past.

In the traditional Han view, the "hand" or Plateau of Tibet belongs to
China and so do its "five fingers." From east to west, these territories are
what the British and Indians called the Northeast Frontier Agency, Bhutan,
Sikkim, Nepal and, far to the west, the northeastern part of Kashmir called
Ladakh. Delhi considers all NEFA – now called Arunachal Pradesh – and all
Kashmir its own, although Pakistan controls Azad or Free Kashmir, and
China occupies the Aksai Chin bulge of Ladakh. Independent India fol-
lowed the Raj in considering the three mountain kingdoms of Nepal,
Bhutan, and Sikkim as protectorates falling in its sphere of influence or
control.

Since the mountain war between India and China in 1962, no one doubts
the Chinese dragon's ability to breathe fire across the Himalayas. Beijing
maintains a number of well-equipped divisions along the higher, northern
ridge of the world's highest mountains, and builds or improves roads providing logistical support. In recent years, the Chinese also have enhanced
airfields and increased the number of missile launchers – and, in all likelihood, nuclear-tipped missiles – in Tibet. What amounts to a Chinese policy
of gradual genocide in Tibet is a classic example of how a larger Asian
power subdues a smaller one and imposes its political, economic, and cultural values.

But the Indian serpent glides slowly and if possible silently along the
southern side of the Himalayas, ever mindful of protecting its lair in the
Gangetic plains, often seeking to tighten its coils around unwary or
defenceless prey that will fatten Bharat Mata: Mother India.

India's foreign ministry has a special section dealing with Himalayan
territories, and so does India's home ministry. Both Jawaharlal Nehru and
his daughter Indira Gandhi paid personal attention to this racially un-
Indian area. India maintains a large standing army along the Himalayas,
exceeded only by its forces confronting Pakistan, to guard against Chinese
expansion.

Nepal is the biggest Himalayan prize. As such, it causes Delhi much con-
sternation. Despite their roots in India, the Nepalese people make no secret
of their deep fear of what they call "brown colonialism." Refusing to recognize Indian overlordship, the remote kings of Nepal have dared to play
off India and China against each other. Its engaging people have miraculously started to make their own form of democracy work, sometimes by
electing Communist-dominated governments. Nepal, one of the world's
poorest countries as well as one of the most strategically located, is desperately trying to maintain its independence.

In the late 1500s, a Rajput family exiled from North India by the Moghuls settled in the town of Gurkha some eighty kilometres west of the present capital of Nepal, taking the name the British later applied mistakenly to all the Nepalese soldiers they recruited. In 1769, Prithvi Narayan, a Gurkha, conquered the Katmandu Valley, made himself the first shah or king of the present dynasty, and declared his mountainous land to be the true Hindustan. It not only eluded the Raj, although the British whittled away much of its territory, but, more importantly, had not fallen under the Moghuls. The disdainful Nepali name for India was Mughland – polluted by Muslims.

Nepal effectively became a British protectorate early in the nineteenth century. It gained full independence only in 1923, although this was twenty-four years before divided India did. For more than a century starting in 1846, however, a powerful Rajput family called the Ranas ruled the country. The Ranas allied themselves with the Raj and reduced Nepal's kings to figureheads while providing both hereditary prime ministers to the country and wives to the kings. Old Rana palaces still grace Katmandu.

Today Nepal is the world's only Hindu constitutional monarchy, and continues to share religious, cultural, and even political traditions with India. It also depends on India almost completely for trade. But, partly because of these ties, inhabitants of Nepal still consider Indians alien. One way the Nepalese show they're different is Katmandu time: it is deliberately set ten minutes ahead of India's single time zone. But differences go deeper. More than 23 million Nepalese really are a mixed lot.

Their Hinduism is blended with erotic Tantric Buddhism. They worship mystical female power although their traditional rulers – both royalty and the Rana families – belong to the Hindu warrior caste. These Rajput rulers from India have had to accommodate people of Mongoloid stock. Racial characteristics vary sharply in a country cut up by virtually impenetrable mountain ranges into narrow self-contained valleys. The remoteness that has attracted many Westerners, and the Nepali version of caste discrimination, are at the root of Nepal's difficulties.

Every morning the woodcutters of Katmandu, small men and women with weathered faces, muscular legs, and bare feet, climb the steep hills around the Valley. They descend hours later with hundred-pound loads of sticks lashed to their backs, cut from ever less numerous trees and offered for sale as firewood that day in Hanuman Dhoka, the dirt-encrusted square of pagoda temples named for a monkey in Hindu mythology. Like the perambulations around the Sleeping Vishnu outside Katmandu, it is primitive. It is unchanging Nepal. But it is also an example of the capacity for hard work of the simple, poor, cheerful people of Nepal. And Nepal is also changing.

This was evident to me as early as the end of 1965, when a Dakota on which I was flying from Delhi literally turned the corner of a mountain and headed down into the green Katmandu Valley. I had flown to Katmandu once before, in mid-1962, when interviews with two leading cabinet ministers, Rishikesh Shah and Tulsi Giri, the first pro-Indian and the other anti-Indian, pointed to Nepal's coming out into the world. Three and a half years later, the country had moved significantly under King Mahendra Bir Bikram Shah Dev, a dour forty-five-year-old monarch who liked hunting and always kept his sun glasses on in public under a high-pointed cotton cap like those worn by most Nepali men with a kurta or long shirt and jodhpur-like trousers. Nepal had become much more than a picturesque, less developed extension of India.

In 1951 Mahendra's father King Tribhuvan, encouraged by India's Prime Minister Nehru and working through the Nepal Congress Party – modelled on and supported by the Indian National Congress – had overthrown the Ranas. When Tribhuvan died in 1955, Mahendra inherited power. In 1959 he permitted Nepal's first democratic election. As Nehru and Delhi had planned, Nepalese Congressmen won and formed a government under B.P. Koirala, a pro-Indian idealist. But King Mahendra abruptly ended Nepal's initial democratic experiment in late 1960.

Taking direct rule back into his own hands, the king jailed Koirala and other Congress politicians who did not escape to India, and set up a non-party panchayat system of indirectly elected councils at three levels similar to Pakistan's basic democracy at the time under Marshal Mohammad Ayub Khan. This was Mahendra's first assertion of independence from India and Nehru, who openly professed dismay. Just as Nepal keeps its time ten minutes ahead of India's, so its new local panchayats had nine members instead of the five (*panch*) on Indian village councils.

But Mahendra went beyond mere symbolism and even domestic political power in defying Bharat Mata. Five years after his royal coup, it was clear in both Katmandu and Delhi that the carefully calculating king was playing with India's security.

He had allowed Chinese technicians, workers, and political overseers to come into Nepal to build a 110-kilometre road north from Katmandu to the Kodari Pass through the Himalayas. It connected an Indian-built road, the first in Nepal, from the North Indian plains to Katmandu, with a road across the Tibetan Plateau from Lhasa, capital of Chinese-subjugated Tibet, to the Kodari Pass. For the first time, it was possible to travel by jeep from Beijing to New Delhi. By the end of 1966, when the Chinese were to complete their first Nepal road, it would be possible to traverse it with a heavy truck – or a column of heavy tanks. Just three years after the Indian defeat in the Himalayan war, Nepal, the centre of the Himalayan wall between India and China, had become a potential invasion route.

Having established close and unprecedented relations with China, Mahendra flew to Delhi in late November 1965 for a twenty-six-day state visit, including Hindu temples where the kings of Nepal have special privileges. Weeks after India had held on to the Vale of Kashmir in its second war with Pakistan, he showed at least that he had not forgotten Nepal's Indian connection, and at most that his country's relations with its southern neighbour still came first. His hosts could do little more at that point than politely hide their exasperation and stress the historic links between the two countries.

It was difficult to know just what the monarch or his people were thinking. Mahendra returned to Katmandu from his long trip to India when I was there for my second visit. The crowds that casually lined the streets to see the monarch exhibited little outward response to him, and he was unsmiling as usual. This may have been partly because it is considered inappropriate for Nepalese to cheer a reincarnation of the Hindu god Vishnu, or for a king of Nepal to show emotion. It may also have been because ordinary Nepalese felt little rapport with their king, or he with them. King Mahendra was the undisputed but unloved boss of Nepal.

High officials at Singha Durbar, the sprawling white palace from which the Ranas had ruled, were potential rivals of Raj Durbar, the royal palace compound surrounded by a high, spiked fence. But political parties were banned and Koirala remained in detention. Following the 1962 Himalayan war, Nehru had stopped raids into Nepal from India by exiled Nepalese politicians. Meanwhile, Mahendra switched his cabinet ministers around so none could challenge him, and the panchayat system put the king's men in key district positions where he wanted them.

Nepal's security was increasingly tenuous, however, under Mahendra and his new policies. There were heavy Indian troop concentrations both east of Nepal in and near Sikkim and west of Nepal in Ladakh, to stop new Chinese advances. But Nepal itself was virtually unprotected against China or India. Selective recruitment of Gurkhas – famed for their fighting skill, kukris or curved knives, and indomitable loyalty – by both the British and Indian armies had left Nepal with a scattered army of 14,000 men, uncertainly trained and equipped and not all wearing exactly the same uniform.

The king was taking a serious risk with his country's survival and his own. Fearful of Indian absorption after the 1962 Himalayan war, by inviting in Chinese road-builders he had persuaded the fuming Indians that Nepal could not be taken for granted. It was as if during the Cold War, to get the attention of the United States, Canada had asked the Soviet Union to build military roads down from the Arctic to Toronto and Montreal.

While India continued to give the most economic aid to Nepal, Mahendra had arranged for assistance not only from China but also from the United States, the Soviet Union, Britain, West Germany, Switzerland, and even Israel. At one time only India had an embassy in Katmandu. Now all these countries but Switzerland did, and also Pakistan and Indonesia. Aid totalled $28 million a year in 1965, with $12 million each from India and the United States, with the latter financing its projects with Indian rupees paid by India for American surplus wheat under U.S. Public Law 480.

Assistance to Nepal, struggling to stand on its own feet and no longer completely remote, ranged from a Chinese shoe factory and a Soviet power project to U.S.-built ropeways for moving supplies across mountains. Several countries would contribute to an east-west road, Nepal's first, through the Terai, the malarial jungle along the Indian border below the mountains. A road network, electric power, and education were what Nepal's then 10 million people, 90 per cent of them illiterate, needed most.

With school enrolment up from a mere 10,000 in 1947 to a still low 340,000, American advisers were setting up an education system almost from scratch. It included a combined demonstration high school, technical institute, and textbook production centre – from writer to binder – near Katmandu. The British planned a school on the Eton model at the behest of Crown Prince Birendra, a graduate. Many hardy members of a group of 200 U.S. Peace Corps volunteers were doing some of the most exciting work in education. They often walked for days to reach their jobs. Malcolm Odell, a Princeton graduate from Shirley Centre, Mass., for one, walked for ten days from Katmandu to Solo-Humbu near Namche Bazaar, the last outpost for mountain climbers intent on scaling Mount Everest. There he taught the Montessori method in a tiny primary school for Nepalese boys and girls at a salary of $55 a month in Nepalese rupees.

Israel, with which neither India nor Pakistan had established diplomatic relations because their relations with Arab countries took priority, had established a foothold in the Subcontinent by offering both private and government aid to Nepal. Israelis owned 49 per cent of the newly created National Construction Company of Nepal, and they supervised projects such as the U.S.-financed education complex. Israeli experts had set up an agricultural resettlement project on the moshav or co-operative model in the Terai, and were planning another. During Hanukkah in December, the roof of the Israeli embassy was ablaze with hundreds of lights burning in oil lamps used by Hindus for Diwali two months earlier.

Of all these new and exotic influences on Nepal, by far the most profound was China's. Mahendra's deliberately lowering his country's natural Himalayan barrier to the Chinese dragon was a good indication of the depth of Nepalese fear of constriction by the Indian serpent. The Chinese were entirely friendly at first. Historically, they weren't really strangers. As traditional Hinduism in Nepal is interwoven with Buddhist beliefs, so Nepal's many racial and ethnic groups, except possibly the Brahmins in the Terai, are largely mixtures of Mongoloid stock and Indo-Aryan characteristics.

Racially, Nepal is one of the world's most fascinating countries. The Newars of the Katmandu Valley, for example, are of Mongolian origin but have changed physically over the centuries through contact with peoples from the south. A proper Gurkha is a member of the Indo-Aryan Kshatriya or warrior caste descended in part from the Rajputs. The Mongoloid features of the Thamangs in central Nepal have hardly altered at all. With east-west movement in Nepal almost impossible, small groups of isolated hill people originally from the north came into contact with the much more accessible south in the form of pervasive Indian civilization. By letting the Chinese through a gap in the Himalayas, King Mahendra opened Nepal to the north again.

When I returned a year later, at the end of 1966, to this land of snow mountains, temples with all-seeing eyes painted on them, and men in little caps ruled by a king in a remote palace, the Nepal fairy tale was beginning to wear thin.

The way Mahendra was playing off one side against the other provoked both anger and envy on the part of the Indians, who would have called his policy non-alignment. But a keenly sensitive Nepalese, Rishikesh Shah, told me in the privacy of his home: "Foreign policy, however successful, cannot itself deliver the goods to the people, nor can it alone achieve the positive ends of nationalism."

Shah knew that his utterances put him in jeopardy. But he had stood up to no less a figure than Nikita Khrushchev at the United Nations in 1960, when he was the only representative of a developing country to tell the Soviet leader from the rostrum of the General Assembly that he had no right banging his shoe on his desk and thereby showing disrespect for an organization that belonged first of all to small nations. When I interviewed him as Nepal's finance minister in 1962, he had carefully explained how his country was trying to develop independently but without undue harm to its traditional ties with India. In 1966, the rotund Shah, out of the king's favour for his outspokenness, paced back and forth in his small house, gesticulating as he talked for hours about the hazards facing Nepal.

The Chinese were speedily completing the Kodari Pass road. The royal government of Nepal had not objected when they insisted on paying for it by depositing $9 million in King Mahendra's personal bank account in London. The government had given the Chinese the go-ahead to build another road northwest from Katmandu 175 kilometres to Pokhara, below Mount Annapurna. This would take their technicians and commissars through the heart of Gurkha country. Gurkha traditions, carried on by some of the best troops in the Indian and British armies, die hard. But it was quite conceivable that hostility to future incursions through the Himalayas by troops of the People's Liberation Army would be softened by the Chinese practice on construction projects of sharing rice equally with local inhabitants.

"De-Brahminize, de-Sanskritize the Gurkhas, or other Nepali hill peoples for that matter, and what have you got?" asked Shah, his voice rising as he alluded to the religious and linguistic pillars of his country's culture. "Mongoloids very much like the Chinese."

The king had recently returned from another long trip, this one to the Riviera for a state visit and holiday in France. Workers were building a new palace for him behind the high fence of Raj Durbar. His bureaucrats were proceeding on paper with popular elections to village councils, whose members would choose zonal councils, whose members would select a national assembly. Some political prisoners had been freed. Land-reform measures were going ahead. Ninety per cent of Nepal's trade was still with India, including the sale of rice that could have fed malnourished Nepalese. But the country's main source of foreign exchange remained remittances from Gurkha mercenaries serving in foreign armies. Communist and Congress agitators had ignited at least two serious outbreaks of violence and harsh police countermeasures. Clearly lacking politically was a sense of common purpose between Mahendra and his people in overcoming poverty, filth, and ignorance.

"The king needs a party, a national front, an organization – something more than he has," pleaded Shah. "Otherwise the gap with the people will continue to widen. But the king is afraid that any organization will turn against him.""

Problems like the Sino-Indian struggle for Nepali hearts and minds and the hazardous state of Nepal's politics didn't bother tourists, bourgeois and beatnik alike, who were beginning to flock to the Himalayan kingdom. Eventually, they provided more foreign exchange than Gurkha remittances.

Many of the foreign tourists with money were royally taken. One of the king's brothers had opened a luxury hotel in Katmandu called the Soaltee with the help of a U.S.-aid loan of $1 million to Nepal's industrial development agency. It charged prices even more fantastic for Nepal than those at the more modest Annapurna, the country's first modern hotel, owned by the king's sister-in-law. A foreign tourist could easily spend in a day the amount earned in a year by an average Nepalese, including many hotel employees – then $57.

Hippies sat in the dirt and, to some, added to the charm of Nepal in the sixties. But the government tried to discourage them from coming. When they weren't smoking marijuana or harder drugs in tiny hotels or eating places in Katmandu's bazaars, many of these sons and daughters of affluent Western families were in the street begging for food or money from impoverished Nepalese. The official English-language newspaper, *The Rising Nepal*, told in these tortured words of the reaction to plans by flower children around the world to descend on the Katmandu Valley for Christmas 1966: "The intelligentsia here are of this opinion that His Majesty's Government must have proper measure to see to it that our young people are not polluted by such gathering of the degenerated dignitaries whom they address themselves as the beatniks."

Nepal's young people were more open to influences from other outsiders. In a country where lapel buttons have been favoured for hundreds of years, university students easily sprouted Mao badges distributed through the Chinese embassy. A year and a half after Rishikesh Shah had expressed his fears for Nepal's future to me, some of them were rapidly being realized.

In mid-1968, I drove more than halfway up the 110-kilometre Kodari Pass road from Katmandu but could not approach the Tibetan border because a landslide temporarily blocked the way. Neither the Chinese nor Nepalese were in an apparent hurry to clear it. Although the Chinese had promised to truck 5,000 Tibetan mountain sheep down the road for ritual sacrifice during a Hindu festival celebrating the triumph of good over evil, there was no sign of the motorized trade that Nepal had cited as justification for the strategic route through the Himalayas.

The hardtop road curved in well-engineered bends around vivid green rice terraces, avoiding all but one town between the pass and Katmandu. Chinese wheelbarrows were scattered about in one spot, a reminder to trudging Nepalese porters that carrying a load on one's back is not the only means of transporting it. A road grader driven by a grinning Chinese, with a pretty Nepalese girl seated next to him, went by at another point. But the Chinese were obviously interested in another kind of conveyance. They had built over the Dologhat River a sturdy bridge supported by concrete and steel that could take vehicles of up to sixty-five tons – the weight of a heavy tank. Overlooking the bridge was one of the two remaining Chinese road camps on the route, festooned with red Chinese banners and well guarded. When I stopped to take pictures of the bridge, several of the guards shouted and rushed my car. I barely got away, unlike the late Frank Moraes, the strongly anti-Communist editor of *The Indian Express*, whom the Chinese had apprehended earlier at the bridge and held for several hours in what became a diplomatic incident.

Nepalese living near the Dologhat bridge said they were sometimes invited to movies at the road camp but the films were in Chinese. The builders of the Kodari highway were keeping a low profile after their first overt venture into Nepal's politics a year earlier, when they had travelled in Nepalese vehicles to Katmandu's airport to join in a raucous anti-Indian demonstration and pass out Mao buttons and little red books. Nepalese authorities had hardly interfered, and Mahendra's government later accepted an insulting Chinese protest note after Nepalese students had staged a counter-demonstration.

Under its agreement with Nepal, China was responsible indefinitely for maintenance of the roads it built in the country. Beijing now planned a ring road around Katmandu and a hydroelectric project near the Kodari route. About 300 Chinese technicians were working at five locations on the new Pokhara road, which, like the Kodari road, would link up with a road north from the Indian plains. In a village in the area, local elders openly scolded Gurkhas walking to an Indian army recruiting centre for misplacing their loyalty, and told them they should be fighting for China instead.

Nepalese officials, reflecting the king's policy, still insisted there was nothing to fear from Beijing. Indian influence in Nepal was still greater than Chinese, and openly feared. But China clearly had won a firm foothold in the central wedge of the mighty Himalayas. Moreover, internal political developments enhanced the position of the Chinese without their having to lift a finger.

In March 1968, King Mahendra, then forty-eight, had suffered a heart attack while he was hunting tigers in the Terai. The attack was officially termed mild, but it was two months before the monarch returned to Katmandu, leaning on a cane, from a district hospital. He appeared weak during his few public outings, and he cut out virtually all his administrative work. A few days before the king's return to the palace, the exiled leader of the outlawed Congress Party, General Subarna Shamsher, put out a statement in Calcutta offering full co-operation to him in fighting "forces of subversion."

This was more than a bid by Subarna, a member of the former Rana ruling class, and other Congress leaders to come back to Nepal and work in the king's panchayat system. By targeting a subversive enemy he was unmistakably referring to Nepalese Communists, particularly the pro-Chinese variety, who also were exiled in India, in Benaras. But informed Nepalese in Katmandu made clear that the inspiration for Subarna's statement had come from Indira Gandhi's government in Delhi. Her ambassador to Nepal, a heavy-handed former information minister named Raj Bahadur, had even informed Mahendra in advance that it was coming.

From India's point of view, the whole ploy backfired predictably. If Mahendra had shown sensitivity to anything, it was dictation from Delhi, whether direct, implied, or imagined. Moreover, he couldn't have taken kindly to a bold statement soon after by Rishikesh Shah and ten other members of the national assembly. Asserting that Nepal was being hurt by economic mismanagement, inflation, and the failure of attempts at land reform, they declared: "The tendency to rule through such tactics as intimidation, terror, and temptation has dealt a heavy blow to the panchayat system. A systematic campaign calculated to make democracy a laughing stock and generate a sense of apathy among the masses is being conducted through the (government-controlled) radio and newspapers ... The people are not being allowed even to make use of fundamental rights ... an atmosphere of fear and distrust still prevails in the country."

The king deliberately delayed replying to Subarna. Before he finally released the ailing Congressman B.P. Koirala after more than eight years in detention, he freed Tulsi Giri, a former non-party foreign minister who had strongly expressed his leftist, anti-Indian beliefs to me back in 1962. Giri had been arrested shortly after the king's heart attack for making disparaging remarks about him, but Mahendra now made him a close adviser. In deliberate contrast, he clapped Shah into jail. This honest advocate of genuine popular democracy in Nepal was later let go but the palace then forced him into temporary exile. In April 1969, Mahendra formed a new government that rode the crest of anti-Indian sentiment on two popular issues: a dispute with India over forty square kilometres where a river marking the boundary between western Nepal and India had changed course, and a clampdown by India on imports of cheap textiles and stainless steel utensils from Nepal.

All this would have come under the heading of intrigue in and out of the royal palace were it not for the Chinese factor in Nepal.

The new prime minister, Kirthinidhi Bista, had made several trips to Beijing as foreign minister and had praised China's communes. Bista's foreign minister had once been dismissed as a civil servant because of Communist leanings. The Bista government dramatically exploited "brown colonialism" – the seeming inability of Indians to rid themselves of the idea that

Nepal is subordinate to them – by revoking a 1965 India-Nepal military agreement and rejecting the Indian argument that the two countries enjoyed a special relationship within a defence community.

Under the agreement, Indians manned wireless stations at fourteen points along the 800-kilometre Nepal-Tibet border, and an Indian military liaison team co-ordinated supplies to Nepal's little army. Nepalese troops had also received some weapons training from Indians, signals assistance from U.S. advisers, and paratroop instruction from Israelis. Along with a 1950 India-Nepal friendship treaty was an unwritten understanding about airlifting of Indian troops to Nepalese airstrips in the event of a Chinese invasion. But now Nepal was demanding that no Indian soldier set foot on its soil. Bista bluntly asserted: "To our way of thinking, it is not possible that Nepal should accept what may be called limited sovereignty for India's so-called security. The theory of special relations for Nepal ... is out of step with modern developments in our relations."

In short, Nepal no longer accepted the idea handed down from the days of the Raj that it was a protectorate of India. Mahendra had permitted Beijing to compete directly with Delhi for leverage on Nepal. This "modern development" served the king's concept of Nepalese nationalism and independence. It also served China's wish, even at the time of the anti-foreign Cultural Revolution, to establish itself as a force in neutral non-Communist Asian countries.

Lacking Nanyang or Overseas Chinese in Nepal, Beijing brought in its own aid technicians. China had edged past the United States as the second biggest giver of aid to Nepal. Whether or not the roads the Chinese were building were eventually used for military purposes, it was evident to all concerned that they could be. China had not only made India more vulnerable, but for the first time in modern history, had made a striking impact on Nepal, historically as well as geographically shielded by the Himalayas from more than limited contact with Tibet.

In January 1972, King Mahendra died at the age of fifty-one from a second heart attack. His son, Birendra Bir Bikram Shah Dev, succeeded him at the age of twenty-six.

In July of that year, the second of the three Himalayan kings, Bhutan's Jigme Dorji Wangchuk, known as the Druk Gyalpo or King of the Dragon People, died at the age of forty-five during a visit to Kenya, also of a heart ailment. His son, Jigme Singye Wangchuk, sixteen, assumed the throne and the title of Fearless Thunderbolt and Master of the Cosmic Powers.

Although the Chogyal of Sikkim was in good health – and Sikkim was still distinct from India although protected by it – the two deaths put in greater jeopardy the struggle of all the Himalayan peoples to emerge with acknowledged national identities in the last years of the twentieth century. For better or worse, the three mountain kings had succeeded over many years in establishing some degree of personal control of their nations' destinies. Now it was more uncertain than ever that popular participation in government and economic progress would come about. It was not known if balances would be upset under inexperienced new monarchs, allowing India and China to manipulate Himalayan politicians for their own ambitious ends.

Birendra, a husky young man with a black moustache, clear glasses, and a confident, outgoing nature in contrast to the impression of suspicion and loneliness conveyed by his father behind dark glasses, quickly took command. Tenth in the line of Shah kings, the only Hindu monarch left in the Subcontinent, he was the first sovereign of Nepal to have been educated outside his country. After being taught by Jesuits at St Joseph's College in nearby Darjeeling, India, he had studied at Eton, Tokyo University, and Harvard.

In two essentials Birendra followed in Mahendra's footsteps. One is that for years he kept a firm, authoritarian hand on Nepal's politics. The other is that he cultivated beneficial ties with both China and India as Nepalese distrust of Delhi rose with the latter's victory over Pakistan creating Bangladesh one month before Mahendra's death, its probable collusion with the Soviet Union in the overthrow of the monarchy in Afghanistan in July 1973, and subsequent Indian action in Sikkim.

In a third essential, Birendra struck out boldly on his own: he made direct contact with his people in working for their rapid uplift from feudal poverty.

On the day of his coronation, 25 February 1975, Birendra declared that Nepal faced the challenge of entering a "new age." The new king told his subjects: "Only a dedication of this breadth and magnitude will enhance the dignity and honour of this Himalayan kingdom, enabling us to hold our heads like the towering peak of Everest itself."

Birendra ordained free primary education for every child, doing away with tuition as a barrier to literacy. He shifted the emphasis in education to scientific and technical training, but required Nepalese students, like their Chinese counterparts at the time, to work in the countryside for a year before receiving their degrees. He shifted the emphasis in development to economic integration, linking fertile areas of the Terai to deprived hill districts. He replaced corrupt palace officials with young Western-educated Nepalese, and travelled by jeep and helicopter to remote villages and hillsides in pursuit of his avowed aim to provide food, clothing, and shelter to every Nepalese. Apparently recalling criticism of his father, he said: "No matter who the leader is, he has got to be in touch with the people." That was a novel notion for Nepal.

Birendra's coronation, however, was a vivid manifestation of the ingrained superstitions and archaic habits that Nepal needs to overcome. Astrologers took months to choose the auspicious moment – 8:37 AM in a private pagoda of Hanuman Dhoka. Before the moment could be consummated, the Eton- and Harvard-educated prince was smeared with mud from an anthill, mud from a Vishnu temple, mud from a prostitute's home, mud from an elephant's tusk, and mud from a confluence of rivers. After these applications had supposedly conferred different manly attributes, Birendra was ritually bathed by representatives of the four Hindu caste groups: in honey from an earthen pot by a Sudra or peasant, in curd from a copper vessel by a Vaishya or craftsman, in milk from a silver pot by a Kshatriya or warrior, and finally in butter from a golden jug by a Brahmin priest.

Whatever he thought of these old Hindu ceremonies, Birendra embraced the ancient concept of princely rule prohibiting criticism of the king. This did not stop interference from Indian and Chinese sources. Congress exiles resumed raids from India. Maoist thought spread among Nepalese university students. Continuing Mahendra's precarious balancing act between Nepal's two huge neighbours, Birendra turned increasingly to the north notwithstanding Nepal's shared heritage with the south.

In December 1973, the young king flew to Beijing, where Chairman Mao Zedong talked with him for more than an hour and a half and Premier Zhou Enlai declared that China supported the Nepalese "in their just struggle against foreign interference." In September 1974, crowds in Katmandu protesting India's takeover of Sikkim attacked the Indian embassy and cultural centre, and Indian shops. India retorted that the "vulgar" demonstrations had "official" backing, and sharply increased the prices of cement, iron, and coal exports to Nepal.

But Indira Gandhi's government continued work on the east-west road through the Terai close to the Indian border, and helped underwrite two hydroelectric projects in northwestern Nepal. Most of the power generated would go to India, setting up a possible pretext for Indian military intervention if the flow were cut. To dampen such temptations, Birendra awarded two bonuses to Beijing when its indefatigable road workers completed the link from Katmandu to Pokhara in 1974.

He curbed the activities of armed tribal Khampa horsemen from Tibet whose CIA-aided clandestine base at Pokhara supported raids into their country from the Mustang bulge of Nepal to the north. When I had flown earlier by Dakota to the Pokhara Valley, where flowers of many colours bloom against a white backdrop of the snows of Annapurna and Dhaulagiri, I was told that wounded Khampas received medical treatment at an undisclosed location near the airstrip. The king also commissioned the biggest Chinese road project yet: a $75-million highway west from Pokhara, extending the roads from the Kodari Pass and Katmandu more than 300 kilometres through rugged hills to Surkhet, near the Terai and Indian border. This increased China's stake in the extraordinary expansion of Nepal's roads from 300 to 3,000 kilometres over twenty-five years. The Chinese also contributed to Katmandu's local transportation system with two dozen odd-looking, green-and-white electric trolley buses.

In April 1976, a glum Nepalese delegation led by Tulsi Giri, the openly anti-Indian politician whom Birendra had named as his prime minister, sat down at a table in Delhi across from a smirking Indian delegation led by Indira and Foreign Minister Yeshwantrao Chavan. The Indians meant to squeeze the Nepalese for their deviationism through a new agreement on the trade and transit of foreign goods. Nepal still depended on India for 90 per cent of its trade, and wholly on India if imported goods came by sea.

But Indira and perhaps even Giri, who was compelled to talk again of a "special relationship" with India, did not wholly bargain on Birendra's tactics. That month the king renewed for another ten years the 1966 China-Nepal trade agreement, although it was much more limited than trade ties with India. In June he returned to China, this time to Chengtu in Szechuan province, where Premier Hua Kuo-feng assured him that China stood beside Nepal in its struggle against "hegemonism and expansionism."

Birendra, alluding to both the Khampas in Nepal and Nepalese Congress politicians in India, responded by declaring: "We will not allow the use of our soil for any activity hostile to any country, and we expect reciprocity in this matter." He reiterated a proposal that Nepal be designated a "zone of peace," and Hua endorsed it. Then the king flew off to Lhasa, the first foreign head of state to be allowed by the Chinese to visit the Autonomous Region of Tibet. Nepal had kept a consulate there after the Indians were forced to leave. Accompanied by two uncles, an aunt, a sister, and a brother-in-law, Birendra toured the old Potala Palace and the new communes of Tibet. As a final reminder to the Indians that his country no longer could be forced to gaze southward only, before he came home he opened the first direct air connection between Nepal and China.

The young king was soon challenged, however, to adopt a more even-handed approach to the two giants on either side of Nepal, and to move closer to the popular democracy abolished by his father. The reasons lay in the startling electoral defeat of Indira in March 1977 as a reaction to her Emergency in India, and the coming to power in Delhi of a more conciliatory government.

Soon after the Janata Party took office, Birendra flew to Delhi to meet Prime Minister Morarji Desai. Perhaps inevitably, considering their ages – Desai was eighty-one, Birendra thirty-one – the prime minister talked to the king as father or grandfather to son, but without the patronizing attitude that Nepalese find irksome in most Indians. Desai made clear his government would not support exiled Nepalese agitating for a return to democracy, or condemn Nepal for its non-democratic system at odds with the revived spirit of liberty in India.

Birendra, who also must have been impressed by the power of the people, responded as he or Mahendra never would have to a hard Indian line. Within six months Tulsi Giri was forced to resign as prime minister, partly on the ground that he had failed to balance relations with India and China. Giri was as well known for his espousal of the royal panchayat system as for his animus against India. The king signalled his intention to loosen the system by asking for and accepting the national assembly's recommendation of Giri's successor, even if its choice was the pro-Chinese Kirthinidhi Bista.

When Desai visited Katmandu in December 1977, he wasn't able to accept the Chinese-endorsed concept of Nepal as a separate "zone of peace." But he did agree to a longstanding Nepalese request for separate agreements on trade with India and the transit of foreign goods through India. Recognizing the huge development potential of the Gangetic plains, the two governments also agreed to joint exploitation of Ganges tributaries in Nepal.

Less than two months later, China's leading pragmatist, Deputy Prime Minister Deng Xiaoping, came to Katmandu. But the man who was to become paramount leader was less forthcoming than Desai had been. He put off Nepalese bids for increased trade with China and joint tourism with Tibet. Beijing had decided earlier to terminate at the end of 1980 an agreement permitting the Nepalese to graze cattle in Tibet. The dragon was no less ambitious in the Himalayas. But its top priority was clearly to keep outside influences away from what it already controlled, namely Tibet.

Prospects for revival of party democracy in Nepal focused at the time on B.P. Koirala, the former Nepal Congress prime minister, and how Birendra treated him.

After he was freed by Mahendra in 1968, Koirala fought his battle for democracy from exile in India, sending armed guerrillas on periodic raids of border towns. Hoping to benefit from an amnesty granted to exiled politicians by Birendra, Koirala returned to Nepal at the end of 1976, at the height of Indira's Emergency in India. The king went back on his word, jailing the aging Koirala again, this time putting him in solitary confinement for seven months and charging him with treason, inciting to murder, arson, and sedition. But when he learned his prisoner was ill, the king sent him posthaste at government expense to the United States for an operation to remove a throat malignancy.

After recuperating, Koirala insisted on returning to Nepal again, and again he was placed in detention. In early 1978, he was acquitted of five of the seven charges against him, and released on bail for further medical treatment in New York City, this time paid for by funds raised by an American defence committee. Operated on again in May 1978, obviously weak, and facing life imprisonment if convicted, Koirala, then sixty-four, nevertheless was determined to follow in the footsteps of his old friend, the ailing Jayaprakash Narayan – JP – who had lived to see the rebirth of democracy in India. BP, as he was known to Nepalese, said hopefully of conditions in Nepal: "I feel the time is propitious for the re-establishment of democracy."

Koirala, one of Asia's great democrats, still expressed this hope when I met him in Katmandu in June 1980. Prematurely aged from the detentions he had endured in the twenty years since democracy was banished, he was not bitter when we talked outside his home in the Valley. The remaining charges against him had been dropped. This was not the reason for B.P. Koirala's kindly smile as he urged a "dialogue on Nepal's future" leading to popular political and economic reforms. The reason was his belief in the healing qualities of human freedom. But democracy did not come back to Nepal for another ten years. And BP did not live to see it. He died in 1982 at the age of sixty-eight.

Democracy returned only when the clash of India and China in the kingdom contributed to widespread unrest that compelled Birendra to give up his absolute powers and allow a constitutional monarchy. The alternative, I found out later in Katmandu, was the king's ruling through an army that had grown to 30,000 soldiers. If he had ended popular protests by force, the monarchy might also have come to an end as the acknowledged symbol of Nepal.

With the Nehru dynasty's return to power in the 1980s, India reverted to intimidation tactics against Nepal as part of a general hardening of policies toward the perceived enemies, foreign and domestic, of Indira and later Rajiv Gandhi. In 1989, alarmed at the Nepalese intent to import Chinese weapons, Delhi exerted its most drastic pressure yet, cutting off the landlocked kingdom's lifeline to the outside world by closing border trading posts. Nepal's always precarious economic plight rapidly grew worse as India ignored entreaties and tightened the screws.

This crisis ignited popular resentment of the corrupt panchayat system – the resentment had begun with the system's failure to bring about changes demanded by voters in a 1980 referendum allowed by the king as a way to buy time. Another factor was news of the successful uprisings against autocratic Communist regimes in Eastern Europe in the fall of 1989. Starting in April 1990, students led angry demonstrations in the Katmandu Valley against Birendra and his personally appointed government with the aim not of having the latter give in to Indian demands but give way to a democratic system. Troops and police shot more than fifty protesters, but the demonstrations continued, bringing banned political parties together in a common cause for the first time.

Birendra was smart enough to realize that the time for palace-sponsored, authoritarian government in Nepal, which had made little or no progress toward his own avowed goal of raising living standards, was up after three decades. Instead of unleashing his army, he pledged to co-operate in the drafting of a democratic constitution and the holding of a democratic election. When he kept his promise, the protests stopped and a wave of high popular expectations began sweeping over Nepal.

In June 1990, India ended its crippling economic blockade with a provisional agreement between a conciliatory Prime Minister Vishwanath Pratap Singh, who had ousted Rajiv Gandhi in a 1989 election, and an interim Nepalese government. This took much of the tension out of Nepal-India relations. But the prices of essential commodities in Nepal remained high, and self-serving Nepalese bureaucrats accustomed to ignoring the poor were still in place. In November, after several false starts under the divided interim government, King Birendra promulgated a progressive constitution. It provided for basic human rights, an independent judiciary, free political parties, and a parliament with a popularly elected lower house and an indirectly elected upper house.

Nepalese men and women voted freely in May 1991 for the first time in thirty-two years. More than 65 per cent of newly registered voters, 7.3 million mostly dirt-poor people, cast ballots for candidates of twenty parties or independents – a tremendously encouraging turnout considering the long delay since the last election and the country's improved but still high illiteracy rate of 80 per cent. International observers found the election generally "free, fair, and open." It was Nepal's healthiest and most promising step toward breaking the shackles of stifling despotism and deadening poverty.

As expected, Nepal's Congress Party won handily, but with nothing like its landslide in the 1959 election. With 38 per cent of the popular vote, it captured a majority of 110 seats in the 205-seat lower house. Its Communist rival, called the United Marxist-Leninist Party since leftist splits had been papered over, did surprisingly well with 28 per cent of the vote and 69 seats. Significantly, a party close to the king and the old panchayat system – one of two groups called the Rastriya Prajantra or National Democratic Party – came in third in the popular vote with 7 per cent although only three of its candidates were elected. The Congress victory was further qualified by setbacks for two of the three party leaders. The third, Girija Prasad Koirala, sixty-seven, a younger and less inspiring half-brother of the late B.P. Koirala, became prime minister when the king asked him to form a government.

G.P. Koirala knew what had to be done, and he had the best of intentions. He was a Nepalese Congressman in the idealistic tradition of the elder Koirala, who never got the chance to return to office and work for the people. During the balance of 1991, the new prime minister made clear that his main goal was reducing poverty. The best he could do at first was to promise to provide safe drinking water to all Nepalese, and to respect the rights of women and children to decent lives. While calling for close relations with both India and China, he went to Delhi in December and won extensions of trade and transit treaties from the new Indian Congress government. He also sought to co-operate with Nepalese Communists and other opposition parties, and went out of his way to try to keep his own party united.

But G.P. Koirala could not dispel a mood of disillusionment and drift that I sensed during a visit to Katmandu in January 1992. In part it was a natural reaction to the high expectations of rapid results accompanying the creation of a democratic constitution and election of a new government. As Bhekh Thapa, a former finance minister and ambassador to the United States, explained as we sat in front of a fire in his modest house on a little hilltop at the end of a Katmandu dirt lane and he kept feeding logs to the fire for heat: "Nepalese people see government as a god and if it fails they lose faith."

The problem, however, went to the reasons for failure. It was reflected in the fact that Thapa, one of the few Nepali experts with the background and international contacts to make economic and social development work in his country, had not at that point been recruited by the new government. Another old friend, Rishikesh Shah, who had first brought Thapa into government, cautioned that the return of democracy he had long fought for did not banish a deep hostility among individuals, racial groups, and political parties growing out of too little for too many. Without a national consensus, "the nation is in trouble," warned Shah, noting that nothing in the new constitution prevented the king from using the army to take absolute power into his hands again, although he added that would mean the end of the dynasty going back to Prithvi Narayan Shah.

Prime Minister Koirala was betrayed at every turn in his efforts to move his country forward. Although Nepal's economy was subject to international guidelines as a condition of loans, the money simply wasn't available to meet humanitarian targets quickly or even to arrest the deterioration of natural resources and the environment. On one hand India was accommodating, on the other it continued to insist that Nepal would have to recognize India's security needs if Nepal wanted its economic concerns addressed. Nepal's Communists supported a damaging strike by civil servants soon after the Koirala government took office, backing off only in August 1991 when the attempted coup in the Soviet Union threw party members into ideological disarray.

All this could have been expected, and probably would have been weathered. But some of G.P. Koirala's Congress colleagues, interested only in their own fortunes or linked to insensitive bureaucrats, also stabbed him in the back.

Former Congress strongman Ganesh Man Singh, personally disappointed in the election results, began sniping at Koirala before the end of 1991 although the prime minister had encouraged a trip by Singh to the United States and other Western countries as an emissary of Nepalese democracy. In July 1994, with popular frustration at the failure to alleviate poverty running higher than ever, thirty-eight Congress dissidents in the lower house voted against the government's annual policy statement, ensuring its defeat and Koirala's resignation. Birendra accepted his recommendation that Parliament be dissolved and another election held in November 1994, a year and a half ahead of schedule.

Like Indira's unnecessary split of India's Congress Party in 1969, the needless breaking apart of Nepal's Congress Party twenty-five years later inaugurated a period of unstable governments and creeping malaise. But differences from India were disturbing and dangerous for democracy. In Nepal, Communists were ready to jump into the breach as an alternative, potentially majority party, and experience with democratic politics was lacking. Economic conditions were worse. Whereas Nehru and Indira had tried to stand above politics while being wholly immersed in politics, Nepal had a king who ostensibly had entirely removed himself from politics. Ironically, the future of democracy in Nepal came to depend increasingly on the tolerance, good faith, and self-interest of a constitutional monarch whose once absolute powers had provoked the return to democracy. Birendra's calculations depended in turn not only on the parlous state of Nepal's politics and economics but also on the chronic threats posed by the Indian serpent and the Chinese dragon.

Turnout for the election was 58 per cent of eligible voters, down sharply from 1991. The Congress share of the popular vote was 33 per cent, also down significantly but still first. The Communist share of the popular vote was up slightly to 30 per cent, still second. But this time the Communists won more seats in the 205-seat lower house than Congress, 88 to 83. With neither party able to form a majority coalition despite vigorous attempts, Communist leader Man Mohan Adhikary, seventy-four, staked a claim to forming a minority government. Two weeks after the voting, King Birendra accommodated him. It was the first time a Communist party came to national power in Asia as the result of a democratic election.

Predictions that the army would not allow the Communists to assume power proved wrong. But Birendra acted in the knowledge that the royalist National Democratic Party, which had won 20 seats with 17 per cent of the popular vote, held the parliamentary balance of power. After the gaunt Adhikary, wearing dark glasses and a Nepalese cap, his shaggy beard trimmed into a goatee, was received at the palace, he emphasized that implementation of "communism as a philosophy" would depend on the "realities of the country." One reality was that Birendra and his supporters held an effective veto over any intended radical policy such as a redistribution of land. Another reality was the fluidity of Nepalese politics, jeopardizing from the outset the life of a minority Communist government in addition to its inability to change Nepalese society.

From the time the king let him form a government, Adhikary manoeuvred for a fresh election that could be expected to give his party a parliamentary majority considering the divisions within Congress. The Communists curried popular favour by taking a hard anti-Indian line in contrast to Congress with its pro-Indian reputation. Adhikary went to Delhi in April 1995 and categorically denounced the 1950 treaty with India as reflecting a "concept of security umbrella dating back to the nineteenth century." Then he flew to Beijing to press Nepal's continuing bid for more trade with Tibet. The Indians responded by again tying their continued trade with Nepal to security assurances. They did not have long to wait for Adhikary's downfall.

In June the prime minister successfully petitioned the king to dissolve Parliament and call a new election – a standard procedure under the British form of parliamentary democracy. But Nepal's Supreme Court ruled in August that Adhikary's move, made without a non-confidence vote like the one in 1994, was unconstitutional. The lower house reconvened in September in extraordinary session and passed a non-confidence motion against the government by a vote of 107 to 88 despite Communist street protests, warnings of violence, and alleged bribes. Adhikary and his badly discredited Marxists were compelled to give way to a coalition government headed by new Congress leader Sher Bahadur Deuba and including all the king's men in the National Democratic Party, which thereby strengthened its hold on the balance of power.

The next change of government before a third election flowed from a realignment of Nepalese political forces that on the surface seemed to make little sense. But a closer look suggested a disquieting logic.

Deuba's government lasted a year and a half, twice as long as the hapless Communist regime. Then the Congress Party lost a non-confidence vote in March 1997 when the monarchists pulled the rug out from under it. This time the new coalition government formed at the behest of the king was led by the small National Democratic Party close to Birendra – and included the Communists it had helped dump in 1995. Prime Minister Lokendra Bahadur Chand named a hardline Communist as his deputy and interior minister and handed ten other portfolios to the Marxists.

This had all the markings of an anti-Congress, anti-Indian alliance under the implicit patronage of the king. If that were so, it could be traced all the way back to Mahendra's dismissal of a Congress government in 1960 and his opening up Nepal to the Chinese. There was nothing new in the royalists in Parliament sharing anti-Indian sentiments with the Communists. What was new was their formally joining with the Communists to topple a Congress-led government and possibly to fight Congress in the next election.

But the strange coalition government of monarchists and Communists lasted only seven months. In October 1997, a Congress-backed non-confidence motion passed by a vote of 107 to 94 in the lower house of Parliament. Chand resigned as prime minister and, again without an election, a new coalition took over combining Congressmen and royalists who had opposed co-operating with the Communists.

This development dampened speculation that Birendra meant to follow his father by dismissing political parties and democracy altogether, and returning to a panchayat system as some monarchists demanded. Even after the installation of the fifth government in six and a half years, this appeared unlikely as long as Nepal's parties could be played off against each other. The king as well as his country, considering the international aid it desperately needed, clearly had an interest in keeping democracy. If democracy in Nepal were to grow more stable, however, Birendra needed to resist undermining Congress, the one major non-Communist party with the ability, notwithstanding its links with India, to keep him a constitutional figurehead in fact as well as in name.

But political confusion only grew worse in 1998, making democracy in Nepal a bad joke and almost impossible to follow. Early in the year the latest prime minister, Surya Bahadur Thapa, a royalist, asked for a new election. The king did not grant his request. This led to Thapa's resignation, and G.P. Koirala taking over again as prime minister. But Koirala resigned before the end of the year when one Communist faction withdrew its support for him. Then Koirala returned as Congress prime minister with the support of another Communist faction. He urged a new popular vote. In January 1999 Birendra finally dissolved the fractious Parliament and Nepal's third election since 1991 was set for May.

With the Communists split and the Maoist United People's Front waging a "people's war" in the countryside, resulting in hundreds of deaths, Nepal's Congress had a good chance to win a clear majority with its promises to restore order and economic development – but only if the party could avoid its own split again. It did so only when G.P. Koirala stood aside to let Krishna Prasad Bhattarai, one of the Congress leaders who had divided the party after the first election, become prime minister. With that agreement in place, Congress won 110 of 205 parliamentary seats, restoring majority rule on the strength of ballots cast by more than 60 per cent of eligible voters. The Communists captured only 68 seats and the royalists 11.

But Congress unity lasted only nine months this time. In February 2000, more than half the party's members of Parliament demanded a change of leadership, and eleven ministers resigned from the cabinet. The next day, Maoist insurgents killed fifteen policemen, their deadliest raid in four years.

As in India for many years, elections worked but many of those elected seemed to lack the will or the ability to reduce grinding poverty and entrenched corruption, and to ensure political stability. Despite all the promises and all the aid that had been given to the people of Nepal, discontent and violence in the countryside were rising. Conditions were so bad that four of every ten children aged five to fourteen worked instead of going to school. China was in a position to exploit popular anger through Nepalese Marxists, and India did not improve matters by exempting a growing number of commodities from free trade with Nepal.

Bhattarai resigned as prime minister in March, and G.P. Koirala took over once again at the age of seventy-six. He openly acknowledged Nepal's many problems and expressed greater determination than ever to overcome them by democratic methods. One of his toughest tasks would be suppressing Communist terrorists while keeping control of abusive police. But after a decade of political fumbling and economic stagnation, Nepal had one more chance to move forward.

That chance seemed to go up in gun smoke at the palace on the night of 1 June 2001.

In killing King Birendra, Queen Aiswarya, seven other members of the royal family, and himself, Crown Prince Dipendra might have come close to killing popular hope and national stability in Nepal. Familiar royal figures suddenly were gone, replaced by suspect interlopers. Nepalese democracy, restarted with high expectations, had turned into little more than a cynical numbers game. Politicians appeared too selfish to break the cycle of poverty, and too paralyzed to take effective action against a Marxist revolution gaining alarming ground in the countryside.

But the Communists, although recognizing that events were rapidly going their way, overplayed their hand. Making impossible demands and carrying out outrageous murders, they lunged for nothing less than a classic takeover of Nepal. This jolted Nepal's new king and a new Congress Party prime minister into declaring a national emergency and ordering the army, grown to 45,000 troops but doing little, to put down the revolt instead of relying on terrorized police. The government even asked India for military assistance, but not in the form of troops. Nepalese troops quickly started to take the initiative away from the insurgents, who had controlled or threatened to control one-third of Nepal's seventy-five districts. Decisive military action did not happen, and might never have happened, with the calculating Birendra as king and the soft-hearted G.P. Koirala as prime minister.

When Parliament convened after the palace massacre, the Communists demanded the Koirala government's resignation on the ground that it had failed to protect the royal family. At the same time, they called for abolition of the monarchy, urged repeal of a new law allowing the arrest of security risks, planned a general strike, and intensified violence in what insurgents called a "people's war" aimed at establishing a Maoist Nepal. On the eve of King Gyanendra's birthday on 7 July, they killed thirty-nine policemen and a civilian in a string of attacks on rural police posts, bringing the death toll since 1996 to nearly 2,000.

China denied giving support to at least 5,000 armed rebels, who called the Beijing government "revisionist." But the Chinese Communists had worked too hard and too long to establish influence in strategically important Nepal for observers to believe they had no meaningful connection to the insurgency. Nevertheless, Nepalese in and out of the government naively put their faith in secret talks with local Communists to reach a compromise and avert civil war. They were apparently unaware that this was a venerable Marxist tactic designed to culminate in complete Communist victory, as was drawing a public distinction between Communists in Parliament and Communists in the hills when they all had the same objective of destroying democracy and institutions upholding it, and coming to power.

On 19 July, Girija Prasad Koirala, the easiest target of Nepalese frustrations and discontents since 1 June, resigned as prime minister. Now seventy-eight, he had served in the position four times, and after his half-brother's death had used the Koirala name to keep the banner of democracy flying in Nepal. He got it right in the end, starting to use the army to rescue policemen taken hostage by rebels, and declaring in a radio-TV address: "The attack by the Maoists is directed not only against the democracy of the country but it is also directed at disturbing national security and integrity." But GP realized he was not the man to lead the counterattack.

Sher Bahadur Deuba, who became Congress prime minister for the second time to head the ninth government since 1990, looked better suited to deal with the Communists. On the basis of early evidence, the same could be said of King Gyanendra as compared to Birendra. The palace massacre could hardly ever be called a blessing in disguise. But Nepal may have been shocked into abandoning drift and turning in a more positive direction under new leaders.

Deuba first tested the Maoists by calling a ceasefire, agreeing to talks, and even releasing prisoners. At the same time, the government outlawed discrimination against Hindu untouchables or dalits, and Gyanendra declared his son Paras the crown prince – both controversial acts but indicating a changing Nepal. With the talks stalled after three rounds, the Communists withdrew from the four-month-old ceasefire. The rebel leader, Pushpa Kamal Dahal, who called himself Prachandra, or Awesome, said they had no reason for continuing it. Two days later, on 23 November, the rebels resumed their armed insurgency with a vengeance, killing at least thirty-seven policemen and soldiers in mass attacks on police posts and army barracks. Gyanendra and Deuba met urgently, and the Congress Party called for a forceful response to the Maoists. On 26 November, the king declared a state of emergency and unleashed the army.

As fighting raged in Solukhumbu district, close to Mount Everest in eastern Nepal and home of the mountaineering Sherpas, and troops advanced toward Communist strongholds in western Nepal, another royal edict may have been as important in enlisting international support for Nepal as the emergency was in making the Nepalese aware of the gravity of the situation. The edict classified the Maoist insurgents as terrorists.

Two and a half months after the 11 September terrorist attacks on the United States, the new king of Nepal authorized the democratic government to detain suspected terrorists for six months without trial, and specified a penalty of twenty years in prison for convicted terrorists. The United States quickly announced its backing for Nepal's military campaign. India, beset in Kashmir by armed terrorists based in Pakistan, had one

more reason besides Nepal's strategic importance to meet Nepal's request
for helicopters and ammunition. Another was connections between Nepal's
Communist rebels and those in the bordering states of West Bengal and
Bihar.

On 18 January 2002, Nepal seemed a little less remote and the Nepalese
felt a little less lonely when Secretary of State Colin L. Powell became the
seniormost U.S. official to fly into Katmandu in thirty-two years (Spiro
Agnew, Richard Nixon's vice president, had visited in 1970). On the way
to India, Pakistan, Afghanistan, and Japan, Powell had told reporters that
the insurgency in Nepal "really is the kind of thing we're fighting against
throughout the world." After meeting separately with King Gyanendra,
Prime Minister Deuba, and Nepalese military officials on his overnight
stay, the former general endorsed "Nepal's right to protect its citizens and
institutions from terrorist attacks." But he also emphasized to the Nepalese
the importance of protecting human rights and creating jobs for young
people so they don't join radical causes: "You have to fight the terrorist[s],
but at the same time you must commit your nation and your government
to good government and to ending corruption, to finding ways to move the
economy forward."

Democracy and unity in Nepal came under new strains, however, before
the end of the year. In early October, King Gyanendra contemptuously dismissed Deuba after the prime minister sought a one-year delay in elections
due in November for fear the Maoists would disrupt them. Having put off
voting indefinitely himself, the king then brought back as prime minister
the monarchist Lokendra Bahadur Chand, who said he would try to open
a dialogue with the rebels. Many Nepalese feared Gyanendra was emulating Birendra in manipulating politics from the palace.

How the Nepalese people feel about democracy remains the key question
about their future. Their expectations are more realistic than at the beginning of the 1990s, when democracy got a second chance in Nepal. If the
kings or the Ranas or the bureaucrats or the panchayats had helped them
overcome poverty without political freedom, they might be excused for giving up on it. But there is nothing in their past to cause them to believe there
can be a better system than democracy in their present and future. There is
compelling evidence that poor Nepalese want to make democracy work
with the tools and under the circumstances at hand.

The danger is that democracy's failure might cause them to lose faith –
and their country – altogether. Still, there is no real alternative for the
largest Himalayan kingdom as it struggles to maintain its identity and
integrity between India and China. But as Bhekh Thapa, who returned to
Washington as Nepal's ambassador in 1995 and later became ambassador
to India, put it to me when I was last in Katmandu: "If democracy is to

survive, it must be able to combine political freedom with the freedom from want that afflicts nearly two-thirds of the Nepalese, who live below the official poverty line bordering sub-human conditions."

Bhutan, the second Himalayan kingdom, also has developed a distinct and legitimate identity of its own. But compared with the status of Nepal, the independence of the beautiful country its 700,000 people call Druk Yul – Land of the Thunder Dragon – is much more constricted. Like Hindu Nepal, Buddhist Bhutan to the east has felt more pressure from India than from China since Han imperialism enveloped Tibet, its mother country, in the 1950s. Unlike Nepal, Bhutan is not in a position to reopen links with the north. The Indian serpent blocks contact with the Chinese dragon.

According to legend, a Tibetan lama riding a flying tigress brought Buddhism to Bhutan 1,200 years ago. It is the erotic Tantric variety of Mahayana Buddhism that influences Nepalese Hindus. In the seventeenth century a warrior lama from Tibet unified Bhutan by defeating rival Tibetan armies. The Bhutanese briefly fought the British in the nineteenth century and ceded land to the Raj. But Bhutan has been recognized as a separate Himalayan state since 1885. The family of the *tongsa penlop*, or governor, became the hereditary royal family in 1907, when Buddhist monks and ordinary Bhutanese elected Ugyen Wangchuk as the first Druk Gyalpo or Dragon King. Today, Bhutan has a limited form of democracy: the king appoints a parliament, it approves his cabinet ministers, and with a two-thirds majority its members can force the king to abdicate.

Bhutan and Britain concluded a treaty in 1910 making the kingdom a protectorate of the Raj. Under a 1949 agreement supplanting this treaty, the foreign policy and defence of Bhutan, as well as access to the country, were made subject to India's guidance. It was not until Jigme Dorji Wangchuk took the sacred Buddhist silk scarf symbolizing Bhutan's throne in 1952 that the inaccessible rugged land the size of Switzerland, hemmed in by the Himalayas to the north and jungles to the south, started to emerge from nearly total feudalism and lack of development.

By the time the progressive Jigme Dorji Wangchuk died suddenly in 1972 at forty-five, the most Bhutan had been able to wring out of the Indians in the way of independence was the right to sell its own postage stamps – almost its only source of foreign exchange – and, more important, to join the United Nations in 1971. India provided the funds for limited economic development and the goods for the bazaars of Paro and Thimpu, the capital. In addition, India protected the ruling Bhutias of Tibetan origin and Nepalese living in the southwestern Himalayan foothills, and determined their relations with other foreigners. Still, Bhutanese continued trading with Tibetans when Chinese Communist troops first moved onto the Tibetan Plateau.

Following the flight of the Dalai Lama to India in 1959, however, Delhi forced Bhutan to close its border with Tibet and to become totally dependent on the south for trade and aid except for small-scale assistance from other foreign countries. Indian bureaucrats "advised" the government, as the 1949 agreement put it. An Indian military mission of more than a thousand officers and men was posted in Bhutan, ostensibly to train the country's tiny army. Delhi periodically asserted its interest in Himalayan border areas not in India itself. When Prime Minister Indira Gandhi visited Nepal in October 1966, India protested to China against four alleged intrusions into Bhutan from Tibet by Chinese troops or Tibetan herdsmen. Other Indian notes to Beijing complained about intrusions into Sikkim by Chinese soldiers.

The king of Bhutan, grateful for Indian aid but wary of the colonial relationship it engendered, was instrumental in bringing his country its first road, its first airstrip, its first money, its first telephones, its first medical facilities, its first schools, and its first parliament despite the power that members could wield against him. By 1968, when the road opened, some 15,000 students were enrolled in a school system started and later expanded by a Canadian Jesuit, the late William Mackey. By the end of the century, it had 100,000 students. All China could do as Bhutan developed was to make clear that in dealings with it, such as settlement of border disputes, Beijing had no intention of recognizing India as an intermediary under the 1949 agreement.

Palace intrigues can be deadly in Bhutan, Indian connivance in them is assumed but difficult to prove. For Westerners, such covert manoeuvres are masked by the exotic charm of the dragon king, of the Tashichodzong or medieval pagoda serving as the country's political and religious centre, of the practice of archery by members of the court, and of strong, handsome Bhutia women who wear their jet black hair short, with bangs.

The less charming side of high Bhutanese society was illustrated by the 1964 assassination of the king's prime minister and brother-in-law, Jigme Dorji Palden, by elements opposing reform, and by the monarch's narrow escape from death in 1965. His son, Jigme Singye Wangchuk, after attending St Joseph's School in Darjeeling like the prime minister's son, went to school in Britain, partly for protection. But his father said in 1967: "He must think, feel, and act like a Bhutanese, or else the people will throw him out." Not altogether surprisingly, on the day before the sixteen-year-old king was to be crowned on 2 June 1974, the Bhutanese government reported a plot to kill him and burn down the Tashichodzong.

The plot, or plots, were understandably murky considering the cast of characters involved as would-be victims or perpetrators, not counting a likely Indian hand. On one side were the fourth Druk Gyalpo, an athletic, independent-minded teenager; the Queen Mother, a Dorji and sister of the late prime minister who had lived and exerted influence apart from the late king; and her until then exiled brother and sister. On the other were a Tibetan concubine of the late king named Yangki who lived in India; a brother of the Dalai Lama of Tibet based in Darjeeling; a deputy home minister; and a police commandant. Nonetheless, the minutely planned Buddhist coronation cheerfully went ahead at the auspicious moment chosen by astrologers, marking as it did a reunion of the two ruling families, the Wangchuks and the Dorjis. The young king calmly accepted from the powerful chief lama the five-colour royal scarf signifying purity. He carefully performed a Bhutanese tea ceremony. Then he offered traditional wine to servers first to make sure it wasn't poisoned.

India permitted a number of foreigners, mainly diplomats stationed in Delhi, to enter Bhutan to attend the coronation. It vetoed representation of Pakistan, and would have kept China out, too. But the Bhutanese government, taking advantage of its proud UN membership, invited the five permanent members of the Security Council to send representatives. To India's chagrin, China gladly accepted, along with the United States, the Soviet Union, Britain, and France.

The teenage king made Indians uncomfortable in another way at the time. Without naming India, he drew obvious contrasts when he observed: "In Bhutan, we are lucky in some ways. We have no population problem. We don't have the gap between rich and poor that you find in other countries. We have no beggars. We are a united people, a very proud people. This unity and pride must remain."

Jigme Singye Wangchuk also announced that he would step up development started by his father, including opening Bhutan to tourists. Before the year of 1974 was out, the first foreign tourists entered the country. By the early 1990s, several carefully located and well-run hotels catered to tourists, and the Bhutanese air line Druk Air flew a jet from Delhi to Paro and back twice a week. But only 3,000 foreigners a year were allowed into the country, and only in groups of four or more at $200 per person per day. Later the limit was increased to 6,000 foreigners, and individuals or couples were permitted if they paid extra.

To mark the twenty-fifth anniversary in 1999 of his coronation, Jigme Singye Wangchuk, then forty-one, even allowed the inauguration of television in Bhutan, and Internet connections followed – risks to any culture. From the beginning of the year, Bhutanese citizens had to pay income tax. But average income had risen to $550 a year, twice as high as Nepal's. Nearly half the population was literate, and free health care reached most

Bhutanese. The government had expelled 95,000 Nepalese to prevent the Bhutias from being overwhelmed.

The handsome dragon king is determined not to let the natural magnificence of his country be spoiled by alien influences. Neither does he want Bhutan to miss the chance of moving ahead at its own pace or to fall back into isolation.

From his coronation day, Jigme Singye Wangchuk, possibly learning from Nepal's kings Mahendra and Birendra, gradually has brought Bhutan farther into the modern world, although his land is still vulnerable to outside influences. Assisted by the four beautiful wives he has taken – all sisters – and encouraging young Bhutanese like himself who want genuine national freedom, he has loosened a little India's coils.

But for the third and smallest Himalayan kingdom, and the most exposed, this was a dream too good to come true.

19

An Unlikely Expression of Hope

When the newest princess of Sikkim was born on 12 February 1968, she was named Hope after the wide-eyed, young Yankee queen of one of the world's smallest countries – but only once Buddhist lamas had come with a string of ancient mystical names from which Hope could somehow be derived.

Sikkim was sort of that kind of place. Whimsical perhaps, a little unreal, an odd mixture of old and new, but most of all an unlikely expression of hope squeezed between Chinese-held Tibet and India. And "sort of" all those things because that was the favourite qualifying phrase of the Chogyal and Gyalmo, the king and queen of Sikkim.

The freckle-faced Gyalmo, the former Hope Cooke of Maine and Sarah Lawrence College, gave birth in a Calcutta nursing home to her second child, who looked like a plump porcelain doll. Her first child, curly-haired Prince Palden, was born in 1964 and named after his father, who had three children, including the heir apparent, from his late first wife.

Chogyal Palden Thondup Namgyal, forty-five, whose family had ruled Sikkim since the fourteenth century, had not only been modern-minded enough to take as his second wife an American woman seventeen years younger than himself; he also had a sense of history. Both attributes are rare in rulers, and both were shared in a rather charming combination with Hope La, the familiar Tibetan designation she had earned for herself.

Together, they were battling odds to maintain and develop Sikkim's distinct identity between two other larger Himalayan kingdoms: Nepal to the west and Bhutan to the east. They couldn't try too hard or their purpose would be defeated. For while Sikkim without Indian defenders would be at China's mercy, Indian defence – more concentrated in Sikkim than in any other sector of the Himalayas – sharply restricted rule by the Chogyal or by Sikkimese generally.

Sikkim was a protectorate of India under a 1950 treaty giving Delhi responsibility for its defence, foreign affairs, and communications. As in Bhutan, the Indians had succeeded the British, who had come to an agreement with China regarding Sikkim in 1886. But Indian combat units were deployed in Sikkim, unlike Bhutan and certainly Nepal, which maintained its independence. Sikkimese led by the Chogyal contended that British connivance had resulted in the loss of a much larger area to Tibet and Nepal. They wanted the treaty with India rewritten so that only defence was a shared responsibility.

This may have been presumptuous on the part of a remote but strategically important country of 7,200 square kilometres and something more than 180,000 people at the time, 70 per cent of them Nepalese. Of the three exotic Himalayan kingdoms squeezed between the Chinese dragon and the Indian serpent, Sikkim was by far the most vulnerable, especially after the 1962 war in the world's highest mountains.

Like Goa in 1961, but more tragically, Sikkim was to become a classic example of what Bharat – India – was prepared to do on its own as the self-perceived centre of the world. In a step-by-step operation different mainly from China's ruthless takeover of Tibet in that it was on a smaller scale – and was hardly noticed by the rest of the world – India's callous and calculated assimilation of Sikkim started by deceit in April 1973 and ended with a show of Indian arrogance in May 1975.

But in June 1968 the Chogyal and Gyalmo – his family from eastern Tibet, hers from the eastern seaboard of the United States – managed in small ways to establish the distinctness of their tiny realm. My wife Pat and I and our three-year-old daughter, Shauna, visited this truly storybook land and were fortunate to spend some time with its rulers before the romantic fairy tale of Sikkim came to a nasty, Indian-dictated end.

When we entered Sikkim on 1 June at the village of Rampo, a young uniformed Sikkimese smilingly stamped our passports. Sikkim's international status was thereby quietly acknowledged – a new procedure insisted on by Queen Hope. On the road to Rangpo, Indian police at two checkpoints had been interested not in passports but in official Indian permits to cross the "innerline" of the Himalayas, the start of the designated "sensitive" area in the disputed mountain borderlands.

After having been turned down in 1966, we had received permits from the Indian foreign ministry, because the Sikkim palace had complained that almost no foreigners were being allowed in. A tourist could obtain an innerline permit for one to three days, and others needed an invitation from the royal family to qualify for a longer stay. We had obtained an invitation before entering Sikkim, and an extension after arriving, so we were able to stay a full week.

Once inside Sikkim, one was likely to be delayed in one's Land Rover or Jeep – the most suitable small vehicle – on the winding road up to Gangtok, the capital, by a train of Indian army mules changing loads, a convoy of Indian army trucks, or the rocks from a landslide or two waiting to be cleared by Indian army bulldozers. In the Gangtok bazaar, a steep hill of mostly Indian-owned shops, olive-uniformed Indian soldiers from the Punjab, Madras, or Indian hill areas were obvious and numerous. They mixed uneasily with the people of Sikkim: Bhutias, from whom the Chogyal's family came; Lepchas, the original inhabitants, reduced to 10 per cent of the population; Nepalese, both born in Sikkim and from Nepal; and Tibetans.

It was and is Sikkim's fate to occupy the most vulnerable part of the Himalayan line between dragon and serpent from India's point of view. The Chinese-held Chumbi Valley in Tibet, part of the land that had been claimed by Sikkim, points like a dagger between Bhutan and Sikkim toward the Siliguri slot, a narrow strip of West Bengal above the top of what was East Pakistan in 1968 and is now Bangladesh. If Chinese troops broke through Nathu La or another Sikkimese pass, they could readily cut off the Northeast Frontier Agency, Assam, Nagaland, and other eastern territories from the rest of India.

Indian and Chinese troops had exchanged heavy fire at Nathu La and Cho La in September and October 1967. But the Chinese had not carried out their threat to come through these Himalayan passes from the Chumbi Valley during the 1965 India-Pakistan war. Sikkim had not been a theatre of operations when Chinese troops did cross the Himalayas, in NEFA and Ladakh, in October-November 1962. India's pervasive military presence in Sikkim dated from that time, however, as did a complete cut-off of Sikkim's trade with Tibet. As early as 1956, trade had been reduced due to Indian and U.S. pressures. Elements of three or four Indian divisions were stationed in Sikkim in 1968, with a full division dug in on high, cold mountain slopes, in some places within yards of Chinese positions.

It was a moot question in Gangtok at the time whether the most important man in Sikkim was the Chogyal, the dewan (Indian political officer) – who lived in a large house on the next hill and at a slightly higher elevation than the palace, and who was then also responsible for Bhutan – or the Indian divisional commander. There was no outward friction between the Chogyal and the Indians. He went out of his way to pay them every respect, as they did him.

But the inescapable fact was that to many Sikkimese, the seen devil – as an Asian considers a foreigner on his soil – was worse than the unseen devil. The Chinese in Tibet were unseen, even if the land they occupied was tied to Sikkimese history. It was impossible to miss the Indians, who were racially and religiously different from the Mongoloid, Buddhist Bhutias and Lepchas, and who also were alien to the Nepalese in Sikkim as in Nepal. Even the Chogyal needed Indian permission to go up to the front line and glimpse the Chinese. While there were 4,000 Sikkimese in the Indian army, there were no Sikkimese units associated with defence of the country, or with defence of India in Sikkim. Even the 300 Sikkim Guards in their medieval dress, a sort of ceremonial palace contingent, had Indian officers.

Although Indian soldiers had been involved in a few incidents with Sikkimese civilians, there was no sign then of a breakdown in Sikkimese society due to the large number of Indian troops. India and Sikkim still saw their interests as complementary, and there was reason to hope that uneasiness on both sides might be overcome by civilized adjustments. But the overwhelming Indian military presence clearly contributed to the solidification of a Sikkimese national spirit. This was no minor matter when Bhutias and Lepchas on one hand and Nepalese on the other were divided by different languages and backgrounds. Encouraged by the Chogyal, a growing popular consensus was bridging this natural division.

He was carrying on Sikkim's long tradition of hands-on benevolent royalty, following the death in 1963 of his father, Chogyal Sir Tashi Namgyal, who had reigned for forty-nine years. India had tried and failed in 1949, soon after attaining its own full independence, to take away Sikkim's limited freedom. A mob led by the Sikkim State Congress – a political party modelled like Nepal's Congress on India's ruling Congress Party and advocating accession to India – stormed the palace. It demanded and got a supposedly popular government, which lasted twenty-nine days. Since then, Sir Tashi and then his son had been responsible for the more important fields of internal administration.

But it had been only in the past year or so that political sniping at the palace had practically ceased. Unlike Nepal at that time and Bhutan, Sikkim had political parties, but none talked any longer of accession to India. In Sikkim's third election in 1967 to the twenty-four-member state council, which then enjoyed limited powers, each of three parties – the National Congress, the State Congress, and the National Party of minority Bhutias and Lepchas – had won a minority of seats. The National Congress was split, and all parties lacked leaders who could challenge the Chogyal.

On the contrary, they were with him on the most burning issue in Sikkim: a revision of the treaty with India so this tiny country could have its own foreign policy – allowing UN membership, as Bhutan enjoyed – could receive aid for mineral and forest development from sources other than India, could put out its own postage stamps, also like Bhutan, and could maintain its own Indian-built roads.

Sikkim, whose average per capita income was double India's, also sought Indian assistance to develop industry and exports. Its main export was cardamom, a spice bought from poor farmers by Indian merchants at low prices and resold at much higher ones. Its industry consisted of an Indian-owned distillery (turning out coloured bottles of liquids ranging from corn whiskey to eau de cologne, and a preparation called Zong wine) and a government-owned fruit cannery (Air India served Sikkimese orange juice on its planes as an Indian product).

Apart from political parties, a group of twenty energetic Sikkimese civil servants had formed what they called the "study forum" with the blessings of the Chogyal. At Indian insistence, his chief administrative officer was still an Indian. But the Sikkimese made up what amounted to an intellectual pressure group for cutting red tape between the government and villagers, and opening up economic and educational outlets for Sikkimese beyond India.

The Indian answer to all these demands was to contend that Sikkim was just a small princely state of India that didn't happen to be integrated in 1947 like the hundreds of others, and the Chogyal was just another maharaja. The most India was willing to consider was to drop the old-fashioned word "protectorate" from the treaty. Indira's government and the pro-Communist press in India were particularly suspicious of the Chogyal's American wife. They intimated that she was really working for the CIA, and recalled that she had once written an essay, half in jest, supporting Sikkim's legitimate claim to the hill station of Darjeeling, where she had met the man who became her husband nine months before his father died.

What India feared was a Himalayan federation, including Sikkim and Bhutan and led by Nepal, where Chinese influence was growing under King Mahendra Bir Bikram Shah Dev. But even Indian officials admitted there had been no attempt by Beijing or pro-Beijing Bengali Communists to gain a foothold in Sikkim. As much as the Sikkimese disliked India's military presence, they did not demand or expect its disappearance. They insisted, however, that accession was the legal test of princely states, and Sikkim had never acceded to India but had kept its special status. Sikkim's best chance for a freer association with India lay in a general loosening of Delhi's grip on border states or territories such as Kashmir, Assam, and Nagaland, as well as the kingdom of Bhutan. This was hardly likely for the time being. What was unimagined, because the consequences were unimaginable, was that the serpent would tighten its grip in the Himalayas, as much as and wherever it could.

Sikkim was special not only for the clean-cut beauty of its forests and mountains, but also for a frontier spirit that would have been refreshing anywhere in the world and amounted to a miracle considering its precarious location. Sikkim was small enough for the Chogyal and the half-serious, half-blithe girl he had taken as the future Gyalmo to give a personal cutting edge to the aspirations of its lively people. The two of them lent a sparkle to Sikkim that was rare in the Subcontinent – and, in retrospect, too bright to last.

The shrewd but lighthearted twelfth consecrated ruler of Sikkim, considered the reincarnation of a high Tibetan lama, held his most important audiences outside the palace, under the trees. He told me as we walked in the fresh air: "We're a small, simple country with the problems of a big country, but still miniature enough to be able to talk about them without a secret service listening in."

As he mixed a very dry Martini before a splendidly prepared lunch of continental delicacies, it really wasn't necessary for the Chogyal to talk about the contrast between perhaps the world's most relaxed palace and the depressing Indian plains far below. He merely observed: "The world is getting too dehumanized."

When he flitted about the hills of Gangtok driving an Austrian Haflinger, sort of a mini-mountain jeep, he acknowledged his self-consciousness in a careless comment: "Frankly, the wheels are a bit small."

Queen Hope didn't quite match her husband in casualness and confidence. During a serious conversation about the intellectual curiosity of Western youth in the 1960s, she was the last of the four of us to slip down on the floor from conventional seats – the Chogyal was the first. News of Robert Kennedy's assassination came to Gangtok while we were there, and Hope nervously twisted the dials of a short-wave radio like any young American far from home.

But her sense of humour complemented his delightfully. When they insisted one evening on going to Gangtok's only movie theatre to see an old Danny Kaye picture spoofing royalty, she gaily explained: "We're very high camp here." When the Indian theatre-owner served drinks in an anteroom with an assortment of suspicious-looking Indian tidbits, she not so discreetly dropped out an open window a little green ball meant to be consumed. (When the tattered film track ran out, four-year-old Prince Palden took our three-year-old Shauna by the hand and they marched out ahead of the royal couple, who were supposed to leave first.)

The Gyalmo of Sikkim spoke softly and studiedly, but less and less in the whisper that had driven some listeners to distraction, and perhaps no longer affectedly. She was actively involved in improving the schools of Sikkim, promoting Sikkimese handicrafts, and preserving Buddhist relics.

She wore colourful *bhakkus*, the form-fitting, full-length Sikkimese jumper with contrasting silk blouse beneath, or flowing skirts down to the ankles with Western blouses.

He held her hand in company and called her darling, and like many affectionate couples they tended mildly to contradict each other. Their palace was simply a rambling yellow bungalow with pleasant grounds. One of their favourite spots in it was a corner of the small living room around a polished tree-slab table. She changed records – French chanteuses, Beatles, all very low – on a portable American-made stereo atop a Tibetan chest, and he sampled fine wines for gourmet repasts served on unique carved Tibetan tables. In the small guest house on the palace grounds where we stayed, full bottles of choice Scotch, cognac, and gin appeared each evening.

In a way it all seemed like a fictional story, illustrated by the Buddhist prayer flags around the palace and the Sikkim Guards in their red medieval uniforms. In another way it was a deliberate, and successful, attempt to be different in an overwhelmingly dreary part of Asia. The Indians lost little chance to portray the royal couple, whose mail they opened, as fatuous and dangerous at the same time. But the Chogyal and his wife were sensitive, concerned individuals, acutely aware that they were holding an important position in a highly strategic area.

What would happen to Sikkim and to them between two predatory giants, and between the larger Himalayan kingdoms of Nepal and Bhutan, was difficult to say when we were their guests in June 1968. It was possible to hope for a happy ending. But the courageous couple were battling daunting odds. Helping a Sikkim Guard set up a projector to show a home movie of his coronation, as drawn curtains closed in a seldom used formal drawing room, the Chogyal half quipped: "Darkness can be created – light cannot be created that easily."

Darkness began to descend on Sikkim on 4 April 1973. Without question, it was created.

Stories from New Delhi that day reported the Chogyal had appealed to India for troops to put down demonstrations against what was said to be his rigging of a new election to the state council the previous January. Whether or not these stories were contrived, they suggested to anyone familiar with Sikkim that much more was involved.

Even if the Chogyal had wanted to fix voting at any time, he would have found it difficult to do so. If he had been forced to call in Indian troops to restore order, it was clear from the outset that Indira Gandhi's government might have other uses for them. If that government had fabricated the request for troops or the reason for requesting them, the

implications were even more troubling. Sikkim, an internationally recognized kingdom rooted in Himalayan history and symbolized by the
Chogyal, was starting to twist slowly in the wind of lies and disinformation invented by Indians, benefitting Indian puppets, and spread by
unquestioning journalists.

The Indians claimed that angry Nepalese in Sikkim's State Congress and
National Congress had massed to protest against the Bhutia-Lepcha
National Party's having unfairly won a majority of seats. Although this was
purportedly happening three months after the election, and there was no
first-hand evidence, most of the Western press rose to the bait. A *New York
Times* dispatch datelined New Delhi reported that "nearly 15,000 anti-
government protesters were poised tonight [6 April] outside Gangtok,
Sikkim's capital, amid rising violence." No non-Indian correspondent was
ever allowed into Sikkim to see for himself what was going on. Two years
before Indira's Emergency, no press dispatch was ever allowed out that did
not adhere to the official Indian line.

The Indian army was already moving into Gangtok, but not in the numbers that were implied, and not to help the Chogyal. From the beginning,
the events leading to Sikkim's liquidation had the markings of an organized
provocation like those staged periodically by Indian authorities in Kashmir
to tighten Delhi's control.

At the same time those angry demonstrators were supposed to be besieg-
ing Gangtok, a telegram to Prime Minister Gandhi was made public in
Delhi as soon as she received it. From an anti-Chogyal organization calling
itself only the Joint Action Committee, it urged India "to intervene quickly
and fully before we are massacred."

Who was "we"? Massacred by whom? The 300 or so Sikkim Guards?
The Chogyal was reported to have ordered the arrest of several political
leaders when violence broke out. These unnamed leaders were said to have
demanded in inflammatory speeches not only changes in the electoral system, which gave the Bhutias and Lepchas a built-in advantage because of
their minority status, but also a revision of the treaty with India, an
expressed objective of the Chogyal.

By 7 April it was reported, again from Delhi, that the Indian army had
taken control of Gangtok at the Chogyal's "request," and the Chogyal and
Gyalmo were under "heavy guard" at the palace. According to Indian officials, the situation was "somber and dangerous." They advanced the
notion, duly reported in *The New York Times*, that Nepalese who had supposedly produced a mob of 15,000 to 20,000 in one place were fleeing in
other places from "armed Tibetan security forces." These forces were not
further identified. Had Sikkim been invaded from Tibet? On the face of it,
the whole story was absurd.

At this time, India's chief pawn in Sikkim emerged in the person of Kazi Lendup Dorji, who had long harboured ambitions at the expense of the hereditary royal family from his Indian base in Kalimpong below Sikkim. Identified now as president of the mysterious Joint Action Committee, he declared in a statement released in the Indian capital that despite the Chogyal's "maladministration" and "oppressive electoral laws," the rights of minorities would be safeguarded. The outlines of an Indian plot to depose the Chogyal and install a puppet were becoming plain.

The first partial non-Indian version of events resulted from telephone calls between the Chogyal, Crown Prince Tenzing Kunzang Jigme Namgyal, and the Chogyal's secretary, all in Gangtok at one end of the line, and *The London Sunday Times*, a friend of Tenzing's in London, and *The New York Times* at the other end.

On 7 April the Chogyal told the British newspaper that the situation in Sikkim was "rather good." He continued: "I don't say I have complete control but we expect to have that within twenty-four to forty-eight hours ... We can go about anywhere, though there are some elements, mainly from outside, who might still try to be violent. I am very sorry that the police had to open fire. It is the first time in our history the police have had to resort to firing on the people." Such shooting is a regular occurrence in India.

Tenzing informed his friend in London that leaders of the two parties defeated in the election had warned villagers their houses would be burned down if they did not take part in demonstrations. Later the twenty-one-year-old crown prince denied that he had personally killed a demonstrator, but admitted that his security guard had shot and wounded two "under extreme provocation" on 2 April, an incident the Indians claimed had provoked widespread riots.

The Chogyal's secretary, Athing Densapa, acknowledged to *The New York Times* that Indian troops had been asked to restore order. But he said there had been "no such thing" as widespread fighting. He confirmed that the royal couple had been able to go outside the palace. He also emphasized that opposition elements had intimidated villagers into joining them. He said one demonstrator had died and 200 had been arrested, but all but about ten were quickly released. He blamed the trouble on neither China nor India, which he called "our protecting power."

When the telephone interviews were published, the Indians cut off communications in the palace. Within hours they made clear what they had in mind in "protecting" Sikkim.

On 8 April, the Indian political officer in Gangtok, Kayatyani Shankar Bajpai, announced that India had taken over administration of the Himalayan kingdom, also supposedly at the Chogyal's "request." Bajpai, who apparently orchestrated the whole takeover and who later became ambassador to Pakistan, said: "India always wanted to be of help to Sikkim." No words could have better summed up India's hypocrisy. The truth was the exact opposite.

Meanwhile, Kazi Lendup Dorji, whose still undefined Joint Action Committee was reported in Delhi to be in control of large parts of Sikkim, declared in another statement that his supporters were "virtually calling for the abdication of the Chogyal." As if on cue, the next night demonstrators demanding the Chogyal's removal started regular marches from the royal polo grounds to the palace. Indian troops – it was learned later that only about 250 of them were on duty in the capital – did not interfere and indeed provided food to the agitators. At the same time, an Indian deputy foreign minister blamed the Sikkimese police for causing many casualties earlier.

Although it was not reported at the time, on 9 April the Chogyal sent a telegram to Indira asserting that India's officials were doing nothing to restore order. Asking for her personal intervention, he said the Indian government had ignored his "repeated warnings" about "impending violence, led particularly by outside elements." He was referring to Nepalese living in India who could have moved into Sikkim only with official Indian connivance. He must have realized by this time that Indira was the chief conniver in Sikkim's downfall.

Two days later, and undoubtedly after receiving information from Sikkim, the Chogyal's sister, Princess Pema Tsedeun Yapshi-Pheunkhang, called a press conference in Hong Kong. She charged that Indian intelligence agents had interfered in Sikkim's internal affairs. She called on Indira's government, which she publicly absolved of blame, to curb their operations. She said these agents had heavily financed the National Congress and State Congress in the election.

The princess emphasized that the counting of votes giving a majority of the state council's twenty-four seats to the National Party – six additional members were appointed by the Chogyal – and seven to the two other parties had been supervised by senior civil servants and magistrates. She pointed out that the Chogyal had asked all three parties to join a new cabinet, but the opposition parties had resorted to "terrorism and lawlessness" instead. Far from committing excesses, she said, the police had tried to maintain law and order after "imported agitators" had entered Sikkim from Darjeeling to loot and burn and take over police posts.

But it was too late for the truth to prevail.

The eerie synchronization of events continued on Friday, 13 April, nine days after the first planted stories had appeared. The demonstrations in

Gangtok suddenly stopped, and the Chogyal suddenly appeared in public to give up.

After meetings with a special Indian envoy, he announced that he had signed an agreement with India promising to meet "most of the political demands" of the demonstrators. The Chogyal's status was left in doubt. The only shred of dignity he was allowed to preserve was a provision that he would act as "mediator" at talks to be held among Sikkim's political parties on the country's future government.

The Chogyal's answers at a press conference obviously had been dictated by the Indian government. He mouthed them because he hoped he could salvage something of his legitimate status. He said quietly but unconvincingly that he had restored "close and confident relations" with the Indian government. He insisted for the record that the movement against him "was not directed by the Indian government nor by any of its agencies," and that "some half a dozen Naxal-type (Maoist extremist) Sikkimese might have been behind the agitation." Even as he spoke, his supporters were being herded into jail, and Indian officials were calling the violence a "popular uprising" against an "outdated monarchy." "

Most observers expected the party talks to last for months. But on 8 May Sikkimese and Indian representatives signed an agreement – whose details were not then made public – providing for the election of a legislative assembly on the basis of equal voting rights for all adult citizens, unspecified protection of the Bhutia and Lepcha minorities, and independence of Sikkim's judiciary. In the past, Nepalese candidates had had to win 15 per cent of the votes of Bhutias and Lepchas to be elected to the state council, and they were limited to the seven seats they had taken earlier that year.

The new arrangement sounded more democratic than the earlier one. If it were all the Indians had in mind, the Chogyal might have continued as something more than a figurehead, and Sikkim might have retained some vestige of the distinct identity that he and the Gyalmo had tried so diligently to enhance. But the agreement was only part of what the Indian government cryptically called the "evolution" of Sikkim. Democracy was not its objective. As the lies and hypocrisy mounted, so did the tragedy.

In July 1973, three months after the meaningful life she and the Chogyal had built together started to collapse around them, Queen Hope returned to New York with their two children and an ailing daughter of the Chogyal from his first wife. Nearly a year later, an aging Chogyal described her as "unhappy." Even if she left Sikkim willingly, the Indians were pleased to see her go. Her departure surely was one of their aims in effectively blowing up the charmingly un-Indian palace in Gangtok. In 1976, the former Hope Cooke applied for repatriation of her U.S. citizenship.

An argument can be made that the Indians only seized on an uneasy situation in Sikkim to bring the Chogyal and Gyalmo down to where they wanted them. It does not hold up. There is compelling evidence that Indira Gandhi and her multifarious agents manufactured, manipulated, and enlarged on events from the very beginning in order to squeeze any pretense of independence out of helpless Sikkim, and to establish the supremacy of the Indian serpent.

In February 1973, the Chogyal had dismissed his Indian chief administrative officer, I.S. Chopra, and taken over his functions himself. In Delhi's probably correct view, this was the most important step in a campaign by the palace to elevate Sikkim's autonomy to a level where, like Bhutan, it could attain UN membership. The Indians, in deliberately creating disorder in Sikkim to prevent this from happening, or in exploiting existing disorder, took two calculated risks.

One was that Chinese forces in the Chumbi Valley would be tempted to intervene, though there probably was no real danger this would happen. But Indian forces never were pulled out of Sikkim's Himalayan passes to restore order in Gangtok. That could be done with relatively few troops notwithstanding the wild reports of army intervention. The other risk had to do with the proximity of a Nepal troublesome to India.

Many Nepalese in Sikkim did want more internal political power. But there was no reason to believe they had given up their joint front with the Chogyal in seeking more independence for Sikkim. Nor was there any reason to suspect that, on their own, most of them would throw their little country into turmoil, inviting Indian intervention, by disgracing their recognized and respected ruler. India may have quickly killed the palace's pretensions – but not Sikkim's. Partly because of Nepal's success under King Mahendra and his son King Birendra Bir Bikram Shah Dev in playing off China and India against each other, Delhi regarded the prospect of Nepalese majority rule in Sikkim with mixed feelings. Not surprisingly, India's next manoeuvre was to turn against Sikkim's Nepalese, the people it ostensibly had helped, and cynically seek the maximum advantage for itself.

That meant nothing short of India's annexation of Sikkim – Delhi's ultimate objective from the outset.

A year after the Sikkim of hope and cheer fell apart, voting supervised by the Indian election commission for the new thirty-two-member legislative assembly returned thirty-one candidates of a single, Nepalese Hindu–dominated Congress Party, virtually shutting out Buddhist Bhutias and Lepchas in their own country. The results were suspect but unchallengeable. In any case it turned out that under the May 1973 agreement an Indian chief executive also presided over the assembly and exercised authority over the Chogyal, and could be removed by neither.

In June 1974, armed Indian police, now present in strong numbers in Sikkim as in Kashmir, stopped a last-ditch attempt by the Chogyal to block the inevitable next step. They removed 500 of his supporters who were surrounding the assembly building. This permitted the compliant members to troop in and, without debate, approve an Indian-drafted constitution formally reducing the Chogyal to a figurehead and creating a paper council of ministers. They also adopted, also without debate, what amounted to a death warrant for the country: a resolution urging "immediate steps to ensure fuller participation of Sikkim in the economic and social institutions of India."

Under the imposed constitution, Sikkim could "seek participation and representation for the people of Sikkim in the political institutions of India and its parliamentary system." Its economy would be run henceforth by the Indian Planning Commission – which had done such a good job of strangling India's economy – and Sikkimese would receive the unwanted services of Indian banking and related facilities.

Alone but still fighting, the Chogyal flew to Delhi to press his argument that the new constitution was undemocratic, violated the 1950 treaty between India and Sikkim as co-equals, and would result in loss of whatever status Sikkim retained. In reality, it would make Sikkim an Indian state like any other, except that it would be vastly smaller than most. Indira kept the Chogyal waiting for four days. When she finally deigned to meet him, she curtly advised him to approve Sikkim's death warrant.

Four days later in Gangtok, the Chogyal announced that he would sign the constitution when the assembly, after hearing a long statement of his views, gave its final approval. Its members had contemptuously refused to listen to him in person. They had warned that if he did not sign, "there would be no more role for him to play in Sikkim."

Soon there would be no more Sikkim for the Chogyal or anyone else to play a role in except as a lackey of Delhi. In August, despite late but rising Chinese criticism of India's moves, Indira announced that the Indian government would seek amendment of its constitution to make Sikkim an "integral part of India" – words usually reserved for Kashmir. Exhibiting a hypocrisy that had lost its ability to shock, a government spokesman pledged with a straight face: "India does not intend to affect or dilute in any way the distinct personality of Sikkim."

The precise opposite was the truth: in every way India was shamelessly trampling on and tearing asunder the legally guaranteed, distinct character of Sikkim.

The Chogyal, whose power had been emasculated on the ground that he was anti-democratic, made a last-gasp appeal for the ultimate democratic test: a free and fair referendum to determine whether or not the people of Sikkim wanted to live in an associate state of India. In cables to Indira, he pleaded that assurances of the protection of Sikkim's separate identity under the 1950 treaty were being "negated by hasty moves in the Indian Parliament for Sikkim's representation without the general consent and knowledge of the Sikkimese people."

The Chogyal's appeal in August 1974 came ten months before the Indian Parliament itself ceased in practice to represent the Indian people under Indira's Emergency. Just as India had coldly ignored calls for years for a free plebiscite in Kashmir, just as Indira later brusquely dismissed critics of her demolition of Indian democracy, she paid no attention now to the Chogyal, the Chinese, an alarmed Nepal and Bhutan, or sharp criticism by some Indian politicians and newspapers of her willful destruction of a small, helpless country.

On 10 September the Lok Sabha or lower house of Parliament approved by a vote of 310 to 7 the proposed constitutional amendment giving Sikkim the status of an associate state of India. Swaran Singh, then foreign minister, turned truth upside down again when he said this "sacrosanct" link gave the Sikkimese people the right to be represented in the Indian Parliament: "This ultimately becomes a solemn proposal made to us and accepted by us." Maintaining that Sikkim retained its own constitution and "system," he said the time for annexation had not yet come: India was "going to the point up to which Sikkim is prepared to go."

Three days later the Rajya Sabha or upper house went along by a vote of 171 to 8, and Sikkim had gained exactly one seat in each house of the Indian Parliament. At the same time, another unsurprising coincidence, Kazi Lendup Dorji reappeared, this time as the head of the evanescent Sikkimese government, and called for the Chogyal's total ouster from his titular position and his family's lands. Oozed Kazi: "I have been overwhelmed to find in India such deep understanding of our problems and aspirations."

The final chapter in what in my experience is one of the most sordid episodes in modern Asian history, began on 9 April 1975, two years and five days after the first.

Without warning, Indian combat troops moved into Gangkok in force. They disarmed the 300 or so Sikkim Guards after a skirmish that left at least 1 dead and 5 wounded. They then surrounded the palace and confined the Chogyal to it.

The next day, the legislative assembly voted unanimously to abolish the monarchy and to seek full statehood for Sikkim in India. With no previous warning, it proclaimed that a referendum on these two steps would be held just four days later, on 14 April. In a classic case of a propagandist accusing a victim of the very kind of conduct of which he and his patrons are guilty, the unscrupulous Kazi Lendup Dorji, who as chief minister had called in the Indian army, said of the defenceless Chogyal: "We have had enough of his intrigues, conspiracies, and illegal behaviour."

With the Chogyal safely out of circulation – and international observers barred along with foreign correspondents – the indecently hurried referendum was run by Indian soldiers, the Indian election commission, Kazi, and other Sikkimese puppets. It was anything but the free and fair referendum urged by the Chogyal. Many Sikkimese did not hear about it until they were told to vote, and none were given a chance to organize opposition. The outcome was fully predictable. Again, India told the world what it wanted the world to believe was happening in Sikkim. The government in Delhi announced that by a vote of 59,637 to 1,496, Sikkimese had rejected a distinct identity and a benevolent ruling family going back more than 500 years, and had chosen to be absorbed into India. About 36,000 eligible Sikkimese voters did not cast ballots, or their ballots were not counted.

Choking back tears as he was allowed to meet Indian journalists, the Chogyal spoke bravely for the Sikkimese people.

"We are not going to be obliterated," he said as if to himself. "I cannot be a party to the liquidation of Sikkim."

Calling the one-sided result of the phony referendum "fantastic" – 120 of every 123 officially recorded votes were for Sikkim's joining India – he observed with more sadness than anger: "Such a victory does not occur in any country except a police state."

The Indian Express commented patronizingly: "One wonders how many of the state's largely illiterate population had time to understand the significance of the issue."

Little more than two months later, the India that had absorbed Sikkim became a police state itself. But on 3 May, the Indian government reacted to the Chinese government's condemnation of the "illegal annexation of Sikkim" – one of Tibet's "five fingers" in the Han view – by accusing Beijing of interfering in India's internal affairs, disturbing the peace of South Asia, and "not understanding ... expression of the will and aspirations of the people of Sikkim."

It was hard to tell who was ahead in hypocrisy and insensitivity – the Indians or the Chinese, who had subjugated Tibet and were obliterating its special character while claiming to liberate it. The outcome in Sikkim was very much the same as the one dictated by the dragon in Tibet.

On 16 May, the serpent finally swallowed its small, tasty supper. On that day the president of India signed another constitutional amendment that had been rushed through Parliament. This one made Sikkim the twenty-second full-fledged state of India. Then the president announced, as if nothing really had changed, that Sikkim's first governor would be the Indian bureaucrat who, on Indira Gandhi's orders, had pushed the Chogyal aside as Sikkim's modern chief executive and historic king.

In April 1974, more than a year before the annexation was complete, Palden Thondup Namgyal talked haltingly about Sikkim's people and its fate as he sat alone in an almost meaningless palace drained of its human magic and happiness. Then fifty-one, the Chogyal had let his white sideburns and beard grow straggly – he had been smooth-shaven at the time of our visit in 1968. In an interview with an Indian journalist, he said:

"How could any of us be happy about the happenings that have shaken our country? ... Twenty years of my efforts to build up amity between the Nepalese and the non-Nepalese, the fragile relationship we have achieved, has been shattered ... We [Sikkim and India] had this special relationship all these twenty-three years [since the treaty], and no one had ever brought up any specific instance of my wickedness ... What choice has Sikkim but to live under the protection of India? The only other choice is China, but any practical-minded person will know that is not in the interest of Sikkim ... All that I said and wanted was that India be the big brother and Sikkim the little brother ... After all, we also want a place under the sun."

In early 1978, the new prime minister of India admitted that Indira's government should not have annexed Sikkim. "It is wrong for a big country to do that," said Morarji Desai in a moment of Indian candour. He quickly added: "But I cannot undo it now."

This was small solace for the Chogyal, who was still living in his yellow palace of pleasant memories, accompanied only by his eldest son, Tenzing. In October 1976, he had lain unconscious for several days after taking an overdose of sleeping pills. He was flown then to Calcutta for emergency treatment at the nursing home where his youngest Hope was born in 1968.

Still kept under virtual house arrest by Indian police in 1978, isolated in his own land, the Chogyal was normally prevented from leaving Gangtok or even seeing other Sikkimese, especially civil servants. Gangtok's handsome little Tibetan museum and its cottage industries centre, both of which the Gyalmo had actively promoted, were no longer even named after the last king of Sikkim. But he was allowed to go to Delhi in July, and it was there that I saw him for the first time since his country had been abolished, and for the last time.

The two of us sat on twin beds in his ordinary room at the Intercontinental Hotel. At fifty-five, just ten years after a vigorous Chogyal and a charming Gyalmo had graciously entertained Pat and me at their palace in Gangtok, he was an old man and the joy was gone. So was his former queen. He talked quietly on the understanding that this was a private conversation.

He was still waiting for a friendly financial settlement with the Indian government after discussing it first with Indira and then with Morarji. In all likelihood this would compel him to leave Sikkim for good and to give up what Desai had called his "disruptive tendencies." The Chogyal noted that India was spending far more on Sikkim than it had when he had tried to run his realm with the help of Sikkimese officials. He didn't have to say much about the "happenings" that had drastically changed Sikkim's status and its character. But he insisted, unemotionally but firmly, that the forced absorption of the kingdom of Sikkim into the Union of India was unconstitutional and illegal. It was hard not to be emotional as we parted as friends.

In May 1980, Pat and I saw Hope Cooke again. The three of us had tea at the fashionable St Regis Hotel in New York. She was still charming but in a less self-conscious way, and also much older.

Engaged in a custody battle with the Chogyal over their two children, who lived with her, she asked if I would support in court her claim to be the more responsible parent. I said I would testify to her being a good mother to Palden and Hope, now fourteen and ten. We also parted as friends. The case never went to court. The Chogyal died soon after. To me, neither he nor she was to blame for anything that had gone wrong. Together, the two of them had tried to make a fairy tale come true. For a while they had succeeded. It was not their fault that Sikkim had vanished along with the bright aura they had created around it.

Hope returned to Sikkim – not hope that it would regain its nationhood, and not Hope Cooke, but Hope Namgyal, daughter of the former Gyalmo and the late Chogyal.

In 1997 a travel writer described in *The New York Times* meeting the youngest Sikkimese princess, now twenty-nine, in Gangtok, where she was living and running a trekking agency for tourists. Dressed like her mother used to dress in Sikkim, Hope told how the cultures of the indigenous Lepchas and the Bhutias were dying now that they were no longer protected, and how the woods and wildlife of what had been a state of India for more than two decades now were fast losing ground to logging and human intrusion.

Hope also recalled Indian troops surrounding the palace in April 1975, when she was seven, and her father running his finger across her forehead with the blood of a slain Sikkim Guard so she would not forget what was happening to her country.

She had not forgotten. In the way she sort of softly erased the line between joy and sadness, she brought back memories of her mother in Sikkim. Neither had Sikkimese forgotten. They called her Semla – "our heart," or "our daughter."

20

Vale of Death

If there be a paradise on earth,
'Tis here, 'tis here, 'tis here!

The Moghul rulers of India dreamt of Kashmir when they inscribed this Persian couplet in gold in their Hall of Private Audience in what is now the Red Fort in Delhi.

In recent years, when India celebrates its independence on the parapets of the Red Fort every 15 August, the simple couplet still describes Kashmir – but with a change of one word:

If there be a hell on earth,
'Tis here, 'tis here, 'tis here!

Kashmir is India's hope and India's shame. Kashmir is meant to demonstrate Indians' devotion to secularism and democracy. Yet Kashmir is where they have done serious harm to their secular ideals and violated their democratic principles. The Vale of Kashmir, perhaps the most beautiful corner of the world, is scarred by India's hypocrisy.

In this deception and tragedy, the Kashmiri Brahmin Nehrus played a special role that still defines predominantly Hindu India's attitude to predominantly Muslim Kashmir. In carrying out a policy of de facto religious discrimination, the Indian army has sullied its honour. The Kashmiri people, the great majority of whom are gentle and patient based on my experience with them, have suffered needless killing and destruction. The soft loveliness of Kashmir has sometimes become a hard killing field. Paradise has become hell. The Vale of Kashmir has often been transformed into a valley of death.

And yet, for old and new reasons, it is impossible to separate Kashmir wholly from India. Almost certainly the Kashmiri people would be worse off if the Vale were controlled not by India but by Islamic Pakistan. This is evident with a glance at the backward area called Azad or Free Kashmir held by Pakistan, the failure of Pakistanis to make democracy work, and Pakistani-backed terrorism in Indian-held Kashmir.

The close connection of the Nehrus to Kashmir accounts for the fact that the best chance for a solution of the Kashmir question, which goes back to the dawn of the post–Second World War era, died with Jawaharlal Nehru in 1964. The Indian army has carried out necessary and even courageous tasks against armed intruders in Kashmir as well as dishonourable excesses against civilians. Indian troops in Kashmir are part of the bulwark against Chinese forces potentially intent on crossing the Himalayas as they did in 1962. Kashmir, bloody as well as beautiful, is too complex for a couplet, original or amended, to sum up.

On a cool, dark night in the Vale of Kashmir in July 1968, boat lights played softly on the still water of Dal Lake. They were so many pale, yellow blobs against an unseen but tangible background of stately trees, stately mountains, and stately people. Suddenly an invisible boatman raised his voice in English above others echoing across the black water.

"Kashmir cannot be ruled by any other country!" he chanted. "Kashmir must have self-determination!"

The chant was surprising and thrilling. It was a small, brave expression of the historic movement among Kashmiris for control of their own destiny. It might have been heard on any night during the twenty-one years before and the more than three and a half decades since. On that memorable evening, it was especially appropriate. For the Lion of Kashmir, Sheikh Mohammad Abdullah, one of the few towering figures left in the Subcontinent then, had come home.

Only Sheikh Sahib, as he was respectfully known to supporters and opponents alike – including, in a secretly personal way, the Nehrus – held the key to a peaceful solution of the Kashmir problem. After years of being held captive by the rulers of India, he had talked to me of Kashmir's future in two long conversations in the sunshine of the rose garden of his house at Soura, in an out of the way part of the Vale.

The only man who could speak for Kashmiri nationalists seemed like the invisible Dal Lake boatman. The Lion's roar was defiant but he had to be careful not to be seen to be clearly tied to any one position. For while he held the key, only India and particularly the Nehrus could use it to open the door to a Kashmir settlement that included Pakistan. This never happened. When the eminently reasonable and peace-loving Lion of Kashmir died in 1983, it was already too late to stop a steady slide into communal emotion, premeditated violence, and unyielding chauvinism as the dominant elements in the Vale. But no future solution, or even acceptance of the status quo by Kashmiris, Indians, and Pakistanis, is possible without going back to what Sheikh Abdullah stood for.

The dwellers in paradise never had much to do with what happened to Kashmir. Its beauty and location in the eyes of others were always more important.

Pristine lakes and sparkling streams, snow mountains and lush meadows, tall chenar trees and bright flower gardens are a pastel postcard come alive. Unbearably cold in winter, Kashmir's climate offers ineffable relief from the North Indian plains during the long hot months. The distant Vale became a cavorting place for the Moghul rulers of India, who made their annual trek from Delhi a grand procession to what they perceived as paradise. But Kashmir is also strategically placed. It is north of the traditional invasion route to India through the Khyber Pass from Afghanistan into the Indus Valley. But it thrusts the Subcontinent into Central Asia. Kashmir touches Xinjiang and Tibet, it points a finger at Tashkent, and it nearly abuts northern Afghanistan.

The British, not surprisingly, are part of the problem. In 1846 the successors to the Muslim Moghuls sold Kashmir outright to a wealthy Rajput for 500,000 pounds. Although roughly three-fourths of its people were Muslim, this meant the ruling princely family was Hindu. When partition and independence of the Subcontinent loomed in 1947, this fact was central in the creation of a dispute that has been at the heart of conflict between India and Pakistan ever since.

Under the Indian Independence Act of 1947 adopted by the British Parliament, the Raj's paramountcy in 562 princely states lapsed and the states became temporarily independent until their assorted maharajas and nabobs acceded to either India or Pakistan. Sardar Vallabhai Patel and V.P. Menon, the archetypal Indian politician and civil servant, respectively, were enormously efficient in pressuring most princes to sign on with Delhi. But Kashmir was a special case: a princely state with a two-thirds Muslim majority, historic connections to the Moghuls, natural geographic and economic links to Pakistan, and a Hindu maharaja in the person of the seemingly indecisive Sir Hari Singh.

In June 1947, a good time of the year to abandon Delhi even temporarily for a cooler clime, Lord Louis Mountbatten, the last British viceroy who had become governor-general of still undivided India, visited Kashmir with the consent of Patel and Nehru. Mountbatten advised the maharaja that he could accede to either India or Pakistan but he should decide before 15 August. Although it wasn't necessary for Mountbatten, Nehru, and the Muslim League's Mohammad Ali Jinnah to abruptly end their negotiations on India after the Raj, this was the date they had arbitrarily set as independence day.

A Muslim prince almost certainly would have opted for Pakistan. As a Hindu, however, Sir Hari did not want to make what was called the state of Jammu and Kashmir part of India. He wanted independence for Kashmir, and he wanted its independence to be guaranteed by both India and Pakistan. To have a chance of getting Kashmiri independence, he had to stall for time.

On 14 August he succeeded in getting Pakistan to sign a standstill agreement, providing an indefinite continuation of essential services. India, however, refused to sign a similar agreement, for good reason from its point of view. If it had, the precedent of equivalent relations could have conceivably led to a special independent status for Kashmir similar to what the maharaja had in mind then; or to what a compromise would have looked like in the 1960s while both Nehru and Sheikh Abdullah were still living; or to what one would conceivably entail at the beginning of a new century. At the time of independence for only India and Pakistan, however, Sir Hari found himself caught between conflicting ambitions on the part of the two new covetous powers he was trying to hold off.

For Pakistan, possession of Kashmir was essential if the dubious two-nation theory of Jinnah, one nation for the Subcontinent's Muslims, one for its Hindus, was going to work in practice. Rawalpindi, the army town that served as the temporary capital of Pakistan, switched tactics when the actual partition didn't budge the stubborn maharaja, who dispatched his Hindu Dogra troops to put down Muslim tribesmen in Poonch in southern Kashmir who were agitating for union with Pakistan. Dropping co-operation with Sir Hari through the standstill agreement, the Pakistanis imposed an economic blockade on Kashmir, and sent marauding armed Pathan tribesmen into the state to intimidate Kashmiris and their maharaja. With his resistance to the first Pakistani-supported invasion of Kashmir collapsing, Sir Hari's only recourse was to ask India for armed assistance. But he still didn't accede to India.

The Indian response, conveyed through Mountbatten, was that Delhi could send troops only if Kashmir gave up its independence and acceded to India. But the British governor-general made clear that India would regard this accession, in the later words of Sheikh Abdullah, as "conditional on the will of the people, as ascertained through a referendum as soon as law and order were restored." After fleeing the Vale, the maharaja of Kashmir agreed, and Mountbatten confirmed the terms of accession, both in writing.

There is a question whether Sir Hari signed the instrument of accession and a letter of agreement to Mountbatten on 26 October, which the official records show, or the afternoon of 27 October, when he reached the winter capital of Jammu. If the latter, the canny Indian official V.P. Menon dictated the terms first, the date of 26 October was added later, and Indian troops intervened in a technically independent state. For on the morning of 27 October, an Indian battalion was flown to Srinagar just in time to save the summer capital from the invading Pakistanis. Whether or not India's action was legitimate, it was an Indian trick that the Pakistanis, and the Kashmiris, could never forget.

Nehru as prime minister, supported by Mahatma Gandhi, constantly reiterated the promise to hold a plebiscite or referendum. "We have declared that the fate of Kashmir is ultimately to be decided by the people," he said over All-India Radio. "That pledge we have given, and the maharaja has supported it, not only to the people of Kashmir but to the world. We will not, and cannot, back out of it."

But the condition attached from the outset to "a reference to the people," in Mountbatten's words, has never been fulfilled. "Law and order" never have been fully restored to Kashmir. Whatever Nehru meant by "ultimately," not once in more than a half-century have Kashmiris had the chance to express their opinion about their future. In all those years, it is fair to say, India has mocked law, order, and free will in Kashmir with oppression, disorder, and denial.

The first war between India and Pakistan dragged on more than a year before it ended with a United Nations–supervised ceasefire effective 1 January 1949. Indian forces then controlled 128,000 square kilometres or more than 60 per cent of Kashmir with 80 per cent of its people – whose number grew to more than 8 million by 2000 – including the all-important Vale. Pakistan, left with less than 40 per cent of the tortured land, called its part Azad or Free Kashmir. Its occupation of even this sparsely populated area was another reason for India to ignore its own pledges and repeated UN resolutions calling for a plebiscite.

Two events in 1954 provided India with further excuses. One was China's quiet uncontested takeover of 38,000 square kilometres of Ladakh or remote northeastern Kashmir, amounting to roughly 20 per cent of the state and reducing the part held by India to a size not much larger than Azad Kashmir. This was where Chinese troops in heavy fighting in 1962 rolled back Indian gains made under Delhi's stealthy "forward policy" in the Himalayas. The other event was Pakistan's becoming a military ally of the United States. In Nehru's view, it "changed the whole context of the Kashmir issue."

Distinguished individuals who had overcome great obstacles in other endeavours, retired Admiral Chester Nimitz, Senator Frank Graham and World Bank president Eugene Black of the United States, diplomats Sir Owen Dixon of Australia and Gunnar Jarring of Sweden, made no headway in attempting to persuade India to honour UN Security Council resolutions and the principle of popular self-determination it had itself originally emphasized. The most India was willing to do was offer Kashmir vague powers of self-rule under article 370 of the Indian constitution. But these were not spelled out much beyond barring the sale of land to non-Kashmiris. As Sheikh Abdullah put it in the spring of 1965, the record up to then on keeping promises to Kashmiris going back to 1947 was "dismal."

At the time, the Lion of Kashmir was trying to keep alive what he realized was the fading best hope for a peaceful solution by inducing Indians, Pakistanis, and Kashmiris to sit down around a table, preferably with a mediator. That hope had emerged with recognition by Nehru in the last few months of his life that the only route to lasting peace between India and Pakistan lay through Kashmir. He had not gotten over the shock of Chinese troops in the Himalayas in the fall of 1962 violently calling the bluff of his high-flown rationalizations. But his late glimpse of possible peace in the Subcontinent had started to overcome his equivocations on Kashmir.

As Abdullah well knew, Nehru had also been torn between two intensely personal considerations. As a Pandit or Kashmiri Brahmin, he had not been able to endure the thought of separating Kashmir from India. But he had had a bond with the Sheikh that I didn't fully realize until I spent some time with Abdullah, who had recently been freed from detention again, in the summer of 1968.

Until Nehru's daughter Indira Gandhi unexpectedly became prime minister in January 1966 upon the death of Lal Bahadur Shastri, however, Abdullah could not play this personal bond again. At most he could appeal for "a great act of faith" on the part of Nehru's successors to reach an agreement with Pakistan that would end Kashmiri "anguish [that] knows no bounds." At least he could hope not to be re-arrested.

As Indian-held Kashmir's first premier – not chief minister, the lesser title given to heads of other state governments – the Sheikh was first jailed in 1953 on suspicion of favouring Kashmiri independence although he had favoured Kashmir's accession to India. With one break, he remained in detention more than ten years while the first of Delhi's puppets in Srinagar, Bakshi Ghulam Mohammad, made traditions of police rule and fraudulent elections in the Vale.

In April 1964, Nehru, ill and aware of his own mortality, dropped conspiracy charges against Abdullah and freed him. Giving the Lion of Kashmir a brotherly embrace, he eagerly explored three options with him: joint rule, joint defence of Kashmir by India and Pakistan, and a loose confederation of India, Pakistan, and Kashmir. He also eased Bakshi from power and had a less corrupt regime installed in Kashmir. Abdullah went to Pakistan to talk about resolution of the Kashmir problem and Hindu-Muslim reconciliation with President Mohammad Ayub Khan. The president listened carefully although the Lion of Kashmir had made clear he was not insisting on a plebiscite and favoured some form of joint Indian-Pakistani rule of Kashmir, including the Vale.

But it was all too late. The prime minister of India and the president of Pakistan never met. The historic agreement they might have produced never saw the light of day. Propagandists in both India and Pakistan never ceased their din against a compromise solution. Nehru died on 17 May 1964. He never quite had the chance to use the key held by Sheikh Abdullah to unlock the door to peace and stability in Kashmir and the Subcontinent.

Indians who had done their best to sabotage reconciliation sought the first opportunity to put the Lion of Kashmir back in a cage. Keen to pursue unhindered an unwritten policy of "integrating" Kashmir with India, they got their chance in May 1965, a year after Nehru's death, when Abdullah spoke with Premier Zhou Enlai of China at an Afro-Asian conference in Algiers. When he returned to Delhi, police took him back into custody as soon as he stepped off the plane. Prime Minister Lal Bahadur Shastri might have prevented Abdullah's re-arrest a month before he himself went abroad for the first time. But tensions were rising in both India and Pakistan barely three months before the outbreak of the second war between them over the paradise dividing the Subcontinent.

I first experienced Kashmir in October 1965. The three-week war seemed over, lost by Pakistan. In reality, the largely suppressed events in the Vale during those bright October days represented the last phase of the war.

A reign of terror by Indian police extended from Srinagar's streets and outlying villages in the Vale into the most holy sanctuary of Kashmiri Muslims. The police countered a student-led uprising that, had its climax coincided with the Pakistani invasion of Indian-held Kashmir in the early days of the war, might have resulted in Muslim capture of the treasured Vale. The hatred of Kashmiri Muslims for India rose to its most fevered pitch until then. But Delhi's brutal police agents broke the back of the legitimate movement for self-determination, which would have mainly benefitted a deeply frustrated Pakistan if it had succeeded.

Soon after arriving in India's capital in September as a correspondent for *The Toronto Globe and Mail*, I had learned from a variety of reliable sources that Indian forces had won a decided victory in the war over surprised Pakistanis. The Indians headed off infiltration of their part of Kashmir by mujahids or Muslim freedom fighters starting in August. They stunned the Pakistani high command under Marshal Ayub by invading Pakistan proper and striking for Lahore when their forces in Kashmir were in danger of being cut off by an attacking Pakistani column. They bested their opponents in the largest tank battle at the time since the Second World War. The prize of the Vale of Kashmir still belonged to India and its Hindu majority. But in mid-October Indian newspapers carried vague reports indicating that Srinagar was anything but calm. Students were marching in anti-Indian demonstrations, schools were closed, and a 9:30 PM to 5:30 AM curfew was in force.

The first thing I learned as soon as my plane landed at Srinagar's little airport was that fact or rumour can travel by word of mouth within minutes through a valley more than 130 kilometres long and 30 to 40 kilometres wide. Small boys scooted up to me and whispered urgently: "To the mosque! To the mosque!" As a foreign journalist, I didn't need to search for a car to take me to Hazratbal Mosque, the centre of Kashmiri religious and political activity, 11 kilometres outside the city on Negin Lake. A Hindustan Ambassador, India's small clunky sedan, was immediately available with a driver who spoke English and knew the ins and outs of Srinagar's winding lanes and Kashmir's politics. Unknown to me, police spies constantly followed the driver and his car and nearly every suspicious activity in the Vale.

Hazratbal is a sprawling, mostly roofless sanctuary containing houses, shops, and a little lakeside bazaar within its walls as well as broad prayer platforms and a holy relic: a strand of hair reputed to have belonged to the Prophet Mohammad. The hair is the most cherished common possession of Kashmiri Muslims.

That day, Monday, 18 October, while hundreds of brown-uniformed police waited outside grasping .303 Lee-Enfield rifles and lathis or long steel-tipped bamboo sticks, the mosque rocked with the mixed prayers and slogans of massed men up front and women wrapped in white or black shawls farther from the platforms. They swayed and chanted in religious devotion and in defiance of the Indian authorities at a meeting organized by the Holy Relic Action Committee, a united front of nine pro-plebiscite Muslim organizations.

By strict, almost universally respected tradition throughout the Subcontinent and all Asia, a religious sanctuary is out of reach of police or troops even if political activities are going on inside. Thousands of worshippers were using Hazratbal for political purposes. But they firmly believed its familiar confines with the sacred relic were safe from alien invasion. The hair of Mohammad had disappeared mysteriously in January 1964, and just as mysteriously had returned to the mosque soon afterward, but no one had seen any intruders.

Now, as I took photographs, a woman in a state of apparent hysteria grabbed my wrist. It was not a hostile act but one beseeching my help for the Kashmiri cause. I realized that a false move on my part as a foreigner, such as trying to jerk away, could easily be misconstrued by similarly excited onlookers as threatening the woman. Male students, who assisted in controlling this moving mass demonstration of Kashmiri Muslim unity, helped me disengage without further incident.

In time, the congregation quieted and most people made their way in orderly fashion to the stone archway forming the front gate of Hazratbal Mosque. There they boarded buses that had come for them from various points in the Vale. This brought the police closer to the gate from a field where they had been waiting. When a group of students came out, some of them shouted slogans and threw stones at forty or fifty policemen who were advancing about a hundred yards away in what appeared to me and another reporter, Barry Farrell of *Life* magazine, to be a deliberate provocation.

The police retreated, threw stones back, reformed, and then lathi-charged the handful of students, who scampered back inside Hazratbal's arch to safety. This incredible scene was repeated perhaps a dozen times. Growing bands of police inched closer to the gate each time on orders from officers in the rear, while young Kashmiris angrily returned volleys of rocks from their tormenters and scored some hits. I wondered why the police hadn't simply gone back to their barracks when the meeting inside the mosque broke up peacefully, or at least stayed out of stone-throwing range while the students dispersed.

Most of the thousands of policemen in the Vale were not Kashmiris. Their shoulder insignia identified them as members of the Central Reserve Police, the Punjab Armed Constabulary, or forces from other Indian states far from Kashmir. Kashmiri Muslim police were armed only with lathis, never with rifles, and they were usually commanded by Hindus. The officer who rushed in a rage at Farrell and me as we stood outside the mosque wall watching the astonishing events in front of the gateway, and angrily grabbed our cameras from our necks, was unmistakably a North Indian Hindu. Earlier, several police officers had beseeched us to leave Hazratbal for our "own safety" and to "relax" at a lakeside resort several kilometres away, an offer we declined with thanks.

Suddenly the ebb-and-flow scene changed. This time the thundering police didn't halt and retreat when they neared the front gate of the sanctuary. They stormed through the archway, chasing the students before them, and now their officers followed close behind.

Flat reports that could only be discharges of tear gas canisters sounded from behind the wall. Then shouts and rifle fire rang out – possibly fifty distinct shots from the venerable Lee-Enfields. Smoke curled toward the clear sky from one part of the mosque grounds.

Police prevented us from re-entering Hazratbal. An awful silence followed the shooting. Then some of the Indian policemen started to stagger out of the holiest Islamic shrine in Kashmir. Two of them, bloodied, collapsed in the grass. Clearly the police had paid a penalty for their unprecedented invasion. What they had done to religious sensibilities, and the small chance of reconciliation in Kashmir and the entire Subcontinent, amounted to a far higher price for maintaining Indian national security. Until heavily armed Indian troops and tanks blasted their way into the Golden Temple of the Sikhs in Amritsar in Operation Blue Star in June 1984, this was the worst intrusion of Indian security forces into a major religious sanctuary. But only two foreign journalists saw it happen, and for days both Kashmiri and Indian authorities blocked dispatches from me as the only daily newspaper correspondent on the scene.

Without question the police at Hazratbal carried out orders to violate the resting place of the holy relic, and so terrorize Kashmiri Muslims into believing they had no refuge from the long hand of Hindu India. Theft of the hair in early 1964 had provoked a near-revolt by Kashmiri Muslims, and strengthened the hand of Indians and Kashmiri Brahmins who argued that it was unsafe to loosen Delhi's tight grip on the Vale even while Nehru was alive. Now Sheikh Abdullah had been back in detention for five months, and the authorities used the fresh Hazratbal incident as a pretext to arrest the last leaders of the Plebiscite Front and other elements of the Holy Relic Action Committee who were still free. Police ransacked, bolted, and placed under guard the committee's offices in Srinagar.

Two days before he was arrested, Ghulam Mohammad Karra, one of the leaders who had addressed the Hazratbal congregation and a man acknowledged by Indian officials to be a moderate, told me the police had deliberately desecrated the shrine containing the strand of the Prophet's hair. Students who had confronted police inside the shrine fully agreed. Glass around the holy relic was smashed and nearby masonry was damaged. To a Muslim, even entering a mosque peacefully with one's shoes on is a desecration.

The students said police also had looted and burned shops inside Hazratbal's grounds. They said they had seen three policemen open fire with rifles. Thirty Muslims had been injured, they reported, and twenty-five policemen hurt, most of them when furious Kashmiris had wrested lathis from them and given them a taste of their own medicine. At the time, they said no one had been killed in the wanton invasion of the mosque.

But since August, the students said, 10 or 12 of their number had been killed by police, and 250 students and others had been arrested. Karra said Indian police and troops had terrorized Muslims in the Vale, committing outrages such as burning homes and raping women, since anti-government demonstrations started on 9 October. The statistics were low compared with what was to come in Kashmir. But Monday, 18 October 1965 marked the beginning of hell in paradise.

The reign of terror then was not over. On Friday, the Muslim holy day, a fresh police curfew prevented prayers at Hazratbal Mosque for the first time in living memory. The next day, police broke up a hartal or general strike called by Muslims in Srinagar to protest desecration of the shrine. They broke open heavy locks on shops with pickaxes and told shopkeepers and bus and horse cart drivers they would lose their businesses or licences if they did not go back to work. Doors grudgingly opened and normal vehicles slowly joined police trucks carrying riflemen who glared at Kashmiris like the occupation troops they were.

Behind this calculated repression of the deprived majority of Kashmiris was a man named Durga Prashad Dhar. Then the home minister of Kashmir, in charge of police, Dhar tried to be suave but was highly nervous. As a Kashmiri Brahmin, he was a natural liaison between the central Indian government and the new Muslim puppet regime in Srinagar headed by Ghulam Mohammad Sadiq, who flew to Delhi when the anti-government demonstrations started and stayed there. Like Sadiq, Dhar had had Communist political connections. But he was more important than the premier as the strongman of Kashmir. And he went on to bigger things: ambassador to the Soviet Union, head of policy planning in the external affairs ministry, and chairman of the Indian Planning Commission as a central cabinet minister.

After zipping up the best part of Kashmir again in India's pocket in 1965, Dhar negotiated the non-aggression pact with the Soviets that effectively ended India's pretense to non-alignment. He planned India's invasion of East Bengal in December 1971 as one of Prime Minister Indira Gandhi's most trusted advisers, manufacturing pretexts for military action in ways that drew on his extensive experience in Kashmir. When the outcome was the creation of Bangladesh, he served as India's proconsul in Dacca. As economic planner in Delhi and a member of the "Kashmir Mafia" of Indira – who like her father was acutely aware of the Nehru family's Kashmiri Brahmin roots – he tied Indian five-year plans more tightly and disastrously to their Soviet counterparts. D.P. Dhar was an undercover operator and habitual liar who specialized in the kind of devious plots that have no place in any democracy.

I met Dhar twice that week in October 1965 in the second-floor bedroom of his home, the real centre of police operations in the Vale. The first time, in early evening, he wore a suit and tie and he sat under a rather good pen portrait of Nehru. Three days later, shortly after noon, he wore rumpled white pajamas and looked older than his forty-five-odd years. He was unshaven, his hair was tousled, and he helped himself to little pills as we talked.

At our first meeting I protested against three government actions: police mistreatment of Farrell and myself outside Hazratbal 18 October, including the confiscation of film (I'd managed to hide an exposed roll of film I'd already removed from my camera); an order to Indian Posts and Telegraphs to "stop as objectionable" my cabled dispatch that night reporting what had happened at the mosque; and the 19 October arrest of a Kashmiri student, Bashir Ahmed, who I had met in the mosque and who had accompanied us on an attempted return to Hazratbal that morning when we were intercepted by a police road block.

Dhar promised on both occasions that the student would be released within a few days. At the second encounter, he answered questions about the Kashmir situation in an affected English accent to the accompaniment of birds, including a raucous crow, singing in the flower garden outside his window. The Kashmiri crow seemed to know exactly when to sound off. For instance, Dhar claimed the police had received strict orders not to enter Hazratbal but, "It would be almost expecting an angelic virtue of police for them not to respond to student taunts." Promptly the crow commented: "Caw, caw!"

Dhar flatly denied the shrine had been desecrated. He smoothly blamed the damage around the shrine on stones thrown at police by students inside the mosque grounds. As a consequence of the Hazratbal incident, he contended, "The Holy Relic Action Committee wanted to re-enact the days when the holy relic was stolen. The Koran was exhibited in processions [in 1964] as a facade for hooliganism and paid Pakistani agents. The game became dangerous [in 1965] when the appeal was not to reason but to religious fanaticism."

Because there were two versions of the October events, Dhar conceded, the Kashmir government had ordered a judicial inquiry (about which nothing was subsequently heard). But he insisted the government had countered armed terrorists inspired by Pakistani infiltration and aggression in order to prevent clashes between Muslims and Hindus. Official figures for violent deaths (five), arrested persons (under forty), and persons injured at Hazratbal (fifteen, all policemen) were lower than new student figures.

After our meetings, I became personally aware of how Dhar's mind worked, and how good his word was, in three ways.

A few hours after the second talk at his home on Friday, 22 October, when Dhar's police were preventing prayers at Hazratbal, I and three other foreign correspondents who by that time had arrived in Srinagar were riding with my faithful Kashmiri driver in the old city's winding lanes. Suddenly a huge Sikh policeman wildly waving a Sten gun stopped us. Without giving any reason, police detained us for several hours at a nearby police station while they literally tore apart the poor driver's car. When they released us after dusk, police said they had been alerted by headquarters to look out for that car on suspicion that it contained a secret radio transmitter.

Dhar, who gave orders at police headquarters, must have known from his spies who was using the car and wanted either to harass us and the driver or stop us from seeing something. Ironically, we all had invitations to a press reception that evening given by the state information minister. We had to arrive late, including the indignant *Times of London* man who had loudly protested his detention on the verandah of a Srinagar police station.

When I flew back to Delhi on the weekend, I discovered that a dispatch I had given Farrell to file for me on his return several days earlier was blocked at the cable office like the one I had filed in Srinagar. I had expected Dhar to stop stories of the Hazratbal outrage from leaving Kashmir. But for cabled press copy to be stopped in Delhi was almost unprecedented. It indicated that his reach extended into the central ministry of home affairs.

I then wrote a long account of the entire week's events in Kashmir, filed it normally, found that it too wasn't transmitted, and informed the central government's chief information officer that I had sent the story out of India by three unspecified unconventional means (air freight, air mail, and diplomatic bag). In a patently phony display of Asian "face," he said the whole story had been held up only because the government objected to a quotation of Karra's charge that Indian security personnel had raped Kashmiri women. I hadn't witnessed any case of rape so I changed the line to read that Karra had alleged general Indian terrorism of many people in the Vale.

Again checking personally at the cable office, I made sure my full story was finally transmitted this time. *The Globe and Mail* featured it on page one – eight days after the police assault on Hazratbal Mosque and my first exclusive, but blocked, story.

If Dhar couldn't repress indefinitely news of police activities in the Vale, even while the UN Security Council was discussing Kashmir following another complaint by Pakistan, he could detain indefinitely Kashmiris he considered undesirable. When my plane landed at Srinagar airport nearly two years later, I happened to see for the first time since October 1965 the student whom Dhar had promised to free in a few days. Bashir said he had been kept in jail for more than a year, including a month in solitary confinement at the beginning, when Dhar was saying his release was imminent.

For his loyal services, Dhar went to the UN General Assembly as an Indian delegate during the fall of 1966. Before he was fully graduated to the international scene, he opened up another bag of dirty tricks in Kashmir in June 1967. They must have been the oddest outgrowth anywhere of the Six Day War in the Middle East.

Early on the morning of 7 June, unidentified sound trucks spread a rumour in the Vale of Kashmir that Israeli planes had bombed Mecca, the holiest city in Islam. The Kashmir government did nothing to counter the potentially explosive rumour. The thousands of police at its command did nothing to prevent a supposedly pro-Arab mob from attacking three churches that day, one after the other over a period of six or seven hours.

Holy Family Roman Catholic Church, located practically next door to both a police station and the premier's official residence, was set ablaze and gutted in late morning. A kilometre or so away, and several hours later in the early afternoon, All Saints Anglican Church and its parsonage were almost completely burned out, and the minister barely escaped with his life. Later in the afternoon, the mob of 4,000 rioters also badly damaged Saint Luke's Anglican Church, the oldest church in the Vale, but was prevented from starting a fire inside by a pistol-waving Hindu. At all three churches, pews were smashed, prayer books were torn, and devotional objects were stolen.

The violent incidents were puzzling and totally uncharacteristic of Kashmiri behaviour. Why should Kashmiri Muslims demonstrate against Israel by assaulting Christian churches, even if there were no Jews or synagogues in the Vale? Why should they wantonly set fire to churches or protest violently at all, when they are known for living at peace with other religious groups no matter what troubles they have experienced, and had shown no enmity toward the Jewish state? Indeed, Sheikh Abdullah appealed later to Kashmiris at Hazratbal Mosque to follow the model of self-reliance set by Israelis – an extraordinary appeal in a Muslim society. Who spread the fantastic rumour about the bombing of Mecca in the first place? And why did police not respond after the first church burning if not immediately?

Durga Prashad Dhar's answers to these questions, when I saw him in Srinagar later that June, strongly suggested that the use of *agents provocateurs* as a political weapon had overstepped even the dangerous bounds previously set by India in Kashmir. He alleged that the "fanatical core" of the pro-plebiscite movement was to blame for the church attacks and the rumours. He said permission had been given for a pro-Arab demonstration on 7 June because it was in line with the Indian government's Middle East policy, but that "something went wrong" and police were caught unprepared to protect the churches.

These lame excuses sounded like a variation on his explanation of police action at Hazratbal Mosque in October 1965, complete with a promise of an investigation. In 1967, Dhar held the title of Kashmir's finance minister but he still coolly gave orders to police officers and took their salutes. Virtually no news of the 7 June church burnings had reached Delhi, let alone the outside world. Indian newspapers had reported only minor damage to two churches. I learned of the latest outrages quite accidentally, when I took my family to the Vale of Kashmir for a vacation.

My initial first-hand source of information was highly perturbed but unimpeachable: Krishna Hutheesingh of Bombay, Prime Minister Indira Gandhi's aunt and Jawaharlal Nehru's younger sister. She rushed over to tell us from the neighbouring houseboat on Dal Lake where she was staying. India, full of people whether or not Kashmir is included, is a small world.

Other informed persons in the Vale said the church attacks were wholly the doing of goondas hired by the government of Kashmir. A lifelong resident of Srinagar who had witnessed the All Saints burning said the mob was divided into groups representing the ruling Kashmir Congress Party, the rival National Conference led now by former Premier Bakshi, and the Plebiscite Front. I found the All Saints Anglican Church and its parsonage looking as if they had been bombed. The mob had cut the telephone line of the minister. When he tried to stop the intruders, they warned him to get out with his family. He fled through the back door of the parsonage as the mob crashed through the front door, spilling gasoline on the floor, setting the house ablaze, and looting what was not destroyed.

Apart from the churches, members of the mob targeted several Europeans. They ripped an Australian woman's clothes. They dragged a Bulgarian diplomat and his wife from their car; he saved himself from injury by shouting "Russian!" but she was hit over the head with a club. Even Mrs Hutheesingh's car was stoned and a window was broken on 7 June; it was doubtful she was recognized personally but she may have been recognized as a high-caste Hindu.

Even if not all the violent demonstrators were recruited by the government, the evidence pointed convincingly to a manipulation or fabrication of events by Dhar and his underlings to permit action – or inaction – suiting their political purpose. It was inconceivable that the large, tightly controlled, mobile police force always in the Vale could not have been deployed to protect other churches even if police had been caught off guard by the first attack on Holy Family. M.R. (Minoo) Masani, the leader of the Swatantra or Free Enterprise Party who visited Kashmir later in June, asserted: "The entire responsibility for these events rests squarely on the shoulders of the state government ... Only a proper investigation will disclose whether the disgraceful failure of the authorities to protect life and property, especially places of worship, was due to connivance or to impotence."

What became all too clear was that not Israel's military victory in the Middle East but Sheikh Abdullah's impending release from detention drove what happened in the Vale of Kashmir.

It was known before 7 June that the Lion of Kashmir, the Dhar-Sadiq regime's number one enemy, would soon be moved to Delhi from Kodaikanal, a South Indian hill station where he had spent the most recent months of his captivity while under treatment for diabetes and high blood pressure. His transfer would be the signal for Indira Gandhi's Congress Party government to decide whether to release him again, as many thinking Indians were demanding. Tied up with this question was whether or not to extend the national emergency dating from India's Himalayan war with China in late 1962 and due to expire on 1 July 1967. "Defence of India" regulations permitted the preventive detention of individuals without charges or trial.

On 8 June Abdullah was flown to Delhi. On 9 June another rumour swept the Vale: he was dead. This time the state government used its mobile loudspeakers to deny the rumour. A few days later, Sadiq, the head of Kashmir's puppet regime who had said his throat was too sore to reply to Mrs Hutheesingh's complaints about the mob violence, talked at length in Delhi to her niece Indira about it. He argued that it was a reason not to release Sheikh Sahib.

Sheikh Abdullah, who still had a slim chance of finding a Kashmir solution along the lines he had explored with Nehru, was not freed at that time. Indira gave in to her negative impulses, and D.P. Dhar had his way: India's state of emergency continued indefinitely.

Just as when the Kashmiri Muslim holy relic was mysteriously stolen in 1964, and as when police invaded and desecrated its shrine at Hazratbal Mosque in 1965, so an unaccountable happening in 1967 in the form of destruction of Christian churches served the aims of Kashmir's ruling minority. Those in power did not deem putting innocent people in jail and repeatedly fixing elections to be enough to bar the people of Kashmir from determining their own future in their own land.

On 23 June, a special Muslim holy day, I returned to Hazratbal and listened with tens of thousands of people to prayers and speeches. Speaker after speaker strongly disavowed organized Muslim responsibility for the church burnings. Their only reference to the Six Day War was a demand that Israel give up possession of Muslim holy places.

Prayers that day included a special entreaty for the safety and health of Sher-i-Kashmir: "O God," the mass of Kashmiris chanted excitedly, "Save him from any trouble."

More than six months later, on 2 January 1968, the Lion of Kashmir was finally released in Delhi. He had been held for more than two and a half years for unspecified and untried crimes against India. This made a total of more than thirteen years in captivity during the last fifteen. Abdullah was then sixty-two years old.

Before letting him go, the government of India took the precaution of putting an anti-secession law through Parliament – after having promulgated an anti-secession ordinance to the same effect – instead of continuing to rely on emergency regulations. For advocating Kashmiri self-determination, which many Indians construed as tantamount to secession, the Sheikh could be put back in jail at any time.

Acutely aware of his predicament, he nevertheless asserted at a press conference that self-determination was the one thing that could not be taken away from the people of Kashmir. He appealed to Indira to "pick up the threads" on Kashmir tenuously woven by her father just before his death nearly four years before. The prime minister, who for a time had shown sympathy for Sheikh Abdullah while he was in detention, replied publicly that it was up to him to resume the dialogue. She made clear privately that he was safe only as long as he did not call for a plebiscite or a change in the by now "integrated" status of Indian-held Kashmir.

Abdullah told me at his small house in Delhi that he no longer considered a plebiscite a final solution. He said he thought that a special international status for Kashmir was the best way out of conflicting claims for a Pakistani, Indian, or independent state, even if Pakistan did not consent to ending the partition of Kashmir. This was an indication that he acknowledged India as the paramount power in the Vale. But he made clear he would not compromise the claim of Kashmiris to first-class citizenship in their own right, reflecting their own nationalism. This indicated that he still had in mind the concept of a distinct identity for Kashmir that he had discussed with Nehru and Ayub, but with India as the greater or sole guarantor following the failure of Pakistani arms in the 1965 war.

The Sheikh was not pessimistic, or dogmatic in either a political or religious sense. He could not afford to be either. If Indian and Pakistani attitudes did not permit a reasonably quick solution, he suggested, perhaps change would come with a diversion of U.S. interest from Vietnam and Southeast Asia, and a revival of Soviet interest in Kashmir.

In March 1968, when unusually heavy snow had been cleared from the royal road of the Moghuls to the Vale, the Lion returned to Kashmir.

Hundreds of thousands of people noisily welcomed him home as a saviour in an unprecedented but peaceful demonstration of love and hope. But most Kashmiris seemed to realize that the Sheikh could not produce miracles. The huge congregations at Hazratbal, relieved at having him again in the midst of Kashmiris, took to listening patiently to Abdullah on Fridays, with less emotion than when his name had been invoked as a prisoner of India. He dared to remind his people – and the world, if it cared to listen – that Indian police and troops still forcibly occupied the Vale.

Each morning during that summer of 1968, Abdullah came out of his three-story house at Soura, thirteen kilometres from Srinagar, into the soothing sunshine of the Vale. He paced back and forth behind the low stone wall of his rose garden, then bent down to pluck a bud. He placed the rose in the third buttonhole of the *achkan* (a long fitted "Nehru" jacket) gracing his six-foot three-inch frame, the way Nehru used to do. When I sat and listened to Sheikh Sahib under a tree in his secluded garden, his resemblance to India's first prime minister, the man who had jailed him for the first ten years, was striking in other ways.

Abdullah was nine inches taller than Nehru had been. But his fine facial features and rarely seen fringe of white hair around a bald pate, usually hidden under a grey lambskin Kashmiri cap as Nehru's had been under a white cotton Congress cap, were amazingly similar. He thought out loud in an unexpectedly high-pitched voice, and he had a habit of expressing what can only be described as high-principled indecisiveness. Both were Nehruvian traits.

If Nehru's presence had been necessary to solve the dilemmas of his own indecisiveness, Abdullah was restrained in trying to solve the Kashmir problem partly because of his own difficulty in making up his mind over the years. The common ideal of the two men in seeking a Subcontinent free from religious bonds had come to grief on the rock of Hindu-Muslim antagonism. Yet there was good reason to share the conviction of many Kashmiris and Indians that this Muslim and this Hindu loved each other like brothers.

The more Abdullah talked earnestly to me in his rose garden in his pensive, self-conscious manner, the more he brought back memories of Nehru. I was persuaded of the veracity of a story heard in both Kashmir and Delhi, although I did not ask him about it. The story is that Jawaharlal and Abdullah had a common father in Motilal Nehru, the master of Anand Bhavan, the palatial family home in Allahabad on the Ganges in northcentral India, where the woman who gave birth to Abdullah was a servant. If the Kashmiri Brahmin who became the first prime minister of India and the Kashmiri Muslim who became the first premier of Kashmir were indeed half-brothers, for both family and political reasons, they could never acknowledge their relationship publicly.

Yet this would account for the obviously close feelings between the Sheikh and the Nehrus over many years. The aging prime minister turned personally and emotionally to his imprisoned adversary in a last bid to find a formula for Subcontinental unity. Abdullah responded in kind despite his years as a prisoner. Later he showed his pain at not finding the response he had hoped for from Nehru's daughter – his half-niece if the story is true – after he was released again in 1968. Indira gave in to pressure that summer to not even invite Abdullah to a meeting in Srinagar of the National Integration Council to discuss "communal troubles" in India. But she could not hide a sensitive remorse when she spoke of the Kashmiri leader as a kind of father figure. And she did finally free him.

Like the rose he plucked each morning, each idea Abdullah tentatively advanced for attaining Kashmiri self-determination wilted and gave way to another. For all the adulation of his people he could finally enjoy, as Nehru had for decades, the Lion was still a caged animal behind his garden wall. The government of India confronted him on one side and Kashmir's Muslims on the other, with Pakistan always peeking through the rose bushes.

The Sheikh insisted only that Kashmir's 1947 accession to India was not final but subject to ratification by Kashmiris in some way. At the same time, he sought to put into practice the secular principle – no state religion, and equality for members of all religions and races – embodied in India's constitution. He never believed in the two-nation theory, the *sine qua non* of Pakistan's existence and its desire for Kashmir. He probably always realized that unconditional independence was impractical, especially after China helped itself to a chunk of Kashmir. But as long as Kashmiri Muslims opposed Indian rule and the Indian government opposed Kashmiri self-determination, Abdullah could easily be accused on one hand of selling out his people and on the other of threatening India's territorial and constitutional integrity.

In searching for a way for Kashmiris to express their self-determination, he talked about an election with himself as the head of a contesting party. But when it looked as if his provocatively named Plebiscite Front would win an election in March 1971, the Indian government outlawed the party and temporarily barred Abdullah and, later, even his wife from setting foot in Kashmir. The record of Kashmiris' never having enjoyed a free and fair election continued intact – enough in itself to set them apart from people living in India's Hindu-majority states.

Sheikh Abdullah nevertheless warmly hailed Indira Gandhi for boldness and courage when she triumphed over her political opponents in the parliamentary election she unexpectedly called at the same time. He seemed to affirm that, as bad as things were, it was necessary to his cause for a Nehru to stay in power. But Kashmir's chance of attaining a special status within India, or even meaningful autonomy, dimmed when Indira and the Indian army tore Pakistan apart in the December 1971 war creating Bangladesh. The reduction of Pakistan did not lead to India's rulers granting a measure of respect to Kashmiri Muslims in a less threatening atmosphere. It encouraged them to pursue a policy of complete domination of Kashmir without regard for anyone else's interests, least of all those of the people living there.

Within a few years Indira's fortunes turned sharply downward. To save her political skin she arbitrarily suspended democracy in all India in June 1975. The popular reaction to Indira's Emergency allowed Sheikh Abdullah to regain at least the foothold he had enjoyed for a few years immediately after India's independence. When the Janata coalition under Morarji Desai swept Indira and the Congress Party from power in Delhi in March 1977, Abdullah and his party – called now by its old name, the National Conference – won the first free election ever held in Kashmir. The Lion of Kashmir came back to power, ironically, when the Nehrus temporarily lost power.

Morarji's government pursued regional co-operation with India's neighbours, including Pakistan, more honestly than any central government headed by a Nehru had, although Hindu nationalists were part of the Janata Party. If it had lasted a full five-year term, it is conceivable that a formula for a distinct international status for Kashmir under India could have been agreed on. But Abdullah's power was limited even with the restoration of article 370 along with the rest of the Indian constitution, and Indira stormed back to power at the beginning of 1980.

Having destroyed the Janata opposition at the centre, she was in no mood to tolerate political opponents in any state, particularly Kashmir and the Punjab. The Sheikh could only keep his head down and wait for another opening. He never found one. His death in 1983 at the age of seventy-five preceded Indira's assassination the following year at the hands of Sikh bodyguards out to avenge the Indian army's desecration of the Golden Temple, part of her campaign to stamp out Punjabi dissidents.

Kashmiri Muslims have never resorted to such extreme retaliation. But the threshold to violence had been steadily lowered. Violence started to become the norm in Kashmir when the Sheikh's successor as head of the state government, his son Farooq Abdullah, a British-educated medical doctor, openly allied the National Conference with the Congress Party of Indira's successor as prime minister, her son Rajiv Gandhi. The two leaders and parties cynically rigged an election in Kashmir in 1987. They ended the brief period of relatively clean politics inaugurated by Sheikh Abdullah a decade earlier. This descent demoralized many Kashmiris who had waited for years with incredible patience for a fair deal from India. It compelled them to conclude that fairness would never come.

During this time, guns began to filter into Kashmir from the war in Afghanistan that had started in 1980 after the Soviet invasion. They were followed by Afghan mujahedeen, who had been armed by the United States via Pakistan, and were looking for an anti-Muslim enemy to fight beyond the Soviets they had forced to retreat from their country. Pakistan was all too ready and willing to provide more arms and training for rebels against unyielding Indian rule of the best part of Kashmir. Rajiv, the last Nehru to hold power, moved more and more troops and police into the Vale, effectively breaking the positive family link with the late Lion of Kashmir.

Sheikh Abdullah's restraining hand was no longer present. His soft voice, like Nehru's, existed only in memory. More than four decades after partition and independence of the Subcontinent, and accession of Kashmir to India only on condition that its people have the final say, the overwhelmingly peaceful struggle of Kashmiris for self-determination gave way to an angry armed insurrection.

A number of militant groups – some ultra-religious, some for union with Pakistan, others favouring the independence of Kashmir – engaged in a guerrilla war against India. They ambushed Indian troops and they killed Kashmiri collaborators with the enemy. They forced 400,000 Kashmiri Hindus to flee the Vale, many of whom settled in refugee camps around Jammu to the south. They caused foreign tourists, 100,000 of whom used to come to Kashmir every year, to stay away. Although they had different aims and they used different methods, thirty-four such groups agreed on one goal when they came together in a new front called the All-Party Hurriyat Conference in 1993: the end of Kashmir's connection to India.

But the force brought to bear and the methods employed by India against the people of Kashmir were more radical. The central government took over the state completely under president's rule in 1989, abolishing the state government in league with Delhi. In March 1994, the Congress Party government of Prime Minister P.V. Narasimha Rao pushed through Parliament a resolution asserting unequivocally: "Jammu and Kashmir has been, is and shall be an integral part of India." While no more than 15,000 armed insurgents challenged this historically flawed proposition, at least 400,000 Indian army troops, paramilitary personnel, and policemen attempted to impose it. The means they used were the most extreme element in the tragic new Kashmir equation.

Indiscriminate abduction and killing, medieval torture, burning of homes and villages, widespread pillage, rape of women, and deliberate desecration of Muslim holy places became the daily rule of behaviour, not the exception, for Indian security forces obsessed by hate and fear of Kashmiri Muslims.

No longer was there any question that Indian soldiers and police made up a cruel and vindictive occupation force in the Vale. They had virtual carte blanche to open fire and therefore knew they would escape punishment for murder. They carried out "cordon-and-search" operations that invariably resulted in dead or imprisoned victims, and were really "catch-and-kill" exercises. Every day they wantonly violated human rights and democratic principles that Indian leaders continued to insist with straight faces they were upholding.

By mid-1996 an estimated 30,000 people had been killed, two-thirds of them civilians and probably most of them innocent Kashmiris. But Indian authorities also fabricated reasons for the toll. They claimed, for example, that 2,000 Kashmiris whose bodies were riddled with bullets and in many cases bore hideous evidence of torture had been caught in "crossfire" between troops and guerrillas. The successors to D.P. Dhar in Kashmir faithfully upheld and proudly built on his legacy of hypocritical ruthlessness.

The first two paragraphs of a painstakingly prepared 126-page Amnesty International report on conditions in Kashmir in January 1995, predictably labelled as biased and inaccurate by the Indian government, summed up a campaign of state terrorism that Kashmiris claimed had "reached genocidal proportions," and certainly went far beyond the terrorist tactics of anti-Indian insurgents:

Torture by the Indian security forces has become routine in the state of Jammu and Kashmir since armed conflict erupted there in 1989. The number of Kashmiris who have died in custody as a result has reached alarming proportions: this report details the cases of 715 detainees allegedly tortured to death or shot outright. The Indian army and paramilitary forces have killed detainees in custody while extracting information about armed secessionist groups, to intimidate the local population or in reprisal for killings of security forces personnel. The international community has largely ignored this escalating human rights crisis.

The entire civilian population is at risk of torture in areas where Indian government forces are engaged in counter-insurgency operations against armed groups fighting for independence or for the state to join Pakistan. Most of the victims are young men detained during 'crackdown' operations to identify armed militants. Typically, the security forces round up hundreds of people in towns or villages. Any that are suspected of links with militants are then taken away. Scores of women claim they have been raped. The relatives of those taken into custody are often not told why they have been arrested or where they are being held. Almost all of those arrested are tortured: many do not survive; others are left mutilated and disabled for life. The severity of torture by the Indian security forces is the main reason for the appalling number of deaths in custody in the state.

Substantiated methods of torture were a grim reflection of both the nature of India's policy in Kashmir and the mentality of the Indians carrying it out: suspending a detainee by his tightly bound feet for hours so that his legs were rendered useless or had to be amputated; electric shocks to moistened ears, eyelids, fingers, and genitals; crushing a victim with a "roller" so that kidney failure and usually death resulted; cutting off of body parts; and, for more fortunate prisoners, repeated kicking, lathi blows, and other abuse.

One of the worst Indian atrocities was the massacre in Sopore, northwest of Srinagar near the border with Pakistani-held Kashmir, on the morning of 6 January 1993. Kashmiri militants had attacked a border security force picket, injuring two men and snatching a light machine gun. An hour later, a platoon of forty Indian border security personnel in armoured trucks drove up to a crowded marketplace more than a kilometre away. They opened fire on civilians without warning, kept shooting for an hour, and set ablaze shops where panic-stricken Kashmiris had fled. They killed 45 people and wounded more than 300.

Indian troops surrounded Hazratbal Mosque in the fall of 1993, claiming militants had taken refuge and stockpiled weapons in the most holy Kashmiri Muslim shrine. For months a repeat of the Golden Temple invasion, with no less disastrous consequences, appeared imminent. Indira Gandhi's successors in Delhi finally backed off from what would have been an incalculably more bloody confrontation than the one I had witnessed at Hazratbal on 18 October 1965.

The heavily armed troops withdrew on 6 August 1994 from thirteen sandbagged bunkers ringing the mosque, and Kashmiri Muslims came out into Srinagar's streets to celebrate. The next day nine people were killed in the centre of Srinagar by the explosion of a bomb that police said Kashmiri militants were transporting but more likely had been planted by government agents. The day after that, the central government extended by another six months its direct rule of Kashmir through nearly a half-million armed men.

Unlike Hazratbal, another sacred Muslim shrine in Kashmir was not fortunate enough to escape destruction in the war between Indians and both Kashmiri and foreign insurgents. In the early morning hours of 11 May 1995, an inferno engulfed the mausoleum of Kashmir's fifteenth century patron saint, Sheikh Nooruddin Wali, at Charar-i-Sharief southwest of Srinagar, and hundreds of the town's charming walnut-wood houses and shops.

Delhi claimed that "terrorists and foreign mercenaries," meaning Pakistanis, had started the fire before trying to escape a two-month siege of Charar-i-Sharief by 12,000 Indian troops. As with the burning of the three churches in the Vale on 7 June 1967, local Kashmiris offered compelling evidence that Indian authorities were responsible for an outrage they were trying to blame on militants. The Kashmiris said that Indian troops had set the fire when they stormed the shrine and killed up to half of about sixty guerrillas who were sheltering nearby. Indian security forces had ignited other fires when they sought to punish or penetrate a Kashmiri town or a part of Srinagar.

Whoever was behind the Charar-i-Sharief catastrophe, it enraged Kashmiris so much against India that the Congress government of Prime

Minister Rao was forced to postpone plans for an electoral exercise in Kashmir. This was hardly to be the popular referendum that India had long rejected. Since central government rule had been imposed on Kashmir in 1989, it was to be the first election of a government in a state that Parliament had decreed at Rao's insistence was "an integral part of India." But the prime minister had vaguely hinted that Kashmiris would be rewarded with a degree of autonomy after voting. Despite article 370, Kashmir with its 70 per cent Muslim majority had less self-government than any Hindu-majority Indian state.

Before the election of a state legislature could happen, or be seen to happen, two more suspicious events occurred. One was the kidnapping in July 1995 of five foreign tourists – two Britons, an American, a German, and a Norwegian – and the beheading of the Norwegian, Hans Christian Ostro, by an avowedly secessionist group calling itself Al Faran. Kashmiris were stunned: "Al Faran has given a terrorist reputation to our movement and that's the last thing we want," said Omar Farooq, chairman of the Hurriyat Conference. But Al Faran was not a member of the front and no one had ever heard of it. Anyone familiar with Indian tactics in Kashmir could not dismiss the possibility that, following the Charar-i-Sharief conflagration, India had created the group and instigated the atrocity it committed precisely for the purpose of smearing Kashmiri Muslims who wanted nothing but to decide their own future. Although unusually brutal, this was the kind of unproven provocation that Indian agents in Kashmir in the Dhar tradition have allegedly been masters at creating.

The second significant event before the state election finally held in September 1996 was more transparent, and also involved voting. As the last stage of India's eleventh parliamentary election, polling for three seats representing the Vale of Kashmir took place on 30 May 1996. At dawn, thousands of Indian troops brandishing rifles and lathis literally forced Kashmiri Muslims throughout the Vale out of their beds to stand in line at voting booths. Many Kashmiris shouted "Azadi!" – Urdu for "Freedom!" – but they were not describing the casting of ballots that a good number of them deliberately spoiled. Every Kashmiri Muslim political group of any relevance boycotted the voting, which a senior Hindu official said marked "a return of peace and democracy." It was actually a trial run for polling in all areas of the state on four separate days in September. This schedule allowed troops, police, and election officials to concentrate in even greater force on getting Kashmiris out to vote for candidates for the long-suspended state legislature.

Worse than the frauds that most past elections in Kashmir had been, this one was a farce even before it took place. Its model was the Punjab election in 1992, when about a quarter of eligible voters cast ballots after police had ruthlessly suppressed a Sikh separatist movement that all but disappeared the following year. With Rao and the Congress Party ousted from power in Delhi in the May 1996 parliamentary election, the weak, leftist governing coalition, dependent on Congress support to stay in power, adopted the Kashmir state election plan and renewed Rao's vague promise of autonomy.

Only forty-six of the Kashmir legislature's eighty-seven seats come from the Vale. So Hindus and Buddhists voting in Jammu and the part of Ladakh held by India brought the overall voting percentage up. But the voting percentage in the heavily Muslim Vale was little more than 10 per cent. Former Premier Farooq Abdullah, showing some of the independence associated with his late father, had termed the May parliamentary vote in Kashmir a "total fraud," and his National Conference boycotted the September state election.

Even so, it captured more than two-thirds of the legislative seats, and agreed to reassume office with a promise to win a restoration of state executive powers. Farooq, now sixty, reluctantly consented to become *wazir* again – the revived title of premier of Kashmir instead of that of chief minister. But he ran the risk of greater popular repudiation than in 1987 for collaborating with Delhi, and even death as a traitor, if Kashmiris did not attain a meaningful measure of autonomy. Later Farooq called this "the only remedy to silence the guns in Kashmir." But on 9 October, the day he was sworn in as wazir, most of the 900,000 people of Srinagar protested by staying home in a general strike called by the Hurriyat Conference.

The Kashmir insurrection was far from crushed. Indeed, members of pro-India militias known as "renegades," recruited by Indian security and intelligence agencies to attack pro-Kashmir guerrillas or to pose as guerrillas threatening voters, had increased the danger of violence during and after the four election days. Such Indian tactics further lessened the likelihood of the state government's becoming credible following the forced voting. The Hurriyat dismissed the whole exercise and warned it would not abide by any political settlement that might follow.

Nothing changed when, shortly after Inder Kumar Gujral became prime minister of the Congress-supported leftist coalition government in Delhi in April 1997, he opened a dialogue on Kashmir with the new Pakistani prime minister, Nawaz Sharif. Later, Gujral invited Kashmiri rebels to take part in unconditional talks to end the eight-year-old civil war. But in two other ways he hoisted his country's familiar colours on Kashmir soon after India observed fifty years of its own independence in August 1997.

Indian artillery engaged in heavy, repeated exchanges with Pakistani gunners on the other side of the forty-eight-year-old Kashmir ceasefire line. And Gujral dragged Queen Elizabeth II into the Kashmir dispute by

contemptuously rejecting during her ceremonial fiftieth anniversary tour of
India an alleged attempt by what he called the "third-rate power" of
Britain to act as mediator.

Kashmir's election in the fiftieth year of India's independence was not a
fitting climax to a healing process of democracy and mutual respect. It was
one of many duplicitous Indian manoeuvres on a road that has led from
paradise to hell, from broken promises to broken bodies and, even worse,
broken hearts. At the urging of the Hurriyat Conference, Kashmiris
observed 15 August 1997, the fiftieth anniversary of India's independence,
as a "black day."

It was the eighth straight Indian independence day marred by violence in
the Vale. Indian troops and police took no holiday then, nor after the September election, from the repression, torture, and murder of Kashmiris. On
13 April, a few days after the outwardly conciliatory Gujral had become
prime minister, Indian troops had stripped naked and gang raped twelve
young Kashmiri Muslim girls near Srinagar in the worst incident of its kind
since 1991.

For too many years, it has not been possible simply to call the Vale of
Kashmir beautiful and remote. Its beauty is permanently scarred. The argument over who should possess it can result in another war or even a nuclear
exchange. The tragedy of Kashmir can begin to end only when the proud
people of the Vale no longer feel they must assail the misty air by shouting:
"Indian dogs, go back!"

But profound political and military changes in the Subcontinent in 1998,
1999, 2000, 2001, 2002, and early 2003 may have made possible a new
and ultimately fair deal for Kashmir. They reflected the failure of desperate
Pakistani Muslims and generals to save their own country, and the rising
power and pragmatism of Hindu nationalists in India.

Testing and Fighting

The breakthrough made by the Bharatiya Janata Party in winning a vote of confidence in the Lok Sabha by thirteen votes on 28 March 1998 led to the decisive victory by the BJP-led National Democratic Alliance in the September-October 1999 parliamentary election. But the breakthrough went beyond Indian domestic politics.

How big it was dawned on the world forty-four days later. At 3:45 in the afternoon of Monday, 11 May 1998, India conducted three underground nuclear tests at Pokharan, the site in the western Rajasthan desert where it had set off its first and until then only nuclear test explosion on 18 May 1974, twenty-four years earlier.

Prime Minister Atal Bihari Vajpayee made the announcement quietly an hour later, without sounding any note of triumph or vindication. Standing on the lawn of his Delhi residence in May's hot sunshine, he read a brief statement to reporters confirming that the BJP in power had executed the party's longstanding and open nuclear policy described to me by his closest associate, Lal Krishna Advani, in early 1992.

Vajpayee's statement reflected a technological difference from the past: one of the three devices tested was "thermonuclear," clearly indicating India's possession of a hydrogen bomb many times more powerful than a Hiroshima-type bomb. The prime minister soon emphasized a historic difference: he said India had become an avowed "nuclear weapons state." At long last, after decades of hypocrisy, the country with more people than any other but one was out of the nuclear closet. Indian nuclear scientists underlined this fact two days later, on 13 May, by carrying out two more underground nuclear tests.

Except for the vast majority of Indians, who cheered their country's new status, most reactions to India's nuclear tests were negative. Considering that India was meeting a perceived threat to its national security from the most populous country, China, the reaction of outsiders was also alarmist, judgmental, and uninformed. Many condemnations of India were as hypocritical and self-serving as the most holier-than-thou pronouncements of earlier Indian governments.

Cries of protest from Pakistan, which in ostensibly copying India's nuclear testing before the end of May lost its best chance to gain international respect, were more screeching than ever. China, which had directly contributed to instability in the Subcontinent by providing Pakistan with nuclear and missile technology – some of it obtained originally from the United States – blithely accepted President Bill Clinton's compliments for supporting nuclear non-proliferation. Little more than a month before Clinton's trip to China in quest of a "strategic partnership" with the Communist dictatorship in Beijing, the United States came down on India as if it were a third-rate authoritarian terrorist country instead of a major democratic regional power.

On 12 May, Clinton's rush to economic sanctions against India, although legally mandated, was eerily reminiscent of another controversial president and another time of momentous change in Asia. In December 1971, two months before he went to Beijing to begin establishing relations and spheres of influence, Richard M. Nixon had intemperately condemned India for breaking up Pakistan and creating Bangladesh. His ordering an aircraft carrier into the Bay of Bengal did more to alienate India from the United States than anything until Clinton's outbursts twenty-seven years later savaging India for making a "terrible mistake." It strengthened the resolve of many Indians to see their country become a superpower.

An angry Nixon and Henry Kissinger feared then that India's unexpected triumph would upset their grand design to create a new balance of power in Asia with China's Communist leaders. A "deeply disturbed" Clinton was anxious now that India's latest surprise not come in the way of a new détente between the United States and dictators in Beijing to whom – in their eyes and in the eyes of other Asians – he was about to kowtow in Tiananmen Square, scene of the June 1989 massacre of pro-democracy students by People's Liberation Army troops and tanks.

For the first time since its war with Pakistan at the end of 1971, India could claim to have made an inescapable impact on the biggest game in the global community. At that time it was the Cold War: following the first decisive election of a strident Indira Gandhi in her own right, India had been effectively allied with the Soviet Union in challenging the presumption of the United States under Nixon and China under Mao Zedong to write the rules of conduct for Asia and the Pacific. In The Greater Game as it was rapidly shaping up in mid-1998, the Indians served unmistakable nuclear notice: following the first undisputed election of the nationalist BJP, India could not be ignored or relegated to a minor role as the United States under

Clinton gave unmistakable signs of acquiescing to Communist China's aim of emerging from Asia's economic and political chaos as the undisputed lord of 60 per cent of the world's population.

Apparently even before the BJP formally took power, it had decided that India would carry out the party's unashamed policy and crash the nuclear club. According to Indian newspaper reports, on 19 March, the day Vajpayee again became prime minister, he met and gave a positive message to senior nuclear officials, including A.P.J. Abdul Kalam, the wholly Indian-educated Muslim who was considered the father of the Indian bomb.

Following India's first nuclear test in 1974, the Hindu nationalists had three reasons for ending the twenty-four-year moratorium: cultural, political and, above all, geostrategic.

The cultural reason was the traditional belief in Bharat or India as the centre of the world, much like China to Chinese is the Middle Kingdom. The Nehru dynasty had disguised this concept by keeping secret India's buildup of up to 200 nuclear warheads following its disastrous loss to China in the 1962 Himalayan war and China's first nuclear test in 1964. But the BJP revived the idea of India as a superpower, incredible to Westerners, as soon as it assumed office.

Politically, India's attaining *Sakti* – power – through a series of nuclear tests was popular among a population nearing one billion. The BJP figured to strengthen its shaky coalition government when Vajpayee honestly revealed India's new status. But calling an immediate new election, widely reported to be the party's strategy, was never a feasible option. Vajpayee didn't want one, and President Kocheril Raman Narayanan in all likelihood would have prevented it. Peace in Asia requires political stability, however, and in India the BJP was the only party now capable of providing that stability.

But the key reason for India's leaving its nuclear ambiguity behind was geostrategic. Its perception that Indian national security was threatened had grown in recent months as China upgraded airfields for fighter-bombers and stockpiled nuclear missiles in Tibet, gave Pakistan continuing assistance with missiles and a Chinese-designed nuclear bomb, and built a naval surveillance base in Burma's Coco Islands in the Bay of Bengal. India's regarding not Pakistan but China as its chief enemy since 1962 was something that Clinton and his advisers found even harder to grasp than earlier U.S. administrations.

But Pakistan's test on 6 April 1998 of a medium-range, nuclear-capable missile in which North Korea had had a hand – and named Ghauri after a Muslim conqueror of India – was what finally provoked the then eighteen-day-old BJP government to tear the camouflage off India's nuclear achievements.

On 4 May Defense Minister George Fernandes, who was not a BJP member and had previously opposed nuclear testing, asserted that China was India's "potential threat number one" and suggested that India declare itself a nuclear-weapons state. Beijing, obviously stung, responded by expressing "utmost regret and resentment" and vehemently denying that it posed a threat to neighbours – a sign that Fernandes was right about China as a major threat. India had its moment of truth on 11 May, just one week after his warning and less than two months after hardline Hindu nationalists had taken responsibility for its destiny.

The Indian tests "came as a complete shock, a bolt out of the blue," maintained a senior Clinton administration official with appropriate dismay. The chairman of the Senate intelligence committee, Republican Richard C. Shelby of Alabama, declared that the CIA's failure to detect Indian preparations for nuclear tests – as it had in December 1995, forcing the then-Congress government to call off testing – was "the intelligence failure of the decade."

But other U.S. officials, and unofficial persons following developments in the Subcontinent, were acutely aware of the nuclear capabilities and likely intentions of both India and Pakistan. The U.S. response before and after India's tests was not so much an intelligence failure as a policy failure. Worse, it was a failure to look at Asia beyond what Clinton wanted to see in China.

Advani had told me in 1992 that a BJP government should avow India's nuclear weapons. When the Hindu nationalists took office in March 1998, they had made no secret of their active consideration of the nuclear option. A month earlier in Washington, a senior State Department official who requested anonymity had informed me that India and Pakistan could then attack each other with short-range nuclear missiles. In his view then, a BJP election victory would create a "really serious problem," increasing the danger of a nuclear confrontation. But he had acknowledged that China was part of the equation for India, and that India's nuclear development was under civilian and scientific control while Pakistan's was under military control.

In late April, the chairman of the BJP's foreign affairs committee had said in Colombo that the government sought talks with the United States on India's security concerns and the prospect of "inducting" nuclear weapons into its armed forces without testing them and thereby avoiding U.S. sanctions. Clinton administration officials, cool to such talks if they did not completely rebuff them, revealed at the same time that India was building a ballistic missile capable of being launched with a nuclear warhead from a submerged submarine, and that Russia had lent assistance to this project for at least three years.

It was true that the tests by India, and later Pakistan, set back efforts to obtain universal approval of a treaty banning all nuclear tests. The Clinton administration was a leader in this campaign although there was widespread opposition to ratification in the U.S. Senate, which on 13 October 1999 was to reject the treaty by a vote of fifty-one to forty-eight, eighteen votes short of the two-thirds majority required for approval. U.S. support of the Nuclear Non-Proliferation Treaty and its extension, opposed by India on the ground that it discriminated in favour of the recognized nuclear powers, was the basis of the 1994 U.S. law requiring economic sanctions against a country violating the NPT, specifically by testing.

But the more immediate issue – and the one most likely to lead to armed conflict – was peace and security in South Asia and, by extension, all Asia and the Pacific. It was with this issue in mind that Vajpayee wrote a respectful letter to Clinton on 11 May, the day India resumed testing. He pointed out: "Although our relations with [China] have improved in the last decade or so, an atmosphere of distrust persists mainly due to the unresolved border problem. To add to the distrust, that country has materially helped another neighbour of ours [Pakistan] to become a covert nuclear weapons state."

The president of the United States, however, was far more interested in communicating and establishing a "partnership" with the Communist dictators of China than with the elected leaders of India. Clinton also set up a special line to Pakistan, going far beyond the usual, and wrong-headed, U.S. treatment of India and Pakistan as equals.

In long, pleading telephone calls to Prime Minister Nawaz Sharif, he promised Pakistan a raft of favours, including the delivery of the F-16 fighters that the U.S. government had legally stopped due to secret Pakistani moves over many years to acquire nuclear know-how and components, if Islamabad did not follow Delhi's example of nuclear tests. Pakistan's foreign minister, Gohar Ayub Khan, more hawkish than his father had been as chief martial law administrator and president, nevertheless blamed the United States for not blocking India's tests after his government had warned in April they were coming. But the Indians had been provoked by Pakistan's test of its Ghauri missile early that month, and infuriated by Clinton's failure to restrain the Pakistanis or constructively engage the BJP government.

One of the few Americans to raise his voice in explanation of India's resort to nuclear testing was John J. Mearsheimer, a political scientist at the University of Chicago known for his geopolitical realism. He wrote in *The New York Times*: "Indian officials are understandably fearful of a hostile encirclement by China and Pakistan, and perhaps even the United States, which has historical ties to Pakistan and is now trying to improve relations with China."

When India completed its series of five tests with two more on 13 May, Vajpayee pointedly asserted: "This was not a political gimmick. For us, the country's security was paramount. These tests were above politics. Approving them was our right, and our duty."

The prime minister repeated his offer of 11 May to consider signing on to some parts of the test-ban treaty, a disarmament measure first proposed by Nehru. But he said calmly that India would face the problems arising from economic sanctions "squarely." In what may have been a tacit acknowledgment that Jawaharlal Nehru had authorized India's clandestine nuclear path soon after independence, Vajpayee added a few days later that the second most populous country had "waited for five decades" before heeding the call of Hindu nationalists and openly "going nuclear."

Clinton, plainly nonplussed by India's defiant refusal to accept his pro-China vision of Asia, responded by imposing sanctions against Delhi while failing to persuade other major powers to do so during a visit to Europe. He also intensified appeals to Pakistan not to respond to what he called India's "irresponsible act." Despite Secretary of State Madeleine Albright's denial, the most powerful democracy painted the most populous one as a pariah among nations.

Pakistan, long regarded as a pariah nation by many, tried to keep the world in suspense before adding to this reputation. Prime Minister Sharif, suddenly the object of Clinton's attention, conveyed the impression he was resisting tremendous political and popular "pressure" to test. Foreign Minister Ayub, keen as his father had been to have another go at India, said repeatedly that testing was only a question of when, not whether. Official Pakistani propaganda characterized India as a country that was falling apart like the former Soviet Union, and its new rulers as "racists" and "fascists."

At a luncheon for a Pakistani delegation visiting Washington and Ottawa, I took strong exception to the easy equation of Vajpayee with Hitler, and pleaded for realism in discussion of a serious situation. Senator M. Akram Zaki, whom I had interviewed in Islamabad when he was foreign secretary and complaining about the undelivered U.S. F-16s, moderated his tone somewhat, and even confided privately, in answer to my question, that planted Pakistani rumours of Israeli nuclear collaboration with India were untrue.

That was a little more than a week after Sharif had announced on television that Pakistan had set off five nuclear explosions on 28 May at a test site in the Chagai hills near its border with Iran, and a sixth on 30 May to go one up on India. "Today, we have settled the score with India," gloated the seemingly indecisive prime minister after the first blasts. "As a self-respecting nation, we had no choice left to us. Our hand was forced by the present Indian leadership's reckless action."

Pakistan did have a choice considering the carrots and the anti-India animus offered by Clinton. If the Pakistanis had refrained from testing, these would have more than made up for China's refusal to offer a guarantee of nuclear protection. Another Pakistani delegation, led by the new foreign secretary, Shamshad Ahmed, and seeking such a guarantee against Indian attack, had come away from Beijing empty-handed a week after India's tests. But the Chinese had already done Pakistan a huge nuclear favour, and in so doing had inevitably raised the level of India-Pakistan hostility.

"If you subtract Chinese assistance from the Pakistani nuclear weapons program, there is no program," observed Gary Milhollin, director of the Wisconsin Project on Nuclear Arms Control. "The Chinese gave Pakistan a tested design using highly enriched uranium. The Pakistanis then went on the world market and bought the components to fit the design."

But apart from the difference in tone between Vajpayee and Sharif in announcing their respective countries' nuclear tests, there was a substantial difference in the nuclear capabilities of India and Pakistan. India had twice as many warheads at a minimum, and possibly fifteen or more times as many. Indeed, experts suspected Pakistan of using up half its warheads in testing, or of carrying out perhaps only half of its six announced tests. India's impressive nuclear establishment had successively tested a thermonuclear device for a hydrogen bomb, something Pakistan's handful of nuclear scientists could only dream of doing. Yet Delhi's steadily developed, demonstrated, and decisive nuclear advantage did not prevent the U.S. and other Western governments, and most Western media, from instinctively equating India and Pakistan as in the past, and thereby putting most of the blame on India for initiating what they called an anachronistic nuclear arms race.

Within weeks, this dangerous habit took a new twist with obviously leaked stories belittling India's ability to create even what Vajpayee called a "minimum deterrent" by fitting its warheads to missiles in a rational, organized, and safe manner. Once more, journalists facilely contrasted India's expensive nuclear ambitions with its hundreds of millions of poor people, as if China with its growing nuclear arsenal did not also have impoverished masses. This combined with U.S. pressure on India not to assemble or deploy actual nuclear weapons. The U.S. deputy secretary of state, Strobe Talbott, stressed this point in a series of talks with Jaswant Singh, at that time Vajpayee's foreign-policy adviser, but India adamantly rejected the U.S. pressure. India was determined not only to protect itself against nuclear-armed adversaries but also to safeguard its nuclear warheads.

Pakistan's tit-for-tat reply to Delhi's tests, by contrast, reflected what the Indians later characterized as a "neurotic" mindset. More dramatically than ever, the Pakistanis showed that their bottom line was not Islam but India. The realization of Zulfikar Ali Bhutto's promised "Islamic bomb," however, increased the chances of Pakistan's rudimentary nuclear capability getting out of control.

Pakistan has started all three of its wars with India, even the one in 1971 that severed Pakistan in half. It lost all three. This was unlikely to stop Pakistani rulers – civilians then, but later generals who, unlike their Indian counterparts, had control of whatever nuclear bombs existed – from launching a fourth war resulting in nuclear catastrophe. Indeed, Pakistan's chronic difficulty in making democracy work became more worrisome with the May 1998 tests. Even with a large parliamentary majority, Prime Minister Sharif declared a national emergency when he announced his country's testing. The given reason was to allow swift measures to counter international sanctions against an economy much weaker than India's. But the move exposed the paramount influence of Pakistan's often bungling generals, especially those in Inter-Services Intelligence who had repeatedly made the bad Afghanistan situation worse by backing Muslim extremists culminating in the medieval Taliban.

Pakistan's irresponsibility was on display even before it completed its tests – India's Defence Minister Fernandes called them "ping pong balls" – and its inability to accept reality re-emerged immediately afterward.

Foreign Minister Ayub said Pakistani warplanes had been armed for attacks on Indian airfields to pre-empt a planned Indian attack on Pakistani nuclear facilities, despite a longstanding agreement between the two countries not to attack each other's nuclear installations. Bombing of Indian airfields by Pakistan had kicked off the 1965 and 1971 wars. In reality, India had an interest in not stopping Pakistani tests of an inferior nuclear stockpile. They undercut U.S. favouritism toward Pakistan, and made India's tests more politically justifiable at home. Indian officials had feared that Pakistan would swallow Clinton's inducements and, by not testing, become a pet of the White House as much as it had been with Nixon.

But after testing, Pakistan, led by Ayub, lost no time in trying to tie the nuclear issue to Kashmir, which his father had failed to win in the 1965 war. At a time when the new BJP government was a step away from fully integrating Indian-held Kashmir into India, the Pakistanis said that minimizing the nuclear danger was contingent on resolving the Kashmir question. They meant that now that they had answered India's tests and created a nuclear standoff in the world's eyes, the Indians should start to hand over Kashmir to them.

When Vajpayee and Sharif met briefly in Colombo in late July at a scheduled South Asian summit, the Indian leader reiterated that both issues

could be considered only within the broader context of India-Pakistan relations. Talks between officials broke down – and the danger of a desperate
Pakistani lunge stayed alive – when Pakistan accused India of taking a
"rigid and inflexible position" on Kashmir. This has been the Pakistani
position for more than fifty years. During the talks, one of the heaviest
exchanges of artillery and mortar fire in years across the line of control in
Kashmir, formerly the ceasefire line, had underlined the hardness of both
sides, and killed more than seventy civilians and soldiers.

But with its nuclear pronouncement India took on not Pakistan but its
share of the responsibility of containing China. Just as the need for broad
popular support among Indian voters has compelled the Hindu nationalists
to give up their narrow domestic agenda, so the need for a wide Asia-
Pacific alliance or coalition among democratic or would-be democratic
countries was forcing the BJP and its supporters to drop the idea of India
as a superpower on its own. The opposition Congress Party nominally led
by Sonia Gandhi, after first seeking a way of faulting the BJP's nuclear policy, had no choice but to go along with it.

This policy is still at odds with the familiar image of India as a poor and
helpless – or aggressive – giant. So international recognition has been slow
in coming or deliberately withheld. But the policy goes far beyond the five
carefully calibrated nuclear tests of May 1998. It includes commitments
other than the immediate 14 per cent increase in India's military budget,
pushing it to $12.4 billion, and increases of more than 60 per cent in spend-
ing on nuclear and missile research, put in place in response to U.S. sanctions. As an avowed nuclear power, even if formally barred at first from the
club consisting of the United States, Russia, China, Britain, and France,
India also pledged not to carry out further tests, not to threaten other
nations with nuclear weapons, and to negotiate a no-first-use agreement
with Pakistan, as well as to work toward improving and signing the universal nuclear test-ban treaty with the aim of limiting all nuclear arsenals.

With India having discarded what Vajpayee called "a veil of needless
ambiguity" – the nuclear legacy of the Nehrus – the prime minister solemn-
ly told Parliament: "Our strengthened capability adds to our sense of
responsibility."

Vajpayee's words did not prevent Presidents Clinton and Jiang Zemin
from issuing a two-page statement in Beijing in June on limiting nuclear
arms in the Subcontinent. Predictably, this joint move elicited a sharp Indian reply accusing China and the United States of interference and
hypocrisy. But for several reasons, U.S. sanctions against India and Pakistan did not bite nearly as hard as many had feared.

Less than a month after Pakistan's tests, the Clinton administration said

it would not block efforts by the International Monetary Fund to prevent
the country's economic collapse. A few days later, Washington did not
stand in the way of a World Bank loan of more than a half-billion dollars
for humanitarian projects in the southern Indian state of Andhra Pradesh.
Then the Senate and House of Representatives, lobbied by American farmers, voted to exempt food exports from sanctions on India and Pakistan.
Finally, a unanimous Senate vote gave Clinton the authority to waive most
remaining economic sanctions on both countries. At the same time, the
withholding of a U.S. visa from the chairman of India's Atomic Energy
Commission, Rajagopal Chidambaram, underlined India's difficulty in
gaining international acceptance as a nuclear power and a major player in
Asia and the world.

On 3 June 1999, when I entered the spacious office of Foreign Minister
Jaswant Singh in New Delhi's South Bloc, where Nehru had once reigned,
India was engaged in a new military conflict with Pakistan. Eight days
before, its forces had launched Operation Vijay: an attack by planes,
artillery, and ultimately mountain troops against armed intruders who had
crossed the jointly recognized line of control into Indian-held Kashmir
along cold Himalayan ridges.

Singh cordially shook hands and immediately put down a terrain map of
the Kargil sector of Kashmir on a coffee table next to a large book entitled
Rajasthan, the name of his home state as a member of a Rajput princely
family. His tall lean frame, accentuated by a dark, open-necked sports shirt
and slacks, seemed to underline the gravity of what he was about to say. As
we leaned over the map, he pointed out the importance of the Srinagar to
Leh road – National Highway One – the intruders were attempting to cut.
Expressing India's determination to drive them out, he assessed Pakistani
motives for the infiltration in force. He explained in turn other elements
making up The Greater Game as India's new ruling party saw them.

Singh stipulated that our interview was off the record. Nevertheless it
was fair to report that he was the architect of a new, not yet fully formed
foreign policy for India. Events in the coming weeks and months supported the main tenets of that policy. They began to change attitudes and
assumptions in a number of capitals, including Washington.

Five points became clear.

First, despite repeated denials, the Pakistani army was behind the intrusion and provided most of the more than 1,500 men involved; others were
Afghan Islamic mujahedeen spoiling to fight infidels.

Second, without escalating combat to full-scale war, Indian forces gradually forged a decisive victory during more than two and a half months of
brutal fighting under extremely difficult conditions, killing at least 700

intruders and forcing complete withdrawal of the survivors while losing 400 Indian troops.

Third, this unqualified military victory contributed immeasurably to the BJP win at the polls, consolidating its power with political allies in India's thirteenth parliamentary election in September-October 1999.

Fourth, the humiliating Pakistani defeat led to a successful military coup on 12 October by General Pervez Musharraf, the army commander who had orchestrated the unsuccessful Kashmir incursion.

Fifth, even before the army seized control for the fourth time in Pakistan's fifty-two-year history of failures, demolishing any pretense of democracy, the United States conveyed its decision to end a policy of "balance" toward India and Pakistan, thereby ceasing the longstanding equation of the two countries.

Consideration of each of these five points dispels some of the myths shrouding the Subcontinent, and suggests a new pattern of policy and performance impacting all Asia and the Pacific.

Prime Minister Vajpayee had taken a potentially fruitful bus ride to Lahore in February, symbolizing the start of a peace process with Prime Minister Sharif. So Indian officials were reluctant at first to blame the Pakistani government for the large-scale incursion across the line of control that divides Kashmir and was recognized by both countries in the 1972 Simla agreement in lieu of the 1949 ceasefire line. The officials also said they had no clear indication of China's involvement. But it was hard to know what was worse: Sharif's being left out of the picture by the army or his secretly colluding with the army. After the fighting had started but before its outcome was clear, both Pakistan and India delivered distinctly different messages directly to China. Following a trip to Beijing by his foreign minister, Sharif personally flew to the Chinese capital to seek support for revival of the Kashmir issue internationally. Then, a few days after my interview with Jaswant Singh, the Indian foreign minister paid a visit to Beijing to make clear India's insistence that the intruders withdraw completely.

Whatever Sharif's part or China's role, the Pakistani army, its notorious directorate for Inter-Services Intelligence, and its commander, General Musharraf, were aware of unavoidable conditions. For one, an international discussion of Kashmir would be difficult at any time. For another, it was virtually impossible with the BJP in power in India. It was out of the question when Indian casualties were mounting on the ridges overlooking the Srinagar-Leh supply route vital to Indian security, and an Indian national election was looming. Moreover, when the Himalayan snows came in September, the intruders would be forced to withdraw if they had not been ousted by then.

So Indian officials concluded that Pakistan's army had instigated the fighting to derail the peace process, to break the calm in the Indian-controlled Vale of Kashmir that had allowed tourists to return for the first time in years, and to make the world again equate India and Pakistan as enemies. Indians from Vajpayee down felt deeply betrayed for these reasons alone. But two larger Pakistani motives were also plausible.

One was that the Pakistani army wanted to embarrass the BJP government and make it vulnerable politically. This would have increased the chances of the election of a Congress Party government led by Sonia Gandhi, who probably would have been softer on Kashmir and certainly would have reverted to Nehruvian opposition to closer Indian ties with the United States.

The other plausible motive had to do with changing the government of Pakistan. In April and May, Musharraf and his colleagues may have put in motion the largest Kashmir infiltration since 1965 as the first direct step toward the coup in October overthrowing Sharif and constitutional government and giving the generals full political control of Pakistan.

The intruders from Pakistan caught an initial break when Indian intelligence and border security forces apparently were slow to detect them. The carefully marked line of control winds for some 725 kilometres through rugged, remote terrain providing easy cover. But by the time the first firefight took place in the Kargil sector on 6 May, and during the following days of the heaviest fighting in the Himalayas since 1962, groups of infiltrators did not advance beyond seven kilometres into Indian territory along a front of 145 to 175 kilometres.

It was not until 26 May, when Indian jets and helicopter gunships attacked intruders dug into mountains and caves, that the world realized how serious the conflict was. The next day an Indian MIG-21 crashed due to mechanical failure and the pilot bailed out, and a Pakistani surface-to-air missile destroyed a MIG-27 and killed the pilot responding to the first plane's distress signal. On 28 May a Stinger missile brought down an Indian helicopter, killing four soldiers. The missile was the kind the United States had provided in bulk to Pakistan's Inter-Services Intelligence for distribution to Afghan mujahedeen fighting Soviet invaders.

Pakistan returned the MIG-21 pilot unharmed but the Indians charged that the returned bodies of six soldiers bore evidence of torture and execution. India buried the bodies of Pakistani soldiers in shallow mountain graves because Pakistan, refusing to acknowledge that regular army troops had crossed the line of control, would not accept them. Both Indian and Pakistani commands copied NATO military briefings at the time on the bombing of Serbia and the Kosovo operation. India's briefers presented evidence that Pakistani regulars were among the intruders, and reported slow but steady progress in driving all the infiltrators out. Pakistan's briefers kept up the pretense of Kashmiri liberation fighters struggling for their land, and reported Indian shelling of villages on the Pakistani side of the line of control. All that most Indians and Pakistanis and the rest of the world saw of the fighting on their television screens was heavy artillery booming on both sides. Indeed, many Indians realized for the first time that Bofors meant not only corruption involving the late Prime Minister Rajiv Gandhi but also long and graceful 155-millimetre guns.

On 13 June Indian troops captured Tololing Peak, the easternmost of three mountains towering above the village of Drass and commanding the Srinagar-Leh road. The beginning of the end of Pakistan's latest attempt to take control of all Kashmir had been preceded the day before by India's shooting down of a Pakistani helicopter, killing eleven military personnel on board, including a brigadier. In hand-to-hand fighting on 21 June, jawans took Peak 5140 – its height in metres – followed by the western-most Tiger Hill. By 12 July Indian forces returned to the line of control, Pakistan agreed to a truce, and India suspended its campaign. But Pakistani artillery resumed shelling the road, Indian forces did not clear the fourth and last battle zone – the Mushko Valley – until 19 July, and India did not declare all the intruders out until 26 July. By then Pakistani tactics had switched to terrorist attacks on border security forces and their families in Kashmir. On 10 August, an Indian fighter downed a Pakistani naval reconnaissance plane with sixteen people on board over the Rann of Kutch. The next day a Pakistani missile missed three Indian helicopters taking journalists to view part of the wreckage.

In early June, Jaswant Singh had anticipated the political fallout in India from fighting the Pakistan-based intruders in Kashmir when he declared: "We are acting not for the BJP but for India – if that means defeat in the election, so be it!"

That was his only flight of rhetoric in our interview, and I took his words to be directly quotable. The foreign minister, and former foreign-policy adviser to Prime Minister Vajpayee, meant that if the government could not claim a clear victory over Pakistan in Kashmir before September, the BJP's chances of winning the crucial parliamentary election then would be significantly diminished. For the first time when India was at war or war was threatened, political opponents were openly criticizing the government. Sonia Gandhi and other Congress Party leaders, and some Indian newspapers, were questioning the government's tactics, indiscreet statements by Defense Minister George Fernandes, and apparent tardiness in detecting the incursion from Pakistan. This was healthy in a democracy. It also posed the danger of Indian instability that the Pakistani generals, as in the past, were trying to promote.

But the BJP government did not make a major mistake, and it did succeed in fully dislodging the intruders. Moreover, it did so without widening or escalating the conflict by giving in to the temptation to cut off Pakistani supply lines by bombing, shelling, or threatening Pakistani-held Kashmir or Pakistan itself.

Vajpayee proved himself a statesman as well as a nationalist. Shortly after the fighting started, he recalled his visit to Lahore and observed: "We still believe in peace, but you cannot clap with one hand." He patiently explained the situation in an address to the nation on 7 June, cautioning that it was "fraught with danger," emphasizing the sanctity of the line of control, and also pledging to "rid our sacred motherland of every single intruder." This promise was kept, and some political analysts said it was not a major factor in the way Indians voted in returning the BJP-led National Democratic Alliance with a solid parliamentary majority. But if Vajpayee's promise had not been kept, without question the BJP would have paid the stiff price foreseen by Singh. India would have, too.

The contrast with Pakistan could hardly have been greater. The existing government and Pakistan itself did pay a stiff price for another loss to India. But the man who had the most to do with the Pakistani failure ended up in undisputed power by taking the law into his own hands. Whether or not this was the way General Musharraf had planned it, Pakistan exposed itself more than ever before as a reckless pariah state dangerous not just to India but to world peace.

At first, Pakistanis in and out of government reacted as they had initially to the 1965 war with India over Kashmir. They thought they had won. They convinced themselves that the major incursion had forced India to overreact, revealed India as an aggressor, and confirmed quick settlement of the Kashmir issue as essential to stability in the Subcontinent. When Foreign Minister Sartaj Aziz flew to Delhi from Beijing on 12 June, he confidently called China a "steadfast friend of Pakistan." At the time of India's nuclear tests, the United States had made a special appeal to Pakistan as a friend.

But Jaswant Singh and Vajpayee made clear that India would accept nothing less from Pakistan than a complete withdrawal of the invaders. The Clinton administration's strong support of this demand shocked the Pakistanis: it was the first time the United States had leaned toward India on the Kashmir question. Along with strengthening India's democratic coalition government, the mini-war in Kashmir brought the United States and India much closer together, in contrast to the nuclear tests a year earlier that had driven them much further apart.

Desperate for good reason, Prime Minister Sharif flew to Washington for three hours of emergency talks with President Clinton on 4 July. Clinton also telephoned Vajpayee. U.S. officials said they expected the intruders to withdraw but weren't sure if the Pakistani military, which they now blamed for the operation, would accept Sharif's order to do so.

The generals did go along with taking out the battered and beaten survivors before the end of July. But they then joined other Pakistanis, including Islamic extremists and opposition parties, in blaming Sharif for the humiliating military defeat. When the prime minister fired Musharraf on 12 October while the army commander was flying back to Pakistan from Sri Lanka, the military executed a pre-arranged plan to take control of the country. Arriving home, Musharraf dismissed Sharif, put him under house arrest, and suspended the constitution and Parliament.

Sharif, like his civilian predecessor Benazir Bhutto, was corrupt. But he had held office legitimately and enjoyed an elected parliamentary majority. Following the fourth military coup in Pakistan's history – generals had held power for twenty-five years – Musharraf did not promise a quick or even gradual restoration of democracy. The question was what bitterly frustrated Pakistani generals would do next with all their collapsing country had left: a meddling army, a handful of nuclear bombs, and bands of armed terrorists looking for ways to wrench Kashmir from India.

The answer came in the last eight days of the twentieth century. On 24 December 1999, five men armed with pistols and grenades hijacked Indian Airlines Flight 814 shortly after it departed Katmandu, Nepal, for Delhi with 184 other people on board. The A300 Airbus then followed an erratic route, landing and taking off four times – in Amritsar, India; Lahore, Pakistan; Kabul, Afghanistan; and Dubai in the Persian Gulf – before coming to rest on the U.S.-built airfield at Kandahar near the southern Afghanistan desert for what would turn out to be an agonizing full week.

In Amritsar, it was learned later, a force of Indian commandos was organizing to storm the plane when the pilot, a hijacker's gun to his head, was forced to take off after only one hour on the ground. In Lahore, it also was learned later, the hijackers talked by cell phone with unidentified Pakistanis. In Kandahar, the home base of the feudal Pakistani-supported Taliban rulers of Afghanistan – who dispatched men to guard the plane – the hijackers received new, more lethal weapons. They had released twenty-seven hostages in Dubai, and later one more. They also had stabbed to death an Indian man who refused to obey an order not to look at them.

As India's government started negotiating with the hijackers, it faced a grim dilemma with no satisfactory way out. The dilemma deepened as the hand of Pakistan's government and the terrorists at its command became increasingly clear to Indians who, as at the beginning of the Kargil conflict, did not at first allege official Pakistani involvement.

In Amritsar India had lost the only opportunity for military action against the hijackers. The Taliban brusquely barred any such action in Kandahar. And a rescue operation anywhere risked high loss of life. Relatives of the Indian hostages demonstrated for their immediate release from unspeakable conditions on the stationery sun-baked plane. But India was sworn not to give in to terrorists, particularly those fighting to detach Kashmir. Any doubt that the hijackers espoused the Kashmir cause disappeared when their demands became known: India's release of extremist Pakistani cleric Maulana Masood Azhar and thirty-six other self-proclaimed mujahids for Kashmir from jail, and payment of a $200-million ransom.

What Jaswant Singh, who led the Indian team of negotiators, called a "terrible crime against humanity" finally ended on 31 December. A plane from Delhi brought Azhar and two members of his Harkat ul-Mujahedeen group to Kandahar and returned with the 155 remaining passengers and crew members on Indian Airlines Flight 814. The Taliban publicly gave the three freed prisoners and the five hijackers ten hours to leave Afghanistan. Vajpayee, sharply criticized by many Indians for compromising, asserted that the hijacking was "an integral part of a Pakistan-backed campaign of terrorism." Jaswant Singh said India had "conclusive proof" from four alleged accomplices arrested in Bombay that the five hijackers were supported by Pakistan. Azhar declared upon reaching Karachi: "Death to India! Death to the United States!"

The two democracies had not been linked before in this bloodthirsty manner, reminiscent of the fanatical slogans of Iran's Muslim militants. But they came to assess blame for the hijacking in much the same way, as they had agreed on who was responsible for the Kargil fighting. In the official U.S. view, the Pakistani army backed the terrorist group responsible for the hijacking – a group close to notorious anti-U.S. terrorist Osama bin Laden. Soon after the prolonged incident, Musharraf rejected a request by three visiting U.S. officials to ban Harkat ul-Mujahedeen and flew off to China.

In early 2000, India sharply increased its military budget again, to $13.5 billion, and its army engaged in war games in Rajasthan near Pakistan. Vajpayee pointedly suggested where the mindset of the generals in Rawalpindi and Islamabad was ultimately leading: "Pakistan is threatening a nuclear war, but do they even know what it means? They think they will drop one bomb and they'll win and we'll lose. This won't happen."

On 19 March, President Clinton arrived in the Subcontinent, the region he and other Westerners were calling "the world's most dangerous place."

The United States and India still disagreed on the nuclear question, and nuclear arms certainly made South Asia dangerous. But Kargil, the coup in Pakistan, and the hijacking had brought Washington and Delhi closer together than ever before.

For weeks, the biggest question hanging over Clinton's repeatedly postponed trip had been whether he would visit Pakistan at all. The Indian government had lobbied strongly against lending respectability to what it considered a terrorist regime. The Pakistani government had laboured frantically to salvage a smidgeon of the equivalence that the United States had granted the two countries for decades. Clinton had finally said on 7 March he would visit Pakistan for "a few hours" after spending five days in India and one day in Bangladesh. On 20 March, the day after his arrival in Delhi, forty to fifty gunmen killed thirty-five men in cold blood in Chati Singhpura Mattan, a Sikh village sixty-five kilometres south of Srinagar in Kashmir. The gunmen remained anonymous, so Clinton could not be specific in joining Vajpayee in condemning this atrocity. But there was little question that the massacre of innocent people was Pakistan's answer to the emerging similarity of views between the United States and India. The president did not cross Islamabad off his itinerary but he was compelled to abandon his wish – and the fervent Pakistani desire – that he mediate between India and Pakistan on the Kashmir question.

When Clinton addressed Parliament in Delhi, he declared: "India and America are natural allies." But members were silent when he called on India to renounce nuclear weapons. They applauded when, in recognition of Vajpayee's insistence on a "credible minimum nuclear deterrent," he added that "only India can determine its own interests." Having given up on mediating on Kashmir, he emphasized that the line of control must be respected – a blunt message to Pakistan. At a state dinner, India's President Narayanan directed a message to Clinton: Characterizations of the Subcontinent as the "most dangerous place" were "alarmist" and encouraged terrorists.

But the declaration called "U.S.-India Relations: A Vision for the Twenty-first Century," signed by Clinton and Vajpayee on 21 March, signalled a historic change in the way the most powerful democracy and the most populous democracy interact with each other on the broad stage of Asia and the Pacific. Considering India's warm ties with the Soviet Union during the Cold War, the Hindu nationalists' old dream of India as a superpower on its own, past U.S. dismissal of India as no more than an equal of Pakistan, and Clinton's discredited but not disavowed bid in June 1998 for a "strategic partnership" with China, the declaration's careful words and clear intent twenty-one months later were nothing short of extraordinary:

"In the new century, India and the United States will be partners in peace, with a common interest in and complementary responsibility for ensuring regional and international security. We will engage in regular consultations on, and work together for, strategic stability in Asia and beyond."

The Vision Statement brought together and went beyond India's new interest in "collective engagement" and America's commitment from Wilson to Reagan to making the world safe for democracy. It noted differences on nuclear weapons but stressed the "common goal" of preventing their proliferation. It even dared to venture that the two nations were "allies" in a worldwide cause: "The true measure of our strength lies in the ability of our people to shape their destiny and to realize their aspirations for a better life. That is why the United States and India are and will be allies in the cause of democracy. We will share our experience in nurturing and strengthening democratic institutions the world over and fighting the challenge to world order from forces such as terrorism."

Finally, the two leaders observed: "For India and the United States, this is a day of new beginnings. We have before us for the first time in fifty years the possibility to realize the full potential of our relationship."

American media paid much more attention to Clinton and his daughter Chelsea gazing at the Taj Mahal in Agra. But images can be as revealing as words. Outside Jaipur, the president revived an old image of India by stalking and finding two Bengal tigers, and cultivated a new image by engaging in a dialogue with village women in colourful dress and rejecting the notion, in answer to a question from one of them, that India is backward. In Hyderabad, he acknowledged the most powerful new symbol of India: its high-tech industry. In Bombay, he visited the stock exchange symbolizing India's growing private enterprise. Even allowing for Clinton's wide-ranging search for a positive presidential legacy – and the apparent contradiction between his strategic alliance with India and strategic partnership with China – his visit to India had a greater impact than those of the U.S. presidents who had gone before him: Eisenhower, Nixon, and Carter.

Now came Clinton's passage to Pakistan. At the insistence of Secret Service agents fearful of a terrorist attack, he took it in a second, smaller plane from Delhi after a decoy Air Force One had landed at Islamabad. This deception also was a powerful symbol – of the new distrustful relationship between the United States and its erstwhile ally Pakistan.

During six hours in the drab capital, Clinton urged General Musharraf and, in a TV address, the Pakistani people to show restraint on Kashmir, to give up nuclear weapons, and to adopt democracy. He delivered one of his best lines anywhere in rejecting armed violation of the line of control as a ploy to provoke talks on Kashmir: "This era does not reward people who struggle in vain to redraw borders with blood." Completing a 180-degree turn on possible U.S. intervention in the Kashmir dispute, he commented: "I'm not going to be dragged into something [like] that." Once Clinton had left Pakistan on Air Force One, Musharraf claimed he and the president had gotten along well. But the general had offered no assurances to Clinton on any of the dangers hanging over South Asia.

Instead, Pakistan persisted on its perilous path despite the sea change in the Subcontinent. There was no attempt at large-scale infiltration of Indian-held Kashmir in the spring and summer of 2000 but Pakistani-backed terrorists and Indian security forces continued to kill in Kashmir, with the toll reaching more than 30,000 over eleven years. Musharraf underlined the military's indefinite hold on political power by making sure Nawaz Sharif, the prime minister he had overthrown and jailed, was convicted – on a charge of attempting to hijack the plane the army commander had returned on to take control of the country! And the generals resorted to a devious new twist when in April India showed a willingness for a Kashmir settlement by freeing some prisoners and offering to talk with the All-Party Hurriyat Conference, the umbrella group for a number of Kashmiri Muslim organizations.

The Hurriyat rejected talks without Pakistan, which India refused to include until terrorism in Kashmir ceased. In June, the National Conference government of Kashmir led by Premier Farook Abdullah unexpectedly entered the picture by pushing through a legislative resolution calling for restoration of Kashmir's special constitutional autonomy before Sheikh Mohammad Abdullah's first arrest in 1953. The BJP-led cabinet in Delhi rejected this proposal because it conflicted with its own peace plan, aimed at granting autonomy only as a final concession for Kashmiri acceptance of Indian rule. Nevertheless, for the first time in a long time there were moves toward a peaceful solution of the fifty-three-year-old Kashmir question.

In late July, Hizbul Mujahedeen, a major Kashmiri militant group close to Pakistan and accounting for perhaps 1,000 of the 2,500 guerrillas in Kashmir, declared a three-month ceasefire and willingness to talk with India. On 2 August, in apparent protest against this ostensible break in ranks, four terrorist attacks in Kashmir resulted in 102 deaths, and Vajpayee blamed Pakistan. But the next day Hizbul representatives sat down with Indian officials, encouraging the belief that Pakistan finally was responding to Clinton's entreaties. Just five days later, however, and following a raid on an Indian army base in Kashmir, Hizbul suddenly pulled out of the talks and ended its ceasefire, citing India's insistence that they be held within the Indian constitutional framework and without Pakistanis. Two days after that, on 10 August, a decoy bomb exploded in Srinagar. When this drew a crowd to the scene, a second, bigger bomb went off, killing nine people. Hizbul Mujahedeen claimed responsibility. There was good reason to believe that the whole sequence of ultimately tragic events was the Pakistani military's way – after the Kargil fiasco and the Indian Airlines hijacking – of jabbing its finger in Vajpayee's eye, and in Clinton's.

More people died in violence in the Vale leading up to India's Independence Day, 15 August, and after it. Indian troops and police still carried out excesses against civilians. India blamed Pakistan for terrorism calculated to prevent or undermine progress toward peace. But the Hindu nationalist government in Delhi continued to seek talks with moderate Kashmiris. In late November, India announced a unilateral cessation of military operations in the Vale during the Muslim holy month of Ramadan. Militant groups and Pakistan immediately rejected this gesture. But then signs of a will toward peace started to appear in several weary quarters if only because, in each, continued violence was less and less sustainable.

Kashmiri Muslims in the Hurriyat Conference, as opposed to outsiders, cautiously welcomed Vajpayee's move. In late December, India said it would extend its unilateral ceasefire for another month. This was followed by an attack on the Red Fort in Delhi by members of a pro-Pakistani militant group that killed three people – and by Pakistan's statement it would pull back its troops "partially" from the line of control. If Pakistan was sending mixed signals on Kashmir as usual, the ruling military's weakness at home was exposed by General Musharraf's decision to exile overthrown Prime Minister Sharif to Saudi Arabia, a surprise move that defused the growing unity among the country's civilian opposition parties. In India, outwardly unrelated surprises suggested a master plan on the part of the shrewd BJP prime minister. Vajpayee indicated he sought separate talks with Pakistan and with Kashmiri Muslims. At the same time, he used the eighth anniversary of the destruction of the Ayodhya Mosque on 6 December to encourage the building of a long-controversial and legally barred Hindu temple on the site. This caused an uproar among Indian opposition parties and some BJP coalition partners. But Vajpayee was willing to risk limited damage to his moderate image by appealing to Hindu militants on the temple issue and thereby softening their opposition to a Kashmir settlement. He quickly made clear that he remained uncommitted to an actual building of the temple. Implicitly, he made equally clear that he was committed to finding a way out of the Kashmir morass.

A Kashmir solution depends partly on Pakistani generals, especially after the late 2001 attacks on Parliament in Delhi and the Kashmir legislature in Srinagar by what India said were Islamic terrorists based in Pakistan and linked to the army's intelligence branch. One of the five men who assaulted the Parliament building had been one of the five hijackers of the Indian Airlines plane flying out of Katmandu one year earlier. The leader of one of the two militant groups that India alleged was behind the attack was none other than Maulana Masood Azhar, the firebrand cleric who had been released from an Indian jail in exchange for the hijackers' release of the plane and passengers at the U.S.-built Kandahar airport, later a major base in the war against terrorists in Afghanistan. Also freed in the deal following the hijacking was Ahmed Omar Sheikh, who was later convicted and sentenced to die by a Pakistani judge for the January 2002 kidnapping in Karachi and brutal murder of Daniel Pearl, the South Asia correspondent of *The Wall Street Journal.*

When Vajpayee ended the Kashmir ceasefires that had lasted six months but had not stopped the violence, he invited Musharraf to Agra in July 2001. But the general played to the media at the summit, the two leaders could not even agree on how to approach the Kashmir issue, and anti-Indian terrorism increased. Pakistani generals apparently refused to read the writing on the wall: pursuit of a terrorist policy was leading to a collapse of what was left of their country. Even when they ostensibly joined the anti-terrorist war in Afghanistan after the attacks of 11 September 2001, they were bitter at not getting the political and military rewards they wanted from the United States, and continued on the self-destructive path of exploiting Kashmir to prop up Pakistan.

But the chance of an eventual breakthrough on Kashmir that both predominantly Hindu India and Kashmiri Muslims could grudgingly accept was likely to increase, not decrease, the more Pakistan distanced itself from civilized dialogue and immersed itself in its own failures. Following an election in Indian-held Kashmir in September-October 2002 that was widely deemed "free and fair," Vajpayee drew down India's military buildup on its borders with Pakistan. With no coercion of Kashmiris to go to the polls as in the past, and a relatively high turnout, voters rejected Farook Abdullah's bid to bring the National Conference back to power. The new and moderate People's Democratic Party formed a coalition government with the support of the Congress Party, and pledged to work toward a peaceful settlement of the Kashmir question. The response of Islamic terrorists based in Pakistan was to invade two Hindu temples in Jammu, Kashmir's winter capital, on 25 November, killing fourteen people and wounding more than forty. In December radical cleric Maulana Masood Azhar was released from house arrest in Pakistan after a brief detention, and Muslim terrorists killed a newly elected Kashmiri legislator, and three young Kashmiri women for the alleged crime of not wearing a veil. Vajpayee had plainly signalled that India would accept as a permanent boundary the line of control dividing the parts of Kashmir held by

India and Pakistan, and would offer meaningful autonomy to Kashmiris –
but only if India's sovereignty over its part, including the Vale, was recognized, and if terrorism was effectively halted or brought under control.

In Washington during the spring and summer of 2000, four well-publicized
leaks of classified conclusions reached by U.S. intelligence underscored the
Subcontinent's relevance for Americans. Two of the leaks appeared calcu-
lated to reinforce doubts in many quarters about the wisdom of the United
States building an anti-missile defence strongly opposed by China and
Russia, and might have come from the White House to justify President
Clinton's 1 September announcement that he would not decide about going
ahead, thereby opening a window of vulnerability to "rogue" missiles.
Whatever the motives of the anonymous sources and the level of accuracy
of the conclusions they disclosed, the classified reports cogently indicated
the growing geostrategic importance of the Subcontinent to all Eurasia and
the Pacific.

   The first leak reported an assessment that U.S. building of an anti-missile defence system would ignite an arms race involving first China, then
India, and next Pakistan. The second leak reported a conclusion that
China was continuing to help Pakistan in the development of long-range
missiles. The third leak claimed that Clinton's warning in Delhi about
nuclear weapons had sprung from an assessment that the chance of a
nuclear war between India and Pakistan had become as high as fifty-fifty
during the Kargil fighting, an estimate many experts would dismiss as
highly exaggerated or even imaginary. The fourth leak, related to the first
and to India's security, reported an assessment that going ahead with a
U.S. anti-missile defence system would prompt China to multiply its number of nuclear weapons by ten, and Russia to put multiple warheads on its
nuclear missiles.

   Atal Bihari Vajpayee came to Washington himself in mid-December
2000, climaxing nearly two weeks in the United States. He suffered the
whole time from persistent pain in an osteoarthritic left knee that was
replaced in Delhi the following month by an Indian-American physician;
later Vajpayee's right knee was also replaced.

   He had crossed verbal swords with Pakistan's Musharraf over Kashmir
and terrorism at the "millennium summit" of the United Nations General
Assembly in New York City. He had addressed the Asia Society, and Indian-American business groups enlisted in India's economic growth and liberalization. He was undoubtedly aware of the leaked intelligence estimates
and how China, intent on producing more nuclear missiles in any case,
might benefit from U.S. indecision and a delay on anti-missile defence. He
met President Clinton, addressed a joint session of the U.S. Congress, and

talked with presidential candidates George W. Bush and Al Gore, all in accordance with the terms of the new Indo-U.S. relationship defined in Delhi six months earlier. In Vajpayee's words then, he moved "beyond a mere intersection of interests to a focusing of our vision." The Indian leader's visit consolidated this historic relationship and pointed it in new directions. But American media paid as little attention to Vajpayee's presence as they had to the Clinton-Vajpayee Vision Statement in March 2000.

On 24 September, before speaking to Congress, the prime minister made probably the most optimistic prediction in years about India's economy. Calling on American "captains of industry" to join in the new "alliance" between the two democracies through investment, he envisioned India's achieving a 9 per cent annual growth rate in the foreseeable future, doubling GNP in ten years.

Senators and Congressmen listened carefully as Vajpayee appealed for American recognition of the dual threats to India from China and Pakistan. He asserted that Pakistani-sponsored terrorism amounted to a "jihad." His blunt words for the Chinese menace in Asia were clearly meant to fall on sympathetic ears: "We do not want the domination of some to crowd out the space for others."

The Hindu nationalist prime minister did more than ask for an "understanding of India's nuclear arms program and security concerns," as his speech was summed up in a two-line photo caption in *The New York Times*. He plainly aimed for a developing alliance between the United States and India against common dangers – the "collective engagement" that had quickly gone from cryptic theory to partial fact.

At the White House on 15 September, both Clinton and Vajpayee were eager to turn what the president called "our common ground" toward the future. Acutely aware that his presidency would end in four months, Clinton said: "It is inconceivable to me that we can build the kind of world we want over the next ten or twenty years unless there is a very strong partnership between the United States and India." Conscious of pressing issues, the prime minister pointed out: "This is a time of new hope and new opportunities in Indo-American ties."

The two leaders talked mainly about regional security. A joint statement afterward, and comments by U.S. officials, including Vice President Gore, reflected advances in some areas and remaining differences in others.

India and the United States pledged to continue their dialogue on nuclear questions and "defense posture" – taken to mean restraint in missile deployment – and the Clinton administration did not publicly criticize India for not going along with a ban on producing fissile material. It was left to Gore to tell Vajpayee after a State Department luncheon that if he were elected president he would make ratification of the Comprehensive

Test Ban Treaty his first foreign-policy priority in Congress, and to urge India to go beyond its voluntary moratorium to formal acceptance. It was not known if this subject had come up earlier when Vajpayee telephoned Bush, who opposed the treaty in its present form as unduly restricting the United States. But Gore, like Bush's foreign-policy advisers, made clear as host of the luncheon for Vajpayee that he was committed to the new relationship with India: "As the world's two leading democracies, we bear a special responsibility to take the lead in meeting the challenges that all democracies face."

Continuing reservations about India as a nuclear power prevented Clinton from fully accepting India as a member of the nuclear club. He also resisted Vajpayee's entreaty to brand Pakistan as a terrorist state, and refused to lift all remaining sanctions on India as well as Pakistan despite House and Senate resolutions calling for their removal. But to his credit Clinton extended U.S. recognition to India as the pre-eminent power in South Asia. The word "tilt," as in toward Pakistan, became archaic in 2000 in both Washington and Delhi.

The joint statement reiterated the U.S. refusal to intervene in the Kashmir dispute, and opposition to the use of violence and terrorism to force talks: "Tensions in South Asia can only be resolved by the nations of South Asia and by peaceful means." Moreover, the United States and India agreed to hold dialogues on Afghanistan and counter-terrorism as well as United Nations peacekeeping. These steps committed the two democracies to fighting terrorism linked to Pakistan, and identified the Taliban rulers of Afghanistan, armed and supported by Pakistan, as a destabilizing force in the region.

A *New York Times* lead editorial, four days after Vajpayee's departure and the day after the U.S. Senate voted to confer permanent trade benefits on China, recognized the "far-reaching ramifications for all of Asia, including China" in Clinton's "embracing India and distancing the United States from Pakistan's military government." It bestowed qualified approval, noting India had "growing importance" and was "a natural American ally on many issues." But, under the inappropriate and misleading headline "A 'Tilt' Toward India," the editorial cautioned Washington not to "incite feelings of distrust" in Pakistan and China by befriending India, and urged Vajpayee to avoid causing "anxiety in Beijing" by failing to practise greater nuclear restraint. Apart from not giving up the discarded idea of U.S. mediation on Kashmir, which would revive the dangerous myth of India-Pakistan equality, the *Times* appeared to accept democratic India as a major player in Asia only on the condition that dictatorial China come first in U.S. calculations.

On assuming the presidency, George W. Bush lost no time in giving greater substance to the new relationship between the United States and India put in place by his predecessor. Months before 11 September 2001, officials from Bush and Vajpayee on down started to explore opportunities for close political, economic, and military co-operation. They began building toward a democratic coalition of Asia-Pacific countries against China's ambitions in the first years of the new century.

This enhanced relationship did not change with 9/11 despite the U.S. need to bring Pakistan onside in the war against international terrorism, and the strains this placed on new U.S. relations with India. When Bush met Vajpayee at the White House on 9 November, his commitment of the United States to a "fundamentally different relationship with India" signalled that he fully accepted India as a responsible nuclear power. His expressed determination at the same time to go after those who harbour terrorists as well as terrorists themselves put the United States and India in the same camp – as the president put it, "Terrorism is terrorism." With the terrorist assault on India's Parliament on 13 December, the Bush administration moved closer and closer to the Hindu nationalist government in demanding that General Musharraf stop terrorist incursions into Indian-held Kashmir and India itself. By the summer of 2002, the Indian and U.S. messages to Pakistan were virtually indistinguishable, although the United States backed up its point by sounding alarms about an India-Pakistan nuclear exchange if the danger of war was not averted.

Americans and Indians not only realize they must learn to get along with each other, something they found hard to do for too many years despite their common commitment to democracy, but together have started to "fight freedom's fight," in Bush's words, on the battlefield pitting civilized nations against ruthless terrorists. The new foreign policy framed by Vajpayee and Jaswant Singh looks not to a conventional or immediate military alliance with the United States and other Asian and Western powers but to "collective engagement" by "allies in the cause of democracy" for the purpose of restraining China in the coming years and, after 9/11 and 12/13, terrorists for as long as it takes.

In his interview with me in mid-1999, Singh did not spell out how this might work in practice. As a realist, he contemplated India and America engaging in strategic co-operation "not emotionally but intellectually." Yet the real challenges thrown up by terrorism now and likely by China soon demand heartfelt as well as rational responses.

The U.S. response to the need for a positive relationship with India also started to emerge in mid-1999. Mathew Daley, then the State Department's senior South Asia adviser, openly consigned to the past "attempts to

impose intellectual constructs such as balance or even-handedness on
American foreign policy toward India and Pakistan."

Singling out the nuclear dialogue between Singh and Strobe Talbott,
Clinton's deputy secretary of state, as "the most comprehensive and intensive exchange of its type in the history of bilateral relations," Daley said the
two countries probably had never had a greater "appreciation and even
sympathy" for each other's views. The contrast with the decades of the
Nehru-Gandhi dynasty did not have to be spelled out. But Daley added
that the new government in India would need to come to a "new strategic
consensus" on China. So would the new U.S. government that took office
on 20 January 2001. With Bush, it is not possible to say, as Clinton officials said at the time of Vajpayee's visit to Washington, that the United
States will not pursue a zero-sum game on China, and India will have to
pursue its own relations with Beijing. The world's only superpower and
South Asia's only major power have acknowledged that they have common
strategic interests as well as common democratic values – interests and values that came into play as early as India's Himalayan war with China in
1962.

For a new overall Indian consensus and a new American consensus to fit
together and join those of like-minded nations, the United States and India
will have to continue building mutual trust. Exceptions like the Singh-
Talbott talks and Vajpayee's talks with Clinton and later Bush will need
to become the rule. Nuclear weapons will be part of a broader dialogue
within a special relationship that in time can turn into a true alliance for
democracy. So will proper regard for neighbours, economic liberalization
and growth, and, above all, respect for the dignity and democratic rights of
individual human beings.

India's overwhelming humanity hit worldwide on 26 January 2001 and
the days following, and again thirteen months later on 27 February 2002
and the days following. The focus of attention each time was the western state of Gujarat, the home of Mahatma Gandhi. But India's contradictions were also at work. The first time, a growing spirit of kindness
and democracy became evident. A year later, a familiar spirit of mean-
ness and intolerance was obvious. It was as if opposite impulses were
competing in the Indian psyche, each struggling to make its mark on
Indian politics.

Minutes before India's stirring Republic Day parade started in New
Delhi on the morning of 26 January 2001, the worst earthquake in independent India's history struck Gujarat. Words and pictures describing a
tragedy that claimed up to 20,000 lives, and an initially inadequate

response, were not surprising. But there was also an unexpected message of hope amidst the chaos in reports of Indians helping one another more than they had in other disasters.

In the remote semi-desert area of Kutch hit hardest by the 7.9 earthquake, whose epicentre was east of the city of Bhuj, whole villages collapsed and no help came for hours or even days. In the modern city of Ahmadabad farther to the east, new, badly-constructed buildings fell while older buildings remained standing. Without a national organization to respond to disasters of this scope, the Indian government threw past pride and policy out the window and asked foreign governments and relief agencies for assistance.

But thousands of Indian troops – not those who marched in the Republic Day parade but many stationed near the border with Pakistan – were quickly on the scene to dig through the rubble and search for survivors. Some bureaucrats, active and retired, threw themselves tirelessly into rescue and relief operations. Most significant, tens of thousands of middle-class Indians – many doctors but also businessmen, shopkeepers, and accountants – travelled voluntarily on their own from Ahmadabad and other cities to lend a helping hand to poor, numbed, homeless villagers. And the BJP government in opening India to the world looked outward, not inward.

"This is the time for people to rally around and fight a calamity which has overtaken us," said Vajpayee. People did. The prime minister spoke to President Bush about the emergency, and thanked General Musharraf for a planeload of Pakistani relief supplies. His government immediately imposed a 2 per cent surcharge on all personal and corporate income to help pay for aid to stricken Indians no matter what their religion or caste, ethnicity or economic status.

In the early morning of 27 February 2002, as the Sabarmati Express pulled out of the station at Godhra in Gujarat, carrying 2,500 chanting Hindus eager to help build a temple on the site of the demolished mosque in Ayodhya far to the east, more than 500 Muslims attacked the train with stones and kerosene. When the flames died away, 58 bodies were found, most of them those of women and children. Vajpayee quickly called on militant Hindus not to retaliate. But the conditions for primitive Hindu-Muslim violence were too classic to prevent retaliation and revenge.

Hundreds of Muslims died in the coming days as extremists encouraged by the World Hindu Council attacked huts and shops belonging to poor people in cities and villages across much of Gujarat. As clashes sputtered on into May, the death toll rose above 1,000, mostly Muslims, and 10,000 Muslims were forced to live in camps. It was the worst communal violence in India since the aftermath of the destruction of the Ayodhya mosque by Hindu fanatics in 1992. It was the worst thing to happen in India in the four years since Hindu nationalists had come to power in 1998.

Army troops sent in by the central government restored order. But witnesses said police under the BJP state government headed by Narendra Modi had stood by as Muslims were killed. It remained unclear why minority Muslims, although they made up roughly half of Godhra's population, had carried out an organized assault on the train when they must have known what to expect next. One explanation was that Hindu pilgrims had taunted Muslim vendors at the railway station. Another was that Pakistani agents had been behind the attack on the train with the aim of embarrassing India and weakening its BJP-led government, but India did not make any such official allegation.

It would be cynical to say there was good news in the sudden explosion of communal hatred. But the violence did not spread beyond Gujarat, which has a long history of religious clashes. And Vajpayee and Home Minister Lal Krishna Advani opposed more strongly than ever the actual building of a temple at Ayodhya. There was no persuasive reason, in short, to believe that the peaceful coexistence of India's many religious groups nationwide was in jeopardy under BJP rule, or that the BJP was abandoning its politically sound moderate policies to return to Hindu revivalism.

In a bid to mollify the BJP's popular Hindu base, Vajpayee did ask publicly, alluding to lawless Muslims: "Who started the fire?" But at the same time he excoriated extremist Hindus: "Have we forgotten our human qualities? ... Madness cannot be answered by [worse] violence." Advani, who had helped lead the Ayodhya movement culminating in the destruction of the mosque, declared: "We will not allow 1992 to be repeated." Both leaders ruled out the building of a temple without Supreme Court and Muslim approval. Fitting action to word, the government put such a large security force into Ayodhya on 15 March that the World Hindu Council could not perform a scheduled ceremony symbolizing a start of construction.

On 1 May, following a fifteen-hour debate, the Lok Sabha defeated by a vote of 276 to 182, with 8 abstentions, an opposition motion to censure the BJP-led government for not dismissing Chief Minister Modi for the violence in Gujarat. It was a decisive victory for the badly bruised Hindu nationalists. But they still needed to mend political alliances and build new ones.

Andhra MPs from Telegu Desam, the BJP's largest coalition partner, walked out of the Lok Sabha before the vote, other Alliance members criticized the Hindu nationalists, and one minister resigned. Congress leader Sonia Gandhi accused "saffron parties," meaning the Hindu nationalists, of favouring "politics of hatred." Although the Congress was still averse to a coalition with other parties, it saw a chance for a national comeback by building on its control of half of India's states and territories, including Delhi most recently. In an important election in the most populous state of Uttar Pradesh, the Congress had remained a minor party but the BJP had done no better than win junior partnership in another government headed by the dalit party of the BJP's former nemesis Mayawati. Following Gujarat's Hindu-Muslim riots, the first political test was an early state election, due after Modi voluntarily resigned as chief minister in July. Before it could take place, Muslim gunmen killed thirty people at a Hindu temple complex in the state capital of Gandhinagar on 24 September in what appeared to be an attempt to provoke renewed religious carnage. This time Advani blamed Pakistan. But there was no Hindu counter-violence, which Vajpayee and Advani had condemned before it could start.

In the December 2002 Gujarat election, the BJP won a landslide victory, capturing 126 legislative seats to only 51 for the Congress. This stopped talk of the Hindu nationalists losing power nationally in a 2004 parliamentary election and started talk of the BJP's taking a big step toward depriving India of its secularism. Neither line of talk was rooted in Indian political reality. India did not "lurch sharply to the right," as *The Guardian* of Britain reported, nor was the democratic outcome a reflection of "fear and terror," as the stunned Congress claimed. With a high voter turnout of 63 per cent, predominantly Hindu Gujaratis opted for stability in a state whose politics had changed since the days of Gandhian idealism. An outspoken defender of Hindutva, Chief Minister Modi insisted that the extent of communal violence had been greatly exaggerated. Whether or not he was right, India had become much too complex politically to make sweeping generalizations about its direction on the strength of the results of one election in one state.

The BJP was still safely ahead of other political forces both in dealing with unforeseen exigencies and preparing for the next parliamentary election due by September-October 2004, when it would seek its third straight national mandate. Some of its moves were predictable but no less effective. Some were surprises and caught off guard its opponents, whose record since the elections of 1998 and 1999 was characterized mainly by obstructionism and unruly conduct in Parliament, sometimes going on for days, whenever there was a chance of making the government look bad.

On the world stage, and particularly in developing India's strategic alliance with the United States, the ruling coalition on one hand took a popular tough stance against Pakistan-based terrorism. On the other hand, it appeared reasonable and responsible in not threatening war over every terrorist incident. Keeping this balance was especially difficult during and after the September–October 2002 Kashmir election, which Pakistan

crudely tried to disrupt despite Western pressures. During two months, up
to and including polling days, Muslim terrorists who had crossed into Indian-
held Kashmir were responsible for nearly 500 deaths, and for intimidating
many Kashmiris in cities into not voting. But overall turnout was still 44
per cent of eligible voters – significantly higher than in elections in Pakistan
at the same time manipulated by Musharraf to ensure continued military
control. And the successful election in India's share of Kashmir, resulting
in a loss by the National Conference of its legislative majority and the
formation of a coalition government, "showed the strength of India's
democracy," in Vajpayee's words, making more likely an eventual political
settlement along the lines he envisioned.

Despite India's new ties with the United States and strong stand against
terrorism, the BJP-led coalition government formally opposed the U.S.-led
attack on Iraq in March–April 2003 to banish the Saddam Hussein regime.
In April and May, Vajpayee once more gave peace a chance soon after terrorists executed twenty-four Kashmiri Hindu villagers, including eleven
women and two children. He gave a speech in Srinagar extending "the hand
of friendship again" to Pakistan, then announced in the Lok Sabha that
India would re-establish full diplomatic ties and air service cut off when Parliament was attacked in December 2001. But he added: "This is the last time
I will be making [such] an attempt." At seventy-eight, Vajpayee seemed to
be emulating Nehru in 1964 in seeking a Kashmir solution. He appeared
confident he would succeed. He (and the United States) not only put Pakistan on the defensive – it would have to give up its claim to the Vale if it
wanted peace – but Vajpayee also planned to visit China in mid-2003,
although a Himalayan border settlement with Beijing was highly unlikely.

In the world of India in the first few years of the twenty-first century, the
BJP performed another balancing act: satisfying secularists and Hindu
nationalists at the same time. Apart from working toward a Kashmir solution without giving up India's vital stake in Kashmir, it did what was necessary to keep the National Democratic Alliance together and simultaneously encouraged what Advani called "enlightened cultural nationalism."
With the religiously sensitive issue that wouldn't go away, this meant
blocking temple-building at Ayodhya in fact and welcoming it in principle.

Individual personalities as well as policies came into BJP strategy in
important ways. On 30 June 2002, Vajpayee announced cabinet changes
that pointed the way to his retirement, Advani's taking over again as party
leader and therefore prime minister if the party remained in power, and
more sweeping economic reforms.

The prime minister, seventy-seven then and in gradually fading health,
formally named Advani, seventy-four, deputy prime minister as well as
home minister. While some looked on Advani as simply a hardliner, his

promotion signalled that he was accepted by the BJP's coalition partners as the next head of the Alliance and wanted in that position by Hindu nationalists. The highly respected Vajpayee was expected to lead the party and coalition in the next election and retire soon after, although he could conceivably leave office sooner.

Apart from putting younger BJP leaders in organizing roles, he also switched the positions of Foreign Minister Jaswant Singh and Finance Minister Yashwant Sinha. The forthright, farseeing Singh would be missed as India's point man with the United States. But he had been the BJP's finance critic before going into international affairs, and as finance minister he would be in a position to make needed economic liberalization broader, deeper, and more politically beneficial. If Sinha, who had an uneven record as finance minister, proved too soft as foreign minister, Vajpayee's longtime national security adviser, Brajesh Mishra, could be counted on to stop any slide away from India's new informal alliance with the United States. When I met Sinha in Ottawa soon after, he blamed American media for not telling people what was really going on in the Subcontinent. But he told me that, like Jaswant Singh before him, he was cultivating close personal ties with the leading figures in the Bush administration.

But the biggest surprise had undercut opposition critics by summing up in one independent individual all that the BJP professed to be striving for: an economically developed, nuclear-armed, communally harmonious, and fully democratic India. The party nominated A.P.J. Abdul Kalam, a Muslim and a rocket scientist popularly revered as the father of the Indian nuclear bomb, to be president of India for the next five years.

On 18 July 2002, Kalam, seventy, had won nearly 90 per cent of the weighted votes cast by members of Parliament and state legislatures, becoming the third Muslim president of India one week later. Born into a poor Tamil family living at the extreme southern tip of India, he had become a scientist at Indian schools and had developed five different missiles to stand up against Chinese and Pakistani missiles. A poet, vegetarian, and bachelor, he had attracted a wide following not only for his technological achievement but also for his eloquently expressed belief in India's potential. Jawaharlal Nehru also had been a believer in the transforming ability of modern technology. But Kalam linked technology to nationalism and ordinary Indians: "Nations consist of people," he wrote in his latest book. "And with their effort, a nation can accomplish all it could ever want."

The Hindu nationalists, challenged to renew their credentials to govern India, hardly could have made a more brilliant political move than choosing Kalam to be constitutional head of state. His election, and his acceptance, also amounted to a common reaffirmation of faith in the future of more than one billion Indians.

22

No Mahatma to Wait For

Shortly before midnight of 14–15 August 1997, Jawaharlal Nehru's voice again magically echoed through the great hall adjoining India's houses of Parliament in New Delhi. As if his words were frozen in time, the Kashmiri Brahmin who was sure of becoming the first prime minister still insisted that "at the stroke of the midnight hour," India would "very substantially" keep "a tryst with destiny" made "long years ago." Despite this moving flashback and worldwide recollections of his historic address at the same time in 1947, memories of fifty years of independence were bittersweet at best for Indians.

Apart from Nehru's paying homage to Mahatma Gandhi's ambition "to wipe every tear from every eye," when a small softness crept into his voice, the recorded words sounded more stiff than spontaneous, more British than Indian. Fifty long years after he delivered them live a few minutes before midnight, the dawn had yet to come to India. Or to Pakistan and Bangladesh, the results of two bloody partitions of once undivided British India. In a sense, time really had stood still. Poverty and hatred, violence and corruption still stalked the Subcontinent. A half-century's tragically wasted decades mocked Nehru's elegant phrases.

India's new president, Kocheril Raman Narayanan, citing his country's achievements on the fiftieth anniversary of its independence, acknowledged the "deterioration" of Indian society caused by "corruption, communalism, casteism, and criminalization of politics." After a successful career as a left-leaning diplomat and as vice-president, Narayanan had been the first Hindu dalit or former untouchable chosen for the presidency, a potentially powerful position the Nehrus had repeatedly belittled or abused for their own political purposes. At almost the same time he received that honour less than one month before what Indians called their "golden jubilee," police in Bombay shot dead ten dalit demonstrators.

Most of the Subcontinent's leaders in the past fifty years – in India, Nehru, his daughter Indira Gandhi, and her son Rajiv over thirty-seven of those years – had failed the Subcontinent's peoples. Not Mohandas K. Gandhi, who had the right ideas about persuading individuals to subordinate their prejudices, come together peacefully, and build from the village up. The dalit and low-caste Hindus who have contended in recent years that the Mahatma's approach was too broad are misguided, although understandably so considering the discrimination they have endured.

But even if he had lived beyond 30 January 1948, when a Brahmin's bullets felled him less than six months after independence, he would have had little influence on free India's direction. He had not been able to stop the profoundly foolish division of colonial India, after all, or to dissolve the sectarian venom behind partition and then his assassination. Nor, despite the respect Nehru professed for Gandhi, could he prevent the permit-licence raj that deadened Indian creativity, limited productivity, and undercut democracy.

In any case, there are no more mahatmas. There is no use waiting for a new mahatma to appear. There have been too many tears and heartbreaks, and there will be many more. There cannot be any more failures. After the first fifty years plus, it is up to the peoples of the Subcontinent – the hungry majorities, hungry for input into building their nations as well as bread – to shape their future. They number 1.3 billion, as many as live in China. Only the more than one billion Indians in all their unbelievable diversity can take the lead. They can define an India that brings about conflict, breakdown, and destruction within the country and the region. Or they can create an India that builds a peaceful, increasingly prosperous, and steadily democratic order.

The Indian people have made their choice. It is not simplistic to say they have opted for freedom, economic growth, and stability. But in the years ahead they will need to work hard to make a free society much more equitable than it has been during the first fifty years and beyond. This is not an easy thing to do, particularly when Pakistani generals and terrorists obsessed with their country's inferiority always wait in ambush, and the threatening colossus of China looms constantly to the north.

In two ways, what will happen in the coming decades and all that has happened in post-colonial India and the Subcontinent in the decades that cannot be taken back make up The Greater Game.

The Great Game the British Raj played with imperial Russia had to do with control of undivided India. Events in independent India and its neighbours have a major impact on the rest of Asia and therefore the rest of the world. It is impossible to cut off the Subcontinent from what Americans and other Westerners increasingly call Asia and the Pacific, including Japan and especially China. It is unwise to succumb to the temptation to do so.

The Great Game was about security and military matters. These remain important. But The Greater Game also embraces economic and political factors. Is a sense of desperation spreading among ordinary people, or a sense of well-being? Are they tired of trying to make democracy work, or are they finally beginning to get responsive, caring regimes? These questions are crucial in South Asia and East Asia alike. The answers will go far to determine whether and how Americans relate to all Asians.

Although few Westerners in recent years have compared the two most populous countries of Asia and the world, India continues to race – perhaps not the best word but still instructive – against China as well as against destiny. Indian answers ultimately will stand against Chinese answers. Independent India started life as a democracy. Since October 1949, Communists have ruled China. Yet the progress and problems of each country are tied to a single dominant political party and a strong central bureaucracy.

The Congress Party of the Mahatma disappeared decades ago in India, and the Congress Party of the Nehrus collapsed almost completely in the last decade of the twentieth century. The Hindu nationalist Bharatiya Janata or Indian People's Party has taken its place as India's only coherent national party, and the only one effectively open at the national level to smaller parties representing pieces of the complex Indian mosaic. In China, the Communist Party of Mao Zedong, Zhou Enlai, and their heirs retains a jealous monopoly on political power. No organized force has yet appeared on the horizon to challenge it or take its place.

Both the Congress and Communist parties are thoroughly corrupt. But one is out of power and the other remains in power. The BJP is not free of corruption but its long-held abhorrence of dishonesty in government is one of the keys to its remaining in power. Authority in both India and China is devolving to state or provincial governments, because politicians and bureaucrats in Delhi and Beijing have failed to allow sufficient or balanced economic growth. India's new coalition politics demands a wide distribution of economic rewards and injects life into a federal system based on the rule of law. In China, there is only one party and it is supreme, and there is no effective rule of law. The risk in either system is national disunity possibly leading to national disintegration.

To avoid this chronically feared outcome in India, with all the repercussions it would have in South Asia and beyond, the nation is redefining the modern expression of itself in a way that is acceptable to hundreds of millions of people who are accustomed to casting ballots. They have done so in thirteen parliamentary elections, the last in September–October 1999, and several hundred state elections.

A redefinition is also increasingly required in China to head off internal conflict that would have an adverse impact on all Asia and the Pacific. Communist cadres and bullets may limit change or provoke it but approval will need to come from hundreds of millions of people who have no experience with democratic methods. The race between China and India is not over and may take unexpected turns.

Broadening the Indian context to all Asia and the Pacific is not easy for many Americans, Europeans, and Asians conditioned to regarding the Subcontinent in isolation. But the momentous events in India since the subdued celebration of the fiftieth anniversary of its independence in August 1997 have opened one door to a wide-ranging alliance of democratic nations – also difficult to imagine but essential to achieve. Other doors to the same goal have opened at the same time in Southeast Asia, Japan, and the United States.

If Southeast Asia does not fully recover from the economic devastation that hit it in mid-1997, if political paralysis continues to grip Japan, if the United States persists in kowtowing to Communist China, these doors will soon close as surely as the Indian door will slam shut if Hindu nationalists are forced to pursue the vision of Bharat as an isolated superpower. Then China, unless it breaks up into warring fragments, will be much more likely to extend its hegemony over most of Asia. The well-founded dream of Asian democracy will fade away. The United States and its navy will retreat eastward across the Pacific.

But a replacement of crony capitalism and dictator-defined "Asian values" in Southeast Asia by democratic capitalism and universal human values, especially in Indonesia, can bring a Pacific community in sight. After several false starts, Japan has an opportunity at the beginning of the twenty-first century to leap into a "third opening" as beneficial as its first and second openings to the world were in the late-nineteenth and post-war mid-twentieth centuries. Under new leadership focused not on personal gratification but on policy fulfillment, the United States can play its historic leadership role in Asia and the Pacific, unashamedly promoting democracy and blocking the expansion of Chinese power and influence. India also has a major constructive role to play in The Greater Game as the largest democratic model in Asia and the natural southern balance to China.

With the end of the Nehru era and the second election of the Hindu nationalists to power in Delhi, India has started to play this role. It is a role ranging from providing village wells to carrying out nuclear doctrine.

What *The New York Times* acknowledged editorially as "Mr. Vajpayee's India" was in better economic shape at the turn of the century than many analysts had expected after the sanctions following the May 1998 nuclear tests, as half-hearted as they were, and the disruptions caused by three national elections in three and a half years. Economic growth was a little over 6 per cent in 1999, a little under 6 per cent in 2001, about 5 per cent in 2002, and projected to be about 6 per cent in 2003, rates lower than expected due to drought and conflict with Pakistan. The rate was nominally one to three percentage points below China's growth rate in each of these years but, considering Beijing's habit of exaggerating, probably roughly equal. There was no question of India's going back to the "Hindu rate of growth" of 3 or 4 per cent. The National Democratic Alliance government aimed to reach and maintain a rate of 7 or 8 per cent, and Prime Minister Atal Bihari Vajpayee boldly predicted 9 per cent growth.

Indeed, 7 or 8 per cent might be too low considering that in 2003 more than 200 million Indians – 20 per cent of the population – were malnourished, and large areas such as virtually all of Bihar and parts of many other states were remote, dust-choked, impoverished wastelands. Yet there were also a growing number of success stories – in villages touched by the Green Revolution, in a mushrooming computer software industry, in industries free of at least some of the red tape that constricted output, exports, and imports for decades.

The central government needs to adopt and implement wider and deeper economic reforms than those initiated by the last Congress government in the early 1990s. It has to attract both Indian and foreign investment in a variety of new enterprises. It has to work with state governments to identify and help villages and areas almost untouched by development. It needs to take political risks by cutting subsidies, raising taxes, and eliminating many public-sector jobs. For humanitarian as well as political reasons, it also has to consider and cushion, if necessary, the adverse effects of liberalization and globalization. All these things it promises to do, and has started to do.

Hard choices are inevitable. In Delhi in late 2000, for example, thousands of workers protested violently when the Supreme Court ruled that the small factories employing them should be closed because they were polluting the atmosphere. Should jobs be protected, or the environment? What is undisputed is that social consciousness as well as political will is necessary to deliver. This is the bottom line of the growing pragmatic alliance between high-caste Hindu nationalists and Indians who belong to low castes, no caste, or other religions.

Shortly after Indian soldiers won the battle of Kargil, and shortly before

Indian voters went to the polls, the caretaker government at the time made public a draft Indian nuclear doctrine. Its timing was a reminder that the BJP considers muscle-flexing to be good politics. More important, the concise statement – meant to be debated, and then adopted by an elected government – was a reflection of BJP determination to establish India not as a global superpower but as a pre-eminent regional power with a "credible minimum deterrence" against nuclear attack.

The document called for India to maintain nuclear weapons in the air, on land, and at sea, along with an early-warning system. While reiterating India's no-first-strike promise of May 1998, it proposed "punitive retaliation" against an aggressor, deployment of nuclear weapons in the "shortest possible time," and giving the prime minister sole authority to launch them. It did not mention the comprehensive nuclear test-ban treaty – soon to be rejected by the U. S. Senate – that the United States was pressing India to sign.

The BJP-led government did not establish a Nuclear Command Authority in line with the proposed nuclear doctrine until April 2002, and did not announce it until January 2003. It still barred "no first use" but served notice that India would respond with nuclear weapons if attacked by biological or chemical weapons. Only the new authority, headed by the prime minister and consisting of a supreme political council, an executive or advisory council, a strategic forces command under an air force officer, and back-up units outside Delhi, could authorize a nuclear strike. India's elaborate nuclear set-up was ominous in a sense, but India's taking its time and not seeing an imminent emergency was reassuring in another sense. Some analysts considered any Indian nuclear doctrine overly ambitious, even presumptuous. Others were aware of Indian intent and Indian capability. Plainly the key common objective should be to bring India's nuclear deterrent into line with the "collective engagement" that Jaswant Singh had told me the government sought for the purpose of restraining China, which, while building up its own larger nuclear arsenal, like Pakistan condemned the Indian framework.

Strains in the alliance between the BJP and regional parties were likely to arise not over the nuclear issue but if economic improvements for ordinary Indians were slow in coming due partly to increased defence spending. But it is hard to envision the Congress returning to power, and a collection of other parties supporting it. There is no evidence that the Congress is capable of overcoming its deep corruption, its unfounded arrogance, and its loss of vision – certainly not if the best it can do is resurrect the Nehru dynasty in a depressing satiric epilogue to a long-playing human tragedy. It is a party of India's past, as it demonstrated once again by re-electing Sonia Gandhi as its leader in November 2000. If by some combination of unforeseen circumstances it gets a grip on India's future, the country is much more likely than under the BJP to become unrecognizable as it breaks into pieces in needless violence.

After the 1999 election, the BJP and its partners were in a good position to make steady progress in breaking down communal barriers and building up one nation through an evolving democratic federalism. India's path will still not be easy. But barring dramatically worse economic problems, the BJP should continue to win elections and strengthen its hold on power – not for the purpose of pushing a Hindu supremacist agenda but in order to continue being the kind of broad-based party that any diverse society needs to make democracy and capitalism work fairly. Then a responsible opposition party or parties also should develop, around or including a reformed Congress without Nehrus.

It is easy to be sceptical about the BJP and the larger Hindu movement of which it is a part, and many Indians and Westerners are, especially after the shocking Hindu-Muslim violence in Gujarat in early 2002. Militants associated with its sister organization, the Rashtriya Swayamsevak Sangh (RSS), are notoriously intolerant of members of lower castes and non-Hindus, to the extent that they have been likened to fascist followers of Hitler. They are opposed to Indian secularism and make no secret of wanting a common culture called Hindutva that all Indians, whatever their religion or background, would be required to accept. To appease them, the BJP-led government has changed textbooks and courses in schools and colleges to emphasize the past glories of Hinduism, and has not been above placing Hindu ideologues in influential positions in the education system.

But there is another side to the Hindu movement in India, and it has been enhanced by the exigencies of modern politics and economics. When the RSS was founded in 1925, its aim was a united and proud Hindu society that rose above caste and regional divisions and left behind centuries of Muslim and British domination. In this sense, despite repeated excesses in the name of Hinduism over many years, the BJP and its roots are modernist. Far from looking back to ancient Hinduism, many party leaders and thinkers look forward to a Hinduism free of caste and even sex discrimination. They do not disavow Indian secularism. There is not a conspiracy but a conflict between the modern BJP and the traditional RSS. Because the Congress Party and the Nehru dynasty failed India and there is no other non-Communist alternative to govern the country, the BJP has accepted coalition politics fully and indefinitely in the knowledge that it cannot promote revivalist Hindu policies and expect to stay in power.

Its choice of A.P.J. Abdul Kalam as the nation's president in mid-2002 reflected the modern side of Hindu nationalism. The irony is that India is finding its destiny not in its first fifty years through the elitist Nehrus with their sweeping pretensions and doctrinaire biases, but in the following years through a party growing out of small-town Hindu shopkeepers and professionals with few pretensions and increasingly irrelevant prejudices. Certainly there are no larger-than-life figures lurking in the wings to emerge at the right moment and save India. But if Indians have no mahatma to wait for, they have themselves to wait for.

They are waiting to make up their minds and hearts definitively on whether or not to entrust India's future and their own to a Hindu party claiming to reflect the Indian soul. Conditioned by Hinduism, the Raj, and the Nehru dynasty – but most of all by their own experiences – Indians are deciding in their own time how and when to keep their own tryst with destiny. Or they may have already quietly decided by voting decisively in late 1999 to reinforce the BJP's mandate, with more such votes of confidence to follow.

For the fiftieth anniversary of their independence, Indians decided to honour Subhas Chandra Bose, who wanted to wage an armed struggle for India's freedom, as well as Mohandas Gandhi, who did win it non-violently. Similarly, a Hindu raj has long seemed un-Indian to many Indians, and its reality or prospect would stir up justified fears. But in order to succeed in holding the country together and making it better, Atal Bihari Vajpayee's Hindu nationalists in power quickly accepted not only the immense diversity of India but also more than a half-century of secularism as represented by the Congress that failed. Undeniably, this was making a virtue of necessity – otherwise, they would not have led the government for long. But it is impossible for them to return to religious or cultural chauvinism without losing the best chance they and India have had for more than two decades, since the Janata government of 1977–79, and possibly for a lot longer.

The Nehrus lost far too much precious time. India is very late in coming to desperately needed economic and political breakthroughs – but perhaps not too late.

At midnight of 14–15 August 1997, its dalit president, Kocheril Raman Narayanan, made an honest admission, amounting to a repudiation of Jawaharlal Nehru's methods if not the man: "We have not been able to abolish poverty, ignorance, and disease from among our people. The massive programs that we have launched in these fields have not yielded the desired fruits."

But, recalling Mahatma Gandhi's prediction that the public would be called upon one day to punish corrupt politicians and officials, he added:

"It seems the people have to be in the forefront of the fight ... to cleanse the system."

That is the meaning of India's race with destiny and China. That, and India's looking to its own security as vital to peace in all Asia and the Pacific. In these ways does The Game become Greater.

Bibliography

NOTE

The following books have informed me in writing this book and should prove useful to others interested in India, both general readers and specialists alike. As noted in the preface, I've written *The Greater Game* as a journalist, relying heavily on first-hand sources in covering events or reconstructing them, and largely avoiding bibliographical references in the text, and footnotes completely. Most of these books, going back many years, cannot be connected to any one chapter; among exceptions are Brij Mohan Kaul's *The Untold Story* and Neville Maxwell's *India's China War*, sources for chapter 16 on the 1962 Himalayan war. Some books are recognized classics, including books by or about Mohandas K. Gandhi and Jawaharlal Nehru, and fiction by E.M. Forster, Rudyard Kipling, John Masters, R.K. Narayan, and Paul Scott. They are cited for the benefit of general readers, young and old, who want to learn about India and its place in Asia and the world, as well as for scholars from other fields, students, and persons in public affairs. The list includes two lectures, an unpublished research paper, and an article in *Foreign Affairs* on India's nuclear policy by Jaswant Singh. In most cases, the title indicates the area addressed: political, economic and social, military, all India, or international. Among books by authors I've known, those by Ambassador Chester Bowles of the U.S. and General Joyanto Nath Chaudhuri complement conversations I had with them over a number of years. This is also true of the lecture by W. David Hopper on economic development. Finally, *The Economist* and *The New York Times* were continuing references, supplementing my own coverage and reporting of India.

– D.V.P.

Ali, Mohammed. *The Afghans*. Kabul: Mohammed Ali, 1965.

Alliluyeva, Svetlana. *Only One Year*. Translated by Paul Chavchavadze. New York: Harper & Row, 1969.

Ayub Khan, Mohammad. *Friends Not Masters: A Political Autobiography*. London: Oxford University Press, 1967.

Bhargava, G.S. *After Nehru: India's New Image*. Bombay: Allied Publishers, 1966.

Bowles, Chester. *A View from New Delhi: Selected Speeches and Writings, 1963–1969*. Bombay: Allied Publishers, 1969.

Brecher, Michael. *Succession in India: A Study in Decision-Making*. Toronto: Oxford University Press, 1966.

Chandrasekhar, S. *American Aid and India's Economic Development*. New York: Praeger, 1965.

– *India's Population: Facts, Problem, and Policy*. Meerut: Meenakshi Prakashan, 1967.

Chaudhuri, Joyanto Nath. *General J.N. Chaudhuri: An Autobiography, as Narrated to B.K. Narayan*. New Delhi: Vikas, 1978.

– *Arms, Aims and Aspects*. Bombay: Manaktalas, 1966.

Chaudhuri, Nirad C. *The Continent of Circe: Being an Essay on the Peoples of India*. London: Chatto & Windus, 1965.

– *The Autobiograpy of an Unknown Indian*. New York: Macmillan, 1951.

– *To Live or Not to Live*. New Delhi: Hind, n.d.

Collier, Richard. *The Indian Mutiny*. London: Fontana Books, 1966.

Collins, Larry, and Dominique Lapierre. *Freedom at Midnight*. New York: Simon and Schuster, 1975.

Dantwala, M.L. *Poverty in India Then and Now 1870–1970*. Delhi: Macmillan, 1973.

Douglas, William O. *Strange Lands and Friendly People*. New York: Harper, 1951.

– *Beyond the High Himalayas*. Garden City: Doubleday, 1952.

Fischer, Louis. *Gandhi: His Life and Message for the World*. New York: Signet Key Books, 1954.

– *The Life of Mahatma Gandhi*. New York: Macmillan, 1966.

Forster, E.M. *A Passage to India*.: London: E. Arnold & Co., 1924.

Fraser-Tytler, W.K. *Afghanistan*. New York: Oxford University Press, 1967.

Gandhi, Mohandas Karamchand. *The Essential Gandhi*. Edited by Louis Fischer. New York: Random House, 1962.

– *The Story of My Experiments with Truth*. Ahmadabad: Navajivan Trust, 1927.

– *All Men Are Brothers*. Ahmadabad: Navajivan Trust, 1960.

Gujrati, B.S. *A Study of Lal Bahadur Shastri*. Delhi: Sterling, 1965.

Hangen, Welles. *After Nehru, Who?* New York: Harcourt, Brace & World, 1963.

Harrison, Selig S. *India: The Most Dangerous Decades*. Madras: Oxford University Press; Princeton University Press, 1960.

Hopper, W. David. "Toward the Well-Being of Rural Peoples." McGill University lecture published by International Development Research Centre, Ottawa, 1972.

Kaul, Brij Mohan. *The Untold Story*. Bombay: Allied Publishers, 1967.

Kipling, Rudyard. *Kim*. London: Macmillan, 1962.

– *Departmental Ditties and Barrack Room Ballads*. Vol. 6. New York: Doubleday and Page, 1916.

Lewis, Oscar. *Village Life in Northern India*. New York: Alfred A. Knopf; Random House, 1958.

Madhok, Balraj. *Indianisation*. New Delhi: Hind, n.d.

Mankekar, D.R. *Twenty-Two Fateful Days*. New Delhi: Vikas, 1978.

Markandaya, Kamala. *Nectar in a Sieve*. Bombay: Jaico, 1955.

Masani, M.R. *Against the Tide*. New Delhi: Vikas, 1981.

– *Bliss It Was in That Dawn ...* New Delhi: Arnold-Heinemann, 1977.

Masters, John. *Nightrunners of Bengal*. New York: Viking, 1955.

Maxwell, Neville. *India's China War*. New York: Pantheon Books, 1970.

Mehta, Ved. *Mahatma Gandhi and His Apostles*. New York: Viking, 1977.

– *The New India*. New York: Penguin, 1978.

Menon, V.P. *The Story of the Integration of the Indian States*. Calcutta: Orient Longmans, 1956.

Moraes, Frank. *India Today*. New York: Macmillan, 1960.

Mosley, Leonard. *The Last Days of the British Raj*. London: Weidenfeld & Nicolson, 1962.

Myrdal, Gunnar. *The Challenge of World Poverty*. London: Allen Lane–Penguin Press; New York: Pantheon, 1970.

– *Asian Drama: An Inquiry into the Poverty of Nations*. 3 vols. London: Allen Lane–Penguin Press, 1968.

Naipaul, V.S. *An Area of Darkness*. London: Andre Deutsch, 1964.

– *India: A Wounded Civilization*. New York: Random House, 1976.

Nair, Kusum. *Blossoms in the Dust*. London: Gerald Duckworth, 1961.

Nanda, B.R. *The Nehrus: Motilal and Jawaharlal*. London: George Allen & Unwin, 1962.

– *Mahatma Gandhi: A Biography*. London: George Allen & Unwin, 1958.

Narayan, R.K. *Waiting for the Mahatma*. Mysore: Indian Thought, 1964.

– *The Guide*. Mysore: Indian Thought, 1958.

Nehru, Jawaharlal. *Glimpses of World History*. New York: John Day, 1942.

– *Toward Freedom*. New York: John Day, 1941; Boston: Beacon Press, 1958.

– *The Discovery of India*. London: Meridian Books, 1956.

– *Nehru: The First Sixty Years*. 2 vols. Edited by Dorothy Norman. Bombay: Asia Publishing House, 1965.

– *India's Foreign Policy*. New Delhi: Government of India, 1961.

Palkhivala, N.A. *We, the People*. Bombay: Tata Press, 1984.

Radhakrishnan, Sarvepalli. *The Hindu View of Life*. London: Unwin Books, 1927.

– "Fellowship of the Spirit." Harvard University lecture published by Cambridge: Harvard University Press, 1961.

Rai, Lajpat. *Shastriji*. New Delhi: New Light, [1966?].

Reid, Escott. *Envoy to Nehru*. Toronto: Oxford University Press, 1981.

Rushdie, Salman. *Midnight's Children*. London: Pan Books, 1982.

Sanders, Sol. *A Sense of Asia*. New York: Charles Scribner's Sons, 1969.

Schlesinger, Arthur M., Jr. *A Thousand Days: John F. Kennedy in the White House*. Boston: Houghton Mifflin, 1965.

Scott, Paul. *The Jewel in the Crown*. London: Granada, 1973.

Segal, Ronald. *The Crisis of India*. Harmondsworth: Penguin, 1965.

Sen, Reeta. "Press and Government in India during Indira Gandhi's Emergency (1975–77) and in the Rajiv Gandhi Years (1984–89)." Master's Research Project, Carleton University School of Journalism, 1991.

Shaha (Shah), Rishikesh. *Heros and Builders of Nepal*. London: Oxford University Press, 1965.

Shirer, William L. *Gandhi*. New York: Simon & Schuster, 1979.

Singh, Jaswant. "Against Nuclear Apartheid." *Foreign Affairs*. September/October (1998): 41–52.

Singh, K. Natwar, ed. *The Legacy of Nehru*. New York: John Day, 1965.

Singh, Khushwant. *Train to Pakistan*. London: Chatto & Windus, 1956.

Singh, V.B., and Shankar Bose. *Elections in India: Data Handbook on Lok Sabha Elections 1952–80*. New Delhi: Sage, 1984.

Spear, Percival. *India, Pakistan and the West*. London: Oxford University Press, 1958.

– *A History of India*. Vol. 2. Harmondsworth: Penguin, 1966.

Stephens, Ian. *Pakistan*. Harmondsworth: Penguin, 1964.

Tagore, Rabindranath. *Gitanjali*. London: Macmillan, 1959.

Thapar, Romila. *A History of India*. Vol. 1. Harmondsworth: Penguin, 1966.

Tully, Mark. *No Full Stops in India*. New Delhi: Viking Penguin, 1991.

Ward, Barbara. *India and the West*. New York: W.W. Norton, 1961.

Wiser, William and Charlotte. *Behind Mud Walls 1930–1960*. Berkeley: University of California Press, 1963.

Zinkin, Taya. *Reporting India*. London: Chatto & Windus, 1962.

– *Challenges in India*. London: Chatto & Windus, 1966.

– *India*. London: Oxford University Press, 1964.

Index